THEODORE CAPLOW

University of Virginia

D1457670

SO-BPO-801

ELEMENTARY SOCIOLOGY

PRENTICE-HALL, INC.

Englewood Cliffs, New Jersey

13-260034-X

Library of Congress Catalog Card Number 70-143582

Printed in the United States of America

Current printing (last number): 10 9 8 7 6 5 4 3 2 1

Prentice-Hall International, Inc., *London*
Prentice-Hall of Australia, Pty. Ltd., *Sydney*
Prentice-Hall of Canada, Ltd., *Toronto*
Prentice-Hall of India Private Limited, *New Delhi*
Prentice-Hall of Japan, Inc., *Tokyo*

CONTENTS

Contents

Part Two SOCIOLOGICAL FIELDS

Part One

Sociological Theory and Research

In Part One you will encounter some of the basic ideas of modern sociology and begin to acquire the vocabulary you need to read about and discuss the findings of sociological research. You will learn something of the methods of social research, partly by considering some landmark studies in sociology, and you will get an introductory look at the ancient enterprise of social theory.

Basic Ideas

Sociology *is the scientific study of human relationships and their consequences.*

It is one of the most interesting of all subjects but not one of the easiest. Human relationships can be exceedingly complex, and the scientific study of them is always hampered by the fact that the most important part of a relationship—the meaning attached to it by the people involved—is invisible, and cannot be directly observed.

The most important unit in sociology is a *social system,* which is composed of a group of living people engaged in some type of collective activity and related to each other in various ways. Social systems may be as small as a pair of lovers, or as large as an army. Some of them last only for a few moments, like the crowd at a street accident, and some endure through many generations, like a gypsy tribe. Every social system generates a certain number of *social facts,* which are regularities of behavior imposed on individuals by the system. In a large and durable system, like a nation, there are millions of social facts to be studied; the only practical way to do this is to divide them up into smaller categories, like population, cities, social classes, work, organizations, family life, crime, war, social change, and so forth. This is what we shall be doing in this book, in order to become familiar with some of the important social facts that have been discovered by research.

WHY STUDY SOCIOLOGY?

As a clearly defined field of study, sociology goes back only about a hundred years, but an interest in human relationships and their consequences is older than civilization; it has been found in a lively form among people who use stone tools and lack a written language. The motives behind this interest are not the same for everybody; not all professional sociologists agree on their ultimate objectives. What you yourself will learn from sociology depends very much on what your purpose is in studying it. You may want, for example:

1. To obtain a clearer picture of our society, how it is organized, and how it works.
2. To escape from the limitations imposed by your own origins and upbringing, and view the social world objectively.

3. To clarify your own values and goals, by examining the social processes by which values are formed.
4. To understand the patterns of social change in the contemporary world and gain some power to predict the future.
5. To understand the structure of social systems in order to improve or reform them.
6. To learn enough about social mechanisms and processes to use them for your personal advantage.
7. To learn enough about social mechanisms and processes to use them in the service of a social movement.
8. To help develop the means of solving a specific social problem.
9. To prepare yourself for a career in one of the social sciences or in a related field such as law, public administration, social work, or practical politics.
10. To satisfy your intellectual curiosity.

Although your interest in sociology may be based on any of these motives, or a combination of them, or have some other basis entirely, you will serve it most effectively by adhering to the scientific procedures that distinguish sociology from gossip, propaganda, mythology, and other nonlogical methods of explaining human relationships and their consequences.

WHAT IS A SOCIAL SCIENCE?

Sociology is a social science. That is, its results are drawn from empirical research conducted according to the ground rules of scientific investigation, including objectivity, the use of numbers wherever possible, the reporting of research failures as well as successes, and acceptance in advance of the need for all results to be checked and confirmed by other investigators.

The subjects taught in the modern college curriculum fall into three broad categories—physical sciences, social sciences, and humanities. The physical sciences are concerned with the scientific study of nature, the social sciences with the scientific study of human behavior, and the humanities with the systematic but generally nonscientific study of cultural products like language and art.

These divisions of knowledge are not sharply separated in either theory or practice. Biology is always counted among the physical sciences, although much human behavior falls within the province of biologists. History can be counted either among the social sciences or among the humanities. Some of the branches of geography fall into each of the three divisions, the formation of rivers belonging to the physical sciences, city growth to the social sciences, and the distribution of architectural styles to the humanities.

In the same way, the differences of method among the three broad divisions of modern knowledge are relative rather than absolute. Although the results obtained by the physical sciences are generally more precise and reliable than those of the social sciences, there are

numerous exceptions. Predictions of the weather based on meteoro-
logical data are generally less certain than predictions of population
growth based on demographic data. Chemistry is sometimes less precise than economics.

The difference of method between the social sciences and the
humanities is even less to be depended on. Some of what passes for
empirical research in sociology is simply propaganda on current issues, whereas, on the other hand, some literary scholars work with
computers. Nevertheless, it remains true in a general way that the
humanities are concerned with cataloging and appreciating the singu-
lar products of human effort, like paintings and symphonies, whereas
the mission of the social sciences is to search for broad general principles that can be used to predict and explain human behavior.

HOW SCIENTIFIC ARE THE SOCIAL SCIENCES?

A generation ago, there was a lively controversy among American
sociologists about the prospects of a truly scientific sociology. George
Lundberg, for example, believed that the methods of sociological research should be modeled on those of physics, emphasizing experimentation and exact measurement. He claimed that there were no
essential differences between physical phenomena and social behavior and that one could be as readily objectified as the other.[1] A somewhat similar position was expressed by the great physicist P. W.
Bridgman, who proposed that those elements of man's interior life not
subject to observation by others should be ignored by the scientifically minded man.[2] The majority of sociologists, however, could not be
persuaded to exclude subjective phenomena, like values and sentiments, from the sociological landscape; and they continued to pursue
their researches and work out their theories without much concern
about finding the basic equations of the social universe.

As we shall see, the methods of modern sociology have been developed by investigators wrestling with the complexity of human experience. What was borrowed from the physical sciences had to be
altered to fit. With each passing year, the methods of social research
improve in scope and accuracy, but it would be hard to demonstrate
that they have moved closer to the methods of the physical sciences.[3]

The most useful way of understanding the relationship between the
physical and social sciences, on the one hand, and the social sciences
and the humanities, on the other hand, is to note that the first two
share certain beliefs about the nature of reality, which we will call the
scientific viewpoint, whereas the latter two share certain features imposed on them by the human material with which they deal.

The Scientific Viewpoint

The scientist's world is composed of elements that can be accurately observed, usually by counting or measurement, and the oberva-
tions can be verified by other scientists using similar procedures. The

Sociological Theory and Research

scientist's world is "consensual"; that is, it relies upon the agreement of the overwhelming majority of mankind that the external world discovered by our senses is real and stable and upon the more refined agreement of an international body of trained men who routinely check each other's observations and are usually able to confirm them within reasonable margins of error.

The scientist accepts in advance the absolute authority of his evidence and agrees to be compelled by it. Whatever preliminary statements he makes about his subject matter before undertaking a study are highly tentative; and whatever conclusions he reaches after his study is completed are understood to be tentative also, subject to the review of his own work by his colleagues, the success or failure of other investigators in replicating his results, and the unending stream of evidence that future studies will produce with the aid of better instruments and more sophisticated ideas.

When he accepts the absolute authority of empirical evidence as interpreted by his peers, the scientist necessarily rejects the validation of knowledge in any of the other ways that are common in human affairs, for example by tradition, authority, revelation or common sense. Thus, the scientific viewpoint, at its first flowering in the seventeenth century, represented a sharp break in the intellectual history of Western man, whose knowledge had been previously drawn from tradition, authority, revelation, and common sense. Most of our familiar knowledge continues to be drawn from these sources. The scientific viewpoint is not completely satisfactory for everyday use, as every student of sociology soon discovers. It is now accepted by nearly all reasonable men nearly everywhere as the correct and appropriate attitude to hold when one is doing any kind of systematic research; but it does not square perfectly with the facts of personal experience, and one is sometimes faced with a choice between abandoning the scientific viewpoint or rejecting direct experience. For example, we experience time as moving faster or slower on different occasions although, from the scientific viewpoint, time runs at a constant rate.

THE SCIENTIFIC PICTURE OF THE UNIVERSE

The universe is assumed to be built out of a relatively small number of elements identified by simple characteristics. All apparently complex phenomena—celestial, physical, chemical, biological, social, and cultural—can be *analyzed;* that is, they can be broken down into their constituent parts and the interrelationship of the parts explained.

The knowledge obtained by observation and analysis is based on external reality and is *verifiable,* which means it can be confirmed by the agreement of independent observers. All men are assumed to have similar experiences of an external world that is solid and real although our senses give us only a partial view of it. If the external world is real and the sensory apparatus of observers is more or less the same, it should be possible for observers to agree most of the time about objects or events set before them. One can even study scientifically phenomena that cannot be directly observed—dreams, for example—by concentrating on their verifiable aspects: the pulse rate or brainwaves of the sleeper, in that instance.

Practically speaking, many people cannot be brought to agree about the objects or events set before them. The company of scientific observers does not include infants, children, mental defectives, primitive tribesmen, or the sages of non-Western cultures. It does not even include the ordinary educated layman, who accepts a scientific statement about relativity or the causes of drug addiction out of sheer faith without any first-hand examination of the data and without being able to follow the analysis. Nevertheless, the practical achievements attributable to science in the past century and a half—a period that extends from the first crude steamboat to landings on the moon—persuade most people living in modernized countries today to accept scientific assertions without much argument, so that paradoxically, the average layman's confidence in the sceptical, empirical, hard-nosed scientific method is founded on hearsay and blind faith.

The scientist himself is a layman outside his own specialty. However, he assumes that the diversity of knowledge in different fields of investigation masks an underlying unity. The universe, as its name implies, is thought to be one system, subject to uniform basic laws. The special principles discovered in one field cannot contradict those discovered in another. There is no fundamental discontinuity between experience on this planet and events in other solar systems. The remotest stars seem to be built of the same familiar chemical elements. Nor is there any fundamental discontinuity between inanimate objects and living things. Life itself is the explicable product of certain molecular arrangements, and something very similar to a living organism can be produced from inanimate materials in the biochemist's laboratory. Likewise, social scientists assume that social and cultural phenomena are built up in an explicable fashion from the biological characteristics of advanced mammals. Within the domain of human action, moreover, the same principles should apply uniformly to all tribes of men at all points in history. Except as it may be affected in the very long run by evolutionary change, human nature is visualized as constant.

Time, as we noted, runs at a uniform rate in the universe known to science. It never stops. It never loops. No part of the past can ever be literally repeated. Nothing in the future can be known with certainty in advance. One year is the same length as another year, regardless of the century in which it falls or the events that happen in it. This special scientific way of viewing time has many consequences, including the implicit denial of fortune-telling, soothsaying, reincarnation, and many other beliefs that have always been cherished by mankind and continue to be stubbornly held even in the age of science and even by practicing scientists.

The scientific conception of time leads directly to the concept of scientific causality. The most advanced philosophers of science are not entirely agreed what it means to say that one event is the cause of another and, as we shall see in a moment, the question is especially difficult in the social sciences, but in spite of these difficulties, scientific analysis depends on the belief that every event is the result of preceding events and the cause of subsequent events and the related belief that similar events have similar causes and lead to similar consequences.

Special Problems of the Social Sciences

The social sciences are as firmly attached as the physical sciences to the scientific viewpoint, but cannot claim the same degree of success with it, at least up to now. The knowledge of social behavior accumulated by the social sciences in the past century is much broader and deeper than what was known before; very few social problems are now left unstudied, and there is a vast repertory of reliable methods on which social research can draw. Nevertheless, it would be presumptuous to maintain that the yield of the social sciences is equivalent to that of the physical sciences. As Ernest Nagel, a leading philosopher of science, points out:

> ... in no area of social inquiry has a body of general laws been established, comparable with outstanding theories in the natural sciences in scope of explanatory power or in capacity to yield precise and reliable predictions. ... "In the social sciences there is nothing quite like the almost complete unanimity commonly found among competent workers in the natural sciences as to what are matters of established fact, what are the reasonably satisfactory explanations (if any) for the assumed facts, and what are some of the valid procedures in sound inquiry.[4]

The special handicap that we face in applying scientific methods to social phenomena can be briefly summarized as follows:

THE RESISTANCE OF THE HUMAN MATERIAL

The natural scientist enjoys a liberty with respect to his subject matter that the social scientist can never hope to attain. Controlled experimentation is the most powerful tool of scientific inquiry, but the experiments that can be undertaken with human subjects in the laboratory cover only a small fraction of the total field of behavior. Many of the phenomena with which the sociologist deals—the problems of urban growth, for example—cannot be fitted into the laboratory at all. Other phenomena that can be miniaturized for experimental purposes, say the relationship between authority and obedience, are necessarily changed in the process so that we can never be quite sure whether the findings of the laboratory experiment are applicable to real life.

The investigator of human behavior is prevented by social norms and by his own scruples from undertaking experiments or even observations that may harm the subject. In most studies, he must gain the consent of his subjects and keep it throughout the investigation. This is never easy; it usually involves concessions and compromises that detract from the value of the data. The consent given by subjects is never unlimited even under ideal conditions; human subjects have reasons for concealing some of their actions and motives. Ideal conditions seldom occur. The social scientist often has as much difficulty as the jury at a criminal trial in ascertaining what *really* happened at a particular time and place, but unlike a court of law, he has no power to summon unwilling witnesses and compel them to testify.

CONTAMINATION OF DATA

It often happens in the physical sciences that the observation of a phenomenon changes its character. However, the danger of contaminating data by observation is less in the physical sciences than in the social sciences. Almost any social event can be modified by being observed. This modification occurs in at least three ways: (a) the presence of an observer changes the character of the situation, for example by destroying its privacy; (b) the subjects change their own behavior—consciously or unconsciously—because they are under observation; (c) the subjects adopt the observer's terms of reference and begin to behave in accordance with them. For example, patients who enter psychoanalysis seem to report dreams that conform to the theoretical expectations of their particular analyst. This last point is related to the peculiar problem of:

SELF-MODIFYING PREDICTIONS

The study of any scientific field produces data that permit the construction of theories, and these theories allow the scientist to predict future events similar to those he has observed. But in the social sciences the predictions themselves enter the field of action, and as often as not, they succeed in undermining themselves. Predictions may be either self-negating or self-fulfilling. For example, a predicted increase in industrial accidents may be self-negating if it leads to installation of new safety equipment; on the other hand, a predicted decline of working hours may be self-fulfilling if it influences workers to press for such reductions.

VALUES AND BIASES

The social scientist, like his subjects, is perpetually interfering with his own results. Sometimes he does this deliberately, in the name of a higher cause; more often accidentally, when unconscious preferences lead him astray. The problem arises because the social scientist as a man and as a member of various groups has a full complement of motives that become entangled with his scientific work and limit his objectivity.

Biases that arise from the investigator's values may appear at any point in his work. The initial selection of problems to be studied is necessarily biased because investigators choose subjects of inquiry with which they can live comfortably and thus automatically exclude other topics that might be more fruitful scientifically. Thus, for obvious and understandable reasons, there have been hundreds of studies of marital adjustment but very few investigations of illicit love affairs, great interest in the causes of juvenile delinquency but relatively little attention to the causes of good conduct, much work on the physician-patient relationship but few studies of medical malpractice. On the other hand, most of the topics that are overlooked come into prominence sooner or later as fashions in research change. The more stubborn kinds of bias appear in the research itself. One of the most important is:

PARTISANSHIP

In any study of a social organization, the scientist will find himself closer to some of his subjects in affiliation and outlook than he is to others, and will be tempted to adopt the viewpoint of his friends to the detriment of his scientific neutrality. A study of a student protest movement sponsored by a university administration is not likely to produce exactly the same findings as a parallel study by an organization of student activists. The ethnologist who studies a cannibal tribe is likely to find himself friendly with those tribesmen who favor modernization and not with those who want to preserve the purity of the old cannibal tradition.

PRIOR COMMITMENTS

The values of the investigator also intrude upon his results. As in the natural sciences, scientific findings in the social sciences can be applied to practical problems, but the attempted solution of a social problem generally touches the social scientist in one of his other human capacities. His view of any social action is necessarily affected by political, moral, and aesthetic values that derive from other and earlier sources than his professional experience. But even professional experience can be a source of bias in a field of action where there is room for disagreement, and where schools of thought have developed to press particular opinions. A member of such a school may be under great pressure not to make discoveries that are inconsistent with its position.

THE PROBLEM OF SUBJECTIVITY

Perhaps the most serious impediment to the application of the scientific method to human experience is the natural division of that experience into overt and covert sectors, the covert sector being shielded from direct observation. Of course, the physical sciences must also deal with many phenomena that cannot be directly observed, for example, the interior transformation of stars or the workings of the endocrine glands in living creatures. Such phenomena can be simulated in the laboratory or examined with new instruments. It is not theoretically impossible that methods will someday be devised that will enable one man to observe the perceptions of another directly. For the time being, however, there are no peepholes in the veil that conceals everyone's inner experience from everyone else. Although sociology and the other social sciences deal largely with the motives of social acts, the feelings and sentiments that accompany them, and the images and concepts to which they give rise, none of these essential elements of social behavior can be observed directly. We must therefore depend on indirect reports, usually given by the actors themselves. Such reports are unverifiable and do not really meet the normal standards for scientific data, but since we have nothing better, we must do what we can to increase their accuracy and reliability.

PSEUDO-SCIENTIFIC BELIEFS ABOUT SOCIOLOGY

One of the most important functions of scientific study is to clear away the tangle of myths, folk beliefs, false reports, and misunderstandings that constitute the popular knowledge of a subject in its prescientific stage. Throughout this book we shall be engaged in undermining ancient fallacies and crude explanations for complex phenomena. New weeds spring upon clear ground, and it is probably inevitable that the progress of modern sociology has stimulated the growth of a new crop of false beliefs almost as fact-resistant as the ones they replace. We will examine these one by one as we move through the sociological specialties, but some of them deserve special notice here because they are widely accepted and because they represent the perversion rather than the application of the scientific method.

The three leading fallacies that masquerade as sociological principles are:

1. All social problems are solvable.
2. Everyone is the product of his environment and therefore cannot be held responsible for his own actions.
3. Since moral principles can be shown to vary from one society to another, it is unscientific to govern one's behavior by moral principles.

Each of these fallacies has a complicated history of its own. What they have in common is a gross exaggeration of the extent to which the invention of social science has transformed the human condition and simplified the choices that men confront. The truth is nearly the opposite. The study of sociology discloses that conflict and discord are inherent features of social structure, that the interests of the individual and his society are never completely reconcilable, that the acceptance of scientific causality does not in any way enable us to dispense with the assumption of human free will, that the basic commitment underlying the moral codes of every tribe is universal, and that every community large or small is held together by the normative sentiments and reciprocal obligations of its members.

The Vocabulary of Sociology

Like all scientific and scholarly fields, sociology has developed a long list of technical terms that refer to the things it studies viewed in a particular way. Such terms have the double function of labeling phenomena and of placing them in position to be analyzed. In addition, many students like to use an argot that identifies them as belonging to an inner circle and in touch with the latest fashions in ideas. A typical form of argot is the use of technical terms as substitutes for common words—for example, "positive" and "negative" for good and bad, "dissensus" for disagreement, and so forth. Even writers who avoid the excesses of argot often develop a professional style that unmistakably identifies them with their discipline. Readers unfamiliar with this style may find it hard to follow at first. Consider the following selection.

> Casual observation suggests considerable variation in the degree to which Santa is used as a child control device, in the degree to which parents tell children that rewards from Santa are contingent upon good behavior. (This variation is limited in two ways. First, the idea that Santa's behavior is contingent upon good behavior is prevalent in the larger culture and manifested in such songs as "Santa Claus is Coming to Town." Children may acquire the belief from other sources than their parents. Second, *in fact* Santa's rewards are generally not contingent upon good behavior; parents who assert otherwise are bluffing.) We need information on the social determinants of these aspects of the behavior of Santa Claus.[5]

The foregoing passage does not contain any technical terms peculiar to sociology but its tone of voice, so to speak, is unmistakably sociological. Contrast it with another excerpt from the same paper.

> Santa Claus, by accepting responsibility for our gifts, allows us to express morally uncontaminated sentiments toward children. He is an especially important figure in American families because of the great emotional importance of the small family group for Americans. Santa Claus is likely to become important in other Western societies to the extent that their family systems become more like the American—to the extent that the power of extended families loses importance and to the extent that the nuclear family becomes the center of the emotional life of all of its members.[6]

This selection, which happens to read more easily than the first, is almost certain to be misunderstood if you try to guess at the meanings of "extended family" and "nuclear family," which are technical terms. Sociological prose has been widely criticized as unclear and awkward. It has been the subject of innumerable tirades by poets and rhetoricians, one of whom describes the sociological style as "almost like Esperanto."[7] Indeed, there is no denying that many sociologists do not write well enough to be read with pleasure or complete understanding either by poets or by other sociologists. There seem to be three reasons for this:

1.   Because almost all the subject matter of sociology is the stuff of ordinary life, the substitution of technical terms for common language is less convincing in sociology than in fields dealing with unfamiliar matters.

2.   For unknown reasons, sociologists have been backward in accepting uniform definitions for their technical terms, so that even experts sometimes misunderstand each other.

3.   When the data of research are put into words, the social scientist's categories do not match the traditional categories of social relationships imbedded in the language. Thus, there is no common word in English that includes brothers and sisters without distinguishing their gender. Since it is almost impossible to discuss kinship systems without such a word, the technical term *sibling,* based on the Anglo-Saxon word for relative, was introduced in 1897.[8] This takes care of part of the problem but leaves us still lacking the terms corresponding to brotherhood, brotherly, fraternal, fraternity. One cannot refer easily to "my favorite sibling." Thus, whenever we talk about sibling relationships in a systematic way, we must resort to elaborate circumlocutions like "reciprocated positive sentiments between siblings" because we cannot say "siblingish love."

ORIGINS OF THE SOCIOLOGICAL VOCABULARY

An actual experiment that tested the ability of high school students to comprehend excerpts from scientific papers in sociology, experimental psychology, psychoanalysis, biochemistry, physiology, and pharmacology did not uncover any significant differences among these six fields in the comprehensibility of their material to untrained readers. All six of the disciplines just mentioned drew somewhat over half of their terms from Anglo-Saxon and Old English and the remainder from foreign, classical, and mixed sources. In another study, the proportion of borrowed words in sociology was found to be 41.7 percent compared to 42.1 percent for all disciplines.[9]

There are only a few neologisms—new words invented for special purposes—in sociology. *Sociology* itself is an example, a hybrid term coined from the Latin root *socius* and the Greek root *logos* by Auguste Comte and first seen in print in 1838. But the typical sociological term is a respectable English word that has been given a new twist of meaning. The sociological meaning of the term generally retains a connection with its original dictionary meaning. *Stratification,* for example, first appeared in the language in Shakespeare's time to refer to the action of depositing something in layers. It was taken up as a geological term late in the eighteenth century and came into general use in sociology only in the 1940's.[10]

The great bulk of sociological writing can easily be understood by any careful reader who has mastered a small number of basic terms and the ideas they express. In the next section, we will examine 20 of the key terms in modern sociology, starting in most cases with an adaptation of the definition given by the *International Encyclopedia of the Social Sciences*[11] and the *Dictionary of the Social Sciences*[12] and showing why the term is useful and how it relates to other key terms.

The 20 Key Terms

1. Social System
   and related terms:
   - 2. Function
   - 3. Integration
   - 4. Group
   - 5. Organization
   - 6. Society

7. Culture
   and related terms:
   - 8. Institution
   - 9. Value
   - 10. Attitude
   - 11. Norm
   - 12. Deviance

13. Interaction
   and related terms
   - 14. Role
   - 15. Socialization
   - 16. Conflict

17. Status
   and related terms:
   - 17. Stratification
   - 19. Mobility
   - 20. Power

---

1. SOCIAL SYSTEM

A social system is a set of persons and activities whose mutual relationships are fairly constant.

This is the most inclusive name for the entities that sociologists study. It includes societies and organizations, groups and institutions. A nation is a social system, so is a baseball game, and so is a pair of lovers. What use can so broad a category have, when the items in it cannot have many features in common?

The fact is, those they do have are extremely important. Every social system maintains boundaries that keep it separate and distinguishable from the environment and develops an equilibrium or balance of activities that permits it to continue in operation.

These fundamental features suggest the starting points for any sociological analysis. Faced with a new social system, the first task is to map its boundaries and to discover the mechanisms by which they are maintained. The second task is to identify its principal activities and to find out how they are related to each other and by what means they are kept in equilibrium.

2. FUNCTION

The function of any element of a social system is the part it plays in maintaining the system.

It is taken for granted nowadays that there is some kind of working relationship among the parts of a social system, so that each part is related in some way to every other and nothing in a social system can be changed without bringing about a whole series of changes elsewhere in the system. This point has been demonstrated so often that it seems entirely obvious, but this was not the case in the early days of social science, when social behavior was often studied without much reference to the system in which it occurred.

A sociologist who emphasizes the interrelatedness of the parts of a social system is called a functionalist. If he is extreme in his views, he may try to show that every part of a social system contributes to the system's survival and is indispensable.[13] The evidence of empirical studies does not seem to support this extreme position. Almost any part of any social system can be shown to have consequences for the whole system, but these consequences are not necessarily beneficial; and it is often possible to show after a change has taken place that a particular usage or belief was not indispensable at all. The functional analyst is liable to fall into confusion unless he carefully specifies the mechanisms through which functions are fulfilled, and the boundaries of the system in which they are fulfilled and—if possible—the functional alternatives or equivalents that could accomplish the same purposes in other ways.

A distinction is often made between manifest and latent functions. The *manifest function* is recognized by the actors involved in the social or cultural pattern. The *latent function* is not recognized by actors in that system and needs to be uncovered by analysis. Thus, for example, the manifest function of cheating on examinations is to improve the cheaters' grades; a latent function is to reinforce the solidarity of student peer groups.

3. INTEGRATION

Integration is the fitting together of the parts of a social system to make it a unified whole.

Integration is a matter of degree. A social system must be integrated to some extent or we would not be able to designate it as a system, but the most casual observation will show differences from one system to another. Some families are much more close-knit than others; some

cultures resist change fiercely, whereas others are open to every passing influence. Even such large amorphous systems as American cities
can be ranked according to their integration[14] and it has been shown
that the less integrated cities have more severe social problems.

Three grand hypotheses are associated with the idea of integration: (1) that it is harder to live in a poorly integrated social system
than a well-integrated one; (2) that a well-integrated system is better able to resist outside encroachment than a poorly integrated
one; (3) that modernization and industrial progress tend to reduce
social integration. These three hypotheses were the life-long preoccupation of Emile Durkheim, whose work we will discuss in the
next chapter, and they have been close to the center of sociological
inquiry since Durkheim published his classic study of suicide in
1897. In that book, the first full-length statistical study in modern
sociology, he assembled a mass of evidence showing that suicide
rates are high where social integration is low.[15]

The principal difficulty we encounter in measuring the integration
of a social system is that no one has ever devised an absolute
measure that would make it possible to compare, let us say, the
integration of a city with that of a church, or the integration of a
family with that of a nation. It is fairly simple to measure the relative integration of units of similar type, like English families selected from a single social class at a particular time and place,[16] or
a series of Mexican communities with the same basic culture but
different degrees of exposure to outside influence.[17] Comparing the
integration of widely separated social systems is a much shakier
procedure. Recent studies have shown less integration in primitive
tribes and more integration in metropolitan neighborhoods than
might be expected.[18]

On the other hand, there can be no serious question that the
twentieth century is characterized by rapid social and cultural
change, which tends to lower the integration of innumerable social
systems. If happiness is more easily attained in integrated systems,
as many studies seem to show, it is not surprising that our era is
not marked by universal contentment.

4. GROUP

*A group is a social system consisting of a number of individuals
who interact with each other and engage in some joint activities.*

It follows from this definition that the "groupness" of a group is a
matter of degree. This observation conforms to everyday experience, in
which some groups, like families or legislatures, are very stable and
other groups, like those at a cocktail party, are so ephemeral that there
is hardly time to note their existence before they disappear.

By a useful convention, a group has at least three members. The
members are living individuals, not collectivities or abstractions. There
is some way of distinguishing them from nonmembers, if only by their
presence at a particular time or place. They are related by interaction,

that is, each of them interacts with others in such a way that all of them are connected by a single network of relationships.

The term *group* is so flexible that it is almost impossible to misuse it, but once in a while, somebody miscalls an aggregate a group. An *aggregate* consists of people who share some common trait but do not interact with each other. Bartenders with red hair are the stock example of an aggregate that is not a group.

5. ORGANIZATION

An organization is a persistent social system with an explicit collective identity, an unequivocal roster of members, a program of repetitive activity directed toward the achievement of explicit goals, and procedures for the appointment of new members.

The unequivocal collective identity is expressed by the organization's name, which is recognized by all of its members and by many outsiders as well. The name often conveys a good deal of information about the organization's purposes, location, and affiliation, and it permits collective action to be taken without confusion. The roster enables an organization to identify its members, and at any given moment, to divide the entire human race into members and nonmembers. The program of activity may be extensive or limited, but it always specifies some definite activities directed toward specific goals and always includes some sort of calendar for arranging activities in advance. Procedures for replacing members provide both for the recruitment of new members and for the transfer of old members from one position to another.

A family, a political party, a work crew, a criminal gang, a regiment, a bank, a government department, a neighborhood church, and a symphony orchestra, are examples of organizations, but one should not leap to the conclusion that all permanent groups are organized. Races, ethnic groups, social classes, and neighborhoods, for example, are *not* organizations.

Organizations have certain fixed features, regardless of the time or place in which they appear, including a *table of organization* that specifies the titles and functions of the principal positions and tells the incumbents of those positions when and how to interact; a *hierarchy* that ranks members in categories from highest to lowest and assigns different duties and rewards to each category; *norms* (informal or formal rules), governing the behavior of members to each other and to outsiders; *rewards and punishments* to obtain compliance; *procedures* for recruiting, promoting, and demoting members; and last but not least, an *inventory* of material objects needed to carry out the organizational program.

6. SOCIETY

A society is a self-sufficient, self-perpetuating social system, including persons of both sexes and all ages.

A society is a group of living people, not a collection of abstract ideas.

One author describes it as "the largest group to which an individual belongs."[19] It is self-sufficient in the sense that it has a complete inventory of procedures for coping with the environment and prolonging its existence indefinitely.

The exact boundaries of a society are almost impossible to draw. As a matter of fact, they are drawn differently for different purposes. It makes reasonably good sense to speak sometimes of American society, sometimes of Western society, and sometimes even of world society, since the communication network of the twentieth century links nearly the whole population of the globe into one group for certain purposes. On the other hand, a complete society, capable of surviving independently, may be very small. Some New Guinea tribes, with their own languages and religions, have less than a thousand people but are nevertheless fully equipped to cope with the environment and to maintain continuity from one generation to the next.

The definition given above describes the usual meaning of society in modern sociological writings, but of course no one has the right to prohibit other uses of the word which you will come across from time to time. The word society is often used to refer to the totality of social relationships, or to some vague, brooding presence that stands behind ordinary customs and enforces them (for example, "Society disapproves of smoking by teenage girls."). Society, with a capital *S,* is used colloquially for an urban upper class.

7. CULTURE

Culture consists of socially acquired and transmitted patterns of activity and the objects associated with them.

What you need to remember about culture is that it always involves know-how: how to plant corn, how to arrange a wedding, how to express futurity by changing the form of a verb, how to take revenge on a defeated enemy, how to catalog a government pamphlet, and so forth, together with the man-made objects that embody this knowledge—the plow, the wedding ring, the grammar book, the trophy, the file card, and so forth. A distinction is sometimes made between small bits of culture, called *culture traits,* and larger units, called *culture complexes.* The wedding ring is a culture trait; the entire set of wedding practices that includes showers, bridesmaids, gown and veil, the license, the ceremony, "something old, something new, something borrowed and something blue," the bridegroom's nervousness, the Mendelssohn wedding march, and the preacher's fee are a culture complex.

8. INSTITUTION

An institution is a distinctive pattern of social activity and values centered upon some major human need and accompanied by distinctive modes of social interaction.

An institution is both a cultural and an organizational phenomenon. It includes a society's accumulated recipes for dealing with some important need plus the people and organizations that are engaged in doing so.

The division of a society into family, religious, economic, political, educational, and recreational institutions is classic and is applicable to any society of any size at any stage of development. These may be thought of as basic institutions.

In addition, there are many types of social activity on a smaller scale that fit the definition given above. For example, science, law, philanthropy, or horseracing may be studied as institutions.

The term *institution* is also commonly used for any large establishment with a permanent staff of workers or inmates under its roof, such as a museum or an orphanage. The great national museum in Washington is called the Smithsonian Institution. In some circles the word institution is a euphemism for any establishment to which it is disgraceful for one's relatives to be sent. Sociologists sometimes speak of a *total institution,* a large establishment whose workers or inmates are subject to a fixed discipline throughout the 24 hours of the day. This interesting category includes prisons, hospitals, monasteries, and military units.

9. VALUE

A value is a conception of what is desirable, which influences the social behavior of the holder.

A value, in other words, is an idea held by an individual but often shared with his friends and relations, which influences his choice of what to do and how to do it by defining what is worthwhile, precious, attractive, or suitable, as the case may be.

Social philosophers have been struggling with the concept of value ever since Plato, who attempted to identify the desirable with the good, and the good of individuals with the good of the community. The underlying problem is that although desiring is the most universal of human reactions, it is not a very steady one.

In both psychology and economics, elaborate systems have been worked out to take account of the fluctuations of value caused by the scarcity or abundance of things desired, the presence or absence of alternatives, and the decrease or increase of satisfaction when a goal is attained. But the concept of value remains one of the most intricate and puzzling ideas in the social sciences. At this point, the student can only be warned to beware of excessively simple explanations of it. Value has something to do with usefulness, but drinking water is not highly valued under ordinary conditions. Value is increased by rarity, but expectant mothers do not yearn for quintuplets. An individual's values are largely derived from his culture but nothing is less certain than the assumption that a value held by a particular group will be supported by all of its members. The prudent sociologist approaches the study of values cautiously and demands solid proof before accepting the statement that a given action or event occurred because a given individual or group held a particular value.

10. ATTITUDE

An attitude is an idea predisposing one to act in a given way in a given situation.

The cluster of beliefs that make up an attitude are held with sufficient conviction, consciously or unconsciously, so that one's response to a situation is determined in advance. Attitudes embody values, most of them derived from one's relatives, friends, and other associates.

The measurement of attitudes has been a flourishing branch of social research for more than forty years. Attitude surveys have been conducted on every conceivable topic from the honesty of chambermaids to the hazards of interplanetary travel. The built-in limitation of an attitude survey is that it gets at an attitude, which is a predisposition to act, by asking the subject how he would respond to a particular situation instead of by watching him do so. (In pre-election polls, and many other types of inquiry, this is a necessary limitation, since the whole point of study is to predict what the voter will do at a later time.) Whenever a description of an attitude is based on the verbal report of its holder, the investigator is faced with three interrelated questions: Is the respondent telling the truth? Does he know what his attitude really is? Can his behavior be predicted from what he says? Attitude measurement is most useful when these questions are answered by combining verbal reports with observations of actual behavior.

11. NORM

A norm is a standard of conduct in a particular group; it enables a person to determine in advance how his actions will be judged by other persons and it provides those other persons with criteria for approval and disapproval.

The important thing about a norm is that it is promulgated by a particular group and based on that group's values. The first scholars who studied norms comparatively were impressed by the fact that an action defined as atrocious by one culture may be regarded as meritorious by another. The duty of a Chinese peasant in a famine year was to keep his aged parents well-fed even at the cost of starving his infant children; the virtuous Eskimo, when food ran short, fulfilled his duty by leaving his old parents alone on the ice to starve in a dignified way. Among the ancient Hebrews, a younger brother had a sacred obligation to marry his older brother's widow and Onan was felled by Heaven for doing it grudgingly, but the theological advisors of Henry VIII concluded that his marriage to Catherine of Aragon was incestuous because she was his older brother's widow. "The mores can make anything right or anything wrong," said William Graham Sumner in his great book, *Folkways.*[20] Since 1906, when that was written, the novelty of the discovery that infanticide can be a sacred duty and kindness to children may be punished as a crime has somewhat worn off. Modern sociologists are more impressed by the universal themes that underly normative systems than by their superficial diversity. For example, all organizations demand loyalty from their members although loyalty may be demonstrated in diverse ways. All social systems seem to distinguish between virtuous and vicious conduct, although the specific act that is virtuous in one system may be vicious in another.

12. DEVIANCE

Deviance is behavior that violates the norms of a social system and provokes corrective efforts by agents of that system.

Deviant behavior has been a major preoccupation of sociology since the pioneer nineteenth-century studies of "crime, vice and misery." The behavior now usually classified as deviant falls into several categories: (1) crime, including the conventional crimes against persons, property, and the state; the modern innovations of white-collar crime and traffic offenses; and some other types of lawbreaking; (2) sexual deviance, such as homosexuality, adultery, and prostitution; (3) deviant forms of consumption, especially alcoholism and drug addiction; and (4) deviant life styles, such as those of Skid Row derelicts, motorcycle gangs, professional gamblers, and high school dropouts.

Deviance is relative, of course, and behavior that violates the norms of one group may conform to the norms of another. Nevertheless, deviant behavior should not be confused with mere nonconformity. It represents a break with the values of a social system from which the deviant cannot completely escape, even when he is surrounded by a group of friends whose values are opposed to those of the larger system.

13. INTERACTION

Interaction is the process by which communicating individuals influence each other's thoughts and activities.

The essence of interaction is *reciprocal* influence. Two persons can be recognized as interacting when the activity of each is affected by the activity of the other. A process of interaction may endure for years or only a few seconds. Human beings interact mostly by means of symbols. A symbol is a sign that has a common meaning for the interacting persons. All words are symbols and so are many gestures and objects.

Interaction is one of the most important concepts in sociology; some sociologists regard it as embracing the whole subject. In practice, the study of interaction must always be approached indirectly because the process itself, involving a contact of minds and a transfer of meanings, is always partly hidden from observation.

14. ROLE

A role is the pattern of behavior expected of the incumbent of a given social position when interacting with the incumbents of other given positions.

It is obvious on reflection that the persons who do most of the expecting are the occupants of the "other positions," and that their expectations are based on two kinds of information; knowledge of the norms that govern the situation and familiarity with the actual behavior of persons in similar situations. These two sorts of information are difficult to separate either in theory or in practice because they blend into each other at every point. The norms that say how a role *should* be played are continuously modified by how it *is* played. Whenever the enactment of a role departs somewhat from expectation, the role is modified to some extent.

Roles may be complementary (as wife is to husband) or identical (as friend is to friend). Both complementary and identical roles have norms of reciprocity built into them; the proper enactment of one role requires the proper enactment of the other, and a careless or indifferent performance by one actor usually seems unfair to the other. Almost everyone has some difficulty in maintaining compatibility among the various roles he is expected to play in the different groups to which he belongs. Another sort of problem arises when the occupants of related positions, say parents and their teenage children, do not agree about their respective roles.

Although the concept of a role is based on an analogy with the stage, it should not be taken too literally. The actor on the stage is playacting, pretending to be someone he is not. The role-player in society is not concealing his real identity but realizing it. A feeling that one is playacting in a significant social role is an indication that something has gone wrong with the performance.

15. SOCIALIZATION

Socialization is the process whereby an individual qualifies to participate in the activity of a group by learning the norms and roles expected and approved by the group.

The process of socialization may be viewed as continuous, since the roles appropriate to a social position are not acquired once and for all when the position is assumed but are learned and relearned throughout the length of a career. Although socialization is usually viewed on its positive side with reference to what is learned, it always implies losses as well as gains, since entry into a new position usually coincides with the abandonment of a former position, and old activities are abandoned as new ones are learned. In order for an outsider to be transformed into a successful incumbent of a social position, capable of enacting the roles associated with it, he must acquire a new image of himself, a new set of associates, new accomplishments, and perhaps new values.

There are certain fundamental modes of socialization that appear in every society; for example, parental training, schooling, apprenticeship, trial and error, imitation, and conversion. *Anticipatory socialization* involves an individual's identification with a group to which he does not actually belong but which he would like to join.

16. CONFLICT

Conflict is a struggle over values, status, power, or scarce resources, in which the aims of the conflicting parties are not only to gain an advantage but also to subjugate their rivals.

Such struggles may take place between individuals or between groups or between individuals and groups. They figure importantly in every social system except a few small-scale utopian communities that are specifically designed to minimize conflict.

Conflict is usually, but not always, accompanied by strong feelings of hostility. Indeed, some conflicts, like beach riots, appear to spring from feelings alone and to have no tactical objectives. Some other conflicts, such as negotiations between management and labor in an industry with a long tradition of unionism, are almost devoid of rancor, and still others, like team games at their best, evoke excitement rather than hostility. The psychology of conflict is more complex than its sociology. Intergroup conflict gives rise to atrociously cruel acts—torture, mutilation, genocide—which cannot be matched by any behavior of the lower mammals and seems to be related in some way to the human monopoly of high ideals. Yet the motivation for the commission of atrocities in the name of a group's values is often difficult to analyze; acts of cruelty are as likely to be based on cool calculations of policy as on anger.

Conflict is regarded by most modern scholars as a necessary feature of social organization for two different, but related, reasons. First, the boundaries of organized groups are maintained by the natural tendency of their members to divide the world into "them" and "us." Without this spontaneous solidarity, the continued existence of most social systems would be jeopardized. Second, the frequency of conflict in modern urban societies divides their citizens along many different lines, so that one's opponents in one contest are one's allies in another, and the society as a whole is held together because no single issue can divide it cleanly in two.

The term conflict is sometimes used in quite a different sense to denote an incompatibility of values or norms that creates emotional tension for individuals. For example, role-conflict describes the predicament of an adolescent whose friends think he is grown up whereas his parents regard him as still a child. Conflict, in this sense, is a phenomenon worth studying, but it is only indirectly (though sometimes closely) related to overt conflict between persons or groups.

17. STATUS

A status is the place of a person or position in the rank order of influence in a social system.

When we say that *A* has higher status than *B*, we mean that some particular group values *A* more than *B*. This preference is usually demonstrated by giving *A* a larger share of the group's resources, more control over its activities, wider rights, and more responsible duties. There are several different kinds of status, including rank in a hierarchy, "sociometric status" in a group, social class, and prestige.

The skeleton of every organization is a hierarchy of ranked positions running from highest to lowest and including all or most members of the organization. The order of such positions is very clear, and the differences in their rights, duties, and privileges rather sharply defined. Sociometric status, or informal leadership, is a related phenomenon that develops spontaneously in unorganized groups. The evolution of a status order based on individual characteristics may be taken as inevitable when any group of equals interacts for any length of time. This tendency is not limited to humans; all of the primates and many of the lower animals develop well-marked status orders, based on such characteristics as sex, age, strength, and assertiveness. People, being more complicated than animals, have a greater number of characteristics on which status differences may be grounded, including membership in other groups, and such intangible traits as beauty, wit, and ambition.

Status was originally a legal term for a set of legal rights and obligations. Such statuses as landlord, mortgagee, guardian, testator, and trustee are still familiar to the law. Later on, the term came to be used more broadly for any type of social position, then it came to mean the ranking of a person or group on some scale of inequality.

The effect of status and status changes on individual behavior has been studied more extensively than almost any other sociological topic, and a great deal is known about it. For example, it has been discovered that the desire to avoid status loss is generally a stronger motive than the desire for status gain. There appears to be a universal preference for status equilibration, that is for the balancing of each individual's statuses in the various social systems in which he participates so that they are mutually consistent, and so that persons who are his inferiors in one system do not become his superiors in another system.

18. STRATIFICATION

Stratification is the arrangement of the members of a social system in graded strata, with varying degrees of prestige, property, influence, and other status attributes.

Most of the current theories about stratification can be traced back either to Karl Marx, who believed that the stratification of any society is almost completely determined by the ownership of the means of production,[21] or to Max Weber, who maintained that stratification rests on several separate bases such as wealth, political influence, and life style.[22] The social classes discussed by Marx in *Capital* were landowners, capitalists, laborers, peasants, and paupers. Weber did not employ such general categories but worked out a particular description of the major strata in each society he described.

One can measure stratification objectively by examining differences in income, education, occupation, consumption, and the like; or subjectively by asking people to rank themselves and others; or by a mixture of the two methods. Systems of stratification can be compared from one society to another with respect to the values on which they are based, their internal consistency, the sharpness of boundaries between strata, whether inequalities are acknowledged or concealed, and what kinds of mobility occur.

19. MOBILITY

Mobility is the movement of individuals, families, and groups from one social position to another.

Three main types of social mobility are recognized: *geographical mobility* is movement from one place to another; *horizontal mobility* is movement from one part of a social system to another; *vertical mobility* is a gain or loss of status. All three types are interesting, but sociological interest has centered on vertical mobility.

Some studies of vertical mobility compare the statuses of parents and their offspring. Others compare the successive statuses of a given individual. Still others describe changes in the status of entire groups.

The measurement of vertical mobility always turns out to be a little more complicated than it first appears. The reason is that as the position of individuals and groups changes within some system of stratification, the system may be changing too. And it is not always possible to be sure of the relative status of positions taken at different points of time. Was the status of movie stars higher or lower in the days of Rudolph Valentino than it is today?

Another problem is that for statuses to be meaningfully compared, they must belong to the same system. The town counselor from Haiti who becomes a pastry chef in a New Orleans restaurant has changed systems as well as positions, and the question whether he has been promoted or demoted is almost meaningless.

Another problem in measuring vertical mobility is how to select the reference points. For example, in comparing the occupational statuses of men with those of their fathers, quite different results will be obtained depending on whether the current occupations of the sons are compared with those held by the fathers when the sons were born, those held when the father was the same age as the son is now, or those held at the peak of the father's career.

Despite these differences, the study of vertical mobility, as expressed in individual careers or in the shifting position of groups, can often tell us more about social change than any other type of inquiry.

20. POWER

Power is the probability that an actor in a social relationship will be able to carry out his own will despite resistance.

Power that is clearly legitimate (that is, supported by norms accepted by those involved in the relationship) is often called *authority*. Power that is exercised informally and without definite mechanisms for overcoming resistance is called *influence*.

Although the power exercised by governments is the principal concern of political scientists, the phenomenon of power is by no means restricted to politics. Power relationships occur in all social systems from the family to the community of nations, and every organization has a power distribution.

There is a certain paradoxical quality about power. Some of the recurrent paradoxes are that:

1. Power is reciprocal; the master can control the slave only if he allows himself to be controlled by the slave to some extent. "There go the people," says a homily attributed to the French statesman, Ledru-Rollin, "I must run and catch up with them for I am their leader."
2. Exercising power and having power are not quite the same thing. The most effective rulers are those who do not have to demonstrate their ability to overcome the resistance of their subjects because they are never resisted.
3. Power is often an illusion but the illusion may persist indefinitely if it is not challenged. The ruler's weakness may not be perceived until some accident shows each of his subjects that he does not command the loyalty of the others.
4. Powerful persons appear to control the means of coercing others, but those means always depend upon the consent of the humble spearbearers who do the final coercing.

Until recently, many sociologists avoided the study of power relationships, either because their interests lay elsewhere or because they did not want to adopt viewpoints that could be characterized as conservative or radical. This is no longer the case. The increased difficulty of maintaining order among nations and within nations in recent years has aroused a great deal of interest in the analysis of power relationships, and in the transformation of power distributions under various conditions.[23]

Special Vocabularies in Sociology

A working knowledge of the key terms just discussed will enable the student to read perhaps 90 percent of the current sociological literature with ease, but there are, of course, a number of specialties in sociology or closely related to it that have their own technical vocabularies. For example, in the chapter on population you will read about *fertility, life expectancy,* and the *sex ratio.* Each of these is a measurement of population and is quite easy to learn and remember when encountered in context.

A number of sociologists, including some of the most influential, have found it necessary to develop an entire set of terms to fit their own ideas, a sort of private vocabulary that must be mastered by their readers.

Some of these private terms ultimately achieve general acceptance, but most of them remain as trademarks of a particular scholar, current among his own disciples and familiar to the readers of his works.

Finally, since sociology enjoys close relations with the other social sciences, or "disciplines," many of the terms belonging to those fields ultimately find their way into sociological writings. For example, when we discuss family patterns in a later chapter, we will distinguish between *consanguineal* relatives (related by common descent) and *affinal* relatives (related by marriage only). These terms are borrowed from anthropology. There are references in the same chapter to neurosis, conditioning, and other terms taken from psychology.

Interdisciplinary Relationships

Aside from problems of vocabulary, the student of sociology is sometimes puzzled to explain the relationship between sociology and anthropology, sociology and history, or sociology and social work. He may find it hard to understand whether social psychology belongs to sociology or psychology and what political sociology has to do with political science. Although the boundaries among these subjects are not fixed once and for all, they are fairly clear in actual practice and are not too hard to understand.

SOCIOLOGY AND ANTHROPOLOGY

The fundamental interests of these two disciplines are very similar, but they are quite different in personnel, vocabulary, and professional atmosphere. Social anthropologists concentrate on the study of remote, unmodernized communities; sociologists do most of their work in today's giant societies. Anthropologists like to make cultural inventories covering such matters as kinship arrangements, religious rituals, folklore, or handicrafts—the whole inventory of ideas and practices inherited from the past by remote tribes and likely to disappear as soon as they cease to be remote. Nowadays, some anthropologists apply their skills to studying the culture of urban, modernized populations; several of the most notable studies of metropolitan life have been accomplished by anthropologists like W. Lloyd Warner and Oscar Lewis. Some sociologists work in villages and even among primitive tribesmen. The two disciplines use each other's findings quite freely, although some of their special fields are very remote from each other. For example, an industrial sociologist is not likely to know much about a physical anthropologist's work with human skulls. The difference in training remains important too. The anthropologist's apprenticeship is likely to be spent in some distant corner of the globe where few strangers ever set foot. He travels to his research site by camel or canoe, and lives for long periods of time in exotic settings.

SOCIOLOGY AND HISTORY

In principle, history is the study of the particular unique events of the past, whereas sociology is concerned with the recurrent, regular, and predictable aspects of social life. In practice, good historians as far back as Herodotus have always sought for underlying regularities in the events they recorded and modern historiography (history writing) includes the search for systematic explanations. The two interests converge very nicely in historical sociology, a borderline field in which sociologists sift through documentary records and historians construct statistical tables to determine the consequences of slavery in the American South or the demographic composition of ancient Athens. The difference between them is one of fundamental intention: the historian has a primary interest in the period he studies, whereas the historical sociologist regards it more as a source of data than as an object of independent curiosity.

SOCIOLOGY AND PSYCHOLOGY

Social psychology is another borderline field, lying squarely between sociology and psychology and sometimes serving as a battleground between them. It is the only branch of the social sciences in which laboratory experimentation is the dominant (although not exclusive) method of research. Social psychology really has two barely distinguishable subject matters: the influence of group life on individual behavior and the behavior of individuals as members of groups. A very sharp eye can discern two separate fields of study here, the former staffed mostly by social psychologists trained in psychology, and the latter by social psychologists trained in sociology, but if a dividing line really exists, it is continually crossed in both directions.

SOCIOLOGY AND SOCIAL WORK

This relationship is difficult to explain and to understand. Social workers are professional people who give advice to handicapped persons and who administer the numerous public and private programs designed to alleviate such social problems as poverty, broken homes, and delinquency. Social workers like to describe what they do as applied sociology, but many sociologists do not recognize this claim. It is undeniable that social workers make use of sociological studies of the problems with which they are engaged, but it is questionable whether they are free to apply sociological principles in dealing with their clients. Only a handful of social workers are independent practitioners; the vast majority are employed by government departments such as municipal departments of welfare or by private agencies such as family welfare services. In most instances, the social worker's duties toward his clients are rather narrowly defined, and he is not free to vary his treatment of them in accordance with sociological principles. It must also be admitted that the sociological principles that would enable the social worker to cope successfully with "the multiproblem family" or "the unmotivated individual" are often lacking and cannot be easily supplied by sociologists approaching the same problems from a different direction. There has recently been a wholesome tendency toward the development of independent social work theories more directly related to the administration of welfare programs.

OTHER BORDERLINE FIELDS

It is characteristic of the social sciences, as of the physical sciences, that a borderline field develops between every two major disciplines when work is done that involves both of them. Thus *political sociology* deals with such topics as the relation between political power and class structure, *economic sociology* with such matters as differences in occupational earnings. Studies of urban minorities by anthropologists or of primitive tribes by sociologists may be described as *social anthropology. Population research* is shared between sociology and biology, and *medical sociology* covers such topics as the effect of the physician-patient relationship on the patient's health. Most of these labels describe clusters of research interests, not independent bodies of knowledge.

Specialization in Sociology

Almost every field of human activity can be considered sociologically, that is to say the relevant institutions can be analyzed, the groups and organizations surveyed, the continuities traced between collective and individual behavior. For example, the sociology of music and the sociology of secret societies have been thoroughly studied. The sociology of sociology has been the topic of several conferences, the sociology of love and the sociology of death were both fashionable areas of research a few years ago. There is an institute devoted to the study of creative altruism, another for socio-drama, and half a dozen for the sociology of language. A recent expedition to climb Mt. Everest included a sociologist who studied the effect of the high-altitude environment on the organization of the climbing party.

This diversity merely reflects the diversity of social activity. On the one hand, it enables a sociologist to study nearly anything; on the other hand, it requires him to specialize. Each chapter of this book, following this one, represents a major specialty in sociology. Each of these has its own literature and its own famous men and will be the subject of separate courses for the student who goes on to further study. The table of contents is not meant to be exhaustive, but it does include most of the major specialties, and the reader who goes carefully through this book to the end will be generally familiar with the current state of sociological knowledge.

1 Sociology is one of the social sciences. It may be studied in order to increase understanding of social institutions and relationships or to make possible the deliberate control of social change.

2 The social scientist shares some assumptions with the physical scientist. He regards the world as real and knowable, obtains information about it by empirical research, analyzes the information with as much objectivity as possible, and allows his results to be inspected and challenged by other scientists.

3 The social scientist has special problems, however, because his subjects are human. He cannot do studies that will harm or offend them, he cannot prevent the people he studies from taking a hand to change his results, and he always has trouble maintaining his own impartiality.

4 Sociology, like all scientific and scholarly fields, has evolved a special vocabulary to describe what it studies, and one must learn the key terms of this vocabulary in order to read sociological writings and understand them.

5 Sociology is closely related to such other disciplines as anthropology, history, psychology, political science, and economics, and shares a borderline field with each of them.

Questions for Discussion / CHAPTER ONE

1 Can you list six social sciences, six physical sciences, and six fields of the humanities and explain what each of them studies?

2 Why is astrology not considered to be a social science?

3 Would you feel yourself qualified to do an objective study of the values and roles within your own family? Why? Why not?

4 Review your understanding of the following terms:

social system	stratification
organization	conflict
interaction	

5 Find a concrete example, drawn from your own experience, of each of the following:

culture complex	vertical mobility

group norm
family role
latent function
hierarchy

deviant life style
attitude survey
total institution

6 The sociology of sociology has been the topic of several conferences. What might be discussed at such a conference?

Recommended Readings / **CHAPTER ONE**

Robert Bierstedt, ed. *A Design for Sociology: Scope, Objectives and Methods.* American Academy of Political and Social Science, Monograph No. 9, April 1969 Admirably summarizes the situation of sociology as a scientific discipline.

Ernest Nagel. *The Structure of Science: Problems in the Logic of Scientific Explanation.* New York: Harcourt, Brace & World, 1961. Explains why sociology is regarded as a science, and what kind of science it is.

Notes / **CHAPTER ONE**

1. George A. Lundberg, *Foundations of Sociology* (New York: Macmillan, 1939).
2. P. W. Bridgman, *The Intelligent Individual and Society* (New York: Macmillan, 1938).
3. An interesting discussion of this question is found in Robert Bierstedt, ed., *A Design for Sociology: Scope, Objectives and Methods* (American Academy of Political and Social Science, Monograph no. 9, April 1969).
4. Ernest Nagel, *The Structure of Science: Problems in the Logic of Scientific Explanation* (New York: Harcourt Brace Jovanovich, 1961), pp. 447–448.
5. Warren O. Hagstrom, "What is the Meaning of Santa Claus?" *The American Sociologist,* I, no. 5 (November 1966), 248–252. The quotation is from p. 251.
6. *Ibid.,* p. 252.
7. This phrase occurs in one of the most extreme tirades against sociological prose, that of Malcolm Cowley, "Sociological Habit Patterns in Linguistic Transmogrification," *The Reporter,* vol. 15, no. 4 (September 20, 1965), pp. 41–43. See also the chapter on "The Behavioral Sciences" in Jacques Barzun, *Science: The Glorious Entertainment* (New York: Harper & Row, 1964).
8. *Oxford Universal Dictionary,* 3d ed., 1955 printing, p. 1887.
9. Frances E. Cheek and Maureen Rosenhaupt, "Are Sociologists Incomprehensible?: An Objective Study," *American Journal of Sociology,* 73, no. 5 (March 1968), 617–627.

10. *Oxford Universal Dictionary,* p. 2037.
11. David L. Sills, ed., *International Encyclopedia of the Social Sciences* (New York: Macmillan and Free Press, 1968), for definitions of culture (vol. 3, p. 528), group (vol. 6, p. 276), interaction (vol. 7, p. 441 adapted), attitude (vol. 1, p. 450), norm (vol. 11, p. 204, adapted), role (vol. 13, p. 547, adapted), social system (vol. 14, p. 583), integration (vol. 7, p. 380), mobility (vol. 14, p. 429, power (vol. 12, p. 406, after Max Weber), conflict (vol. 3, p. 232), deviance (vol. 4, p. 148, adapted).
12. Julius Gould and William L. Kolb, eds., *A Dictionary of the Social Sciences,* compiled for UNESCO (New York: Free Press, 1964), for definitions of society (674), culture (165), institution (338, adapted), value (743, after Kluckhohn), function (278, after Radcliffe-Brown), stratification (695, adapted), and socialization (672, adapted).
13. The most forceful exponent of this position was the Polish anthropologist Bronislaw Malinowski. See especially his article, "Anthropology," *Encyclopaedia Britannica,* 13th ed., s.v. "anthropology."
14. See Robert Cooley Angell, "The Moral Integration of American Cities," *American Journal of Sociology* 57, no. 1, pt. 2 (July 1951), 1–140.
15. Émile Durkheim, *Suicide: A Study in Sociology* (New York: Free Press, 1963). Originally published as *Le Suicide* (Paris, 1897).
16. Elizabeth Bott, *Family and Social Network: Roles, Norms and External Relationships in Ordinary Urban Families* (London: Tavistock, 1957).
17. Robert Redfield, *The Folk Culture of Yucatan* (Chicago: University of Chicago Press, 1941).
18. The first point is illustrated by Oscar Lewis, *Life in a Mexican Village: Tepoztlán Restudied* (Urbana, Ill.: University of Illinois Press, 1963); the second by Herbert J. Gans, *The Urban Villagers: Group and Class in the Life of Italian Americans* (New York: Free Press, 1965).
19. Arnold W. Green, *Sociology: An Analysis of Life in Modern Society,* 3d ed. (New York: McGraw-Hill, 1960), p. 31.
20. William Graham Sumner, *Folkways: A Study of the Sociological Importance of Usages, Manners, Customs, Mores, and Morals* (Boston: Ginn, 1940).
21. Karl Marx, *Capital: A Critique of Political Economy* (New York: Modern Library, 1936).
22. Max Weber, *The Theory of Social and Economic Organization (Wirtschaft und Gesellschaft),* trans. A. M. Henderson and Talcott Parsons (New York: Free Press, 1966).
23. See, for example, Thomas C. Schelling, *The Strategy of Conflict* (Cambridge, Mass.: Harvard University Press, 1960); and Theodore Caplow, *Two Against One: Coalitions in Triads* (Englewood Cliffs, N. J.: Prentice-Hall, 1968).

LOOKING FORWARD

Here in Part One we are becoming familiar with the concepts that are used in the sociological analysis of individual and collective behavior. We have just reviewed the fundamental assumptions of sociology and a list of key terms that you must learn in order to understand sociological writings.

Next we take up the research methods that have been developed to get accurate, first-hand information about social phenomena, first reviewing the landmarks of social research in the past half-century and then going into the details of how to plan a research project, design and test appropriate instruments, gather empirical data and code, tabulate, and analyze it, and, finally, make sense out of the results. Then we will take a historical tour of social theory and observe the attempts of various scholars to grasp and explain the social universe, beginning with Aristotle and ending with men who are still alive and at work.

Part Two treats seven of the most important subdivisions of sociology, each of which you will meet later, in separate courses, if you go on with the study of sociology. These subdivisions (or substantive fields of sociology) are population, the city, stratification, work, organizations, the family, and deviance.

Part Three is about macrosociology, which literally means "big sociology" and is concerned with the study of the large issues that haunt the contemporary world: local and international conflict, the positive and negative aspects of large-scale social change, and the prospects for a social technology that might simplify the task of improving the conditions of life in modern societies.

Research Methods

Introduction

Social research is the systematic observation and recording of human behavior in social systems for the purpose of developing and testing social theories. It is the principal activity of the working sociologist, and the one to which his training is chiefly directed. Most of the higher degrees awarded in sociology are for dissertations or theses reporting the results of social research.

The unit of research is the "study" or "project"—usually conducted under the auspices of a university or a research institution, and supported by a grant of funds from a government agency, a foundation, or some other large organization. A research project normally has a fixed duration, although extensions of time are common. Its results are usually published.

The plan of a typical research project is prepared by a principal investigator who acts as the project's entrepreneur throughout its existence. In addition to specifying a field of investigation, a theoretical model, and a set of questions to be answered (or hypotheses to be tested), an adequate project plan also includes a description of the methods to be used for collecting and analyzing data, a summary of the results obtained in previous investigations of similar topics, and a statement of the relationship between the project's hypotheses and some larger body of theory, together with a budget and a time schedule.

Some projects are undertaken by a lone investigator who works all by himself. Others are of much larger scale. For example, the plan of a recent study of some social aspects of narcotics addiction called for a principal investigator, a co-investigator, a project director, three research associates, four research assistants, two coders, a field supervisor, a statistician-programmer, a librarian, a messenger, 20 interviewers, several secretaries and typists, outside consultants, and an advisory committee.

Although social research projects are launched for all sorts of reasons, the formal goal of the investigator is always to increase scientific knowledge. It is expected that he will publish his results without concealment or distortion and that he will provide enough information about his methods so that other investigators can repeat the study if they wish. Studies conducted under rules of secrecy by military or commercial organizations do not count as scientific research unless their results are ultimately published. Some projects have dual purposes, scientific and practical. For example, a project may be undertaken as part of a program of institutional reform. This is known as *action research;* it often has interesting consequences.

The project form of organization has a number of inherent disadvantages. It requires intellectual problems to be treated discontinuously, picked up at one time and abandoned later, to be taken up again under different auspices somewhere else. The choice of problems is always somewhat dependent on the availability of funds, and research effort is easily distracted from important projects that are hard to finance to trivial projects that are easy to finance. The necessity of finishing a study within a predetermined period may lead the investigator to concentrate on the more accessible surface of a problem rather than to explore it in greater depth. Finally, the project format sometimes makes it difficult for an investigator to stop if he does not obtain interesting results or to change his approach drastically after he has reached the data-gathering stage. Large-scale projects are sometimes pursued doggedly to the end by investigators who have lost interest in the problem or have no confidence in the results.

Despite all of these defects, it is difficult to devise a workable substitute for the project form of organization, and the overwhelming majority of sociological investigations continue to be cast in this mold.

QUANTIFICATION

The data gathered in a research project may be qualitative (expressed in words) or quantitative (expressed in numbers) or both. The accumulation of statistical information is always an early essential step in the study of a large social system, and many studies of small systems also employ statistical procedures. There was formerly a school of sociologists who believed that no information could be used for scientific purposes until it was expressed numerically.[1] Although this restriction now seems absurd, it is indisputable that the refinement of verbal categories into numerical measures is a major preoccupation of sociologists. Perhaps 9 out of 10 sociological studies make extensive use of quantitative data. The methods of quantification are not necessarily complex. Only a minority of investigators construct mathematical models or employ the more elaborate techniques of measuring associations between variables. There can be no question, however, of ignoring the quantitative aspects of the sociological literature. The student who wants any real acquaintance with the subject must acquire a basic knowledge of statistics and the habit of examining tables of data before accepting someone else's interpretation of them.

The Five Stages of a Research Project

Every research project, large or small, may usually be divided into five stages, with certain characteristic problems at each stage.

1. Planning the project
2. Designing procedures
3. Gathering data
4. Analyzing data
5. Reporting results

Students preparing doctoral dissertations are sometimes advised to follow an old rule of thumb that says an individual project should take 2,000 hours to complete and that these hours should be divided evenly among the five stages, allowing 400 hours for each stage.

Like most such rules, this is too simple. It is obviously impossible to fit diverse projects into so rigid a mold. But the rule reminds the inexperienced investigator that each stage of his project is equally important. The results of hasty planning or incomplete testing of procedures is to extend the time required for each of the later stages. An hour's work skipped in an early stage may lead to weeks or months of extra work at a later stage trying to patch up defective data.

First Stage / Planning the Project

The planning stage of a research project begins with a preliminary statement of the research topic and a preliminary description of the purposes of the project, followed by a thorough review of the work of previous investigators, which leads to a restatement of the problem and a refinement of the purposes. The two basic tasks of the investigator in the planning stage of a research project are (a) to formulate the problem and (b) to select the method or methods he will use for gathering data.

FORMULATING THE PROBLEM

The sociological apprentice undertaking his first independent research may discover, to his consternation, that the very first step of a research project is the hardest. In principle, he is free to pick anything out of the infinite variety of social experience and study it by any method he can manage in order to answer any question that happens to come into his mind. This boundless freedom is almost intolerable. It discourages some from ever starting.

The range of choice is much narrower for an investigator in a specialized research institute, or in a commercial research agency, but he too must decide exactly what to study and how to study it.

More research projects go astray at the beginning than at any subsequent stage. The questions asked may be too trivial to be worth answering or too broad to be answered at all. The proposed field of investigation may be badly defined or inaccessible. The method selected may be unsuitable to the problem. It is easy to waste months and years of hard work on a badly planned project before its defects are fully apparent. Hence, the formulation of the problem demands the best thought the investigator can give it and as much good advice from colleagues, from experts in the field, and even from respondents as he can possibly obtain.

The major elements in the formulation of every research problem are a field of investigation, a theoretical model, and a set of questions (or hypotheses). These elements are closely interrelated, but there are no fixed rules for assembling them. Many studies start with a generally recognized social problem. The investigator develops an interest, let us say, in the long-term rise of the divorce rate, and begins to consider what theoretical model (see below) would be appropriate for studying divorce trends. In other instances, the theoretical model comes first. The investigator wants to test a theory about interpersonal conflict and discovers that divorce is "a good area" for that purpose.

The investigator is not required to account for his selection of a particular problem or to explain the personal motives that led him to it. He may have undertaken to study the relationship between family interaction patterns and divorce because his own parents were divorced and he regards the prevention of divorce as an urgent social necessity; or because he has never known any divorced people well and is curious about them; or because he has constructed a model of organizational integration and does not have the resources to test it on large-scale organizations; or because he can obtain a grant for any project related to marriage and the family; or because he works part-time as a marriage counselor and can combine the study with his professional activity; or because he wants to try out a new method of analyzing trends; or for no discernible reason other than that the problem seems "interesting." The results of scientific research have a public, objective, and impersonal character, but the investigator's selection of a problem is an arbitrary choice, somewhat resembling courtship.

The investigator who knows what he wants to study has not formulated his problem but is ready to begin doing so. Is his field of investigation to be local, regional, national, cross-national? Limited to present time or extending over several time periods? Limited to one cultural and social type or generalized? Including what behavior? Thus, in the study of divorce, one investigator might define his field very broadly and use cross-cultural data to examine the relationship between the relative dominance and subordination of husbands and wives in 200 societies described by ethnologists, and the patterns of divorce in those same societies. Another investigator will restrict his inquiry to middle-income, white-collar, urban families having one to three children and less than 10 years of marital experience.

An equally wide choice of *theoretical models* is available. The concepts that will be used to organize information may be drawn from psychoanalysis or from organization theory; from Durkheim or Freud; from a long series of cumulative studies, or from the investigator's imagination. Whatever its origin, the theoretical model must satisfy the criteria of *relevance, completeness, range* and *usefulness.*[2]

A relevant theoretical model is one that fits the data sufficiently well for predictions generated in the model to be confirmed in the field. For example, a relevant theoretical model that explains the relationship between family interaction patterns and divorce ought to predict reasonably well which families in a field sample will be broken by divorce.

A model is complete if it provides terms for all the phenomena we want to describe, and all the concepts we need for classifying them. The model provided by interaction pattern analysis would be appropriate for the study of divorce only if it could be extended to cover long-term as well as short-term interaction, and if it made provision for the rupture of a relationship as a consequence of interaction.

The range of a model describes the number and variety of situations to which it is applicable and the scope of the general statements that the model can generate. A model that explained divorce as the outcome of quarreling and arrayed the causes of marital quarrels in rank order of disruptiveness would be very narrow. Even if valid, its range would be limited to families of a given type in a given culture at a particular time. A model based on interaction process analysis or on a theory of organizational integration would have much more range. Oddly enough, experience in sociological research does not indicate that an increase of range must always be paid for by a decrease of precision. On the contrary, widening the range of a model often increases its accuracy.

Finally, a theoretical model must be useful in at least one of two ways. *A model is scientifically useful if it enables us to make sense out of a great many facts and to generate significant new questions to guide the gathering of additional facts. It is practically useful if it suggests ways of applying sociological knowledge to the solution of social problems.*

A good theoretical model for the relationship between family interaction patterns and divorce would enable us to bring a great many facts about marriage and family life under the same umbrella, so to speak. It would also raise new questions for research; for example, whether the relationship between political interaction patterns and revolution resembles the relationship between family interaction and divorce. And it might suggest to the marriage counselor or to the legislator how divorce can be prevented.

Perhaps the most important step in formulating a research problem is the framing of questions or hypotheses. *A hypothesis is a statement of a possible relationship between elements in a system stated in a form suitable for testing by empirical research.* It is customary, although not obligatory, for research reports to include a list of the initial hypotheses on which the study was based. In the case of controlled experiments, the listing of formal hypotheses is nearly indispensable. Nevertheless, the inexperienced investigator may be fooled by the oversimplified account of a research project that begins with the statement of a major hypothesis, followed by a listing of propositions derived from the hypothesis, followed by evidence for and against each proposition. In real life, the relationship between a project and its major hypothesis is much more complicated. It is seldom possible to state a hypothesis in final testable form until a great deal of exploratory work, including pilot research, has been done. It often happens that the data do not fit the original hypothesis at all and a new hypothesis has to be worked out during the analysis of the data. Moreover, simple propositions that can be flatly proved or disproved are rare in social research, the results of which must usually be expressed as complex statements of association and interdependence.

It is often preferable to phrase one's propositions as a series of simple questions, especially in the planning stage of a project. "Simple questions" are those that can be understood by anyone interested in the problem without any special familiarity with the investigator's terms or methods. Any intelligent layman should be able to understand the simple questions that a research project undertakes to answer. If they cannot be explained to him, they should be progressively simplified until he can understand them. Inscrutable research questions are not likely to elicit important, new knowledge. It is surprisingly easy for the investigator to lose track of his purpose as he wrestles with the details of data gathering and analysis; and the failure to pose simple questions is the reason why some large-scale research projects do not produce any meaningful results.

A research question should be real, not nominal, that is, it should permit a definite answer. Instead of asking, "What is the relationship between patterns of family interaction and divorce?" we need to ask something like, "Can we detect any consistent difference between the interaction patterns of families that will eventually be broken by divorce and the interaction patterns of nondivorcing families in the same environment?" Or, "How long before an actual separation can we identify couples approaching divorce by examining their family interaction patterns?" The adequate research question can be recognized by two features. First, it calls for a definite answer. Second, the answer makes a difference; it is more than a vague claim that "insight has been increased," or that "the results point the way to further research."

SELECTING THE METHOD OF GATHERING DATA

There are only a limited number of possible ways for the sociologist to obtain information about human activity in social systems. He may observe the actors or question them or examine already existing records of their activity. If he questions them, the questions and answers may be oral or written. The wording of oral or written questions may be standardized or spontaneous; the answers may be brief or extensive, coded or uncoded. The activity may be described in its entirety, or by means of a representative sample, or by means of a typical specimen.

Social research projects obtain their information from one or more of the following sources:

1. Official statistics
2. Interviews
3. Questionnaires
4. Observation
5. Documents

6. Experimentation
7. Special devices

Analysis of the papers published in major sociological journals in the United States and Europe shows that in recent years, the great majority of research projects have obtained their data from *one* of these sources; most often interviews or questionnaires. Studies using standardized interviews or questionnaires are known as surveys, and the survey method has largely replaced direct observation as the fundamental method of gathering data. The survey method permits the mass production of data—rapidly, cheaply, and reliably—but just for that reason, it is sometimes used in place of other methods that would be more appropriate for a given research problem.

In the pages that follow, we shall briefly describe methods used to obtain data from the seven sources listed above, and try to indicate the principal advantages and disadvantages of each.

1. *OFFICIAL STATISTICS*

Modern governments and other bureaucratic organizations produce a great quantity of sociological data in the course of their normal operations. As technology advances, the scope, content, and accuracy of official records increase with no apparent limit.

The *Statistical Abstract of the United States,*[3] published annually, contains more than 1,200 tables on topics ranging from air travel to prison management, from the birth rate to veterans' affairs, from the share of national income received by the poor to the distribution of books translated from foreign languages.

The government of every other sizable country in the world, with the possible exceptions of North Vietnam and North Korea, publishes some kind of statistical yearbook containing similar kinds of information. The United Nations, other international agencies, and innumerable private institutions collect and publish comparative statistics on population, the labor force, health, occupations, trade, religion, education, literacy, communications, and many other subjects that concern the working sociologist. It is now possible to obtain up-to-date comparative figures for most of the countries of the world on such matters as the number of children in school at various ages; the per capita use of telephones, newspapers, and radios; the number of motor vehicles and the distances they travel; the average daily consumption of food calories, and of mechanical energy; and even the distribution of political liberties.[4]

An official source is not necessarily governmental. Professional baseball, for example, generates an enormous volume of official statistics, issued by a special section in the office of the National Baseball Commission. Nearly all large enterprises issue official reports containing quantitative information on operations, finances, personnel, and other aspects of their activities.

An enumeration is a count or measurement of the incidence of a specific phenomenon in a specific population at a stated time or during a stated time interval. Some enumerations, like the decennial census of the United States, are field inquiries conducted for the sole purpose of obtaining information. Other enumerations, like the annual statistics of exports and imports, are derived from administrative procedures maintained for other purposes. Still others, like crime statistics, are obtained by combining the separate enumerations of many local public bodies.

Official statistics are ordinarily printed or mimeographed and made available to interested persons. The cost of obtaining information of this type is negligible, and for that reason the sociological investigator ought to make extensive use of it, particularly at the beginning of an investigation.

For example, a study of juvenile gangs in an urban slum in a northern city might well begin with the published reports that contain detailed information about the population, housing, and labor force characteristics of each small district in the city (called a census tract) and enables it to be compared with adjacent census tracts; or with the city, state, or nation; or with itself at earlier dates.

It is often possible to go beyond the published statistics and to obtain more detailed data from the office responsible for the enumeration. For example, the Bureau of the Census is able and willing to provide the same items of information that are published for census tracts for the individual blocks *within* a census tract.

A review of the published statistics is the first step in the conduct of many inquiries, and it is often unexpectedly rewarding, since official statistics are issued in such vast quantity that they are seldom fully analyzed, and even very striking patterns and trends may go unnoticed. Many studies can be completed using these sources alone. Under those circumstances, the data-gathering stage of the investigation, ordinarily costly and arduous, is reduced to almost nothing.

The principal drawback of official statistics for sociological purposes is that they are not always designed to answer the questions posed by sociological inquiry, and it may be awkward or impossible to make the adaptation. A secondary drawback is that most collections of official statistics contain mistakes and inaccuracies, which may be particularly difficult to identify when the investigator is not in a position to review the procedures by which the data were collected and arranged. The student must remind himself continually that the official character of a figure does not guarantee its accuracy. Although a clock in the lobby of the Commerce Building in Washington ticks off a change in the population of the United States every few seconds and shows the total population at any given moment, to nine digits, the true figure may differ from that shown on the clock by as much as 5 million. In this case, the difficulty arises from the technical problem of conducting a comprehensive census in a country that lacks a civil register and does not require its citizens to carry identification papers. But official records also contain more serious flaws, including outright fabrications. With the passage of time and with an improving technology, these defects tend to disappear. The larger the quantity of statistical information that is available on a particular topic, the higher its quality is likely to be.

2. INTERVIEWS

In an interview survey, interviewers personally question a representative sample of a pre-selected population according to a pre-planned procedure in order to obtain information about the population as a whole. The persons questioned, called *respondents,* respond voluntarily to a research inquiry with the understanding that their answers will be anonymous or will have no personal consequences.

The interview is a characteristic modern form of communication and by no means restricted to social research. Interviewing is an important technique for journalists, lawyers, social workers, physicians, personnel men, and bureaucrats of every description. But these other cases are clearly distinguishable from the survey interview either because the interview has consequences for the respondent, as in applying for a job, or because participation is obligatory, as in the taking of legal testimony, or because the responses are used to describe an individual rather than a population, as when a celebrity is interviewed by reporters.

As mentioned above, the interview survey has become the leading method of sociological research. The advantages that explain its popularity appear to be as much operational as intellectual. Unlike observation, experimentation, documentary analysis, or even the use of data from official sources, the interview survey permits the investigator to delegate most of the actual labor of data-gathering to assistants, without losing control of the project design. Not only is his personal time saved in this way; by engaging more assistants and arranging a more intensive division of labor among them, the time necessary to complete a project can be reduced almost at will.

These advantages are shared, of course, by the (written) questionnaire survey, but there are two reasons why interviewing is preferred in most research projects if the available resources permit. First, the questionnaire survey usually has such a high rate of nonresponse that its sample ceases to be representative. Second, the amount of attention respondents are willing to give to a questionnaire is only a fraction of what they will accord to an interview on the same subject.

Hundreds of thousands, perhaps millions, of research interviews are conducted every year in the United States and in western Europe, and an uncounted additional number in the remoter parts of the globe. The theory and practice of research interviewing have been exhaustively studied, and the interview situation is probably as well understood as any other form of social interaction. It has been repeatedly shown that nearly everyone can be interviewed by a skillful interviewer on nearly any topic, without external incentives. A properly conducted interview is rewarding in itself; the average respondent enjoys the experience of conversing with a stranger who hangs on his every word, never hurries him, and never contradicts or disputes what he says. Long ago, Kinsey demonstrated that respectable old ladies would gladly reveal their sexual fantasies to a sympathetic interviewer. In other surveys, physicians have calmly estimated for an interviewer the number of patients they have killed by mistake and students have willingly described their cheating on examinations.

These almost magical effects require certain definite conditions in the interview situation. The interviewer must be a stranger, interested in the respondent as a member of a population and not as an individual, able to guarantee the respondent's anonymity and his own detachment. If any of these conditions is breached, the interviewer cannot expect full and truthful responses; he may not even be permitted to finish his questions. Whenever the respondent sees possible consequences for himself in answering one way or another the necessary conditions for a research interview are absent. If the respondent recognizes the interviewer as a friend, neighbor, or associate, as an organizational superior or subordinate, as one who has power over him or who must placate him, the interview will probably have little value for research purposes.

Even when conditions are favorable, certain types of information may be difficult or impossible to obtain. It is the universal experience of survey interviewers that high-status Americans will cheerfully discuss the most intimate aspects of their personal lives with an interviewer, but will balk at any question about their incomes. Since the Internal Revenue Service offers cash rewards to informers, the interviewer becomes potentially threatening whenever he poses a question whose answer might interest a tax collector.

Even under optimum conditions, the information obtained through interviewing is subject to various distortions arising out of the interaction between interviewer and respondent and affected by their social characteristics. It is a foregone conclusion that white interviewers studying interracial attitudes will obtain somewhat different responses from a given population than black interviewers; and it is likely that responses will be somewhat affected by the interviewer's race even in a study that has no ostensible connection with race relations.[5]

Interviews are used to obtain information that varies from "very hard" to "very soft." *Hard information has an objective character. It does not change from one day to the next and can be empirically verified. Soft information is subjective, changeable, and impossible to verify.* A respondent's report of his age, marital status, number of children, occupation, church membership, education, and residential history is hard information. His account of the feelings he would experience if confronted with a hypothetical situation is soft information. In general, and with numerous exceptions, the hard information obtained in research interviews is less subject to interviewer effects and other types of situational distortion. Questioning a respondent about his overt behavior usually produces harder information than questioning him about the overt behavior of others, which in turn produces harder information than questions about his attitudes and opinions.

A single interview often demands information ranging from very hard to very soft. The following questions were all asked in the same preelection poll.

Question	"Hardness" of information
Are you a registered Republican?	Very hard
For whom did you vote in the last Presidential election?	Hard
Do you intend to vote a straight party ticket in this year's election?	Soft
If Johnson were the Democratic candidate and Rockefeller the Republican candidate in this year's election, how would you vote?	Very soft

An unstructured interview has no fixed set of questions or fixed wording or order of questions. This does not mean that respondents are interrogated at random. The questioning may be centered on a particular incident or topic, or it may be based on a checklist of topics to be covered or on a list of questions that the interviewer modifies as he goes along.

The usual reason for using an unstructured interview is that the investigator does not know enough about the field of investigation to design a structured interview. A pilot study with unstructured interviews based on a checklist of significant topics is commonly undertaken in the planning stage of a large-scale interview survey. Indeed, the use of unstructured interviews for exploratory purposes is a self-evident procedure.

However, some investigators prefer unstructured to structured interviews for *any* purpose. They argue that a structured interview always distorts the thoughts and actions of the respondent by imposing the investigator's frame of reference upon them. For example, a respondent interviewed about his family relations is forced to think in terms of a category labled "family relations" although in his own daily life he may think of his relationship with his parents as entirely separate from his relationship with his wife. The structured interview often calls on the respondent to give opinions on issues he has never thought about and to express attitudes he has never bothered to formulate. Explaining his use of unstructured interviews in a study of a southern town, John Dollard wrote, "The informant was invited to talk about his life in his own way beginning where he chose and saying what he chose. It was stressed that the researcher would use this material in no way to the detriment of the informant and that communication of more than ordinary freedom would be appropriate. I explained that I would not ask set questions because I could not know in advance what questions would bring out the important information about the informant; surely that was something which only he could know, and I might spoil his chance to give an account of himself if I intruded with inappropriate questions."[6]

The unstructured interview, of course, has certain disadvantages that limit its use in large-scale research. First, the answers obtained by this method are always difficult and sometimes impossible to code; and when more than one interviewer is involved, any coding at all is open to criticism. Second, it is difficult to insure coverage of the same topics from one interview to the next unless the checklist used is so elaborate that it approaches an ordinary structured interview. Third, the interviewer's personal perspective is certain to change in the course of a series of interviews, and as he acquires increasing familiarity with the material and develops new attitudes toward it, the questions he puts will no longer be quite the same. Whenever a large number of persons of relatively homogeneous characteristics are to be studied, the structured interview, with its repetition of fixed questions within a fixed framework, is likely to be preferable. On the other hand, the unstructured interview recommends itself whenever the number of respondents is small and they occupy positions so different that it would make no sense to ask them identical questions.

3. QUESTIONNAIRES

The written questionnaire survey is generally regarded as a cheap substitute for the interview, and it is often selected by an investigator for the sole reason that he lacks the time or money or personnel to undertake interviews along the same lines. The basic difference between the two forms of inquiry is that most persons find the experience of being interviewed rather agreeable but do not like to fill out questionnaires. Consequently, a questionnaire survey must anticipate a high refusal rate, even after numerous follow-up requests to nonrespondents. A refusal rate as high as 30 or 40 percent is considered a satisfactory showing in many questionnaire surveys. The nonrespondents almost always differ significantly from the average of the sample, so their absence from the final sample implies a serious bias in the findings. To make response to a questionnaire compulsory solves this problem, but introduces many others.

A questionnaire survey must ordinarily content itself with a lower per capita yield of information than an interview survey and a much higher degree of ambiguity and nonresponse from question to question, because people are less willing to spend time on a questionnaire than in an interview. With many populations, it is not possible to obtain any satisfactory results from open questions in a questionnaire survey that require the respondent to compose his own answers. The investigator is limited to multiple-choice questions or similar devices —a limitation that restricts his perspective in many ways.

Nevertheless, under certain circumstances, questionnaires may be more productive than interviews. When respondents are personally interested in the survey and eager to assist its progress (for example, if they are members of an association engaged in self-examination as part of a major reform), the refusal rate may be low and the responses to a questionnaire may be more extensive than those that could be obtained through interviewing because the respondents are willing to take time to prepare their written statements. Surveys whose respondents are collectivities, such as the separate branches of a large enterprise, often rely on questionnaires for this reason.

The two weaknesses of the questionnaire survey, the high refusal rate and the low per capita yield, are linked in such a way that one can sometimes be overcome if the other is accepted. It is sometimes possible to design a useful mail questionnaire that requires the respondent to do no more than make two or three checkmarks on a stamped and addressed postcard. A questionnaire about the adoption of a new drug sent by mail to physicians contained only two questions:

---

1. Have you prescribed drug X _____today
_____in the past week
_____in the past month
_____more than a month ago
_____never
2. Do you intend to prescribe drug X in the future?
_____often
_____occasionally
_____perhaps
_____never

This simple inquiry, requiring only two checkmarks on the return half of the stamped and addressed postcard, drew responses from well over 90 percent of the large sample of physicians to whom it was sent. Since many characteristics of each respondent—his age, sex, specialty, rural-urban location, volume of practice, and type of practice—were known in detail and entered in advance on the coding form, the investigation produced considerable information about the prescription of the drug by different categories of physicians.

Conversely, a high yield of written information can sometimes be elicited from a few respondents if the investigator is willing to settle for refusal by a large majority. After the disorders that accompanied the Democratic National Convention in Chicago in 1968, one research institute advertised for participants in the demonstrations who had witnessed instances of police violence and were willing to prepare written reports according to a prescribed outline. This is called an *open questionnaire*. It somewhat resembles an essay examination. To produce satisfactory responses, the respondents must be literate, well-informed on the topics covered, and eager to cooperate. The open questionnaire cannot be precoded; indeed, the absence of precoding is its defining characteristic, but there is no reason why a code cannot be devised after the responses have been examined and their recurrent themes have been identified.

4. OBSERVATION

Observation is perhaps the most important method of sociological research, but it is currently somewhat neglected. There is no complete substitute for the personal involvement of the investigator in his field of investigation; no other method is so productive of new ideas. It is difficult to imagine any serious study of social behavior in which observation does not play a part. Even the most mechanized and impersonal forms of survey research are presumably based on earlier first-hand observations; otherwise the investigator would have no mental picture of what he was studying. If the preliminary observations were superficial, the introduction of sophisticated measurements in the later stages of the project is not likely to overcome the limitations of perspective introduced at the outset.

The history of social research furnishes abundant testimony about the importance of observation. Most of the landmark studies reviewed in Chapter Three relied heavily on the principal investigator's first-hand observations—including the great nineteenth century surveys, most of the ecological studies of the Chicago school, the Middletown, Tikopia, and Yankee City projects, the Hawthorne experiments, *Street Corner Society,* and the case studies of bureaucracy, for example.

In recent years, as we have said, observation has fallen into relative disfavor. Many interview and questionnaire surveys are designed without any systematic observation at all; in other projects, the observational phase is brief and casual.

The reasons for this neglect are not hard to discover. Of all methods of sociological research, observation is the most demanding. It requires a great deal of training and practice, and it places the observer under emotional and intellectual strain. The work is time-consuming and expensive, and although an assignment can be delegated or shared, the coordination of multiple observers is much more difficult than the coordination of a team of interviewers. Observation is a kind of handicraft operation compared to interview or questionnaire surveys, which have all the advantages of mass production.

It must be conceded that observation does have one serious drawback compared to more impersonal methods of sociological inquiry. No matter what the observer is observing, he must do so from a fixed position in physical and social space, with a limited field of vision. Only part of the social situation or system that he examines will be visible from his position, perhaps a very small part. The nature of the situation or system may prevent his shifting position in order to get a better view. For example, it is seldom possible for the observer of large-scale conflict to move freely from one side to the other.

The observation of a social situation or a system may be *detached* or *participant, overt* or *covert. The detached observer remains outside the situation or system he is studying; the participant observer assumes a role and engages in social activity within the situation or system he is studying. The overt observer is identified as an investigator by the persons observed; the covert observer is not.* The two classifications cross-cut each other; detached observation may be either overt or covert, as may participant observation.

The ethnologist studying a primitive people is an overt participant observer. The three social psychologists who studied a millenarian cult by pretending to join it were covert participant observers.[7] The investigator who sat at a desk facing the wall at the back of the Bank Wiring Observation Room in the Western Electric plant was an overt detached observer.[8] Henle and Hubble, who hid under beds in dormitories to record students' conversations were covert, detached observers.[9]

Detachment and participation are matters of degree. In some instances the participant observer is one of the principal actors in the situation being studied; this is characteristic of "action research" wherein the observer defines himself as a "change agent."[10] On the other hand his participation may be almost entirely passive, consisting, for example, of attendance at otherwise private meetings. The overt observer may make a public announcement of his purposes and methods; or, at the other extreme, he may go no further than letting it be known that he is engaged in some sort of study.

Although covert observation has been practiced in various forms since the beginning of the social research tradition, it is difficult to name a study in which it produced important results. The sociological problems amenable to covert observation are relatively minor. The movement of crowds, the content of telephone conversations, and the reaction of drivers to traffic signals are some of the topics that have been investigated in this way. When covert observation is directed to less public forms of social interaction, and especially when it requires the tools of espionage—concealed microphones, telescopic lenses, and the like—it begins to raise serious ethical questions.

On the other hand, overt observation always involves some elements of situational distortion attributable to the presence of the observer. As a participant, he may act in such a way as to change the outcome of a situation. As a detached observer, his mere presence can prevent the pattern of social interaction that would otherwise occur. To take an elementary example, it would not be feasible to undertake a study of lovers' conversations in parked cars by placing an observer in the back seat of each car.

Besides the observer's impact on the situation he observes, there is the problem of the situation's impact on the observer. Experienced participant observers have repeatedly testified to the difficulty of conserving one's neutrality in the midst of a friendly group. As the observer gets to know his subjects better, he engages in more interaction with them, and he would be less than human if his own ideas and sentiments were not influenced, and less than normal if his own self-image was not modified in the process. Morris S. Schwartz describes an experience of this kind, during the initial stages of his work as an overt, detached observer in a mental hospital.

During the first weeks of the project it became clear to me that I could not look upon the hospital participants as objects of investigation, a view that we are taught to strive for; that it would not suffice to identify myself only as a sociologist with a specific training and problem to investigate. Such a role delineation would ignore the importance of relating as a person to other persons rather than as an observer to objects. Thus, early in the project, I recognized that I had to relate to others in the hospital as one human being (called researcher) to another (where he was more unfortunate he was called patient; where he was less unfortunate he was called staff member). However, it took some weeks before the full impact of this recognition and its implications penetrated my everyday working relations and before I could use this insight effectively in my work. Thus the "I" that was doing the observing, encountering the other and being engaged and observed by the other was first a personal one, and only secondarily a role performer. The human person had to precede the role person before I could accept myself, or be accepted, in the role of sociologist. When I accepted the patients' (and staff's) and my own common humanity, when I felt our similarities were greater than our differences and that these similarities were more important in the human condition than were the differences, I could then confidently differentiate myself from the observed into the special role of observer-investigator.[11]

It is almost impossible for a low-status observer to obtain a comprehensive view of a stratified social system. With a few exceptions,[12] participant observers have enjoyed relatively high status within the systems they observed. The archtypical participant observer, the ethnologist who lives in a tribal village, is dangerously powerful and incalculably rich in the eyes of the local people. If he is adopted into the tribe, it will be by a high-ranking family, and the native viewpoint he acquires will be closer to that of a chief than to that of a slave or water carrier. The point need not be labored; participant observation is very susceptible to status bias.

Another problem of participant observation is more subtle but equally pervasive. As the observer takes on the behavior and attitude of his new milieu, his own frame of reference shifts and he begins to take things for granted that would have called for explanation when he was an outsider.

It sometimes happens that the observer is unable to bring his roles as a sociologist and as a participant into harmonious conjunction. Some investigations have been abandoned because the investigator could not resolve the kind of cross-pressures encountered by Schwartz in the mental hospital. In some other instances, the participant has displaced the observer. Some ethnologists have gone native. One well-known criminologist turned to a life of crime in the course of his observations and another, having voluntarily entered a penitentiary in order to study its social organization, developed so much resentment as a prisoner that he abandoned sociology and devoted the remainder of his life to campaigning for prison reform. A reverse effect occasionally transforms the observer's principal informants from normal participants to amateur sociologists.

5. DOCUMENTS

In literate societies, a great deal of information about every individual is written down from the moment of his birth. Under favorable conditions, fragments of these writings survive for many centuries. Every community, association, and corporate body produces a huge mass of documents relating to every phase of its collective activity. "For even an isolated community," the author of *Plainville, U.S.A.* remarked, "there exists so vast a body of relevant printed or other documentary material that no one could read it all in a lifetime."[13]

Documentary analysis is the special business of historians, and manuals of historiography (history writing) discuss the handling and interpretation of documents in detail.[14] The methods of historiography differ somewhat from those of sociological research, although they meet and overlap in the borderline field of *social history* or *historical sociology*.[15] As a rule, the historian tries to recreate the significant events of the past and to place them in a meaningful relation to the present, whereas the sociologist attempts to extract generalizations about social behavior from a representative sample of past events. The military historian who studies the battles of the Civil War attempts to describe a sequence of events and to weigh the evidence about disputed points. Did Longstreet doze during the Battle of Gettysburg? Who was primarily responsible for the failure of the federal forces to win a decisive victory at Antietam? The sociologist handling the same documents is likely to pursue a more abstract type of question. What was the relationship between battle casualties and morale? What were the organizational differences between the two armies? Even studies that combine both approaches, like Jones' reconstruction of the socioeconomic structure of ancient Athens,[16] will be read somewhat differently by historians and sociologists. For the historian, such a study provides background for the interpretation of individual events, like the decline of the Athenian empire. The sociologist may use the same data as evidence about a general relationship, such as that between new forms of stratification and the weakening of a traditional social order.

Types of Documents Sociologically relevant documents about the individual include letters, diaries, autobiographies, and newspaper clippings; birth, baptismal, marriage, divorce, and death certificates; school records, applications, examinations, diplomas, references, and recommendations; job applications, personnel tests, personnel files, and letters of appointment and dismissal; licenses, certificates, and permits; account books, ledgers, bank records, and tax returns; membership lists, minutes of meetings, newsletters, and speeches; medical and hospital records; wills, depositions, contracts and affidavits; legal and medical case records; military records, awards of decorations, and pensions; entries in directories, and many others.

The individual records just described are relevant, taken collectively, for the study of a *community,* together with posters, proclamations, newspapers, advertisements, circulars, ordinances, invitation lists, the programs of ceremonies, maps, censuses, tax rolls, graffiti, folklore, records of costumes and customs, popular songs, and inscriptions on monuments and tombstones.

Among the important documents to be examined in the study of *organizations* are charters, constitutions, bylaws, rules, resolutions, rosters of members and officers, tables of organization, financial records, personnel records, inventory and property lists, catalogs, contracts, and operating reports. Special types of organizations generate special types of documents. A legislature, for example, has records of the votes taken on various measures, copies of bills submitted, withdrawn, amended passed and rejected, records of the seating and expulsion of members minutes and reports of its committees, and verbatim records of its debates.

Private documents are intended to preserve information for the writer's own use, or to convey information to a small number of interested persons. Diaries, notebooks, and personal correspondence fall into this category. *Public documents are intended to be shown to the world at large.* Books, newspapers, directories, maps, and popular songs are examples.

Attested documents are documents with which special pains have been taken to guarantee the accuracy of the information recorded and to insure its preservation. Among the devices used for attestation are oaths, endorsement by witnesses, special seals and forms of signature, and entry in an official register. Deeds, wills, marriage certificates, diplomas, commissions, patents, and passports are examples of attested docuents.

A traditional way of classifying documents is as *primary* or *secondary*. A primary document contains information the writer obtained from personal experience or first-hand observation; a secondary document contains information derived from other documents. A moment's reflection will show that there is really a continuum extending all the way from the notes of a competent, well-informed observer taken in the immediate presence of a phenomenon to an account of the same phenomenon set down in another language at another time and place by an unknown author whose information passed through an unknown number of intermediaries. The most important rule of documentary analysis is to prefer primary to secondary sources whenever primary sources are available, that is, to get information about an event from records as close to the event as can be found.

Finally, documents may be written, graphic, or oral. *Written documents* consist of words and other symbols inscribed on paper or parchment or painted on wood or baked in pottery or engraved in stone. Most of the primary documents that have survived from ancient civilizations come in the more durable of these materials. One way of attesting a document among the ancient Greeks was to carve it in small letters on the stone walls of the temple enclosure at Delphi, where thousands of inscriptions still remain in a good state of preservation. Other written records have been preserved on birchbark, tombstones, coins, mummy wrappings, and tablets of baked clay.

Graphic documents contain information about social behavior and cultural pattern in pictorial form—from Neolithic cave paintings, whose bright colors were laid down about 8,000 years ago, to documentary films produced in conjunction with social research projects. The sociological analysis of graphic documents has not kept pace with the enormous expansion of graphic materials, although there have been a few tentative efforts in that direction, like Fourastié's attempt to describe past trends in the European standard of living by examining paintings of peasant life from different periods.[17] No one has yet undertaken, for example, a sociological study of the thousands of Greek vase paintings, carrying a wealth of descriptive detail, that have survived from antiquity and that modern photography makes it possible to assemble and compare. Nor has there been any serious effort to use the millions of feet of film covering violent conflicts for the sociology of conflict.

The use of the motion picture camera in sociological research has been marginal so far, although there have been a few interesting studies of expressive movements, gesture systems, and crowd patterns.[18] Until recently, sound cameras were bulky, expensive, and complicated to operate (while silent film is not very useful for the study of social interaction). The development of videotape opens vast new opportunities for social research. It permits an entire social situation, rather than its verbal component alone, to be recorded and examined repeatedly at leisure. But the forms the use of this new instrument will take are not yet clear. The tradition of the sociological documentary film, with its sentimental and hortatory style, is perhaps more a hindrance than a resource. The sociological cinematographer, like any other sociologist, will find that the quality of his results depends upon the quality of his theoretical model.

Oral documents are a new class of documents dating from the invention of the phonograph (followed by the tape recorder and the sound camera), which made it possible to preserve spoken words and other sounds indefinitely. Massive archives of recent history are now being assembled in several places under the name of *oral history.* [19] Persons who have played important historical roles or have witnessed important events record their recollections on tape, often at great length, and usually with the understanding that the material will be kept under seal for a period of years before it is made available to future scholars.

6. EXPERIMENTATION

Experimentation can be described as "observation under controlled conditions." When observation alone does not disclose the connection between one element and another, the observer resorts to manipulation, that is, he modifies some element in the field of observation and records the consequences of his action. By doing this, the observer becomes an experimenter.

In principle, an experiment involves only three steps: observation of

Figure 2-1   THE CONTROLLED EXPERIMENT

	Step 1	Step 2	Step 3	Step 4	Step 5
Experimental Group	Measurement of Entire Sample	Separation of Experimental and Control Samples	Treatment	Measurement	Estimation of Experimental Effect
Control Group			No Treatment		

an initial situation, modification of the situation by the experiment, and observation of the consequences. In practice, however, an experiment must have certain other features in order to be instructive: (a) the situation observed must be representative of a class of natural situations; (b) only one modification at a time is introduced; the introduction of several at once would make it difficult to allocate the consequences; (c) in order to be certain that the consequences observed would not have occurred in the absence of the modification introduced by the investigator, it is normal practice to divide the field of observation into two parts, as nearly identical as possible, and to introduce the modification in only one part of the field, leaving the other part as a *control.*

The successive steps of a controlled experiment are shown in Figure 2–1. First, a sample of some kind is drawn. (It may be a sample of rock, of living tissue, of experimental animals, or of social situations, depending on the field of inquiry.) The things in the sample are carefully measured and then divided into an experimental sample and a control sample, making them as nearly identical as possible. The experimental sample is then manipulated in some way by the experimenter, while the control sample is carefully left untouched. Both samples are measured again. The experimental effect is estimated from changes that have taken place in the experimental sample and have not taken place in the control sample.[20]

The controlled experiment is the classic method of research in physics and chemistry. Biology has both experimental and nonexperimental branches. Astronomy and geology are largely nonexperimental.

Experiments involving human subjects are frequently carried out in pharmacology and other medical sciences, and in several branches of psychology. Sociologists, too, have been attracted by the possibilities of experimentation ever since the days of Auguste Comte, who was in close touch with John Stuart Mill, the English philosopher who worked out the logic of the experimental method[21] in the 1840s and decided only very late and reluctantly that controlled experimentation was impracticable in the social sciences.[22]

Laboratory Experiments *A laboratory is a room or other enclosed space under the control of an investigator, containing equipment for carrying out the procedures and measurements required in a particular type of scientific research.* The laboratory environment is, by definition, artificial. It reproduces those features of the natural environment the investigator wants to take into account, while excluding other features that he considers irrelevant or distracting. He can never be sure that this process of selection has not introduced unanticipated changes in the environment, and experienced laboratory investigators in every discipline take for granted that the processes observed in the laboratory are never really identical with those that occur in a natural environment.

Most of the laboratory work on social processes falls within the domain of social psychology, a borderline field between sociology and psychology. The typical social psychological laboratory is a medium-sized room in a university building or research institute, equipped with tables, chairs, and screens that can be combined in various patterns; microphones, cameras, and other recording devices; a soundproof observation room, separated from the experimental room by a one-way mirror; and a variety of electronic devices for registering subjects' reactions.

A large proportion of social-psychological experiments use college students as subjects; they are easily accessible and likely to be intelligent and cooperative. Modern social psychology has occasionally been criticized as "the science of sophomore behavior"; the criticism is justified in some respects, but many of the investigations undertaken in the social-psychological laboratory deal with rather universal processes, like group learning or coalitions in games, and do not seem to require representative samples of the population.

Laboratory groups are usually composed of unrelated individuals. Their social relations are constructed *ad hoc* in the course of the experiment, and it depends on the skill of the experimenter to make them real rather than illusory. When differences of status or relations of solidarity are successfully established in the course of an experiment, they are likely to be rather weak replicas of the status differences or group loyalties that occur in real life. Nonetheless, the element of surprise in the laboratory situation and the concentration it demands from the subject often produce situations of surprising intensity during experimental sessions that last only an hour or two.

In a number of studies, real-life relationships have been imported into the laboratory and subjected to experimental procedures there. For example, in a famous study, Fred L. Strodtbeck selected a sample of families from different cultural backgrounds—each composed of father, mother, and adult son—and examined their modes of resolving disagreements in a laboratory experiment.[23]

It should be noted in passing that many of the experiments performed in the social-psychological laboratory do not conform precisely to the model of the controlled experiment. The most common deviation is that instead of an experimental group and a control group, as called for by the model, a social-psychological experiment is likely to have two or more experimental groups subjected to different treatments and no control group at all. The reason for this departure is simple and logical. The duration of an experimental session seldom exceeds two hours and the measurements are often a large part of the experimental procedure. Under these circumstances, the measurement of a control group before and after a nontreatment would appear futile, and the investigator finds it more meaningful to compare the differing effect of two or more treatments on two or more experimental groups.

Field Experiments   Under ideal conditions, a field experiment does not differ essentially from a laboratory experiment; in the rare instances when ideal conditions prevail, the field becomes a kind of extended laboratory. These ideal conditions are too rare, however, to have much practical importance. Usually the investigator is unable to meet the requirements (Figure 2–1) and must settle for some type of imperfect experiment (Figure 2–2).

Figure 2-2   TYPES OF IMPERFECT EXPERIMENT

a. Uncontrolled experiment

	Step 1	Step 2	Step 3	Step 4
Experimental group	Measurement	Treatment	Measurement	Estimation of experimental effect
Control sample		No control sample		

b. Cross-sectional experiment

	Step 1	Step 2	Step 3	Step 4
Experimental sample	Treatment or no treatment	Identification of experimental and control groups	Measurement	Estimation of experimental effect
Control sample			Measurement	

c. Partial experiment

	Step 1	Step 2	Step 3	Step 4	Step 5
Experimental sample	Separation of experimental and control samples	No Measurement	Treatment	Measurement	Estimation of experimental effect
Control sample		No Measurement	No Treatment	Measurement	

d. Ex post facto experiment

	Step 1	Step 2	Step 3	Step 4
Experimental sample	Treatment or	Measurement	Construction of experimental and control samples by matching cases	Estimation of experimental effect
Control sample	no treatment			

The difficulty of arranging a controlled sociological experiment under field conditions may be shown by considering what would be required to substitute a controlled field experiment for one of the nine imperfect experiments described by F. Stuart Chapin in his *Experimental Designs in Sociological Research*.[24] Let us use the example of an attempt to determine whether the rehousing of New Haven slum families in low-rent public housing reduced the incidence of juvenile delinquency among their children.

In order to set up a controlled experiment, the investigator must start with a random sample of families living in slum housing. Before any family is selected for rehousing, the investigator must enumerate all of the children in the selected families, ascertain reliably what police records they have, and obtain whatever other information about the selected families will be needed later in the experiment. At a minimum, information will be required on parental age, race, nativity, education, occupation, religious affiliation, income, marital history, and criminality, along with other factors relevant to the local situation. The next step is critical. The experimenter must be able to divide his sample into two equal groups, either by random assignment or by pairing each family in the sample with the family it most resembles and then splitting the pairs. Ideally, the two groups should be selected *before* one of them is designated as the experimental sample. The experimenter must then be able to assign every family in the experimental sample to a unit of public housing almost simultaneously and to make sure that none of the control sample families is rehoused. The experiment will be invalidated if any significant number of families refuse the offer of public housing or leave the housing project before the experiment is completed, or if their departure from the slum neighborhood changes its character substantially (for example, by reducing overcrowding) or if any substantial number of families in the control sample depart from the slum neighborhood in other directions, or if many families in either group break up, or are lost sight of, or refuse to cooperate. If many of these contingencies occur, it is nearly certain that the families lost will differ from those remaining so that their departure will have biased the sample and compromised the experiment.

Supposing these steps to be accomplished, the investigator must now wait a reasonable length of time—perhaps three years as a minimum—before observing the results of his treatment. The experimental design will be jeopardized not only by the loss of any families from either sample during this period, but also by any significant change in the environment of either group—for example, an increase in unemployment, or the construction of a new high school in the slum neighborhood. If environmental conditions remain unchanged, the investigator will still have to seek reassurance on two important points: that police practices with respect to juvenile delinquents are approximately the same in the slum neighborhood and in the housing project; and that police records are sufficiently accurate and complete so that he can obtain valid delinquency rates for both the experimental and the control samples. If this turns out to be feasible, he will be left with the further problem of determining whether a delinquency rate based on reported offenses reflects the real incidence of delinquent behavior in his two groups.

The mere recital of the necessary conditions for a controlled experiment tells us why few controlled experiments are attempted in the evaluation of social action programs[25] and why even fewer succeed. It must be pointed out that even if the investigator completes this experiment successfully and discovers a dramatic decline in delinquency among the rehoused families, that result will not demonstrate a general relationship between improved housing and reduced delinquency. The experiment would need to be repeated in many localities with populations of varying characteristics before any conclusions about the relationship of housing and delinquency could be established.

Given the difficulty or impossibility of conducting a controlled experiment in the field, it is understandable that most investigators, faced with a problem like that of determining the effect of rehousing on juvenile delinquency, will adopt some form of the imperfect experiment, which will be much cheaper and easier. The results will be admittedly uncertain, but no more so than the results of a controlled experiment contaminated in one way or another. The investigator may resort to the uncontrolled experiment by ascertaining the rate of juvenile delinquency in a population of slum families before and after their relocation in a public housing project. He can greatly shorten the time required for his study by a cross-sectional experiment (see Figure 2–2) in which he compares an experimental sample of families selected from the population in public housing units and a control sample selected from a slum neighborhood to match the experimental sample on such characteristics as race, education, income, and family size. He may undertake a partial experiment by examining the delinquency rates in an urban area before and after a slum is cleared and replaced by public housing, recognizing the fact that the "before" and "after" populations are not composed of the same families. He may undertake a more ambitious ex post facto experiment by selecting a contemporary experimental group of families in public housing, matching them with a control group of families in slum housing and examining retrospectively, as far as the records permit, the delinquency rates of each group prior to the rehousing of the experimental group.

None of these substitute methods is entirely satisfactory, but the fault is not really the investigator's. It resides in the data themselves. Sociological experimentation is always handicapped to some extent by (a) the difficulty and impropriety of manipulating human subjects; (b) the tendency of human subjects to modify any environmental stimulus by redefining its meaning; (c) the impossibility of keeping any human environment unchanged for more than a very short time.

Under the circumstances, the field experimenter in sociology deserves more praise for his intellectual courage than censure for the shortcomings of his method.

7. SPECIAL DEVICES

This last category of methods for obtaining sociological data is a grab-bag of novel and unusual devices. It includes any procedure that does *not* involve official records, interviews, questionnaires, direct observation, documentary analysis, or experimentation. Some devices register data about human behavior in nonverbal form or mechanically. They are often amusing. Francis Galton, one of the founders of modern statistics, suggested measuring interpersonal attraction in a seated group like a dinner party, by putting strain gauges on the legs of the chairs and noting how each participant shifts his weight toward or away from his neighbors.[26] The authors of *Unobtrusive Measures,*[27] a mine of information about unusual research devices, suggest that the popularity of museum exhibits with visitors of various ages might be measured by the number and height of noseprints on the specially sensitized glass of display cases. The counting of toilet room inscriptions, the content analysis of garbage cans in different sections of a city, or the use of a lie detector in the study of deviant behavior verge on frivolity, even though the investigator who uses them may be perfectly serious. They have not so far made any indispensable contribution to sociological knowledge. There are however, two types of device that have produced important results in the past and are likely to be much further developed in the future. These are: (a) staged episodes, and (b) nonverbal tests.

An example of the staged episode is Richard T. LaPiere's classic 1934 study, "Attitudes vs. Actions."[28] With a Chinese couple, he visited a large number of restaurants whose operators had previously reported by questionnaire that they would refuse to serve Chinese customers. Their actions turned out to be much less discriminatory than their attitudes. This study has been replicated frequently, usually with the same results; overt behavior toward minority groups is less hostile than the attitudes reported in surveys. To take another example, staged episodes have been used frequently in the study of rumors, both to demonstrate the distortion of information in an unstructured situation and to demonstrate the accurate transmission of information through the grapevine of a structured organization.[29]

Nonverbal tests of various kinds are used extensively by psychologists and social psychologists. Almost everyone has heard of projective tests, like the Rorschach Ink Blot Test or the Thematic Apperception Test, which require subjects to react to ambiguous nonverbal stimuli. Other tests have been devised, especially in the study of learning processes, which involve nonverbal responses to nonverbal stimuli. Although such methods are relatively rare in sociological research, they are not unknown, and are occasionally very useful.

Second Stage / Designing Procedures

Once the problem has been formulated and the method chosen, the investigator moves to the design (which includes the testing) of the research procedure to be used. During this second stage, a time schedule, a workplan, and a detailed budget for the project are prepared, and the specific instruments for collecting data are designed, tested, and repeatedly modified.

In most projects, a sampling scheme must be developed and checked for soundness and feasibility. The procedures for obtaining entrée and for gaining the cooperation of subjects are worked out, scrutinized for bias, and tested in advance, if possible.

When circumstances permit, the design stage includes a small-scale dress rehearsal of the entire project, called a *pilot study,* complete with its own data-collection and analysis stages, and a miniature final report. Under less favorable circumstances, the procedures of a project may have to be tested piecemeal, but pilot work in some form is always required. The required operations are described at length in manuals of social research methods.[30] Our discussion here will be limited to three important problems encountered at this stage of a research project: (a) the design of valid and reliable instruments (questionnaires, interview schedules, classifications, indexes, and so forth); (b) the construction of standardized scales to measure attitudes and behavior; and (c) the selection of a representative sample.

RELIABILITY AND VALIDITY

The *reliability* of an instrument is its ability to deliver an unchanged measurement when applied repeatedly to an unchanged phenomenon. Thus, a questionnaire designed to measure permanent attributes of personality is reliable if respondents answer the same way when the questionnaire is readministered at long intervals. An index that measures socioeconomic status of families by assigning weights to their material possessions is reliable if any trained observer is certain to assign about the same score to a given family as any other trained observer would. One usually determines the reliability of an instrument by correlating two or more sets of measurements of the same subjects taken at different times, or by correlating two or more measurements of the same subjects by different observers taken at the same time.

Unreliability can occur in any kind of sociological data. As previously noted, even census enumerations can be unreliable. Interviews, questionnaires, observations, experiments, and nonverbal devices each have their characteristic types of unreliability, so that regardless of the method he uses, the investigator must be constantly aware of reliability as a problem.

The *validity* of a research instrument is its ability to measure what it purports to measure. It is more difficult, both philosophically and practically, to establish validity than to establish reliability. An instrument can be reliable but invalid; in that case, it will give consistent results that do not mean what they are supposed to mean. An instrument cannot be nonvalid; if it is unreliable, it cannot measure anything adequately.

The difficulty of establishing the validity of an instrument can sometimes be bypassed by what is called an *operational definition,* that is, a definition of the thing measured in terms of the operation by which it is measured. For example, instead of asking whether a given intelligence test is a valid measure of intelligence, we can define intelligence as the score achieved on that particular test, and support the definition by pointing out that such a score will predict the future achievement of pupils in a school as well as or better than any other "so-called" intelligence test. We may even say the test measures "Stanford-Binet Intelligence," and try to avoid any reference to intelligence-in-general.

The operational definition was devised in the physical sciences, where it resolves some difficult questions of definition that appear when extremely sensitive instruments are used to measure entities that are far removed from everyday experience.[31] It is perhaps less useful in the social sciences, where the rejected nonoperational definition is likely to sneak back in disguise. No matter how hard we try to think of what the test measures as "Stanford-Binet Intelligence," we cannot quite succeed in forgetting the usual definition of intelligence as mental ability or the fact that the test was originally devised to measure intelligence as mental ability.

The sociological investigator is never very far from the issue of validity. Even the direct observation of behavior raises the issue in several different ways: "Can the behavior under study be observed from the observer's vantage point?" "Does the observer correctly interpret what he sees?" "Does the presence of the observer transform the observed behavior into something different from what it would be if unobserved?"

Validity is especially difficult to establish in attitude research when the data are drawn from paper-and-pencil tests whose relation to the respondent's actual behavior is unknown. Ideally, soft data, like expressions of attitudes, should be validated by hard data, that is, by showing a close correspondence between a given pattern of verbal expression and a matching pattern of overt activity. The experimenter can validate a scale of racial prejudice, for example, by showing that respondents who score high on the scale engage in many acts of racial discrimination, whereas those who score low engage in few or no such acts. In practice, such validation is often impossible, and perhaps for this reason, its desirability is often forgotten, so that even when the circumstances of an investigation make it feasible to validate soft data with hard data, the opportunity is often ignored.

Aside from the question of external validation, a good many structured interviews and sociometric scales exhibit problems of internal validity because they are constructed in such a way that no definite meaning can be attached to individual responses or because it is self-evident that a given response will not have the same meaning for every respondent. In one recent study, a sample of unmarried girls attending a state university were asked to respond to a standardized rating scale in order to determine whether they held traditional or modern beliefs about female personality traits.[32]

The complete scale read as follows:

1. Women are more emotional than men.
2. Men are better leaders than women.
3. Men are more aggressive than women.
4. Women are more sympathetic than men.
5. Women are more moral than men.
6. Men are better able to reason logically than women.
7. Women are more artistically inclined than men.
8. Men are more inclined toward intellectualism than women.

Although this scale looks straightforward enough, it contains numerous elements of ambiguity. First, there is no way of telling whether "women" in this context refers to all the women of the world, American women, women known to the respondent, adult women in contrast to college girls, or the college girls of the respondent's own milieu. The reader may find it instructive to answer these questions for himself, first thinking of one of these populations and then thinking of another. Second, it is not at all clear from the scale whether a respondent who agrees with the statement that women are more emotional than men is saying that all women are more emotional than all men; that most women are more emotional than most men; that typical women are more emotional than typical men; or that the average emotionality of women is higher than the average emotionality of men. Third, the key term "emotional" is itself ambiguous. Some respondents may take it to mean depth of feeling, while for others it refers to the habit of expressing feelings openly. A popular stereotype regards men as more emotional in the former sense and women in the latter. Since the questions can mean different things to different respondents, the scores obtained with this scale cannot possibly measure the single dimension they purport to measure. Nonvalidity is built into the scale.

This is not an uncommon situation and it is not always so detectable. The scores obtained from nonvalid scales often correlate quite well with the characteristics of respondents and with other pencil-and-paper measurements, both valid and nonvalid. Common sense and ordinary logic are the best remedies for problems of this kind.

SCALE CONSTRUCTION

The structured interview schedule or questionnaire is composed of questions that have been provided with precoded answers. The question with precoded answers is variously described as objective, structured, or closed. Nearly any question can be converted to this form provided that the questioner knows the general pattern of possible responses in advance and has settled on the categories of response that interest him.

For example, a closed question on education might read:

How much formal education have you had?
Please circle the last year of school you have completed:

$-8 - 9 - 10 - 11 - 12 - 13 - 14 - 15 - 16 - 16+$

Even a question that elicits highly variable responses can be expressed as a closed question.

What was your principal reason for leaving school when you did?

a. graduation
b. lacked financial resources to continue
c. dissatisfied with own progress in school
d. attracted by outside opportunity
e. other reason

A *scale* is a set of closed questions arranged to produce one or more scores based on the respondent's combined responses to all the questions in the set. A true-false test is a simple scale. Its score may be the number of right answers, the number of right answers minus the number of wrong answers, the ratio of right to wrong answers, or the ratio of right answers to the number of questions.

Some scales have been developed to describe overt activity;[33] others to describe physical characteristics of individuals[34] or configurations of cultural objects.[35]

Here, for example, is a scale to measure the amount of interaction between neighboring families, a type of overt activity:

Neighborhood Interaction Scale

Scale Value	Description
0	Do not know their names or faces.
1	Recognize them on the street, but have only a greeting acquaintance.
2	Stop and talk with them outside regularly (involving at least one adult from each family).
3	Stop and talk with them outside regularly (all adults involved).
4	Mutual aid and/or common activities (involving at least one adult from each family).
5	Mutual aid and/or common activities (involving all adults).
6	Mutual visiting and entertaining in each other's houses, including drinking and dining.[36]

But the greater number of scales used in sociological research measure *attitudes* (or opinions) rather than visible activities or things. Here, for example, is the Srole Scale of Anomie,[37] which has been used in scores of studies to describe the attitudes of respondents toward the society in which they live.

Beyond *reliability* and *validity,* a good scale should have *unidimensionality, reproducibility,* and *equal intervals.* An ordinary yardstick is

```
┌─────────────────────────────────────────────────────────────────────┐
│                          Scale of Anomie                            │
├─────────────────────────────────────────────────────────────────────┤
│   1   There's little use in writing to public officials because often they │
│       aren't really interested in the problems of the average man.  │
│   2   Nowadays a person has to live pretty much for today and let   │
│       tomorrow take care of itself.                                 │
│   3   In spite of what some people say, the lot of the average man is │
│       getting worse, not better.                                    │
│   4   It's hardly fair to bring children into the world, the way things │
│       look for the future.                                          │
│   5   These days a person doesn't really know whom he can count on.  │
└─────────────────────────────────────────────────────────────────────┘
```

a measuring tool that satisfies all these requirements. It is reliable within about a quarter inch: repeated measurement of an unchanging object, or measurements of the same object by different persons using the same yardstick will not often disagree by more than that amount. It is unquestionably valid: it does not differ by more than a small fraction of an inch from a standard yard incised on a platinum bar at the National Bureau of Standards and can be used to measure length in yards, feet and inches, which is what it purports to measure. The unidimensionality of the yardstick is obvious. The length of a straight line on a plane surface is a homogeneous variable under the conditions of ordinary experience and the reading on the yardstick is not affected by other properties of the measured object, provided, of course, that we measure a straight line on a plane surface. The intervals of the yardstick, within the limits set by the accuracy of calibration, are equal, every foot and inch being the same length as every other. Finally, the yardstick has the property of reproducibility: when an object has been measured as 15 inches long, we know that it is shorter than any greater length and longer than any lesser length.

There are three established methods for the construction of attitude scales, each identified by the name of its inventor: Thurstone, Likert, Guttman.[38] All three of the methods attempt to satisfy the criteria enumerated above, but their emphases are a little different. A Thurstone scale emphasizes equal or equal-appearing intervals. A Likert scale emphasizes unidimensionality. A Guttman scale emphasizes reproducibility.

The constructor of a Thurstone scale prepares a large number of cards, each carrying a statement (or question) that seems to be related to the attitude he wants to measure, and asks a large number of "judges" to distribute the cards into a number of piles arranged from the statement expressing the most favorable attitude to the statement expressing the least favorable attitude and corresponding to the number of intervals into which the scale is to be divided (usually 11). The dispersion (scatter) of the judges' ratings of each item is then computed and statements with a wide dispersion of ratings (signifying that the judges did not agree about the item's favorableness or unfavorableness) are discarded. The process is continued until a number of items, usually about 20, can be evenly spaced out along the continuum from "most favorable" to "least favorable."

The scale is now ready to administer. The 20 items are arranged in random order, and the respondent is asked to agree or disagree with each. The scale values of the items (the average ratings each received from the judges) with which he agrees are added together and their average becomes his score. Ideally, the respondent to a Thurstone scale will agree to only a single item, the statement which most nearly expresses his own position on the scale. In practice, almost all respondents agree to several items and if the scale values of these form a cluster, the instrument is considered valid. The Thurstone method of scale construction has fallen into partial disuse because: (a) it is extremely laborious, and (b) there is considerable doubt as to whether the equal-appearing intervals it produces can ever be treated as equal for statistical purposes.

The Likert method was designed to reduce the work required by the Thurstone method and its risk of failure. The scale constructor begins with a large pool of items. These are tried out on a large sample of respondents—not judges. The investigator decides, on the basis of his own judgment, whether agreement with each particular item is to be scored as favorable or unfavorable. Each response is then assigned a score ranging, for example, from 7 for the most favorable response to 1 for the least favorable response; and the scores of all the items are then added together to get a total score. The scores obtained by the whole sample of respondents on each separate item are then correlated with the total scores obtained by the same respondents on the aggregate of all the items in the pool. The items that correlate closely with the total score are retained; others are discarded. The resulting scale consists of questions with a high degree of mutual consistency, that is, a respondent is fairly likely to give the same or similar responses to all of the retained questions. The scale is ready for use when it has been reduced to a limited number of highly interconsistent items. The investigator computes the score of an individual to whom the scale is then administered by adding up the scale values (1 to 7) of his responses and dividing by the number of responses. The resulting average places him at some point on the original seven-point scale, ranging from most favorable to least favorable with respect to the attitude in question.

The Guttman method of scale construction is designed to obtain a reproducible scale that will also be reliable, valid, and unidimensional. It need not have equal or equal-appearing intervals. Again, the constructor starts with a pool of statements or questions and a sample of respondents on whom he tries them out. As in the Thurstone method, these items usually call for a binary response: *agree* or *disagree, yes* or *no, true* or *false*. The number of items tested may be very large or very small, but the final scale seldom contains more than eight or nine items. The object of the analysis is to arrange a series of items in such an order that a respondent who agrees with item 4 but disagrees

Figure 2-3 SCALOGRAM OF RESPONSES TO A PERFECTLY
REPRODUCIBLE SCALE

Ten Respondents Arranged by Their Responses	X — Agree O — Disagree				
	Q1	Q2	Q3	Q4	Q5
A	X	X	X	X	X
B	X	X	X	X	X
C	X	X	X	X	X
D	O	X	X	X	X
H	O	X	X	X	X
F	O	O	X	X	X
G	O	O	X	X	X
H	O	O	O	X	X
I	O	O	O	O	X
J	O	O	O	O	X

with item 5 will almost always agree with items 1, 2, and 3 and disagree with items 6, 7, and 8. The work of sorting the responses to the original items to bring out such patterns can be very tedious, but two mechanical shortcuts are available. The items can be arranged in the order of maximum reproducibility by means of a scalogram board, a special device for this purpose, or by computer procedures. A perfectly reproducible scale would produce a triangular pattern of responses like that shown in Figure 2–3.

In principle, a scale is devised with a test sample of respondents, validated with another sample, refined with additional samples; and then added to the repertory of standardized scales available for sociological research. But deviations from this procedure are very common. The same sample is often made to serve for the development, validation, and application of a scale. And it is often necessary to modify a scale developed in one project before it can appropriately be used for the somewhat different purposes of another project.

SAMPLING

Next to the design of his instruments, the principal technical problem the investigator meets in the design stage of his project is the selection of a sampling scheme. There are a few studies in which sampling is not a problem, either because a population is studied in its entirety or because only a single case is available for analysis. But the great majority of sociological projects involve the drawing of a representative sample from a larger population, and the subsequent use of that sample to obtain information about the larger population from which it was drawn. The idea of drawing a sample to represent a larger population is so commonplace in the modern world that it is difficult to realize that the procedure is comparatively recent and depends on certain mathematical discoveries made in the last century.

The cornerstone of sampling theory is the empirical observation that when repeated samples are drawn from a given population of people or things for the purpose of measuring the frequency of an attribute in that population, the frequency of the attribute in the samples will vary. These variations are called sampling errors, and they are obliging enough to follow two natural laws. First, as the size of the samples increases, the size of the sampling errors decreases in a regular and predictable way; second, if a sufficient number of samples of the same size are drawn from the same population, the sampling errors will arrange themselves according to the famous bell-shaped distribution discovered by Gauss and known as the "normal curve" (see Figure 2–4). This extraordinary fact makes it possible to calculate how far a sample of given size is likely to diverge from the population it represents (by chance alone). It tells us, in other words, how much reliance can be placed on quantitative information about a population obtained from a sample.

There are two points about sampling that often confuse even advanced students of social research. First, the accuracy with which a sample represents the population from which it is drawn depends on the size of the sample. It is not ordinarily affected by the size of the population or by the ratio of sample size to population size. A carefully drawn sample of 300 United States residents will estimate the proportion of cigarette smokers in the United States no better and no worse than a carefully drawn sample of 300 local residents will estimate the proportion of cigarette smokers in Camden, Maine.

Second, the entire theory of sampling rests on the assumption that the individuals in the sample are drawn *at random* from the larger population. Although it is permissible to split the larger population into sections for sampling purposes, it always remains essential that the individuals drawn from each section be selected at random. A nonrandom sample is no sample at all. It tells us practically nothing about the larger population from which it is drawn. It cannot be used to represent that population, since the mathematical theory that underlies the use of samples to describe larger populations is applicable only to samples that have been randomly selected.

The identifying characteristic of a random sample is that every individual in the population had an identical chance of being chosen for the sample.

A *simple random sample* can be drawn by listing and numbering all the individuals in a population and then selecting the required number of individuals for the sample by means of random numbers (from a table of random numbers). An equivalent procedure would be to write the names of every individual in the population on a small slip of paper, place all the slips in a revolving drum of the type used in lotteries, and

Figure 2-4 SOME TYPES OF DISTRIBUTION CURVES

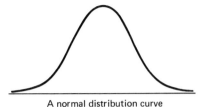

A normal distribution curve

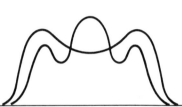

A bimodal and a trimodal distribution. A sociological example is found in the exercises.

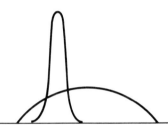

Two examples of kurtosis. *Leptokurtosis* (tall, narrow peak) and *platykurtosis* (flattened out hump, shortened tails).

A rectangular distribution. Here every class has the same frequency. An example will be found in the sampling experiments in Chapter 9.

Two skewed distributions. Most continuous distributions of interest to sociologists are more or less skewed. The curve with the hump to the left is positively skewed. The other is negatively skewed.

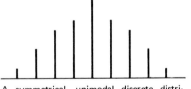

A symmetrical, unimodal discrete distribution

Source: Morris Zelditch, Jr., *A Basic Course in Sociological Statistics* (New York: Holt, Rinehart & Winston, 1959), p. 26.

take the number of slips required for the sample out of the drum one by one.

A *systematic random sample* is often a satisfactory substitute for a simple random sample. One draws it by listing all the individuals in the population alphabetically, chronologically, by location, or according to some other unitary principle, and then drawing every fifth or tenth or thousandth name. Under most circumstances, this is a very close approximation to a simple random sample, although it has certain peculiarities. For example, if we were drawing a sample of infants from a chronological file of birth certificates, we would never find a pair of twins in the sample.

To draw a *stratified random sample,* the investigator first divides into strata on the basis of some known characteristic and then takes a random sample of each stratum separately. The main purpose of this procedure is to allow the sampling ratio (the ratio of sample size to population size) to be varied so that the stratum of particular interest to the investigator can be viewed under higher magnification, so to speak. Thus, in a study of physicians' attitudes and practices regarding birth control, a stratified random sample was drawn that contained 5 percent of the Protestant and Jewish physicians in a given area and 20 percent of the Catholic physicians, the attitudes and practices of the latter being of special interest to the investigators.

It is sometimes impossible to obtain a listing of the population to be sampled, as random sampling requires. The population may be too large or too widely scattered for the investigator to enumerate. Some European countries have civil registers of the entire resident population, but these are not always available to the sociologist. The United States has no civil registers, and census records do not come in a form that would permit such a listing to be made. Many countries have neither civil registers nor adequate censuses. Other types of population are difficult or impossible to list for a variety of reasons. It would not be easy to list the total population of stamp collectors, sadists, blacks who have "passed" as whites, women who have had illegal abortions, or scientists who have just missed being awarded the Nobel prize.

The question to be asked when the total population cannot be listed is whether its subdivisions can be listed. If the answer is affirmative, and the sizes of the subdivisions are known, it may be possible to draw a reasonably good sample. Although we cannot list the population of the United States, we do have lists of the states, counties, and minor civil divisions into which the country is divided, and we know their approximate populations. A *cluster sample* is obtained through two or more successive sampling operations. A random sample of the subdivisions of a population is drawn first, then a random sample of individuals is drawn in each of the selected subdivision, and these are combined to make a sample of the total population. Thus, in surveys of public opinion in the United States, it is common practice to draw a random sample of counties first; then to draw a random sample of small areas within each county; then to enumerate all the families in each small area in order to obtain a list from which to draw a random sample of families; then randomly to select a respondent from each family. Even when the listing of the total population would not be impossible, cluster samples are often used to reduce the extraordinary trouble and expense of finding and interviewing a sample of individuals scattered over a large area.

False samples are nonrandom samples of various kinds. Among the most common are volunteer samples, quota samples, and samples with high refusal rates. A volunteer sample might consist, for example, of students in a high school selected by the principal as "typical." Quota samples are often used by careless or unskilled investigators. Each interviewer is instructed to find, for example, so many males, so many females, so many married persons, so many single persons, so many whites, and so many blacks. The selection of respondents by this system is always easy at first and becomes progressively more difficult as each category fills up and the interviewer finds himself looking for an unmarried female Negro college graduate over 60, or other persons with unusual combinations of social characteristics. What remains of a random sample after a high proportion of refusals is also considered a false sample. Those who refuse to participate in a study generally differ significantly from those who agree to participate. If enough information can be obtained about those who refuse, the remaining sample can sometimes be redefined or corrected in such a way as to make it usable, but when, as is normally the case in surveys, very little is known about those who refuse, it is impossible to consider the remaining sample as representing any known population.

The question of what minimum sample size should be set for a given study is fairly complicated, because it depends both upon the degree of accuracy sought and the distributions of the relevant measurements in the population.[39] If we want results accurate to 1 or 2 percent, the sample will have to be very much larger than if results only need to be accurate within 5 percent. If we are counting attributes present in 40 or 50 percent of the population, a modest sample (say, 200 cases) may provide an adequate estimate, but if we are studying rare attributes that appear in perhaps one out of 100 cases, an enormous sample (say, 20,000 cases) will be needed for a comparable estimate. The reader is referred to any good statistical manual for further instructions.

Small samples (under 30 cases) present special problems, and even when they are carefully drawn to be random, the estimates obtained from small samples remain doubtful. They should be avoided as far as possible in sociological research. A rule of thumb sometimes used by experienced research organizations is to set the total sample size so that the smallest subdivision of the sample about which any information will be wanted will exceed 30 cases. Another rule of thumb is to refuse to use percentages (that is, frequency per 100 cases) to describe frequencies in any subdivision having less than 100 cases. Using this rubric, the investigator determines in advance the subdivisions of his sample for which he will want percentage distribution and sets the size of the total sample large enough to be sure that each such subdivision will contain at least 100 cases.

Generally speaking, a carefully drawn sample of moderate size is always more useful than a big, careless sample. Except under special circumstances, enormous samples are not very useful in sociological

Research Methods

research. The time and effort required to obtain and tabulate 10,000 completed questionnaires would be better spent, as a rule, in minimizing the refusal rate in a carefully drawn sample of 500.

Third Stage / Collecting Data

The third stage of a research project is often the most satisfying for the investigator. As he leaves the office for the field, the difficult choices lie behind him. The problems that now present themselves are manageable, operating problems. After the long period of preparation, he has the pleasure of watching the data pile up day by day. Surrounded by the fruits of his intellectual harvest, he does not yet have to labor at processing them.

It is in this stage that irretrievable mistakes are most often made and that carelessness or inattention are likely to ruin the whole project. Throughout this stage, the investigator must maintain the cooperation of his respondents and the quality of the incoming data; he must be on the lookout for breakdowns in the sampling procedure and keep an eye on the refusal rate. In addition, he must attend to the handling, checking, and filing of data; the preservation of confidentiality; and, in a large-scale project, the continuous supervision of the staff. Just as he rehearsed and tested his data-gathering procedures during the design stage, the careful investigator will rehearse and test his analytical procedures as soon as he has enough data in hand to begin coding and tabulating.

Two major problems are encountered in the data-gathering stage of nearly every project—allowing for the investigator's role and maintaining the quality of data.

ALLOWING FOR THE INVESTIGATOR'S ROLE

"Give me a place to stand," said the Greek philosopher, Archimedes, "and I can move the world." The sociologist might almost say the same. Willy-nilly, he becomes part of the social system he wants to study; his own role in the system affects his perceptions and deforms his data. The participant observer who comes into a factory under the auspices of management will see and hear different things than the participant observer whose study is sponsored by a union. The physician who is interviewed by a young married woman from a nearby university will answer her questions in the language he reserves for his patients, many of whom are young, married, college-educated women. Interviewed by a middle-aged male Ph.D., he will answer the same questions in the language he uses with his colleagues, most of whom are middle-aged men called doctor. The institutionalized narcotics addict, asked for his life history, will probably identify the social investigator as a social worker and shape his answers accordingly. The investigator who attempts to study the system of selection whereby ladies are admitted to garden clubs, or lawyers in large firms advanced to partnership, is likely to find that he must strike a bargain with his respondents and promise them his silence on some topics in exchange for information on other topics. The ethnologist surveying an exotic community sets about making friends as the first step in gaining familiarity and local knowledge, but he cannot take on the obligations of friendship without also acquiring enemies, the old enemies of his new friends.

The taint of partisanship, the marks of identification with one viewpoint or another, the affinities and hostilities built into the investigator's situation, cannot be removed by any effort of will or dissolved in the purity of scientific motives. They need to be taken into account, recognized, stated openly, and corrected whenever possible by the juxtaposition of other perspectives. Even so neutral and seemingly impersonal a branch of research as the sociology of modernization is marked by powerful biases. Studies of modernization are invariably conducted by persons from an advanced industrial society who in effect appraise a less developed society as better or worse according to whether it resembles their own.

MAINTAINING THE QUALITY OF DATA

In sociological research, as in other occupations, there are good workmen and bad; but the quality of workmanship is not always immediately apparent in the finished product. Good workmanship in the data-gathering stage involves an unremitting search for errors of all kinds; errors of entry, enumeration, and transcription; mistaken identifications; typographical and filing errors; losses of material; cheating by interviewers and observers; false and careless responses; factual inconsistencies. Any one of these sources of error, if not attended to, can ruin a project by obscuring real relationships or by creating spurious relationships.

The careful workman verifies everything, repeats observations, and readministers questionnaires to maintain a running check on reliability; verifies field information whenever possible; and remains constantly on guard against new sources of error. He never accepts information uncritically, and all of his data are presumed guilty until proven innocent. His codes and tabulations are repeatedly inspected, and all of his statistical calculations are double- or triple-checked.

The careless worker (his number is legion) goes merrily along, secure in the knowledge that his final report will be too long and complicated to be scrutinized line by line. If his interviewers omit questions and fabricate responses, he takes care not to find them out. If respondents falsify information, so much the worse for them. If the data from two different samples seem to be contradictory, better to abandon one set of data than to waste time in tedious comparisons. When respondents refuse to be interviewed, the careless workman substitutes cases from his reserve roster and thinks no more about it. The results he obtains are likely to be either useless or misleading but, as he says in his final report, they "point the way to further research."

The two fundamental procedures of the sociological investigator for collecting data in the field are *interviewing* and *observation*. Some of the accepted practices of interviewing and observation are set out in simplified form below, to guide the student who wants to try his hand at these interesting operations. Needless to say, they are not absolute rules, and they do not apply with equal force to every type of research project.[40]

INTERVIEWING PRACTICES

There is no set duration for a research interview, but as a practical matter, a structured interview with respondents who have no special reason for wanting to participate in the study can seldom be extended much past an hour without inducing fatigue and arousing some resistance. Since the time it will take to cover a given set of questions differs from one interviewer to another and from one respondent to the next, an interview designed to allow for this normal variation cannot ordinarily average more than about 30 minutes. Excessive length is a common fault in the design of interview schedules; it encourages skipped questions, hasty and frivolous responses, and cheating by interviewers.

The amount and quality of information obtained depends upon the personal skill of the interviewer. Some interviewers elicit much better responses than others. Even in highly structured interviews, the quality of information varies for different interviewers. Moreover, in most surveys the interviewer must approach a pre-selected respondent and obtain his consent to be interviewed. The rate of refusal (by respondents) may range from 0 percent to nearly 100 percent under externally similar conditions.

The talent for interviewing seems to be partly inborn, but it can be developed by training and practice, and even persons without much natural inclination for the work can become very competent interviewers. There are numerous handbooks for the beginner,[41] and the following pointers may be helpful.

Preparation

1. Be thoroughly familiar with the objectives of the research before you go into the field.
2. Memorize the questions, their order, and all accompanying instructions, even when working with a printed interview schedule.

Approach

3. Develop a simple, standard approach to respondents by experimental approaches to similar persons outside the sample.
4. Follow the set procedure for the selection of respondents literally, carefully, and without exceptions.

5. Make a full record of every refusal, giving as much detail as possible about the circumstances.

Introduction

6. Explain the purposes of your interview briefly and politely to the respondent.
7. Make sure the respondent understands that his responses will be anonymous, confidential, or protected, as the case may be.
8. Do not begin an interview in the hearing of other persons, or when the respondent is incapacitated (for example, by intoxication or illness), or when the time available for the interview is insufficient to complete it.

Questioning

9. Ask each question clearly and slowly. Repeat rather than explain if the question is not immediately understood. Listen attentively to the response.
10. Keep your curiosity alert. Do not accept ambiguous or implausible responses without further probing. Each question should be pursued until the response makes sense to you personally.
11. Never lead the respondent by suggesting which response is expected, preferred, obvious, or easy.
12. Never force a response into a category it does not quite fit.

Note-Taking

13. Always record responses in the first person, and as nearly as possible in the respondent's words.
14. Never mingle your own impressions with the words or actions of the respondent.
15. Never report a response that was not made, even when you are quite sure it would have been.
16. Always review your notes immediately after leaving the respondent, adding additional material that is still fresh in your mind. If you discover serious omissions, inconsistencies, or illegible entries, do not hesitate to go back to the respondent again.
17. Always allow enough time between scheduled interviews so that you are not forced to skip or delay the review of your notes.

Interaction

18. Be ready to answer any reasonable question put by the respondent, but do not consent to give him your own responses to any of the interview questions.
19. Never gossip with a respondent by repeating information obtained from other respondents.

20. Confine your emotional reactions during the interview to expressions of curiosity and mild approval, as far as possible.
21. Never argue with a respondent or advise or admonish him about the behavior or attitudes he reports.
22. Do not accept responses that appear to be frivolous, incomplete, or deliberately inaccurate. The uncooperative respondent should be offered a choice between discontinuing the interview or continuing it in a responsible manner.

Termination

23. If an interview is interrupted by circumstances, try to arrange to complete it at the earliest opportunity. Do not skip questions to cover the main points.

OBSERVATIONAL PRACTICES

Pencil and paper are the principal tools of the sociological observer. His training is necessarily concentrated on the note-taking process. The observer learns first as an article of faith, later as a conclusion from his own experience, that what he sees and fails to write down will be forgotten or remembered too imperfectly to be useful for scientific purposes.

The standards for field notes are much the same in sociology as in zoology or archeology. Notes must be made as quickly after the observation as possible and they must include the journalistic essentials— who, what, when, where, why, how—together with relevant background information. The beginner is often startled to find that note-taking occupies more of his time than observation. This is as it should be. Looking and listening are only part of a work sequence whose end product is an entry in a notebook or on a card. The sociological observer must learn to notice the time of day and the persons present, the state of the weather and the temperature of a room. He must learn to look at people's hands and at their shoes, to observe gestures, watch comings and goings, and above all, to listen to what is actually said. With practice, some observers develop an almost uncanny ability to watch a number of persons simultaneously and to recall long sequences of conversation. But this takes long experience and self-discipline.

To become a good observer, one must sharpen one's eyes and ears, listen to others instead of reacting directly to them, and be constantly on guard against the daydreaming and the lapses of attention that occur so frequently in normal social interaction. The rewards, of course, are correspondingly great. The trained observer sees more and hears more than the people around him and the sensitivity he gains in the course of his work makes everyone in his field of observation more interesting.

The following pointers on sociological observation bear a family resemblance to those given above for interviewing. This is not surprising if one thinks of interviewing as a special type of observation. The differences, however, are as important as the similarities.

Approach

1. Before going into the field, the observer should be thoroughly familiar with the objectives of the research.
2. The procedures of observation and note-taking should be designed in advance and rehearsed as necessary, to make sure that it will be feasible to obtain notes of adequate quality in the field.
3. Before beginning any period of observation, the observer should memorize a checklist of the items he proposes to observe.

Procedure

4. Observations should be converted to written notes at the time they are made if circumstances permit; otherwise, as soon as possible.
5. The allowable lapse of time between observation and written entry is measured in minutes, or under unusually difficult conditions, in hours. Observations kept in the observer's head overnight should be regarded as "spoiled."
6. The division of the observer's time between observation and note-taking will be regulated by the nature of the research, but note-taking should not be scanted to permit longer periods of observation.
7. The observer should remember to include himself as a subject of observation and to note down his own overt actions during the period of observation.

Content

8. An observation note should include the date, time, and duration of the observation; the exact place (with maps, photographs, or sketches, if necessary); the nature of the occasion; the persons present and their roles; the role attributed to the observer; the furniture and equipment involved; the relevant aspects of the physical environment (temperature, lighting, noise, and so forth); and any changes in these elements that occur during the period of observation.
9. Unverifiable evaluations, inferences, and characterizations should be excluded from observation notes (see box).
10. Conversations and dialogue should be recorded in the first person, never in the third person. Even when full recording is impossible, summaries of speech should be noted down in the first person.
11. The opinions and inferences excluded from observation notes

should be written down separately in a research log or diary at regular intervals.

Follow-up

12. Observation notes should be reviewed as soon as possible so that necessary corrections and additions can be made.
13. Observation notes should be classified by some predetermined system before filing, and the classification(s) clearly marked on each note.

Wrong	Right
It appeared from his excited manner that he had participated in the riot himself.	His face was flushed and he spoke rapidly as he described the riot.
He reassured me with a friendly smile.	He looked at me and smiled.
He was dressed like a miner.	He wore blue coveralls, a brown leather jacket, and brown Army shoes.
The rioters were in an ugly mood, having lost all fear of the police.	About 10 of the rioters shouted at the police, repeating, "Cops go home" and some inaudible phrases.

Observational studies build up an incredible mass of material in a relatively short time. A participant observer who makes five pages of notebook entries every day—a very modest quota—will accumulate a thousand pages in a little over six months. Careful classification is essential in order to retain control of so much material. It is good practice to number and file field notes chronologically, and to cross-index them to a card file. In most sociological studies, the first type of cross-indexing is by name. A card is made for each person observed or discussed and every reference to him is recorded on that card by the date and number of the note in which it occurs. Additional types of cross-indexing will be required according to the nature of the study, unclassified notes being nearly useless.

Fourth Stage / Analyzing Data

In every research project there comes a moment when the investigator is no longer limited to trial runs but has accumulated enough information for full-scale analysis. The basic processes in this stage are coding, tabulation, and interpretation of findings.

Coding is the reduction of the information gathered in the field to a standardized form. It may involve the conversion of qualitative to quantitative data, as in Figure 2–5a; the sorting of qualitative data into a limited number of categories, as in Figure 2–5b; or the reduction of quantitative data to a simpler quantitative form, as in Figure 2–5c. Cod-

SELF-CODING ITEMS FROM A FACULTY QUESTIONNAIRE

A. How adequate *for your purposes* are the computer facilities available to you?

(Circle one.)

1	2	3	4	5

More than Adequate   Adequate   Very Inadequate

B. What sort of control is exercised over the content of courses?

(Circle all that apply to your department.)

The university sets guidelines	1
The department faculty sets guidelines	2
A faculty committee sets guidelines	3
Colleagues let you know what's expected	4
Everything is up to the person(s) actually teaching the course	5
Students let you know what's expected	6
Other (specify) _____	7

C. Your salary for the current academic year is:

(Circle one.)

Below $7999	1
$8,000–$10,999	2
$11,000–$13,999	3
$14,000–$16,999	4
$17,000–$19,999	5
$20,000–$24,999	6
$25,000–$29,999	7
$30,000 and over	8

Source: Questions 27, 34, and 64 from Project on University Organization, "Faculty Questionnaire," (Ithaca, N.Y.: Cornell University, n.d.).

ing, like data collection, invariably involves the twin problems of reliability and validity.

A code is invalid if it puts unlike phenomena into the same category or assigns the same values to attitudes or acts that differ significantly within the frame of reference of the project. For example, the coding of "professional age" as the number of years elapsed since the completion of professional training may be valid for male professionals, whose careers are generally continuous, but invalid for female professionals whose careers have been intermittent.

A code is unreliable if different coders do not obtain identical or

Figure 2-6	POPULATION OF THE UNITED STATES BY AGE AND SEX, 1964			
		Sex		
Age	Male	Female	Total	
Under 30	50,166,000	49,412,000	99,578,000	
Over 29	43,824,000	47,967,000	91,791,000	
Total	93,990,000	97,379,000	191,369,000	

Source: Based on Keyflitz and Flieger, *World Population* (Chicago: University of Chicago Press, 1968) p. 162, table 7.

nearly identical results when coding the same data. The criteria for a reliable code are much more rigorous than the criteria for a reliable test or questionnaire. There are many legitimate reasons why a respondent may answer the same question a little differently on different occasions and why similar individuals may not give similar responses, but there are no good excuses at all for variations in coding—either the code is defective or the coders are careless. It is standard procedure to code sociological data at least twice and to revise the code or the accompanying instructions until a very high level of reliability is achieved.

All coding involves some loss of information, and it is always a matter for concern to the careful workman to retain as much information as possible in his code and to recover the lost information by other means. For example, when questionnaires or interviews containing open questions are coded for electronic tabulation, it is often useful to reproduce the original uncoded responses to each question on a *transfer sheet,* classified by respondent characteristics, so that the thematic patterns that might be obscured by coding can be examined directly.

Tabulation is the arrangement of data according to two or more codes simultaneously. A tabulation may involve two, three, four, or more variables, but the most common and useful form is the simple *cross-tabulation* involving two variables, one independent and the other dependent; as in Figure 2–6.

The designation of independent and dependent variables is particularly crucial when a long series of tabulations is to be made. The independent variable is the one in which we are *not* interested, in other words, the variable used to group the population so that the effects of that grouping on the dependent variable can be inspected. What makes a variable independent in a particular tabulation is that we want to know what it does to the dependent variable or variables. The distinction, of course, applies only to a given tabulation. Elsewhere, in the course of the same project, we may want to tabulate the same variables the other way around.

Figure 2-7   SOME CONSEQUENCES OF THE INDEPENDENT-DEPENDENT DISTINCTION

	Independent variable	Dependent variable
For ordering tables from the tabulator	write first the independent variable	then the dependent variable.
For "running" tables	sort first on the independent variable	then on the dependent variable.
For presenting tables	put the values of the independent variable horizontally.	put the values of the dependent variable vertically.
For percentaging tables	percentage vertically, with basis in the values of the independent variable.	read off horizontally, from the values of the dependent variable.
For making diagrams	put the values of the independent variable along the horizontal axis.	put the frequency along the vertical axis, make one curve for each dependent value of any interest.

Source: Johan Galtung, *Theory and Methods of Social Research* (New York: Columbia University Press, 1967), Table 5.1.2, p. 392.

The investigator who fails to identify the independent variable in any tabulation will soon find himself hopelessly confused. The consequences of the independent-dependent distinction are neatly summarized in Figure 2–7.

Analyzing a body of data means finding answers to three separate but linked questions: (a) What relationships have been found among the variables tabulated (or among the qualitative classifications compared? (b) How much confidence can be placed in the relationships discovered, that is, how high is the probability that they did not occur by chance? (c) With how much confidence can the relationships found be projected to the population from which the sample was drawn or to other populations?

To answer the first of these questions, the investigator examines his tabulations, looks for patterns, recodes, rearranges, retabulates, shifts and shuffles his data until, so far as he can tell, all of their important interrelationships have been exposed. In this process, he uses his eyes, his native intelligence, his knowledge of the empirical field, his recollection of other studies, and a battery of statistical devices that measure the association and interdependence of his variables. These range from simple four-cell tables sketched in pencil at the bottom of a tabulation to complicated programs of factor analysis that can be performed only on a late-model computer.

The second question can sometimes be answered by common sense if the relationships between variables are unusually strong or if they have an all-or-nothing character. But in most cases, a statistical measure of significance is required. Measures of significance come in various forms, some simple and some relatively complex. Selecting the appropriate measure for a particular statistical situation may itself be a challenging problem, but all such measures do essentially the same job. They provide a numerical value of the probability that a given relationship between variables could (or could not) have occurred by chance, that is, without any cause and effect connection between the variables. A relationship is described as "significant at the 1 percent level" if the computed probability of its occurring by chance alone is less than 1 percent, or "significant at the 5 percent level," if that probability is less than 5 percent. Acceptable levels of significance vary from one area of social research to another. In the study of modernization, for example, relationships between variables are often significant at the .001 percent level, but an investigator examining the causes of juvenile delinquency may be happy to turn up a relationship significant at the 10 percent level. In most areas it is reasonable and prudent to require that relationships be significant at the 1 percent level to be taken seriously.

A common fault in data analysis is embodied in such statements as "The relationships between variable A and variables 1, 2, 3, and 4, respectively, although not individually significant, are consistent and in the same direction and may therefore be taken as confirming the hypothesis that changes in variables 1, 2, 3, and 4 are attributable to changes in variable A." Such a statement is nonsense. One cannot evade a test of statistical significance by combining nonsignificant findings in this fashion, and a genuine examination of such consistent patterns by multiple correlation or factor analysis usually shows the investigator's optimism to be unfounded.

The third question, whether the relationships found can be projected from the sample to other populations, cannot be answered without taking into account the results obtained by previous studies and without a retrospective appraisal of the entire research process with special emphasis on sampling flaws, refusal rates, internal inconsistencies, and other sources of bias. These suggest caution in projecting the findings to other populations or warn us that they should not be projected at all. At this point in the project, the need for further research is likely to be real, and deeply felt.

QUANTITATIVE ANALYSIS OF NONQUANTITATIVE MATERIALS

A quantitative analysis of nonquantitative materials is an analysis that permits the investigator to extract statistics describing behavior in a social situation or system from nonquantitative materials such as unstructured interviews, open questionnaires, observational notes, or archival records. The usual requirements of reliability, validity, and representative sampling apply to these as much as to any other statistical data. Reliability becomes particularly important if, as often happens, the materials analyzed are relatively difficult to find or to decipher, so the investigator has a special responsibility to make sure that the procedures for extracting numerical data are reliable.

One form of quantitative documentary analysis deserves special mention. *Content analysis is the analysis of themes in written or spoken communications.* Its principal inventor was Harold D. Lasswell, a political scientist whose interests included psychoanalysis and political sociology. During World War II, Lasswell and his associates used content analysis to study enemy propaganda. Essentially, the procedure consisted of breaking down a piece of political literature into its component statements and counting the appearances of certain themes that were regularly found. The frequencies of such themes in a piece of suspected propaganda could be compared with the frequencies of the same theme in publications known to be pro-Axis.[42]

Content analysis has also been used to study religious literature, popular culture, the thematic content of suicide notes, and the authorship of the Federalist Papers,[43] among many other fascinating topics. Data collection is easy and inexpensive. The data can be analyzed repeatedly, if necessary, to improve the reliability and validity of the results. The most serious problem is how to disassemble the text of a document into component units that can be counted. Most investigators use the "statement" as a unit; but "bits of information," words, sentences, and even entire works have been counted as units. Some minor problems arise from incomplete sampling, difficulties of translation, and different literary styles, but these are more easily overcome.

Content analysis can also be used to quantify information obtained from open questionnaires and unstructured interviews. It is often more effective in revealing the ideas and images held by a population than are standardized scales based on the ideas and images of the investigator.

Under certain conditions, the results obtained by content analysis may be highly objective; when, as in propaganda analysis, the model to which a text is to be compared is known in advance, the number of themes is limited, and the style of writing makes it easy to divide the text into units. When none of these conditions is met, for example, in the predictions of scientists about future scientific discoveries, a content analysis may appear subjective and arbitrary. Nevertheless, such an analysis usually provides much more information than will be obtained by a reader who attempts to summarize the same material without the formalities of classification and counting.

QUALITATIVE ANALYSIS

In an analysis of this kind, both the raw data and the results of analysis are expressed in nonquantitative form, although rough quantification may be implied by such statements as "Most of the documents mention X"; "Y is almost never found"; "Z is very frequent." An investigator may choose to analyze a collection of materials qualitatively because he knows that they are a nonrandom and possibly nonrepresentative sample of some larger group of materials he cannot obtain, or because he is looking for invariable elements or patterns of elements, or because the relationships he wishes to study are too complex to reduce to numerical form, or because he regards his qualitative evidence as sufficiently persuasive by itself.

Even the "anecdotal method" (citing a series of anecdotes from unrelated documents) can sometimes be justified. It has been used, for example, to show that famine was a familiar event in seventeenth-century Europe, and that birth control was practiced in ancient Rome.[44]

In some studies, the refusal to use numbers has a numerical aspect. By analyzing a large number of diverse documents and showing how certain elements recur continually, the investigator establishes the high incidence of these elements without ever counting them. This was the method used with great success by Thomas and Znaniecki in *The Polish Peasant*.[45] They showed how the key phenomena of individual and social disorganization could be identified in different sorts of documents—letters, newspaper stories, court records—and in a great number of individual cases.

Fifth Stage / Reporting Results

There is no sharp break between the analysis of data and the reporting of results. In any well-managed project, the investigator will find it necessary, while writing his report, to engage in further analysis of the data from time to time. But for convenience, the final stage of a research project may be said to begin at the same time as the preparation of the research report. In most sociological projects, this is a fairly lengthy document, containing both textual material and statistical tables, together with a summary of previous research, a restatement of the problem, a clear account of the procedures followed in data-gathering and analysis, a full presentation of findings, and a summary and interpretation of them. It is customary to include questionnaires, interview schedules, rating scales, and other source material necessary for a full understanding of the results in the report, or in an appendix.

To satisfy these requirements, the research report often must be a very long document that makes dull reading. It is customary to prepare an abridged report suitable for public consumption as a brief paper or journal article. The reduction of a 400- or 500-page report to a journal article of 10 pages or less requires such drastic condensation that the resulting reports are often difficult to understand and impossible to evaluate without further information. Yet this is the only form in which the results of the average project can expect to reach a large audience.

Figure 2-8 SPECIFICATIONS FOR SOCIOLOGICAL REPORT RATING

	Defective	Substandard	Superior
Statement of problem:			
1. Clarity of statement	Statement is ambiguous, unclear, biased, inconsistent, or irrelevant to the research.	Problem must be inferred from incomplete or unclear statement.	Statement is unambiguous and includes precise description of research objectives.	Statement is unambiguous and includes formal propositions, and specifications for testing them.
2. Significance of problem	No problem stated, or problem is meaningless, unsolvable, or trivial.	Solution of the problem would be of interest to a few specialists.	Solution of the problem would be of interest to many sociologists.	Solution of the problem would be of interest to most sociologists.
3. Documentation	No documentation to earlier work, or documentation is incorrect.	Documentation to earlier work is incomplete or contains errors of citation or interpretation.	Documentation to earlier work is reasonably complete.	Documentation shows in detail the evolution of the research problem from previous research findings.
Description of method:			
4. Appropriateness of method	Problem can not be solved by this method.	Only a partial or tentative solution can be obtained by this method.	Solution of the problem by this method is possible, but uncertain.	Problem is definitely solvable by this method.
5. Adequacy of sample or field	Sample is too small, or not suitable, or biased, or of unknown sampling characteristics.	The cases studied are meaningful, but findings can not be projected.	Findings are projectable, but with errors of considerable, or of unknown, magnitude.	Results are projectable with known small errors, or the entire universe has been enumerated.
6. Replicability	Not replicable.	Replicable in substance, but not in detail.	Replicable in detail with additional information from the author(s).	Replicable in detail from the information given.
Presentation of results:			
7. Completeness	Relevant results are suppressed or omitted.	Relevant results are presented in summary form.	Relevant results are presented, partly in detail, partly in summary form.	Relevant results are presented in detail.
8. Comprehensibility	Results are incomprehensible, or enigmatic.	Comprehension of results requires special knowledge or skills.	Close study is required for comprehension.	Results are fully understandable at first careful reading by average professional reader.
9. Yield	No contribution to solution of problem.	Useful hints or suggestions towards solution of problem.	Tentative solution of problem.	Definitive solution of problem.
Interpretation:			
10. Accuracy	Errors of calculation, transcription, dictation, logic or fact detected.	Errors likely with the procedures used. No major errors detected.	Errors unlikely with the procedures used. No errors detected.	Positive checks of accuracy included in the procedures.
11. Bias	Evident bias in presentation of results and in interpretation.	Some bias in interpretation, but not in presentation of results.	No evidence of bias.	Positive precautions against bias included in procedures.
12. Usefulness	Not useful.	Possible influence on some future work in this area.	Probable influence on some future work in this area.	Probable influence on all future work in this area.

Source: E. William Noland et al., "Proceedings of the 53d Annual Meeting. American Sociological Society: Report of the Committee on Research," *American Sociological Review* 23, 6 (December 1958). p. 706.

Recognizing that many research reports are seriously defective in one way or another, the Research Committee of the American Sociological Association developed some years ago the set of specifications[46] for sociological report rating reproduced in Figure 2–8. It deserves careful study by anyone who has to prepare such a report.

HOW TO PRESERVE INTELLIGIBILITY

Most projects in the final stage, it has been said, need the help of an intelligent 12-year-old, without special training in sociology, to whom each section of the research report is read as soon as it is drafted. If there is any section he cannot understand, it ought to be revised until it becomes intelligible to him. Many of the ultimate readers of the report, although better educated in sociology, will be less willing to puzzle out difficult material than our young collaborator. The text of a report should be complete in itself—since many readers never examine statistical tables in detail. The tables of a report also should be complete in themselves; otherwise, no reader will be able to appraise the investigator's interpretation of his findings.

The investigator's narrative of his research experience should be a full and true account of what he did and how and why he did it. The practice of tidying up the history of a project so that, for example, the original hypotheses are revised retrospectively to match the findings, is as deplorable as the falsification of data.

Finally, the investigator has an obligation to preserve the continuity of his science by making it possible for an interested reader to check his analysis and to replicate his field work. Every research report, however condensed, should inform the reader where the original forms and procedures can be found and where the raw data have been filed. The last, indispensable step in the final stage of a sociological research project is the orderly arrangement of the files and their disposition in a dry, safe place where they can lie undisturbed indefinitely, to be available if they are needed again.

1   The unit of social research is the *project,* undertaken to increase scientific knowledge of some social phenomenon. The work of a project may be divided into five stages: planning the project, designing procedures, gathering the data, analyzing the data, reporting the results.

2   Sociological data may be obtained from the following sources: official statistics, interviews, questionnaires, direct observation, documents, experiments, and special devices.

3   In formulating a research problem, the investigator first develops a theoretical model to describe the situation he wants to study. The model is used to frame hypotheses that can be tested empirically. These, in turn, largely determine the choice of data-gathering methods.

4   In designing procedures, particular attention must be given to the reliability and validity of instruments, and to sampling. Reliable instruments give consistent measurements. Valid instruments measure what they are intended to measure. Representative sampling requires that all the cases included in a sample be selected from the original population by a random procedure.

5   In the data–collection stage of a project, elaborate precautions are taken to insure that the information obtained is complete and correct, is recorded accurately, and is not distorted either by the investigator's biases or the subject's reaction to being studied.

6   In the data analysis stage of a project, the information obtained from the field is coded and tabulated, and the patterns of association that then appear are examined in relation to the theoretical model with which the research began.

7   In the reporting stage of a project, the conflicting requirements that the project report be comprehensive and that it be readily intelligible are usually met by the preparation of a complete report for fellow specialists, and a brief summary of results for a wider audience.

Questions for Discussion / CHAPTER TWO

1   Suppose you are interested in studying the relationship between racial segregation and academic performance in elementary schools. What might be a suitable theoretical model?

2 Using your answer to the previous question, state two hypotheses (or research questions) suggested by your model.

3 Using your answer to the previous question, indicate the method you would use to test these hypotheses, and explain why.

4 "Long ago, Kinsey demonstrated that respectable old ladies would gladly reveal their sexual fantasies to a sympathetic interviewer." How do you account for this? What if they had been asked to fill out and mail in a questionnaire on the same topic?

5 You have an assignment to observe how the local police handle arrests for drunkenness. Which method of observation would be most suitable? How would you go about obtaining access to the situation?

6 Make a list of all the attested documents you can think of in which your own name appears.

7 A new law permitting physicians to perform abortions at the patient's request is described in the newspapers as a "social experiment." What type of experiment would this be? Can you diagram its steps?

8 Is the suicide rate a valid measure of the amount of unhappiness in a given population? Is it a reliable measure? Explain.

9 Could a representative sample of the living alumni of your college be obtained by taking from the files the names of all alumni beginning with the letter M?

10 Review your understanding of each of the following items:

> operational definition
> content analysis
> independent variable
> random sample
> attitude scale

Recommended Reading / **CHAPTER TWO**

Theodore R. Anderson and Morris Zelditch, Jr. *A Basic Course in Statistics: With Sociological Applications,* 2d ed. New York: Holt, Rinehart & Winston, 1968; Robert S. Weiss. *Statistics in Social Research: An Introduction.* New York: John Wiley, 1968. Two manuals that explain statistical methods in a sophisticated way with a minimum of mathematical apparatus.

Bernard Berelson and Gary A. Steiner. *Human Behavior: An Inventory of Scientific Findings.* New York: Harcourt, Brace & World, 1964, abridged paperback, 1969. The best available inventory of accumulated research findings in sociology and related fields.

Arthur J. Vidich, Joseph Bensman, and Maurice R. Stein, eds. *Reflections on Community Studies.* New York: John Wiley, 1964. Describes the techniques and problems of sociological observation and the personal experiences of research sociologists in the field.

Stephen A. Richardson, Barbara Snell Dohrenwend, and David Klein. *Interviewing: Its Forms and Functions* New York: Basic Books, 1965; Raymond L. Gordon. *Interviewing: Strategy, Techniques and Tactics.* Homewood, Ill.: Dorsey, 1969. Two manuals of research interviewing that are suitable for beginners.

Harold Garfinkel. *Studies in Ethnomethodology.* Englewood Cliffs, N.J.: Prentice-Hall, 1967. Introduces a new way of studying social interaction.

A. H. M. Jones. *Athenian Democracy.* Oxford: Basil Blackwell, 1966. A superb example of the use of historical documents for sociological purposes.

Charles M. Bonjean, Richard J. Hill, and S. Dale McLemore. *Sociological Measurement: An Inventory of Scales and Indices.* San Francisco: Chandler, 1967. Lists and classifies the scales and indices referred to in American research reports from 1954 to 1965.

Notes / CHAPTER TWO

1. George A. Lundberg, *Foundations of Sociology* (New York: Macmillan, 1939).
2. For a more detailed set of criteria for theories, see Johan Galtung, *Theory and Methods of Social Research* (New York: Columbia University Press, 1967), pp. 458–465. The relationship of theoretical models to research results is clearly explained by Robert Dubin, *Theory Building* (New York: Free Press, 1969).
3. U.S. Department of Commerce, Bureau of the Census, *Statistical Abstract of the United States* (Washington, D. C.: Government Printing Office, published annually).
4. See, for example, United Nations Statistical Office, Department of Economic and Social Affairs, *United Nations Statistical Yearbook,* published annually; and *United Nations Demographic Yearbook,* also published annually. Among the best of the unofficial collections of official statistics is Bruce M. Russett et al., *World Handbook of Political and Social Indicators* (New Haven: Yale University Press, 1964).
5. A thorough discussion of interviewer effects and of methods for minimizing them will be found in Herbert H. Hyman et al., *Inter-*

viewing in Social Research (Chicago: University of Chicago Press, 1954).

6. John Dollard, *Caste and Class in a Southern Town,* 2d ed. (New York: Harper & Row, 1949), p. 25.

7. Leon Festinger, Henry W. Riecken, and Stanley Schachter, *When Prophecy Fails* (Minneapolis: University of Minnesota Press, 1956).

8. F. J. Roethlisberger and William J. Dickson (with Harold A. Wright), *Management and the Worker* (Cambridge, Mass.: Harvard University Press, 1939).

9. M. Henle and M. B. Hubble, "'Egocentricity' in Adult Conversation," *Journal of Social Psychology,* 9 (1938): 227–234.

10. A classic report of action research is Elliott Jaques, *The Changing Culture of a Factory* (New York: Dryden Press, 1952).

11. Morris S. Schwartz, "The Mental Hospital: The Research Person in the Disturbed Ward," pp. 85–117, in *Reflections on Community Studies,* ed. Arthur J. Vidich, Joseph Bensman and Maurice R. Stein (New York: John Wiley, 1964). This volume is an outstanding source of information about the personal experience of sociological observers.

12. The study of homeless men has been an exception, perhaps because their status order is so amorphous. For reports of low-status participant observation on Skid Row, see Nels Anderson, *The Hobo: The Sociology of the Homeless Man* (Chicago: University of Chicago Press, 1923); Thomas Minehan, *Boy and Girl Tramps of America* (New York: Crosset Publishing Co., 1934); Theodore Caplow, "Transiency as a Cultural Pattern," *American Sociological Review,* 5, no. 5 (October 1940): 731–739; Theodore Caplow, Keith A. Lovald, and Samuel E. Wallace, *A General Report on the Problem of Relocating the Population of the Lower Loop Redevelopment Area* (Minneapolis: Minneapolis Housing and Development Authority, 1958); Samuel E. Wallace, *Skid Row as a Way of Life* (Totowa, N. J.: Bedminster Press, 1965).

13. James West (pseudonym of Carl Withers), *Plainville, U.S.A.* (New York: Columbia University Press, 1945), p. xiv.

14. One such manual by the French historians Langlois and Seignobos had a considerable influence on the development of empirical sociological research in the United States. It was used in the early 1900s by Franklin H. Giddings of Columbia as a textbook for the teaching of research methods. Two of the students exposed to this instruction, William F. Ogburn and F. Stuart Chapin, went on to found schools of sociological research based on the doctrine that objectivity in the description of human behavior is possible and highly desirable. Charles V. Langlois and Charles Seignobos, *Introduction to the Study of History,* trans. G. G. Berry (New York: Barnes and Noble, 1966). Originally published 1898.

15. An admirable collection of studies in this borderline field will be found in Werner J. Cahnman and Alvin Boskoff, eds., *Sociology and History: Theory and Research* (New York: Free Press, 1964).

16. A. H. M. Jones, *Athenian Democracy* (Oxford: Blackwell, 1966).
17. Jean Fourastié, *The Causes of Wealth* (New York: Free Press, 1960), pp. 64–65.
18. For example, Jurgen Ruesch and Weldon Kees, *Nonverbal Communication: Notes on the Visual Perception of Human Relations* (Berkeley: University of California Press, 1956). Other Photographic studies are cited by Ray L. Birdwhistell, "The Kinesic Level in the Investigation of Emotions," in Peter H. Knapp, *Expression of the Emotions in Man* (New York: International Universities Press, 1963). pp. 123–139.
19. A full account of this movement may be found in Louis Starr, *Oral History: The First Twenty Years* (New York: Columbia University, Oral History Research Office Annual Report, 1968).
20. For the authoritative discussion of such procedures and other aspects of experimental design, see Sir Ronald Aylmer Fisher, *The Design of Experiments,* 8th ed. (Edinburgh: Oliver and Boyd, 1966). For more detailed instructions, see Donald T. Campbell and Julian C. Stanley, *Experimental and Quasi-Experimental Designs for Research* (Skokie, Ill. Rand McNally, 1966).
21. John Stuart Mill, *A System of Logic, Ratiocinative and Inductive: Being a Connected View of the Principles of Evidence and the Methods of Scientific Investigation* (London: Longmans, Green, 1961). Originally published 1879.
22. The term "social experiment" may be casually applied to any institutional innovation or indeed to any program of action whose outcome is in doubt. For example, such utopian communities as New Harmony, Aurora, and Oneida—founded on various principles in nineteenth-century America—were described as experiments; or, take a more recent example, the various rearrangements of school districts that have been worked out in large cities in the hope of reducing racial segregation are often described as experiments. Such innovations are always interesting and often instructive, but they have only a remote connection with controlled experiments. A good historical account of sociological experimentation can be found in Ernest Greenwood, *Experimental Sociology: A Study in Method* (New York: King's Crown Press, 1945).
23. Fred L. Strodtbeck, "The Family as a Three-Person Group," *American Sociological Review* 19, no. 1 (February 1954): 23–29; a similar experiment is reported by John F. O'Rourke, "Field and Laboratory: The Decision-Making Behavior of Family Groups in Two Experimental Conditions," *Sociometry* 26, no. 4 (December 1963): 422–435.
24. F. Stuart Chapin, *Experimental Designs in Sociological Research* (New York: Harper & Row, 1947).
25. In a book on methods of research for evaluating public service and social action programs, Suchman gives less than two pages to the evaluative experiment. Edward A. Suchman, *Evaluative Research: Principles and Practice in Public Service and Social Action Programs* (New York: Russell Sage Foundation, 1967).

26. Francis Galton, "Measurement of Character," *Fortnightly Review,* n.s. 36 (1884): 179–185.

27. Eugene J. Webb et al., *Unobtrusive Measures: Nonreactive Research in the Social Sciences* (Skokie, Ill.: Rand McNally, 1966).

28. Richard T. LaPiere, "Attitudes vs. Actions," *Social Forces* 13, no. 2 (December 1934): 230–237. A later study demonstrating the same point is B. Kutner, Carol Wilkins, and Penny R. Yarrow, "Verbal Attitudes and Overt Behavior Involving Racial Prejudice," *Journal of Abnormal and Social Psychology* 47 (1952): 647–652.

29. See the section on "Rumor" in Gardner Lindzey and Elliot Aronson, eds., *The Handbook of Social Psychology,* 2d ed. (Reading, Mass.: Addison-Wesley, 1969).

30. Among the most useful of these are Herbert Hyman, *Survey Design and Analysis: Principles, Cases, and Procedures* (New York: Free Press, 1955); Galtung, *Theory and Methods of Social Research;* Abraham N. Oppenheim, *Questionnaire Design and Attitude Measurement* (New York: Basic Books, 1966); and an old but still useful manual by William J. Goode and Paul K. Hatt, *Methods in Social Research* (New York: McGraw-Hill, 1952).

31. See P. W. Bridgman, *The Intelligent Individual and Society* (New York: Macmillan, 1938), for a discussion of some of the issues involved. Also, Harry Alpert, "Operational Definitions in Sociology," *American Sociological Review* 3, no. 6 (December 1938): 855–861.

32. Kenneth Kammeyer, "Birth Order and the Feminine Sex Role Among College Women," *American Sociological Review* 31, no. 4 (August 1966): pp. 508–515.

33. For example, Diana Crane, "Scientists at Major and Minor Universities: A Study of Productivity and Recognition," *American Sociological Review* 30, no. 5 (October 1965): 701–702, including part of fn. 18.

34. For example, Howard E. Freeman, David Armor, J. Michael Ross, and Thomas F. Pettigrew, "Color Gradation and Attitudes Among Middle-Income Negroes," *American Sociological Review* 31, no. 3 (June 1966): 365–374. See p. 367.

35. For example, Louis Guttman, "A Revision of Chapin's Social Status Scale," *American Sociological Review* 7, no. 3 (June 1942): 362–369.

36. This scale, together with a list of some studies in which it has been used, will be found in Theodore Caplow, Sheldon Stryker, and Samuel E. Wallace, *The Urban Ambience: A Study of San Juan, Puerto Rico* (Totowa, N. J.: Bedminster Press, 1964), pp. 68–69.

37. Originally presented in Leo Srole, "Social Integration and Certain Corollaries: An Exploratory Study," *American Sociological Review* 21, no. 6 (December 1956): 709–716. The version produced here is from Curtis R. Miller and Edgar W. Butler, "Anomia and Eunomia: A Methodological Evaluation of Srole's Anomia Scale," *American Sociological Review* 31, no. 3 (June 1966); 400–406.

38. Louis L. Thurstone and E. J. Chave, *The Measurement of Attitudes*

(Chicago: University of Chicago Press, 1929); Rensis Likert, "A Technique for the Measurement of Attitudes," *Archives of Psychology,* no. 140 (1932); Louis Guttman, "The Basis for Scalogram Analysis," in *Measurement and Prediction,* ed. Samuel A. Stouffer (Princeton, N. J.: Princeton University Press, 1950). The best elementary exposition will be found in Oppenheim, *Questionnaire Design and Attitude Measurement.*

39. An excellent summary of the technical aspects of sampling will be found in Philip J. McCarthy, "Sample Design," in Marie Jahoda, Morton Deutsch, and Stuart W. Cook, *Research Methods in Social Relations, Part Two: Selected Techniques* (New York: Dryden Press, 1951), pp. 643–680.

40. The rules of interviewing are always subject to modification by the requirements of a particular situation. For a classic example of such an adaptation, see the section on "Technical Devices in Interviewing," in Alfred C. Kinsey, Wendell B. Pomeroy, and Clyde E. Martin, *Sexual Behavior in the Human Male* (Philadelphia: Saunders, 1948), pp. 47–59.

41. One of the best is Stephen A. Richardson, Barbara Snell Dohrenwend, and David Klein, *Interviewing: Its Forms and Functions* (New York: Basic Books, 1965).

42. Harld D. Lasswell, Nathan Leites, and associates, *The Language of Politics: Studies in Quantitative Semantics* (New York: Stewart, 1949).

43. Louis Schneider and Sanford M. Dornbush, *Popular Religion: Inspirational Books in America* (Chicago: University of Chicago Press, 1958); Shiso no Kagaku Kenkyukai, *Japanese Popular Culture: Studies in Mass Communication and Cultural Change,* ed. and trans. Hidetoshi Kato (Rutland, Vt.: Tuttle, 1959); Charles S. Osgood and Evelyn G. Walker, "Motivation and Language Behavior: A Content Analysis of Suicide Notes," *Journal of Abnormal and Social Psychology* 59, no.1 (July 1959): 58–67; Frederick Mosteller and David L. Wallace, *Inference and Disputed Authorship: The Federalist* (Reading, Mass.: Addison-Wesley, 1964).

44. The successful use of the anecdotal method in a field whose documentation is sparse and fragmentary is illustrated by the history of family limitation practices by Helénè Bergues et al., *La Prévention des Naissances dans la Famille: Ses Origines dans les Temps Modernes* (Paris: Presses Universitaires de France, 1960).

45. William I. Thomas and Florian Znaniecki, *The Polish Peasant in Europe and America,* 2 vols. (New York: Knopf, 1927); republished in facsimile ed. (New York: Dover, 1958). Originally published 1918–1920.

46. From E. William Noland et al., "Proceedings of the 53d Annual Meeting, American Sociological Society: Report of the Committee on Research," *American Sociological Review* 23, no. 6 (December 1958): 704–711.

Landmarks
of Social Research

Introduction

In this chapter, we shall review a small number of research reports that represent high points of social research during the first half of the twentieth century. They are part of the intellectual background of the working sociologist and you will find many references to them in your later reading. Many of these studies were carried out by American investigators; until recently, social research was organized on a much larger scale in the United States than elsewhere and much of the innovative work was done in this country. Only in recent years was there a comparable development of social research in France, England, West Germany, Italy, Poland, Yugoslavia, India, Japan, and other countries.

Early Studies

The great development of empirical social research in the United States after World War I and in nearly every country in the world after World War II had many sources. The remoter sources include the "Political Arithmetick"(a kind of descriptive sociology) that flourished in seventeenth-century England with the encouragement of the Royal Society,[1] the remarkable socioeconomic surveys undertaken by French officials under the *ancien régime*,[2] the introduction of national and local censuses after the middle of the eighteenth century,[3] and the work of the Belgian scientist Adolphe Quetelet (1796–1874), who called attention to the stability of various social rates over time and promoted the concept of "social physics."[4] Other influences were such monumental nineteenth-century surveys as Booth's *Life and Labour of the People in London*,[5] Villermé's *The Physical and Moral State of Workmen Employed in the Manufacture of Cotton, Linen and Silk*,[6] Parent-DuChâtelet's two-volume study of prostitution in Paris,[7] LePlay's case studies of family life among European workers,[8] and the almost innumerable surveys of urban, industrial, and family problems in the United States that appeared around 1900.

Much of this early work has been undeservedly neglected; only recently has the history of social research in Europe begun to be uncovered.[9] It is sometimes startling to discover the energy and sophistication

Table 3-1 A SCHEME OF THE INCOME, AND EXPENCE, OF THE SEVERAL FAMILIES OF ENGLAND; CALCULATED FOR THE YEAR 1688

Number of Families	RANKS, DEGREES, TITLES, and QUALIFICATIONS	Heads per Family	Number of Persons	Yearly Income per Family	Total of the Estates or Income	Yearly Income per Head	Expense per Head	Increase per Head	Total Increase per Annum
				£ s.	£	£ s.	£ s. d.	£ s. d.	£
260	Temporal Lords	40	6,400	2,800 —	448,000	70 —	60 — —	10 — —	64,000
26	Spiritual Lords	20	520	1,300 —	33,800	65 —	55 — —	10 — —	5,200
800	Baronets	16	12,800	880 —	704,000	55 —	51 — —	4 — —	51,000
600	Knights	13	7,800	650 —	390,000	50 —	46 — —	4 — —	31,200
3,000	Esquires	10	30,000	450 —	1,200,000	45 —	42 — —	3 — —	90,000
12,000	Gentlemen	8	96,000	280 —	2,880,000	35 —	32 10 —	2 10 —	240,000
5,000	Persons in Offices	8	40,000	240 —	1,200,000	30 —	27 — —	3 — —	120,000
5,000	Persons in Offices	6	30,000	120 —	600,000	20 —	18 — —	2 — —	60,000
2,000	Merchants and Traders by Sea	8	16,000	400 —	800,000	50 —	40 — —	10 — —	160,000
8,000	Merchants and Traders by Land	6	48,000	200 —	1,600,000	33 —	28 — —	5 — —	240,000
10,000	Persons in the Law	7	70,000	140 —	1,400,000	20 —	17 — —	3 — —	210,000
2,000	Clergymen	6	12,000	60 —	120,000	10 —	9 — —	1 — —	12,000
3,000	Clergymen	5	40,000	45 —	360,000	9 —	8 — —	1 — —	40,000
40,000	Freeholders	7	280,000	84 —	3,360,000	12 —	11 — —	1 — —	280,000
140,000	Freeholders	5	700,000	50 —	7,000,000	10 —	9 10 —	— 10 —	350,000
150,000	Farmers	5	750,000	44 —	6,600,000	8 15	8 10 —	— 5 —	187,000
16,000	Persons in Sciences and Liberal Arts	5	80,000	60 —	960,000	12 —	11 10 —	1 10 —	40,000
40,000	Shop-keepers and Tradesmen	4½	180,000	45 —	1,800,000	10 —	9 10 —	— 10 —	90,000
60,000	Artizans and Handicrafts	4	240,000	40 —	2,400,000	10 —	9 10 —	— 10 —	120,000
5,000	Naval Officers	4	20,000	80 —	400,000	20 —	18 — —	2 — —	40,000
4,000	Military Officers	4	16,000	60 —	240,000	15 —	14 — —	1 — —	16,000
511,586 Families.		5¼	2,675,520	67 —	34,495,800	12 18	12 — —	— 18 —	2,447,100
									Decrease.
50,000	Common Seamen	3	150,000	20 —	1,000,000	7 —	7 10 —	— 10 —	75,000
364,000	Labouring People and Out Servants	3½	1,275,000	15 —	5,460,000	4 10	4 12 —	— 2 —	127,500
400,000	Cottagers and Paupers	3¼	1,300,000	6 10	2,000,000	2 —	2 5 —	— 5 —	325,000
35,000	Common Soldiers	2	70,000	14 —	490,000	7 —	7 10 —	— 10 —	35,000
849,000 Families.		3¼	2,795,000	10 10	8,950,000	3 5	3 9 —	— 4 —	562,000
	Vagrants		30,000		60,000	2 —	3 — —	1 — —	60,000
849,000		3¼	2,825,000	10 10	9,010,000	3 3	3 7 6	— 4 6	622,000
	So the GENERAL ACCOUNT is:								
511,586 Families;	Increasing the Wealth of the Kingdom	5¼	2,675,520	67 —	34,495,800	12 18	12 — —	— 18 —	2,447,000
849,000 Families;	Decreasing the Wealth of the Kingdom	3¼	2,825,000	10 10	9,010,000	3 3	3 7 6	— 4 6	622,000
1,360,586 Families.	Net Totals	$\frac{1}{20}$	5,500,520	32 —	43,505,800	7 18	7 11 3	— 6 9	1,825,100

Source: Gregory King, "Natural and Political Observations and Conclusions Upon the State and Condition of England, 1696" in Alexander Chalmers, ed., *Estimate of the Comparative Strength of Great Britain* (Piccadilly: J. Stockdale, 1802), pp. 424-425.

of early investigators. For example, Table 3–1, from Gregory King's seventeenth-century study, is an attempt to arrange the entire population of England in 1688 by socioeconomic status, family size, and income.

Twentieth Century Studies

Although the studies we are going to review are the modern classics of sociological research, not all of them were produced by sociologists. Anthropologists, psychologists, and amateur investigators have made important contributions. The social sciences have never been sharply differentiated with respect to research interests. Anthropological descriptions of simple societies continue to furnish material for sociological analysis. Data are exchanged between psychology and sociology continuously and as a matter of course; the line between political and sociological research cannot be sharply drawn.

The studies to be reviewed are arranged in rough chronological order according to the date of their first published reports, but this chronology is subject to two sorts of error. First, a considerable span of time, more than ten years in some instances, may have elapsed between the gathering of data and the publication of the report. Second, a major research project often provides enough material for multiple reports, which may be widely spaced.

The summaries that follow are necessarily too brief to do full justice to any of the projects and can only serve as introductions to them. The history of research, like the history of theory, must be learned from the original sources. Another limitation of these summaries is that they do not take full account of the critical literature that has grown up around each project, because our present purpose is to understand why each of them survived the gantlet of criticism and made a permanent contribution to sociological knowledge.

The Polish Peasant / William I. Thomas and Florian Znaniecki

In 1908 Professor William I. Thomas of the University of Chicago obtained a large grant from a private foundation to study the problems connected with European immigration to the United States. Soon afterwards, he decided to concentrate on Polish peasants; they were well represented in Chicago's foreign-born population and notably problem-ridden. On one of his trips to Poland, Thomas discovered Znaniecki, a poet and philosopher, and arranged for him to come to the United States and work on the project. Their collaborative report was published just after World War I.[10]

The raw data consisted of a vast collection of documents—personal letters, newspaper stories, applications to an immigration society, parish histories, accounts of Polish-American associations, case records from courts and social agencies. It is not known how many documents were collected in all, but more than a thousand of them are reproduced in *The Polish Peasant in Europe and America*, including the long, erotic autobiography of an immigrant named Wladek. The authors regarded personal life records as "the *perfect* type of sociological material."[11] Their principal method was a type of content analysis—searching their documents for evidence of the attitudes and values held by the persons to whom the documents referred.

Attitudes and *values* were the key terms in this study. Social values, for Thomas and Znaniecki, were something like Durkheim's social facts. A social value is anything, tangible or intangible, that is useful to the members of some social group and has a meaning for them on which they unthinkingly agree. An attitude, by contrast, is a process of individual consciousness that determines the social actions of an individual. It is the private and subjective counterpart of a social value. Like Simmel, but unlike Durkheim, Thomas and Znaniecki regarded social actions as dual by nature, the result of social forces outside the individual actor and of private impulses within him. They denied the validity of any sociological explanation that left either social facts or individual motivations out of account. *"The cause of a value or of an attitude,"* they proclaimed ·in italics, *"is never an attitude or a value alone, but always a combination of an attitude and a value."* [12]

The combination of individual attitudes and social values is realized in every individual by a great number of *wishes*, which can only be satisfied in a social setting. Four general patterns of wishes are enumerated:

1. The desire for new experience
2. The desire for recognition—including sexual response and general social appreciation
3. The desire for mastery—including ownership and political power
4. The desire for security—including the support and company of one's fellows.

These famous "four wishes" are better known in Thomas' later formulation[13] in which the desire for mastery disappears and the basic wishes are for *new experience, recognition, response,* and *security.*

As its title suggests, *The Polish Peasant in Europe and America* analyzes the situation of the Polish peasant on both continents. The emphasis, if any, is on Europe, but social change is the focus of interest for both situations. In the traditional Polish village, the family group had been the principal social actor, and individuals were subordinated to it as far as possible. The duties of family members toward each other were matters of obligation rather than sentiment. Marriage was an arrangement between families; sexual life was denied any independent value. The family was practically the only organized social group to which the peasant belonged. Its relationships with neighboring families were not especially close, but there was considerable solidarity in each village because all of the peasants held the same views about their roles and relationships and the same beliefs about religion and magic. In its traditional form this society was remarkably isolated from outside influences; there was no landowning aristocracy above it and there were few cities nearby.

Thomas and Znaniecki show how this pattern was disrupted by economic changes and other outside influences that weakened the solidarity of the family and village, allowing individuals to develop new attitudes in opposition to familistic values, and introducing differences of opinion, belief and economic orientation into the village. They define *social disorganization* as a decrease of the influence of group norms upon individual members of the group, and show how this characterized every aspect of peasant society in Poland after 1900 and how it led to *reorganization.* In the family, hedonistic values and attitudes were substituted for family solidarity. In the village, the pursuit of success and economic advantage replaced the old, conservative collectivism. The larger society in Poland witnessed the growth of a new middle class, the intensification of nationalism, the modification of religious beliefs, the appearance of revolutionary movements, and the increasing diffusion of new ideas through education and the press.

A more drastic form of disorganization occurred when peasants emigrated to the United States, leaving the Polish villages behind them, and often detaching themselves from their families as well. Thomas and Znaniecki point out that the immigrants did not enter American society directly. Their first associations were almost exclusively with other immigrants, the world they entered was that of the Polish-American immigrant, not that of the native American. Here, too, disorganization was followed by reorganization and by the emergence of new attitudes and values. Immigrant societies, the Polish parishes, benefit societies, the parochial school system, and Polish-American associations sprang up and partly replaced the group anchorages the immigrant had lost. But these new secondary groups could not fully substitute for the old primary groups. Among Polish peasants in the United States there was a great deal of *individual disorganization,* defined by Thomas and Znaniecki as the loss of the individual's ability to organize his life for the realization of his own goals. Individual disorganization is not the same thing as social disorganization, although related to it. Some individuals become disorganized when social disorganization is prevalent, but others are stimulated to invent new and successful patterns of action.

The characteristic forms of individual disorganization among the Polish peasants in the United States were economic dependency, breakdown of the conjugal relationship, murder, and juvenile delinquency. The way that Thomas and Znaniecki account for behavioral problems by examining the attitudes and values underlying them is illustrated by the following excerpt, in which they discuss the results of efforts by the courts and social agencies to prevent the breakup of immigrant families.

After a careful study of many hundreds of cases we have not found a single instance where official interference strengthened the conjugal bond. The explanation of this is easy. The social control to which a marriage-group in the old country is subjected by the families and the community bears upon this group as a unit and has the interests of this unit in view. The role of the social milieu is not to step between husband and wife and arbitrate between their personal claims as those of separate individuals, but to uphold their union when threatened by the action of either. The misbehaving individual is made to feel that he sins against the sacredness of marriage, not that he is wrong in his contest with another individual. Therefore the control of the old social milieu increases the institutional significance of the conjugal bond. On the contrary, the interference of the American institution means an arbitration between husband and wife, who are treated, officially and unofficially, as contesting parties, as individuals between whose claims a just balance should be established. This, for the consciousness of the immigrant, puts the whole matter at once not upon the basis of solidarity but upon that of fight where each party wants to get the best of its opponent by whatever means possible.[14]

The Polish-Americans of today are, for the most part, third or fourth generation natives who do not exhibit any distinctive problems, but the foregoing analysis is still applicable to some of the newer immigrants and migrants who now reside at the bottom of the urban social heap.

The Ecology of Chicago / Chicago School

Robert E. Park, who inspired this large group of studies and supervised many of them, came to the University of Chicago at the age of 50 after a long career as a newspaper reporter, race relations expert, and world traveler. His only instructor in sociology had been Simmel, and like Simmel, he was perpetually fascinated by the variety, complexity, and pathos of metropolitan life. Park once remarked that he had probably covered more ground in cities in different parts of the world than any other living man.[15] In 1916, he wrote a notable paper for *The American Journal of Sociology,* "The City: Suggestions for the Investigation of Human Behavior in the Urban Environment,"[16] in which he called for the study of urban life and culture by a number of methods: direct observation, statistical analysis, case studies, descriptions of vocational types, examination of governmental processes, and the analysis of what are now called deviant subcultures.

In the ensuing years, this program was put into effect with unparalleled enthusiasm in a long series of studies of Chicago carried out in Park's department, and published by the University of Chicago Press. The following is a partial list.

Additional studies in the same series dealt with cities other than Chicago[17] or extended the Chicago findings to urban areas in general.[18]

The investigators of the Chicago school were known as *urban ecologists* because of the resemblance they saw between the relationships of various populations in the city and the relationship of species of trees and plants on uncultivated land. Borrowing terms from botany, they spoke of *succession* when one population replaced another in a neighborhood, *symbiosis* when unrelated populations were found in the same area, or *dominance* when outlying districts were influenced by conditions at the urban center. They also made use of a broader set of terms derived from the study of group interaction. Group relationships, they held, could take the form of *competition, conflict, accommodation,*

Nels Anderson	The Hobo	1923
Ernest Mowrer	Family Disorganization	1927
Frederic M. Thrasher	The Gang	1927
Louis Wirth	The Ghetto	1928
Ruth Shonle Cavan	Suicide	1928
Harvey Warren Zorbaugh	The Gold Coast and the Slum	1929
Clifford Shaw	Delinquency Areas	1929
Paul G. Cressey	The Taxi Dance Hall	1932
E. Franklin Frazier	The Negro Family in Chicago	1932
Walter C. Reckless	Vice in Chicago	1933
Robert E. L. Faris & H. Warren Dunham	Mental Disorders in Urban Areas	1939

or *assimilation*. In competition, groups struggle impersonally for similar goals. In conflict, they seek to achieve their goals by removing each other as obstacles. In accommodation, groups with incompatible goals work out a stable, mutual adjustment. Assimilation is the merger of two groups so that they no longer have separate goals.

These processes were used by the ecologists to explain patterns of urban growth. For example, the competition for favored sites in the center of the city is regulated by the price of land. Conflict between older and newer immigrant groups accounts for the rapid turnover of population, as each new group invades the territory occupied by earlier arrivals. Accommodation is the uneasy peace that prevails where the Gold Coast meets the slum on Chicago's Near North Side. Assimilation occurs when the descendants of immigrant groups move to the suburbs, develop a common middle-class culture, and erect barriers to shield themselves from the poor of the central city.

The methods used in the Chicago studies were rather casual by modern standards. In almost every instance the investigator first acquired a thorough knowledge of his subject by participant observation. Later, he added whatever additional materials he could obtain—official records, census data, private enumerations, documents and life histories, interviews, questionnaires, newspaper articles, and the reports of qualified informants. Some of the studies dealt with deviant behavior (crime, delinquency, suicide, prostitution, and mental disorders), and these relied increasingly on statistical measures, culminating in Faris' and Dunham's demonstration that even so individual an ailment as schizophrenia was highly concentrated in a few ecological areas. Describing this work of the Chicago school, John Madge speaks of

"its determined concern with locality, its faith in human betterment, and an intrinsically American hatred of deviation and radicalism which cohabits strangely with the school's grasp of the wonderful richness and variety of human institutions."[19]

The principal findings of the Chicago studies may be briefly summarized:

1. The metropolitan community is not dominated by a single unified culture but exhibits a variety of subcultures, each reflecting a separate history and a distinctive set of interests.

2. The metropolitan community is not a unified social system; it comprises a cluster of subcommunities, each with its own pattern of opportunities and limitations.

3. The metropolitan environment allows great social distances to develop with little physical separation. The social distance between groups is greater in the metropolis than in smaller cities because of the impersonality of metropolitan life and because segregated groups in the metropolis are large enough to be self-sufficient.

4. The internal compartmentation of metropolitan communities does not preclude individual mobility. Indeed, it encourages mobility, because the individual who moves into a new group or a new stratum is automatically insulated from his former associates.

5. Through the combined effects of differentiation and mobility, many city dwellers become more or less desocialized and learn to live without recognition or response from others. Desocialized (or *anomic)* persons are often found in each other's company—in rooming house districts, residential hotels, skid rows, and trailer camps, for example—but they do not develop strong social bonds among themselves. Such districts typically show high rates of suicide, mental disorder, malnutrition, and ill health.

6. The metropolis is characterized by a high incidence of crime against persons and property, and of other behavior defined by the larger society as illegal, immoral, or both—alcoholism, drug addiction, prostitution, homosexuality, gambling, truancy, vandalism, and dependency, for example. The Chicago studies were first to disclose that much of this behavior develops in conformity with the norms of subcommunities that encourage and reward deviant behavior.

7. Every significant form of deviant behavior that occurs in the metropolis is highly concentrated. Although prostitutes and drug addicts appear throughout the metropolitan area, the majority of them can be found in a few locations, sometimes in a single census tract. There are ecological correlations among the various forms of deviant behavior (they tend to concentrate in the same places) and poverty, dependency, and unemployment.

8. The ecological structure of an American metropolis at any given moment is much less permanent than it appears. It is the product of a rapid development that is still under way. Patterns of settlement and land use seldom persist for more than a single generation. The child who has grown up cannot go back to his old neighborhood and expect to find it intact.

9. The expansion process goes by the clumsy name of *centralized decentralization.* The population and the structural complexity of the metropolitan area continue to increase. The growth of suburbs and the extension of urban influence to a larger hinterland is accompanied by

an intensified concentration of functions in the central business district, and by many changes in the character of intervening districts.

Many of the topics first explored by the Chicago school—for example, neighborhood interaction, juvenile gangs, the slum family, homeless men—are now studied nearly continuously, and nearly everywhere, from Chicago to Osaka and Ibadan.

Social Mobility / Pitirim Sorokin

Sorokin's *Social Mobility* [20] contains a vast collection of statistical material from many different sources, countries, epochs, and types of inquiry, together with the results of the investigator's own statistical studies and some nonquantitative material, all imbedded in a long, interpretive discussion.

Sorokin was a Russian intellectual, originally trained in psychology, who played a moderately prominent part in the early phase of the Russian Revolution as a member of the national council and as secretary to the prime minister. He fell into disfavor under the Communist regime that replaced the first revolutionary government and left Russia in 1922 as a political refugee. While holding a temporary appointment at the University of Minnesota he wrote *Social Mobility,* the first of his many books in English. Its importance was recognized immediately, and it set him on the road to a professorship at Harvard and a long, distinguished academic career that continued without interruption until his death in 1968.

Sorokin defined *social mobility* as the shifting of individuals or classes within social space, [21] and identified two principal types of social mobility—horizontal and vertical. *Horizontal mobility* is movement from one position to another within the same social stratum. It includes migration, occupational shifts, and changes of affiliation. *Vertical mobility* is a movement from one social stratum to another, an ascent or descent in a hierarchical social structure. Sorokin's study deals with vertical mobility and social stratification; horizontal mobility is mentioned only in passing.

He begins with a demonstration that systems of stratification in historical times have tended to fluctuate in a cyclical way; for example, average wealth and income vary within the same society from one period to another; the diffusion of property alternates with the concentration of property; and political stratification "seems to fluctuate in space and time without any perpetual trend." [22] There follows a long discussion of the channels of vertical circulation in various societies, leading to the conclusion that some degree of economic, political, and occupational opportunity exists in even the most rigid system, although no system is so open as to permit absolutely free mobility.

The most useful sections of the book are those dealing with physical and mental differences between persons occupying different strata of modern societies and with the factors that maintain a continuous process of vertical circulation within Western society. Sorokin resurrected dozens of forgotten studies by physicians and anthropologists to demonstrate that in many, if not all, societies there is an appreciable correlation between class status and such physical indicators as height, weight, head circumference, absence of abnormalities, beauty, longevity, health, bodily strength, resistance to disease, and infant survival; as well as the more familiar correlations between status and intelligence, school achievement, and occupational achievement. How much these differences are due to unequal endowments and how much to unequal opportunities for personal development, Sorokin was not able to determine.

Middletown / Robert and Helen Lynd

Robert Lynd was trained to be a Presbyterian minister. In the early 1920s he and his wife undertook to survey the religious activities and practices of a typical American community. The place they selected was Muncie, Indiana, a small manufacturing city with a population of about 40,000, quite close to Robert Lynd's birthplace. Its identity was partially concealed by an alias, "Middletown." The study soon outgrew its original purpose and was extended to all the major aspects of institutional life, which were grouped under six headings: getting a living, making a home, training the young, using leisure, engaging in religious practices, and engaging in community activities. Each of these institutional categories was further subdivided; for example, the discussion of community activities in *Middletown* [23] covers the machinery of government, keeping healthy, caring for the unable, getting information, and "things making and unmaking group solidarity."

The Lynds and their assistants opened an office in a local building and gathered data for 18 months. During that period, they participated as fully as possible in all phases of community life, and their final report was based on a combination of formal data and informal impressions. The study was organized around a point-by-point comparison of contemporary Middletown (1924 and 1925) with the Middletown of an earlier generation (1890).

In addition to obtaining information by participant observation, they examined documentary materials, compiled statistics, conducted interviews, and administered questionnaires. Each of these methods elicited several types of material. Among the written documents examined were census reports, city and county records, court files, school records, state reports and yearbooks, newspapers, minutes of meetings, personal diaries, scrapbooks, local histories, directories, maps, chamber of commerce brochures and high school annuals. The interview program included casual conversations, planned interviews with strategic informants, and a survey of a sample of working-class families and another sample of business-class families.

Middletown was the first sociological bestseller. It went through six printings the year it appeared, and was hotly discussed throughout the United States—and with special intensity in Middletown. Its authors became famous overnight. To some readers, the book seemed to expose the narrowness and futility of life in the hinterland; H. L. Mencken called it "A Study of Moronia." To others, including the opinion leaders of Muncie, it seemed to demonstrate the strength and adaptability of the American way of life. For his part in the work, Lynd was awarded a doctorate by Columbia University and appointed professor of sociology in 1931.

Meanwhile, the Great Depression had overtaken the United States and all of its Middletowns. In 1935 the Lynds returned to Muncie with a larger staff to study the impact of the Depression and to examine the changes that had occurred in each institution. The methods of this second investigation were much more summary than those of the first, and *Middletown in Transition*[24] was published only two years later. The investigators had changed as much or more than the community. In the interim between the two studies they had come to accept a Marxist view of social structure and now believed that the relationships involved in getting a living determined the structure of the five other institutions as well as the prevailing values and beliefs. Their old confidence in the Middletown way of life had been severely shaken—much more than the confidence of the inhabitants had been. They not only pictured Middletown in 1935 as considerably changed but as we shall see, they also modified their picture of Middletown in 1925, so that its negative features became more conspicuous.

The principal finding of the earlier study was the sharp division of the community into a business class, drawing most of its income from work with people, and a working class, drawing most of its income from work with things. The two classes were more sharply separated than their members realized. Their life chances, their routines, their family relationships, and to a lesser extent their religious and political beliefs were different. In some respects, the habits of the working class resembled those of the business class of the previous generation. New culture traits appeared first in the business class and filtered slowly down.

Not only were the two classes unevenly affected by social change. The young were more sensitive to social change than their parents; women, especially in the business class, more than men. There even seemed to be a rough hierarchy with respect to the speed of social change in the six institutional categories; change was most rapid in economic activity, followed by leisure, education, community activities, family patterns, and organized religion, in that order. For the system as a whole, adjustment to rapid social change was *the* problem.

> Middletown's life exhibits at almost every point either some change or some stress arising from failure to change. A citizen has one foot on the relatively solid ground of established institutional habits and the other fast to an escalator erratically moving in several directions at a bewildering variety of speeds. Living under such circumstances consists first of all in maintaining some sort of equilibrium.[25]

The men of the business class had found it somewhat easier than the workers to maintain such an equilibrium in 1925, although their confidence was shaken by the restlessness of their wives and the rebelliousness of their teenage children. Moreover, they could not ignore portents of trouble in the business system itself. Their response to this uneasiness was the "booster spirit," an ideology that combined local solidarity, political conservatism, the idealization of business activities, and an insistence on conformity. The working class, although not entirely happy with this ideology, did not openly challenge it in 1925.

In 1935 Middletown was just beginning to recover from the decline of manufacturing, the mass unemployment, and the losses of property and savings that occurred during the five previous years. The economic progress of the community had been totally interrupted. About a quarter of its families were supported on public relief, marriages and births declined, and new construction ceased. The business system was transformed by federal regulations and by the unionization of labor; and the latent conflicts in Middletown's values, for example, between the ideals of individualism and of collective responsibility, began to work their way to the surface.

The overall effect of the Depression, however, was to decelerate social change. The map of Middletown's culture showed much the same contours in 1935 as in 1925. The public relief program was the only new feature in the institutional configuration. The greatest difference between the two periods seemed to be in the minds of the inhabitants—in their awareness of a growing incompatibility between reality and the symbols they used to explain it.

The Lynds' own disenchantment ran a parallel course. They discovered unpleasant features of life in Middletown that they had overlooked or understated in 1925. Discussing prostitution, the earlier study had recorded its decline and stated that only two or three furtively conducted houses of prostitution remained. Ten years later, the investigators discovered that Middletown had been the prostitution center of a large region in 1925, and that they had failed to notice an extensive red light district just across the tracks from the business section. Similarly, they became aware that a large proportion of the population lived in dilapidated housing without plumbing facilities or adequate heating, that heavy drinking had been common in 1925, that prejudice against Negroes was endemic, that the local press was subject to manipulation, and that the river was badly polluted.

Most important, they revised their earlier view of the class structure to take into account the role of an influential family, the X's, who owned the principal local industry and exercised some measure of control over the entire community by means of strategic connections with the leading banks, the law firms, the school board, philanthropic organizations, the churches, the press, and both political parties. This control seemed to have been strengthened by the Depression, and the investigators identified an emerging upper class composed of wealthy manufacturers, bankers, local managers of national corporations, and a few well-to-do dependents of these groups. They now subdivided the business class into an upper-middle class of manufacturers, merchants, professionals and executives and a lower-middle class of small retailers, clerical workers, civil servants and employed professionals. They also divided the working class into a labor aristocracy of foremen, craftsmen and skilled machinists, a much larger stratum of machine operators and semiskilled laborers, and a bottom stratum of unskilled and irregularly employed workers, many of them poor whites from the neighboring mountains. The Lynds did not conclude from these sharpening divisions that class war was imminent; it seemed to them more likely that Middletown would continue its customary middle-of-the-road course, adapting reluctantly to necessary changes and shaping its future by means of compromise and expediency. In the last sentence of *Middletown in Transition* they quoted a phrase of Tawney describing the aftermath of the French Revolution: " . . . they walked reluctantly backwards into the future, lest a worse thing should befall them."[26]

Tikopia / Raymond Firth

Raymond Firth is a social anthropologist from New Zealand. He began his study of the Tikopia, a Polynesian people on a small Pacific island (the people and the island go by the same name) with a year of field work in 1928–1929. In 1952, Firth made a second expedition to the island, accompanied by a younger colleague, and in 1966 a third expedition. His first report of the project was *We, the Tikopia,* published in 1936; others have been issued at intervals since. *The Work of the Gods in Tikopia* and *Tikopia Ritual and Belief* were first published in 1967, and at least one more report was then in progress. Thus, this single research project occupied its principal investigator for more than 40 years.[27]

From its earliest beginnings, modern sociology has been much preoccupied with what used to be called *primitive* and are now called *preliterate* or *preindustrial* peoples. As "living ancestors" they figure in nearly every discussion of social origins; Durkheim examined the totemic practices of the Arunta in order to explain the development of religion in civilized societies.[28] As "societies in a bottle" they have been used by nearly every sociologist since Comte to define the limits of variation in human behavior, to demonstrate the relativity of social values, to analyze social change, and to examine the functional interdependence of the elements of social systems.

Each generation of sociologists has had its favorite ethnologists and its preferred primitives: The Australian aborigines at the turn of the century,[29] the Northwest Indians studied by Franz Boas in the following decade,[30] the Trobrianders studied by Malinowski (Firth's teacher) in the 1920s.[31] A little later Margaret Mead demonstrated the relationship between socialization practices and personality types in Samoa and in three New Guinea societies;[32] Ruth Benedict, pursuing a similar theme, identified opposing social values among the Southwest Indians;[33] Robert Redfield described the secularization of folk societies in Mexico.[34] Firth's *Tikopia* did not become a favorite ethnographic source for sociologists until the appearance, in the early 1950s, of two major works that drew heavily on it, George C. Homans' *The Human Group*[35] and

William J. Goode's *Religion Among the Primitives.*[36] Since then, Tikopia has become nearly as familiar to students of sociology as Chicago or Middletown.

It is an admirable example of an isolated, miniature society. The island stands alone in the Pacific Ocean, 70 miles from the nearest dot of land and hundreds of miles from any important neighbor. It is only 3 miles long and had a population of only 1,200 in 1928. Contact with the outside world was minimal; a missionary vessel called once a year. Although half the population were nominally Christian, no white man had ever lived on the island for more than a few months. The people are Polynesian—tall, fairly light-skinned, and handsome by European standards. The island has been totally self-supporting since time immemorial. Its miniscule territory includes a good-sized mountain, an interior lake, swamps and desert places, beaches and coral reefs. Within its tiny compass, Tikopia in 1928 displayed a cultural and social structure elaborate enough for a major civilization. It had its own language (related to Maori), its own oral literature and mythology, its own pantheon of gods, and a cycle of religious ceremonies and rituals that occupied the leading men throughout most of the year.

The population was divided into two classes, chiefs and commoners, with finer gradations of status in each class and provision for upward and downward mobility. It was further divided into four clans, each with its own chief and distinctive rituals and customs. Each clan was divided into *houses,* household units larger than a single family. The population was clustered in two rival districts on the opposite coasts of the island, one predominantly Christian and the other pagan.

Even the division of labor was complex. The Tikopia fished both offshore and on the reef. Each type of fishing requires widespread cooperation, technical expertise, the division of proceeds between capital and labor, and arrangements for the manufacture, maintenance, and storage of equipment. As agriculturists, they cultivated taro, breadfruit, coconut, banana, sago, and yams, each major crop being under the protection of one of the clan chiefs, who was responsible for supervising the sacred and secular procedures appropriate to that form of cultivation and maintaining production at an optimum level. Although the Tikopia had no money, they had an elaborate system of property rights and procedures for renting, borrowing, and exchanging commodities.

The family relationships of the Tikopia are fairly similar to our own. Descent is patrilineal, and real property (but not personal property) is inherited only in the male line. Marriage is generally monogamous, although polygamy is allowed. The balance of authority between husbands and wives and between parents and children is about what we are used to, although special relationships, such as that of a boy with his mother's brother, and special kinship arrangements, like the substitution of a mother's cousin when no mother's brother is available, are more important among the Tikopia.

All the institutional aspects of Tikopian society were closely integrated. The chief of the clan was simultaneously a social planner, the head of an extended family, the high priest of a private cult, the foreman of large working parties, a justice of the peace, and everyone's rich uncle. Rank, religion, and economic production were closely interwoven.

Tikopia was perhaps the last of the idyllic Polynesian societies of the Great South Sea to maintain its sacred character in the face of the massive European invasion that began with Captain Cook's expedition at the end of the eighteenth century and has continued ever since. This immunity was due to its extraordinary isolation, the lack of a secure anchorage for ships, and a reputation for inhospitality.[37] Between 1929 and 1952, however, the external contacts of Tikopia multiplied as young men went abroad as laborers and brought back European tools, household utensils, and clothing in large amounts. Money came into use. The missionary effort intensified. A disastrous hurricane in 1952 threatened the population with famine and shook the social structure to its foundations. After an epidemic in 1955, the three pagan clan chiefs adopted Christianity and the old religion came to a sudden end. By the time of Firth's last visit in 1956, Tikopia, although still remote and picturesque, was no longer isolated, sacred, or self-sufficient. A sense of irremediable loss pervades the ethnographer's carefully noncommital account of the transition.

Firth's studies of Tikopia show the best traits of the modern social anthropologist—his willingness to live with his people, learn their language, participate in their ceremonies; his ceaseless patience in observing, questioning, counting, and recording every feature of the native life around him. The significance of these studies for sociologists is that we have a more complete description of Tikopian society than of any other, and that it is a society comprehensible to us.

Taken as a *representative* simple society, the case of Tikopia leads us to a number of conclusions that may or may not be correct. First, there seems to be no such thing as a primitive mentality. The Tikopia react as we do to social snubs, dirty jokes, and political speeches; they are perhaps more subtle than most of us in their perception of personal relationships. Second, the presence of class distinctions seems to be compatible with social solidarity, indeed, with the unparalleled integration of a society in which everyone knew everyone else and violence was effectively tabooed. Third, a society is held together by bonds of reciprocal obligation between husband and wife, parents and children, young and old, chiefs and commoners, and it conserves this equilibrium as long as both parties to each reciprocal transaction accept their obligations and are capable of carrying them out. Fourth, all the institutions of Tikopia can be shown to be interdependent; the forms of production do not determine religious beliefs or vice versa, but each influences the other. Fifth, the interdependence of institutions does not imply that social change must be an all-or-nothing process. Traditional religion has disappeared among the Tikopia, whereas the social structure and family system remain intact for the time being.

The Hawthorne experiments, also known as the Western Electric studies, were carried out at the manufacturing plant of the Western Electric Company in the Hawthorne section of Chicago from 1927 to 1932, under the joint supervision of company officials and a team of Harvard investigators directed by Elton Mayo. The definitive report of the project, *Management and the Worker*,[38] was published in 1939 by F. J. Roethlisberger and William J. Dickson, but a summary of findings had appeared several years earlier in Mayo's *The Human Problems of an Industrial Civilization*,[39] and a long statistical report by T. H. Whitehead had also been issued previously.[40]

Although Mayo presented a simplified version of the findings, he placed them in broad perspective, showing their relevance to Durkheim's concept of anomie, Pareto's stress on the importance of nonlogical theories in everyday human affairs, the ecology of Chicago as described by the Chicago school, the early results of the Yankee City study, the psychological theories of Janet, Freud, and Piaget, and the behavior of Australian aborigines and Trobrianders. Mayo combined themes from these varied sources with the findings of the Hawthorne experiments to support his central argumer   at industry needs a very high level of administrative ability and knowledge in order to maintain the close communication and cooperation necessary for efficient production and equally essential for the personal happiness of the workers.

Western Electric is a manufacturing subsidiary of the American Telephone and Telegraph Company; it manufactures most of the equipment used by the parent company. The Hawthorne Works was and is a huge plant engaged in the mass production of telephone equipment. At the time of the study, a large proportion of the work force were foreign-born or the children of immigrants. There was an ineffectual company union, but no serious attempt at unionization had been made.

The Hawthorne experiments consist of five separate studies, each with different methods and results, all tending to the conclusion that the output of workers is largely determined by the nature of their social relationships with fellow workers and supervisors. The five studies are referred to as:

1. the illumination experiments
2. the relay assembly test room
3. the mica-splitting team
4. the interview program
5. the bank wiring observation room

We will discuss three of them here.

The Illumination Experiments These early experiments were conducted by Western Electric people before the arrival of the Harvard team. They were designed to reveal the relation of illumination to industrial efficiency. In the first experiment, the level of illumination was increased by easy stages in three departments engaged in different tasks. In two of the three departments, efficiency increased as the lighting improved; the third department showed no effect. In the next experiment, a single group was chosen to work under variable illumination. It was carefully matched with a control group for whom illumination was maintained as nearly constant as possible. The results were startling. Both groups showed appreciable and almost identical production increases. In the third illumination experiment, both the test group and the control group were placed in artificial light to exclude variations in daylight. The level of illumination in the test group enclosure was gradually decreased. Again, the efficiencies of the test group and the control group increased at about the same rate. Not until the test group's illumination was reduced to about the level of moonlight, so that they could barely see their materials, did their output begin to decrease.

It appeared from these experiments that illumination had only a minor influence on output and that the observed increases during the experiments must have been caused by some other factor that had unintentionally been brought into play. This mysterious factor was later identified as the effect of the investigation itself, and labeled the Hawthorne Effect. According to this interpretation (which was not fully accepted by the original investigators), workers who are placed in an experimental program, and given personal attention in connection with the program react so favorably to the change from the indifference and social distance of their usual relationships with management that they work much harder, and output tends to increase regardless of how working conditions are manipulated by the experimenters. The Hawthorne Effect has been observed in schools, offices, hospitals, prisons and other places as well as in factories.

The Interviewing Program   The interviewing program at Western Electric grew out of a supervisory training program that disclosed a lack of information about morale and also out of the discovery of a relationship between supervision and morale in the test room. The interviewing program consisted of two phases: a pilot study conducted in one branch of the company between September 1928 and February 1929, and a continuous program involving about 20,000 interviews with company employees in 1929 and 1930. The program was discontinued in 1931 because of the same decline in manufacturing activity that halted the other experiments, but it was revived in 1936 and became a permanent feature of personnel management at the Hawthorne Works under the name of personnel counseling.[41]

At the outset of the program, the interviewers followed a checklist of topics thought to be associated with morale, such as heating, ventilation, lockers, accident hazards, fringe benefits, and promotion opportunities. The interviewers had trouble keeping their respondents to these topics, and the material turned up when the interview strayed away was often more significant and interesting than responses when they followed the outline. After much discussion, they adopted a new interviewing procedure which they called *the indirect approach;* it is now better known as *nondirective interviewing.* The respondent was allowed to choose his own topics, and the interviewer followed the respondent's train of thought without any attempt to change the subject or to control the conversation. The change in procedure had the immediate effect of lengthening the average interview from 30 to 90 minutes and the average interview report from about 4 pages to about 10 pages. The opportunity to talk with a noncritical interviewer during working hours and to reveal personal problems in strict confidence to this sympathetic stranger seemed to have an independent favorable effect on the morale of the workers. This was the finding that attracted the most attention, and when the interviewing program was later reinstated at the Hawthorne Works, it was primarily for this purpose. However, the original program had other ends in view. From the interviews conducted during 1929, the "analyzing department" of the project extracted about 80,000 comments and classified them according to their urgency and their favorable or unfavorable tone—the first large-scale content analysis ever performed. The comments involving complaints were classified by a system reminiscent of Pareto, into Class A or Objectively Verifiable Complaints, Class B or Subjective Complaints, and Class C or Nonlogical Complaints. This classification led the investigators to discriminate between the *manifest content* and the *latent content* of complaints and to conclude that the latent content (the underlying attitude of the complainer) was often as significant as the manifest content (the grievance he expressed). The employee who on one occasion complained about the lunchroom and on another occasion about his supervisor might be expressing the same underlying attitude in each instance.

The principal finding of this extensive analysis was that the whole working environment of the industrial employee—and presumably that of any other worker—is permeated with social significance. To understand the worker's complaints and grievances, as well as his sources of satisfaction, it is necessary to take account of four separate classes of facts: the social organization in which the work takes place; the events, objects, and persons in the environment of the worker; his own position within the organization; and the outside social systems that surround his work.

The Bank Wiring Observation Room   The final Hawthorne experiment consisted of a detailed study of a shop situation from a sociological point of view. It was designed to reveal the effects of social interaction on employee behavior. As the study progressed, it came to focus on the restriction of output by an informally organized peer group.

A group of male workers were taken out of their regular department and placed in a separate room to continue the same work under observation. Their task was to wire banks of terminals for telephone switchboards, and the group was composed of 14 men—9 wiremen, 3 soldermen, and 2 inspectors, plus an observer whose behavior was rigorously controlled so that he would not slip into a quasi-supervisory role. This final experiment lasted from November 1931 to May 1932, when it was terminated for lack of business.

The men's wages and hours remained the same. The wage incentive system set a "bogey" or standard of 7,200 connections, but the operators had fixed on 6,600 connections as a daily norm, and most of them managed to report a daily output very close to this figure, although to do so required continuous adjustment of the pace of work and considerable tinkering with the figures. Except for one or two individuals who were not fully integrated into the group, the men were able to report nearly uniform straight-line output. This meant that some men reported less work than they actually did, some reported more, and the group as a whole accomplished much less than it was capable of.

The internal social organization of the bank wiring room during the short term of its existence was much more elaborate than anything observed in the smaller women's work groups of the previous experiments. Not only did the group develop its own set of norms, centered on the stabilization of output at the desired level and the maintenance of solidarity against supervisors and outsiders, but it was divided into two cliques, one clearly superior to the other and each with its own pattern of internal interaction. This subminiature society was brilliantly analyzed some years later by George C. Homans[42] to show how social systems in general maintain themselves against external pressures and develop an internal balance of sentiments and activity that insures conformity to group norms, a proportioning of social reward to social rank, and the achievement of common goals.

The Yankee City Series / W. Lloyd Warner

The Yankee City study was a direct outgrowth of the Hawthorne experiments, in which W. Lloyd Warner, an anthropologist who had turned his attention from primitive to modern societies, participated briefly. The Western Electric investigators had planned to study the relationship of the Hawthorne Works to the surrounding community. Closer consideration revealed some of the obstacles to studying a city as large as Chicago, and a search was launched for a small manufacturing community in which the problems of factory workers could be examined in their total social context. Warner wanted a community less disorganized than the industrial districts of Chicago, one where social patterns would be relatively stable and resistant to change. This appeared to limit his choice to New England or the Deep South. The place eventually selected was Newburyport, Massachusetts, a small coastal city with a long, continuous history. It had about 17,000 inhabitants during the time it was under observation.

The field work began in 1931 and was completed in 1935. The results of the project were presented in five large volumes[43] that appeared between 1941 and 1959, in accordance with the original project plan. These volumes cover the general pattern of social life in Yankee City; a more particular analysis of the status system; the situation of eight ethnic groups in the community (Irish, French-Canadians, Jews, Italians, Armenians, Greeks, Poles, and Russians); the evolution of the local shoe industry as expressed by a significant strike; and the political, historical, and religious symbols current in Yankee City. In preparing them, Warner was helped by an exceptionally able group of collaborators and assistants, many of whom went on to do important research of their own.

The Yankee City project resembled the first Middletown project in many respects. Once again, a young, enthusiastic group of investigators moved into a community, informed the local people of their general purposes, and set about gathering a huge mass of information by a variety of methods—participant observation, mapping, statistical enumeration, interviews, questionnaires, case histories, public documents, newspapers, diaries, and reminiscences. As in Middletown, the earliest important discovery was the existence of a well-defined system of social classes that affected the lives of the inhabitants in every aspect and, as in Middletown, the presence of the investigators had a considerable impact on the social awareness of the people being studied. (Warner and his study appear in fictionalized form in a novel about Newburyport by John P. Marquand.)[44]

But the differences between the two studies are as important as the similarities. The focus in Middletown was on the social changes that occurred between 1890 and 1925; in Yankee City, change was studied continuously over a much longer period. Middletown could be considered as a sample of American society or at least of the American Midwest; Yankee City, although not unique, represented a much less typical slice of American life. The Yankee City project is pervaded by an interest in particular places and persons. The most important procedural difference between the two projects is that the groups in Middletown were treated as aggregates, whereas the data gathered in Yankee City were arranged by individual names. The principal part of the analysis consisted of tracing the associations and relationships of individuals, using a filing system that accumulated information individually for nearly every living inhabitant of the city.

A *class order,* according to Warner, consists of:

two or more orders of people who are believed to be, and are accordingly ranked by the members of the community, in socially superior and inferior positions. Marriages within the same order are preferred although the values of the society permit marriage up and down. A class system also provides that children are born into the same status as their parents. A class society distributes rights and privileges, duties and obligations, unequally among its inferior and superior grades. A system of classes, unlike a system of castes, provides by its own values for movement up and down the social ladder. In common parlance, this is social climbing, or in technical terms, social mobility. The social system of Yankee City, we found, was dominated by a class order.[45]

That class order was composed of six classes—or of three major classes, each divisible in half. In local parlance they were given names based on districts of the town (Hill Streeters, Side Streeters, and River-brookers, for example), and these designations served as euphemisms for class labels. In Warner's terminology, the six classes were upper-upper, lower-upper, upper-middle, lower-middle, upper-lower, and lower-lower. The upper-uppers were the old families whose ancestors had maintained a leading position in the town through at least three generations. Below them were newer families (lower-upper) whose style of life was identical but more recently acquired. The upper-middle class consisted of business and professional men with some degree of independence; the lower-middle class of small shopkeepers and white-collar workers. The predominant element in the upper-lower class were the factory workmen. The lower-lower class were the intermittently employed Riverbrookers, who got an uncertain living from casual labor, clamming, fishing, and odd jobs.

The Yankees (persons descended from the early English settlers of New England) were the dominant group, and Yankees of local origin made up about half the population; they were numerous in all six classes, but especially in the highest and the lowest. About a quarter of the population belonged to the several ethnic groups that had begun to settle in Yankee City in the 1840s. They were found in every class except the upper-upper. Each of the ethnic groups seemed to be gaining steadily in status at the time of the study as the proportion of its native-born members increased and its cultural separation from the dominant population diminished.

Although Warner occasionally refers to the "organization" of life in Yankee City, the class system is not an organization in the sociologist's usual sense; it is not, that is, a social system with explicit collective goals. Until the investigators came along, no one in Yankee City had full knowledge of the class system, although everyone in town had some picture of it. It was a spontaneous pattern that had gradually evolved out of historical circumstances and was able to continue because Newburyport had a relatively immobile population of almost fixed size, and was not subject to any extreme pressure from the outside.

Although the Yankee City class system was ultimately based on the ownership of capital and on access to positions with different earning opportunities, it could not be fully explained by economic factors. People in each class were wealthier on the average than those in the class below, but there was a time lag, sometimes a very long time lag, between any change in the economic position of a family and a corresponding change in its status, so that some members of the upper-upper class lived in near poverty and some lower-middle-class individuals had high incomes. The mainspring of the class system was not the comparison of incomes but an intricate, subtle, highly ramified set of rules by which persons were chosen or rejected for particular types of association. The memberships that mattered in Yankee City were in families, cliques, associations, and economic groups. Each of these collectivities had its own class pattern: the members of the same family ordinarily belonged to the same class, the members of a clique belonged to one or two adjacent classes, the members of an association belonged to a configuration of classes depending upon its nature, and the members of an economic group were sharply differentiated along class lines.

The system was remarkably effective in enforcing itself, perhaps because dissatisfied individuals migrated elsewhere and those who remained were those accepting the values of Yankee City. Within the community, any sort of upward mobility was contingent upon the willingness of persons in the next upper stratum to associate with the aspirant for higher status. On the other hand, each class, even the upper-upper, was large enough so that no single person or clique could monopolize access to it and the candidate for membership turned away at one entrance was free to seek another. Thus the dowagers of Yankee City spent their lives in an inexhaustible network of parlor intrigues, and every social gathering could be interpreted, either by the investigators or by less professional gossips, as one round of a perpetual game played for status points. The game was followed most intensely at the top of the scale where the rewards were greatest and played in a rougher, more careless style among the underprivileged.

Like the Middletown studies, the Yankee City project expanded the view that Americans had of their own society and showed how much local diversity underlies the apparent uniformity of our institutions. This insight was not gained without a price, however, since the class system that flourished in Newburyport was by its nature a clandestine, unacknowledged, and illegitimate departure from the prevailing American ideals of democracy and personal equality. By making the system explicit, the investigators may have changed its character to some extent, validating the pretentions of those who claimed superior status, and making it difficult for middle and lower groups to claim the same theoretical equality as before. By the 1960s, the existence of a class system in the United States was universally taken for granted and the six-class system that Warner had found in Newburyport was assumed without further inquiry to be present in other communities.

Street Corner Society / William Foote Whyte

Another strange country close to home was discovered by William Foote Whyte, a Harvard graduate student, when he studied an Italian slum neighborhood (Cornerville) in Boston between 1937 and 1940.[46] Whyte's study had some relation to the Yankee City project. He learned his field work techniques from Conrad Arensberg and Elliott Chapple, who had acquired their art in Yankee City, and he enjoyed Warner's advice in preparing his report.

The great contrast between the two studies is that Whyte worked almost entirely alone (except for minor help from a fellow student and from his wife) and relied almost exclusively on the method of participant observation. The population of Cornerville at the time of the study was somewhat larger than that of Yankee City; it had about 20,000 inhabitants. Whyte did not pretend to study its institutions exhaustively; indeed, he scarcely mentioned the family, the church, the schools, and the legitimate sector of the local economy. The topic of inquiry was the interrelationship of the voluntary associations of young men in Cornerville with organized gambling and with politics. In the first section of his book, Whyte describes the development of two associations in which he participated, a street corner gang called the Nortons and a small association called the Italian Community Club. The members of the Nortons were "corner boys" whose ambitions and opportunities were limited to the local scene. The members of the Italian Community Club were "college boys," eager to make places for themselves in the larger society.

Street Corner Society has a remarkable dramatic quality; no other work in the sociological literature contains so much skillful characterization, drama, and pathos; few other works have been so much quoted. Much of this quality must be attributed to the author's emotional involvement with the people he studied. Somewhere he remarks that he nearly turned from being a nonparticipating observer to being a nonobserving participant. He was much closer to the Nortons than to the Italian Community Club. Doc, the leader of the Nortons, was his first informant and became his close friend, almost his collaborator. The story of the Nortons is largely the story of Doc, first in the days of his glory, later as a declining leader whose continued unemployment made it impossible for him to meet the obligations of leadership and led him at last to break up his own gang. The contrasting story of the Italian Community Club was largely the story of its leader, Chick Morelli, an unprincipled opportunist with a superior understanding of Cornerville's social structure. It is a struggle, in miniature, between Pareto's lions and foxes; Whyte's sympathies are all with the hapless lions (see Chapter Four).

The second section of the report is a study of the social structure of racketeering in Cornerville. The racketeers controlled the numbers game, maintaining a delicate accommodation with the police and close relations with the political structure that satisfied ethnic loyalties and local needs. The particular merit of Whyte's study was to show this system from the bottom up. One long chapter tells how a tiny social and athletic club was partly taken over by a racketeer and how it played a small but appreciable part in an aldermanic election. The clarity of Whyte's style, his close description of events, and his extensive use of direct quotation provide the reader with a sense of personal involvement.

There is another dramatic element in *Street Corner Society*. Although Whyte studied a slum area toward the end of the Great Depression and was ostensibly concerned with the seamy side of its life—unemployment, poor housing, police payoffs, political corruption, election frauds, limited opportunities—his enthusiasm led him to describe Cornerville as a place without violence, malice, or real suffering. He performed his task of gaining entreé so well that he fell in love with his subjects and they with him. He found a second home in the family of a local restaurant keeper, learned Italian, achieved high status in the Nortons, made friends with racketeers, worked in election campaigns, and even brought his new bride to live in Cornerville. He sometimes forgot neutrality and took sides on local issues.[47] On occasion, he went further than his friends expected to conform to their norms, for example, by voting several times on election day. He may have carried his preference for nondocumentary, nonstatistical, first-hand information further than was necessary in order to emphasize the importance he attached to direct personal interaction.

Among the regularities of behavior that Whyte discovered in Cornerville were that the corner boys held "local values" and the college boys held "cosmopolitan" values. That is, the corner boys maintained the indigenous virtues of their own circumscribed society, whereas the college boys, abetted by social workers and other agents of the larger society, neglected their obligations to each other in a race for upward mobility.

In each of Cornerville's hierarchies Whyte discerned a three-level system made up of little people, big people, and intermediaries. The corner boys were little people, the racketeers and politicians were big people, and the leaders of the corner gangs were intermediaries who bridged the gap between them. The pattern even extended to the supernatural hierarchy, in that the worshipers, as little people, approached the intermediary saints to intercede for them with the "big people" in Heaven.

But stratification in Cornerville involved more than these broad gradations. Each of the Cornerville associations Whyte observed, no matter how simple and informal it appeared at first, had an elaborate status order of its own. He was always able to show the dependence of status on a network of obligations within the group so that an individual's status measured his relative ability to conform to group values.

In every case, the leader was the focal point of the group's structure, its representative to the outside world, its internal arbiter, and the initiator of its collective activities. The leader's significant relationships were with his lieutenants, not with the rank and file (see Figure 3-1). When changes of leadership occurred, they were by shifts in the relationships between the men at the top of the structure, never by an uprising of the men at the bottom. Such changes are likely to be upsetting to those concerned. The deposed leader and some of his orphaned followers might even fall ill when the group's equilibrium is disturbed.

Perhaps the best remembered of Whyte's findings is the bowling score effect. One of the principal activities of Doc's gang was bowling, and considerable importance was attached to performance in that game. Whyte at first supposed that an individual's skill in bowling contributed to his status in the group, but he concluded, after prolonged observation, that the reverse was more nearly true. The status

Figure 3-1   HIERARCHIES IN CORNERVILLE

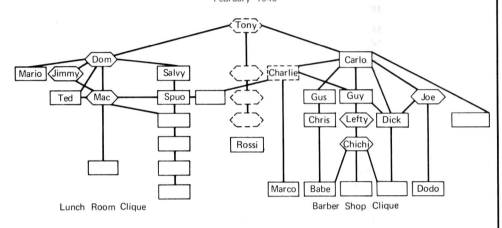

Informal Organization of the Cornerville S & A Club
February 1940

Lunch Room Clique

Barber Shop Clique

☐ Corner boy

⬡ Member of racket organization

----- Infrequently present

——— Line of influence

Positions of boxes indicate relative status

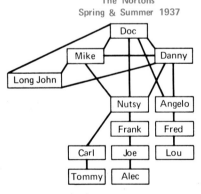

The Nortons
Spring & Summer 1937

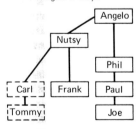

Angelo's Boys

Source: William Foote Whyte, *Street Corner Society: The Social Structure of an Italian Slum.* Chicago: University of Chicago Press, 1955), pp. 13, 49, 184.

of a group member determined his bowling skill, at least on those occasions when the entire group was assembled for an important match. The performance of lower-ranking members was depressed by both subtle and crude group pressures, and the performance of leaders was sustained in similar ways. Whyte reports this phenomenon as a subjective experience too:

> Here was the social structure in action right on the bowling alleys. It held the individual members in their places—and I along with them. I did not stop to reason then that, as a close friend of Doc, Danny, and Mike, I held a position close to the top of the gang and therefore should be expected to excel on this great occasion. I simply felt myself buoyed up by the situation. I felt my friends were for me, had confidence in me, wanted me to bowl well. As my turn came and I stepped up to bowl, I felt supremely confident that I was going to hit the pins that I was aiming at. I have never felt quite that way before—or since. Here at the bowling alley I was experiencing subjectively the impact of the group structure upon the individual. It was a strange feeling, as if something larger than myself was controlling the ball as I went through my swing and released it toward the pins.[48]

The combination of objective and subjective elements in *Street Corner Society* makes one wonder what another observer of different temperament would have found in the same situation. More than any other study in the sociological literature, *Street Corner Society* seems to call for replication. It is almost inexplicable that no such replication has been attempted. The superficially similar study of Negro street corner men by Elliot Liebow[49] is concerned with occupational and family problems, and covers a quite different sector of experience.

An American Dilemma / Gunnar Myrdal

The Myrdal study of the situation of the American Negro was initiated by the Carnegie Corporation in 1937. The field work was carried out with remarkable celerity between 1938 and 1940.

It was designed to be a comprehensive study of the Negro in America, and comprehensive it was. Myrdal, a Swedish social economist of international reputation, was selected to direct the project because he came from a country that had no appreciable nonwhite population and no history of colonial involvement. He brought an assistant, Richard Sterner, with him from Sweden and they began their work by traveling extensively through the South. Although he returned to Sweden early in 1940, Myrdal came back to America to prepare the final report in 1941 and was largely responsible for its leading ideas.

This project was the largest cooperative venture undertaken up to that time by American social scientists. Nearly 150 of them participated in the study as consultants, advisers, investigators, and writers. The roster included a large proportion of the eminent sociologists then alive. Three volumes on social aspects of the Negro situation[50] appeared before the project report[51] had been completed. Several books drawing on its data appeared later,[52] and dozens of other manuscripts prepared for the project remain unpublished. The scope of inquiry was wide enough to include Negro history; the origin, composition, and physical characteristics of the Negro population; intelligence and personality tests; a review and critique of census data; questionnaire studies; psychiatric case histories; analyses of stereotypes and ideologies among whites regarding Negroes; crime and prejudice; the Negro role in manufacturing, agriculture, private business, education, and government; differential wages; racial legislation, and many other matters. Despite this complexity of detail, the central theme of *An American Dilemma* is quite simple; it is set forth in italics in Myrdal's introduction to the project report:

> The American Negro problem is a problem in the heart of the American. It is there that the interracial tension has its focus. It is there that the decisive struggle goes on. This is the central viewpoint of this treatise. Though our study includes economic, social, and political race relations, at bottom our problem is the moral dilemma of the American—the conflict between his moral valuations on various levels of consciousness and generality. The "American Dilemma" referred to in the title of this book, is the ever-raging conflict between, on the one hand, the valuations preserved on the general plane which we shall call the "American Creed," where the American thinks, talks, and acts under the influence of high national and Christian precepts, and, on the other hand, the valuations on specific planes of individual and group living, where personal and local interests; economic, social and sexual jealousies; considerations of community prestige and conformity; group prejudice against particular persons or types of people; and all sorts of miscellaneous wants, impulses, and habits dominate his outlook.[53]

This formulation implies that the causes of the American Negro problem are to be sought in the beliefs and actions of the white majority, not those of the black minority—the same conclusion reached by the National Advisory Commission on Civil Disorders nearly a generation later after an investigation of Negro rioting in the summers of 1965–1967.[54] Indeed, the Myrdal study foreshadowed many events. For example, it assumed the continued migration of southern Negroes to northern cities, perceived the critical role of the white policeman in the Negro neighborhood, detected the pent-up aggressions later expressed by black nationalists, and even predicted that improved opportunities might lead some Negroes to favor self-segregation rather than integration.

The common denominator of the American race problem, as Myrdal saw it, was the nearly unanimous refusal of white Americans to consider amalgamation with the black population and their reliance on segregation to prevent the friendly contacts that might lead to intermarriage. He noted what he called the white man's rank order of discrimination—the relative importance attached to each type of discrimination by whites—and asserted that the Negroes' rank order—the relative importance they attached to the removal of each form of discrimination—was almost precisely opposite. The white man's rank order of discrimination began with the ban against intermarriage and sexual intercourse with white women followed by barriers to close social contact, segregation in public facilities, political disenfranchisement, discriminatory treatment by public agencies, and economic discrimination, in that sequence. The Negro's rank order began with the removal of economic discrimination.

Myrdal was much struck by the partial resemblance of the Negro's situation to that of other populations banned from full participation in the economy. Women were one example, poor whites another. He pointed out that the underprivileged strata of the American labor force did not unite against the ruling class in Marxian style but instead exhibited mutual hostility and kept each other subdued.

The mechanism whereby Negroes are kept underprivileged is described as the principle of *cumulation*. "White prejudice and discrimination keep the Negro low in standards of living, health, education, manners and morals. This, in its turn, gives support to white prejudice. White prejudice and Negro standards thus mutually 'cause' each other."[55] Myrdal took it for granted that all the factors of deprivation were interrelated, but with his primary interest in economics he emphasized the economic forms of deprivation to which Negroes were, and still are, subjected. He characterized the economic situation of American Negroes as pathological, noting that they owned little property, their household goods were inadequate, their incomes were low and irregular, Negro farmers were concentrated in the least productive sectors of agriculture, Negro nonfarm workers were concentrated in the worst-paid service and lowest industrial occupations, unemployment among Negroes was disproportionately high, and the rise of unionism in the 1930s had injured rather than improved their relative position.

Myrdal believed strongly (and still does) that a value-free social science is pointless, that the social scientist owes his audience not cold objectivity but a clear statement of the *value premises* that enter into his work. The basic value premise of *An American Dilemma* is stated with the utmost clarity. "We assume that it is to the advantage of American Negroes as individuals and as a group to become assimilated into American culture, to acquire the traits held in esteem by the dominant white Americans."[56] Although this value premise has lately been challenged by many black spokesmen, it continues to be widely accepted on both sides of the color line together with Myrdal's prescription for reversing the principle of cumulation by improving the condition of the Negro population step by step and institution by institution, using for this purpose the powers of government, the initiative of private organizations, and the consciences of individuals. He maintained that the solution of the race problem in the United States is inextricably joined to the relationship between the white and nonwhite populations of the globe and that the white population, facing a colored majority, will "either have to succumb or to find ways of living on peaceful terms with colored people."[57]

The People's Choice / Paul F. Lazarsfeld and Others

In the Presidential election of 1940, the voters of Erie County, Ohio had to decide whether to vote for the incumbent President Franklin D. Roosevelt for a third term or for the Republican challenger Wendell Wilkie, or to stay away from the polls. Lazarsfeld, the founder of the Bureau of Applied Social Research at Columbia University, undertook to discover how they made up their minds. The resulting research report[58] was less than 200 pages long, but it had far-reaching effects on the theory and practice of politics in the United States, and it set a fashion in political surveys that has since produced an enormous literature on the factors that determine the outcome of elections in democratic countries.[59]

The Erie County project grew out of the extensive use of public opinion polls to estimate trends in voter sentiment in the election campaigns of the 1930s and out of the audience research undertaken by radio networks and national magazines at about the same time to augment the impact of their advertising. A national magazine and a polling service provided most of the necessary funds.

The data were obtained by interviewers who called on a statistical cross-section of the population and obtained their responses to a standardized questionnaire. This study was far more elaborate than the usual public opinion survey, however. An interviewer visited every fourth house in Erie County in order to draw a sampling roster of approximately 3,000 voters, matched to the total adult population of the county by age, sex, residence, education, telephone and car ownership, and nativity. From this roster four samples of 600 persons each, matched on the same criteria, were then selected. One of these became the main sample, and the persons in it were interviewed monthly from May to November, the first interview taking place before the nominating conventions and the last after the election. The persons in the other three samples were interviewed at different intervals. These three samples served as control groups to test the effect of repeated interviewing on the main sample.

The study focused on the respondent's intended vote in the November election and the changes that occurred in that intention from one interview to the next. Whenever a respondent changed his voting intention in any way, he was questioned closely about his reasons and about the accompanying circumstances. A careful record of each respondent's exposure to campaign propaganda was kept. The text of the questionnaire was not included in the printed report, but we are told that it contained "voluminous information about each respondent's personal characteristics, social philosophy, political history, personality traits, relationships with friends and relatives, organization affiliations, religion identification and his opinions on current issues."

The principal finding of the study was that the electoral choice of a

Figure 3-2   POLITICAL PREDISPOSITION

High SES level, affiliation with the Protestant religion, and rural residence predispose a voter for the Republican party; the opposites of these factors make for Democratic predisposition. Summarized in an index of political predisposition (IPP), their effect is illustrated by the high correlation with vote intention.

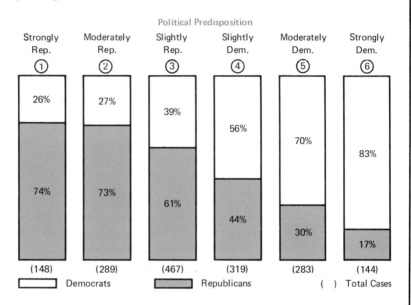

Political Predisposition

Strongly Rep. ①	Moderately Rep. ②	Slightly Rep. ③	Slightly Dem. ④	Moderately Dem. ⑤	Strongly Dem. ⑥
26%	27%	39%	56%	70%	83%
74%	73%	61%	44%	30%	17%
(148)	(289)	(467)	(319)	(283)	(144)

☐ Democrats   ▨ Republicans   ( ) Total Cases

Source: Paul F. Lazarsfeld, Bernard Berelson, and Hazel Gaudet, *The People's Choice: How the Voter Makes Up his Mind in a Presidential Campaign* (New York: Duell, Sloan and Pearce, 1944), chart 8, p. 26.

large majority of the voters could be predicted from only three social characteristics: socioeconomic status, religious affiliation, and rural or urban residence. High status, Protestantism, and rural residence predisposed voters toward the Republican candidate; low status, Catholicism, and urban residence predisposed them toward the Democratic candidate. Using these factors alone, the investigators were able to construct an index of political predisposition whose high predictive power is shown in Figure 3–2. This result was achieved even though the measurement of the three characteristics was rather crude. The rating of socioeconomic status, for example, was based on the interviewer's subjective assessment of the homes, possessions, appearance, and manner of speaking of the people interviewed. The respondent's statement of his religious affiliation was not controlled by church attendance or any other test of involvement.

Aside from social characteristics, the voter's choice was constrained, in a sense, by his own political history. For example, virtually all the Republicans who had voted for Landon against Roosevelt in the lean Rupublican year of 1936 voted for Wilkie in 1940. To take another type of example, most new voters followed the party preferenes of their parents when they voted for the first time.

The net effect of these various regularities was to reduce the number of voters whose decisions could be affected by the Presidential campaign to a relatively small minority of the voting population. These uncommitted voters have since become the principal targets of every sophisticated political campaign. But, as the Erie County study demonstrated, they are not easily reached. The voters who are most interested in an election, who participate in campaign events, and who expose themselves to political communications are likely to make their voting decisions well in advance of the election, or even before the nominating conventions have met. Among undecided voters there are disproportionate numbers of women, the young, the poor, and the uneducated; if their interest flags slightly, they may not vote at all.

But it is not only the apathetic voter who delays his decision. Voters are subject to cross-pressures when they belong to groups with incompatible voting tendencies; rich Catholics, for example, are pushed in opposite directions and tend to delay their decisions as they wait for events to resolve the conflicting pressures. Of all the cross-pressures the investigators identified, the one most likely to delay a decision was a lack of agreement within the voter's family. Some voters hesitated until they were actually inside the voting booth, but it is significant that they generally resolved the cross-pressures by voting the same way as their closest relatives did. One of the most interesting discoveries of this research was that the same factors that predisposed a voter to an early decision for one candidate or the other continued to operate when he was unable to make an early decision. Even under these circumstances, his eventual choice was influenced in the usual direction by his social characteristics.

All these findings tend to cast doubt on the rationality of the political process and on the relevance of the arguments with which candidates and parties attempt to influence voters. The doubt is deepened when we discover that exposure to campaign materials is determined in much the same way as the voting decision itself. The more interested and better-informed voters make up their minds earliest; they are also the most exposed to campaign materials and most likely to limit their exposure to the campaign materials of the candidates they have already selected. Even people who have not yet decided how to vote expose themselves more to the propaganda of the party toward which they are predisposed by the usual background factors.

Lazarsfeld and his associates were convinced that rational persuasion had very little to do with the way the voter makes up his mind:

> Arguments enter the final stage of the decision more as *indicators* than as *influences*. They *point out*, like signboards along the road, the way to turn in order to reach a destination which is already determined. ... The political predispositions and group alle-

giances set the goal; all that is read and heard becomes helpful and effective insofar as it guides the voter toward his already "chosen" destination. The clinching argument thus does not have the function of *persuading* the voter to act. He furnishes the motive power himself. The argument has the function of *identifying* for him the way of thinking and acting which he is already half-aware of wanting. Campaigning for votes is not writing on a public *tabula rasa;* it is showing men and women that their votes are a normal and logical and more or less inevitable expression of tendencies with which each has already aligned himself.[60]

The final section of *The People's Choice* discusses the political homogeneity of social groups and explains how the correlations previously demonstrated rest upon the general likelihood that people who work or live or play together will vote for the same candidate, either by an original spontaneous choice or because of the exercise of personal influence. The usual outcome of the political conversation that occurs throughout a campaign among friends, neighbors, and relatives is to augment the majority opinion within each social group, a bandwagon effect that corresponds to the bandwagon effect in the electorate at large. People expect the candidate they favor to win, and the reverse is also sometimes true—they sometimes favor a candidate because they expect him to win.

American politics were never the same again. *The People's Choice* concluded that the side "which can mobilize grass roots support in an expert way" has a great chance of success, and the practitioners of the expert way rose as if on a signal and flourished in the land. By the 1960s, the discoveries of this study had been so thoroughly incorporated into the political process that in the television announcements of election results, breakdowns of voting tendencies by income, religion, age, race, occupation, union membership, and other predisposing factors were given as a matter of course along with the election returns. Fortunately, the insights provided by voting research were equally available to every political contestant, and therefore did not change the competitive character of election campaigns as much as they might otherwise have done.

The American Soldier / Samuel A. Stouffer and Others

Shortly before the Japanese attack on Pearl Harbor, Samuel A. Stouffer, an eminent sociologist, was appointed civilian director of a newly formed Research Branch in what later became the Information and Education Division of the United States Army. The division was commanded by Major General Frederick Osborn, a former businessman who was also a social scientist. The Research Branch, as Stouffer noted later, existed to do a practical engineering job, not a scientific job. Its function was to undertake attitude surveys among the troops whenever higher headquarters became aware of problems that required survey information. It was asked, for example, to analyze the factors that made soldiers in the South Pacific theater reluctant to use atabrine as a prophylactic against malaria, to find which of two kinds of huts men preferred in Alaska, to examine the laundry situation in Panama and the attitudes of the troops toward the Chinese in the India-Burma theater. Many assignments were trivial, but some were of major importance. For example, the point system used to assign priorities to individual soldiers in demobilizing the armed forces at the end of the war was designed by the Research Branch. Its studies also provided the informational basis for veterans' benefit legislation, particularly the G.I. Bill of Rights, which permanently expanded the American system of higher education.

By the time World War II was over, the Research Branch had interviewed more than 500,000 persons using more than 200 different questionnaires, and had prepared several hundred reports of its findings for various military purposes. The scientific value of this enormous mass of material, however, had not been exploited at all. The task was assigned to a special committee of the Social Science Research Council, under the chairmanship of General Osborn, and carried out under the direction of Professor Stouffer, with a grant from the Carnegie Corporation, in the five years following the war. Thus the Research Branch, under the same leadership, was transformed into a scientific research team under civilian auspices. The results of its work were published in the four volumes of *Studies in Social Psychology in World War II*,[61] better known as *The American Soldier* from the title of the first two volumes.

Like the Myrdal project, it was a cooperative venture on a huge scale. The list of professional and administrative personnel runs to 134 names; the title pages of the four volumes show 15 principal authors. No subsequent piece of social research has equalled this one in scale.

Although it draws upon several disciplines, especially psychology and social psychology, *The American Soldier* is primarily sociological in its method—the attitude survey—and in the character of its results. Most of the reinterpretation and further analysis that followed its publication focused upon the sociological implications of the data, and not on their psychological, historical, or administrative significance.

Volume 1 of the report is devoted to the personal adjustment of soldiers, particularly the great mass of civilian soldiers who served temporarily in the Army during World War II. Volume 2 is concerned with the special problems of combat and its aftermath. Volume 3 investigates the reaction of military audiences to orientation films and other propaganda material; it stands somewhat apart from the rest of the work. Volume 4 is a thorough treatment of the theory and practice of attitude scaling and of three sophisticated methods that were developed for analyzing survey data—scalogram analysis, latent structure analysis, and the use of survey responses for predictive purposes.

The material in these four volumes is so vast and so loosely connected that subsequent interpretation has followed the general procedure of the blind men of Hindustan who went to view an elephant and found it to resemble a wall, rope, tree, fan, or snake according to the part they happened to touch. Thus, Edward A. Shils, in his famous essay, seems

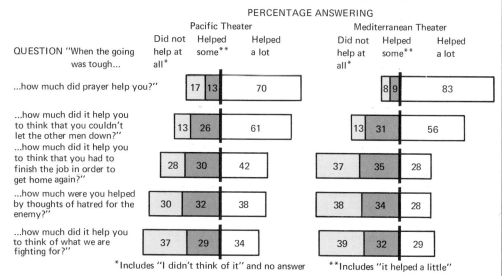

Figure 3-3 THOUGHTS WHICH ENLISTED MEN SAID WERE HELPFUL WHEN THE GOING WAS TOUGH (VETERAN ENLISTED INFANTRYMEN IN THE PACIFIC AND MEDITERRANEAN THEATERS)

Thoughts That Enlisted Men Said Were Helpful When the Going Was Tough

PERCENTAGE ANSWERING

	Pacific Theater			Mediterranean Theater		
QUESTION "When the going was tough...	Did not help at all*	Helped some**	Helped a lot	Did not help at all*	Helped some**	Helped a lot
...how much did prayer help you?"	17	13	70	8	9	83
...how much did it help you to think that you couldn't let the other men down?"	13	26	61	13	31	56
...how much did it help you to think that you had to finish the job in order to get home again?"	28	30	42	37	35	28
...how much were you helped by thoughts of hatred for the enemy?"	30	32	38	38	34	28
...how much did it help you to think of what we are fighting for?"	37	29	34	39	32	29

*Includes "I didn't think of it" and no answer   **Includes "it helped a little"

Pacific: Four divisions surveyed, March-April 1944, S-100. Unweighted average of four divisions. Numbers of cases in the four divisions were 1,428, 1,299, 1,364, and 643, respectively. Mediterranean: Four divisions surveyed in Italy, April 1945, S-177. 1,766 cases. In Italy the wording of the last question was: "... how much did it help you to think of the meaning of what we are fighting for?"

to suggest that the morale of the combat soldier was primarily dependent on his primary group attachments in the Army,[62] and seems to minimize the dependence of combat morale on prayer, which, as Figure 3-3 shows, was a more important support than comradeship for the combat soldier.

Similarly, emphasis was placed by several distinguished analysts on the effects of relative deprivation (for example, Negroes in northern camps made a worse general adjustment than those in southern camps, because in both the South and the North the soldier's basis of comparison was the local civilian, and the relatively worse condition of the Negro civilian in the South counterbalanced the objectively worse treatment of Negroes in southern camps). This emphasis has displaced attention from some interesting findings about absolute deprivation, especially the discovery that military units begin to disintegrate when exposed to combat or to other forms of hardship for excessively long periods.

The analysts' emphasis on the effects of role and position in modifying attitudes—"Differences in role and position lead not only to differences in attitude but to misunderstandings and mistaken judgment of one group by another"—have obscured the salient finding that the wartime Army was pervaded with resentment about the abuse of the privileges of rank, and that this sentiment had highly adverse effects on morale, except in the Air Force, where different conditions prevailed.

The American Soldier is perhaps the most devastating critique of a large-scale organization that has ever been prepared by its own members. In contrast to earlier community studies and later organizational studies, which find most people reasonably content with the social systems in which they find themselves, the data of *The American Soldier* reveal the remarkable case of millions of men engaged in a desperate struggle for the sake of ultimate social ideals while great numbers of them have no real commitment to their cause, no confidence in their leaders, and nothing but contempt for the norms that regulate their lives. Three out of five men with overseas combat service had doubts, as of 1945, whether the war was worth fighting.[63]

The American Army in World War II consisted largely of men who had been drafted for the task of winning a war of which the ideological purposes always remained a little vague to them. The third volume of the series shows, without quite intending to, how this situation arose and why very little could be done about it. Much of the experimentation reported in that volume concerns the reaction of soldier audiences to the superb film series called *Why We Fight,* which recounted the events leading up to the war as if the soldiers to whom the films would be shown had never heard of those events or formed opinions about them at the time they occurred. This may explain why the message of the films was so readily accepted by the military audience and why it had so little effect on their attitudes toward the war.

Other experiments in communication had to do with propaganda pure and simple. For example, two kinds of radio programs were prepared after the end of the war in Europe to persuade soldiers that there was no basis for their optimism about an early peace in the Pacific (as later events proved, their optimism was justified). The question studied was whether a program presenting only the arguments for the official (pessimistic) position was more persuasive than a program that presented the arguments on both sides and attempted to refute the arguments opposed to the official position. At first, the two programs appeared to be equally effective. The opinions of nearly half the audience in each case changed in the desired direction. But when the audience was divided into subgroups, sharp differences in the programs' effects appeared. The program that presented both sides was much more persuasive for men who initially opposed the official position and much less persuasive than a one-sided presentation for men who originally favored the official position. The one-sided program was more effective with less educated soldiers, whereas the presentation of both sides was more effective with high school and college graduates. When initial opinions and educational level were taken into account simultaneously, the differences in effect were startling. For example, among more educated men initially opposed to the official position, the two-sided presentation had the net effect of persuading 44 per cent of the audience in the desired direction; among less educated men initially favorable to the official position, the same program had a negative net effect.

Such experiments were undertaken quite openly in the hope of teaching the military authorities how to manipulate the opinions and sentiments of the rank and file. The Research Branch, as Stouffer repeatedly pointed out, was established for social engineering as an arm of military management, and the wholehearted commitment of the investigators to the war effort enabled them to support the managerial objectives of higher headquarters without qualms. When serious flaws in the system of military management were discovered, they were treated as morale problems. The possibility of reforming the military system in appropriate ways was not considered by the Research Branch, since such reform did not fall within the competence of the commanders the Research Branch was trying to assist. The improvements accomplished as the result of the research findings were not impressive. The complaints of infantrymen that they were unfairly treated compared to men in other branches of service were met by the introduction of honorific insignia. The discovery that the Army's system for reporting abuses of authority through the confidential channels of the Inspector General's office had broken down led the investigators to propose that new procedures be introduced *in peacetime*. This one-sided viewpoint was severely criticized after the report appeared in print, but none of the critics took advantage of the opportunity provided by the mountain of data in *The American Soldier* to develop a systematic program for improving military institutions. The principal reforms introduced in the Army after World War II were initiated internally and concerned military justice, a topic not covered in *The American Soldier*.

The Kinsey Reports / Alfred C. Kinsey

Dr. Alfred C. Kinsey, a quiet, shy zoologist at Indiana University, who had labored for years on a monumental study of wasps, decided about 1938 to investigate human sexual behavior. By 1948 Kinsey and his staff had interviewed more than 12,000 Americans of every age and both sexes using a sexual history questionnaire that contained 521 items. The answers were recorded in a special code devised by a cryptographer, and the files of the project were guarded as if they contained military secrets.

For many years Kinsey himself did most of the interviews, and he never had more than a handful of collaborators. They seem to have achieved an unprecedented level of sophistication and skill as they administered the standard interview, during a long period of years, to thousands of persons drawn from every region, occupation, socioeconomic level, and personality type—to convicts and nuns, sex offenders and old maids, bankers and pimps, housewives and psychiatrists. Their purpose was to construct a cross-section of the American population, and despite some major flaws in sampling procedures, they seem to have accomplished it.

Included in the Kinsey interview was all sexual behavior, that is, any type of physical activity causing sexual arousal. His categorization of sexual behavior may be described as behaviorist; that is, with only a few exceptions, the manifestations with which he was concerned had to be overt and physiological. Sentiments and emotions are largely excluded from this perspective—it has often been remarked that the word *love* does not appear in the index to either of the two major reports—but on the other hand, the category of sexual activity is expanded far beyond ordinary heterosexual activity to include homosexual contacts, masturbation, nocturnal emissions, and animal contacts.

Kinsey's principal discoveries were that:

1. The principal forms of illegal sexual activity are not rare, but are very widely diffused throughout the society
2. Males on the average have an earlier, more intense, more uniform, more continuous, and more promiscuous sex drive than females
3. Individuals of the same age, class, and social type vary greatly in the variety and frequency of their sexual activity
4. The frequency of sexual activity is strongly influenced by age, sex, religious affiliation, educational level, rural or urban residence, and occupational level
5. There was no clear trend of increasing sexual nonconformity at the time of the study.

The findings regarding the wide diffusion of forms of sexual activity that were nominally banned in the United States by law, by religious precepts, or by the mores, not unexpectedly attracted the greatest attention, since they drastically modified the picture of sexual life held by most observers—including habitual nonconformists. Most of the persons interviewed believed their own behavior to be more deviant than it really was. They were aware of their own unconventional sexual activities, but underestimated the extent to which others engaged in similar activities.

Kinsey found that 50 percent of the married women in his sample had engaged in premarital coitus, about half of them with a man who was not their future husband and about a tenth of them with six or more partners. Among men at the highest educational level, more than two-thirds engaged in premarital coitus; among those at the lowest educational level, virtually all. In the higher educational groups, intercourse was replaced to some extent by "petting" to orgasm, in which 39 percent of the women and 31 percent of the men had engaged by age 25. The women engaged in petting reported an average of eight partners. Twenty-six percent of married women and 50 percent of married men reported at least one episode of extramarital coitus, although not necessarily during the active phase of the marriage.

Homosexuality was found more frequently among men than among women. At least one homosexual experience leading to orgasm was reported by 37 percent of the men and 13 percent of the women. The frequency was much higher in prisons and other segregated places. About 4 percent of the men had only homosexual contacts.

Masturbation to orgasm was reported by 58 percent of the women and 92 percent of the men, but the frequency among men was much higher, and in a large number of cases, masturbation continued during a sexually active marriage.

Animal contacts involving orgasm were reported by 4 percent of the women and 8 percent of the men in the sample.

Impressive as this evidence of nonconformity is, it does not indicate —as some careless readers of the Kinsey reports have inferred—that the prevailing norms were generally ineffective. Half the women in the sample were virgins at marriage; half the remainder had lost their virginity to their future husbands. More than half of all husbands and more than three-quarters of all wives had been faithful to their spouses up to the time of the interviews. Most homosexuality occurred in the form of adolescent experimentation, or under special circumstances; the majority of both sexes had no such experience at all.

The "male" report appeared in 1948 and the "female" report in 1953,[64] to the accompaniment of worldwide excitement. Dr. Kinsey died in 1956. The two further volumes by his collaborators that have since appeared, *Pregnancy, Birth and Abortion* in 1958 and *Sex Offenders: An Analysis of Types* in 1965, attracted much less public attention although they too contain a great deal of previously unavailable information.

The publication of the reports marked a major turning point in social research, not only by providing a mass of data about sexual activity but also by bringing the topic within the perspective of social research and demonstrating once and for all that the most intimate and guilt-ridden types of human behavior could be investigated by survey methods. The numerous checks on reliability in the project itself included the reinterview of several hundred subjects, the comparison of responses given by spouses, and the matching of interview reports with external evidence. By all of these tests, the data appeared to be generally reliable. It is surprising that no major replications have been attempted in other countries; the comparative results would be interesting.

Later Landmark Studies

The last volume of *The American Soldier* was published in 1950; the second Kinsey Report in 1953. Since that time, no single research project has commanded the universal attention of social scientists, although the amount of social research has increased spectacularly and hundreds of important studies have been reported. During the 1950s and 1960s, the funds available for social research increased sharply from year to year; dozens of new research institutes were established; the number of working sociologists increased sixfold. There were similar increases in neighboring disciplines; and social research was transformed from a largely American enterprise to a cooperative effort involving most of the world's countries.

The natural consequence of this explosive growth was specialization. The typical sociologist ceased to take all of social experience for his province, and began to limit himself to one or two special fields.

The stream of sociological research results that, as late as 1950, found an adequate outlet in two or three major journals now occupies scores of specialized periodicals, some dealing with subjects as narrow as minority problems in urban elementary schools or the reaction of physicians to pharmaceutical advertising. Publications reporting sociological research results are now too numerous to be skimmed by any single reader.

The communication of research results tends to become less effective as the number of projects increases. Even the largest and most significant of current studies do not attract as much notice as did those we have just discussed.

Many of the recent studies are comparatively modest in their intentions. They illuminate a particular sector of social activity, such as the workings of a criminal court or of a racetrack,[65] without attempting ambitious generalizations. At the same time, vast new bodies of work have appeared on topics like socioeconomic development and human sexual behavior, which are relevant to sociology but somewhat outside it.

For these reasons, it is not possible to identify the landmarks of recent social research with the same assurance as the earlier ones. The contemporary landscape is dotted by many more projects, but none of them looms high against the horizon.

In the two sections that follow, we discuss two *areas* of research, small-group experiments and case studies of bureaucracy, to illustrate the way landmark studies now appear on a smaller scale in more specialized fields; there are at least a score of other fields of current sociological interest that could be described in the same way.

SMALL-GROUP EXPERIMENTS

In the field of psychology, laboratory experimentation with small groups of subjects has a long history going back to the nineteenth century. However, the study of social relations by laboratory methods did not develop extensively until after World War II, at first stimulated by the work of Kurt Lewin and his followers in "group dynamics," and later by the work of Robert F. Bales and others in "interaction process analysis." The former group was identified as psychologists; the latter as sociologists. Together they contributed to the borderline field of social psychology, which subsequently grew so large that it almost dwarfed its parent disciplines.

It would be quite impracticable to summarize the results of small-group experimentation here. The subject has handbooks and textbooks of its own.[66] A few studies of special significance for sociologists will be mentioned, however, to show what kind of results have been obtained by laboratory methods.

In 1950, Bales published his *Interaction Process Analysis,*[67] based on a program of experimental work at the Harvard Laboratory of Social Relations. The name refers to a method Bales devised for scoring interaction in small discussion groups. The observers, concealed behind one-way mirrors, divide the discussion into single "acts." An "act" is speech or gesture with an ascertainable social meaning. Every "act" is scored by each observer on a moving tape calibrated in small intervals of time so that the tapes of separate observers can later be compared with each other and with verbatim transcripts of the same session. The observers' code is a complex form of shorthand learned through intensive training. Each "act" is scored in one of 12 categories, ranging from positive to negative in social-emotional response. The categories used are shown in Figure 3–4. The scoring of each act also shows which member of the group originated the "act" and toward whom it was directed; and there is a way of coding group acts, the acts of an individual toward the group as a whole, and self-directed acts. The categories are symmetrical: positive emotional reactions are at the top, negative emotional reactions are at the bottom, and there is a "task area" of questions and attempted answers in the middle. Each pair of categories extending out from the middle represents one of six types of problem that every group must solve continuously in order to achieve collective goals. The influence of Parsons, with whom Bales had been closely associated, is seen clearly in the emphasis on social acts, their positive and negative forms, and the functional requirements of a social system.

Among the results obtained by this method was the discovery that the rank order of initiation of "acts" corresponds very closely, often perfectly, with the rank order of reception. In other words, those persons who speak most in group meetings are also the most spoken to and the most influential. Another interesting discovery was that small experimental groups tend to develop two leaders rather than one: a task or "instrumental" leader who contributes the most to accomplishing the group's collective tasks, and an emotional or "expressive" leader, who is most influential in maintaining group solidarity. The task leader is generally the most respected member of the group but not the best liked. On the basis of this experimental finding, Parsons and Bales developed a theory of family structure as a balanced system in which the father is normally the instrumental leader and the mother the expressive leader.

A notable study in the Lewinian tradition of small-group experimentation is Stanley Schachter's *The Psychology of Affiliation,* published in 1959.[68] Schachter, a gifted experimenter who likes to use the results of each experiment to design the next experiment in a coherent sequence, began in this case with a study of the effects of complete isolation on individual subjects. Student volunteers were locked up alone in sound-insulated windowless rooms for considerable periods of time. To the surprise of the investigator, who expected that solitary confinement

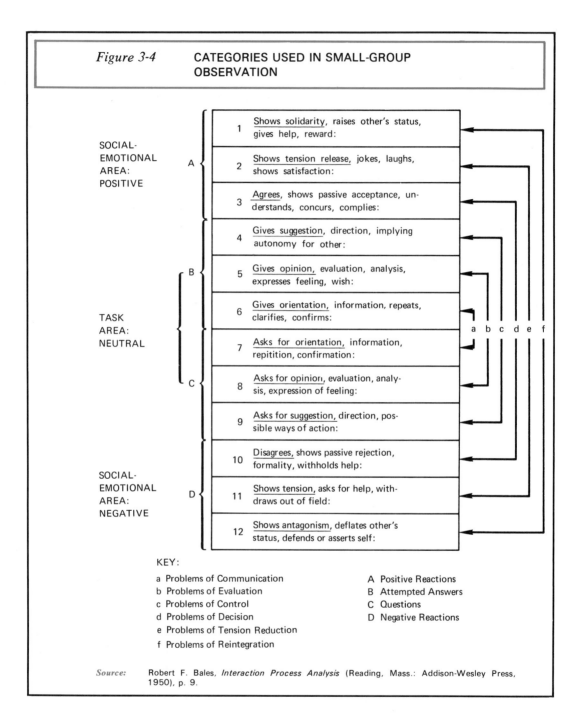

Figure 3-4 CATEGORIES USED IN SMALL-GROUP OBSERVATION

SOCIAL-EMOTIONAL AREA: POSITIVE

A

1 Shows solidarity, raises other's status, gives help, reward:

2 Shows tension release, jokes, laughs, shows satisfaction:

3 Agrees, shows passive acceptance, understands, concurs, complies:

TASK AREA: NEUTRAL

B

4 Gives suggestion, direction, implying autonomy for other:

5 Gives opinion, evaluation, analysis, expresses feeling, wish:

6 Gives orientation, information, repeats, clarifies, confirms:

C

7 Asks for orientation, information, repitition, confirmation:

8 Asks for opinion, evaluation, analysis, expression of feeling:

9 Asks for suggestion, direction, possible ways of action:

SOCIAL-EMOTIONAL AREA: NEGATIVE

D

10 Disagrees, shows passive rejection, formality, withholds help:

11 Shows tension, asks for help, withdraws out of field:

12 Shows antagonism, deflates other's status, defends or asserts self:

a b c d e f

KEY:

a Problems of Communication
b Problems of Evaluation
c Problems of Control
d Problems of Decision
e Problems of Tension Reduction
f Problems of Reintegration

A Positive Reactions
B Attempted Answers
C Questions
D Negative Reactions

Source: Robert F. Bales, *Interaction Process Analysis* (Reading, Mass.: Addison-Wesley Press, 1950), p. 9.

would cause his subjects to suffer, their typical reaction was boredom rather than distress. The experiment suggested that isolation from all human contact does not produce anxiety when there are no other threatening elements in the isolate's situation. Schachter then went on to a series of group experiments in which the subjects were told that they faced various unpleasant experiences and chose whether to remain alone or to join a group before and during these ordeals. The experimenter introduced physical stress by having some subjects skip meals before the experiment. In the presence of a threat, anxiety was generally higher among isolated individuals. Most subjects chose to meet a threatening situation in company. The introduction of hunger as an additional stress increased both the level of anxiety and the desire for group protection. In the course of these experiments, some subjects showed a much stronger need for protective affiliation than others. After trying out various other possibilities, Schachter discovered that the subject's ordinal position in his family of origin accounted for much of the difference. Subjects who had been first-born or only children were much more likely to seek the protection of a group under high-anxiety conditions. They were more susceptible to anxiety and less tolerant of pain, and they became more anxious and fearful than later-borns when exposed to an anxiety-producing situation. Moving outside the experimental framework, Schachter discovered that a good deal of evidence already existed for the greater social dependence of first-born individuals. First-borns are more likely, for example, to accept psychotherapeutic treatment and to be closely attached to parents and teachers; they are less likely to become alcoholics or to succeed as fighter pilots.

One of the most remarkable studies in the experimental literature is the experiment conducted by Muzafer Sherif and his associates[69] at a summer camp in Oklahoma. The subjects were grade-school boys about 11 years old, all white, middle class, and Protestant, as homogeneous a sample as careful selection and psychological testing could obtain. Soon after their arrival at the camp they were split into two experimental groups matched for athletic ability, personality characteristics, and prior acquaintance. The two groups were then placed in a series of competitive situations in which their interests were opposed and each group was an obstacle to the goals of the other. In the course of the camp season, a state of miniature war evolved. Each group developed its own status order and political style. The two social systems that emerged were strikingly different. Their mutual hostility, although it fell within the experimental design, was quite real, and the investigators were nearly unable to prevent the eruption of violence. Having created a social conflict experimentally they set about experimenting with peace and discovered that it could be achieved when both groups were persuaded to pursue "a superordinate goal," which could not be achieved by the efforts of either group alone. Reluctant cooperation under these conditions dissipated some of the tension aroused by their previous conflict, although the camp season ended too soon to determine the ultimate effects of peace on the internal structure of each group.

In recent years both psychologists and sociologists have pursued the investigation of coalitions in triads by means of laboratory experiments.[70] A triad is a social system containing three related members in a persistent situation. It is one of the most familiar phenomena in human experience. The members of a triad need not be individual persons; they may be collectivities acting as units. In most of the laboratory experiments conducted on coalition formation, the experimental group consists of three volunteer subjects who are taught to play an experimental game that allows two players to combine forces against the third.

The tendency of triads to split so that two members combine against the third was first noted by Georg Simmel in his analysis of the changes in group activity associated with changes in group size. Simmel was also the first to glimpse the basic mechanism whereby strength is transformed into weakness and weakness into strength by the formation of coalitions in triads. Indeed, certain configurations of power in a triad make such a transformation nearly inevitable. For example, in a triad in which *A* is stronger than *B* and *B* is stronger than *C,* but *A* is not stronger than *B* and *C* combined (Figure 3–5), the formation of any of the three possible coalitions (*AB, BC,* or *AC*) will upset the previously existing distribution of power. Laboratory experiments have repeatedly shown *BC* to be the most likely coalition when the conditions of the game are such as to encourage coalitions. Thus, the superior strength of *A,* compared to that of the other two players individually, virtually insures his defeat.

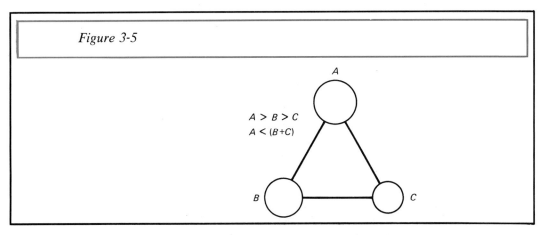

Figure 3-5

$$A > B > C$$
$$A < (B + C)$$

The laboratory work on triadic games shows the formation of coalitions to be so orderly a process that the formation of a particular coalition can often be predicted with a high degree of probability. It provides a particularly clear example of the potential usefulness of laboratory experiments. Large triads made up of collectivities—factions, political parties, nations—can be shown to behave like small experimental triads with respect to coalition formation; and the results obtained in laboratory games can be applied to the analysis of large-scale situations in which direct experimentation would not be feasible.

Beginning in the early 1950s, Weber's concept of bureaucracy[71] provided the theoretical framework for a number of field investigations of bureaucratic organizations. The combined result of these researches has been the expansion and clarification of the concept. On the one hand, there is no longer room for doubt that a bureaucracy functions very much as Weber supposed—as a kind of large, impersonal machine for the coordination of human effort and the adjustment of social relationships. On the other hand, the studies have shown that bureaucracies are human, so to speak; they never run exactly by their own rule books, they are subject to numerous perversions of function and style, and they develop features that are totally unplanned. Some of these findings, of course, were foreshadowed in the Hawthorne experiments and even earlier, but the recent studies go much further.

For example, Alvin W. Gouldner's *Patterns of Industrial Bureaucracy*,[72] is a study of values, norms, and norm enforcement in a gypsum mine and in the executive and clerical offices connected with the mine. It cast new light on the enforcement of social norms in organizations, and on the changes that occur when one man replaces another in a key organizational post. Gouldner discovered that the form and content of a norm do not tell us very much about the way it is activated. The enforcement of any norm is the outcome of a complicated transaction between the group that promulgates norms and the group controlled by them. Some norms, the utility of which is accepted by both groups, such as the prohibition of smoking where explosives are stored, are obeyed literally and perfectly. Other norms, such as the prohibition of smoking in certain safe working places, are "mock" enforced; a kind of collusion between the two groups conceals the infractions that occur. Still other norms, representing a clash of unresolved interests between groups, are entirely unenforceable. With respect to succession, Gouldner was able to show how and why a change in the incumbency of an important position was likely to be accompanied by changes in the administrative style, the normative system, and the status order of the organization affected.

Another influential case study of bureaucracy was Peter M. Blau's *Dynamics of Bureaucracy*,[73] based on the author's direct observation of the behavior of officials in two government agencies in 1948–1949. One agency was a branch of a state employment service that interviewed applicants and placed them in jobs in the clothing industry. The other was a federal department responsible for the enforcement of certain laws regulating business (apparently minimum-wage laws). The two agencies differed greatly in function and atmosphere, but both of them were found to have unofficial structures that had grown up in response to the social needs of their officials and were not part of the prescribed organization or entirely consistent with its aims.

In the state employment service, there were elaborate procedures for limiting work output and for maximizing the apparent performance of interviewers, sometimes at the cost of sacrificing the interests of clients or leaving the work unperformed. In this agency, as in many other welfare agencies that have been studied since, there was considerable hostility between officials and clients.

In the federal agency, the divergence from official expectations took an entirely different form. Although each agent was expected to handle his cases independently, an elaborate system of joint effort had appeared instead. In this instance, the departure from official norms may have led to a higher level of efficiency than would have been possible otherwise. The agents formed a close, cohesive group with an informal status order based on technical competence. Within that group help and advice were freely exchanged, and the agent was protected against the mistakes he might have made by following his unaided judgment since he drew upon the pooled knowledge of the entire group. At the same time, there was evidence—somewhat understated by the investigator—that these arrangements allowed the agents to change the substance of the law they were enforcing in order to suit their collective convenience.

Michel Crozier's study of bureaucracy in France,[74] which appeared about a decade later, focused directly on the diversity of bureaucratic experience that previous studies had disclosed and analyzed the reasons for divergent adjustment to bureaucratic systems. Crozier studied three government agencies in France, in each case taking the whole agency for his field of observation. Although the increase of scale entails a loss of detail, the study shows clearly how structural differences develop in bureaucratic units intended to be identical.

The most interesting of Crozier's agencies is a state-owned industry with large manufacturing plants scattered throughout the country. In these plants, potential conflict is reduced by drawing each level of personnel from a separate source of recruitment and maintaining separate career lines for each level. Thus, all managing directors are promoted by seniority rather than merit from the ranks of assistant directors, all of whom are recruited from a famous engineering school. No managing director ever rises from the ranks. The two other classes of high officials, technical engineers and comptrollers, are likewise separate, each having a prescribed preparation and promotion by seniority. A similar separation of levels prevails among the manual workers on the shop floor. Foremen, maintenance men, and machine operators are recruited from different sources and remain separate and noninterchangeable throughout their working lives. The reduction of conflict between management and labor is effectively achieved but at the cost of low efficiency, poor communication, and low morale. Crozier is able to trace the relationship of this type of organization to certain fixed elements in French society and culture.

Studies of hospitals by participant observation provide additional information about the possible variations of the bureaucratic pattern. The first major work was Stanton and Schwartz's *The Mental Hospital,* a study of a private psychiatric institution published in 1954.[75] Several other notable studies of mental hospitals[76] and a number of important studies of general hospitals[77] and of medical training in hospitals[78] have since appeared. An astonishing diversity of structure has been discovered, and successive investigators have enlarged the catalog of possible departures from formal rationality in therapeutic institutions without being able to set limits to the process or to predict the development of a particular informal structure in a given type of hospital.

The two great discoveries common to all of the hospital studies are: (1) Illness (especially, but not exclusively, mental illness) is a social phenomenon, and its symptoms and manifestations in a hospital are always conditioned by the social interaction among patients, between patients and staff, and among members of the staff. One recent hospital study even seems to show that patients are pronounced dead partly on sociological rather than physiological evidence. (2) Although a hospital is often visualized as consisting of two populations—patients who submit passively to treatment and doctors, nurses, technicians, and attendants who administer treatment—actual observation of the modern hospital discloses a single social system in which staff members and patients are both—and almost to the same extent—subjects and objects, capable of initiating action and responsive to each other's initiatives, despite the vast differences of status and power between patients and staff that are inherent in this form of organization.

Summary / CHAPTER THREE

1. The origins of social research go back to the seventeenth century, but the sociological research project, which involves a combination of theorizing and fact-gathering, is a comparatively recent invention. The first good example was Durkheim's *Suicide,* published in 1895. Most of the landmark projects in the sociological research tradition were carried out in the United States during the past half-century.

2. Thomas and Znaniecki's *Polish Peasant in Europe and America* was a study of Polish immigrants, the society from which they came in Poland, and the Polish-American society to which they went, based on a vast collection of letters and other documents. The attitudes and values of both societies were in a state of flux, with a general movement away from traditional family solidarity toward unregulated individualism.

3. The Chicago School, under the leadership of Robert E. Park, produced a large number of careful studies of urban life and culture based on miscellaneous empirical methods. Among their topics were family disorganization, suicide, prostitution, mental disorder, delinquency, juvenile gangs, homelessness, and many types of urban neighborhoods, from the richest to the poorest. The findings were set in a theoretical framework based on plant botany, and called *urban ecology.*

4. The Lynds studied *Middletown,* a small Indiana city, in the early 1920s and again in 1935, in order to describe in detail the changes that were taking place in its major institutions. The first study traced changes from 1890 to 1925 retrospectively; the second study examined changes from 1925 to 1935 and especially the effects of the Great Depression. The central feature of the community, according to the Lynds, was its class system.

5. *Tikopia* is an isolated society on a tiny island in the Pacific, studied by Firth in three widely spaced expeditions. Because the material drawn from these expeditions is exceptionally clear and complete, it has been heavily drawn on to support the theories of other sociologists. During the period covered by the study, the traditional culture of Tikopia has been heavily eroded by contact with the outside world.

6. *The Hawthorne experiments* were a well-known series of studies carried out at the Western Electric Company from 1927 to 1932 by a large team led by Elton Mayo. In various ways, these studies showed that the productivity of industrial workers was influenced by their social relationships on the job as much or more than by objective working conditions.

7   *Yankee City* is a small New England city with a long, continuous history, studied by Warner and others in the early 1930s. He discovered a six-class system and an intricate web of status relationships, interwoven with local beliefs and practices.

8   *Street Corner Society* is the report of Whyte's participant observation study of an Italian-American slum in the late 1930s. He showed how the young men of the community adapted to a situation of limited opportunity and how their lives came to be centered on close interaction with their peers.

9   Myrdal's *An American Dilemma* was a comprehensive study of the situation of Negroes in the United States on the eve of World War II. Myrdal documented a cycle of discrimination, deprivation, and poverty that he attributed to the inconsistent beliefs and actions of the white majority.

10   *The People's Choice* by Lazarsfeld and others showed how the social characteristics of voters in an Ohio county influenced the way they voted in a Presidential election. It was followed by a long line of similar studies, which have had a considerable effect on political practices.

11   A large team of investigators directed by Stouffer studied *The American Soldier* in World War II, obtaining information primarily from attitude surveys. The results provided a mine of data for organizational theorists, particularly as concerned the effect of organizational position on morale.

12   *The Kinsey reports,* based on extensive interviewing of a sample of more than 12,000 respondents, summarized the patterns of sexual behavior of males and females in the United States, cross-classified by such factors as age, education, occupation, religion, and marital status. The statistical incidence of various types of unconventional behavior was charted with what appears to be reasonable precision.

13   In recent years, there has been a vast increase in the number of research projects undertaken, so that individual projects no longer stand out as distinctly as before. Among the many fields in which important research has been done, small-group experiments on various types of social process and case studies of bureaucratic organizations were singled out for discussion.

1 Which of the studies described in this chapter would it be most useful to repeat at regular intervals? Why do you suppose this has not been done?

2 Which of these studies would it be impossible to repeat under current conditions? Why?

3 If you were studying stratification in your home community, would you take an approach closer to the Lynds or to Warner? Explain.

4 What would you like to know about life in an Italian slum that is *not* covered in *Street Corner Society*? Could that information be obtained through participant observation?

5 What effects might the publication of the Kinsey Report have had on patterns of sexual behavior in the United States? How could one find out whether such effects actually occurred?

6 What does it mean to say that "illness is a social phenomenon?" What do you learn by applying this concept to the most recent illness in your own family?

7 Do you think that the widespread use of survey methods to predict election results helps or hinders the democratic process?

8 In what ways are studies of American society carried out in the 1920s or 1930s still useful today? What are their limitations?

9 Find an illustration of each of the following concepts in your own experience:

> the "bowling score effect"
> the "Hawthorne Effect"
> relative deprivation
> a coalition in a triad
> social disorganization
> expressive leadership

Recommended Reading / **CHAPTER THREE**

Bernard Lécuyer and Anthony R. Oberschall. "Sociology: Early History of Social Research," *International Encyclopedia of the Social Sciences,* ed. David L. Sills. New York: Free Press and Macmillan, 1968, 15: 36–51. An excellent account of the early history of social research.

John Madge. *The Origins of Scientific Sociology.* New York: Free Press,

1962. Presents in more detail many of the landmark studies included in this chapter.

Notes / CHAPTER THREE

1. One of the best examples is Gregory King, "Natural and Political Observations and Conclusions Upon the State and Condition of England, 1699" in Alexander Chalmers, ed., *Estimate of the Comparative Strength of Great Britain* (Piccadilly: J. Stockdale, 1802).
2. The outstanding example is Sébastian LePrestre de Vauban's *Projet d'une Dîme Royale,* originally published in 1707.
3. The first national census reports were produced in Sweden around 1750, although local censuses had been made much earlier in various parts of the world.
4. Quetelet's contribution to social research is summarized by Paul F. Lazarsfeld, "Notes on the History of Quantification in Sociology: Trends, Sources and Problems," *Isis,* 52 (1961): 277–333.
5. Charles Booth et al., *Life and Labour of the People in London,* 2 vols. (London: Williams and Norgate, 1889–1891).
6. Louis R. Villermé, *Tableau de l'État Physique et Moral des Ouvriers Employés dans Les Manufactures de Coton, de Laine et de Soie,* 2 vols. (Paris: Renouard, et cie., 1840). There is no English translation, but a partial summary of Villermé's findings is contained in Jean Fourastié, *The Causes of Wealth,* trans. and ed. Theodore Caplow (New York: Free Press, 1960).
7. Alexandre B. Parent-Duchâtelet, *On Prostitution in the City of Paris,* 3d ed., 2 vols. (London: Burges, 1857).
8. Frédéric LePlay, *Les Ouvriers Européens,* 6 vols. (Tours: Mame, 1877–1879).
9. See Lazarsfeld, "History of Quantification in Sociology;" and Bernard Lécuyer and Anthony R. Oberschall, "Sociology: Early History of Social Research," *International Encyclopedia of the Social Sciences,* vol. 15, 36–53.
10. William I. Thomas and Florian W. Znaniecki, *The Polish Peasant in Europe and America,* 2 vols. (New York: Knopf, 1927). Republished in facsimile (New York: Dover, 1958). Originally published 1918–1920.
11. *Ibid.,* p. 1832.
12. *Ibid.,* p. 44.
13. In William I. Thomas, *The Unadjusted Girl: With Cases and Standpoint for Behavior Analysis* (Boston: Little, Brown, 1964). Originally published 1923.
14. Thomas and Znaniecki, *The Polish Peasant,* pp. 1747–1748.
15. Robert E. Park, *Human Communities: The City and Human Ecology* (New York: Free Press, 1952), p. 5.

16. Robert E. Park, "The City: Suggestions for the Investigation of Human Behavior in the City Environment," *American Journal of Sociology* 20, no. 5 (March 1915): 577–612.

17. For example, Roderick Duncan McKenzie, *The Neighborhood: A Study of Local Life in the City of Columbus, Ohio* (Chicago: University of Chicago Press, 1923); Pauline V. Young, *The Pilgrims of Russiantown* (Chicago: University of Chicago Press, 1932).

18. For example, Norman S. Hayner, *Hotel Life* (Chapel Hill: University of North Carolina Press, 1936); E. Franklin Frazier, *The Negro Family in the United States* (Chicago: University of Chicago Press, 1939); Clifford H. Shaw and Henry D. McKay, *Juvenile Delinquency and Urban Areas* (Chicago: University of Chicago Press, 1942).

19. John Madge, *The Origins of Scientific Sociology* (New York: Free Press, 1962), p. 125.

20. Pitirim Sorokin, *Social Mobility* (New York: Harper & Row, 1927).

21. *Ibid.,* p. 3. Another definition, which provides for the mobility of objects and values as well as people, is presented at the beginning of Chap. 7 of *Social Mobility,* but Sorokin makes no further use of it.

22. *Ibid.,* p. 84.

23. Robert S. Lynd and Helen Merrell Lynd, *Middletown: A Study in American Culture* (New York; Harcourt Brace Jovanovich, 1929).

24. Robert S. Lynd and Helen Merrell Lynd, *Middletown in Transition: A Study in Cultural Conflicts* (New York: Harcourt Brace Jovanovich, 1937).

25. Lynd and Lynd, *Middletown,* p. 498.

26. *Ibid.,* p. 510.

27. Disregarding journal articles, the principal reports in this long series are: Raymond Firth, *We, the Tikopia: A Sociological Study of Kinship in Primitive Polynesia* (London: Allen & Unwin, 1936); *Primitive Polynesian Economy* (London: Routledge & Kegan Paul, 1939); *Social Change in Tikopia: Re-Study of a Polynesian Community after a Generation* (New York: Macmillan, 1959); *History and Traditions of Tikopia* (Wellington, New Zealand: The Polynesian Society Incorporated, 1961); *Essays on Social Organization and Values* (London: University of London, The Athlone Press, 1964); *The Work of the Gods in Tikopia* (London: University of London, The Athlone Press, 1967); *Tikopia Ritual and Belief* (London: Allen & Unwin, 1967). Another volume, *Rank and Religion in Tikopia,* is said to be forthcoming.

28. Emile Durkheim, *The Elementary Forms of the Religious Life,* trans. Joseph Ward Swain (London: Allen & Unwin, 1915) and (New York: Macmillan, 1915).

29. Durkheim relied principally on Sir Baldwin Spencer and Francis James Gillen, *The Native Tribes of Central Australia* (New York: Macmillan, 1899); and *The Northern Tribes of Central Australia* (New York: Macmillan, 1904).

30. Franz Boas, *The Kwakiutl of Vancouver Island* (New York: Stechert, 1909); *Race, Language and Culture* (New York: Macmillan, 1940).

31. Bronislaw Malinowski, *Argonauts of the Western Pacific: An Account of Native Enterprise and Adventure in the Archipelagoes of Melanesian New Guinea* (New York: Dutton, 1922).

32. Margaret Mead, *Coming of Age in Samoa: A Psychological Study of Primitive Youth for Western Civilization* (New York: William Morrow, 1928); *Growing Up in New Guinea: A Comparative Study of Primitive Education* (New York: William Morrow, 1962).

33. Ruth Benedict, *Patterns of Culture* (Boston: Houghton Mifflin, 1934).

34. Robert Redfield, *Tepoztlán, a Mexican Village: A Study of Folk Life* (Chicago: University of Chicago Press, 1930); *The Folk Culture of Yucatan* (Chicago: University of Chicago Press, 1941).

35. George C. Homans, *The Human Group* (New York: Harcourt Brace Jovanovich, 1950).

36. William J. Goode, *Religion Among the Primitives* (New York: Free Press, 1951).

37. For an account of the Tikopians' unfriendly reception of casual visitors, see Captain and Mrs. Irving Johnson, *Westward Bound in the Schooner Yankee* (New York: Norton, 1936), pp. 182–186.

38. F. J. Roethlisberger and William J. Dickson (with Harold A. Wright), *Management and the Worker* (Cambridge, Mass.: Harvard University Press, 1939).

39. Elton Mayo, *The Human Problems of an Industrial Civilization,* 2d ed. (Boston: Division of Research, Graduate School of Business Administration, Harvard University, 1946), originally published 1933 (New York: Macmillan). The project grew out of previous research on industrial fatigue at the Harvard Fatigue Laboratory. The director of the laboratory at that time was Lawrence J. Henderson, a biochemist who occasionally offered courses in sociology, and who occupies an extraordinary place in the history of social research in the United States. He encouraged and guided the early work of Parsons, Whyte, Barnard, Warner, Arensberg, and Homans, among others. Mayo came to Harvard and began his collaboration with Henderson in 1926; the Western Electric Project was launched the following year.

40. Thomas North Whitehead, *The Industrial Worker: A Statistical Study of Human Relations in a Group of Manual Workers,* 2 vols. (Cambridge, Mass.: Harvard University Press, 1938).

41. A description of the interviewing program at the Hawthorne Works two decades later may be found in Jeanne L. Wilensky and Harold L. Wilensky, "Personnel Counseling: The Hawthorne Case," *American Journal of Sociology* 57, no. 3 (November 1951): 265–280.

42. George C. Homans, *The Human Group,* Chaps. 3–6.

43. W. Lloyd Warner and Paul S. Lunt, *The Social Life of a Modern Community* (New Haven: Yale University Press, 1941); W. Lloyd Warner and Paul S. Lunt, *The Status System of a Modern Community* (New Haven: Yale University Press, 1942); W. Lloyd Warner and Leo Srole, *The Social Systems of American Ethnic Groups* (New

Haven: Yale University Press, 1945); W. Lloyd Warner and J. O. Low, *The Social System of the Modern Factory: The Strike: A Social Analysis* (New Haven: Yale University Press, 1947); W. Lloyd Warner, *The Living and the Dead: A Study of the Symbolic Life of Americans* (New Haven: Yale University Press, 1959).

44. John P. Marquand, *Point of No Return* (Boston: Little, Brown, 1949).

45. Warner and Lunt, *The Status System of a Modern Community,* p. 82.

46. William Foote Whyte, *Street Corner Society: The Social Structure of an Italian Slum* (Chicago: University of Chicago Press, 1943); enlarged ed., 1955.

47. See Whyte's account of his personal experiences in the enlarged edition of *Street Corner Society, ibid.;* and in Arthur J. Vidich, Joseph Bensman and Maurice R. Stein, eds., *Reflections on Community Studies* (New York: John Wiley, 1964).

48. Whyte, *Street Corner Society,* enlarged ed., pp. 318–319.

49. Elliot Liebow, *Tally's Corner: A Study of Negro Streetcorner Men* (Boston: Little, Brown, 1967).

50. Melville J. Herskovits, *The Myth of the Negro Past* (New York: Harper and Brothers, 1941); Charles S. Johnson, *Patterns of Negro Segregation* (New York: Harper & Row, 1943); and Richard Sterner, *The Negro's Share: A Study of Income, Consumption, Housing and Public Assistance* (New York: Harper & Row, 1943).

51. Gunnar Myrdal with the assistance of Richard Sterner and Arnold Rose, *An American Dilemma: The Negro Problem and Modern Democracy* (New York: Harper & Row, 1944).

52. Especially Otto Klineberg, ed., *Characteristics of the American Negro* (New York: Harper & Row, 1944).

53. Myrdal, *An American Dilemma,* p. xlvii.

54. *Report of the National Advisory Commission on Civil Disorders* (New York: Bantam, 1968).

55. Myrdal, *An American Dilemma,* p. 75.

56. *Ibid.,* p. 929.

57. *Ibid.,* p. 1018.

58. Paul F. Lazarsfeld, Bernard Berelson, and Hazel Gaudet, *The People's Choice: How the Voter Makes Up His Mind in a Presidential Campaign* (New York: Duell, Sloan and Pearce, 1944).

59. Later studies of Presidential elections in the United States include Bernard R. Berelson, Paul F. Lazarsfeld, and William N. McPhee, *Voting: A Study of Opinion Formation in a Presidential Campaign* (Chicago: University of Chicago Press, 1954); Angus Campbell, Gerald Gurin, and Warren E. Miller, *The Voter Decides* (Evanston, Ill.: Row, Peterson, 1954); Heinz Eulau, *Class and Party in the Eisenhower Years: Class Roles and Perspectives in the 1952 and 1956 Elections* (New York: Free Press, 1962); Ithiel de Sola Pool, Robert P. Abelson, and Samuel L. Popkin, *Candidates, Issues and Strategies: A Computer Simulation of the 1960 and 1964 Presidential Elections* (Cambridge, Mass.: M.I.T. Press, 1965).

60. Lazarsfeld, Berelson, and Gaudet, *The People's Choice,* pp. 83–84.
61. *Studies in Social Psychology in World War II,* 4 vols.: Vol. 1, Samuel A. Stouffer et al., *The American Soldier: Adjustment During Army Life* (Princeton, N.J.: Princeton University Press, 1949); Vol. 2, Samuel A. Stouffer et al., *The American Soldier: Combat and Its Aftermath* (Princeton, N.J.: Princeton University Press, 1949); Vol. 3, Carl I. Hovland, Arthur A. Lumsdaine, and Fred D. Sheffield, *Experiments on Mass Communication* (Princeton, N.J.: Princeton University Press, 1949); Vol. 4, Samuel A. Stouffer et al., *Measurement and Prediction* (Princeton, N.J.: Princeton University Press, 1950).
62. Edward A. Shils, "Primary Groups in the American Army," pp. 16–39 in *Continuities in Social Research: Studies in the Scope and Method of "The American Soldier,"* ed. Robert K. Merton and Paul F. Lazarsfeld (New York: Free Press, 1950).
63. See Stouffer et al., *Studies in Social Psychology in World War II,* vol. 1, chart II, p. 440.
64. Alfred C. Kinsey, Wendell B. Pomeroy, and Clyde E. Martin, *Sexual Behavior in the Human Male* (Philadelphia: Saunders, 1948); Alfred C. Kinsey and others, *Sexual Behavior in the Human Female* (Philadelphia: Saunders, 1953). When Dr. Kinsey died in 1956, his work was carried on by his collaborators, but their subsequent publications have been addressed to specialists more than to the general public.
65. For example, Abraham Blumberg, *Criminal Justice* (Chicago: Quadrangle Books, 1967); Marvin B. Scott, *The Racing Game* (Chicago: Aldine, 1968).
66. Excellent summaries of the results of small-group experiments may be found in Gardner Lindzey and Elliot Aronson, *The Handbook of Social Psychology,* 2d ed. (Reading, Mass.: Addison–Wesley, 1968); and in Alexander Paul Hare, Edgar F. Borgatta, and Robert F. Bales, rev. ed., *Small Groups: Studies in Social Interaction* (New York: Knopf, 1965).
67. Robert F. Bales, *Interaction Process Analysis: A Method for the Study of Small Groups* (Reading, Mass.: Addison–Wesley, 1951). For a reappraisal of the method, see Nancy E. Waxler and Eliot G. Mishler, "Scoring and Reliability Problems in Interaction Process Analysis," *Sociometry* 29, no. 1 (March 1966): 28–40.
68. Stanley Schachter, *The Psychology of Affiliation: Experimental Studies of the Sources of Gregariousness* (Stanford, Calif.: Stanford University Press, 1959).
69. Muzafer Sherif et al., *Intergroup Conflict and Cooperation: The Robbers Cave Experiment* (Norman, Okla.: University of Oklahoma Institute of Group Relations, 1961).
70. Partially summarized in Theodore Caplow, *Two Against One: Coalitions in Triads* (Englewood Cliffs, N.J.: Prentice-Hall, 1968), Chap. 3.
71. See the discussion of Weber's work in Chapter Four of this book.
72. Alvin W. Gouldner, *Patterns of Industrial Bureaucracy* (New York: Free Press, 1954).

73. Peter M. Blau, *The Dynamics of Bureaucracy: A Study of Interpersonal Relations in Two Government Agencies,* rev. ed., 1963 (Chicago: University of Chicago Press, 1955).

74. Michel Crozier, *The Bureaucratic Phenomenon* (Chicago: University of Chicago Press, 1964).

75. Alfred H. Stanton and Morris S. Schwartz, *The Mental Hospital: A Study of Institutional Participation in Psychiatric Illness and Treatment* (New York: Basic Books, 1954).

76. For example, Ezra Stotland and Arthur L. Kobler, *Life and Death of a Mental Hospital* (Seattle, Wash.: University of Washington Press, 1965); Robert Rubenstein and Harold D. Lasswell, *The Sharing of Power in a Psychiatric Hospital* (New Haven: Yale University Press, 1966).

77. See especially, Rose Laub Coser, *Life in the Ward* (East Lansing, Mich.: Michigan State University Press, 1962); and Temple Burling, Edith M. Lentz, and Robert N. Wilson, *The Give and Take in Hospitals: A Study of Human Organization in Hospitals* (New York: Putnam's, 1956).

78. For example, Robert K. Merton, George G. Reader, and Patricia Kendall, eds., *The Student Physician: Introductory Studies in the Sociology of Medical Education* (Cambridge, Mass.: published for the Commonwealth Fund by Harvard University Press, 1957); and Howard S. Becker et al., *Boys in White: Student Culture in Medical School* (Chicago: University of Chicago Press, 1961).

Social Theory

Introduction

Social theory has three major purposes: it tells us how to visualize the social universe, how to obtain knowledge about it, and how to put that knowledge to use. The three purposes are inseparable, but a particular theory may not give them equal emphasis. Although any system of describing social reality suggests certain strategies of research, some very good theorists, like Georg Simmel, have been quite satisfied with the data provided by ordinary experience. Similarly, although the use of any research method implies some picture of the reality being studied, nothing compels the investigator to develop the picture in detail. Similar considerations apply to the applications of social theory. Every program of individual conduct or of social reform necessarily relies upon some image of the social universe and some way of obtaining usable knowledge about it, but these need not be fully developed. It seems to be a distinguishing mark of great theorists, however, that they provide reasonably full answers to each of the basic questions with which the sociologist approaches any social system: What is the nature of the system? How can I learn more about it? How can I use what I learn to achieve desirable goals?

Social theory is a great deal older than sociology. It is found in the Old Testament, in the Hindu Vedas, and in the works of the Chinese sages, all of which are still influential in some parts of the world today. Even if we restrict our attention to theories that have a direct connection with modern social science, we must go back 2,400 years to ancient Athens to find their origins.

The treatment of social theory in this chapter will be divided into five sections. In the first section, we will consider the Ancients—the prescientific social philosophers who developed new ways of describing society, culture, and institutions, and who identified fundamental social problems and proposed solutions to them. In the second section, the Age of Discovery, we touch briefly on the sociopolitical theories that were stimulated by the European exploration of the world and discuss in some detail the optimistic social theory of Adam Smith and Thomas Malthus' pessimistic one.

The third section will describe the forerunners: Auguste Comte, who combined a Greek root with a Latin root and invented the word *sociology;* Herbert Spencer, with his evolutionary theories; Karl Marx and Friedrich Engels, with their theories of class conflict and historical inevitability; and Vilfredo Pareto, whose destructive analysis of nonlogical theories led into his own nonlogical theory of social change.

In the fourth section, we will take up the founders: Emile Durkheim, Max Weber, and Georg Simmel. These three men, in their prime around 1900, provided most of the basic ideas for modern sociology. Their influence has increased rather than declined; they are probably more widely read now than ever before.

The fifth section touches on social theory in the United States, with special attention to the period after World War II, and to a pair of American theorists, Talcott Parsons and Robert Merton, who were influential both at home and abroad. At least a dozen other major theorists can be identified among contemporary sociologists, but the student of elementary sociology will probably find it useful to begin his study of recent social theory with these two leading figures, whose work will be briefly summarized at the end of the chapter.

The Ancients

PLATO

Plato (427–347 B.C.) was an Athenian, born at the height of the Golden Age, when the institutions of the Greek city-state had reached their highest development and the artistic and commercial preeminence of Athens was acknowledged throughout the Mediterranean world. By the time he came of age, Athenian prosperity had crumbled and the social structure had been undermined as the result of a senseless and costly war with Sparta. Plato seems to have been repelled by the terrorism of the conservative government led by his own relatives after the defeat of Sparta, and by the excesses of the democratic government that took its place and executed Socrates for "corrupting the youth." He decided to devote himself to a search for fundamental solutions to the social disunity and individual demoralization that he saw all around him.

In a long series of dialogues,[1] each in the form of a conversation between a central character and a small circle of friends or opponents, Plato drew together and unified most of what the Greeks knew about philosophy, science, mathematics, art, psychology, and sociology and added a program for further inquiry. His other great achievement was the founding of a school called the Academy for the instruction of advanced students and for philosophical and scientific research. It continued in operation for just over nine hundred years and was largely responsible for the great progress in mathematics and physical science that occurred soon after its founding. The Academy was the world's first university, and the model that was consciously followed when "academic" institutions were revived in Europe in the thirteenth century. The members of the Academy, like the members of a modern faculty, went all over the known world advising governments on jurisprudence, social reform, and financial policy. They wrote constitutions for small city-states and conducted tactical research for Alexander the Great.

Most of Plato's sociological ideas are found in two very long dialogues, *The Republic* and *The Laws. The Republic* is an early work; its principal speaker is Socrates, Plato's teacher. (Socrates left no written work behind him but his teachings were independently recorded by several Greek writers.) *The Republic* analyzes the problems of existing societies and lays down the conditions for an ideal society whose rulers would be brought up and fitted for their tasks in a very special and unusual way. *The Laws,* a much later work, is a nonutopian development of the same or similar principles; it seems to be intended for practical application. The principal speaker is an unnamed Athenian who probably stands for Plato himself.

These dialogues are largely devoted to sociological issues, especially those connected with the problem of social disunity.[2] Plato was a conservative, but only in the limited sense that he valued stability more than change. The ideal societies described in *The Republic* and *The Laws* are highly integrated, highly stratified, externally warlike but internally peaceful. The institutional arrangements proposed for the ruling class of Guardians in *The Republic* were radically novel. They were to practice absolute communism, have no personal property or private lives, hold their women and children in common, and ignore individual parentage. In *The Laws,* this proposal was given up for practical reasons, but still defended as an ideal.

Plato perceived an inherent conflict of interests between the individual and the community and proposed to resolve it in favor of the community by abolishing—at least for the rulers—the institutions on which private interests are based: property, the nuclear family, sexual love, art, and party politics. It was a large order, particularly in fourth-century Athens, where the community's power over a citizen was rather limited.

Plato's philosophy is so closely interwoven with all subsequent Western thought that it would be pointless to attempt an assessment of his influence on contemporary social science, but a few themes that are still with us deserve particular mention. Plato maintained that: (1) social ends as well as means can be rationally selected; (2) the stratification of a society ought to be determined by its division of labor and not the other way around; (3) the degree of correspondence between natural ability and class position is the test of any system of stratification; (4) individual happiness depends on social order; (5) the lack of integration in a society is the cause of deviant behavior in individuals.

ARISTOTLE

Aristotle (384–322 B.C.) was born in a small town near the Macedonian frontier. He studied under Plato at the Academy and later founded a similar institution called the Lyceum. He traveled extensively outside of Greece and for a time tutored the young Alexander the Great. He wrote extensively on a variety of subjects. Most of his surviving works[3] seem to have been prepared as textbooks for courses he gave at the Lyceum in his later years.

Aristotle took all knowledge for his field and impressed an outline on it that is still visible. It was Aristotle who developed the idea of a science, the logic that underlies scientific investigations, the interrelationship among the sciences, the continuity of animate and inanimate nature, the study of living forms, and the systematic investigation of human behavior. His discussion of the problem of achieving precision in the social sciences is more sophisticated than that of some recent research manuals. His insistence that the study of human behavior must be focused on values is startlingly up to date, and his study of the constitutions of 158 city-states was the first large-scale social research project in all history. It led him to the modern-sounding conclusion that the opposition of interests between the rich and the poor can only be conciliated in a state with a large, influential middle class.

The writings of Aristotle were never completely lost, even in the Middle Ages, but were studied piecemeal so that, although his influence on medieval philosophers and theologians was profound, they were able to ignore his scientific and sociological principles. To the men of the Renaissance and the Reformation, the founders of modern science, Aristotle's name stood for an intellectual method founded on blind obedience to authority and indifference to the real world. He was held responsible for the worst features of medieval scholarship—its tendency to empty verbalism (opium induces sleep because of its dormitive power) and its habit of looking for practical knowledge in books (a legendary medieval scholar was expelled from the University for counting the teeth of a live horse instead of looking up the number in Aristotle.) Not until late in the nineteenth century did Aristotle's importance as a philosopher of science and the original discoverer of the scientific method come to be recognized. Even now the extraordinary quality of sociological analysis in his works, especially in *The Nicomachean Ethics* and *The Politics,* is not fully appreciated. Consider, for example, the following piece of analysis, with its acute discrimination of motives and roles.

Benefactors are thought to love those they have benefited, more than those who have been well treated love those that have treated them well, and this is discussed as though it were paradoxical. Most people think it is because the latter are in the position of debtors and the former of creditors; and therefore as, in the case of loans, debtors wish their creditors did not exist, while creditors actually take care of the safety of their debtors, so it is thought that benefactors wish the objects of their action to exist since they will then get their gratitude, while the beneficiaries take no interest in making this return. ... But the cause would seem to be more deeply rooted in the nature of things; the case of those who have lent money is not even analogous. For they have no friendly feeling to their debtors, but only a wish that they may be kept safe with a view to what is to be got from them; while those who have done a service to others feel friendship and love for those they have served even if these are not of any use to them and never will be. This is what happens with craftsmen too; every man loves his own handiwork better than he would be loved by it if it came alive; and this happens perhaps most of all with poets; for they have an excessive love for their own poems, doting on them as if they were their children. This is what the position of benefactors is like; for that which they have treated well is their handiwork, and therefore they love this more than the handiwork does its maker. The cause of this is that existence is to all men a thing to be chosen and loved, and that we exist by virtue of activity (i.e., by living and acting), and that the handiwork is in a sense, the producer in activity.[4]

This comes very close to sociological theory in the modern sense. The meticulous observation of social activity in many different settings leads to general statements about the interaction of individuals and groups. Moreover, these statements are tentative and one can improve and refine them by gathering more information and analyzing it further.

OTHER ANCIENT WRITERS

Just as Thales and Hero and Archimedes nearly became physicists in the modern sense, so Plato and Aristotle and a few of the ancient writers who followed them were nearly social scientists.[5] For example, Polybius (about 200–118 B.C.) wrote a history of the rise of Rome to world dominance in which he explained the expansion of Roman power[6] by a close analysis of the social structure and the major institutions of Rome based on official records, private files, and thousands of interviews. Strabo (about 63 B.C.–23 A.D.) continued the work of Polybius on the rise of Rome and added to it a long geographical treatise in which he examined the effects of the physical environment on communication, migration, and culture contact; the influence of mobility on culture change; the characteristic forms of rural and urban settlement; the origin of stratification systems; and the causes and consequences of group conflict.[7]

But these promising beginnings led nowhere. Although the later classic philosophers speculated about human nature and social relationships, they did not reach their conclusions by observing behavior in a systematic way or by comparing the institutions of different societies. Their statements about social reality are based on little more than common sense observations and ethical platitudes.

With the ascendance of Christianity the content of social doctrine changed, but its method remained the same. From St. Augustine (354–480 A.D.) to St. Thomas Aquinas (1225–1274 A.D.) the Christian Fathers proposed various social doctrines that drew on their interpretations of the Gospel and on "first principles"—assertions about human nature or social order that were held to be self-evident. However, their primary concern was with salvation, not with sociological analysis.

The first writer after the ancient Greeks to return to sociological theory was Ibn Khaldoun (1332–1406), whom the *Encyclopaedia Britannica* calls an "Arab historian and sociologist." The title of sociologist, applied to a man who died half a century before the invention of printing, is amazing but appropriate. Among other topics, he discussed the fundamental forms of human association, the effect of contact between dissimilar social systems, the diffusion of culture traits, the influence of climate on culture, and the effects of urbanization and population growth on political systems. In many respects Ibn Khaldoun was half a millennium ahead of his time in the history of social theory. However, he left no disciples behind him and his writings were almost unknown until quite recently; some of them were translated for the first time in the 1950s.[8]

The Age of Discovery

The sixteenth, seventeenth, and eighteenth centuries witnessed the exploration of the world by Europeans and their colonization of the Western Hemisphere, the Protestant Reformation, the rise of science, the emergence of the nation-state, and the development of commerce, warfare, information, and bureaucracy on an unprecedented scale. Throughout those busy centuries many men observed the changing world about them and theorized about the possibilities and limitations of social development. Among them were Machiavelli, Bodin, Hobbes, Locke, Rousseau, Vico, and Montesquieu. None was a sociologist in the modern sense—their aims were too large and their methods too rough—but they changed the way men thought about social events and ultimately acted; each of them is still represented in our current inventory of ideas and images.

It was not until the latter part of the eighteenth century that works of social theory began to appear that were essentially modern in style, involving the construction of theoretical models and an ultimate reliance on empirical data. Among the numerous representatives of this tendency, at least two, Smith and Malthus, are still influential today.

ADAM SMITH

Few men who ever lived seem to have had so few personal problems as Adam Smith (1723–1790) or to have taken so optimistic a view of society. A lifelong bachelor, the only son of a widowed mother, he had an early successful academic career, becoming professor of moral philosophy at the University of Glasgow at the age of 28. He resigned some years later to become tutor to a young duke; through that connection, he was employed as an economic expert by the British government, returning to Scotland in 1778 with a lucrative official appointment that he held for the rest of his life. Smith believed that most men are basically happy, like himself; he even favored an increase in the population on the grounds that it would increase the aggregate national happiness. He is best known as the principal founder of modern economics and the advocate of free trade and free enterprise. But his two great works,[9] *The Theory of Moral Sentiments* and *The Wealth of Nations*, represent important steps in the development of sociology.[10]

The *Theory of Moral Sentiments* was the first systematic explanation in modern terms of how social norms develop out of interaction and how the individual personality is formed in the process of socialization. As the following excerpt illustrates, it anticipates the essential features of the symbolic interaction model developed by George Herbert Mead around 1900, from which many of our current assumptions about human nature and society are derived.

> The principle by which we naturally either approve or disapprove of our own conduct, seems to be altogether the same with that by which we exercise the like judgments concerning the conduct of other people. We either approve or disapprove of the conduct of another man, according as we feel that, when we bring his case home to ourselves, we either can or cannot entirely sympathize with the sentiments and motives which directed it. And, in the same manner, we either approve or disapprove of our own conduct, according as we feel that, when we place ourselves in the situation of another man, and view it, as it were, with his eyes and from his station, we either can or cannot entirely enter into and sympathize with the sentiments and motives which influenced it. We can never survey our own sentiments and motives, we can never form any judgment concerning them, unless we remove ourselves, as it were, from our own natural station, and endeavor to view them as at a certain distance from us. But we can do this in no other way than by endeavoring to view them with the eyes of other people, or as other people are likely to view them.[11]

Smith discusses at length the relationship between the imaginary spectator (Mead's "generalized other") and the real spectators from whom the values of the imaginary spectator are taken and by whose reactions the judgments of the imaginary spectator are corrected. In vivid language he portrays the conversion of the judgments of "the man within your breast" into a set of habits and opinions by which the actor estimates the social value of his own conduct even when there is no possibility of external observation. This process, now called the internalization of norms, is perhaps as well explained by Smith as by any of the numerous modern scholars who have described it.

The Wealth of Nations, published in 1776, introduced several other themes that now occupy a central place in sociological theory. Adam Smith was the first observer to realize that the European exploration of the world and the development of the factory system had launched Great Britain on a course of unprecedented economic development. At a time when other authors were struggling with curious theories about the divine right of kings, Smith was calmly describing the main outlines of the modern world, urbanization, population growth, continuous inflation, the business cycle, the division of labor, increasing per capita productivity, the changing distribution of the labor force, the consequences of social mobility, and the conflict of interest between capital and labor. His most important achievement was to identify the increasing division of labor as the mainspring of social change and to trace its connections with the improvement of technology, the growth of a market economy, the rise of nationalism, and the development of world trade. In effect, he prophesied the history of the following two centuries, but with his customary optimism, he omitted the negative consequences of the division of labor—such as large-scale mechanized war —that came hand-in-hand with the benefits of progress.

THOMAS MALTHUS

The absence of any serious foreboding in Adam Smith's vision of the future was amply compensated by the pessimism of Thomas Robert Malthus (1766–1834), an English clergyman who spent most of his life teaching history and economics at the company college of the East India Company and revising his essay on *The Principle of Population,* which began as a pamphlet in 1798 and grew into a monumental tome in the course of successive edition.[12]

The "principle" to which the title refers is that population increases geometrically if unchecked, whereas the means of subsistence can increase only arithmetically.

> In the northern states of America, where the means of subsistence have been more ample, the manners of the people more pure, and the checks to early marriages fewer than in any of the modern states of Europe, the population has been found to double itself, for above a century and a half successively, in less than twenty-five years.

And a little further:

> A thousand millions are just as easily doubled every twenty-five years by the power of population as a thousand. But the food to support the increase from the greater number will by no means be obtained with the same facility. Man is necessarily confined in room. When acre has been added to acre till all the fertile land is occupied, the yearly increase of food must depend upon the melioration of the land already in possession. This is a fund, which, from the nature of all soils, instead of increasing, must be gradually diminishing.[13]

Thus, as Malthus saw it, every improvement in agricultural productivity, including the discovery or extension of arable land, would be quickly canceled out by the pressure of population growth unless that pressure were limited by either positive or preventive checks. The positive checks include all the consequences of poverty that shorten the duration of human life—unwholesome occupations, exposure, malnutrition, accidents, diseases, war, and famine. The preventive checks consist of two kinds: moral restraint and vice. Moral restraint is "restraint from marriage which is not followed by irregular gratifications," that is, either celibacy or late marriage without any extramarital sexual activity. The preventive checks that come under the heading of vice are, "promiscuous intercourse, unnatural passions, violations of the marriage bed, and improper arts to conceal the consequences of irregular connections." By this latter phrase, Malthus apparently meant abortion; he associated it only with irregular connections, and it did not occur to him that married women in England also practiced "improper arts" to limit the size of their families. But he did know something about contraception, which was being rapidly improved in his time, and it was his particular blind spot that having identified population pressure as the chief cause of human misery he set himself firmly against contraception on the shaky ground that it would reduce the incentives of workers and the even weaker argument that it might stunt population growth.

> Indeed I should always particularly reprobate any artificial and unnatural modes of checking population, both on account of their immorality and their tendency to remove a necessary stimulus to industry. If it were possible for each married couple to limit by a wish the number of their children, there is certainly reason to fear that the indolence of the human race would be very greatly increased, and that neither the population of individual countries nor of the whole earth would ever reach its natural and proper extent.[14]

It is hard not to dislike Thomas Malthus as a moralizing hypocrite who devised high-minded excuses for selfishness and irresponsibility. By arguing on the one hand that population pressure was necessary to maintain the incentives of the labor force and on the other hand that it condemned the poor to perpetual misery, he was able to oppose any attempt to relieve the misery, while advocating those forms of population control whose ineffectiveness could be depended upon.

Moreover, it is clear that Malthus misinterpreted much of the population data that he gathered from all the corners of the globe. The worldwide population pressure that he was the first to detect was a consequence of the commercial and industrial revolutions, and not the normal condition of previous societies. Indeed, it seemed for a while that Malthus might have been mistaken about his basic principle also. Throughout the nineteenth century and well into the twentieth the population of the world increased geometrically but the means of subsistence more than kept up, and the standard of living rose, although at unequal rates, almost everywhere. It was only after World War II, with the global population above 3 billion and predicted to double in less than 40 years that a catastrophic confirmation of Malthus' principle began to seem possible.

AUGUSTE COMTE

Although Malthus and his contemporaries treated sociological topics they did not identify sociology as a distinct branch of knowledge. This important step was taken by Auguste Comte (1798–1857), who might be called the godfather of sociology. He gave the field its name and its initial program, although most of his specific ideas were later discredited.

Comte was a philosophical crank who believed that he alone had discovered the secrets of the universe. Nevertheless, he was taken seriously by some of the most serious men of his time. John Stuart Mill was his disciple in a sense, and Durkheim drew heavily on Comte for some of the basic concepts of his *Rules of Sociological Method.*

The early part of Comte's career was spent at the École Polytechnique, teaching mathematics and what was then called social physics. In 1842, he gave up teaching, abandoned his family, and spent the rest of his life attempting to establish what he called the positive philosophy as a new religion. He even designed a calendar, a catechism, and appropriate vestments for it.

The secret that Comte thought he had discovered was that the universe, including every aspect of human life, is completely explicable by science, which can provide not only rational understanding of cause and effect but rational guidance for individual conduct and for social policy. As Comte explained it in his principal work,[15] *The Course of Positive Philosophy,* published in six volumes between 1830 and 1842, all human existence can be divided into three stages—the theological, the metaphysical, and the positive or scientific. Each of the three stages is divided into a number of substages and all of these occur in a fixed order in the life of every individual and in the development of every society. The theological stage, for example, begins with cannabalism and universal fetishism and works up to star worship, polytheism, and monotheism. The positive stage begins with an understanding of astronomy, and the other sciences then develop in a fixed order, beginning with physics and ending with sociology. Attached to each stage or substage of mental development are characteristic institutions, customs, and habits. In the final stage, which Comte believed himself to be ushering in, all humanity would be brought under one rational scientific order, united in the worship of the "Great Being" (humanity itself), and all social problems would be solved by applied sociology. Lacking both the common sense of his contemporaries and the ethnographic data accumulated later in the nineteenth century, Comte simply invented most of the facts he needed to discuss social evolution, and defended them by pointing out how plausible they were.

It is plain that the settled abode of agricultural peoples must fix their speculative attention upon the heavenly bodies, while their labours remarkably disclosed the influences of the sky: whereas, the only astronomical observations to be expected of a wandering tribe are of the polar star which guides their nocturnal course. Thus there is a double relation between the development of fetichism and the final establishment of agricultural life.[16]

Despite his delusions, Comte left an indelible impression on the history of social thought because he emphasized and reemphasized that social phenomena could be scientifically studied. He perceived the importance of the division of labor in determining social structure and thereby paved the way for Durkheim's greatest work, and he anticipated Simmel in identifying "elementary subordination" as the essential element of social organization. He also introduced the distinction between theoretical and applied sociology and between the study of social structure, which he called *social statics,* and the study of social change, which he called *dynamical sociology.*

HERBERT SPENCER

Herbert Spencer (1820–1903), constructed another system of sociology as elaborate as Comte's, even more influential in its day and as quickly forgotten. Spencer was the very model of an eminent Victorian. After an early career as a railroad engineer, he retired on an inherited income and devoted himself to the gigantic project that he called the synthetic philosphy (meaning all-embracing, not artificial). This included a philosophy of science and treatises on the principles of biology, psychology, ethics, and sociology.[17] Spencer's *The Study of Sociology,* published in 1873, was the first sociology textbook used in college courses in the United States.

As a theorist he had two leading ideas: that a society is very much like a giant organism; and that the process of evolution, which produces different species of flora and fauna and arranges them in an orderly hierarchy from the lowest amoeba to the highest type of man, also operates in the social sphere to establish a sequence of development from the simplest primitive tribe to the most advanced civilization.

Spencer was also responsible for a project that anticipated the present-day data files in collecting facts from a great number of societies and arranging them in a standard format for comparative purposes. The results of this project were published in eight large folio volumes from 1873 to 1881 under the title of *Descriptive Sociology;* when Spencer died in 1903, he provided funds for a second series of volumes completed in 1934. Unlike Comte, who seems to have derived most of his data about primitive society from introspection, Spencer was genuinely interested in ethnography and accumulated a great deal of empirical knowledge about societies in different stages of development. His basic conception of social evolution is firmly grounded on empirical data:

The many facts contemplated unite in proving that social evolution forms a part of evolution at large. Like evolving aggregates in general, societies show *integration,* both by simple increase of mass and by coalescence and re-coalescence of masses. The change from *homogeneity* to *heterogeneity* is multitudinously exemplified; up from the simple tribe, alike in all its parts, to the civilized nation, full of structural and functional unlikenesses. With progressing integration and heterogeneity goes increasing *coherence.* We see a wandering group dispersing, dividing, held together by no bonds; the tribe with parts made more coherent by subordination to a dominant man; the cluster of drives united in the political plexus under a chief with sub-chiefs; and so on up to the civilized nation, consolidating enough to hold together for a thousand years or more.

Simultaneously comes increasing *definiteness.* Social organization is at first vague; advance brings settled arrangements which grow slowly more precise; customs pass into laws which, while gaining fixity, also become more specific in their applications to varieties of action; and all institutions, at first confusedly intermingled, slowly separate, at the same time that each within itself marks off more distinctly its component structures. Thus in all respects is fulfilled the formula of evolution. There is progress toward greater size, coherence, multiformity, and definiteness.[18]

However, it is not always easy for a modern student to read Spencer's work appreciatively. He represented a high-water mark of Victorian complacency and took for granted the superiority of his own era and his own social type to everything that preceded it. This frame of mind is now difficult to recapture. Discussing esthetic progress Spencer wrote: "From necklaces of fishbones we advanced to dresses, elaborate, gorgeous and infinitely varied; out of discordant war chants come symphonies and operas; cairns develop into magnificent temples; in place of caves with rude markings there arise at length galleries of paintings; and the recital of a chief's deeds with mimetic accompaniment gives origin to epics, dramas, lyrics, and the vast mass of poetry, fiction, biography, and history."[19]

When these lines were written, the great discoveries of ancient jewelry in the tombs of Mycenae and of Egypt had already been made; it was somehow possible to group them with fishbones. The neolithic cave paintings at Altamira, which represent the motions of animals better than any nineteenth century painting, were only "rude markings" to Spencer. The *Iliad* and *Odyssey* were primitive efforts that could only culminate in the Victorian novel after a long sequence of evolution. Coupled with this cultural chauvinism went a middle-class complacency that makes Malthus seem humanitarian. Spencer interpreted Darwin's theory of the improvement of species through natural selection to imply that any interference with natural selection would be harmful to the species. He took for granted that the wealthy and educated classes in English society were the fittest and the lower classes less fit and argued that the state ought to do nothing to relieve the condition of the poor lest it retard the elimination of unfit strains from the population. This reactionary bias is not a mere quirk in Spencer's philosophy but nearly its raison d'être. One of his books is mostly remembered today because of the remark of a United States Supreme Court justice that "the Fourteenth Amendment does not enact Mr. Herbert Spencer's *Social Statics.*"[20]

Spencer's place in the history of sociology turned out to be marginal, but in his time he was largely responsible for popularizing the subject and introducing it to a generation of scholars whose work overshadowed his own. By the time he finished his *Principles of Sociology* in 1896, the three real founders of modern sociology, Durkheim, Simmel, and Weber, had already brought out their early important essays. We will turn to these shortly after a brief look at two great figures, Marx and Pareto, who stood to the left and right of them, respectively.

KARL MARX

Karl Marx (1818–1883) was born and educated in Germany, receiving a doctorate in philosophy from the University of Jena at the age of 23, but spent most of his life as a political exile in London where he wrote huge books,[21] helped to establish the international socialist organizations from which twentieth-century Communism claims descent, and worked as a freelance correspondent for American newspapers.

Marx's intellectual partner, Friedrich Engels (1820–1895) was co-author of *The Communist Manifesto,*[22] and edited and rewrote the second and third volumes of *Capital,* Marx's definitive work. Engels' *Condition of the Working Class in England* (1844) was the earliest social survey of a slum community.[23] Engels also collaborated with Marx in his political activities, helped support his family, and served as his literary executor.

The social theories of Marx, which were closely linked to his political doctrines, are maintained in countries of the Soviet bloc as a kind of official, dogmatic sociology committed to "the revolutionary struggle" and permanently opposed to the "bourgeois" ideal of the objective, dispassionate analysis of social phenomena. But Marx's theories have also played a large part in the development of bourgeois sociology; among those strongly influenced by Marxism were Pareto and Weber, and in the United States Thorstein Veblen, Albion Small, and C. Wright Mills, each of whom adopted some of the assumptions of Marxist sociology without arriving at the same conclusions.

The sociological and partly sociological writings of Marx were voluminous, well-informed, eloquent, and not always consistent; they are difficult to summarize briefly.[24] The central concept is the *class struggle.* "The history of all hitherto existing societies," proclaimed the *Communist Manifesto,* "is the history of class struggles."

Class membership, in the Marxian sense, is determined by the ownership of property under various conditions—the capitalist owns the means of production, the proletarian owns only his own labor, which he is forced to sell to the capitalist in order to live. Marx and Engels acknowledged the existence of other classes in modern society but dismissed them as irrelevant in one way or another to the great forthcoming struggle between the capitalist and proletariat classes. They assumed that minor property owners—small farmers, storekeepers, people with savings—were gradually being dispossessed and merged with the proletariat; that professionals and managers, as well as statesmen and government officials, were merely agents of the capitalists without separate interests of their own; and that the lowest class, the *lumpenproletariat,* without regular employment, would be recruited as capitalist "tools."

The interests of capitalists and proletarians are conceived as irreconcilable and not subject to compromise. Everything that is produced is produced by the labor of the proletarians but out of the product they receive only the minimum necessary for survival; the remainder—the surplus value—is expropriated by the capitalists, who perform no useful social function. The worker, lacking a real interest in the outcome of his work and unable to express himself freely because of the discipline of the industrial system, becomes alienated. In this desocialized condition, he requires fantasies to sustain his morale, and these fantasies—including religion, patriotism, art, and politics—are deliberately provided by the capitalists to distract the proletarian from class consciousness and to persuade him to accept exploitation.

It is a central proposition of this system that economic relations are basic to any social system and everything else is derivative. The "relations of production" are the foundation of a society; law, politics, knowledge, morality, even family relationships are part of the "superstructure." They change whenever the modes of production are modified by technology but do not exercise any reciprocal influence on production.

Consistent with this view, Marxism defines the state as an instrument of the ruling class to maintain its dominance over the exploited workers and predicts the disappearance of the state after the proletarian revolution. Marxism is both revolutionary and apocalyptic. Capitalism arose by overthrowing feudalism; feudalism displaced earlier forms of oppression. Each state of society arises naturally and *inevitably* from the one preceding it. No strategy adopted by a ruling class can prevent the inexorable upward movement of society. But, although all preceding history is the history of class struggles, the impending proletarian revolution against European capitalism was, for Marx and Engels, the end of the line. It would usher in a classless, stateless society without private property, without inequality or exploitation, without any need for the worker to endure constraint. This condition is difficult to visualize—and perhaps for this reason neither Marx nor Engels nor any of their later disciples ever attempted to describe it in detail. The political appeal of Marxism, after a hundred years and after many triumphs, continues to lie in its negative utopianism, its complaint against the widespread misery and inequality to be found in capitalist society and not in its specification of alternatives. The national societies constructed on Marxist principles appear to have lessened inequality and to have alleviated the extremes of misery but, far from disappearing after the revolution, the state becomes all-powerful and the constraint exercised over the worker seems to be greater than before. Indeed, in a somewhat paradoxical way, the Marxian theory that the forms of production determine the other elements of a social system is partly confirmed by the persistence of political, bureaucratic, and moral problems in industrial societies without capitalists.

VILFREDO PARETO

Vilfredo Pareto (1848–1923) was another great theorist whose work encompassed both economics and sociology, but coming a generation later than Marx, he treated them separately, in the modern fashion. His *Course of Political Economy,* published in 1896, was an important contribution to mathematical economics. *The Mind and Society: A Treatise on General Sociology,* published in 1916, is one of the permanent landmarks of sociological theory.[25]

Pareto belonged to a rich Genoese family. His father was a famous railroad engineer and a passionate liberal active in public affairs, and Pareto at first followed in his footsteps. He graduated from an engineering school with a brilliant record in mathematics, became a successful engineer, and was engaged before the age of 30 as manager of a mining enterprise near Florence. In 1882, after an unsuccessful try at public office, he retired from business to work on his system of mathematical economics, and in 1894 he became professor of that subject at Lausanne in Switzerland, where he taught and wrote for most of the rest of his life.

The Mind and Society resembles no other book, ancient or modern. It is more than 2,000 pages long and touches on nearly every subject under the sun. Pareto was a scholar of unmatched erudition. He was thoroughly familiar with the documents of ancient Greece and Rome, and to this classical knowledge he added a thorough grounding in modern mathematics and physical sciences, in the history of religion, modern European politics, money and banking, linguistics, botany, anthropology, and popular literature. The casual reader, dipping into Pareto, must prepare himself to move easily from a discussion of human sacrifices among the Aztecs to the drinking habits of modern statesmen. Because of the sheer length of his books, the variety of topics treated in them, his somewhat unfamiliar vocabulary and his use of mathematical diagrams and notations, Pareto is often regarded as a difficult author to read. But his fundamental ideas are simple, straighforward, and important, and they have left an indelible impression on American sociology through the works of a few men, like Talcott Parsons and George Homans, who have studied them carefully.

For Pareto the most important thing to know about a society was how its members perceive reality, what *theories* they hold about the natural universe, the supernatural, and their own actions. Almost any mental manifestation is a theory in Pareto's sense and every social act is based on such theories. Some theories are "logico-experimental," that is, they start from empirically ascertainable facts and proceed by logical reasoning to conclusions that follow from the facts and can be verified objectively. Logical actions can be based on logico-experimental theories; the relationship of the action to a desired end is established in the actor's mind by a scientifically verifiable theory or, if he does not know the theory, the efficacy of his behavior is nevertheless demonstrable by such a theory. The effect of a logical action as seen by the actor coincides with what would be seen by a detached scientific observer.

Logical action is normal in the experimental sciences, engineering, industrial production, military strategy, and a few other special fields. But most human action is nonlogical (not *illogical,* as Pareto repeatedly explained). Nonlogical actions are based on imaginary or incorrect facts, on fallacious reasoning, or on conclusions that cannot be verified, or on some combination of these. Pareto was surely not the first theorist to note the importance of nonlogical action in human affairs (Sigmund Freud was busy at the same time developing a much more influential theory of nonlogical action.) However, he was the first to chart and classify types of nonlogical action and to demonstrate the nonlogical character of most of the prevailing political, religious, and moral beliefs of Western society, including especially the beliefs of such earlier social theorists as Rousseau, Comte, and Spencer.

Pareto pointed to the many kinds of social actions that can only be explained in terms of persistent tendencies for socialized beings to act and think in peculiar ways. Among these he identified a tendency to invent new combinations of the elements of human experience; a tendency for socially recognized aggregates or patterns to persist; the need to express sentiments in action, a whole set of sentiments connected with sociality, such as the desire for conformity, self-sacrifice, and the need of group approbation; a tendency toward the maintenance of individual integrity; and so forth. All of these are what Pareto called *residues;* they are what is left after the reasoning that supports a theory or belief is removed.

Pareto does not offer any explanation for the appearance of the residues in human behavior. He does not think that any explanation is needed, because, in his own view, a logico-experimental theory rests on observed facts, and he is able to demonstrate that the behavior corresponding to each of the residues can be observed in the societies he studied. But even if we refrain from asking where the residues come from, we are almost compelled to inquire how they are distributed, and this brings us to the second and somewhat less satisfying theme in Pareto's sociology. The residues are thought to be universal, that is, all observed societies and their inhabitants manifest all of the same residues—but not in the same proportion. The sentiment of self-sacrifice is more conspicuous in one society or social class than in another. The desire for conformity was an obsession among the Spartans but only a weak impulse among the Athenians. A given social class dominated by a particular residue will differ from another class in the same society dominated by another residue.

Armed with this formulation, Pareto set out to refute Marx and Engels.[26] He accepted their definition of a class as a group within a society having the same economic interests, and he agreed with them in ignoring minor class distinctions and dividing every society into the rulers (whom he called the elite) and the ruled. He was perhaps even more emphatic than they had been in insisting that every society, regardless of its form of government, has a small ruling class and that political ideologies are devices to persuade the subject class to support the interests of the rulers in preference to their own. But he disagreed with them in his identification of the ruling and subject classes in modern society. According to Pareto, European societies were divided between a "plutodemocratic" ruling class composed of industrialists and their unionized workmen, and a subject class composed of farmers, small merchants, government employees, pensioners, professionals, soldiers, and small investors.

Marx and Engels had pictured the march of history as a progression from one class struggle to the next, leading upward in an evolutionary fashion to the final class struggle between capitalists and proletarians, to be followed by the victory of the proletariat and the emergence of a classless society. Pareto saw the class struggle as continuous, cyclical, and permanent, an alternation of "lions" and "foxes." The lions are ruling classes inspired primarily by the residue of persistence. They are conservative, traditional, and committed to the use of force. The foxes are moved primarily by the residue of combinations, which leads them to seek technological progress and social change. They rule by persuasion and propaganda. Either group will be overthrown when in power, unless it accommodates itself to the pressures for change that inevitably develop by admitting talented members of the subject class, bearing the other residue, to its ranks. If this process continues, the fundamental characteristics of the ruling class are transformed and the foxes turn into lions or the lions into foxes. Otherwise, the accumulating pressures lead to revolution and the installation of a new ruling class as the brave lions replace the corrupt, scheming foxes, or the forward-looking foxes do away with the brutal and reactionary lions. This process Pareto called the "circulation of elites."

The Founders

Marx and Pareto are huge figures in the history of sociological theory but they stand somewhat aside from its mainstream. The intellectual framework of modern sociology is largely the work of three European scholars whose major works appeared between 1890 and 1910: Durkheim, Simmel, and Weber. They were almost exact contemporaries, and it is still difficult to say, half a century after their deaths, which of them exerted the greater influence.

EMILE DURKHEIM

Emile Durkheim (1858–1917) was born in the small, ancient town of Epinal on the Moselle River in eastern France. His parents intended him to be a rabbi, but during his early adolescence he moved away from Judaism to Catholicism and thence away from any religious faith. His later life was spectacularly uneventful. Trained for university teaching at the Ecole Normale Superieure, a famous school then at the height of its reputation, he taught for a few years in provincial high schools, moved to the University of Bordeaux, married, had two children, was promoted to professor, was called to the Sorbonne, edited a journal, attended international conferences, lost his son and several favorite students in the war, and died of a heart attack at the age of 59. He wrote four important books: *The Division of Labor* (1893); *The Rules of Sociological Method* (1895); *Suicide* (1897); and *The Elementary Forms of the Religious Life* (1912).[27] All of them develop his favorite theme that society is "a reality *sui generis,"* that is, a natural entity greater than and different from the sum of its parts and not explainable in psychological or biological or purely rational terms. Durkheim was not the first to maintain that man is a product of society—the point had been made as far back as Aristotle—but he went much further along that line than anyone before him, and identified all the principal forms of human experience as social products evolving over the course of many generations and combining the individual experience of innumerable men.

All of his works are variations on this theme. In *The Division of Labor,* he explained morality as an expression of a collective conscience that is founded on group experience and reflects group interests. In his introduction to the first edition, omitted from later editions, he rejected all of the previous theories that attempted to base morality on religion, natural law, reason, or social utility, maintaining that the forms taken by the collective conscience develop unpredictably and not in accordance with any general principle of ethics. In *The Rules of Sociological Method,* he defined sociology as the study of *social facts,* that is, of the external constraints that society imposes on the individual. In *Suicide,* he undertook to show that the constraints accounting for suicide were real:

> But whatever they are called, the important thing is to recognize their reality and conceive of them as a totality of forces which cause us to act from without, like the physico-chemical forces to which we react. So truly are they things *sui generis* and not mere verbal entities that they may be measured, their relative sizes compared, as is done with the intensity of electric currents. ... [28]

In his final work, *The Elementary Forms of the Religious Life,* Durkheim went much further and identified the fundamental attributes of human awareness—perceptions of time, space, categories, and causality—as collective representations arising from social experience.

> Society supposes a self-conscious organization which is nothing other than a classification. This organization of society naturally extends itself to the place which this occupies. To avoid all colli-

sions, it is necessary that each particular group have a determined portion of space assigned to it: in other terms, it is necessary that space in general be divided, differentiated, arranged, and that these divisions and arrangements be known to everybody. On the other hand, every summons to a celebration, a hunt or a military expedition implies fixed and established dates, and consequently that a common time is agreed upon, which everybody conceives in the same fashion. Finally, the co-operation of many persons with the same end in view is possible only when they are in agreement as to the relation which exists between this end and the means of attaining it, that is to say, when the same causal relationship is admitted by all the co-operators in the enterprise. It is not surprising, therefore, that social time, social space, social classes and causality should be the basis of the corresponding categories, since it is under their social forms that these different relations were first grasped with a certain clarity by the human intellect.[29]

Thus, Durkheim shifted the ground on which all previous social theorists had stood. Where they had sought to explain social phenomena by reference to religion or natural law or reason or human nature or biological evolution, Durkheim insisted on regarding all of these as "collective representations" produced by society out of social experience, manifestations of group behavior; results, not causes of group behavior.

Durkheim, like Comte, had unlimited confidence in the scientific method; he believed that it was theoretically possible to establish individual morality and social policy on a scientific basis and that continued social progress could almost be taken for granted. Unlike Comte, Durkheim was highly aware of strains and flaws in the structure of modern society; he emphatically denied that social progress is synonymous with individual happiness.

In *The Division of Labor,* which was a revised version of his doctoral dissertation, Durkheim presented his own greatly simplified model of social evolution. In the earlier stages, societies are made up of small groups of people who resemble each other physically and mentally, have nearly identical skills and aptitudes, and share a single set of collective ideas. They are bound together by "mechanical solidarity," having nearly everything in common and sensing their resemblance to each other and their dissimilarity to everybody else. As population increases and interaction within and between groups intensifies, the division of labor begins to differentiate individuals by occupation, class, interests, norms, and values. Mechanical solidarity is transformed into "organic solidarity." The social system is now held together by complicated relations of interdependence and reciprocity. In a famous preface to the second edition of *The Division of Labor,* Durkheim proposed the revival of the guild system in a modern form to overcome the lack of integration between industry and society and between management and labor.

The Rules of Sociological Method is Durkheim's shortest book. Hardly more than a long essay, it became the declaration of independence for modern sociology. He started by defining *social facts;* they are "ways of acting, thinking, and feeling, external to the individual, and endowed with a power of coercion, by reason of which they control him." Thus defined, social facts include legal and moral regulations, mores, folkways, customs, creeds, rituals, bureaucratic procedures, informal norms, and indeed any regularities of collective behavior that have "an external power of coercion." The fundamental rules for the observation of social facts are to consider social facts as things, to examine them without any preconceptions, to identify them by external, verifiable characteristics, and to concentrate on uniformities of behavior rather than individual variations.

There follows a rule for distinguishing between normal and pathological social conditions—a pathological condition is one that interferes with the survival of a social system. Thus crime is normal, not pathological, under ordinary circumstances; it becomes pathological only when it increases to the point of jeopardizing society's survival. Another set of rules has to do with the classification of societies (Durkheim proposes to measure the "degree of organization" of each specimen), and the final chapter explains how to prove sociological postulates by Durkheim's preferred method of "concomitant variations"—what is now called correlation.

Suicide, published in 1897, was one of the earliest in a long line of statistical studies of social problems, but it is by no means crude. Durkheim and his students collected a huge mass of information about the incidence of suicide in various populations. Although the statistical methods were simple and the handling of figures occasionally careless, the analysis was subtle and profound. Durkheim established that the suicide rate differed greatly from one European country to another but was extremely stable in each country over long periods of time; that the tendency to suicide increases regularly from childhood to old age; that suicide is not correlated with climate; that suicide rates increase from January to June and decrease from June to December, that most suicides occur in the daytime and more on weekdays than on weekends. Suicide rates are much higher among Protestants than Catholics, but Catholics in Protestant countries and Protestants in Catholic countries show rates influenced by the majority. Suicide is positively correlated with education. It is lower for women than for men, for married than for single persons, for parents than for childless married persons. It declines in wartime and during other periods of crisis. From these regularities, Durkheim concluded that suicide varies inversely with the degree of religious, domestic, and political integration, and in general that "suicide varies inversely with the degree of integration of the social groups of which the individual forms a part."[30]

Note
Refer
All of the foregoing regularities reflect the phenomenon of *egoistic suicide,* which occurs when individuals detach themselves from social life, and their own goals become preponderant over those of the community. There is less suicide in integrated societies partly because an integrated society "holds individuals under its control, considers them at its service and thus forbids them to dispose wilfully of themselves,"[31]

partly because the members of integrated groups have common goals that distract them from their personal troubles. The egoistic state is traumatic in itself.

But Durkheim recognized that suicide often occurs, especially in tribal societies, under conditions just the opposite of egoism, when the integration of a social group is so strong that its members willingly commit suicide out of a sense of duty. Examples are the suicides of Polynesian men on the threshold of old age, the suicides of Hindu widows at the funerals of their husbands, and the suicides of African tribesmen after the death of their chief. These suicides are sacrifices imposed by society for social ends. They reflect a very high degree of integration and Durkheim classifies them as *altruistic suicides.*

The third type is *anomic suicide.* Durkheim's explanation of anomic suicide is often confused with his explanation of egoistic suicide.[32] Indeed, it is not uncommon to read that the substitution of individual for collective goals is the cause of anomie.

Durkheim begins his discussion of anomic suicide by demonstrating that market crashes and financial crises increase the suicide rate but that it is also increased by rapid, unexpected rises in prosperity and even by expositions and world fairs: "Every disturbance of equilibrium, even though it achieves greater comfort and a heightening of general vitality, is an impulse to voluntary death. Whenever serious readjustments take place in the social order, whether or not due to a sudden growth or to an unexpected catastrophe, men are more inclined to self-destruction."[33]

The whole sense of Durkheim's discussion of anomic suicide is intensely conservative. In the old days, he says in effect, men were content with the stations to which they had been called and achieved happiness by accepting their places in the social hierarchy. There is no way of avoiding a hierarchy, since even if inheritance were abolished, differences of natural talent would continue to give rise to differences of social worth. What matters more than the particular form of a social system is the confidence that its members have in its rightness and permanence. When this is shaken in any way, by social change or technological progress, by increasing wealth or by a depression, by mobility or class conflict, then the possibility of individual happiness declines (as the increase in suicide demonstrates) and institutional reforms are needed to restore the lost equilibrium.

Fifteen years elapsed between *Suicide* and *The Elementary Forms of Religious Life.* In the interim, Durkheim steeped himself in the literature of ethnology and became familiar with everything that was then known about primitive man. *The Elementary Forms* is an analysis of the whole phenomenon of religion, using the totemic religion of the Australian aborigines, the most primitive people known, as a case in point.

Totemism is a system whereby a tribe is divided into kinship groups named for an animal, or more rarely for some other natural phenomenon. This *totem* is surrounded by special prohibitions and observances that apply to members of the totemic group and only to them, and which the natives explain as means of controlling *mana,* the invisible force with which the totem is imbued. *Mana* can be either helpful or harmful to the worshipper; he never regards it with indifference. The Australian aborigines have neither gods nor devils, although they do venerate the souls of ancestors and other spirits. In Durkheim's view, the emergence of gods would represent a more advanced stage in the individualization of religion, but the essential religious element would remain the same: the division between a sacred realm, whose objects and personages have *mana,* and a secular realm, lacking that unseen force. But *mana,* he concludes, after a long analysis of Australian aboriginal beliefs and practices, is nothing more than an emanation of the social group, an expression of its collective force. The totem is sacred because it symbolizes the kinship group as a collectivity, the social experience that creates, sustains, and disciplines the individual. Whatever is worshipped in any religion is always society in disguise. The "reality, which mythologies have represented under so many different forms, but which is the universal and eternal objective cause of these sensations *sui generis* out of which religious experience is made, is society."[34]

GEORG SIMMEL

Georg Simmel (1858–1918) was born in Berlin, studied at the University of Berlin, and taught there until he moved to the University of Strasbourg, late in life. He was of Jewish ancestry but was raised as a Lutheran.

Simmel was much more of a loner than Durkheim. Although his lectures and his writings were very popular, he had few friends among his colleagues and attracted only a few disciples. In a famous entry in his diary he wrote, "I know that I shall die without intellectual heirs—and that is as it should be. My legacy will be, as it were in cash, distributed to many heirs, each transforming his part into use conformed to *his* nature: a use which will reveal no longer its indebtedness to this heritage."[35] And that is exactly how it turned out. American sociology, with its emphasis on social interaction, roles, stratification, urban problems, and group conflicts, is particularly indebted to Simmel. Albion Small, the founder of *The American Journal of Sociology,* translated chapters from Simmel's *Soziologie,*[36] which appeared one by one in that journal during the formative years from 1896 to 1906. Robert E. Park, who studied with Simmel for a year, promulgated more of his ideas through the "Chicago school" of urban sociology. More recently, Simmel's ideas on conflict and on coalitions in triads have had more influence than ever before.[37]

Simmel's books and articles were very numerous, many of them on topics in philosophy and art criticism that were only remotely connected to sociology, but almost all his sociological ideas are set forth in *Soziologie,* published in 1908.[38] The book has never been completely translated into English but copious excerpts from it are included in collections of Simmel's writings.[39]

Durkheim, it will be remembered, described sociology as the study of "social facts external to the individual which have the power to constrain him"—what we now call norms. Simmel described sociology as the study of social interaction, particularly the study of certain patterns of interaction that appear again and again in different settings. Simmel was willing to leave the analysis of current events and the solution of social problems to others, while he studied the basic processes of human association, conceived almost as abstractly as geometry. He saw no need for empirical research, believing that the information needed for the analysis of social interaction is available to any thoughtful man with ordinary powers of observation. It is therefore a kind of paradox that Simmel's ideas have turned out to be extraordinarily fertile in stimulating empirical research and in suggesting solutions to problems of social engineering.

The central theme in Simmel's analysis of the "pure forms of socialization" is that all social experience is essentially two-sided. Human nature is not, as Durkheim supposed, a social product; it has both a social and a nonsocial aspect. Conflict between groups in a society is not accidental or pathological but a necessary condition of social integration. Good and evil, cooperation and competition, friendship and jealousy are opposite sides of the same coins. Indeed any social situation may be resolved into positive and negative tendencies. The most important thing about a social situation is the way these opposing tendencies are reconciled.

Society is not a creation of independent individuals, nor is it a vast organism in which individuals are cells. Human existence, like human nature, is partly social and partly individual. It is "the synthesis or simultaneity of two logically contradictory characterizations of man— the characterization which is based on his function as a member, as a product and content of society; and the opposing characterization which is based on his functions as an autonomous being, and which views his life from its own center and for its own sake."[40] Although every social system demands that its members conform perfectly to its norms, they never do so; and although men constantly seek immunity from social control, they never achieve it. No collective program is ever carried out exactly as planned; it is always modified by the private purposes of individuals. At the same time, these private purposes are continuously checked by society. The opposition between the individual and society is permanent and irreducible. The individual's conscience is always grounded on two incompatible virtues—submission to group norms and defiance of them. Everyone is faced with a lifelong choice between conformity and autonomy, but the circumstances of human existence do not permit us to choose finally between them.

Simmel was the first sociologist to identify superordination and subordination as the most important forms of social interaction and to perceive that every organization is built around a framework of graded statuses. He was also the first to describe the ambivalent character of the status relationship and to understand that authority is never a one-way street but always confers some ability on the subordinate to control the behavior of the superior. Every status relationship involves elements of cooperation toward common objectives and measures of defense against common enemies, but it also involves the resistance of each to the influence of the other, and the opposition of peer groups to those above and below them. The integration of an organization depends in part on its opposition to outsiders but is always threatened by the internal strains generated by its own status order.

The interplay of conflict and cooperation is the basis of Simmel's geometrical model of social interaction. He conceived of interaction as occupying or seeming to occupy space; although he drew no diagrams himself, modern methods of representing social relationships by "sociograms" and of representing group relationships in terms of "territories" and "boundaries" are derived from Simmel. A *boundary*, according to Simmel, is an imaginary line that appears around groups in contact with other groups and enables them to maintain their separate identities. The boundary informs both members and outsiders what degree of intrusion would provoke a conflict and where the battleground for that conflict would be located.

The dualism that is Simmel's trademark is equally conspicuous in every part of his sociological theory. Indeed it pervades his entire view of human existence as a precarious balance between absolute and contradictory necessities—cooperation and conflict, obedience and rebellion, permanence and change. Unlike most nineteenth-century sociologists, Simmel did not attach much importance to social evolution or to the idea of progress, and he did not believe that the human condition at the end of the nineteenth century was dramatically different from what it had been in former eras. Simmel was inclined to view "the pure forms of association" as fixed, recurrent patterns that could not be much affected by technology. The modern world, in his view, had two important peculiarities—an increase in the size and number of groups and a tendency for groups to overlap and intersect to a greater extent than before. In medieval times, for example, the groups to which an individual belonged formed a series of concentric circles—family, guild, town, province. Under modern conditions, the individual chooses many of his memberships—for example in occupational or political organizations—and they are no longer mutually determining. These diverse affiliations expose modern man to the pressure of conflicting norms and to a good deal of psychological stress, but they increase his freedom by allowing him to pick and choose among the norms of the groups to which he belongs. This freedom is not unlimited, however. The individual cannot sustain more than a certain number of relationships without reverting to unrestrained egoism, and the group cannot expand indefinitely without losing its hold on its members. Thus, the sociological expansion that follows from the increasing scale and complexity of modern society needs to be balanced by the development of intermediate groups large enough to make themselves heard but small enough to recognize their individual members.

MAX WEBER

Max Weber (1864–1920) was born in Erfurt, the son of a prosperous and influential lawyer who was active in politics. Like his friend Simmel, Weber was brought up in Berlin. He studied law, history, economics, and philosophy and achieved early recognition, becoming a professor at the age of 30. Then he suffered a nervous breakdown which forced him to give up teaching. After he recovered, he spent most of his life in private study. His writings were extensive; although many volumes have been translated into English, a considerable amount remains untranslated. His work falls into four major categories; for the advanced student of sociology, practically everything in the first three categories is required reading:

1. Studies in the sociology of religion. He began in 1904 with a famous essay, *The Protestant Ethic and the Spirit of Capitalism*.[41] This was followed by detailed studies of the religion of China, the religion of India, ancient Judaism and the long section on the sociology of religion that is part of *Economy and Society*.

2. *Economy and Society (Wirtschaft und Gesellschaft.)* This is a large, unfinished work that was not published until after Weber's death.[42] Besides the sociology of religion it deals with the nature of sociology, the varieties of social organization, the sociological aspects of economics, political authority and forms of government, the causes and effects of bureaucracy, and the sociology of science.

3. A large number of sociological studies on such diverse topics as urban growth, music, European politics, the methodology of the social sciences, and American culture.

4. A body of nonsociological writings on general economic history, law, administration, and politics.

Weber is generally acknowledged as the greatest of sociologists. He knew more about the organization of civilized societies, ancient and modern, Western and Oriental, than anyone else has ever known. The problems he took up—the origins of capitalism, the relationship of religion and science, the effect of stratification on government, the growth of bureaucratic organization, the limits of social rationality, and the connections among values, emotions, and actions—appear even more important now than when he identified them.

His work is too rich and voluminous to be adequately summarized in the space available here but a few of his leading ideas can be noted. Like Simmel, Weber believed that the same forms of social organization develop independently in different cultures, and his enormous historical knowledge enabled him to demonstrate the one point again and again. The following sentence is typical of Weber's style; he is discussing religious congregations and the balance between preaching and pastoral care in such congregations. "Among those religious functionaries whose pastoral care has influenced the everyday life of the laity and the behavior of political officials in an enduring and often decisive manner have been the counseling rabbis of Judaism, the father confessors of Catholicism, the pietistic pastors of souls in Protestantism, the directors of souls in Counter Reformation Catholicism, the Brahminic *purohitas* at the court, the *gurus* and *gosains* in Hinduism, and the *muftis* and dervish *shaykhs* in Islam." [43]

One of Weber's lifelong concerns was to show how the major segments of a society influenced each other in their historical development. His first important work, *The Protestant Ethic and the Spirit of Capitalism,* demonstrated how the religious values held by the Puritan sects of the Reformation, especially their asceticism and their belief that God arbitrarily elects certain souls for salvation, contributed to the development of industrial capitalism in England and northern Europe by providing motives for hard work, austere living, and the accumulation of wealth. Although it was not his sole purpose, Weber refuted Marx's contention that all beliefs and values were mere superstructure, explainable by reference to the organization of production, by showing that beliefs and values could be equally well used to explain the development of a system of production.

Because he provided an alternative explanation of the rise of capitalism and a different set of predictions about its future, Weber has been called "the Marx of the bourgeoisie." But his historical analyses go far beyond this one point; he was able to show the mutual dependence of economic systems, forms of government, social stratification, and religious beliefs in Greece and Rome, in the Middle Ages, in the ancient Near East, in India, China, Japan, and medieval Russia, indeed wherever civilization had left written records.

For Weber, sociology is as much a science as physics or chemistry but with very different materials and methods. Sociology is founded on "meaning," "understanding," "comprehension." Being human, the sociologist can get closer to his subject matter than the natural scientist, and Weber saw this as an advantage, not a drawback.

> Sociology . . . is a science which attempts the interpretative understanding of social action in order thereby to arrive at a causal explanation of its course and effects. In "action" is included all human behaviour when and in so far as the acting individual attaches a subjective meaning to it. . . . Action is social in so far as, by virtue of the subjective meaning attached to it by the acting individual (or individuals), it takes account of the behaviour of others and is thereby oriented in its course.[44]

Unlike some sociologists who take the natural sciences as a model, Weber did not want to create a value-free sociology. Values, insofar as they give meaning to social action, are essential for any understanding of it. But this does not free the sociologist from the need to be objective. Weber distinguishes between value judgments, which are the values accepted by an actor, and value references, which are the same values dispassionately considered by the sociologist.

But it would be a mistake to suppose that all forms of social action are equally affected by value judgments. Weber distinguishes four types of action—rational action directed toward goals, rational action in support of values, action based on immediate emotions, and habitual action. For example, a manufacturing process is a rational action in relation to its goals, a religious ceremony is a rational action in support of a value, a family argument is an emotional action, and shaking hands when introduced is an habitual action. Corresponding to the types of action are types of government and social organization. The rational exercise of power, either in pursuit of a goal or in support of a value, leads to bureaucratic forms of organization, such as a modern government bureau or business enterprise. Social systems based on emotion have charismatic leaders, endowed by their followers with magical charm and invincibility. Social systems based on habit or tradition, like the family, embody forms of social action that are presumably efficacious because they have worked in the past but whose exact relation to goals and values cannot be determined. Weber is quick to point out that these types of social action cannot often be observed in pure form; there are many traditional elements in the organization of a factory and many rational elements in the organization of a family.

The *ideal type* is a means of understanding the complex pattern of causation of a social phenomenon by developing a simplified, sharpened version of the phenomenon to which real instances can be compared and their deviations noted. Thus, in setting out the characteristics of "bureaucracy" or "feudalism" Weber was not suggesting that every bureaucratic organization or every feudal system has exactly the same characteristics. On the contrary, he assumed that no bureaucratic organization or feudal system exactly represents the ideal type. He described the ideal type in order to understand a recurrent pattern of cause and effect and also in order to explain deviations from the pattern.

Weber developed dozens of ideal types, but the one to which he devoted the most attention and the one that has had the most influence on later sociologists was the ideal type of *bureaucracy*. He analyzed this form of organization more thoroughly than any social phenomenon had ever been analyzed before, and it occupies a central place in his description of the modern world.

Bureaucracy is not an exclusively modern form. Weber identifies large and well-developed bureaucracies in Ancient Egypt during the period of the New Empire; in the later Roman Empire, especially under Diocletian; in Byzantium; in the Roman Catholic church after the Crusades; and in China "from the time of Shi Hwangti" but its purest embodiment is to be found in the modern Western state and in the large business enterprise.

The predominance of bureaucracy is closely associated with increases of population, the decline of religion and the growth of science, constitutional government, large-scale production, improvements in machinery and communication, the concentration of control over the means of production in a few hands, the separation of the worker from the final product of his work, the increase of written records and quantitative measurements, and the other characteristic features of an advanced industrial system. The reason for the growth of bureaucracy under these conditions, according to Weber, is its "technical superiority" to other forms of organization; indeed, it stands in the same relation to other forms of organization as machine production to handicraft methods.

Weber's idea of bureaucracy is precisely opposite the popular notion of a clumsy, slow-moving system, entangled in its own red tape, although he did not fail to consider the reasons why some bureaucracies break down in this way. In the ideal type of bureaucracy, operations are marked by "precision, speed, unambiguity, knowledge of the files, continuity, discretion, unity, strict subordination, reduction of friction and of material and personal costs."[45] A bureaucracy consists of officials who occupy permanent positions arranged in a hierarchy under fixed rules. The regular activities required for the purposes of the system are distributed among these positions as official duties, together with the limited authority necessary for carrying out these duties. Bureaucratic management is based on written documents, carefully arranged and preserved in the files. The management of every office follows general rules, which cover most of its operations and need to be learned. Hence, the official must be trained first for his career and then for the duties of each position. He is appointed, not elected, and expects to serve for life, advancing to higher positions with increasing age as his talents and opportunities permit. He receives a regular salary and an old-age pension. The salary is sufficient to support him in comfort, and he normally enjoys life tenure but does not acquire any vested interest in the position he holds; he cannot sell or bequeath it as he might do in a nonbureaucratic system. Indeed, the most fundamental trait of bureaucracy is a sharp distinction between the position and the man who holds it. His office is completely separated from his home, and the hours he must spend in the office are specified. His conduct as an official is not supposed to be influenced by his personal traits or affiliations or by the personal traits and affiliations of the people he deals with. The whole purpose of the bureaucratic system is to establish working relationships that are impartial, dispassionate, predictable, and uniform.

Weber was not in the least insensitive to the problem of how to lead a humane existence in an increasingly bureaucratized society. Indeed, he considered it to be *the* problem of modern man. But he did not believe that the progress of bureaucracy could be arrested in the foreseeable future or that it could be reversed by a socialist revolution. He insisted that a socialist regime would be more bureaucratized than a capitalist system because of its greater need for centralized control and coordination of the economy.

As Weber saw it, the subjection of the individual to the giant organizations of a large-scale industrial society cannot be avoided, and the sense of alienation which results from it cannot be completely cured. The individual has no power to reverse the "disenchantment of the world" by science and technology. On the other hand, bureaucracy is an instrument, not an end in itself; it does not create the values it serves. The individual retains the right to choose between competing values, to commit himself to one goal or another, and to lead a life of fully human choices outside of office hours, so to speak.

Sociology, Weber thought, could not offer any easy solution to the dilemmas of modern existence or protect anyone from the necessity of hammering out his own choices among irreconcilable attitudes toward life, among what he called the "warring gods." He wrote hopefully that knowledge is pursued for something more than its own sake. " ... if we are competent in our pursuit (which must be presupposed here) we can force the individual, or at least we can help him, to give himself an *account of the ultimate meaning of his own conduct.* This appears to me as not so trifling a thing to do, even for one's own personal life."[46]

Social Theory in the United States

Durkheim died in 1917, Simmel in 1918, Weber in 1920, and Pareto in 1923. Durkheim's best students were killed in World War I. The development of the social sciences in Germany was interrupted by the social disorders of the twenties, and then halted altogether by the Nazi purge of the universities. Pareto was hailed as the philosopher of fascism and ceased to be read.

Meanwhile, sociology in the United States was thriving.[47] The first generation of American sociologists came to prominence in the closing years of the nineteenth century; some of its leading figures were Lester F. Ward, sometimes known as the American Aristotle; William Graham Sumner of Yale, who gave a course on Spencer's principles of sociology as early as 1875; Franklin H. Giddings of Columbia, a lifelong theorist who taught his students to do careful empirical research; Albion W. Small of the University of Chicago who founded the *American Journal of Sociology,* co-authored the first American textbook of sociology, and was largely responsible for the early growth of the American Sociological Society; and Thorstein Veblen, an influential radical theorist.

The leading figures of the second generation of American sociologists, Charles Horton Cooley, Robert E. Park, W. I. Thomas, and E. A. Ross, were all born around the end of the Civil War and did most of their work after 1910. All but Cooley studied in Germany, traveled widely, and involved themselves in public affairs. They wrote voluminous theoretical works that are seldom read now and helped to develop a tradition of empirical research that has grown beyond their wildest expectations. Somewhat apart from this group, but contemporary with them, was the philosopher George Herbert Mead, who analyzed the way the "self" is shaped by the anticipated or actual reactions of other people in the process of social interaction.

Their immediate successors were numerous, but only two of them, Pitirim Sorokin and Howard Becker, produced theoretical work of marked originality. It was not until after World War II, when Europe was rather painfully relearning sociology from American textbooks and visiting lecturers, and students were flocking from the remote corners of

Asia, Africa, Latin America, and the Balkans to study social research methods in the United States, that two American theorists, Parsons of Harvard and Merton of Columbia, attained an influence comparable to that of Spencer or Durkheim.

TALCOTT PARSONS

Talcott Parsons, born in Colorado in 1902, was educated at Amherst, the London School of Economics, and Heidelberg, where he took his doctorate in 1927. He has taught at Harvard for more than 40 years, beginning as an economics instructor but changing to sociology early in his career. He has been chairman of the Department of Sociology (renamed Social Relations) for much of that time, and is a leading figure in the American Sociological Association. He has published more pages than any other social theorist, including such voluminous writers as Montesquieu, Marx, Pareto, and Weber. Among his best-known books are *The Structure of Social Action* (1937), *The Social System* (1951), *Towards a General Theory of Action* (with Shils, 1951), *Essays in Sociological Theory* (1949 and 1954), *Working Papers in the Theory of Action* (with Bales and Shils, 1953), *Family Socialization and Interaction Process* (with Bales, 1955), *Economy and Society* (with Smelser, 1956), *Structure and Process in Modern Societies* (1960), *Social Structure and Personality* (1964), and *Sociological Theory and Modern Society* (1967), together with almost innumerable papers. Throughout these works, Parsons has labored with remarkable single-mindedness to construct a "general theory of social action." [48]

The heart of Parsons' work is an intricate system for classifying social phenomena in terms of social actors and the systems within which they act. His concepts of actors and systems were derived originally from an exhaustive comparison of the works of Weber, Durkheim, Pareto, and the classical economist, Alfred Marshall. Parsons distinguishes four kinds of systems in which humans are involved—cultural, social, psychological, and biological, all of them analytically separate and noninterchangeable. The two focal points of his theory are the relation of the individual actor to a system and the interdependence of systems and subsystems. Every social system, according to Parsons, has an internal and external situation and supports two kinds of activities, those that are instrumental to goals and those that are ends in themselves. Every system must solve the problem of adapting to the external environment, attaining its goals, maintaining its patterns of internal operation, and keeping itself integrated. The solution to these problems is accomplished, either for an individual actor or a system, through a pattern of choices in the five major dilemmas that always confront human actors: affectivity versus affective neutrality, diffuseness versus specificity, particularism versus universalism, quality versus performance, collectivity-orientation versus self-orientation. Among the other central concepts in the Parsonian system are values, norms, beliefs, sentiments, status roles, power and authority, boundary maintenance, system linkage, social control, socialization, sanctions, and facilities. (There is no shortcut to the mastery of the special meanings that Parsons gives to each of these terms.)

Parsons has attracted a great many enthusiastic disciples and as many fervent critics. Elements of his theory have been used successfully in the analysis of political, economic, occupational, scientific, religious, and family systems. Parsons himself has written on nearly every important current issue—civil rights, economic planning, international relations, teenage culture, voting behavior, marital conflict, and the future of higher education, among other topics. The ability of his theory to generate new insights and to provide a framework for empirical research can hardly be questioned. The principal objections of his critics are first, that the theory cannot be confirmed or disproved (in the words of one critic, it consists of directives for theorizing rather than statements about the real world); and second, that his emphasis on the maintenance of social systems and the way they induce the appropriate motivations in individuals leads Parsons to minimize the unfavorable features of modern society and to regard contemporary American institutions with more complacency than they deserve.

ROBERT K. MERTON

Robert K. Merton was born in Philadelphia in 1910, educated at Temple and at Harvard, where he was closely associated with Parsons. He has been at Columbia since 1941 and is largely responsible for the extraordinary influence of that department. Like Parsons, Merton has been showered with academic honors; he was the first sociologist to be elected to the National Academy of Sciences. Unlike Parsons, his great reputation rests mainly on a single book, *Social Theory and Social Structure,* first published in 1949 and revised in 1957 and again in 1968.[49] It is a collection of loosely related papers, which were not originally intended as chapters of a single volume but have somehow acquired a coherent pattern. It is divided into four sections: theoretical sociology, studies in social and cultural structure, the sociology of knowledge and mass communication, and the sociology of science. In the first two parts, especially, there is hardly a page that has not had a measurable influence on the development of American sociology.

One reason for this is that American sociology has specialized almost from its beginning in empirical research of limited scale, to which Merton's theory is closely related. Unlike other major theorists, he advocates what he calls *theories of the middle range,* lying somewhere between the working hypotheses that develop in the course of a particular research project and the grand theories that attempt to explain all the observed uniformities of those phenomena. Middle-range theory is intended to guide empirical research, and Merton's own formulations have been widely used for that purpose. He has several not entirely consistent objections to grand theories—that they have been tried in the past and generally proved ineffective in explaining or predicting events; that sociological knowledge is not yet sufficiently advanced to provide the necessary foundations; and that grand theories must rise naturally out of the convergence of middle-range theories, as the history of science illustrates.

Merton is usually identified as a *functionalist,* which means that he interprets patterns of social behavior by showing how they contribute to (or detract from) the functioning of social systems. Similar viewpoints are familiar in biology and psychology. But Merton's functionalism is both elegant and subtle. He is never tempted into the functionalist fallacies that what is good for the system is necessarily good for the individual or that a system in equilibrium is worth preserving or that conformity is somehow more valuable than nonconformity. He is largely responsible for the distinction between the manifest functions of a social system, those that are recognized by the participants, and its unrecognized, latent functions, and for establishing the expectation among sociologists that latent functions can be discovered in every system. Merton insists that nonconforming behavior is as much a product of social pressures as conforming behavior and his famous analysis of types of nonconformity (innovation, ritualism, retreatism, and rebellion) explains how the attempt of individuals to adapt to inconsistencies between the means and goals offered by a social system bring about various kinds of deviant behavior. Most individuals have statuses in several groups at the same time (the *status set*), and even as incumbents of a single status position, they have various partly incompatible roles toward other persons in the group (the *role set*). An individual's behavior may conform to the norms of a group to which he belongs, may even be imposed on him by group pressure, yet violate the norms of another group to which he belongs.

Mertonian subtlety goes even further into the heart of social affiliation. Social pressure is not an entirely objective phenomenon. The individual constructs his self-image by comparing himself with a *reference group* and shapes his behavior in accordance with the group's norms but he need not actually belong to his own reference group. It may be one he hopes to join eventually, or one he can never join but has nevertheless selected as the source of his own standards. To make matters more complicated and to increase the range of individual choice, there are negative as well as positive reference groups and reference individuals as well as groups.

Merton's own middle-range theories often pick some single typical pattern out of the flux of social experience and highlight it with amazing sharpness. Thus he uses the notion of the self-fulfilling prophecy—a false description of a situation that induces the behavior which brings reality into line with the false description—to explain ethnic and racial conflict in the United States, showing how the belief of whites in the intellectual inferiority of Negroes leads to a denial of educational opportunities for Negroes, which produces statistical evidence of their inferiority. His concept of *serendipity* in science, the discovery of a new principle unrelated to what the scientist was looking for as the result of unanticipated research findings, has sensitized an entire generation of social scientists who look for such findings. His investigation of simultaneous discoveries in the physical and social sciences has done a great deal to strengthen the connection between theory and research. Few important ideas, he points out, are entirely original, but the greatest value of the classics lies in their capacity to be reinterpreted in the light of new knowledge. "For, just as new knowledge has a retroactive effect in helping us to recognize anticipations and adumbrations in earlier work, so changes in current sociological knowledge, problems, and foci of attention enable us to find *new* ideas in a work we had read before."[50]

1. Social theory has three major purposes—it tells us how to visualize the social universe, how to obtain knowledge about it, and how to put that knowledge to use. Most great theorists have provided reasonably full answers to all three of these questions.

2. The story of social theory begins with the ancient Greeks, who were the first to examine social phenomena with a view to understanding and changing them. Aristotle came closer to being a social scientist than anyone else who lived before the nineteenth century; other ancient writers like Polybius even did field research; but these promising beginnings led nowhere. Interest in sociological questions died out early in the Christian era and did not revive until about 1,500 years later.

3. During the Age of Discovery—from about 1492 to about 1776— curiosity was rekindled in Europe by contact with strange cultures all over the world and by the social changes taking place at home. Many speculative theories about the essential nature of society and the individual's relationship to it were worked out. At the end of this period, Adam Smith developed a theory of social interaction and described the major trends of the modern world, and Thomas Malthus forecast the population explosion.

4. The forerunners of modern social theory include Auguste Comte, the first man to call himself a sociologist, Herbert Spencer, who developed a sociological system based on Darwin's theory of evolution, Karl Marx, who formulated the ideology of international Communism, and Vilfredo Pareto, the analyst of nonlogical social actions.

5. The principal founders of sociology were Émile Durkheim, Georg Simmel, and Max Weber. They lived at about the same time, and their major works appeared between 1890 and 1910. Durkheim studied the mechanisms by which society shapes and molds the individual in its own image. Simmel investigated the permanent, universal patterns of human association. Weber described the origins of contemporary institutions, and the principles that govern social change.

6. After World War I, the center of influence in social theory shifted from Europe to the United States. Among the many American theorists whose work has been influential are Talcott Parsons, best known for his comprehensive theory of social action, and Robert Merton, who advocates theories of the middle range to explain limited fields of social phenomena.

1 Would you enjoy living in a community organized like Plato's *Republic?* Why? Why not?

2 "Marxism defines the state as an instrument of the ruling class to maintain its dominance over the exploited workers and predicts the disappearance of the state after the proletarian revolution." What is the *Marxist* explanation of the persistence of the state in contemporary Communist countries?

3 Compare the ideas of Pareto and Durkheim with respect to social change. Which set of ideas has more contemporary relevance?

4 What might Simmel have to say about the slogan, "Do your own thing"?

5 In the light of Weber's theory of bureaucracy, how can the impersonality of large modern organizations like a university or a telephone company be modified?

6 Parsons and Merton are sometimes said to be "theorists of the status quo." What does this mean? Is it a good or bad thing for a theorist to be?

7 Find a concrete example, drawn from your own experience, of each of the following:

> a nonlogical belief
> a social fact
> ambivalence in a status
>   relationship
>
> anomic behavior
> rational action in support
>   of a value
> a reference group

Recommended Reading / **CHAPTER FOUR**

Alvin W. Gouldner. *Enter Plato: Classical Greece and the Origins of Social Theory.* New York: Basic Books, 1965. Reinterprets the work of Plato in relation to modern sociology.

John Plamenatz. *Man and Society: Political and Social Theory.* 2 vols. New York: McGraw-Hill, 1963. Describes and explains the work of important social theorists from Machiavelli to Marx.

Raymond Aron. *Main Currents in Sociological Thought.* New York:

Basic Books, 1967. Describes and explains the sociological theories of Durkheim, Pareto and Weber.

Charles P. and Zona K. Loomis. *Modern Social Theories: Selected American Writers.* Princeton, N.J.: Van Nostrand Reinhold, 1961. Describes and explains the work of seven modern American theorists (Becker, Davis, Homans, Merton, Parsons, Sorokin, and Williams).

Raymond P. Cuzzort. *Humanity and Modern Sociological Thought.* New York: Holt, Rinehart & Winston, 1969. Contains particularly readable summaries of a number of current sociological theories.

Notes / CHAPTER FOUR

1. Plato, *Works,* with an English translation (Cambridge, Mass.: Harvard University Press, The Loeb Classical Library, 1952).
2. In his remarkable sociological critique of Plato, Gouldner notes that most of the factors that would now be considered in relation to social disunity are taken up by Plato as, for example, the disorganizing effects of war and the importation of foreign beliefs; the effects of internal invention; demographic shifts and changes; social stratification and the unequal distribution of wealth and power; the integration between individual personalities and socially prescribed roles; and the norms regulating property, sex, and kinship. See Alvin W. Gouldner, *Enter Plato: Classical Greece and the Origins of Social Theory* (New York: Basic Books, 1965).
3. Aristotle, *Works,* with an English translation (Cambridge, Mass.: Harvard University Press, The Loeb Classical Library, 1937).
4. From *Nicomachean Ethics,* bk. 9, chap. 7, pp. 506–507 in Richard McKeon, *Introduction to Aristotle* (New York: Modern Library, 1947).
5. "Had Aristotle held to the course he in part so admirably followed, we would have had a scientific sociology in his early day. Why did he not do so? There may have been many reasons; but chief among them, probably, was that eagerness for premature practical applications which is ever obstructing the progress of science . . . " From Vilfredo Pareto, *The Mind and Society: A Treatise on General Sociology,* Vol. I, par. 277, p. 185 (New York: Dover, 1963).
6. Polybius, *The Histories of Polybius,* trans. Evelyn S. Shuckburgh, 2 vols. (Bloomington, Ind.: Indiana University Press, 1962).
7. Strabo, *The Geography of Strabo,* trans. Horace Leonard Jones, 8 vols. (Cambridge, Mass.: Harvard University Press, Loeb Classical Library, 1959–1961).
8. Ibn Khaldoun, *The Mugadimmah: An Introduction to History* (New York: Pantheon, 1958).
9. Adam Smith, *The Theory of Moral Sentiments* (New York: Augustus M. Kelley, 1966); *An Inquiry into the Nature and Causes of the Wealth of Nations,* 6th ed., 2 vols. (London: Methuen, 1950).

10. Adam Smith, together with the contributions of his colleagues and friends in Scotland. The sociological importance of this school has only lately been appreciated. A good summary of their contribution may be found in Louis Schneider, ed., *The Scottish Moralists on Human Nature* (Chicago: University of Chicago Press, 1967).

11. Smith, *Moral Sentiments,* p.161.

12. Thomas Robert Malthus, *An Essay on the Principle of Population,* 7th ed. (London: Reeves and Turner, 1872).

13. *Ibid.,* pp. 3–4.

14. *Ibid.,* p. 512.

15. Harriet Martineau, trans. and ed., *The Positive Philosophy of August Comte,* 3 vols. (London: G. Bell, 1896).

16. *Ibid.,* vol. 3, p. 22.

17. Herbert Spencer, *The Study of Sociology* (Ann Arbor, Mich.: University of Michigan Press, 1961); *The Principles of Sociology,* 3 vols. (New York: D. Appleton and Company, 1883–1909).

18. Spencer, *Principles of Sociology,* vol. 1, pp. 617–618.

19. *Ibid.,* vol. 1, p. 15.

20. Justice Oliver Wendell Holmes in his dissenting opinion in Lochner *v.* New York, 1905.

21. Karl Marx, *Das Kapital,* published piecemeal from 1867–1894. See *Capital: A Critique of Political Economy* (New York: Modern Library, 1936).

22. Karl Marx and Friedrich Engels, *The Communist Manifesto* (New York: Washington Square Press, 1965).

23. Friedrich Engels, *The Condition of the Working Class in England* (Oxford: Blackwell, 1958).

24. They are anthologized in T. B. Bottomore and Maximilien Rubel, eds., *Karl Marx: Selected Writings in Sociology and Social Philosophy* (New York: McGraw-Hill, 1956). For an admirable summary and critique of these theories, see John Plamenatz, *Man and Society: Political and Social Theory,* 2 vols. (New York: McGraw-Hill, 1963), vol. 2, *Bentham through Marx,* pp. 269–408.

25. Vilfredo Pareto, *The Mind and Society: A Treatise on General Sociology,* trans. by Andrew Bongiorno and Arthur Livingston (ed.), published through the sponsorship of the Pareto Fund (New York: Dover, 1963). Originally published by Harcourt, Brace & Co., 1935. The first part of the title *(The Mind and Society)* is Livingston's, not Pareto's, but it describes the book very well. This edition is itself a masterpiece. The erudition of the editor matches that of the author. Numerous long quotations that Pareto translated from other languages, especially Greek and Latin, into Italian were retranslated by Livingston from the original into English, and hundreds of obscure citations were verified.

26. Pareto, in the last part of *The Mind and Society,* but also in other writings, especially *Les Systèmes Socialistes* (Paris: M. Giard, 1926).

27. Emile Durkheim, *The Division of Labor in Society,* trans. George Simpson (New York: Free Press, 1960); *The Rules of Sociological*

Method, 8th ed. (New York: Free Press, 1968); *Suicide: A Study in Sociology* (New York: Free Press, 1951); *The Elementary Forms of the Religious Life,* trans. Joseph Ward Swain (New York: Free Press, 1965).

28. Durkheim, *Suicide,* pp. 309–310.

29. Durkheim, *The Elementary Forms of the Religious Life,* p. 492.

30. Durkheim, *Suicide,* p. 209.

31. *Ibid.,* p. 209.

32. Although one recent critic maintains that they *are* identical: See Barclay D. Johnson, "Durkheim's One Cause of Suicide," *American Sociological Review,* 30, no. 6 (December 1965). 875–886.

33. Durkheim, *Suicide,* p. 246.

34. Durkheim, *The Elementary Forms of the Religious Life,* p. 465.

35. Quoted in Lewis A. Coser, ed., *Georg Simmel* (Englewood Cliffs, N.J.: Prentice-Hall, 1965), p. 24.

36. Simmel's work appeared at intervals in the *American Journal of Sociology* from 1896 to 1957. These papers are listed in "Simmel's Writings Available in English," pp. 379–382, Kurt H. Wolff, ed., *Georg Simmel: 1858–1918* (Columbus, Ohio: Ohio State University Press, 1959).

37. See, for example, Lewis A. Coser, *The Functions of Social Conflict* (New York: Free Press, 1964); Theodore Caplow, *Two Against One: Coalitions in Triads* (Englewood Cliffs, N.J.: Prentice-Hall, 1968).

38. Georg Simmel, *Soziologie: Untersuchungen über die Formen der Vergesellschaftung* (Leipzig: Duncker and Humblot, 1908), plus later editions.

39. Nicholas J. Spykman, *The Social Theory of Georg Simmel* (Chicago: University of Chicago Press, 1925). Kurt H. Wolff, trans. and ed., *The Sociology of Georg Simmel* (New York: Free Press, 1950).

40. Wolff, *Georg Simmel, 1858–1918,* pp. 350–351.

41. Max Weber, *The Protestant Ethic and the Spirit of Capitalism,* trans. Talcott Parsons with an introduction by R. H. Tawney (New York: Scribner's, 1930).

42. Max Weber, *Wirtschaft und Gesellschaft: Grundriss der Verstehenden Soziologie* (Tübingen: Mohr, 1956). Two versions of this work are available in English: *The Theory of Social and Economic Organization,* trans. A. M. Henderson and Talcott Parsons (New York: Free Press, 1957); *Economy and Society,* ed. G. Roth and C. Wittich (Totowa, N.J.: Bedminster Press, 1968).

43. Max Weber, *The Sociology of Religion,* trans. E. Fischoff (Boston: Beacon Press, 1963), p. 76.

44. Weber, *The Theory of Social and Economic Organization,* p. 88.

45. Hans H. Gerth and C. Wright Mills, *From Max Weber: Essays in Sociology* (New York: Oxford University Press, 1946), p. 214.

46. Weber's personal attitude toward life is magnificently set forth in his paper, "Science as a Vocation," from which these lines are taken. See Gerth and Mills, *From Max Weber,* p. 152.

47. For a fuller account, see Howard W. Odum, *American Sociology:*

The Story of Sociology in the United States through 1950 (New York: Longmans, Green and Co., 1951); and Don Albert Martindale, *The Nature and Types of Sociological Theory* (Boston: Houghton Mifflin, 1960).

48. The best attempt at a concise summary is "Talcott Parsons' Social Theory" in Charles P. and Zona K. Loomis, *Modern Social Theories: Selected American Writers* (Princeton, N.J.: Van Nostrand Reinhold, 1961). It occupies 115 pages.

49. Robert K. Merton, *Social Theory and Social Structure* (New York: Free Press, 1968), enlarged edition.

50. *Ibid.,* p. 37.

Part Two

Sociological Fields

In Part II, we turn from the discipline of sociology taken as a whole to some of its important subdivisions, taken one at a time. The following seven chapters deal respectively with population, the city, stratification, work, organizations, the family, and deviance. These are sometimes called "substantive fields," in contrast to "general fields" like social theory or methodology. The seven fields we will consider do not exhaust the possibilities, but each is undeniably important. Each has its own literature, its own core of specialists, and its own affinities with other branches of social science. Together, these seven fields cover a large part of the sociological landscape.

Population

Introduction

The study of population in its narrow sense is called *demography* and involves the statistical analysis of changes in the size, composition, and distribution of human populations. In its broad sense, the study of population includes the study of factors that affect fertility and mortality, patterns of migration, and the two-way relationship between population changes and changes in social institutions.[1]

The significance of the study of population as a sociological field is too obvious to require much explanation. Any social behavior takes place within a population, and it can nearly always be shown that a given pattern of behavior is influenced by the characteristics of the population within which it occurs. The era in which we live is marked by the most dramatic population changes since the dawn of human experience and, for reasons that will be explained presently, the tempo of these changes is likely to accelerate within the next few years.

THE CONCEPT OF A POPULATION

A population is an aggregate of persons identified by one or more characteristics which all of them have in common. The simplest common characteristic is residence within a given territory at a given moment in time. For example, the United States Census enumerates all persons residing within the boundaries of the 50 states and the District of Columbia at the beginning of April in every tenth year. The territorial characteristic may be qualified by any number of other characteristics to define a smaller aggregate, for example, the population of U.S. married white women having two or more children under the age of five. Although it is possible to designate a population without using a territorial characteristic (for example, all the living graduates of a college), nonterritorial populations are rarely studied by demographers.

The size of a population is simply the number of individual persons it contains at a given moment in time. The size of a territorial population is affected only by births, deaths, and migration.

The composition of a population is the assortment of individual traits within it. The basic demographic traits are age, sex, race, and marital status; other traits often counted are occupation, education, income, birthplace, language, and religion.

The distribution of a population is its spatial arrangement within its territory. The aspects of distribution most often taken into account are the numbers of persons living in various types of settlements (farms, villages, cities, suburbs), and variations in the density of settlement from one part of the territory to another.

LIMITATIONS OF DEMOGRAPHIC DATA

Because the data of population studies are in numerical form, they are often given more credit for validity and reliability than they really deserve. Even so accurate an enterprise as the decennial census of the United States fails to enumerate a sizable fraction of the population, counts many persons twice, and is rather unreliable in distinguishing among single, divorced, and married persons. In underdeveloped countries and in remote parts of developed countries, census data may provide only a rough approximation of population size. As recently as 1954, it was estimated that about 20 percent of the world's population had not been enumerated in any census during the previous 10 years.[2] Underenumerations of 50 percent or more are not uncommon in some parts of Latin America, Asia, and Africa.

Even when population data are of good quality, they often come in a form that does not permit comparison from one country to another. There are hardly any two countries in the world whose demographic statistics can be compared without making major adjustments.

The theoretical importance of a demographic datum does not insure its availability. Infant mortality statistics are almost indispensable for estimating potential changes in the rate of population growth, but for various reasons, reliable statistics on infant mortality were available for less than half the world's countries in the 1960s. The United States has always had relatively poor records of birth, death, marriage, and divorce.

Despite a worldwide improvement in population statistics in recent years, there are still many populations about whom practically nothing is known. Even with steady progress in census-taking and the registration of vital statistics, it will be many years, at best, before all these gaps are filled in. Meanwhile, the student of population, like any other sociological analyst, must be constantly critical of his raw data.

Demographic Measures and Processes

The sex ratio is the number of males per 100 females in a given population. Thus, a high sex ratio (over 100), means there are more males than females in the population. A low sex ratio (under 100) means that there are more females. The fundamental biological conditions affecting the sex ratio in most human populations are that more males than females are born and that females are hardier from infancy to old age.

As Table 5–1 shows, the *birth sex ratio (males born per 100 females born)* in the United States is comparatively stable in the neighborhood of 105, which means, of course, that there are 105 boy babies for every 100 girl babies.

Table 5–2 shows the birth sex ratio for a number of countries selected

Table 5-1   BIRTH SEX RATIO UNITED STATES

Year	Males Born per 100 Females Born
1940	105.5
1955	105.1
1966	104.9

Source: Based on *Statistical Abstract of the United States, 1968,* table 57, Excludes Hawaii and Alaska for 1940 and 1955 figures.

Table 5-2   BIRTH SEX RATIO, VARIOUS COUNTRIES, 1965

Country	Males Born per 100 Females Born
Australia	105.6
Bulgaria	106.3
China (Taiwan)	106.6
Finland	105.1
Honduras	108.6
Netherlands	105.9

Source: Based on Nathan Keyfitz and Wilhelm Flieger, *World Population: An Analysis of Vital Data* (Chicago: University of Chicago Press, 1968), table 1.

Table 5-3   DEATH RATE BY SEX, UNITED STATES, 1900/1965
(DEATHS PER THOUSAND LIVING
PERSONS)

Year	Death Rate: Males	Death Rate: Females
1900	17.9	16.5
1920	13.4	12.6
1940	12.0	9.5
1966	11.0	8.1

Source: Based on *Statistical Abstract of the United States, 1968,* table 69.

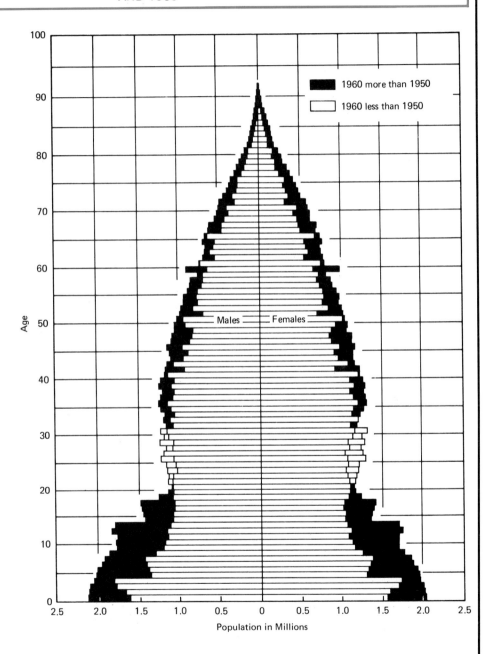

Figure 5-1   POPULATION OF THE UNITED STATES, BY
SINGLE YEARS OF AGE AND SEX: 1950
AND 1960

1960 more than 1950
1960 less than 1950

Males   Females

Age

Population in Millions

Source: Warren S. Thompson and David T. Lewis, *Population Problems* 5th ed., (New York: McGraw-Hill, 1965), Fig. 5-5, p. 100.

for diversity. These also cluster in the neighborhood of 105, with some inexplicable variations.

Table 5–3 compares the annual death rate (deaths per thousand living persons) of males and females in the United States population since 1900. As the rates for both sexes have declined, the advantage of females has increased. The effect of this advantage operating through the entire life span is that by extreme old age, there are nearly twice as many females as males surviving. Table 5–4 shows the sex ratio for the population over 85 in the United States and some other countries.

No one knows what biological mechanisms are at work to produce the excess of males at birth and the excess of male deaths at each stage of life. We have no way of knowing whether these phenomena reflect modern living conditions in some way or are constant for the human species. It is likely that in former centuries, when the risks of childbearing were greater, women in the childbearing ages had much higher death rates than men. However, the propositions that more males are born and that females are hardier appear to apply to every contemporary population for which we have accurate information.

The sex ratio of a given population is affected not only by these fundamental tendencies but also by immigration, migration, and war casualties. In general, young populations tend to have high sex ratios, which reflect the excess of male births. Old populations tend to have low sex ratios, reflecting the greater survival of females. As Table 5–5 shows, the sex ratio of the U.S. population has fallen sharply in the past half-century. The population grew older on the average during this interval, the female advantage with respect to survival increased, and the proportion of foreign-born immigrants—predominantly male—greatly declined.

AGE DISTRIBUTION

The median age of a population is that age which divides it exactly in half, with the same number of persons older and younger. It is the simplest available measure for comparing the age of two populations.

A population pyramid (Figure 5–1) *is a diagram that shows the relative numbers of persons at each age level in a population, usually divided by sex.* Modern populations often have irregular pyramids. The population pyramid furnishes some of the essential information for predicting short-run changes in population.

The median age varies greatly among territorial populations and sub-populations. It can change dramatically in the same population from one era to another. Generally speaking, technological advancement tends to raise the median age of a population, for reasons that will become more apparent later in our discussion. As Table 5–6 shows, the median age of the United States population has advanced from under 17 in 1820, the earliest year for which we have accurate information, to over 30 in 1950, since when it has receded by more than two years. In the 1820 population, which is thought to have aged considerably from colonial times, more than half of the total population consisted of children and adolescents. The same is true today in many parts of Africa, Asia, and Latin America and in the West Indian islands; at the other extreme, the larger countries of western Europe have median ages over 35.

Variations in median age occur not only among national populations but also among segments of the same population. As Table 5–7 shows, American females are older than American males, and the white population of the United States is much older than the black population. There are striking variations among the several states. As Table 5–8 shows, the median age in New York in 1960 was more than 10 years higher than the median age in Utah. Other components of the American population show even more extreme variation: the median age of foreign-born whites in 1960 was 57; the median age of Puerto Ricans living in the United States was 18.

Table 5-4	SEX RATIO OF AGED POPULATION, VARIOUS COUNTRIES, 1965

Country	Males over Age 85 per 100 Females over 85
Australia	49.9
Bulgaria	68.2
China (Taiwan)	33.3
Finland	44.2
Honduras	75.8
Netherlands	76.8
United States	61.9

Source: Based on Keyfitz and Flieger, *World Population*, table 1; and *Statistical Abstract of the United States, 1967*, table 8.

Table 5-5	SEX RATIO, UNITED STATES, 1910/1966

Year	Sex Ratio
1910	106.2
1930	102.6
1950	98.7
1967	95.6

Source: Based on *Statistical Abstract of the United States, 1968*, table 23.

Table 5-6   MEDIAN AGE, UNITED STATES, 1820/1967

Year	Median Age of Total Population
1820	16.7
1860	19.4
1900	22.9
1930	26.4
1950	30.2
1967	27.8

Source: Based on *Statistical Abstract of the United States, 1968,* table 21.

Table 5-7   MEDIAN AGE BY RACE AND SEX, UNITED STATES, 1967

Segment of Population	Median Age
White females	30.0
White males	27.9
Negro females	22.4
Negro males	18.9

Source: Based on *Statistical Abstract of the United States, 1968,* table 26.

Table 5-8   MEDIAN AGE IN SELECTED STATES, 1960

States	Median Age
New York	33.1
Massachusetts	32.1
Iowa	30.3
Michigan	28.3
North Carolina	25.5
Utah	22.9

Source: Based on *Statistical Abstract of the United States, 1968,* table 24.

Table 5-9   MEDIAN AGE IN SELECTED COUNTRIES, 1965

Country	Age in Years
Australia	28.3
Bulgaria	32.0
China (Taiwan)	17.5
Finland	28.4
Honduras	14.6
Netherlands	28.5
United States	27.9

Source: Based on Keyfitz and Flieger, *World Population*, table 1.

Excluding the effect of migration, which is significant only in exceptional cases, the median age of a national population (see Table 5–9) is determined by the birth and death rates that have prevailed in the years since the birth of the oldest living person. It is obvious that any rise in the birth rate tends to lower the median age of the population by increasing the proportion of persons under the median age, while any decline in the birth rate tends to raise the median age by decreasing that proportion.

It is less obvious but equally true that low death rates are associated with young populations and that a falling death rate usually has the effect of lowering the median age of the population very rapidly. To understand why this happens, we must look a little more closely at the pattern of mortality characteristic of human populations.

Mortality

The death rate is the number of deaths in a calendar year per thousand persons alive in a given population at the beginning or the middle of that year. It is determined partly by the health of the population and partly by its age and sex composition.

An age-specific death rate is the number of deaths per thousand living persons in a given age group during a given year. A sex-specific death rate is a rate for males or females considered separately. Refined or adjusted death rates are death rates based on some other population than the one in which they occurred, for example, on a hypothetical stable population.

The infant mortality rate is the number of deaths of infants under one year old per 1000 live births in a calendar year. It is probably the best single measure for comparing the health of two different populations, and for that reason it can be used to measure the level of modernization a country has achieved.

We have already taken note of one of the basic facts about mortality —that females have lower mortality at every age and in every population, with the possible exception of a few localities where childbearing is exceptionally hazardous. There are two other basic facts about mortality to be taken into account.

The first year of life is by far the most vulnerable. In a technologically advanced country like the United States, with comparatively low mortality at every age, the death rate falls abruptly after the first year and does not return to the same level until past the age of 65. In a technologically backward country, like Peru, where infant mortality is staggeringly high and the remaining years of early childhood are hazardous too, the age-specific death rate does not return to the infant level until past the age of 80. Within the first year of life, the first month is by far the most vulnerable and within the first month, the first few hours of life. In the United States, more than half of all infant deaths occur in the first month and about half of these within 24 hours after birth. Even in the most advanced population, infant mortality accounts for a substantial proportion of total deaths. Under primitive conditions, there may be more deaths of infants than of persons at all the later ages combined.

Mortality tends to decline with *modernization,* which may be defined as the process whereby a contemporary society improves its control of the environment by means of an increasingly competent technology applied by increasingly complex organizations. The effects of climate, race, and natural environment on the collective health of a population are so slight compared to the overwhelming influence of modernization that they can be almost disregarded. Originally felt only in Europe, the effect of modernization in reducing the death rate is now universal. In every country for which we have information, with the possible exception of Egypt, the infant mortality rate declined appreciably from 1955 to 1965.

Modernization not only reduces mortality; it also improves mortality statistics. In order to have good mortality statistics, it is necessary to have a reliable census of the population, for births and deaths to be witnessed by a doctor or certified by an official functionary, for literacy to be sufficiently widespread so that vital events can be recorded in every village and age accurately reckoned throughout the population. These conditions are met only in fairly modernized societies. As a result, our knowledge of past mortality trends is very scanty, and even as late as 1971 it was still impossible to obtain a complete picture of mortality rates in any of the large countries of Asia or Africa, or in all but a few of the countries of Latin America. The general downward trend of mortality, however, is universal and unmistakable.

The most complete mortality statistics are from Sweden, extending from 1778 to the present. Table 5–11 shows the crude death rate of Sweden at 20-year intervals from 1778 to 1962. It declined steadily from the beginning of the nineteenth century to the second half of the

Table 5-10   MALE AGE-SPECIFIC DEATH RATES FOR THE UNITED STATES AND FOR PERU, 1961

Age	U.S.	Peru
0	29.2	176.3
1-4	1.1	17.0
5-9	0.5	7.0
10-14	0.5	2.5
15-19	1.2	4.5
20-24	1.7	6.3
25-29	1.7	7.0
30-34	2.0	7.4
35-39	2.8	8.4
40-44	4.5	10.4
45-49	7.3	13.6
50-54	12.4	18.4
55-59	17.9	25.2
60-64	27.9	35.8
65-69	41.4	53.0
70-74	57.4	76.3
75-79	83.4	114.9
80-84	128.3	190.6
85 and over	219.6	278.7

Source: Based on David M. Heer, *Society and Population* (Englewood Cliffs, N.J.: Prentice-Hall,), 1968, table 4-1, p. 35.

twentieth century, when less than 1 percent of the population died each year.

The only American state that has accurate vital statistics going back more than a century is Massachusetts. Its crude death rate at 20-year intervals from 1860 to 1960 is shown in Table 5–12. The sharp rise from 1860 to 1880 is probably due to the incomplete enumeration of deaths in 1860. The trend is otherwise very much like Sweden's.

Table 5–13 shows the trend in the crude death rate of a country with very different conditions, India, for the decades from 1901 to 1961. It is not as reliable as the series for Sweden and Massachusetts, but there is no doubt about its general pattern. As late as the decade 1941–1951, the Indian rate was still above the Swedish rate of 1778–1782, but in the following decade it fell to about the same level as the Swedish rate of 1878–1882, accomplishing in a decade the reduction that had taken a full century in Sweden at an earlier time. Moreover, even after the crude death rate of the Indian population had been cut in half in the single generation from 1921–1931 to

Table 5-11	CRUDE DEATH RATE, SWEDEN, 1778-1962

Years	Crude Death Rate
1778-1782	25.9
1798-1802	25.9
1818-1822	24.9
1838-1842	21.7
1858-1862	19.9
1878-1882	17.6
1898-1902	16.2
1918-1922	14.2
1938-1942	11.1
1958-1962	9.8

Source: Based on Keyfitz and Flieger, *World Population,* p. 36.

Table 5-12	CRUDE DEATH RATE, MASSACHUSETTS, 1860-1960

Year	Crude Death Rate
1860	18.7
1880	19.8
1900	18.4
1920	13.8
1940	11.9
1960	11.0

Source: Based on *Historical Statistics of the United States,* 1957, Series B155-162; and *Statistical Abstract of the United States, 1968,* table 70.

Table 5-13	CRUDE DEATH RATE, INDIA, 1901-1961

Years	Crude Death Rate
1901-1911	43.1
1911-1921	48.6
1921-1931	36.3
1931-1941	31.2
1941-1951	27.4
1951-1961	18.0

Source: Based on *Hindustan Yearbook* and *Who's Who,* 1965, p. 107.

Table 5-14	INFANT MORTALITY RATE, SWEDEN, 1778/1962

Years	Infant Mortality Rate
1778-1782	211.6
1798-1802	249.0
1818-1822	206.7
1838-1842	184.6
1858-1862	150.8
1878-1882	131.3
1898-1902	106.8
1918-1922	46.4
1938-1942	31.3
1958-1962	15.6

Source: Based on Keyfitz and Flieger, *World Population*, p. 36.

Table 5-15	INFANT MORTALITY RATE, MASSACHUSETTS, 1860/1966

Years	Infant Mortality Rate
1860-1864	142.5
1880-1884	161.3
1900-1904	141.4
1920-1924	78.7
1940-1944	34.3
1966*	20.7

*whites only

Source: Based on *Historical Statistics of the United States*, 1957, Series B113; *Statistical Abstract of the United States, 1968*, table 75.

1951–1961, it was still not much below the levels of Sweden or Massachusetts a hundred years before, so that a comfortable margin remained for continued reduction. In Ceylon, formerly part of India, where demographic conditions began to improve at an earlier date, the crude death rate was down to 8.5 by 1962. Such unprecedentedly rapid reductions in mortality occurred all through the "Third World" of underdeveloped countries immediately after World War II and led, within a very few years, to an unprecedented increase in population.

The reduction of the infant mortality rate has followed the same trend as the reduction of the crude death rate. Indeed, it is the other side of the same coin since a large part of the decline in the crude death rate is due, especially in the early stages of improvement, to the decline in infant mortality. Table 5–14 shows the infant mortality rate of Sweden at 20-year intervals from 1778 to 1962. At the beginning of this period, more than one out of five babies died before reaching their first birthday. At the end, fewer than one out of 60 babies failed to survive. The trend in Massachusetts (Table 5–15) is again very similar, except for its last entry. Infant mortality in Massachusetts in 1965 was nearly 50 percent higher than infant mortality in Sweden a few years before (see Table 5–14), if attention is restricted to white infants only. In the nonwhite population, the 1965 infant mortality rate in Massachusetts was 38.5, or two and a half times the Swedish rate. These differences are thought to reflect the relative shortage of medical services in the United States and the persistence of acute poverty in some sectors of the population.

There are no long series of infant mortality rates for any large Asiatic or African country or, indeed, for any of the underdeveloped countries in which spectacular improvements in mortality are known to have occurred in recent years. Table 5–16 shows the infant mortality rates of Bulgaria, a relatively backward European country, from 1950 to 1965, a 15-year period during which the infant mortality rate declined by more than two-thirds. Table 5–17 provides additional examples of dramatic improvement in infant mortality during the past generation.

These statistics represent a fundamental change in the human condition. As Heer observes:

> Contemporary citizens of developed nations rarely encounter death, except among the aged. This is in great contrast to the situation which prevailed in these nations in former times. To illustrate how different the situation was in our own country during the past, let us note some of the bereavements suffered by three of the noted presidents of the United States, and their families. George Washington's father died when George was only 11. Upon her marriage to George, Martha Washington was a 26-year-old widow. She had already borne four children, two of whom had died in infancy; of her two surviving children, one died at age 17 and the other in early adulthood. Thomas Jefferson lost his father when Tom was only 14. His wife Martha had also been previously widowed when she married Jefferson at the age of 23, and died herself only 11 years later. Of the six children that Martha bore to Tom, only two lived to maturity. Abraham Lincoln's mother died when she was 35 and he was nine. Prior to her death she had three children; Abraham's brother died in infancy and his sister in her early twenties. Abraham Lincoln's first love, Anne Rutledge, died at age 19. Of the four sons born to Abraham and Mary Todd Lincoln, only one survived to maturity.[3]

Table 5-16	INFANT MORTALITY RATE, BULGARIA, 1950/1965

Years	Infant Mortality Rate
1950-1952	103.9
1953-1955	88.6
1956-1958	66.1
1959-1961	47.8
1963	36.4
1965	31.7

Source: Based on Keyfitz and Flieger, *World Population*, pp. 32-33.

Table 5-17	INFANT MORTALITY RATES, SELECTED COUNTRIES, 1930/1965

Country	Infant Mortality Rate	
	Around 1930	Around 1963
Hungary	152.5	42.9
Mexico	131.6	76.7
Japan	124.5	23.8

Source: Based on *United Nations Demographic Yearbook 1951*, table 14; and Keyfitz and Flieger, *World Population* Tabular Summary of Contents.

CAUSES OF REDUCED MORTALITY

The causes of reduced mortality are not as crystal-clear as one might suppose. Five separate factors contribute to the net effect, but there is considerable disagreement among demographers and other experts as to the relative contribution of each factor. The factors are improved nutrition, control of famine, improved public health measures, improved medical care, and changes in living and working conditions.

Improved nutrition is one of the first favorable results of modernization. Increasing per capita income is used to buy more and better food. It is one of the paradoxes of the twentieth century that the average nutritional level continues to improve in nearly every country of the world at the same time that this abundance of food contributes to the increase of population, which, in turn, presses on the agricultural resources of the globe.

Improved nutrition may be an especially important factor in the decline of infant mortality. One field experiment in Guatemala[4] reduced the death rate of infants between 1 and 11 months old from the very high rate of 113 per 1,000 to the comparatively low rate of 19 per 1,000 merely by feeding them a high-protein dietary supplement. Prior to the modern era, all but a few infants were dependent on the natural milk supply of their mothers, and if that failed for one reason or another, the infant died. The worldwide introduction around 1940 of safe and nutritious substitutes for mother's milk, made of cow's milk or soy bean extract, rendered infants independent of the maternal milk supply and at the same time eased the strain of child-bearing on the health of mothers. Although breast-feeding is still regarded as favorable for both mother and child under ideal conditions, more than 9 out of 10 infants in the modernized countries with low infant mortality rates are now raised on substitute milk products, often fortified with additional proteins, vitamins, and minerals.

The *control of famine* may be even more important than the improvement of nutrition in the growth of world population that accompanies modernization, although the two factors are closely related. In the preindustrial era, a crop failure in an isolated region or a series of poor crops in a larger region led inexorably to famine. The same isolation and lack of organization in these regions that caused famines make them very difficult to study, but there is no doubt that they were frequent and dreadful. According to one source, there were 1,828 famines in China between 108 B.C. and 1911 A.D., an average of nearly one per year.[5] Writing of the tenth and eleventh centuries in western Europe, a medieval chronicler counted more years of scarcity than plenty:

> In the annals of the tenth and eleventh centuries, the word famine appears repeatedly. According to Raoul Glaber, 48 years of scarcity were counted between 970 and 1040. Nor is this surprising. The decline of commerce having reached a maximum in the tenth century, it was enough for the weather to bring about a bad harvest or for a district to be ravaged by war, for the most elemental necessities to be scarce. . . . The chronicler reports that in many places the people, prey to atrocious suffering, went as far as to "eat not only the flesh of animals and of the filthiest reptiles, but also even that of women and children."[6]

The last great famine in the western European area was the Irish potato famine of 1845–1848, in which more than a million people died out of a total population of some 8 million and huge numbers were driven to emigrate.[7] Within the present century, there have been great famines in China and in the Soviet Union.

The improvement of communication and transportation networks has now progressed to the point where the failure of the food supply in any region can usually be overcome by the importation of emergency supplies from other regions or even from other continents. Only when the relief routes are blocked by military action or deliberate political measures, is a real famine likely to occur under modern conditions, as happened in the seceding Nigerian province of Biafra in 1968 and 1969.

The diminishing role of famine in human affairs does not mean, of course, that the problem of adequate nutrition has been solved for all the world's population. Outside of Europe, North America, and Oceania, there are many areas of chronic malnutrition. Some populations, like the homeless families of the larger Indian cities, seem to live continuously on the edge of starvation.

Improved *public health measures* and *medical care* have virtually eliminated some epidemic diseases, like smallpox; reduced others, like diphtheria, to relative unimportance; and greatly reduced the mortality associated with such widespread diseases as malaria and tuberculosis.

Prior to the Industrial Revolution, epidemics were largely responsible for the prevention of long-term population growth. For example, the Black Death, the great epidemic of bubonic plague that broke out in Europe in 1348, is estimated to have killed a quarter of the total population in that year alone. Some districts were nearly depopulated. The smallpox brought to the West Indies and Central America by the Spanish conquistadors and the measles and syphilis introduced into the South Pacific by the English explorers carried off millions of the native inhabitants and destroyed some populations completely. Modern epidemics are trivial by comparison. Although the influenza epidemic of 1918, the most severe of the twentieth century, spread over the globe and killed several million people, it had hardly any perceptible effect on population growth.

Infectious diseases are controlled by purification of water and effective sewage disposal; the elimination of rats, lice and mosquitoes; use of vaccines, antibiotics, and antiseptics; the quarantine of infected individuals; the protection of food supplies; and presumably, to some extent, by more intensive contacts among different regions, which prevents the endemic diseases of one region from wreaking havoc among the nonimmunized population of another. It would be absurd to claim that modern populations are no longer threatened by disease. Even in the most advanced countries, a considerable number of deaths and a large number of disabilities are caused by disease. Moreover, the use of antibiotics and other chemical agents sometimes produces new and stronger bacteria and viruses that have been selectively bred, in effect, to resist existing drugs. The possibility that some new form of epidemic disease, more dangerous than any previous disease, will be developed in this fashion cannot be entirely excluded. For the time being, it is undeniable that the ravages of infectious disease are being steadily reduced from year to year throughout the world.

Changes in working and living conditions also help to explain the universal reduction of mortality. Among the significant improvements in living conditions that seem to diminish pressure of the natural environment upon the human organism are central heating, air conditioning, indoor toilets, running water, electric lighting, mechanized transportation, paved roads, warm clothing, waterproof footwear, and hundreds of other items provided by an industrial society. Although some deleterious influences, like air pollution, are introduced at the same time, the balance is overwhelmingly favorable.

Some of the changes in working conditions that accompany the later stages of modernization have a similar character. Work places in modernized countries are better protected from the weather, better ventilated, and better lit. A good deal of work that formerly involved unusual exertion, such as excavating, or peculiar discomfort, such as cleaning chimneys, or special health risks, such as blowing glass, is eliminated or mechanized. Children and aged persons, particularly vulnerable to occupational hazards, are gradually taken out of the labor force. Fatigue and over-exertion are countered by shorter work days and weeks, longer rest periods and vacations.

Improvements in child-bearing conditions include the availability of contraception to prevent ill-timed pregnancies or an excessive number of pregnancies; dietary supplementation and appropriate care during the prenatal period; the disappearance of the dangerous magical practices that surround childbirth in many traditional societies; the establishment of antiseptic conditions for childbirth and the care of newborn infants; and the availability of medical procedures to cope with emergencies occurring during and after delivery. From 1930 to 1966 in the United States, the risk of maternal death—in childbirth or from complications of pregnancy—fell from 1 out of 150 to fewer than 1 out of 3,000 births.

Life Span and Life Expectancy

The belief that modernization has increased the duration of life is almost universal, but many of those who hold it have never stopped to consider what it means.

In fact, the duration of human life seems to have extended in one sense but not in another. Modernization enables an increasingly large number of persons to avoid premature death from infection, accidents, or malnutrituion, and to die of old age or of a malady like arteriosclerosis that is closely related to the aging process. *The life span is the maximum age that can be reached by an individual who lives his entire life in wholesome conditions and ultimately dies of old age.*

Individuals vary in their life spans; it seems to be an inherited characteristic. There are persons who manifest signs of senility around the age of 50 and others who are capable of a full day's work at 90. But, in general, the range of variation is rather narrow. The overwhelming majority of the human race are apparently capable of surviving to 65 but not capable of reaching 85.

So far as the evidence goes, the average life span has not increased under the influence of modernization. It may even have declined slightly. About one person in 30,000 celebrates his or her hundredth birthday. Survival much beyond that age is a rare and dubious phenomenon. The last survivors of the millions of men who fought in the Union Army in the American Civil War reached the apparently authentic ages of 112 and 116. There does not seem to be a single case of authenticated survival beyond the age of 120, despite the claims made from time to time on behalf of ancient peasants from Bolivia or Albania.

The reasons for the inexorable wearing out of the human body are not fully known, and the possibility that physiological research will discover means of slowing down or reversing the process cannot be presently assessed. The search for the fountain of youth continues under the aegis of modern science. Even a small measure of success would have sweeping consequences for population composition and the structure of social institutions. For the time being, however, the life span continues to impose a fixed term on individual existence.

What *is* changed by modernization is life expectancy. *Life expectancy is an estimate of the average survival of a cohort of individuals of the same age if the specific mortality rates observed at a given date prevailed throughout their lives.* This sounds complicated and it is. Although the measure is useful for summarizing the state of health of a population, it readily lends itself to misinterpretation. Life expectancies are obtained from life tables.[8] In order to construct a life table, the demographer takes a hypothetical population of newborn infants at a given time and place (usually a population of 100,000 in order to simplify the computation) and constructs a table showing how many of these infants would survive to each successive age if the age-specific death rates prevailing at that time and place remained unchanged throughout their lifetime. When the number of survivors at each age has been calculated according to these assumptions, it is possible to compute the total number of years remaining to be lived by the entire cohort from any given age, and if this total is divided by the number of persons remaining in the cohort at that age, the result is the life expectancy.

Table 5–18 shows one of the first life tables ever constructed, from an early nineteenth century study of the French textile industry. Table 5–19 shows part of the life table for a much healthier population, white females in the United States 1949–1951. If you have grasped the principle of the life table from the brief explanation above, you should be able to explain why the life expectancy in the older table rises sharply from age 1–5 whereas in the more recent table it falls slightly but steadily between those ages.

The most important thing to note about these life tables is that except for the mortality rates in column 1 of Table 5–19 (they are not shown in Table 5–18), none of the figures refer to real people. Each table is based on the arbitrary assumption that the age-specific and sex-specific death rates prevailing in the population at the time the cohort was born would continue unchanged until the last member of the cohort had died. Under contemporary circumstances this assumption can never be even approximately realistic, since specific death rates have been falling continuously for a long time and will probably continue to do so. Consequently, the life table does not represent either the actual or the probable experience of any real persons. When we say that a female infant

Table 5-18   MORTALITY BY AGE IN THE DEPARTMENT OF
HAUT-RHIN, 1814-1833

Observed Living	Total Population Estimated Life Expectancy	
	years	months
216,095	13	5
178,439	30	5
167,723	34	6
156,129	38	11
141,660	43	7
132,979	45	9
127,042	46	7
122,798	46	11
111,051	45	5
106,642	41	8
101,682	38	8
95,183	34	10
89,478	31	2
83,898	27	5
77,935	23	9
71,428	20	2
64,572	16	10
56,224	13	9
47,282	10	10
36,226	8	6
25,395	6	7
15,088	5	1
7,433	4	1
2,749	3	4
697	3	4
158	2	3
9	2	3

Source: Jean Fourastié, *The Causes of Wealth* (New York: Free Press, 1960), Table XXXVI, p. 221.

born in the United States in 1949–1951 had a life expectancy at birth of 72.03 years, we are establishing a measure that enables us to compare the general health of the female population of the United States at that point in time with the general health of any other population. We are not predicting that the female infants born in those years will die at an average age of 72.03. If present trends continue, their median age at death should be considerably higher, but we cannot be sure that the

Table 5-19   LIFE TABLE FOR WHITE FEMALES, UNITED STATES, 1949-1951[a]

Year of age x	Rate of Mortality per 1,000 — Number dying between ages x and $x + 1$ among 1,000 living at age x $1,000q_x$	Of 100,000 Born Alive — Number surviving to exact age x l_x	Number dying between ages x and $x + 1$ d_x	Number of years lived by the cohort between ages x and $x + 1$ L_x	Total number of years lived by the cohort from age x on, until all have died T_x	Average number of years lived after age x per person surviving to exact age x[b] e_x
0	23.55	100,000	2,355	97,965	7,203,179	72.03
1	1.89	97,645	185	97,552	7,105,214	72.77
2	1.12	97,460	109	97,406	7,007,662	71.90
3	0.87	97,351	85	97,308	6,910,256	70.98
4	0.69	97,266	67	97,233	6,812,948	70.04
5	0.60	97,199	59	97,169	6,715,715	69.09
6	0.53	97,140	52	97,114	6,618,546	68.13
7	0.48	97,088	46	97,065	6,521,432	67.17
8	0.44	97,042	43	97,020	6,424,367	66.20
9	0.41	96,999	39	96,980	6,327,347	65.23
.	.	.	.	.	.	.
.	.	.	.	.	.	.
.	.	.	.	.	.	.
100	388.39	294	114	237	566	1.92
101	407.52	180	73	143	329	1.83
102	426.00	107	46	84	186	1.74
103	443.67	61	27	48	102	1.66
104	460.76	34	16	26	54	1.59

[a]Based upon recorded deaths in the United States during the three-year period 1949-1951, recorded births for each year from 1944 through 1951, and the census of population taken April 1, 1950; for details, see U.S. Public Health Service 1959, pp. 149-158.

[b]Represents complete expectation of life, or average future lifetime.

Source: Mortimer Spiegelman, "Life Tables," *International Encyclopedia of the Social Sciences*, 1968, Vol. 9, p. 293.

Table 5-20	LIFE EXPECTANCY OF MALES AT AGE 80, SELECTED COUNTRIES, AROUND 1964

Country	Expectation of Life at Age 80
Costa Rica	6.4 years
United States	6.2
Japan	5.2
Jordan	5.1
Czechoslovakia	5.4
Netherlands	6.0

Source: Based on *Demographic Yearbook of the United Nations 1967,* table 29.

present trends will continue, and, as a matter of fact, we simply do not know how long they are likely to live.

Life expectancy can be a particularly confusing statistic in under-developed countries with high infant mortality rates, since a rapid reduction of infant mortality may increase life expectancy at birth from, say, 35 to 50 years even though the average age of death for adults remains unchanged. This confusion can be reduced, however, if we examine life expectancy at ages 30, 40, and 50, in conjuction with life expectancy at birth. In general, modernization *does* improve life expectancy in the intermediate adult ages, although not as dramati-cally as life expectancy at birth. With advancing age, the differences between modernized and underdeveloped countries become pro-gressively smaller until extreme old age, when, as Table 5–20 shows, life expectancies are about the same in countries at any level of modern-ization.

Fertility

The fertility of a population is its actual reproductive performance during a given period.

The simplest and most useful measure of fertility is the *crude birth rate, the number of births per thousand living persons in the total popu-lation of a given territory in a calendar year.* Since the crude birth rate has the same base as the crude death rate, one can calculate the natural increase or decrease of a population by subtracting the smaller from the larger of the two measures. The United States, for example, had a crude birth rate of 19.6 and a crude death rate of 9.3 in 1965, a natural increase of 10.2 per thousand per year, or 1.02 percent.

An *age-specific fertility rate is the number of live births per thousand women of a given child-bearing age in a given population in a calendar year. The gross reproduction rate is a measure calculated somewhat like life expectancy, by computing the total number of girl babies a given cohort of women would produce from age 15 to age 44 if the age-specific birth rates prevailing in the population in a given year remained unchanged from the time the cohort reached 15 until all of its members passed 44. The net reproduction rate measures the replacement of a generation of child-bearing women by their child-bearing daughters a little more elaborately by taking account of mortality among the mothers or the daughters or both.*

The biological limitations that govern fertility are easily stated. Women are capable of childbearing roughly between the ages of 15 and 44, although both these markers are occasionally passed. Out of 4 million births in the United States in 1964, about 8,000 were attributed to girls from 10 to 14 and about 5,000 to women from 45 to 49. Not a single birth was attributed to a girl under 10 or a woman in her fifties in that year, although such cases have been recorded. Under modern conditions, a substantial majority of women giving birth in any year are in their twenties.

Pretty nearly all healthy women appear to be potentially fertile, (the technical term is *fecund*). When native white rural farm women, aged 45 to 49, who had been married before the age of 18 were asked about their child-bearing experience in the census of 1940, 97.6 percent reported that they had borne one or more children.[9]

The maximum number of children ever born to one woman is not known; it may have been as high as 35. Families of 20 children born to the same couple are rare but not unknown, even in modernized countries. Among American women who were bearing children about a century ago (women born between 1835 and 1839 and surviving to 1910), 15 percent reported in 1910 that they had borne 10 or more children.[10] Among Hutterite women, members of a pietistic Protestant sect settled in farm communities in the Dakotas, Montana, and Canada, a sample of married women past child-bearing age reported bearing an *average* of 10.6 children, although they had married relatively late.[11] A number of Caribbean countries currently approach the Hutterite fertility level, and one country, Costa Rica, exceeds it, if the statistics can be trusted. Nevertheless, fertility anywhere near the biological capacity of a population is an unusual and transient phenomenon. The reasons why this is so will appear when we examine some of the numerous factors that influence birth rates.

Practically all fertility is attributable to women who are married or living in stable consensual unions. Although the rate of illegitimacy in the United States more than tripled between 1940 and 1964, illegitimate births accounted for only 7 percent of total births in 1964, and a considerable proportion of these probably involved unmarried women living in relatively stable consensual unions, especially among the nonwhite population, which accounted for the majority of illegitimate births in 1964.

Table 5-21 shows the crude birth rate in Sweden, again the only country for which a reliable long series is available, from 1778 to 1962. From the middle of the eighteenth century to the middle of the nine-

Table 5-21	CRUDE BIRTH RATE, SWEDEN, 1778/1782

Years	Crude Birth Rate
1778-1782	34.5
1798-1802	31.2
1818-1822	34.3
1838-1842	30.5
1858-1862	34.1
1878-1882	29.5
1898-1902	26.8
1918-1922	21.0
1938-1942	15.8
1958-1962	14.0

Source: Based on Keyfitz and Flieger, *World Population*, p. 36.

teenth century, there was no consistent trend, but from the middle of the nineteenth century to the middle of the twentieth, the rate fell steadily from around 34 per thousand to around 14 per thousand. The latter rate is one of the lowest in the world but since death rates also declined to an unprecedentedly low level, the population continued to increase at a moderate rate even with the birth rate at 14. Indeed, the net reproduction rate, although much lower now than it was in the latter part of the nineteenth century, is about the same as it was in the eighteenth century.

Table 5–22 shows the trend of the birth rate in the United States from 1800 to 1960. This series too shows a steady decline, but it starts and finishes on a much higher level than the Swedish series. The crude birth rate of 54 per 1000 in 1800 is one of the highest ever recorded for any population, and it was not until 1900 that the American rate fell below the highest of the Swedish rates. Other important measures of the American series are the sharp drop between 1920 and 1940 and the upward trend that appeared after 1940.

The long-term decline in the American birth rate is almost entirely attributable to the decreasing size of families. So far as the evidence goes, the average age at which women marry has not increased at all from 1800 to the present; at the same time, the proportion of women who remain unmarried has greatly declined. These trends must have tended to raise the birth rate, but their effects were trifling compared to the massive shift in family patterns that occurred simultaneously. Table 5–23 shows the number of children ever born to married women in the United States who entered the child-bearing cycle at various points in time. The most significant information in the table is that only 16 percent of the women who reached child-bearing age about

Table 5-22	CRUDE BIRTH RATE, UNITED STATES, WHITE POPULATION, 1800-1960

Year	Crude Birth Rate
1800	55.0
1820	52.8
1840	48.3
1860	41.4
1880	35.2
1900	30.1
1920	26.9
1940	18.6
1960	22.7

Source: Based on *Historical Statistics of the United States,* 1957, Series B19-30; and *Statistical Abstract of the United States, 1968,* table 55.

the time of World War I eventually produced five or more children, compared to the 54 percent of their grandmothers' generation producing that many.

Crude birth rates in the contemporary world vary greatly from one region to another. Table 5–24 shows the crude birth rate for a number of Caribbean countries around 1960, together with their annual natural increase and the number of years required for the population to double if these rates remained unchanged. Costa Rica has the highest crude birth rate ever recorded for any country. At its 1960 rate of increase, its population would double in 15 years and quadruple in 30. Table 5–25 shows a group of European countries under Soviet domination which have very low crude birth rates. The rate for Hungary is far below the lowest rate ever recorded in Sweden or the United States. Although these countries show some natural increase, their gross reproduction rates are very close to 1.0, which implies that if their present rates of mortality and fertility continue indefinitely, their populations will remain approximately stable.

Theoretically we can visualize four extreme conditions, a high birth rate and a high death rate, a low birth rate and a high death rate, a high birth rate and a low death rate, a low birth rate and a low death rate. The first condition was probably that of most populations before the Industrial Revolution. Such a population remained stable or slowly increased or slowly decreased, depending on the exact relationship between the two rates and their fluctuations from time to time. No sizable population in the modern world remains in this condition, so far as is known.

The low birth rate-high death rate condition occurred very fre-

Table 5-23	COMPLETED FAMILIES OF MARRIED WOMEN, UNITED STATES, VARIOUS DATES

| | | Percent Bearing: | |
Of Women Reaching Childbearing Age in:	No Children	1-4 Children	5 or More Children
1855-1859	7.9	38.0	54.0
1875-1879	9.5	44.4	46.1
1895-1899	16.7	55.4	27.9
1915-1919	20.4	63.9	15.6

Source: Based on *Historical Statistics of the United States,* 1957, Series B69-75.

Table 5-24	A GROUP OF CARIBBEAN COUNTRIES WITH HIGH BIRTH RATES, AROUND 1960

Country	Crude Birth Rate	Annual Increase	Doubling Time (at this rate)
Honduras	42.4	3.0%	23 years
Venezuela	43.4	3.6	19
Mexico	46.1	3.5	20
Costa Rica	55.5	4.7	15

Source: Based on Keyfitz and Flieger, *World Population,* pp. 26-30.

quently among native populations during the European colonization of the world, sometimes because of social disorganization, sometimes because of epidemic diseases imported by the colonizers. This condition, if continued, leads to extinction. We have detailed descriptions of one such dying population, the Marquesans, and of the curious social structure that developed as children became increasingly rare.[12] (They were spoiled beyond belief.)

The high birth rate-low death rate condition is a phenomenon of the twentieth century. So far as we know, it could not have occurred anywhere prior to 1900, but it is now the characteristic condition of most of the countries of Asia, Latin America, and Africa. It leads to rapid

Table 5-25	A GROUP OF EUROPEAN COUNTRIES WITH LOW BIRTH RATES, AROUND 1960	

Country	Crude Birth Rate	Annual Increase
Bulgaria	17.6	0.9%
Czechoslovakia	15.9	0.7
Rumania	18.9	0.2
Hungary	14.6	0.2

Source: Based on Keyfitz and Flieger, *World Population,* pp. 32-36.

increases of population size and rapid shifts in the distribution of population, the full implications of which cannot yet be foreseen.

The low birth rate-low death rate condition appeared first in the advanced industrial countries after World War I and was expected to usher in a phase of stable or declining population. This expectation proved illusory. The death rate continued to fall and the birth rate rose sufficiently after World War II to generate substantial population growth in western Europe, the United States, and the former British dominions. The widespread introduction of pharmaceutical contraceptives in the 1960s may check the growth of these populations, but it is still too early to be sure. At the present time, for undetermined reasons, the European countries within the Soviet sphere of influence exhibit the most extreme version of the low birth rate-low death rate condition.

Factors Influencing Fertility

The generally accepted classification of factors affecting fertility was developed by Kingsley Davis and Judith Blake,[13] starting with the basic observation that every birth requires (1) that sexual intercourse has occurred; (2) that the intercourse has resulted in conception; and (3) that the resulting pregnancy has been brought to successful term. From this they inferred that any variable affecting fertility must do so by affecting this sequence of events, and they developed a classification of such variables. (See Figure 5–2.) In effect, this is a classification of the factors reducing human fertility below the maximum fertility that might be observed if all the females in a population were married as soon as they were capable of child-bearing, remained married throughout the child-bearing years, and conceived and bore as many children as possible. No population meets these hypothetical requirements, but under modern conditions of mortality, some, like the Caribbean countries described in Table 5–24, come surprisingly close.

Figure 5-2   INTERMEDIATE VARIABLES AFFECTING
FERTILITY

I. Factors Affecting Exposure to Intercourse

  A. Those governing the formation and dissolution of unions in the reproductive period

    1. Age of entry into sexual unions

    2. Permanent celibacy; proportion of women never entering sexual unions

    3. Amount of reproductive period spent after or between unions

      a. when unions are broken by divorce, separation or desertion

      b. when unions are broken by death of husband

  B. Those governing the exposure to intercourse within unions

    4. Voluntary abstinence

    5. Involuntary abstinence (from impotence, illness, and unavoidable but temporary separations)

    6. Coital frequency (excluding periods of abstinence)

II. Factors Affecting Exposure to Conception

    7. Fecundity or infecundity, as affected by involuntary causes

    8. Use or non-use of contraception

      a. by mechanical and chemical means

      b. By other means

    9. Fecundity or infecundity, as affected by voluntary causes (sterilization, subincision, medical treatment, and so forth)

III. Factors Affecting Gestation and Successful Parturition

    10. Foetal mortality from involuntary causes

    11. Foetal mortality from voluntary causes

Source: Kingsley Davis and Judith Blake, "Social Structure and Fertility: An Analytic Framework," *Economic Development and Cultural Change* 4, no. 3 (April 1956): 212.

AGE AT MARRIAGE

The average age of women at marriage, which has an obvious effect on fertility, varies considerably among nations, from about 16 in India to about 26 in Ireland around 1960. However, strangely enough, some of the most fertile populations, like the Hutterites studied by Eaton and Mayer,[14] marry comparatively late; and modernization does not exert a consistent influence on age at marriage, which seems to fluctuate according to local conditions. On the other hand, in most of the modernized countries a very high proportion of females are married. Fewer than 1 in 20 American women remain single throughout the child-bearing years. The overwhelming majority of them bear children, as do a fair number of those who remain single.

BIOLOGICAL FACTORS

The biological factors influencing fertility are perhaps the least well understood. Among married couples in good health, living together uninterruptedly, there is known to be considerable variation in the frequency of sexual intercourse, and there may be equal or greater variation in the incidence of conception at a given level of sexual activity. It was formerly supposed that civilization, urban life, the education of women, and excessive or insufficient exercise had adverse effects on fertility, but the more the subject is studied, the less seems to be known about it. Even in the absence of contraception, some populations appear to be relatively infertile, and other populations that are normally fertile seem to go through infertile phases.

SOCIAL FACTORS

The most important social factors affecting the fertility of modern populations appear to be number 8 in the Davis-Blake list, the use or nonuse of contraception, and number 11, fetal mortality from voluntary causes, which is their way of referring to abortion.

The history of birth control presents certain mysteries that may never be dispelled. It is plain from historical records that small families have been the rule in many historic populations, and the practice of limiting family size seems to have been followed throughout history, even in societies where abortions were condemned and the exposure of unwanted infants was apparently unknown. The same may be said for many of the preliterate peoples observed by ethnographers; in some cases, the facts reported suggest the use of contraceptive methods unknown to science. Malinowski, for example, who studied the sexual behavior of the Trobrianders in great detail, was quite unable to account for the nonoccurrence of pregnancy among unmarried Trobriand girls, who were encouraged to engage in sexual liaisons but who would have been severely punished for an illegitimate pregnancy.[15]

It is an almost inescapable conclusion from early European statistics that birth control in some form was widely practiced by the middle of the nineteenth century. France, for example, had a crude birth rate around 23 in 1851, which suggests that birth control was nearly as extensive then as now, but despite some plausible hypotheses, it is not entirely clear how this was accomplished.[16] Condoms seem not to have come into general use until the end of the nineteenth century and diaphragms much later. Various chemical devices were introduced after World War I, but it was not until 1959 that the first oral contraceptives were made available to the general public.

The novel feature of the Pill, as it came to be internationally known, was its infallibility. Earlier methods of contraception all had substan-

| Table 5-26 | CRUDE BIRTH RATE BY COLOR, UNITED STATES, 1960-1966 |

| | Crude Birth Rate | |
Year	White Population	Nonwhite Population
1960	22.7	32.1
1961	22.2	31.6
1962	21.4	30.5
1963	20.7	29.7
1964	20.0	29.2
1965	18.3	27.6
1966	17.4	26.1

Source: Based on *Statistical Abstract of the United States, 1968,* table 54.

tial failure rates, that is, they prevented conception in most but not in all cases. The failure rate of oral contraceptives is negligible.

Following the introduction and rapid diffusion of oral contraception, there was a precipitous decline in birth rates, which may reflect a reduction of unplanned conceptions. Table 5–26 shows the downward trend in the crude birth rate in the United States from 1960 to 1966. Although the birth rate of the nonwhite population was much higher than that of the white population in 1960, the two rates declined in parallel.

At about the same time that oral contraceptives were coming into general use in the more advanced countries of the world, a mechanical intrauterine device (IUD) was perfected and distributed on a large scale in a few of the underdeveloped countries with high rates of natural increase. Although these devices have relatively high failure rates, they are extremely cheap and require less effort than other procedures.

Sterilization, a surgical operation on either males or females that prevents conception without interfering with sexual activity, continues to be advocated here and there by medical experts, but it has not had a major influence on the fertility of any large population and is not likely to do so in the near future.

Until the introduction of oral contraception, abortion was the only certain method of preventing the birth of unwanted children. Abortions are illegal in most countries, except under special medical or legal circumstances. Although common in many of the countries in which they are illegal, they are dangerous when performed by unqualified operators. With modern techniques, abortion in the early months of pregnancy is relatively safe and simple. It was the principal means of reducing the birth rate in Japan, where the restriction of population growth was adopted as a national policy after World War II and in the Communist countries of Central Europe, where elements of the social structure appear to discourage large families. The delegalization of abortion in Roumania in 1965 led to a sudden sharp increase of the birth rate, which had been for some years among the lowest in the world.[17] The legalization of abortion in the United States was well under way by 1970.

Young and Old Populations

A young population contains a large proportion of young persons and has a low average age, whereas an old population has a high average age and a high proportion of old people.[18] In recent years demographers have become increasingly aware of the importance of this classification in determining the possible future growth of a population.

Table 5–27 shows the aging of the male population of the United States from 1800 to 1950. (The age of females was not obtained in the earliest censuses.) In 1800, when the American republic was still brand new, it had one of the youngest populations in the world. Nearly half the people in the country were children under 15. The proportion of old people was negligible. By 1950, children were only about a fourth of the population, whereas the proportion of old persons had more than tripled. The United States today has a moderately old population.

Table 5–28 lists a number of countries in the neighborhood of the Caribbean Sea that have very young populations, about as young as the population of the United States in 1800. Nearly half the people in these countries are children, and the proportion of old people is very low. We do not know whether these are the youngest populations in the world. They are the youngest for which there are reasonably good census statistics, but it is possible that the populations of some of the underdeveloped countries that do not have good censuses may be even younger.

The second column of Table 5–28 presents a very useful figure called the *dependency ratio. It is the ratio of the combined population of persons under 15 and persons 65 or over to the population, aged 15 to 64;* in other words, the ratio of the dependent population, needing to be supported, to the economically active population capable of supporting dependents. The total dependency ratio for the Caribbean countries in Table 5–28 ranges from .92 to 1.03. Honduras, for example, had a ratio of 1.00 in 1959–1961. This means that the combined number of children and old persons in the Honduran population was exactly equal to the number of persons 15 to 64, and it implies that there was a child or old person needing support for every able-bodied man and woman.

Table 5–29 shows those western European countries having the oldest populations. In every one of these, less than a fourth of the people are children, barely one in five in Germany and Luxembourg. The dependency ratios are around .50, which means that there is only one dependent child or old person for every two economically active adults.

Table 5-27 AGE DISTRIBUTION, WHITE MALES, UNITED STATES, 1800-1950

Year	Percent 0-14	Percent 15-64	Percent Over 65
1800	48.0	49.7	2.3
1850	41.4	56.3	2.4
1900	34.0	62.0	4.0
1950	27.6	64.6	7.7

Source: Based on *Historical Statistics of the United States*, 1957, Series A71-85.

Table 5-28 CARIBBEAN COUNTRIES WITH VERY YOUNG POPULATIONS AROUND 1960

Country	Percent Under 15	Total Dependency Ratio
Costa Rica	46.4	.96
Dominican Republic	47.3	1.03
Honduras	47.3	1.00
Mexico	44.4	.92
Venezuela	45.2	.93

Source: Based on Keyfitz and Flieger, *World Population*, pp. 26-31.

The dependency ratio is only an approximation, of course. On the one hand, the older populations are found in highly modernized countries where people enter the labor force rather later and retire from it rather early. On the other hand, the inferior health conditions of under-developed countries imply that more of the people in the 15–64 age group will be physically incapacitated. Nevertheless, the general correlation is unquestionable. In countries where an active worker earns less, he is likely to have more mouths to feed.

The populations described in Table 5–29 are among the oldest and healthiest populations the world has ever known. The age of a population is largely a function of its present and recent fertility. All the

Table 5-29	WESTERN EUROPEAN COUNTRIES WITH VERY OLD POPULATIONS AROUND 1960

Country	Percent Under 15	Total Dependency Ratio
Belgium	23.5	.55
East Germany	21.1	.53
West Germany	21.3	.47
Luxembourg	20.7	.46
Sweden	22.4	.52
England and Wales	22.9	.54

Source: Based on Keyfitz and Flieger, *World Population,* pp. 32-39.

populations of former times must have had higher birth rates than those now prevailing in western Europe, or they would have rapidly become extinct, given the high mortality that appears to have prevailed in all preindustrial societies.

To visualize the effect of high fertility on the age distribution of a population, let us think of a population with a net reproduction rate of 2.0, which was not an unusual rate around 1970. A rate of 2.0 means that each woman of child-bearing age will be replaced by two child-bearing women in the next generation. To achieve this result, the majority of women must bear children, and the average number of children must be well over four. It is obvious that children will be more numerous than adults of parental age and that if this level of fertility has persisted for some time, those in turn will be much more numerous than their own parents. The proportion of old people in the population will be very small. The reverse is true in a population that experiences prolonged low fertility. Such a population will contain about as many children as adults of parental age, and these, in turn, will be few in relation to their parents. The proportion of children in the total population will be relatively small and the proportion of old persons will be relatively large.

As Coale[19] has pointed out, whereas an increase in fertility lowers the average age of the population, a decrease of mortality does not raise the average age of the population as might be expected. The reason is that mortality is not evenly distributed throughout a population, but is highest among infants and old people. The reductions of mortality recorded in nearly every country of the world during this century have saved many more infants than old people, with the odd result that they have tended to *reduce* the average age of the population.

Even under primitive conditions, mortality is very low between the end of childhood and the early twenties. Under modern conditions, the mortality of females from 15–25 is almost negligible. Since most births are attributable to women in their twenties, a young population with a high proportion of children almost invariably has a high proportion of women of child-bearing age. Such a population will continue to have a high natural rate of increase for some time, even if its fertility should suddenly decline; on the other hand an old population, which necessarily has a rather small proportion of women of child-bearing age, will not increase very rapidly when its birth rate rises.

The very young populations of Asia, Africa, and Latin America, produced by two generations of declining mortality and sustained or rising fertility, are pre-set for further expansion. Even if the widespread adoption of birth control should cause their fertility to decline dramatically, to the point where women have only a sufficient number of daughters to replace themselves in the next generation, the populations of those countries would continue to increase appreciably until about the end of the present century.

Differential Mortality and Fertility Within Nations

Up to this point, we have been discussing fertiltiy and mortality as if they were uniformly distributed within the geographical and social divisions of each nation. Nothing could be further from the facts. There is hardly any significant division of a population that does not reveal differences in birth rate, death rate, age distribution, marriage, divorce, survivorship, and other demographic measures.

The most important of such divisions from the sociological standpoint are residence, social class, religion, and ethnicity. The conventional expectations with regard to these four types of division may be summed up as follows:

1. Rural populations will be younger than neighboring urban populations.
2. A lower-class population will be younger than an upper-class population in the same nation.
3. A Catholic population will be younger than a Protestant population in the same nation.
4. A nonwhite population will be younger than a white population in the same nation.

Since young populations normally have a greater rate of natural increase than old populations, such differentials, when they exist, imply the rapid growth of the younger population relative to the older and, if long continued, the gradual replacement of the one stock by the other.

The younger subpopulation, of course, is the one with higher fertility. It may or may not have higher mortality as well; but as noted above, the median age of a population is largely a function of its fertility.

Table 5–30 shows the development of a hypothetical population divided into two equal subpopulations, one younger and one older. The younger subpopulation has been assigned a gross reproduction rate of

Generation	Younger Subpopulation (Net reproduction rate = 1.5)	Older Subpopulation (Net reproduction rate = 1)
First	1000 women aged 15-44	1000 women aged 15-44
Second	1500 women aged 15-44	1000 women aged 15-44
Third	2250 women aged 15-44	1000 women aged 15-44
Fourth	3375 women aged 15-44	1000 women aged 15-44

Table 5-30   GROWTH OF A HYPOTHETICAL POPULATION

1.5, and the older subpopulation has been assigned a gross reproduction rate of 1. As the table shows, if these differences continue for several generations, the women of the fourth generation in the younger subpopulation (who come to maturity about 80 years later) will outnumber the women of the older subpopulation by more than three to one.

Table 5-31 shows the number of children ever borne by women in the United States who were over 45 in 1964 by the educational level of these women, and Table 5-32 shows the number of children ever born to them by their family income of 1963. Assuming that about 48 percent of the children these women bore were girls, we can estimate that the gross reproduction rate varied from about 0.8 for women college graduates to about 1.8 for the least educated group; from just over 1.0 in the high-income group to about 1.6 in the low-income group. There was a difference of fertility of the same order of magnitude between farm and city women (Table 5-33) and an appreciable, but much smaller, difference between whites and Negroes (Table 5-34) and between Protestants and Catholics (Table 5-35).

Differences in mortality among contemporary subpopulations are generally less spectacular than differences in fertility, and most of them are diminishing rapidly. Table 5-36 shows the trend of the crude death rate for whites and nonwhites in the United States from 1900 to 1965. In 1900 and 1930, the death rate of nonwhites was about 50 percent higher than that of whites. By 1965, the difference had virtually disappeared, even though nonwhites were not as well fed, housed, or doctored as whites. This change is part of a worldwide reduction of death rates after World War II. Differential mortality between unequal social groups has nearly disappeared in modernized countries. It was not always so:

> . . . Villermé notes, as part of a remarkable study that he conducted at Mulhouse concerning mortality in the period 1823 to 1834, that the life expectancy at birth was 28 years among the rich, and

Table 5-31	DIFFERENTIAL FERTILITY BY EDUCATIONAL LEVEL, UNITED STATES, 1964

Educational Level of Women Over 45	Average Number of Children Ever Born to These Women
Elementary school not completed	3.61
High school graduates	2.06
College graduates	1.68

Source: Based on *Statistical Abstract of the United States, 1968,* table 64.

Table 5-32	DIFFERENTIAL FERTILITY BY FAMILY INCOME, UNITED STATES 1963

Family Income of Women Over 45	Average Number of Children Ever Born to These Women
Under $3,000	3.23
$5,000-$7,999	2.40
Over $10,000	2.21

Source: Based on *Statistical Abstract of the United States, 1967,* table 58.

Table 5-33	DIFFERENTIAL FERTILITY BY RURAL AND URBAN RESIDENCE, UNITED STATES, 1964

Residence of Women Over 45	Average Number of Children Ever Born to These Women
Farms	3.58
Suburban areas	2.47
Central cities	2.31

Source: Based on *Statistical Abstract of the United States, 1968,* table 64.

Table 5-34   DIFFERENTIAL FERTILITY BY COLOR, UNITED STATES, 1964

Color of Women Over 45	Average Number of Children Ever Born to These Women
White	2.65
Negro	3.01

Source: Based on *Statistical Abstract of the United States, 1968*, table 64.

Table 5-35   DIFFERENTIAL FERTILITY BY RELIGIOUS AFFILIATION, UNITED STATES 1957-1958

Religious Affiliation of Adult Women	Percent Childless	Percent Having Three or More Children
Protestant	43	22
Catholic	39	27

Source: Based on Survey data from Bernard Lazerwitz, "A Comparison of Major U.S. Religious Groups," *Journal of the American Statistical Association* 55, no. 295 (September 1961).

Table 5-36   DIFFERENTIAL MORTALITY BY COLOR, UNITED STATES, 1900-1966

Color	Crude Death Rate		
	1900	1930	1966
White	17.0	10.8	9.5
Nonwhite	25.0	16.3	9.7

Source: Based on *Statistical Abstract of the United States, 1968*, table 69.

—one cannot write this without a feeling of revolt—*one year and three months* among the "simple weavers." We should like to be able to say that Villermé had made an error of calculation. Not at all. For every 100 births among these workers whose level of living we previously described, there were 30 deaths in the first six months and 20 deaths in the nine months following. Of the 100 infants, only 27 reached age 10; 17 age 20; 6 age 40, and only one reached the age of 60.[20]

There are two important types of differential mortality that remain, but they affect individuals rather than families. Certain occupations exposed to special hazards continue to have high death rates. As Table 5-37 shows, at least two broad occupational groups in the United States, service workers and nonfarm laborers, had death rates significantly higher than other occupational groups as late as 1950. Marital

---

Table 5-37   DIFFERENTIAL MORTALITY BY OCCUPATIONAL LEVEL, UNITED STATES, 1950

Occupational Level	Specific Death Rate, Men 45-64
Professional, technical	9.7
Clerical	9.6
Craftsmen, foremen	10.3
Operatives	10.6
Service workers	14.8
Nonfarm laborers	18.9
Farmers and farm laborers	10.0

Source: Based on *Demographic Yearbook of the United Nations 1967*, table 28.

Table 5-38   DIFFERENTIAL MORTALITY BY MARITAL STATUS, UNITED STATES, 1960

Marital Status	Specific Death Rate Men 45-54	Specific Death Rate Women 45-54
Single	15.7	6.4
Married	8.6	4.7
Widowed	21.0	8.5
Divorced	25.9	7.2

Source: Based on *Demographic Yearbook of the United Nations 1967*, table 28.

---

status, especially the marital status of men, has a dramatic influence on mortality (Table 5–38). It has been known for more than a century that single persons have much higher death rates than married persons of the same age. This difference cannot be explained by the supposition that single persons in poor health are less likey to marry, because widowed and divorced persons have the highest death rates of all. The conclusion is nearly inescapable that marriage is a biologically wholesome condition for men and, to a lesser extent, for women.

Implications of Differential Fertility

Whenever there are age differences between two subdivisions of a national population, a younger, more fertile subpopulation can be visualized as displacing the older and less fertile subpopulation. This is the aspect of fertility that attracted the attention of scholars in the latter part of the nineteenth centrury. Two of them, Francis Walker and Francis Galton, were men of strong opinions and great influence; the interpretation they gave to differential fertility persisted for many years and had profound effects on population policy in some countries.

Francis A. Walker (1840–1897) was the superintendent of the United States censuses of 1870 and 1880 and the founder of the *Statistical Abstract of the United States*. He had been a Civil War general at the age of 25, and became professor of political economy at Yale, president of the Massachusetts Institute of Technology, and president of the American Economic Association. In the course of his work with the census, Walker discovered that the immigrant population of the United States was younger and more fertile than the native-born population of primarily English descent, whose fertility had declined sharply during the nineteenth century. On the basis of these facts, Walker reached the rather sweeping conclusion that immigration had not contributed to the growth of the population but had merely altered its composition.[21] He based this belief on the assumption that, had there been no immigration, the fertility of the native-born population would not have declined. The alarm raised by Walker led eventually to a reversal of the traditional American policy of open immigration and to the enactment of a quota system designed to encourage immigration from the British Isles and Germany and to discourage immigration from other parts of Europe and the world.

Francis Galton (1822–1911) was one of the great Victorian intellectuals, a contemporary of Huxley and Darwin. He made significant contributions to geology, geography, meteorology, and psychology; and he may be considered the father of modern statistics. The statistical laboratory he founded at the University of London was for a long time the most important in the world, and his successors there, Karl Pearson and R. A. Fisher, invented many of the fundamental procedures of statistics. Galton began the systematic study of intelligence by using the normal curve to grade intellectual ability. In the course of his inquiries into intelligence, Galton became aware (a) that intellectual ability is apparently inherited; (b) that the average intellectual ability of the upper classes in England was higher than that of the lower classes; and (c) that the lower classes were more fertile. It seemed to him only a short step from this pattern of facts to the conclusion that the intellectual ability of the population was declining from one generation to the next and that the ultimate prospect was a nation of morons, if the existing trend were allowed to continue. In 1883 Galton introduced the term "eugenics" to describe the improvement of the human stock by selective breeding—which would mean encouraging raising the fertility of biologically superior families and lowering the fertility of biologically inferior families. In light of the evidence available when Galton published his book, *Human Faculty*,[22] the conclusions were perhaps reasonable, but subsequent research has thoroughly undermined them.

The belief that the quality of human population, particularly its mental quality, was declining progressively because of differential fertility went almost unchallenged for 50 years. As late as 1934, the leading American textbook on population estimated that average I.Q. in the United States was declining by about one point per generation.[23] A few years later, a series of empirical studies in the United States and elsewhere indicated that the general intelligence of the population was *rising* and showed that persons of low intelligence have remarkably low fertility, because many of them remain unmarried and if married, many of them never have children.[24]

It has also been repeatedly demonstrated that intelligence tests do not measure innate intelligence, as was originally supposed, but a combination of hereditary and environmental factors that cannot be disentangled. Without having been flatly disproved, the Galtonian belief that the English upper class represented a biologically superior stock now seems absurd. It rested upon the unstated assumption that the biological identity of social classes is easy to determine and relatively fixed, but everything that has been learned about mobility since Galton's time contradicts this assumption. Social mobility is so rapid in the English-speaking world that among the fairly recent ancestors of Queen Elizabeth II, there were an innkeeper, a toyman, and a London plumber.[25]

In addition to the movement of individuals and families through the class structure, the structure itself changes so rapidly from one generation to the next that no long-term theory of biological circulation is very plausible. The views of society held by Walker and by Galton were influenced by the milieus in which they passed most of their lives. The Victorian era in England was marked by an extraordinary concentration of talent in the lower-upper class and, indeed, among a group of related families among whom the Darwins, the Galtons, the Arnolds, and the Huxleys were conspicuous. This historical accident made the idea that intellectual ability was a simple inherited biological characteristic more plausible than it might otherwise have been. Walker lived in New England at a time when a sudden influx of immigrants and the rapidly increasing wealth of the native population created so wide a separation between the two groups that for a generation or two it was easy to visualize them as separate human types.

Under ordinary circumstances, any attempt to follow a distinct segment of a larger population through time is defeated by the simple arithmetic of human ancestry. Every living soul has two parents in the first ascending generation, four grandparents in the second, eight great-grandparents in the third, more than a thousand direct ancestors in the tenth ascending generation, and more than a billion in the twenty-first ascending generation—five or six hundred years back, a number several times greater than the population of the whole world around 1400. This apparent impossibility is accounted for by multiple ancestries. When first cousins marry, their children have six individual persons to fill the eight great-grandparent positions. Nearly every man and woman who marry are, in fact, remote cousins. According to one genealogical estimate, no two persons of English descent are likely to be further apart than tenth cousins. The practice of reckoning descent in the male line impels us to pick out a single chain of ancestors about which we may have some information from the huge number of other chains, and to ascribe our genetic inheritance to the single chain labeled with the same surname, but in fact, we have no way of identifying the persons who figure most conspicuously in our ancestral trees by occupying multiple positions. No person of European descent can trace his total ancestry back more than six or seven generations, and in the rare cases where that much is possible, the information available about the physical and mental characteristics of most of these ancestors is negligible.

The pyramid of descendants is as difficult to trace as the pyramid of ancestors. If we take any generation of adults in a given population, it is clear that some of them will have no children, some will have children but no grandchildren, some will have grandchildren but no great-grandchildren. In short, some lines of descent will become extinct in every successive generation so that the number of ancestors in the original cohort is steadily reduced with the passage of centuries. We do not know how far this process goes, but it is likely that of all the persons alive in the time of Julius Caesar, only a minute fraction have living descendants today, and that, among that minute fraction, some unknown couples are the ancestors of millions or hundreds of millions of persons now alive. The beginnings of this process are illustrated by the number of descendants of the Twenty-Nine Founders of the Ramah Navaho population as shown in Table 5–39. This table is based on one of the rare genealogies that covers an entire population for the better part of a century. Of course, it somewhat understates the amount of selection that took place, because its construction started with the descendants and those persons in the generation of the founders whose lines died out before the arrival of great-grandchildren are omitted from the table. The amount of selection that occurred is nevertheless impressive. The three ancestors numbered 1, 2, and 3 in the table had more descendants after three and a half generations than all the ancestors numbered 10 through 29.

| Table 5-39 | NUMBER OF DESCENDANTS OF RAMAH NAVAHO "FOUNDERS" BY DESCENDING ORDER OF NUM- BER OF DESCENDANTS |

| Descendant's Generation | | | | | Total | Percentage |
Founder	1	2	3	4	Descendants	of Total
1	9	66	230	106	411	14.18
2	23	107	123	57	310	10.69
3	12	71	162	46	291	10.04
4	4	30	83	86	203	7.00
5	8	40	60	58	166	5.73
6	8	67	66	5	146	5.04
7	21	53	57	11	142	4.90
8	12	35	79	5	131	4.52
9	2	21	42	65	130	4.48
10	8	63	53	5	129	4.45
11	6	17	50	37	110	3.79
12	6	32	68	...	106	3.66
13	8	32	57	...	97	3.34
14	12	35	30	...	77	2.66
15	7	16	34	...	57	1.97
16-29	37	108	182	66	393	13.56
Totals	183	793	1376	547	2899	100.01

Source: J.N. Spuhler, "Physical Anthropology and Demography," in Philip M. Hauser and Otis Dudley Duncan, *The Study of Population: An Inventory and Appraisal* (Chicago: University of Chicago Press, 1959), table 70, p. 743.

Differential Fertility and the Demographic Transition

The demographic transition is the name given to the worldwide process whereby preindustrial populations with high mortality and fertility are transformed into modernized populations with low fertility and mortality after passing through an intermediate phase of rapidly declining mortality and slowly declining fertility accompanied by spectacular natural increase. This transition was well under way in western Europe by the end of the eighteenth century and may be taken as virtually completed in most of the technologically advanced countries of the world. The developing countries, on the other hand, are found for the most part in the intermediate phase and a few, isolated, very backward populations have barely begun the transition.

Recent studies have suggested the possibility that differential fertility and mortality may be more marked in the intermediate phase of the demographic transition than either before or afterwards. On the one hand, differences in mortality among social classes and occupational groups seem to be disappearing in all of the highly developed countries and differences in fertility to be diminishing at the same time. Indeed, there is some evidence in both European and American data for the period after World War II to indicate that under fully modernized conditions, with effective contraception available to the entire population, the upper stratum of a population may be the most fertile.

On the other hand, there is evidence that in some countries, still in the early phase of the demographic transition, the expected differentials seem to be lacking or even reversed. In Egypt, for example, the population in large cities appears to be younger than in smaller cities, the populations of which in turn are younger than the rural population, urban and rural fertility being approximately at the same level and urban mortality lower.[26] Somewhat similar fertility conditions have recently been found in central India.[27]

Migration

Migration is a change of residence from one place to another. When it takes place across national boundaries, it is often described as *emigration* (from the standpoint of the sending country), or *immigration* (from the standpoint of the receiving country.) Movement over very short distances, as from one part of a city to another, is often called *residential mobility.* Temporary or *seasonal mobility,* like the employment of mountain peasants as laborers on coastal plantations or the annual movement of Mexican field hands into California to assist with the harvest, is not the same as migration, nor is the movement of nomads and other persons who have no fixed residence.

The systematic study of migration began with five "Laws of Migration" proposed by Ravenstein in two papers submitted to the Royal Statistical Society in the 1880s.[28] For the first of these papers, Ravenstein used data from the British Census of 1881; for the second, he obtained information from more than 20 other countries. The five laws may be briefly summarized as follows:

1. Most (internal) migrants proceed only a short distance to a local center of absorption; most long-distance migrants go to great cities.
2. Therefore, migration takes place by stages from country districts to small towns to larger towns to cities.
3. Each mainstream of migration produces a compensating counterstream, that is, a smaller number of people moving in the opposite direction.
4. An urban population is less migratory than the nearby rural population.
5. Females predominate among short-distance migrants and males among long-distance migrants.

The Ravenstein model appears to hold up surprisingly well for the pattern of migration within a continuous territory, like that of Great

Britain or the continental United States. It is less valid for voluntary resettlement across international boundaries, and it does not apply at all to political resettlements or forced migrations. A revised and expanded version of Ravenstein's Laws was published in 1966 by Lee.[29]

Another general model of migration was proposed by Stouffer in 1940.[30] His theory of intervening obstacles proposes that the volume of a stream of voluntary (internal) migration will be directly proportional to the amount of opportunity at the destination and inversely proportional to the amount of opportunity in the intervening areas between the origin and the destination. This formula, entirely consistent with Ravenstein's, is moderately successful in predicting the movement of population between pairs of American cities.

There are four different types of migration that need to be taken into account: urbanization, population drift, voluntary resettlement, and political resettlement.[31]

Urbanization is the movement of population from farms to cities and from small cities to larger cities that can be observed everywhere in the modern world. Population drift is the tendency for residential mobility within a territory to produce a net displacement of population in certain directions. Voluntary resettlement is the free movement of individuals and families from one country to another or from one region to another, with corresponding changes of occupation or social identity. Political resettlement is the more or less simultaneous movement of large groups of persons from one area to another either to escape political persecution in the old area or to achieve political goals in the new area. In the sections that follow, we shall discuss each type of migration as it affects the world as a whole and the United States in particular.

URBANIZATION

The worldwide movement from farms to cities and from small cities to large cities is one of the most certain indications we have that history is not merely repeating itself in the twentieth century but has taken a new direction. There are various ways of drawing the line between urban and rural settlements, but wherever we draw it, the results are much the same.

Until 1950, in the United States, incorporated places with over 2,500 people were classified as urban and all other places as rural. Table 5–40 shows the proportions of the population living in urban and rural places from 1790 to 1960, using this classification. Even with this definition, which tends to exaggerate the urban proportions, the country was intensely rural in the early days of the Republic— nearly 95 percent rural in 1790—and although the cities and towns grew steadily all through the nineteenth century, there was still a slight rural predominance as late as 1910. By 1960, however, city people outnumbered country people about two to one.

Table 5–41 shows the urban proportion of the whole world's population from 1800 to 1950, considering the residents of cities of

Table 5-40 URBAN PROPORTION, UNITED STATES, 1790-1960

Year	Percent of Population in Incorporated Places Over 2,500
1790	5.1
1850	15.3
1900	39.5
1960	63.0

Source: Based on *Historical Statistics of the United States, 1957,* Series A34-50 and *Statistical Abstract of the United States, 1967,* table 13.

Table 5-41 URBAN PROPORTION, THE WORLD, 1800-1950

Year	Percent of Population in Cities of 20,000 or More
1800	2.4
1850	4.3
1900	9.2
1950	20.9

Source: Based on Kingsley Davis, "The Origin and Growth of Urbanization in the World," *American Journal of Sociology* 405, no. 5 (March 1955): 433.

Table 5-42 METROPOLITAN PROPORTION, THE WORLD, 1800-1967

Year	Percent of Population in Cities of 1,000,000 or More
1800	0.0
1850	0.3
1900	1.3
1950	3.3
1967	8.9

Source: Based on *Demographic Yearbook of the United Nations 1967,* table 6; and Warren S. Thompson and David T. Lewis, *Population Problems,* 5th ed. (New York: McGraw-Hill, 1965), table 6-2.

20,000 or more as urban. The urban proportion rose from about one in forty to about one in five in a century and a half, approximately doubling every fifty years.

While the urban proportion of the world's population has been increasing in relation to the rural proportion, the larger cities have been growing faster than the smaller cities. The metropolitan proportion of the world's population (the proportion in cities or urban agglomerations over one million) is shown in Table 5–42. It was zero in 1800 because there were no places of that size at that date anywhere, although ancient Rome at the height of its glory, and Chiang-An, the capital of China in the eighth century, may have exceeded one million. By 1850 there were two metropolitan cities in the world, London and Paris, the twin capitals of the Industrial Revolution. By 1900 there were 10, including New York, Chicago, and Philadelphia. By 1950, the number had grown to 29 and by 1967 to 126, including 30 in the United States, 15 in China, 10 in Latin America, and 8 in the Soviet Union. Figure 5–3 is the full list. It will be a rare reader who does not find some unfamiliar names in the list. It is an interesting fact that each of these places outranks in size most of the greatest cities of the past.

The motives for the great urban migration have not been as closely studied as one might suppose, perhaps because they seem obvious. The first step in analyzing a current of migration is to determine whether it is caused by a "push" or "pull" or both. In the case of urbanization, the push is derived from the presence of a large surplus population in rural areas, partly due to the modernization of agriculture, which reduces the demand for agricultural labor, and partly due to the large natural increase characteristic of rural populations in modern times.

The pull might be described as the lure of the city. It is compounded of economic opportunities, opportunities for social mobility, the relaxation of traditional constraints, and an enlargement of the horizons of individual experience. The lure of the city, for the time being, is universal and irresistible. People flock to metropolitan centers as fast as they can be absorbed into the metropolitan labor force, and sometimes faster. In the course of these transitions, it is not unusual for the peasant to abandon his rural livelihood for unemployment in the big city.

Many of the metropolitan centers that have sprung up recently in underdeveloped countries are ringed with bidonvilles—squatters' colonies, hardly deserving the name of slums. Some metropolitan centers in Asia have permanent sidewalk populations of people who have migrated to the city but have been unable to find a home there. Even in highly developed countries, the standard of living offered to recent rural migrants often compares unfavorably with the conditions they left behind. In the long run, however, the migrants who endure this initiation appear to be correct in their expectation that they and their children will ultimately be absorbed into the metropolitan labor force and acquire an urban outlook and standard of living. Some migrants,

Europe (26)

Vienna	Berlin	Amsterdam	Stockholm
Brussels	Athens	Rotterdam	Birmingham
Prague	Budapest	Warsaw	Leeds
Copenhagen	Milan	Bucharest	Liverpool
Paris	Naples	Barcelona	London
Hamburg	Rome	Madrid	Manchester
Munich	Turin		

Soviet Union (8)

Baku	Kharkov	Leningrad	Odessa
Gorky	Kiev	Moscow	Tashkent

North America (35)

Montreal	Buffalo	Kansas City	Philadelphia
Toronto	Chicago	Los Angeles	Pittsburgh
Havana	Cincinnati	Miami	St. Louis
Guadalajara	Cleveland	Milwaukee	San Bernadino
Mexico	Dallas	Minneapolis	San Diego
Anaheim	Denver	Newark	San Francisco
Atlanta	Detroit	New Orleans	Seattle
Baltimore	Houston	New York	Washington
Boston	Indianapolis	Paterson	

South America (10)

Buenos Aires	Recife	Santiago	Montevideo
Belo Horizonte	Sao Paulo	Bogota	Caracas
Guanabora (Rio)		Lima	

Asia (42)

Nagoya	Istanbul	Shenyang	Hyderabad
Osaka	Saigon	Sian	Kanpur
Tokyo	Canton	Taiyuan	Madras
Yokohama	Chengtu	Tientsin	Djakarta
Pusan	Chungking	Tsingtao	Surabaya
Seoul	Harbin	Wuhan	Teheran
Karechi	Nanking	Taipei	Baghdad
Lahore	Peking	Ahmedabad	Kitakyushu
Manila	Port Arthur-	Bangalore	Kobe
Singapore	Dairen	Calcutta	Kyoto
Bangkok	Shanghai	Delhi	

Africa (4)

Casablanca	Alexandria
Johannesburg	Cairo

Oceania (2)

Melbourne	Sydney

Source: Based on: *Demographic Yearbook of the United Nations 1967,* Table 6.

Table 5-43   RESIDENTIAL MOBILITY, UNITED STATES, 1966-1967

Mobility in Twelve Months	Percent of Total Population*
None	80.2
Moved within county	12.7
Moved within state	3.3
Moved to another state	3.3
Living abroad	0.5
	100.0

*Excluding infants under 1 year.

Source: Based on *Statistical Abstract of the United States, 1968*, table 37.

Table 5-44   DISTRIBUTION OF POPULATION BY REGIONS, UNITED STATES 1790-1965

Year	Northeast	Percent of Total Population North Central	South	West	Total
1790	50	—	50	—	100
1830	43	13	44	—	100
1860	33	29	36	2	100
1890	28	35	32	5	100
1920	28	32	32	8	100
1965	25	28	31	16	100

Source: Based on *Historical Statistics of the United States*, 1957, Series A95-122, and *Statistical Abstract of the United States, 1967*, table 20.

of course, sink into the culture of poverty and abandon all hope of advancement. But even for these disadvantaged people, the attraction of metropolitan life remains strong; as far as can be determined, very few of them regret moving off the land or ever attempt to return to it.

POPULATION DRIFT

If we examine the movements of families from house to house within a large city, we discover that such moves take place in all directions,

Figure 5-4

CENTER OF POPULATION FOR COTERMINOUS UNITED STATES, 1790 TO 1960

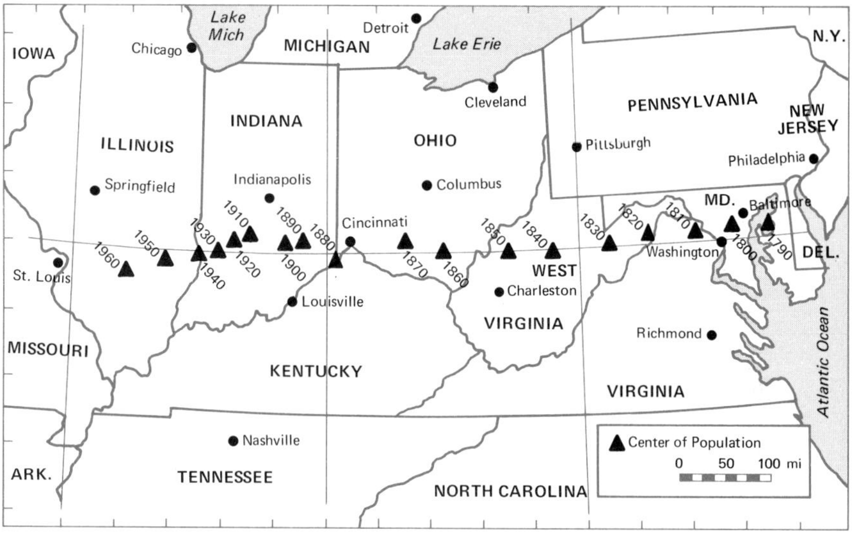

Year	North Latitude			West Longitude			Approximate Location
	°	′	″	°	′	″	
1790	39	16	30	76	11	12	23 miles east of Baltimore, Md.
1850	38	59	0	81	19	0	23 miles southeast of Parkersburg, W. Va.
1900	39	9	36	85	48	54	6 miles southeast of Columbus, Ind.
1940	38	56	54	87	22	35	2 miles southeast by east of Carlisle, Haddon Township, Sullivan County, Ind.
1950	38	50	21	88	9	33	8 miles north-northwest of Olney, Richland County, Ill.
1960	38	37	57	88	52	23	4 miles east of Salem, Marion County, Ill.

Source: *Statistical Abstract of the United States 1968*, p. 10.

but sometimes away from the center of the city and sometimes toward it. However, when we sum up the effect of all such moves during a given period, we discover that moves in various directions do not quite cancel each other out. Since there are somewhat more moves outward than inward, the net result is a displacement of population toward the suburbs.[32] This particular drift is one of the constant features of contemporary urban experience in the United States, western Europe, and Latin America; the use of automobiles for mass transportation permits a vast and continuous process of suburbanization, which has gone so far in the United States that in several of the larger cities the popula-

Table 5-45   DISTRIBUTION OF THE NEGRO POPULATION BY REGIONS, UNITED STATES, 1860-1960

A. Percent of Negro Population

Year	Northeast	North Central	South	West	Total
1860	4	5	92	0.1	(100)
1880	3	6	91	0.2	(100)
1900	4	6	90	0.3	(100)
1920	6	8	85	1.0	(100)
1940	11	11	77	1.0	(100)
1960	16	18	60	6.0	(100)

B. Number of Negroes

Year	Northeast	North Central	South	West
1940	1,369,875	1,420,318	9,904,619	170,706
1960	3,028,499	3,446,037	11,311,607	1,085,688
Change	+121%	+142%	+14%	+540%

Source: Based on *Historical Statistics of the United States*, 1957, Series A95-122; and *Statistical Abstract of the United States, 1967*, table 27.

tion of the city proper is declining while the suburbs grow at nearly astronomical rates.

The residential mobility of modern populations is so high that even a relatively small imbalance in one direction or another is sufficient to create a major population drift. Table 5–43 shows the proportion of the United States population over a year old who moved from one permanent address to another within a single 12-month period from mid-1966 to mid-1967. More than one-fifth of the total population changed addresses, and more than one-third of these moved across a county line. The main currents of population drift can be traced out for each region and each community separately; the process is continuous and continuously interesting. For the United States as a whole, there has always been a westward tendency. As Figure 5–4 shows, the center of population has moved almost directly west along the 39th parallel of latitude from each census to the next since 1790.

Table 5–44 shows the regional drift of population in another way. In 1790, the American population was evenly divided between the South and the North (now the Northeast). Through most of the nineteenth century, these two regions lost population to the north central states, but since about 1890 they have held their own, reinforced by foreign immigration to the Northeast and by a high rate of natural increase in the South. The West, meanwhile, has gained steadily, mostly at the expense of the north central region. The legend that all good Iowans die in California symbolizes a set of demographic facts.

Another population drift that has been under way for more than a century is the movement of the black population out of the South into the three other major regions of the country (Table 5–45). This drift was at first directed toward the northeast, but it has swung increasingly westward. Since 1940, the black population of the South (south Atlantic, east south central, and west south central states) has gained slightly in absolute numbers but declined relative to the southern white population. Meanwhile the black population of the northeast (New England and the middle Atlantic states), the north central region (east north central and west north central), and the West (mountain and Pacific states) has increased spectacularly in absolute numbers and in proportion to the white population, especially in the large metropolitan centers toward which most black migration is directed.

Population drift is, by definition, a phenomenon internal to each nation. It seems to occur in every nation where the free movement of population is permitted. In Great Britain, for example, the long-term population drift is southward, toward London. In Italy it is northward, toward the industrial districts of Lombardy.

VOLUNTARY RESETTLEMENT

The most significant form of voluntary resettlement is the permanent movement of individuals and their families across national boundaries in search of better living conditions. One of the most important examples of voluntary resettlement in history has been the great movement of Europeans to the Western Hemisphere, which continued on a small scale from the fifteenth to the eighteenth centuries, assumed enormous proportions in the nineteenth century, and persists in a modest way today.

Table 5–46 shows the total immigration into the United States from 1820 to 1966 by 30-year periods (the last period is five years short). The number of immigrants averaged less than 100,000 a year in the first period. It rose greatly after 1850 and reached its peak in the 30 years from 1881 to 1910, when more than 17 million persons entered the United States, most of them through the famous portal of Ellis Island in New York Harbor, with the announced intention of taking up permanent residence. Immigration was severely checked by restrictive legislation in the 1920s and further discouraged by the Great Depression. The annual figure for 1924, the last year of unrestricted immigration, was 707,000. By 1934 immigration was down to 29,000, the lowest figure since 1827. Through the remainder of the thirties and until the end of World War II, immigration remained highly restricted. After the war, however, it became the practice to make exceptions in

Table 5-46	IMMIGRATION INTO THE UNITED STATES 1820-1966

Period	Number
1820-1850	2,464,000
1851-1880	7,725,000
1881-1910	17,730,000
1911-1940	10,371,000
1941-1967	5,685,000
Total	43,975,000

Source: Based on *Statistical Abstract of the United States, 1968,* table 125.

the national quota system for various categories of immigrants—displaced persons, skilled technicians, relatives of citizens, and some others. Later the quota laws were liberalized, and though the procedures for entering the United States remain exceedingly rigid, complicated, and time-consuming. More than 5 million immigrants were admitted from 1946 to 1966.

Table 5–47 shows the major sources of immigration into the United States from 1820 to 1966. (Although we do not have annual figures for immigration from 1789 to 1820, the total for that period could not have much exceeded 100,000.) The vast majority of immigrants came from Europe, and the vast majority of these from six countries—Germany, Italy, Ireland, Austria-Hungary, Great Britain and Russia—in that order. Although Great Britain had furnished most of the original colonial population, and the descendants of Englishmen continued to dominate the public affairs of the United States, Great Britain accounted for less than one-tenth of the total number of immigrants after 1820.

No reliable statistics on the religious affiliation of the nineteenth century immigrants are available, but the majority seem to have been Catholic, including almost all the immigrants from Ireland, Italy, and Austria-Hungary, and a large proportion of those from Germany. Most immigrants from Russia were either Greek Orthodox or Jewish.

It is possible that the figures given in Tables 5–46 and 5–47 somewhat overestimate the amount of resettlement that occurred, since substantial numbers of immigrants ultimately returned to their countries of origin either because they were disappointed in America or because, having prospered, they went home to enjoy their wealth. There are no reliable figures for the total number of returnees, but they must have been an appreciable fraction of the total. On the other

Table 5-47	MAJOR SOURCES OF IMMIGRATION INTO THE UNITED STATES 1820-1967

Last Permanent Residence	Number in Thousands
Germany	6,879
Western Hemisphere	6,881
Italy	5,096
Ireland	4,709
Austria-Hungary	4,289
Great Britain	4,735
Russia (present area of USSR)	3,346
Sweden	1,264
Asia	1,300
All others	5,477
Total	43,976

Source: Based on *Statistical Abstract of the United States, 1968,* table 127.

hand, a considerable amount of illegal immigration is known to have occurred, especially after 1924, and this may be taken as an offsetting factor.

One recent current of immigration, the entry of Puerto Ricans into the United States, is not counted at all. Puerto Rico, an island in the West Indies acquired by the United States as a trophy of the Spanish-American war, enjoys a special status as an associated commonwealth *(estado libre asociado)* of the United States. Citizens of Puerto Rico are considered to be citizens of the United States and may enter the country at will. About a million Puerto Ricans, upwards of one-third of the island's population, reside in the United States at any given time, but movement back and forth is so frequent and easy that it is often impossible to determine whether an individual or family has migrated permanently.

The voluntary resettlement of Europeans was never, of course, limited to the United States. Similar movements on a smaller scale have occurred in many other parts of the world. In recent decades, for example, there has been substantial European immigration to Australia and to Brazil, Chinese immigration to the islands of Oceania, Russian immigration into the developing areas of Siberia, and West Indian immigration to Great Britain. However, in the twentieth century, every large-scale movement of population has political implications, and currents of immigration are more likely to depend upon governmental than private initiative.

As in the case of urbanization, the pushes and pulls that lead to voluntary resettlement are not hard to identify. The pull is again a compound of economic, social, and psychological opportunities. All through the nineteenth century and well into the twentieth, "America" was a golden word in the vocabulary of the European peasant. It stood for political freedom, social equality, and fabulous wealth. The push was likely to be a crisis in the home country that made difficult conditions intolerable. The political repression that followed the German revolutions of 1848, the famine due to the failure of the Irish potato crop in the 1840s, the anti-Semitism that swept western Russia in the late 1880s, the partition of Germany in 1945, the revolution in Cuba in the late 1950s, and similar events persuaded thousands of people who might otherwise have remained at home to join an already existing current of migration as fast as they could dispose of their household goods and obtain transportation.

POLITICAL RESETTLEMENT

Political resettlement occurs in three forms—the transfer of population as part of a political program, the displacement of population in the presence of an invading army, and the planned settlement of an area under a governmental program. In this case, as in other types of migration, the movement of population may be due to a push or to a pull or to both at the same time.

Involuntary migration has occurred throughout history but never before on so large a scale as recently.[33] The large-scale movements of the twentieth century began with the Balkan Wars of 1912–1914. The political changes of the interwar period occasioned major movements of population in central Europe, the Soviet Union, China, and Africa. The Nazi regime first uprooted and then killed about six million Jews together with large numbers of forced laborers, political opponents, and innocent victims from each of the countries occupied by Germany in the early phases of World War II. During the same period, the Nazis moved a considerable German-speaking population into western Poland and began a program of settling Germans in the Ukraine. Later in the war, all of these migrants plus several million Germans from East Prussia and former Polish territory were forced back into West Germany, together with a large number of refugees and homeless persons from other countries in the Soviet zone of occupation.

The partition of British India into India and Pakistan in 1947 led to a mass exchange of population. Some 10 million Hindus migrated from Pakistan to India and 7 or 8 million Moslems from India to Pakistan. The establishment of the state of Israel and the series of wars between Israel and the Arab countries led to a large-scale displacement of the Arab population formerly settled in Palestine and the almost total displacement of the Jewish communities in Arab countries. The apartheid program in South Africa involved massive shifts of the nonwhite population into "designated, protected areas." The failure of the secessionist movement in Nigeria forced the defeated Biafrans out of the territory they formerly occupied into a small defended enclave, where many of them died of starvation. During the Vietnam war, the populations of villages and entire districts suspected of collaboration with the Viet Cong were removed from their homes by United States forces and transferred to other areas for eventual resettlement. There has even been one instance of the political resettlement of an entire population in the United States. During World War II, persons of Japanese ancestry were removed en masse from the West Coast and confined in resettlement camps for most of the duration of the war.[34]

The repatriation of colonists is another type of political resettlement. The independence of Indonesia forced some two million Dutch citizens to return to the Netherlands or to seek homes elsewhere in the East Indies. The independence of Algeria led to the repatriation of nearly a million Frenchmen, some of them from families settled in Algeria for more than a century.

Altogether, more than 100 million people have been forced unwillingly out of their homes and their native places in the present century by national governments bent on eliminating minorities or improving the shape of their frontiers or gaining a military advantage. The concentration camp and the collective mess hall are as typical of the twentieth century as rockets and computers.

The Population Explosion

Despite the massive scale of these migrations, they have not had much effect on the worldwide distribution of population. The scale of growth is such as to reduce the effect of migration almost to insignificance. It is conventional to cry out in superlatives when describing the contemporary phenomenon of population growth, because the numbers involved are of a new order of magnitude and because the consequences are difficult to predict in the absence of any comparable episode in human history.

From 1960 to 1967, according to the United Nations, the population of the entire world increased at an annual rate of 1.9 percent. Philip M. Hauser, a leading American demographer, discusses the significance of this rate and shows why it cannot possibly continue:

> With an initial population of three billion, the present rate of world population growth would give a population of fifty billion in 142 years. . . .
> A continuation of the 2 per cent rate of world population growth from the present population of about three billion would provide enough people, in lock step, to reach from the earth to the sun in 237 years. It would give one person for every square foot of land surface on the globe, including mountains, deserts and the arctic wastes, in about six and one-half centuries. It would generate a population which would weigh as much as the earth itself in 1,566 years. . . .

Projections of this type, of course, are not to be interpreted as predictions. They merely help to indicate the meaning of the present rate of growth. They also permit another firm conclusion— namely, that the present rate of world population growth cannot possibly persist for very long into the future.[35]

It is generally accepted by demographers that the world population grew from about half a billion in the middle of the seventeenth century[36] to about one and a half billion around 1900 and thence to around three billion in 1960, taking about 250 years to double the first time, and about 60 years to double again (Table 5–48). If present rates of population growth do not change dramatically, it will take less than 30 years to double the next time, reaching a population of six billion around 1990. Although figures for world population before 1900 are highly speculative, there seems to be no question that the rate of population growth in the world as a whole has accelerated very sharply in the present century.

The first reasonably reliable estimates of the world population as a whole date from 1930. Table 5–48 shows the increase of population by continents for the ensuing 30 years (separating the Soviet Union, as has become customary, from both Europe and Asia). In this 30-year period, approximately equal to one generation, the population of the whole world increased by nearly half, as did the populations of North America and Asia. Latin America and Africa had growth rates much higher than the world average; Europe, including the Soviet Union, much lower. Since the population of the earth is very unevenly distributed, it is interesting to examine the effect of these changes on the density of settlement. In the five major continents, the vast disparities in both the earlier and later densities are shown in Table 5–49. The density of the world and of the continents increased, of course, by the same proportion as their respective populations, bringing Africa,

Table 5-48	GROWTH OF POPULATION, WORLD, 1930-1960		
Area	1930 Population	1960 Population	30-Year Increase
World	2,070,000,000	3,004,000,000	46%
Africa	164,000,000	278,000,000	69
North America	134,000,000	199,000,000	49
Latin America	108,000,000	213,000,000	97
Asia	1,120,000,000	1,660,000,000	48
Europe	355,000,000	425,000,000	20
Soviet Union	179,000,000	214,000,000	20

Source: Based on *Demographic Yearbook of the United Nations, 1967,* table 1.

North America, South America and the U.S.S.R. to about the same level—approximately ten persons per square kilometer or 26 per square mile—while Europe rose to the unprecedented density of 238 per square mile, and Asia increased to an overall density nearly as high as the European density in 1930 without coming anywhere near the European living standards of 1930.

Table 5–50 shows the growth of the United States population by 30-year intervals from 1790 to 1970. Several surprising features of this trend should be noted. First, the rate of growth up to 1880 averaged considerably more than 100 percent per generation. Second, the great immigration of 1880 to 1910 was accompanied by a decline in the *rate* of population growth. Third, even in the lean years 1910 to 1940, which included the restriction of immigration, a dramatic decline of family size, and the low fertility of the Great Depression, the rate of growth was nearly as high as the rate of growth in Asia from 1930 to 1960. In the following period, 1940 to 1970, it was much higher than the Asian rate.

The causes of population growth are extremely complex, and demographers cannot predict future population growth with any certainty. Modernization increases population both by reducing the death rate and by raising productivity per acre and per capita so that a larger population can be fed, housed, clothed, and educated. Although the world's population is now growing so rapidly, per capita income is still rising nearly everywhere in the world and even if population growth has retarded the rise of the standard of living in many countries, it has not yet prevented it from rising, except in a few scattered districts.[37] The capacity of the earth to support further increases of population is not seriously in question, but it is perfectly plain that the present rate of population growth cannot be maintained indefinitely. What bothers demographers is their inability to visualize the process by which the birth rate in relatively underdeveloped countries can be reduced to

Table 5-49	DENSITY OF POPULATION PER SQUARE MILE BY CONTINENTS, 1930 AND 1967	
Area	1930	1967
World	38.8	64.7
Africa	12.9	28.5
North America	15.5	25.9
Latin America	12.9	33.7
Asia	103.6	178.6
Europe	186.4	238.2
Soviet Union	20.7	28.5

	GROWTH OF POPULATION, UNITED STATES	
Table 5-50	1790-1970	

Year	Population	30-Year Increase
1790	3,929,000	—
1820	9,638,000	140%
1850	23,192,000	141
1880	50,156,000	116
1910	91,972,000	83
1940	131,669,000	43
1970	205,395,000	57

Source: Based on *Statistical Abstract of the United States, 1967,* table 7; *Statistical Abstract of the United States, 1968,* tables 1 and 5, and from Bureau of the Census.

approximately the same level as the very low death rates these countries have already achieved by the grace of modern science.

Until about 1950, most demographers accepted without question the theory of "the demographic transition," which was based on a few long series of vital statistics in such advanced countries as Great Britain, France, Sweden, and the United States. In these countries, all in the forefront of the Industrial Revolution, the statistical curtain rises in the late eighteenth century, when birth rates were very high, as they had probably been since time immemorial, but death rates had begun to fall in relation to birth rates and the population was already growing rapidly. For two or three generations thereafter, the death rate continued to decline faster than the birth rate and growth accelerated, but eventually the birth rate began to catch up. By 1930 it was nearly equal to the death rate in most of the advanced countries and they began to worry about the "problem of small families." The great English demographer, Alexander Carr-Saunders, wrote in 1936:

The perfect contraceptive, cheap, easy to use, and infallible, may be invented any day. Therefore, if things remain as they they are, the reproduction rate will fall, and the prospect will be a reduction of the population to less than a quarter of its present size a century from now. But the coming of this catastrophic decline will be masked for a time by the fact that in any case the fall will not be large during the next two decades. The [British] population will decline at the most by three or four millions in the next twenty years. This fall will be welcome to the many who believe that unemployment is due to over-population. Meanwhile people will come to think that they are rendering positive service by keeping their families small. All the habits connected with the small family system will harden into custom. Any suggestion that more births are desirable will meet with the impassioned opposition of birth-control enthusiasts. The prospects of so catastrophic a fall makes it urgent that steps should be taken at once.[38]

After World War II, demographers were startled to observe an increase of fertility in the United States and in most of the countries of western Europe. At first this was attributed to a backlog of births delayed during the war years, but as time went on, it became apparent that people in the advanced countries were having more children for no obvious reason. At the same time the course of events in less modernized countries also diverged from what was expected. The death rate, instead of falling slowly in response to technological progress, declined precipitously all over the world. Some underdeveloped countries registered greater improvement in mortality from 1950 to 1960 than the advanced European countries had achieved throughout the nineteenth century. Simultaneously there were indications that the birth rate might refuse to decline in a rapidly modernizing country or might decline too slowly to put a brake on population growth.

The spectacular case of Puerto Rico, the most densely settled country in the world, illustrated the possibility that the demographic transition might fail to occur even after intense modernization. Before 1940, Puerto Rico was an area of desperate poverty. After World War II massive American assistance and a brilliantly successful program of economic planning led to a pattern of modernization unmatched in the world. Only 3 percent of Puerto Rican families had incomes of over $1,000 in 1941; in 1960 more than half had incomes over $3,000. In the same interval of time, the birth rate declined from 39.8 to 32.3, but since the death rate declined even faster, the natural increase rose from 21 per thousand per year to 26 per thousand per year. Even today it remains above the level of 1941.[39]

In the case of Puerto Rico, the cultural and psychological factors associated with high fertility have been thoroughly investigated.[40] Birth control clinics were established there as early as 1937, and birth control programs have expanded steadily over the years. Puerto Rico was the testing ground for oral contraceptive pills; they were available on that island several years before they were introduced elsewhere in the world. Sterilization is encouraged and abortion is legal. In addition, there is convincing evidence that many Puerto Rican women desire smaller families than they have. But none of these influences has induced a major decline in fertility. The principal reasons for this failure appear to be the lack of communication between husband and wife on sexual matters, the ignorance and isolation of young women in their early child-bearing years, the high value that men attach to large families and particularly to male children as signs of their virility, the timidity of wives in relation to their husbands, and the fears induced by the atmosphere and procedures of birth control clinics. In sum, although Puerto Rican women are willing or eager to have fewer children, their husbands are not necessarily of the same opinion, and in the Hispanic culture of Puerto Rico it is the husband who makes the decision.

There is some reason to believe that attitudes about fertility in other countries with very high birth rates resemble those found in Puerto Rico. Studies in Peru, Lebanon, Jamaica, and India have shown that lower-class women in these very fertile societies do not want large families but are somehow unable to put their preferences into effect. Examining this pattern in relation to the relative failure of birth control programs in these same countries, Stycos proposes that the character of such programs ought to be changed,[41] removing them from the influence of the urban middle-class women who have initiated them and the medical personnel who have operated them, since both of these groups intimidate the potential clientele. Instead, he proposes that birth control programs should give as much or more attention to men, emphasize male rather than female contraceptive techniques, put more resources into nonclinical systems of education, distribute materials through retail channels and voluntary organizations, make use of magazines and newspaper publicity, and try to reach young couples in the early stages of marriage. He would base campaigns for limiting family size on the social and economic advantages to be gained, rather than on the health hazards of rapid childbearing. Finally, he believes that sterilization and probably abortion should be offered to people who have already had as many children as they want.

It would be a mistake, however, to reduce the problem of population growth to the question of how the ignorant masses of underdeveloped countries can be persuaded to adopt contraceptive practices. The real problems are more fundamental and may be briefly summarized as follows.

Although the control of population may be advantageous for individual families, and a necessity for the world as a whole, it is not necessarily advantageous for a particular nation, or for a particular ethnic or religious group. In countries as advanced and densely settled as England and France, cries of alarm are heard on all sides whenever the birth rate falls and the continued growth of population seems to be jeopardized. The Catholic Church, whose Latin American communicants are the fastest growing sector of the world's population, reaffirmed its opposition to contraception in 1968, although not without arousing considerable opposition from its own clergy and laity. The United States, although now willing to export contraceptive advice and materials to Asiatic countries, has no large-scale program for discouraging the growth of its own population.

In the world as it is presently constituted, a rising national population is equivalent to increasing political influence and military potential. The expansion of the national market sustains the demand for labor and commodities of all kinds; up to a point it is nearly a guarantee of continued prosperity. Most large-scale organizations are so constituted as to regard expansion as a signal of success and contraction as a signal of failure. Continued population growth underwrites the future of many large-scale organizations.

When this expansion is accompanied by a continuous rise in per capita income, large-scale organizations are able to expand at a hectic rate. As we saw from Table 5–50 nearly 80 million people were added to the American population between 1940 and 1970, a number about equal to the combined populations of France and Spain. Under these circumstances, the cities and their suburbs spread over the adjacent countryside, highways multiplied and their traffic multiplied faster. New airports, shopping centers, marinas, colleges, office buildings, football stadiums, summer resorts, and innumerable other facilities sprang up across the land and were used to capacity almost as soon as their paint was dry. Although economists have labored long and hard to develop the concept of an optimum population,[42] the practical optimum from the standpoint of many government officials and businessmen is the largest population obtainable.

From another standpoint, of course, universal expansion is a universal tragedy. The countryside disappears, places of interest and recreation become too crowded to serve their purposes, the rivers are polluted, the air over the cities becomes poisonous, the overburdening of social networks impedes their operations at every point. The old houses, the tall trees, the quiet valleys, the peaceful habits are swept away in the path of development. However much one regrets the relative serenity of a less crowded world, economic and political forces encourage continuous growth.

There is one more issue that needs emphasis, since its presence is always felt in any practical discussion of population problems. When Malthus first identified population growth as a problem, it was the potential growth of the rude and uneducated part of the English population that concerned him, not the increase of respectable persons like himself. This attitude found a clearer expression in the work of Galton and the eugenicists who feared that the "better people" were being outbred by inferior stock. It continues to haunt demographic discussions today. The American population, as Tables 5–48 and 5–49 showed us, has grown somewhat faster than the population of Asia in recent decades but we are more likely, when discussing the population explosion, to think of the teeming masses of Asia than of the teeming suburbs of southern California. Even within the United States the population problem is perceived by many people as an increase in the proportion of blacks rather than as an overexpansion of the total population. These attitudes do not go unperceived by the persons toward whom they are directed, and it is easy to understand why the contraceptive assistance offered by advanced countries to underdeveloped countries is often regarded with suspicion and identified with "colonialism" and "racism." The problem of checking the growth of the world's total population is gradually forcing itself upon anyone who can count, but the question of whose growth should be checked to obtain the desired result will remain troublesome for some time to come. Very few of the world's large groups can repress the conviction that the ideal population trend would be one that produced more of *us* and fewer of *them*.

Summary / **CHAPTER FIVE**

1. The study of population begins with the size, composition, and distribution of territorial populations. The size of such a population is affected only by births, deaths, and migration. Its composition is described principally in terms of age, sex, race, and marital status. Its distribution takes account of types of rural-urban settlement and their density.

2. The sex ratio is the number of males per 100 females in a given population. It is affected by the fundamental conditions that more males than females are born and that females are hardier than males at every age.

3. The modernization of the world during the past two centuries has been marked by rapid population growth. Modernization induces some reduction of fertility but a much greater reduction of mortality, particularly infant mortality. The reduction of mortality can also be expressed as an increase of *life expectancy;* it is attributable to improved nutrition, the control of famine, public health measures, medical care, and changes in working and living conditions. The maximum *life span* is not affected by these influences, however.

4. The median age of populations varies greatly. High fertility over a period of years lowers the age of a population and creates a potential for further, rapid increase. Median age is correlated with rural-urban residence, social class, religion, ethnicity, and level of modernization.

5. The forms of migration include international migration, internal migration, and residential mobility. The most conspicuous effect of migration throughout the world is a transfer of population from rural to urban places and from smaller to larger cities, with a spectacular increase from decade to decade in the number of metropolitan centers.

6. The growth of the world's population has been accelerating. It doubled from 1900 to 1960, and if present rates of growth continue, it will double again from 1960 to 1990, from three billion to six billion. An increase of this magnitude is entirely outside historical experience and represents a fundamental change in the human condition.

Questions for Discussion / **CHAPTER FIVE**

1 Country *A,* with a median age of 18 has 109 males to every 100 females. Country *B* with a median age of 28, has 91 males to every 100 females. Without knowing anything else about these countries, how might you account for the difference in sex ratio?

2 Country *A* has an infant mortality rate of 50. What does this tell you about Country *A*? Where might it be located?

3 An infant is born today in a population with a life expectancy at birth of 70.0 years. What do we know about his probable age at death? Assuming that he dies a natural death, is it more likely to be at an older or younger age than 70?

4 "The age of a population is largely a function of its present and recent fertility." Explain.

5 Your grandfather probably had at least twice as many siblings as you have. How many different reasons for this probability can you find?

6 Can you estimate the median age of the Mulhouse weavers from the figures on mortality given in the quotation from Villermé?

7 "The immigration of foreign-born males to the United States in the nineteenth century had no serious effect on the growth of the American population." Does this statement make sense? Why? Why not?

8 Why did Galton suppose that the greater fertility of the lower classes in England would lead to a decline in the average intelligence of the population? What was wrong with his argument?

9 Can you give five reasons why the metropolitan proportion of the world's population is not likely to stabilize in the near future?

10 What was the "demographic transition?" What happened to it after World War II?

11 Review your understanding of the following terms:

> net reproduction rate
> metropolitan city
> differential mortality
> population drift
> birth/sex ratio

Recommended Reading / **CHAPTER FIVE**

Thompson, Warren S. and David T. Lewis. *Population Problems.* 5th ed. New York: McGraw-Hill, 1965; Petersen, William. *Population,* 2d ed. New York: Macmillan, 1969; Bogue, Donald J. *Principles of Demography.* New York: John Wiley, 1969. Three excellent textbooks in this field.

Hodge, Patricia Leavey and Philip M. Hauser *The Challenge of America's Metropolitan Population Outlook—1960 to 1985.* New York: Praeger, 1968. Recent and useful studies of the population explosion.

Mayer, Jean. "Toward a Non-Malthusian Population Policy," *Columbia Forum* 12, no. 2 (Summer 1969): 5–13. A short and simple summary of the long-range world population outlook.

U.S. Bureau of the Census, Department of Commerce. *Statistical Abstract of the United States.* Washington: Government Printing Office, published annually with about a 1-year lag; and U.S.Bureau of the Census *Historical Statistics of the United States: Colonial Times to 1957.* Washington: Government Printing Office, 1960, rev. ed., with yearly supplements. The basic American reference books for students of population.

Keyfitz, Nathan, and Wilhelm Flieger. *World Population: An Analysis of Vital Data.* Chicago: University of Chicago Press, 1968. An accurate reference work on world population based on computer analysis of data from many sources.

Malthus, Thomas Robert. *On Population.* New York: Modern Library, 1960. This classic work of the early nineteenth century is the best single source of pre-modern population data.

Notes / **CHAPTER FIVE**

1. For a systematic description of formal demography and its relationship to broader population processes, see N. B. Ryder, "Notes on the Concept of a Population," *American Journal of Sociology* 69, no. 5 (March 1964): 447–463.
2. For an inventory of available demographic data by continents and countries as of some years ago, see Forrest E. Linder, "World Demographic Data" in *The Study of Population: An Inventory and Appraisal,* ed. Philip M. Hauser and Otis Dudley Duncan (Chicago: University of Chicago Press, 1959), pp. 321–360.
3. David M. Heer, *Society and Population* (Englewood Cliffs, N.J.: Prentice-Hall, 1968), p. 43.
4. *Ibid.,* p. 41.
5. Quoted in Warren S. Thompson and David T. Lewis, *Population Problems,* 5th ed. (New York: McGraw-Hill, 1965), p. 390, from a paper by Walter H. Mallory who, in turn, quoted a study by unnamed investigators at the University of Nanking. Note the hearsay character of famine data.
6. From Jean Fourastié, *The Causes of Wealth,* trans. Theodore Caplow (New York: Free Press, 1960), pp. 65–66, quoted from Glotz quoting Flèche quoting the medieval chronicler Raoul Glaber.
7. See Marston Bates, "Role of War, Famine, and Disease in Controlling Population," in *Population in Perspective,* ed. Louise B. Young (New York: Oxford University Press, 1968), pp. 30–49.

8. For a brief but authoritative explanation, see Mortimer Spiegelman, "Life Tables," *International Encyclopedia of the Social Sciences*, ed. David L. Sills (New York: Free Press and Macmillan, 1968) 9, 292–299.

9. Wilson H. Grabill, Clyde V. Kiser, and Pascal K. Whelpton, *The Fertility of American Women* (New York: John Wiley, 1958), p. 291.

10. U.S. Bureau of the Census, *Historical Statistics of the United States: Colonial Times to 1957* (Washington: Government Printing Office, 1957), Series B69–75.

11. Joseph W. Eaton and Albert J. Mayer, "The Social Biology of Very High Fertility Among the Hutterites: The Demography of a Unique Population," *Human Biology* 25, no. 3 (1953): 206–264.

12. Ralph Linton, "Marquesan Culture," in *The Individual and His Society: The Psychodynamics of Primitive Social Organization*, ed. Abram Kardiner (New York: Columbia University Press, 1939), pp. 137–196.

13. Kingsley Davis and Judith Blake, "Social Structure and Fertility: An Analytic Framework," *Economic Development and Cultural Change* 4, no. 3 (April 1956): 211–235.

14. Eaton and Mayer, "The Social Biology of Very High Fertility Among the Hutterites."

15. Bronislaw Malinowski, *The Father in Primitive Society* (New York: Norton, 1927).

16. Hélène Bergues et al., *La Prévention des Naissances dans la Famille: Ses Origines dans les Temps Modernes* (Paris: Presses Universitaires de France, 1960).

17. Roland Pressat, "La Suppression de l'Avortement Légal en Roumanie: Premiers Effets," *Population* 22, no. 6 (November-December 1967): 1116–1118.

18. This definition is taken from Ansley J. Coale, "How a Population Ages or Grows Younger," in *Population: The Vital Revolution*, ed. Ronald Freedman (Chicago: Aldine, 1964), pp. 47–58.

19. *Ibid.*

20. Fourastié, *The Causes of Wealth*, pp. 219–220.

21. Francis A. Walker, *Statistics, Natural Growth, Social Economics*, Vol. 2 of *Discussions in Economics and Statistics* (New York: Henry Holt, 1899).

22. Francis Galton, *Inquiries into Human Faculty and Its Development* (London: J. M. Dent, 1908), originally published 1883.

23. Frank Lorimer and Frederick Osborn, *Dynamics of Population: Social and Biological Significance of Changing Birth Rates in the United States* (New York: Macmillan, 1934).

24. Carl Jay Bajema, "Estimation of the Direction and Intensity of Natural Selection in Relation to Human Intelligence by Means of the Intrinsic Rate of Natural Increase," *Eugenics Quarterly* 10, no. 4 (December 1963): 175–187.

25. Sir Anthony Richard Wagner, *English Ancestry* (London: Oxford University Press, 1961), p. 93.

26. Janet Abu-Lughod, "Urban-Rural Differences as a Function of the Demographic Transition: Egyptian Data and an Analytical Model," *American Journal of Sociology* 49, no. 5 (March 1964): 476–490.

27. Edwin D. Driver, *Differential Fertility in Central India* (Princeton, N.J.: Princeton University Press, 1963).

28. Ernest George Ravenstein, "The Laws of Migration," *Journal of the Royal Statistical Society* 48, pt. 2 (June 1885): 167–227; and another paper with the same title in *Journal of the Royal Statistical Society* 52 (June 1889): 241–301.

29. Everett S. Lee, "A Theory of Migration," *Demography* 3, no. 1 (1966): 47–57.

30. Samuel A. Stouffer, "Intervening Opportunities: A Theory Relating Mobility and Distance," *American Sociological Review* 5, no. 6 (December 1940): 845–867.

31. A somewhat different typology of migration is proposed by William Petersen in "Migration: Social Aspects," *International Encyclopedia of the Social Sciences,* Vol. 10, pp. 286–292.

32. Theodore Caplow, "Home Ownership and Location Preferences in a Minneapolis Sample," *American Sociological Review* 13, no. 6 (December 1948): 725–730.

33. Malcolm J. Proudfoot, *European Refugees 1939–1952: A Study in Forced Population Movement* (Evanston, Ill.: Northwestern University Press, 1956); John G. Stoessinger, *The Refugee and the World Community* (Minneapolis: University of Minnesota Press, 1956).

34. A sociological study of one such camp is available: Alexander Leighton, *The Governing of Men: General Principles and Recommendations Based on Experience at a Japanese Relocation Camp* (Princeton, N.J.: Princeton University Press, 1945).

35. Philip M. Hauser, "The Population of the World: Recent Trends and Prospects," in Freedman, *Population: The Vital Revolution* (Chicago: Aldine, 1964), pp. 17–18.

36. The accepted estimates of world population prior to 1800 are based primarily on the work of Walter F. Willcox, *Studies in American Demography* (Ithaca, N. Y.: Cornell University Press, 1940); and A. M. Carr-Saunders, *World Population* (Oxford: Clarendon Press, 1936). Both sets of estimates are highly speculative, as are those presented for a longer historic span by Edward S. Deevey, Jr., "The Human Population," *Scientific American,* Vol. 203, no. 3 (September 1960): 194–205.

37. The only countries reporting a decline in per capita national income from 1958 to 1965 were Algeria, Mauritius, Brazil, Costa Rica, and the Dutch West Indies. All of these cases reflect special situations: the impact of decolonization in Algeria and Mauritius, and in Brazil; a currency too unstable in 1965 to permit a reliable calculation of per capita income. In Costa Rica, the country with the highest natural increase in the world, and in the Dutch West Indies, population appeared to be outrunning the means of subsistence in Malthusian fashion. But most countries with rapid population growth showed *substantial* increases of per capita income

during this period. United Nations Statistical Office, *United Nations Statistical Yearbook* (New York: United Nations, 1967), table 185. For a masterly analysis of the current relationship between world population and world resources, see Jean Mayer, "Toward a Non-Malthusian Population Policy," *Columbia Forum* 12, no. 2 (Summer 1969): 5–13.

38. Carr-Saunders, *World Population,* pp. 258–259.
39. Data from Richard L. Meier, "Puerto Rico," pp. 284–302, in Young, *Population in Perspective,* table 1, p. 286; and from Theodore Caplow, Sheldon Stryker, and Samuel E. Wallace, *The Urban Ambience: A Study of San Juan, Puerto Rico* (Totowa, N.J.: Bedminster Press, 1964), p. 8.
40. See especially, J. Mayone Stycos, *Family and Fertility in Puerto Rico: A Study of the Lower Income Group* (New York: Columbia University Press, 1955).
41. J. Mayone Stycos, "Obstacles to Programs of Population Control: Facts and Fancies," *Marriage and Family Living* 25, no. 1 (February 1963): 5–13. See also his "Social Class and Preferred Family Size in Peru," *American Journal of Sociology* 70, no. 6 (May 1965): 651–658.
42. For a summary of efforts to determine the optimum size of populations, see Alfred Sauvy, "Population Theories," and Joseph J. Spengler, "Optimum Population Theory," *International Encyclopedia of the Social Sciences,* Vol. 12, pp. 349–358, and 358–362, respectively.

The City

Introduction

A *city is a large, permanent assemblage of buildings and people; it is at the same time a commercial, productive, political, cultural, and ceremonial center.*

Among the characteristic institutions of the city are markets, shops, wharves, warehouses, banks and merchant associations, offices, factories, law courts, archives, property taxation, and police. Its institutions for the preservation and transmission of culture include libraries, museums, theaters, observatories, and schools. For ceremonial activities it has parks, plazas, parade grounds, citadels, temples, arenas, and auditoriums. The city offers specialized services to residents and outsiders by providing such facilities as hospitals, fire brigades, rental services, pawnshops, brothels, gymnasia, public baths, laundries, funeral establishments, beauty salons, and hotels. Every one of the institutions just enumerated existed in ancient Athens, imperial Rome, and medieval Venice; and all of them are found in every large, modern city.

There is no exact population figure that separates cities from villages and small towns. Some settlements with populations as small as 2000–3000[1] contain all of the usual urban institutions, whereas an industrial or mining town of 10,000–15,000 inhabitants may lack most of them.

What Cities Have in Common

All cities, wherever situated in space or time, seem to show certain common features.

1. No city is self-supporting with respect to food and raw material. The presence of a city implies the presence of farmers somewhere in the neighborhood, who grow enough for their own needs and have a surplus left to feed city dwellers.

2. Every city or urban agglomeration is the capital of a region from which it draws people and raw materials and for which it provides a great variety of services.[2] The size and importance of a city is necessarily related to the size and importance of its hinterland.

3. Every city is located at an intersection of roads or routes that connect it to more than one external region. Such intersections are

often marked by a "break in transportation," that is, a change from one form of transportation to another—water to land, or road to railroad, for example. The size and importance of a city is greatly affected by the volume and importance of the traffic intersecting there.

4. Each city is a node in a network of cities to which it is connected by its intersecting roads and routes. Most cities stand in a dependent relationship to some larger center whose hinterlands include theirs.

5. The division of labor in a city is always more intricate than in the surrounding hinterland. More occupations are followed in the city, and those occupations that are shared with the hinterland are more specialized in the city.

6. The inhabitants of the city are more differentiated than the inhabitants of the hinterland; they are usually more diverse in their origins, physical characteristics, religious beliefs, political attitudes, daily habits, costumes, possessions, and modes of recreation.

7. Every city requires policing, and most cities have a great deal of internal disorder.

How Cities Differ

Many cities, particularly of middle size, specialize in one kind of activity, although the whole range of urban institutions is present. Among the familiar types of specialized cities are political capitals like Washington and Bonn, industrial cities like Pittsburgh and Liverpool; shrine cities like Mecca and Lourdes; commercial cities like Geneva and Amsterdam; museum cities like Venice and Antigua Guatemala; resort cities like Miami and Nice; university cities like Madison and Oxford; and port cities like Duluth and Barranquilla.

Besides the differences in specialization and those attributable to size, cities differ in many other ways. Some are incredibly beautiful; others are ugly. Some are planned; others chaotic. Some cities have flowers everywhere; in other cities in the same region, hardly anything is allowed to grow. There are spotlessly clean cities and filthy, bedraggled cities; cities whose inhabitants regard themselves as singularly fortunate and cities in which it is disgraceful to be born.

Theories of Urban Life

Because urban life has so many facets, no single theory provides a broad enough base for all the branches of urban sociology. A standard textbook of the subject includes chapters on the origin and development of cities, the conditions of city growth in historic times, urbanization, ecological processes, the metropolitan region, urban institutions, leisure patterns, the adjustment of migrants, intergroup relations, communication and public opinion, housing and redevelopment, city planning, and some other topics.[3] Nevertheless, there is a fairly definite sociological approach to the city, shaped by a small number of theorists, especially Georg Simmel, Max Weber, and Robert E. Park.

GEORG SIMMEL / THE URBAN MENTALITY[4]

Simmel described the type of mentality that develops in the modern metropolitan city because of its intricate division of labor, which differentiates the individual from his fellows but keeps him dependent upon them. The psychological basis of the metropolitan personality is the "intensification of nervous stimulation" resulting from the number and diversity of images, messages, situations, and impressions to which the metropolitan man is exposed and to which, in self-defense, he reacts with his head instead of his heart.

Intellectual sophistication is closely connected with the money economy, which permits social interaction to be rationalized, standardized, quantified, and kept anonymous. Metropolitan life is also tied to the clock and the integration of individual activities and personal relations into a stable and impersonal time schedule.

In the face of these relatively inhuman demands, the city man reacts with an attitude that Simmel calls reserve, neutralizing personal contacts by indifference and a slight antipathy that protects him from emotional involvement. This mode of interaction protects him against others' demands, and despite the physical and social constraints of urban life, gives the metropolitan man a large measure of personal freedom.

This freedom is as much a burden as a privilege. The difficulty the individual experiences in asserting his own personality within the metropolitan environment threatens his sense of his own identity and drives him to various forms of behavior designed to attract attention and make him stand out from the crowd. Reduced to a negligible quantity by the overwhelming concentration of people and talents in the metropolis, he is driven to exaggerate whatever distinguishing features he can find in himself in order to preserve the core of his personality.

MAX WEBER / THE URBAN COMMUNITY[5]

Max Weber made use of his fantastic erudition to survey the history of city development throughout the world. He concluded that cities in the economic sense had appeared nearly everywhere at one time or another, as had garrisons and shrines surrounded by a settled population, but that the urban community—the city as a fundamental form of social organization—was a Western invention whose development began with the Greek city-states and ran through the Roman Empire and its towns, the fortified settlements of the Middle Ages, and the city-states of the Renaissance to the European and American cities of the twentieth century. An urban community is a settlement predominantly engaged in trade and commerce, which displays certain features:

1. a fortification
2. a market
3. its own law court

4. a local political structure
5. considerable autonomy.

In broadest outline, the history of the Western city has consisted of a slow and irregular expansion of the self-governing part of the community, which, in earlier periods, was limited to a minority of patricians or burghers but has gradually and irregularly grown to include nearly the whole population.

ROBERT E. PARK / URBAN ECOLOGY[6]

Robert E. Park was the founder and principal figure of the Chicago school, whose numerous studies of urban institutions were described in Chapter Three. He was not the only theorist of this school—others were Roderick Duncan McKenzie, Ernest W. Burgess, and Louis Wirth —but it was Park who laid the foundations of what he called *urban ecology*.

According to Park, an urban community is only a special case of the symbiotic community that develops whenever several populations of plants or animals or people occupy a given habitat for whose resources they compete. Competition regulates the number of individuals and preserves the balance between competing species. It gives the community something of the character of an organic unit with a structure and life history of its own. Over a period of time, competition establishes a "balance of nature," or stable equilibrium, in which competition is superseded by cooperation. If the equilibrium is disturbed by some intrusive factor, competition again operates to restore equilibrium and bring about a new division of labor.

According to this view, the city is a part of nature, a biological unit that emerges from the universal struggle for existence. As in the forest or on the sea bottom, certain areas are dominated by certain populations at a given time, but there is an orderly sequence of change through which the community passes during its development. In the course of this sequence, the pattern of the community changes owing to the succession of new species and new functions.

In the urban community, competition is expressed in terms of land values, and one can explain patterns of domination and succession by examining changing patterns of land values. Park recognized, of course, that human societies are more complex than plant or animal communities and that their customs and institutions limit competition to some extent. But he believed, nevertheless, that most of the ties that hold a territorial settlement like a city together are "physical and vital, rather than customary and moral."

The Great Dichotomy

Whereas some sociologists, like those just discussed, have tried to understand the city as a unique phenomenon, others have focused their attention on the relationship between the rural and urban components of the same society, or on the progression farm/village/small town/small city/large city/metropolis.

A large part of traditional sociological theory is concerned with the distinction (sometimes called the Great Dichotomy) between two distinct modes of social life that can be roughly identified as rural and urban. Its earliest version dates from 1861, when Sir Henry Maine distinguished between a rural-traditional society based on *status* and an urban-impersonal type of society based on *contract*.[7] A more influential version was set forth by Ferdinand Tönnies in 1887, in a famous book called *Gemeinschaft und Gesellschaft*.[8] A *Gemeinschaft is a community based, so to speak, on togetherness. A Gesellschaft is an association rationally designed to achieve particular goals*. It is purposive, relatively impersonal, and held together by the common interests of its members.

Emile Durkheim's[9] version of the Great Dichotomy uses terms that at first sight séem reversed. The primitive village is held together by *mechanical solidarity,* the modern city by *organic solidarity*. The first type of solidarity is called mechanical because the human parts of such a system are practically identical and cling together without any need for mutual adjustment. Social systems based on an advanced division of labor are made up of highly differentiated interlocking parts, and each part is necessary for the functioning of the whole system. It is in that sense that Durkheim described the solidarity of a modern, large-scale society as organic.

Other terms for the Great Dichotomy that have been employed by more recent scholars are "sacred and secular" (Howard Becker), "traditional and modern" (Daniel Lerner), "community and society" (R. M. MacIver) and "folk and urban" (Robert Redfield).

All of these, of course, are ideal types. Even Maine and Tönnies were quick to point out that pure examples of their two types are seldom found in real life, and few of their successors have overlooked the point. Indeed, in the formulations currently used, the two extremes serve mainly as points of anchorage for a scale (or continuum) that extends all the way from the most traditional type of village life to the most highly modernized type of metropolitan life.

THE FOLK-URBAN CONTINUUM

Robert Redfield's study, *The Folk Culture of Yucatan,* published in 1941, illustrates the empirical application of a model of social alternatives derived from the Great Dichotomy.[10] In the Mexican province of Yucatan around 1930, Redfield selected for study four communities widely spaced out on the urban-rural continuum: the city of Merida with 96,000 inhabitants; the town of Dzitas with 2,400; the village of Chan Kom with 250; and the isolated tribal village of Tusik with a population just over 100. Merida was the hub of road and railroad transportation in the province; Dzitas was located on a branch line of the railroad and had one passable automobile road and a number of cart roads. Chan Kom was located in the deep bush, a day's walk from the railroad; it had a network of paths and trails but all transportation was on foot or by horse and mule. Tusik was isolated in the forest; its inhabitants did not recognize the Mexican government, and the few paths leading to the settlement were carefully concealed.

Most of the inhabitants of Merida spoke Spanish and were literate; only about a third of those in Dzitas ordinarily spoke Spanish; fewer than a fifth of those in Chan Kom and nobody in Tusik spoke Spanish. The proportion of the population wearing Indian costumes, having Indian surnames, and speaking Mayan increased steadily from Merida to Tusik.

Merida in 1930 had banks, wholesale houses, insurance agencies, department stores, automobile dealers, modern hotels, a power plant, a brewery, factories, apartment houses, a highly centralized state government, a university, the offices of political parties, a daily newspaper, a heterogeneous population, and a clearly defined upper class.

Dzitas had a railroad station, a law court, a public school, a newspaper agency, a post office, an electric-light plant, several small mills, saloons, bakeries, two inns, a plaza with a little park and bandstand, a town hall, a jail, and a movie theater.

Most of the inhabitants of Chan Kom made their living by growing maize for their own consumption and for sale. It was sold to traveling merchants or carried to nearby towns. Some livestock was raised for profit and lesser crops were grown for local consumption. When the study began, Chan Kom had an elementary school, one or two little stores, a bakery, a midwife, a bone setter, several shaman-priests of the native cult, and reciters of Catholic prayers. It was growing rapidly. A little later, there was a plaza, a municipal building, a small open-air theater, a post office, a civil registry, a cemetery, and a Protestant mission.

Tusik had its own tribal government with a council of chiefs and a Mayan priesthood, but there were no storekeepers, no artisans, and no public institutions except the well, the public space around it, and the village church.

The attitudes and beliefs found in the four communities formed a scale parallel to their social and material structures.

In Tusik the outlook on life which one man has is very like that of any other, making allowances for temperamental differences. Even in Chan Kom this may still be said, in spite of the differing degrees to which influences from the city have modified the ideas and practices of individuals. In Dzitas the heterogeneity of mental worlds and of corresponding overt behavior is much greater, while in Merida the range of interest, knowledge, belief, and general sophistication is so wide that in describing the life of the city it is necessary to deal with one social class or interest group at a time, and even then general statements as to the thoughts and behavior of any one of these are more approximate than are corresponding statements for the entire subtribe . . . [11]

At the same time, Redfield is careful to point out that not all of the differences run in the expected direction. It happened by chance that Tusik was the newest of the four settlements; it was founded only 50 years before the study was carried out. Chan Kom was slightly older. Merida was founded at the time of the Spanish conquest, and Dzitas goes back to the pre-Colonial era. Witchcraft and sorcery were virtually unknown in Tusik in 1930; their importance increased from Chan Kom to Dzitas to Merida. All four of the communities were changing at the time of the study and not necessarily in the same direction. Redfield also noted the striking inconsistency of his findings with those of studies of certain Indian villages in Guatemala where the use of money and exposure to outside influences had been deeply rooted in village life since before the Spanish conquest. He concluded that, "A consideration of Yucatan, set against a background of general impressions as to the primitive societies on the whole ... indicates that in the absence of a money economy, isolated, homogeneous societies tend to have well-organized cultures and to be sacred and collectivistic."[12]

RECENT CRITICISM OF THE GREAT DICHOTOMY

The conventional picture of the folk society as small, isolated, nonliterate, homogeneous, solidary, ideologically unified, animistic, personalized, and without a money economy or a complex division of labor or written documents has been sharply criticized by Oscar Lewis, Philip Hauser, and others[13] on the following grounds.

1. The Great Dichotomy identifies the city as the source of social and cultural change but there is some evidence that isolated societies not exposed to external influences may also change rapidly.

2. There is considerable evidence that some of the traits associated with folk societies, for example, extensive kinship networks, superstition, and the predominance of traditional over utilitarian goals are found in some urban populations, as recent studies by Gans[14] and others have shown, whereas characteristics associated with the urban end of the continuum—for example, impersonal monetary transactions, a complex status structure, alienation, and role conflict—occur in isolated and even in primitive communities.

3. The assumption that contemporary folk societies resemble the societies from which contemporary urban societies developed is quite arbitrary. The folk society is not a sociological fossil. It has as long a history as the urban society and may have undergone as much change.

These criticisms do not seem to have completely demolished the Great Dichotomy, but they have considerably diminished its scope. The student of urban-rural differences is now compelled to recognize that the differences he discovers between urban and rural life at a given time and in a given place are not likely to be found in identical form at other times or in other places.

The description of contemporary rural-urban differences in the United States is not as simple as one might suppose. Since the coming of the automobile, American cities have expanded in such a way that they are no longer separated from their hinterlands by definite boundaries. Many of the people who work in any large city and use its facilities live in nearby smaller cities, in newly founded suburbs, in adjacent towns and villages, and even in the open country. Indeed, the process is now so far advanced that more people live on the fringes of large cities than within them.

The Bureau of the Census has discovered that cities are now so differently shaped from what they were in the past that it is impossible to devise a single classification of rural and urban places that gives a picture of the present population distribution and at the same time permits the study of historical trends. By way of compromise, the 1960 census made use of three separate classifications. The oldest of these simply counts the population within the legal boundaries of every incorporated city, town, and village. Incorporated places with populations of 2,500 or more are counted as urban; places with less population are rural. By this criterion, the United States was 63 percent urban in 1960, a considerable rise from the 46 percent urban reported in the census of 1910. In 1950, for the first time, the census used a revised urban definition, which involved drawing informal boundaries for "urbanized areas" containing central cities of 50,000 or more, to include their suburbs and densely settled fringes; new boundaries were also drawn for many unincorporated places with urban characteristics. Under the revised definition, 70 percent of the American population lived in urban places in 1960. Still another census classification is based on standard metropolitan statistical areas (SMSA's). Each SMSA includes at least one county containing a central city of at least 50,000 inhabitants plus any contiguous counties that are densely settled or heavily industrialized or contain large numbers of commuters, or can otherwise be shown to be dependent on the central city. According to this classification, 64.5 percent of the American population lived in metropolitan areas in 1966 (Table 6–1). In comparing the urban and rural populations as they now exist, we are almost compelled to use this last classification to avoid mixing genuine rural districts and small towns with the thinly settled suburbs that surround all large cities to a considerable distance. However, the solution remains imperfect, because a certain number of farmers and villagers who are not closely connected with any urban community are then counted in the metropolitan population.

Obviously metropolitan areas differ from smaller communities in being more densely settled, and having a more intricate division of labor and a wider range of communal facilities. Similar differences are found when smaller cities and towns are compared to farms and villages. There are a number of other noteworthy differences.

1. The metropolitan population is older than the small-community population, which, in turn, is older than the rural population.
2. Metropolitan fertility is lower than small-community fertility, which is lower than rural fertility.
3. Both family income and per capita income are higher on the average in metropolitan areas than in small communities and in small communities than on farms.
4. Average prices and wages are higher in metropolitan areas than in small communities and rural areas.
5. The average level of education is considerably higher in metropolitan areas than in small communities and higher in small communities than in rural areas.
6. Crimes against property are much more frequent in metropolitan areas than in small communities and much more frequent in small communities than in rural areas.
7. Crimes against the person are more unevenly distributed, but the highest rates are found in the central cities of metropolitan areas.
8. Alcoholism and drug addiction appear to be more frequent in metropolitan areas than in small communities and more frequent in small communities than in rural areas.

With respect to other forms of psychological disturbance, the evidence is unclear. Commitments for mental disorders are much more frequent in metropolitan areas, but it is not certain that this reflects a real difference in the incidence of psychoses.

Participation in voluntary associations, religious observance, and political participation do not show consistent rural-urban differences for the country as a whole. Small communities and rural areas may exhibit either very high or very low rates of social participation compared to the metropolitan average.[15]

Table 6-1	POPULATION OF UNITED STATES LIVING IN METROPOLITAN AREAS, 1966		
Residence		**Number**	**Percentage**
Standard metropolitan statistical areas		125,232,000	64.5
Central cities		59,418,000	30.6
Outside central cities		65,815,000	33.9
Nonmetropolitan areas		68,915,000	35.5
TOTAL		194,147,000	

Source: Based on *Statistical Abstract of the United States, 1968,* table 17, p. 18.

Since cities first appeared, they have been centers for the importation and invention of new cultural traits and the diffusion of new traits through the surrounding territory.[16] By contrast, the relative immobility of the countryside and the traditionalism built into agricultural operations tended to preserve old costumes, customs, dialects, artifacts, and beliefs long after they had disappeared from urban centers. The city dweller has usually been able to visit his grandfather's world, or at least an approximate replica of his grandfather's world, by going into the country; and by visiting the remoter villages of the hinterland, he could travel even further back in historic time. Conversely, the peasant who visited the city had a preview of the life his children or grandchildren would lead.

Some elements of this situation survive in the United States today. New England and Virginia are full of little towns that have more eighteenth century buildings than New York or Washington. There are still a few towns to which cowboys ride their horses on Saturday nights and a few places where barefoot children go to school in a one-room schoolhouse, but most of these vestiges of the past are rapidly disappearing.

Beginning 50 years ago with the mail order catalog and the weekly magazine, and continuing today with radio and television and innumerable varieties of printed matter, the mass media bring urban styles and innovations within the reach of the farmer and the villager with a lag that must be measured in months or weeks rather than, as formerly, in decades. Where rural and small-town life continues to have an archaic character, it is more likely due to an economic base—like sheepherding or lobstering—which preserves some of the conditions of an earlier era than to effective isolation from metropolitan influence.

City Growth in the Nineteenth Century

The first half of the nineteenth century witnessed the appearance of the steamship, the railroad, mechanized factories, the mass production of products with interchangeable parts, central heating, paved highways, steel and petroleum, photography, and industrial chemistry. The second half added the telegraph, the telephone, the automobile, the high-speed printing press, electric lighting, antiseptic surgery and, in embryonic form, the radio and the airplane, together with a spectacular, unprecedented improvement of the tools and methods of agriculture.

Cities grew as they had never grown before. They grew upward, inward, and outward. In the central districts of large cities, buildings became taller and more massive. The Crystal Palace in London, the world's first great exhibition hall, was completed in 1859; the Flatiron Building, the first New York skyscraper with a steel frame and curtain walls, in 1902. The density of central residential districts was multiplied by the construction of tenements and the filling in of open spaces. Every city of any consequence burst its boundaries and spilled over. In cities that had been fortified, the walls were torn down and the moats filled in. Everywhere, the suburban zone spread over the surrounding countryside, absorbing the villages and towns in its path. By the end of the century, some of the suburbs of Chicago were more than 50 miles from the city center. Some European cities had expanded more than tenfold in area during the century. These forms of expansion have continued unabated ever since.

In the last years of the nineteenth century, while the systematic study of population was still in its infancy, two extraordinary demographers appeared in the United States. Working without the aid of computers or international statistical agencies, they analyzed trends very effectively. One of these was Walter F. Willcox, who presented his last scientific paper in 1962 and died in 1964 at the age of 103; the other was his student, Adna Ferrin Weber, who was 94 in 1964. Weber's masterpiece, *The Growth of Cities in the Nineteenth Century,* published in 1899,[17] was a comprehensive study of what he called "the most remarkable social phenomenon of the present century"—the concentration of population in cities.

Drawing upon figures from a dozen countries, Weber was able to show that by the end of the nineteenth century cities everywhere were showing a considerable excess of births over deaths and that this natural increase was contributing as much to their growth as migration from rural areas, or even more. He was also able to show that although it was the growth of agricultural productivity and the decline of both the absolute and relative numbers of the farm population that made urbanization possible, the concentration of the urban population in large cities had a multiplicity of causes. These included the growth of manufacturing, mechanical power, the extension of long-distance commerce, centralized government, the concentration of facilities for education and amusement, the economies of large-scale distribution, and the mechanization of urban services. Writing before the turn of the century, Weber was already aware of what he called the "submerged tenth" of city dwellers, mostly recent migrants, who lived in substandard conditions. Even more surprising, he was already concerned about what is now called the population explosion and discussed such possibilities as extracting large quantities of food from the ocean. His book shows that the double problem of the concentration of national populations in large cities and the dispersion of city population into suburban and fringe areas were already obvious to a skilled observer more than 70 years ago.

City Growth in the Twentieth Century

Urban growth in the twentieth century has followed the trends laid down in the nineteenth century. Table 6–2 which combines A. F. Weber's data for 1800 and 1890 with information assembled by the Statistical Office of the United Nations for 1960, shows how continu-

| Table 6-2 | PERCENT OF TOTAL POPULATION LIVING IN CITIES OF 100,000 OR MORE* | | | |

Country	c. 1965	c. 1890	c. 1850	c. 1800
England and Wales	72.2	31.8	22.60	9.73
United States	64.0	15.5	6.00	0.00
Netherlands	47.3	16.6	7.30	11.50
Denmark	37.9	17.3	9.60	10.90
Switzerland	37.0	0.0	0.00	0.00
Scotland	35.1	29.8	16.90	0.00
France	35.0	12.0	4.60	2.80
Austria	32.9	8.0	2.80	2.60
Spain	32.6	6.8	4.40	1.45
Sweden	30.6	7.3	0.00	0.00
Ireland (North and Eire)	30.3	10.6	3.90	3.00
Italy	27.9	6.9	6.00	4.40
Hungary	25.5	3.2	1.35	0.00
Norway	23.2	7.6	0.00	0.00
Belgium	14.9	17.4	6.80	0.00
Portugal	13.0	8.8	7.20	9.50

*For 1965 column, "urban agglomeration" as defined in the source table has been used where available.

Source: Based on *United Nations Demographic Yearbook*, 1967, table 6, for 1965. All other data from Adna F. Weber, *The Growth of Cities in the Nineteenth Century* (Ithaca, N.Y.: Cornell University Press, 1963), table cxii.

ous the process of growth has been. The concentration of population in great cities, limited to the highly industrialized countries in 1890, can now be observed nearly everywhere.

Perhaps the only new factor in the situation is the private automobile, which has made possible the continuously wider extension of suburban areas and at the same time has decreased the safety and comfort of life in the central cities, thereby further encouraging suburbanization, which increases automobile traffic even further. Until World War II, the traffic jam was an exclusively American phenomenon. By 1970, traffic jams were part of the urban way of life from Zagreb to Zamboanga. In many of the cities newly endowed with automobile transportation, automobiles circulated in the central districts at peak hours at a lower speed than pedestrians. This did not seem to discourage other citizens from buying automobiles, moving to the suburbs, and entering the traffic stream.

Since the bombing of Hiroshima in 1945, residence in large cities has carried the risk of total destruction, without warning, at any time. So far, at least, this is a cause without consequences. The vulnerability of metropolitan cities to nuclear attack does not seem to have influenced their recent development in any important way.

The current urban situation in the world is marked by an astonishing uniformity of pattern. Nearly everywhere:

1. The size of the rural population continues to decline and the size of the urban population continues to increase.

2. The number of metropolitan cities and agglomerations continues to increase, and the population of those already existing continues to increase.

3. The total area occupied by metropolitan agglomerations increases faster than their populations, as suburbs, industrial districts, and such urban fringe facilities as airports and cemeteries move further out into the surrounding country. The average density of population in metropolitan areas actually declines while "traffic density" increases.

4. As metropolitan areas expand, some of them run into others and form metropolitan clusters, which in certain respects resemble supercities.[18]

5. The metropolitan cities of the twentieth century share a nearly universal culture. Among the traits of this culture are the automobile, high-rise construction, central heating, air conditioning, telephones, television, daily newspapers, jet planes, automated commodity distribution, the cinema, the restaurant, and the department store. A nearly universal style of dress and nearly universal styles in furniture, decoration, and architecture accompany the larger patterns.

6. The metropolitan culture is diffused from each metropolitan center to the smaller settlements and rural districts of its own hinterland where the local, indigenous culture still survives. In advanced industrial countries, where the process of metropolitanization has been under way for several generations, villagers and farmers participate in the metropolitan culture, that is, they use the same equipment and express the same attitudes as metropolitan people. In countries where metropolitanization is more recent, there are startling contrasts between the city dweller who drives a car, watches television, and sends his children to high school and his country cousin who goes naked, hunts with a spear, and follows the old tribal customs.

7. The material equipment of the metropolitan household improves from year to year in the normal course of events, although it may lag occasionally. The number of households having the basic items of urban equipment—central heating, indoor plumbing, television, a telephone, an automobile, and mechanical appliances—increases steadily until virtually all households are equipped with each item. Meanwhile, new items are invented, and the cycle begins again.

8. The collective equipment of the metropolitan city also tends to improve over time but not as steadily or predictably as the equipment of individual households. The combination of territorial expansion, unregulated population growth, and traffic crowding may overburden public facilities almost to the point of collapse and create what appear to be insoluble problems with respect to slums, water and air pollution, and public transportation. Nevertheless, the actual collapse of a

metropolitan community is unlikely. With contemporary technology, any such community contains more than the minimum resources required for its continued operation.

Urban Ecology

Urban ecology is the study of the relationship between the city as a social system and the city as a landscape.

Every landscape occupied by a settled population is transformed by human effort. The geography of settled areas is the joint product of nature and man. In a metropolitan city, the part attributable to nature is less and the part attributable to man is greater than in other places. The architectural forms of the modern metropolis are less dependent on the natural environment than any architecture of the past. Nevertheless, the study of urban ecology properly begins with a consideration of natural sites.

Almost everywhere in the world, the largest cities are found wherever they happened to be located at the beginning of the modern era. There does not seem to be a city anywhere that, having had a population of over 100,000 in 1850 or 1900 or 1950, has since declined. Any site capable of supporting a large city before the advent of the automobile is capable of supporting a much larger city now. The modern metropolis lives to a great extent by taking in its own washing; its presence on a given site must usually be explained by conditions that prevailed one, two, or three centuries ago. In the United States, for example, the growth of cities in the eighteenth and early nineteenth centuries was almost entirely determined by the availability of water transportation. After 1850, city growth was greatly affected by the intersection of water and railroad routes, the latter being largely determined by the natural topography of the country. After 1900, river and canal traffic ceased to have much influence on city growth, but highway location became important.

Early city building in this country was subject to severe geographical constraints. There is, for example, only one water route which connects the Great Lakes to the East Coast and it has only a single coastal terminus, New York harbor. There is only one navigable connection between the Great Lakes and the Mississippi River system—a canal starting at Chicago. There are only two feasible railroad routes from the Great Plains to California; they terminate, respectively, at San Francisco and Los Angeles, and are now paralleled by superhighways.

In other times and places, the location of cities has been determined by other combinations of factors. In Spanish America, several important colonial capitals—Mexico City, Guatemala City, Lima, Bogotá were located on high plains surrounded by fertile agricultural districts and remarkably isolated from the territories they governed and from the seaports which connected them with the outside world. (As recently as 1910, Bogotá in Colombia was a two weeks' journey away from its principal seaport, by the fastest available transportation.) The prevalence of malaria in the lowlands of these countries was one reason for this pattern. Once established as a capital, each of these highland cities became the center of a vast network of roads and trails, in apparent defiance of topography.

Many of the coastal cities of the ancient Mediterranean world were located on defensible hilltops far enough from the sea to be safe from surprise attack, and with separate subsidiary towns as ports. Mycenae and Troy were such cities, and the pattern may still be observed in Athens and Rome.

On the northwest coast of Europe, ever since the revival of trade in the late Middle Ages, the size and importance of cities has been strongly affected by the shifting of the currents and channels of the navigable rivers. Thus, commercial supremacy in the Rhine delta passed from Bruges in the thirteenth century to Antwerp in the fifteenth century to Amsterdam in the seventeenth century and to Rotterdam, now the largest port in the world, at the beginning of the twentieth century; as channels shifted, old harbors silted up, new canals were dug, and the average size of ships and barges increased. It is interesting to note that the recent shift of maritime traffic from Amsterdam to Rotterdam has led to an enormous expansion of Rotterdam's population, but without any compensating decline in Amsterdam's. Both cities continue to grow.

CRESCIVE AND PLANNED CITIES

The foregoing example is partly deceptive, however, because all city growth in the Netherlands is planned and the population of each major center is held within predetermined limits by means of the simple device of restricting the construction of new housing units so that no more than the desired increase in population can be accommodated from year to year. By contrast, the growth of every large American city, except Washington, D.C., was spontaneous until about 1920, the size and the population and the pattern of settlement being determined by millions of individual decisions. Beginning in the early 1920s, city planning, zoning, slum clearance, public housing, urban renewal, and freeway construction have affected American cities in various ways, but have not deliberately interfered with their growth.

Of course, few cities are completely planned or completely spontaneous. The planned city needs a steady inflow of voluntary migrants to keep up its planned rate of growth, and it is affected by numerous unforeseeable events. The spontaneous city requires a network of public services—streets, public transit, water supply, and sewage disposal, which must necessarily be planned, even if the plans are separate and provisional. Nevertheless, the differences between predominantly planned and predominantly spontaneous cities are important.

In their early development, North American cities were typically spontaneous; most Latin American cities were planned. They form an interesting contrast.[19]

THE NORTH AMERICAN CITY TO 1920: SPONTANEOUS GROWTH

The North American city began with a few wooden buildings around a landing place or at a road intersection. The very first structure was sometimes a log fort or a trading post, sometimes a mill or a saloon or a settler's shack, at first indistinguishable from dozens of neighboring settlements, but in a more favored location. In a few months or years, it had perhaps a hundred cabins, half a dozen well-built houses, a church, a general store with a post office, a blacksmith's shop, a one-room school, a bar, a bank, a cemetery, a jail, a livery stable, and a doctor. Most of the houses would be within a stone's throw of the main intersection, but a few straggling cross streets would already have appeared. In a decade or two, the town had a rough gridiron of streets, a few mansions with large gardens, a volunteer fire company, a public library, a theater, a town hall and a county courthouse, one or two houses of prostitution, a druggist and a variety store, several competing churches, and a railroad station. Around the railroad yard the first slum had already appeared. As growth continued and the town grew into a city, most of the original structures would be swept away and replaced by bigger structures of more expensive materials and swept away and replaced again in the next generation. The street plan of the central area would remain nearly intact, however, and the center of traffic seldom shifted more than a few hundred feet from the point of original settlement. Meanwhile, the entire settlement continued to expand at the periphery and each interior zone continued to expand at its own periphery, so that commercial and industrial establishments continuously encroached on older residential areas, tenements invaded the territory of former suburbs, new suburbs devoured the surrounding farmland.

Land use in the American city is essentially temporary. Although New York was a thriving town in 1650, not a single seventeenth-century structure still survives on its original site in Manhattan, and there are only a handful of eighteenth-century buildings. In some districts of Manhattan, not a single structure dates back as far as 1900. There are sites in Manhattan that have borne 10 successive buildings. Even a relatively young American city like Minneapolis, founded well on in the nineteenth century, has sites now occupied by "fifth generation" buildings.

The pattern of growth takes the following course. Land value is the basic device for distributing population and functions in the growing city. The price of land is highest at the center and declines more or less regularly all the way out to open country. It rises steadily with the growth or anticipated growth of the city's population. As the value of a plot of land rises, the owner's property tax, which is a percentage of the value, rises correspondingly, and owners are forced to convert their land to more profitable uses, for example, by tearing down a private house and building a hotel or apartment building. In the process, many landowners are enriched.

Rich families live in large houses on large grounds near the periphery of the city in places where the price of land is low enough to permit its lavish use, but from which the central district is fairly accessible. A small number of rich families continue to live in the central district, mostly in apartment buildings where the cost of land has been reduced to manageable proportions through putting more families on the same lot. Middle-income families have a choice between multiple housing on fairly expensive land fairly close to the center or single-family housing on cheaper land further out. The poor are usually found in obsolete buildings on moderately expensive land, or in densely populated housing projects on moderately expensive land, or on patches of cheap land near railroad tracks or in other undesirable locations, or on equally cheap land on the urban periphery. As the value of land changes from decade to decade, there are frequent shifts in the residential pattern, as tenants, owners, builders, and speculators perceive opportunities of various kinds.

The higher the value of urban land rises, the more its use is circumscribed. When land in central business districts is sold for $100,000 a front foot, it is necessarily reserved for intense commercial and administrative use, and the dispersed residential population is drawn in and out of the central district with great force. Some two million persons enter the square mile of the Chicago Loop, which has virtually no residential population, every working day. In addition to the mainstream of white-collar workers commuting to and from their jobs, there are vast subsidiary currents of shoppers, truck drivers, sightseers, and theatergoers that swell the diurnal migration.

THE BURGESS MODEL

Until the early 1920s, there was virtually no deliberate interference with the operation of the land-value mechanism. In 1923, Ernest W. Burgess, a prominent member of the Chicago School of urban sociology, wrote his classic description of the spontaneous pattern of the American city as he thought it might appear in the absence of any local distorting factors. The pattern was composed of five major concentric zones, as follows:

Zone I: The Central Business District. At the center of the city as the focus of its commercial, social, and civic life is situated the Central Business District. The heart of this district is the downtown retail district with its department stores, its smart shops, its office buildings, its clubs, its banks, its hotels, its theatres, its museums, and its headquarters of economic, social, civic, and political life. Encircling this area of work and play is the less well-known Wholesale Business District with its "market," its warehouses, and storage buildings.

Zone II: The Zone in Transition. Surrounding the Central Business District are areas of residential deterioration caused by the encroaching of business and industry from Zone I. This may therefore be called a Zone in Transition, with a factory district for its inner belt and an outer ring of retrogressing neighborhoods, of first-settlement immigrant colonies, of rooming-house districts, of homeless-men areas, of resorts of gambling, bootlegging, sexual vice, and of breeding-places of crime. In this area of physical deterioration and social disorganization our studies show the greatest concentration of cases of poverty, bad housing, juvenile delinquency, family disintegration, physical and mental disease. As families and individuals prosper, they escape from this area in Zone III beyond, leaving behind as marooned a residuum of the defeated, leaderless, and helpless.

Zone III: The Zone of Independent Workingmen's Homes. This third broad urban ring is in Chicago, as well as in other northern industrial cities, largely constituted by neighborhoods of second immigrant settlement. Its residents are those who desire to live near but not too close to their work. . . .

Zone IV: The Zone of Better Residences. Extending beyond the neighborhoods of second immigrant settlements, we come to the Zone of Better Residences in which the great middle-class of native-born Americans live, small business men, professional people, clerks, and salesmen. Once communities of single homes, they are becoming, in Chicago, apartment-house and residential-hotel areas. Within these areas at strategic points are found local business centers of such growing importance that they have been called "satellite Loops." . . .

Zone V: The Commuters' Zone. Out beyond the areas of better residence is a ring of encircling small cities, towns, and hamlets, which, taken together, constitute the Commuters' Zone. These are also, in the main, dormitory suburbs, because the majority of men residing there spend the day at work in the Loop (Central Business District), returning only for the night. Thus the mother and the wife become the center of family life. If the Central Business District is predominantly a homeless-men's region; the rooming house district, the habitat of the emancipated family; the area of first-immigrant settlement, the natural soil of the patriarchal family transplanted from Europe; the Zone of Better Residences with its apartment houses and residential hotels, the favorable environment for the equalitarian family; then the Commuters' Zone is without question the domain of the matricentric family . . . [20]

Figure 6–1 is the famous diagram that Burgess drew to illustrate the application of the concentric zone hypothesis to the Chicago metropolitan area around 1920. The irregular line that runs vertically through the diagram represents the shore of Lake Michigan, so that the five zones are concentric half-circles rather than concentric circles. The diagram is not scaled and it is not really a map. It is the graphic representation of a theory. Since it first appeared, innumerable authors have pointed out that it does not apply at all to some American cities, that it greatly understates the influence of topography, and that urban growth takes place in patches and sectors and never in smooth homogeneous bands. All these criticisms are justified, but the diagram contains enough information to have kept a powerful hold on the imagination of urban sociologists.[21]

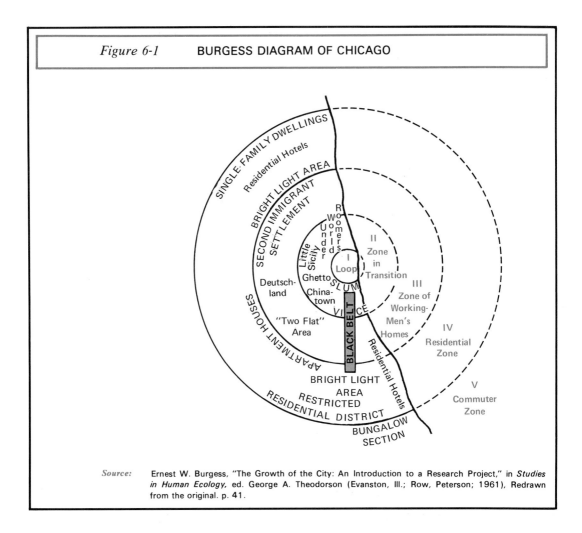

Figure 6-1   BURGESS DIAGRAM OF CHICAGO

SINGLE-FAMILY DWELLINGS

Residential Hotels

BRIGHT LIGHT AREA

SECOND IMMIGRANT SETTLEMENT

Little Sicily

Ghetto

Deutsch-land

China-town

"Two Flat" Area

APARTMENT HOUSES

Roomers

Women Under World

SLUM

VICE

BLACK BELT

I Loop

II Zone in Transition

III Zone of Working-Men's Homes

IV Residential Zone

Residential Hotels

V Commuter Zone

BRIGHT LIGHT AREA

RESTRICTED RESIDENTIAL DISTRICT

BUNGALOW SECTION

Source: Ernest W. Burgess, "The Growth of the City: An Introduction to a Research Project," in *Studies in Human Ecology*, ed. George A. Theodorson (Evanston, Ill.; Row, Peterson; 1961), Redrawn from the original. p. 41.

THE LATIN AMERICAN CITY TO 1920: PLANNED GROWTH

Most of the colonial cities of Spanish America were built in accordance with a single master plan promulgated by the King of Spain early in the colonial period. The resulting pattern differed from the spontaneous North American pattern in several important respects. Land value had only a minor influence on land-use; the plan itself indicated where each function and each social class belonged. There was no marked gradient of density, because buildings were limited in height, were more or less uniform in style, and were seldom torn down and replaced.

Every city was divided into residential neighborhoods called *barrios,* and the plan of the *barrios* reproduced the plan of the city in miniature; each had its own small marketplace, its central plaza was a church and government building, and it could be further subdivided into parishes.

Once the plan had been established and the territory occupied, further growth took place by the addition of entire new *barrios* while the older sections of the city remained substantially intact.

Rich and powerful families lived near the main plaza at the center of the city. Middle-income families lived near the subsidiary plazas of the *barrios.* Poor families occupied crowded settlements at the edge of the city.

The original plan was contained in a royal decree issued in 1573 and labeled "ordinances for new settlements." It specified a gridiron street plan with a main plaza from which four main streets diverged. The size and shape of the plaza, the width of the streets, and the orientation of the plan were specified in some detail. Smaller plazas were to be laid out at the center of each district. The location of public buildings, churches, hospitals, and tanneries and slaughterhouses was also indicated. Finally, settlers were enjoined "to make all structures uniform as far as possible for the sake of the beauty of the town."[22]

Figure 6–2 is a plan of Guatemala City around 1870. It shows that the colonial plan was still virtually intact at that late date.

Urban Nuclei

Before we consider the recent developments that have changed both of the foregoing city types, it may be useful to examine a classification of ecological patterns that is nearly as important as the distinction between spontaneous and planned cities.

Cities may be nucleated, polynucleated, or unnucleated. Nucleated cities, like Chicago or Guatemala City, are tightly concentrated around a single center. Most of the city's internal traffic moves toward or away from the center, and the use of land at any point can be understood only with reference to the distance and direction of that point from the center. Unnucleated cities, like Paris or New York, are not organized around a single point of maximum concentration. Instead, they have vast central areas in which public institutions are interspersed with residential districts. The polynucleated city, like Algiers or modern Berlin, consists of separate quarters or compartments, each with its own central district and its own ecological patterns. These distinctions are relative, not absolute. Even the most tightly nucleated city has important subsidiary centers that are not entirely dependent on the central nucleus. Almost every metropolitan city has some segregated districts that lead a life of their own—Harlem in New York, for example.

RECENT CHANGES IN URBAN PATTERNS

In the past 50 years, North American and Latin American cities have been subject to common influences that have brought their ecological patterns much closer together than before. The spontaneous North American city has been overtaken by planning in many forms. Zoning regulations divide it into districts reserved for separate uses such as

Figure 6-2 GUATEMALA CITY, ABOUT 1870

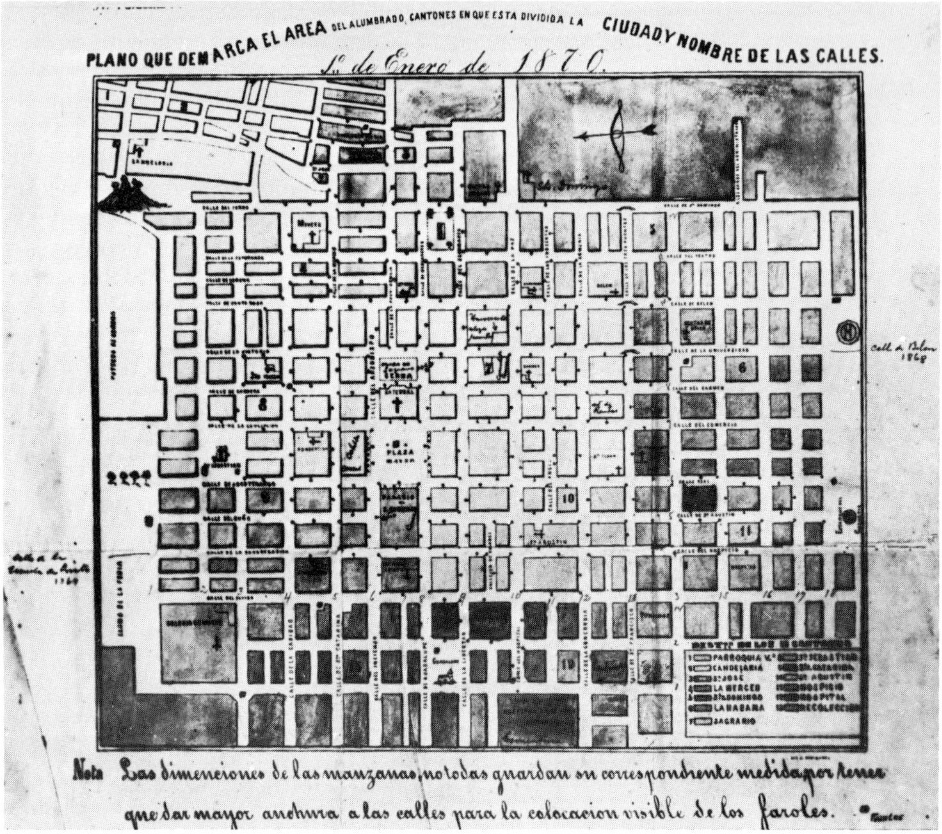
PLANO QUE DEMARCA EL AREA DEL ALUMBRADO, CANTONES EN QUE ESTA DIVIDIDA LA CIUDAD Y NOMBRE DE LAS CALLES.
1° de Enero de 1870.
PLAZA MAYOR
Nota Las dimenciones de las manzanas, no todas guardan su correspondiente medida por tener
que dar mayor anchura a las calles para la colocacion visible de los faroles.

commercial, industrial, multiple dwelling, or single dwelling; they were almost universally adopted in the 1920s together with elaborate building codes to regulate construction methods and the use of structures. Slum clearance and public housing were introduced in the 1930s, followed after World War II by urban renewal, the construction of civic centers, much closer control of new subdivisions, and a vast program of urban freeways. Each of these new procedures reduced the influence of the land-price mechanism and tended to freeze existing patterns of land use in areas not directly involved in redevelopment. During the same era, the planned Latin American city was overtaken by rapid commercial development, a spectacular increase of population, and an even greater expansion of the middle class, which finally shattered the rigid framework of the colonial plan. Land values became highly variable, modern skyscrapers rose around the old plazas and traffic congestion became very severe. The rich moved from their traditional locations near the main plaza to elegant, remote suburbs far out on the urban periphery, and the poor flocked into the slums that now surround the central district. Elsewhere in the older parts of the city, old buildings are being replaced at an accelerated pace and freeways have begun to set the course of future growth.

Ecological Areas

Although the simple arrangement of concentric circles designed by Burgess was too abstract and oversimplified to be of much use in empirical research, it taught sociologists to divide cities and urban agglomerations into ecological areas.[23] *An ecological area is a district within a city that has a distinct history, recognizable boundaries, and a distinctive configuration of architectural and social characteristics.*

Most cities can be divided into a relatively small number of ecological areas. It depends on the investigator how many ecological areas he will recognize and whether noncontiguous settlements with similar social characteristics are grouped together—whether, for example, all the new middle-class suburbs around a city shall be treated as a single ecological area.

Maurice R. Davie, in his classic study of New Haven, identified 25 ecological areas, each of them a distinct territory.[24] On the other hand, Robert E. Dickinson was able to describe nearly all European cities as composed of only three areas, a pre-modern central zone, a middle zone built up in the nineteenth and early twentieth centuries, and an outer zone dating from after World War I.[25] In the study of San Juan, Puerto Rico described below, only six ecological areas were needed to describe a rather diverse city.

There are two reasons why the identification of ecological areas has become a fundamental technique of urban sociology. First, it forces us to recognize the enormous diversity in life style and experience among the people in each ecological area of a city. In many respects, a slum area of New York resembles a slum area of Rio de Janeiro or Johannesburg more than it resembles a suburb 10 miles away. Second, urban social problems are conveniently localized by ecological area, as the following example shows.

THE ECOLOGICAL AREAS OF SAN JUAN, PUERTO RICO[26]

San Juan is a Latin American city that has been exposed to a great deal of direct North American influence, and in many ways it represents a combination of the two types of city discussed above. Its six ecological areas are:

1. *The Old City,* on the site of the walled colonial town founded in the sixteenth century. The street plan has not changed in nearly three centuries; it is a gridiron of less than 10 blocks long in either direction,

organized around two plazas. The oldest buildings go back to the original settlement but have been almost continuously remodeled. The newest buildings date from the present century but follow the colonial style. The residential population is a cross-section of the social pyramid, with the poor very numerous and the rich very rich.

2. *The Beachfront,* a string of districts running along the sea beach at the northern edge of the city. It was not settled until the 1920s, when a few rich families began to move from the Old City to landscaped villas in a park-like district near the beach. After them came the related institutions of luxurious living—clubs, restaurants, private schools, hospitals, and hotels. Eventually, the upper-income families were joined by middle-income families seeking the same style of life on a more limited scale. There has recently been another wave of new construction—tourist hotels and cooperative apartment houses.

3. *The Central District,* a highly heterogeneous area that occupies the neck of the peninsula that connects the Old City and the Beachfront. It resulted from the expansion and merger of a dozen tiny villages between 1900 and 1940. Neither the architectural styles nor the arrangement of public spaces shows any consistent pattern. The mixture of functions is extraordinary. All levels of the population are present, often in the same block. The entire area is crowded night and day by automobile traffic.

4. *The Slum Belt,* a crowded, poverty-stricken district along a canal that serves as the main sewer of the urban area. It was founded as a squatters' colony early in this century, but its chief growth occurred during the 1930s. In 1964, it was five miles long and housed about a fifth of the total metropolitan population.

5. *The Old Suburbs,* which occupy a large tract of ground south of the older parts of the city. There is a scattering of structures dating back as far as the nineteenth century, but most buildings were constructed after World War I. Two great avenues run through the area, lined with a variety of commercial and cultural establishments. Most of the side streets are exclusively residential. The houses in each small neighborhood have a family resemblance because they were part of the same developments. Their style is predominantly North American. Traffic is light, and there is little street life.

6. *The New Suburbs,* which lie south and east of the Old Suburbs on land that was open country only a few years ago. They consist of subdivisions of uniform, single-family homes built in clusters of hundreds or thousands. There are few schools or public buildings of any kind, fewer offices or factories, hardly any theaters or shopping centers. Most families do not have automobiles and are linked to the outside world only by bus transportation. At the time of the study, the total population was roughly equal to that of the Slum Belt but growing very much faster.

We can get a rough idea of the difference it makes to live in one ecological area or another by comparing the Old City and the Beachfront with respect to a few statistical indicators. (See Table 6–3.)

Table 6-3   COMPARISON OF TWO ECOLOGICAL AREAS IN SAN
JUAN, PUERTO RICO, 1960

Indicator	Old City	Beachfront
Population density	70.6	22.8
Sex ratio	118	74
Median family income	$2,054	$8,439
Percent of households with automobiles	11.4	73.0
Percent of population on welfare	19.0	0.4

Source: Theodore Caplow, Sheldon Stryker, and Samuel E. Wallace, *The Urban Ambience:* A Study of San Juan, Puerto Rico (Totowa, N.J.: Bedminster Press, 1964), tables 1-24, pp. 53-63.

OBTAINING ECOLOGICAL AREAS BY CALCULATION

In the foregoing examples, the boundaries of the major ecological areas were established by inspection of the terrain and of maps showing the distribution of various characteristics. Another method is to divide a city into a great many small units, measure their characteristics, and then identify an ecological area as a cluster of units with similar characteristics. One of the first investigators to use this method was Clifford R. Shaw, who divided Chicago into 113 small areas and calculated delinquency rates for each small area before combining them.[27]

Since the census of 1930, the U.S. Bureau of the Census has followed the practice of dividing major cities into census tracts containing approximately equal populations. A typical census tract has about 4,500 inhabitants on about 400 acres. Census data are tabulated and published separately for each of these tracts; this greatly simplifies the statistical construction of ecological areas. Other countries with good censuses have similar units called by a variety of names—wards, police districts, precincts, and so forth.

A number of standard techniques for grouping and combining census tracts have been devised. The best-known and most widely used of these is the technique of "social area analysis," originally designed by Shevky for an ecological study of Los Angeles[28] and later revised for general application by Shevky and Bell.

According to this technique, each census tract is measured on three scales—social rank, urbanization, and segregation. Social rank is a composite measure based on the occupational and educational distribution of the tract population. Urbanization is a composite measure based on fertility, the proportion of working women, and the proportion of single-family homes. Segregation is a measure of the proportion of nonwhites, and of recent immigrants from certain countries, in the tract population. Experience has shown that these measures are not interchangeable, although social rank and segregation show substantial negative correlations in many cities.[29]

THE BLACK GHETTO AND THE WHITE SUBURB

These are the two ecological areas that have attracted the most interest in recent discussions of American urban problems. They are found in every sizable American city and in recent years have grown faster in population than other areas. Moreover, the increases are linked. As white families move out of the row houses and tenements of the central city, they are replaced by black families. When the replacement of a white by a black population has begun in an established residential area, it tends to be cumulative; as the proportion of white families declines, the rate of movement tends to accelerate. In a mere six years, between 1960 and 1966, the black population of the central cities of SMSAs in the United States increased by 24 percent. During the same period, the white population of the SMSA districts but outside the central cities, increased by more than 20 percent.[30] These extraordinary figures are for all metropolitan cities lumped together. In many localities, the shifts were even more dramatic.

The black ghetto and the white suburb are alike in having relatively young populations and a high proportion of children and in wanting new schools and other public institutions. They are both rather homogeneous with respect to income, occupation, education, and style of life. Children in both areas grow up with an extraordinarily limited view of urban life. Most of the people they meet resemble themselves or their own families, and except for the information they obtain through the mass media, they have little knowledge of their fellow citizens in other ecological areas. In both cases, the school is the principal public institution; and the high school supports a special culture of its own.

The differences between the black ghetto and the white suburb are equally important. The standard of living is much higher in the white suburb; houses, furniture, clothing, equipment, and food are of greatly superior quality. There are more health hazards of all kinds in the black ghetto. Crime is much more frequent; drug addiction, gambling, prostitution, and domestic violence are part of the daily environment. Although both areas have high rates of desertion and divorce, the family institution is much stronger in the suburb, where the overwhelming majority of the population live in single-family households composed of two parents, their children, and no other persons. In the ghetto, a large number of families are headed by women, a large number of households contain multiple families or fragments of several families, and a large number of adults live alone or in households without children. Identification with the local community is strong in both cases, but participation in local associations runs higher in the suburb. People in both places are alienated from the city's traditional political structure, but for different reasons and in different ways. In the ghetto, the welfare machinery is an important and uncontrollable factor in the lives of many families. The police and other municipal functionaries are regarded as hostile intruders, against whom the ordinary citizen is powerless. In the suburb, the residents are able to control their immediate local affairs, but disenfranchised with respect to the larger urban community in which they work and helpless to change those features of it that threaten them.

City Planning

Although the development of American cities is still largely spontaneous, *city planning—the design of the physical structure of a city or part of a city in order to realize particular social values—*has become an important factor in every sizeable community. Its principal devices are these:

1. MASTER PLANS AND ZONING ORDINANCES

A master plan is a document prepared by a group of architects, usually with the assistance of economists, lawyers, and sociologists. It describes a desirable pattern for the city that might be achieved at some definite date in the future if the growth of the city in the intervening period could be made to conform to guidelines established in the plan. By itself, a master plan has no legal force, but it often becomes the basis for zoning ordinances that assign space for industrial and commercial expansion and determine what types of construction and occupancy will be allowed in residential districts. A master plan is also likely to influence the public acquisition of land for parks, freeways, schools, and housing projects and the requirements imposed on new subdivisions.

2. MASS TRANSIT FACILITIES

The great expansion of American cities before World War I occurred within a framework established by elevated railroads, streetcars, and subways in the larger cities and by local and interurban streetcars in the smaller cities. In addition, many of the early suburbs were linked to the central cities by commuter railroads and ferries. The expansion of these systems continued at a reduced rate in the 1920s and 1930s; new subway systems were inaugurated in Philadelphia and Chicago as late as the 1950s but after World War II almost all street railways were abandoned, bus lines failed to keep pace with urban expansion, many of the elevated railroads were torn down, and most of the ferries and the commuter railroads were discontinued. The abandoned public facilities were replaced by private automobiles. An automobile passenger occupies about 10 times as much road surface as a bus passenger and requires at least 100 times as much terminal space at his destination. A railroad track can carry about 44,000 passengers per hour, compared to 3,000 or 4,000 for a highway lane. Proposals for the construction of new, high-speed public transit facilities have been widely discussed in recent years and appear to offer the only real solution to urban traffic congestion. For a variety of reasons, most such projects—monorails, high-speed commuter trains, hydrofoil ferries—are still in preliminary planning stages. Meanwhile, the federal government has been proceeding steadily with the construction of the 41,000-mile freeway system authorized by the Federal Aid Highway Act of 1956. By the late 1960s expenditures on highways and street construction in the United States came to more than $10 billion a year, and almost every major American city had been transformed by the construction of freeways through its central district. Among the side effects of freeway development are the destruction or blighting of numerous neighborhoods, an increase in both traffic congestion and business activity at the urban center, expansion of the urban periphery and of the total size of the metropolitan area, improved intercity transportation, increases in land value, and shifts of land use along freeway routes.[31] From the sociological standpoint, the most important effect of freeway development has been to accelerate the movement of middle-income families out of the central city and their replacement by low-income (mostly black) families.

3. SLUM CLEARANCE, PUBLIC HOUSING, AND URBAN RENEWAL

The federal programs intended to remove slums and to provide low-rent public housing for families who would otherwise live in slums began with a single sentence in the National Recovery Act of 1933. About 50 projects of moderate size, combining slum clearance with the construction of publicly owned apartment houses, were undertaken under this clause. Experience with these early projects led to the policy established in the Housing Act of 1937, whereby projects are initiated, constructed, and operated by local public housing commissions with funds provided by the federal government, which establishes the standards and requirements for such projects and changes them frequently. Subsequent housing acts passed by the Congress broadened the scope of the federal programs to include renewal of blighted areas, housing research, subsidies to cooperative and private low-rent housing projects, redevelopment of slum areas for nonresidential use, relocation of persons displaced by highways and other public construction, and a special housing program for elderly retired persons. Nevertheless, public housing in the United States is still fairly modest in scale. The total value of residential construction undertaken under public auspices in 1967 was only $700 million compared to nearly $24 billion of private residential construction.[32] The total number of low-rent housing units under public management in the same year was 673,000—slightly over 2 percent of the total number of dwelling units in the country.[33]

The results of these programs have been much criticized and as hotly defended. In order that public housing not compete with private housing, public housing legislation generally provides for construction at minimum cost and with minimum facilities, which gives many projects a drab and inhuman aspect. Most public projects impose rigid income ceilings on their tenants. This has the weird effect of forcing families whose situations improve in accordance with the goals of the program to move out as soon as the improvement is noted. Moreover, income ceilings have had a tendency to lag behind increases in average income. These regulations turn many public housing projects into segregated enclaves, populated almost exclusively by families on welfare or those headed by women. In many European cities, very large public housing projects coexist happily with private housing, but the terms and conditions of the American formula appear to be self-contradictory.

4. FEDERAL SUBSIDIES FOR PRIVATE HOUSING

The influence of federal policy on urban development has been exerted to a greater extent through the Federal Housing Administration (FHA) program, which subsidizes private residential construction by guaranteeing the repayment of mortgage loans. This makes it easy for builders to secure loans for most (sometimes all) of the cost of new houses and apartments. The Veterans' Administration (VA) program guarantees the repayment of mortgages issued to veterans of the armed forces, mostly for the purchase of new single-family houses. In the typical case, the effect of these subsidies lowers the monthly cost of buying a single-family house on installments below the rent of a similar house.

These two programs largely account for the rise in the proportion of owner-occupied dwelling units in the United States from 44 percent in 1940 to around 67 percent in 1970, of which somewhat more than half were mortgaged. Taken together, the FHA and VA programs affected nearly one-fifth of the private housing units constructed in the 1960s as well as a considerable number of existing dwellings that were purchased or remodeled under the same programs. In general, the policies of the two agencies favor ownership over rental, construction on new land over construction on previously used land, suburban locations over central city locations, purely residential districts over mixed residential districts, large multiple dwellings over duplexes or row houses, and homogeneous over heterogeneous neighborhoods. They are clearly reflected in recent patterns of suburban expansion.

5. SUBDIVISION CONTROL

Virtually all American cities, most towns, and many villages regulate new construction by means of building codes that specify the acceptable materials and modes of construction for a given type of building and the standards to be met in regard to stability, waterproofing, plumbing, wiring, fire resistance, insulation, ventilation, land coverage, and like matters. These codes differ greatly from place to place. They have a reasonable purpose but often lag behind innovations in construction technology and sometimes have the unintended effect of conferring a monopoly upon local builders who alone know how to meet the requirements of a particular code. It is at the local level, too, that control is exercised over the conversion of open lands to residential use and the concurrent establishment of new streets, water and sewer lines, and other public services. The multiplicity of local regulations has retarded technological improvement in the construction industry and kept house-building in the hands of numerous small and medium-sized firms adapted to their own localities. On the other hand, the advantages of mass production, compared to the construction of dwelling units one-by-one, have increased with the increasing amount of mechanical equipment required for a standard home.

The result of these conflicting tendencies has been the appearance of the *residential subdivision* as the vehicle of urban expansion. Subdivisions range in size from a few to a few thousand dwelling units, all of approximately the same type, size and cost, similarly equipped, and designed for families of similar social and demographic characteristics. The subdivision is planned, built, and occupied in a short interval. The builders dispose of their interest as quickly as possible and retire from the scene, leaving the newly created community to fend for itself. How well it can do so depends on the adequacy of local procedures for the approval of subdivision plans. In many cases, when a subdivision is built on vacant land outside an established community, no provisions are made for schools, sewage disposal, bus transportation, and other public facilities. In other cases, all these problems are carefully worked out in advance.

6. REGIONAL PLANNING

Unlike most other modernized countries, which have more or less orderly pyramids of governmental authority extending from localities to districts to provinces up to the national government, the United States has an unbelievable patchwork of local government agencies distributed almost haphazardly across the landscape. In 1962, the United States had 1 federal government, 50 state governments, and 91,185 local governments![34] Many of the local governments have overlapping jurisdictions, and each of the largest metropolitan areas, like New York, Chicago, and Los Angeles, includes *thousands* of local governments—cities, counties, municipalities, townships, towns, boroughs, villages, school districts, and special districts.

Regional planning in the United States was an outgrowth of the Great Depression,[35] and its initial successes had to do with rural development in major river valleys.[36] However, the conception was soon extended to the larger metropolitan centers, and in some cases—the Port of New York Authority is a notable example—regional planning bodies went beyond planning to the construction and operation of bridges, tunnels, terminals, toll roads, and airports. So far, most regional planning in the neighborhood of large cities has been concerned with transportation, water supply, and parks, the facilities that are hardest to provide through multiple, local governments.

The Sociology of City Planning

The essential elements of a city plan are:

1. The description of an existing set of conditions in an existing territory
2. A set of values proposed to govern the future development of the territory
3. The description of a set of future conditions embodying the desired values
4. Specification of the successive steps required to achieve the set of conditions
5. A budget and a calendar for the operation

The sociological analysis of a plan usually concentrates on the second of these elements—the values the plan is intended to realize—and poses questions like the following:

1. Who (persons, classes, groups, organizations) supports these values? Who is indifferent to them? Who is opposed to them? Why?
2. What existing values are excluded or rejected by the plan? Who supports and who opposes the excluded values? Why?
3. What ideology connects the desired values with the concrete proposals intended to realize them? Is the connection rational, empirically demonstrable, or both, or neither?
4. What contingencies external to the plan are likely to affect its realization? How vulnerable is the plan to changes in population size, population composition, traffic flow, and personal preferences? What elements of self-adjustment are built into the plan? What possible consequences have not been anticipated?

When city plans are subject to this sort of analysis, several major conflicts of interest come to the fore.

INNOVATION vs. STABILITY

The bankers, merchants, and real estate men of the central business district; the land developers, shopping center operators, and industrial managers of the suburban zone; together with the federal and state roadbuilding agencies and the numerous persons and enterprises who profit directly from their operations, all have a vested interest in the continuous rapid expansion of metropolitan population, the continuous commercial and industrial development of the urban periphery, and the continuous improvement and enlargement of traffic links between the periphery and the center. By contrast, the great mass of urban residents, particularly those settled in built-up residential areas, have a vested interest in stability. Their neighborhoods are already equipped with an appropriate complement of public and private services, and almost all the changes that accompany large-scale planning affect them adversely, either by raising their taxes to pay for facilities in newer neighborhoods, or by overcrowding established routes of public transportation, or by leading additional traffic past their houses, or by eliminating open land, or by forcing neighborhood merchants out of business, or by an increase in noise and air pollution. The problem is not limited to the United States. European cities like Paris and Florence probably suffer more severely from traffic blight than any American city. During the past generation, the forces of innovation have been completely in the ascendant, and for the moment, it is almost impossible for an urban population anywhere to maintain a secure, comfortable residential environment on the same site for a long period of time.

URBAN vs. SUBURBAN

The central facilities of a large metropolitan area—its theaters, department stores, museums, parks, colleges, railroad stations, warehouses, public markets, and innumerable other installations—are used by the entire metropolitan population of whom a large minority, and in some cases the majority, live in the suburbs. Every central installation involves overhead costs for the central city—police and fire protection, the maintenance of streets and sidewalks, and many other expensive services down to inspecting restaurant kitchens and rounding up stray dogs. Most of these costs are borne by those who live in the inner city. Even when city income taxes or sales taxes are imposed, they apply alike to urban and suburban residents and do not really ease the unequal burden on the urban taxpayer. Many of the urban facilities that are particularly useful to the suburban population—museums, art and music centers, colleges and universities, and convention buildings, for example, are tax-exempt and make no contribution to the overhead expenses they generate.

Meanwhile, the number of urban taxpayers has been declining rapidly in relation to the total metropolitan population. The effect is cumulative—with each rise in urban taxes, there is a further incentive for families and businesses to migrate to the suburbs. The flight of the middle-income stratum of the population from the inner city and their partial replacement by low-income families simultaneously reduces the city's potential tax revenue and imposes a large new burden of welfare and special services. New York City had a total population of approximately eight million in 1968, and in that year, the number of residents receiving welfare payments passed one million. The population of the suburban and satellite communities surrounding New York was approximately the same as the city's, but their combined welfare population was very much smaller.

What came to be known in the late 1960s as "the crisis of the cities" is mostly traceable to this particular conflict of interest. Most of the country's larger central cities are deep in debt; some are nearly bankrupt. Of the 25 largest cities in the United States in 1966, only three (Washington, San Francisco, and Boston) had standing debts smaller than their annual revenues.[37] The public debt of a city is not like that of a national government; it does not generate additional credit, and its interest charges represent a pure loss to the city. It is not surprising that urban public services are deteriorating in many places.

CONCENTRATION vs. DISPERSION

The city planners of this century have had difficulty deciding whether the concentration of national populations in metropolitan cities and the daytime concentration of metropolitan populations in central districts were desirable or undesirable phenomena. Some of the most distinguished planners have put forth what appear to be contradictory proposals. The giant of American architecture, Frank Lloyd Wright, at one time proposed a Broad Acre City whose density would not be allowed to rise above semirural levels. At another time, he advocated mile-high skyscrapers to relieve crowding in central districts. Le Corbusier's 1922 formula for the Radiant City—a contemporary city with a population of three million—envisaged the entire population housed in skyscrapers covering only 11 percent of their sites, with vehicular traffic underground, and the ground surface left entirely to pedestrians.[38] His point, which has greatly influenced the design of modern housing projects, was that such an arrangement would permit much higher density of population than conventional construction—about 1,000 persons per hectare compared to 800 in the most densely populated quarters of Paris.

Some planners have explored the possibility of emancipating the single-family dwelling from the network of urban services. Pushing the logic of the individual automobile to an extreme conclusion, they envisage an individual dwelling powered by its own generator, heated by solar energy, with its own water supply and sewage disposal system.[39] Some existing house trailers come close to realizing this particular dream. A more influential opinion, particularly among younger architects, favors an overall increase in the residential density of cities, obtained by means of high-rise construction, more effective use of smaller open spaces, and the use of "air rights" to make new sites over highways, railway yards, reservoirs, and existing buildings.[40] The effects of residential and traffic density on human adjustment have not been much studied by sociologists or psychologists. Although it is clearly established that residential overcrowding (more than two persons per room, for example) has deleterious effects, it is uncertain whether the same is true of residential density. Expensive and highly sought-after residential districts, like Park Avenue in New York, Lakeshore Drive in Chicago, and Nob Hill in San Francisco, have higher densities per acre than many of the worst slums in the same cities.

The net effect of population growth and suburbanization in most

American cities has been a *decline* in the overall density of settlement, often accompanied by an apparent increase of density because of the disappearance of open spaces, and always accompanied by spectacular increases in miles of local travel per capita.

HOMOGENEITY vs. HETEROGENEITY

For more than 60 years, city planning in the United States was dominated by the goal of replacing the typical heterogeneity and disorder of urban districts by more homogeneous, geometrical, and rational arrangements. This movement took two general forms—the construction of housing projects and subdivisions for homogeneous populations of predetermined characteristics, and the design of clusters of monumental public buildings—civic centers, cultural centers, commercial complexes, industrial parks. The values that underlie such efforts are largely derived from the work of Ebenezer Howard, an English planner who in 1898 proposed to halt metropolitan concentration by building "garden cities," surrounded by green belts, in the countryside for industrial workers. A few such communities were actually built, including Radburn, New Jersey, and Greenbelt, Maryland, but Howard's ideas were principally influential through the writings of his disciples, Sir Patrick Geddes and Lewis Mumford, both passionately opposed to existing forms of city life.[41] Another current of influence can be traced back to Daniel Burnham, the Chicago architect who introduced the idea of the City Beautiful as the theme of the Chicago Exposition of 1893. His vision of great clusters of harmonized baroque buildings to replace the crowded central districts of modern cities was elaborated by such men as Frank Lloyd Wright and Le Corbusier.

Thousands of residential suburbs and scores of government, commercial, and cultural complexes have been built under the spell of these ideas, but in the early 1960s they began to be widely challenged by critics who discovered overlooked advantages in heterogeneity, diversity, and spontaneous growth, and who looked upon the efforts of conventional planners to replace the natural city by a more symmetrical pattern as vandalism. The two contrasting viewpoints are well represented, for example, by Clarence Perry's description of the Neighborhood Unit Plan, published in 1933, and Jane Jacobs' eloquent manifesto in favor of urban diversity, published in 1961.

PERRY'S NEIGHBORHOOD UNIT PLAN[42]

Clarence Perry envisaged the ideal form of urban settlement as a compact, self-enclosed residential neighborhood centered around a primary school. The Neighborhood Unit Plan is a formula for the construction of neighborhoods, not a rigid design. It is adaptable to urban or suburban conditions, to single dwellings or apartment houses or both, and to rich or poor districts. Its six essential elements are:

1. An elementary school population of about 600 (a number determined by the contemporary standards of metropolitan school systems) corresponds to a residential population of about 5,000 people and about 1,200 to 1,500 households within the neighborhood unit. The requirement that even the smallest child be able to walk to and from school imposes a maximum radius of about a quarter mile for a neighborhood unit, which implies a maximum area of about 160 acres. At 10 families per acre, a tract of this size can accommodate low-density settlement in single-family houses. The basic requirements could also be met by apartment houses on a much smaller site. A 10-acre site housing 150 families per acre in multiple dwellings would still permit most of the surface area to be left open.

2. As much as possible of the neighborhood's land is planted in grass, trees, and shrubbery, to encourage outdoor recreation, improve the view, and protect the health of the inhabitants.

3. The neighborhood is bounded on all sides by arterial highways or express streets, so that it is always easier for through traffic to bypass the unit than to enter it.

4. The school around which the neighborhood is organized is located close to the center of the site and any other local institution, like a community hall or a church, whose service area coincides with the boundaries of the neighborhood is placed nearby.

5. The neighborhood is provided with the shops and services required for its daily needs so that housewives, like school children, can make their daily rounds without crossing any heavy stream of traffic. The location of retail establishments (grocery, drug store, laundry, and so forth) at an exterior corner enables them to be supplied by trucks that do not penetrate the neighborhood and to attract outside customers as well. When groups of neighborhood units are built together, larger-scale service centers, including, for example, theaters and department stores, can be established where the boundaries of three or four neighborhoods intersect.

6. The neighborhood has an internal street system that does not match the surrounding external streets. It is adapted to the terrain and the streets wind and curve. The streets and sidewalks are reserved for exclusively local use.

Although few neighborhoods correspond perfectly to the Neighborhood Unit Plan, the six elements of the formula and some of its tacit assumptions (uniformity of architectural style, homogeneity of population) are represented in the design of most of the suburban subdivisions built in the United States after World War II, as well as in the design of low-rent public housing projects.

THE DEFENSE OF DIVERSITY

Jane Jacobs' *The Death and Life of Great American Cities* [43] shook the foundations of American city planning, and its influence began to appear in practice soon thereafter. It opens with a study of the conditions that assure public safety on the sidewalks or urban districts and shows how safety is the product of the casual, round-the-clock surveillance of a public area by a multitude of loosely interconnected persons whose normal business brings them routinely onto the sidewalks and into contact with each other.

> The other day an incident occurred on the street where I live, and it interested me because of this point.
>
> My block of the street, I must explain, is a small one, but it contains a remarkable range of buildings, varying from several vintages of tenements to three- and four-story houses that have been converted into low rent flats with stores on the ground floor, or returned to single family use like ours. . . .
>
> The incident that attracted my attention was a suppressed struggle going on between a man and a little girl eight or nine years old. The man seemed to be trying to get the girl to go with him. By turns he was directing a cajoling attention to her, and then assuming an air of nonchalance. The girl was making herself rigid, as children do when they resist, against the wall of one of the tenements across the street.
>
> As I watched from our second-floor window, making up my mind how to intervene as it seemed advisable, I saw it was not going to be necessary. From the butcher shop beneath the tenement, had emerged a woman who, with her husband, runs the shop; she was standing within earshot of the man, her arms folded and a look of determination on her face. Joe Cornacchia, who with his sons-in-law keeps the delicatessen, emerged about the same moment and stood solidly to the other side. Several heads poked out of the tenement windows above, one was withdrawn quickly and its owner reappeared a moment later in the doorway behind the man. Two men from the bar next to the butcher shop came to the doorway and waited. On my side of the street, I saw that the locksmith, the fruit man and the laundry proprietor had all come out of their shops and that the scene was also being surveyed from a number of windows besides ours. That man did not know it, but he was surrounded. Nobody was going to allow a little girl to be dragged off, even if nobody knew who she was.[44]

In urban neighborhoods designed in accordance with the Neighborhood Unit Plan, this network of casual observers[45] is lacking; the streets are at best, vacant, and at worst, dangerous. The inner courtyards and open spaces of housing projects are not protected by the presence of diverse activities, and they are too secluded to be adequately protected by guards or policemen. The contact of strangers and residents, the maintenance of the delicate boundary between public and private affairs, the round-the-clock surveillance that comes from a mixture of functions and a variety of timetables assure safety not only in the streets, but in urban parks, apartment houses, and public buildings. Turning some of the time-honored assumptions of planning upside down, Jacobs argues for the superiority of sidewalks over playgrounds for children's play, the need for small blocks and numerous intersections, the advisability of discouraging the flow of private automobiles to and from the city center, the advantages of mixed residential and commercial occupancy, and the value of dilapidated buildings that provide niches for marginal enterprises. She is particularly opposed to massive slum clearance, as undertaken under the Federal programs for urban redevelopment and low-rent public housing, because the original operation destroys the social fabric of an existing neighborhood, suppresses hundreds of independent small services, and disperses forever a population that had formed a viable community. The replacement of such communities by huge apartment houses whose residents are surrounded by unusable open spaces but deprived of the small daily interchanges of city life may be a form of blight more serious than the structural deterioration of slum dwellings. So far as the empirical evidence goes, the rehousing of slum families in large-scale projects does not appear to have lowered crime rates, increased family stability, or raised educational achievement as was hopefully expected. On the other hand, a number of urban neighborhoods, like Boston's North End and Chicago's Back of the Yards, have transformed themselves from slums to thriving residential districts without external intervention and without massive transfers of population.

Whether better city planning methods can be founded on these new principles remains to be seen. The obstacles are both fiscal and sociological. In the United States, and nearly everywhere else, it is much easier to obtain funds for the construction of new buildings than for the rehabilitation of old ones, much easier to undertake large-scale construction than small-scale reconstruction. It is doubtful that the movement of urban population to the suburbs can be halted, or that efforts to preserve the city's inner residential districts against traffic blight will have more than limited success. But it is likely that the urban residential projects of the future will be better adapted to the needs of their residents than those built in the recent past.

1   All cities, wherever situated in space and time, have many features in common and many of the same institutions. The contrast between urban and rural styles of life is one of the permanent features of human society.

2   Nearly everywhere in the modern world, the urban population has been increasing in relation to the rural population for many years, and the metropolitan population has been increasing in relation to the population of smaller cities. These trends are likely to continue until most of the population in most regions is settled in metropolitan cities.

3   Cities differ in their modes of growth (some grow spontaneously and others are planned); in their patterns of centralization; and in the number and type of distinctive districts, or ecological areas, they contain. In all cities, the conditions of life differ enormously from one ecological area to another.

4   In recent years, planning has become increasingly important in the growth of American cities, but there is a great deal of disagreement about the goals toward which planning ought to be directed and about the characteristics of a desirable urban neighborhood. Hence, some of the current programs for solving urban problems are self-contradictory.

Questions for Discussion / CHAPTER SIX

1   Select a small city with which you are familiar and identify the road, rail, and water routes at whose intersection it stands. Can you see any ways in which the location of these routes influenced the internal growth of the city?

2   Taking the same city, can you describe its ecological patterns around 1900 by observing it now, without using any old maps or documentary evidence? What was the principal effect of the automobile on the 1900 pattern?

3   Why does the growth of suburbs around a metropolitan city tend to increase racial segregation in the central city?

4   Professor Edward Banfield writes, "The range of feasible measures for dealing with the serious problems of the cities is much narrower than one might think. Moreover, within this range hardly any of the measures are acceptable." What does this statement mean? Would you agree or disagree with it?

5 Why is the public debt of a city unlike the public debt of a national government?

6 Plot on a map the distribution of fires, old age assistance cases, and crimes of violence obtained from the municipal administration in a small city with which you are familiar. How do you account for the relationship among the three distributions?

7 How might a city plan for heterogeneity?

8 What are the principal obstacles to the reduction of urban traffic congestion? Of racial violence in cities?

Recommended Reading / CHAPTER SIX

McKelvey, Blake. *The Emergence of Metropolitan America, 1915–1966*. New Brunswick, N.J.: Rutgers University Press, 1968. Traces the development of contemporary urban problems.

Stewart, Cecil. *A Prospect of Cities: Being Studies Towards a History of Town Planning*. London: Longmans, Green and Co., 1952. An unsystematic but fascinating introduction to the history of European cities.

Boskoff, Alvin. *The Sociology of Urban Regions,* 2d ed. New York: Appleton-Century-Crofts, 1970; and Gist, Noel P. and Sylvia Fleis Fava. *Urban Society,* 5th ed. New York: Thomas Y. Crowell, 1964. Two excellent textbooks of urban sociology.

Jacobs, Jane. *The Death and Life of Great American Cities.* New York: Random House, 1961. An eloquent introduction to current urban problems and proposals for solving them.

Banfield, Edward C. *The Unheavenly City: The Nature and Future of Our Urban Crisis.* Boston: Little, Brown, 1968. Presents an unconventional view of the current urban crisis.

Liebow, Elliot. *Tally's Corner: A Study of Negro Streetcorner Men.* Boston: Little, Brown, 1967; Taeuber, Karl E. and Alma F. Taeuber. *Negroes in Cities: Residential Segregation and Neighborhood Change.* New York: Atheneum, 1969; Clark, Kenneth B. *Dark Ghetto: Dilemmas of Social Power.* New York: Harper & Row, 1965; Moore, William, Jr. *The Vertical Ghetto: Everyday Life in an Urban Development.* New York: Random House, 1969; Hannerz, Ulf. *Soulside: Inquiries into Ghetto Culture and Community.* New York: Columbia University Press, 1969; and Schultz, David A. *Coming Up Black: Patterns of Ghetto Socialization.* Englewood Cliffs, N.J.: Prentice-Hall, 1969. A series of readings on the black ghetto.

Dobriner, William M. *Class in Suburbia.* Englewood Cliffs, N.J.: Prentice-Hall, 1963; Gans, Herbert J. *The Levittowners: Ways of Life and Politics in a New Suburban Community.* New York: Pantheon, 1967;

Berger, Bennett M. *Working-Class Suburb: A Study of Auto Workers in Suburbia*. Berkeley: University of California Press, 1960; Gordon, Richard E., Katherine K. Gordon, and Max Gunther. *The Split-Level Trap*. New York: Bernard Geis Associates, 1961. A series of readings on the white suburb.

Notes / CHAPTER SIX

1. See Marvin Harris, *Town and Country in Brazil* (New York: Columbia University Press, 1956) for a description of a tiny, remote Brazilian settlement with characteristics of a city.
2. An early and very interesting study by Galpin showed that villages and towns in Wisconsin were surrounded by clearly defined "trade areas." See Charles Josiah Galpin, *Rural Life* (New York: Century, 1918).
3. Noel P. Gist and Sylvia Fleis Fava, *Urban Society,* 5th ed. (New York: Thomas Y. Crowell, 1964).
4. Georg Simmel, "The Metropolis and Mental Life," in *The Sociology of Georg Simmel,* ed. Kurt H. Wolff (New York: Free Press, 1950), pp. 409–424.
5. Max Weber, *The City,* trans. Don Martindale and Gertrud Neuwirth (New York: Free Press, 1958).
6. Robert Ezra Park, "Human Ecology," *American Journal of Sociology* 42, no. 1 (July 1936): 1–15.
7. Sir Henry James Sumner Maine, *Ancient Law: Its Connection with the Early History of Society and Its Relation to Modern Ideas* (New York: Dutton, 1960). Originally published 1861.
8. Ferdinand Tönnies, *Community and Society (Gemeinschaft und Gesellschaft),* ed. and trans. Charles P. Loomis (East Lansing: Michigan State University Press, 1957). Originally published 1887.
9. Émile Durkheim, *The Division of Labor in Society,* trans. George Simpson (New York: Macmillan, 1933). Originally published 1893.
10. Robert Redfield, *The Folk Culture of Yucatan* (Chicago: University of Chicago Press, 1941).
11. *Ibid.,* p. 110.
12. *Ibid.,* pp. 368–369.
13. For summaries of these criticisms, see Oscar Lewis, "Further Observations on the Folk-Urban Continuum and Urbanization with Special Reference to Mexico City," and Philip M. Hauser, "Observations on the Urban-Folk and Urban-Rural Dichotomies as Forms of Western Ethnocentrism," in *The Study of Urbanization,* ed. Philip M. Hauser and Leo F. Schnore (New York: John Wiley, 1965), pp. 491–502 and 503–518, respectively.
14. See especially Herbert J. Gans, *The Urban Villagers: Group and Class in the Life of Italian Americans* (New York: Free Press, 1965).
15. Murray Hausknecht, *The Joiners: A Sociological Description of*

Voluntary Association Membership in the United States (Totowa, N.J.: Bedminster Press, 1962), particularly p. 26.

16. The early origins of cities are described in Gideon Sjoberg, *The Preindustrial City: Past and Present* (New York: Free Press, 1960), especially Chaps. 2 and 3; Eric Lampand, "Historical Aspects of Urbanization," in Hauser and Schnore, *The Study of Urbanization,* pp. 519–554; and Jean Comhaire and Werner J. Cahnman, *How Cities Grew: The Historical Sociology of Cities* (Madison, N.J.: Floreham Park Press, 1959).

17. Adna Ferrin Weber, *The Growth of Cities in the Nineteenth Century: A Study in Statistics* (Ithaca, N.Y.: Cornell University Press, 1963). Originally published 1899.

18. The somewhat fanciful notion that the Eastern seaboard of the United States from Washington, D.C. to Boston comprises one "megapolis" has been publicized by Jean Gottman. See his *Megapolis: The Urbanized Northeastern Seaboard of the United States* (New York: Twentieth Century Fund, 1961).

19. For an authoritative review of the evidence for the existence of contrasting patterns of city growth in North America and Latin America, see Leo F. Schnore, "On the Spatial Structure of Cities in the Two Americas," in Hauser and Schnore, *The Study of Urbanization,* pp. 347–398.

20. Ernest W. Burgess, "The Growth of the City," paper prepared for the annual meetings of the American Sociological Society, 1923. Reprinted in Schnore, *ibid.,* pp. 349–351.

21. For an excellent selection of these criticisms, see Section B, "Criticisms of the Classical Position," in George A. Theodorson, ed., *Studies in Human Ecology* (Evanston, Ill.: Row, Peterson, 1961), pp. 77–126.

22. *Bulas y Cedulas para el Gobierno de las Indias* (Madrid: Archivo Nacional de Espana, ms. 3017), trans. Zelia Nuttall, "Royal Ordinances Concerning the Laying Out of New Towns," *Hispanic American Historical Review* 5 (1922): 249-254.

23. Sometimes called "natural areas," not because they are determined by the terrain but because they are unplanned.

24. Maurice R. Davie, "The Pattern of Urban Growth," in *Studies in the Science of Society,* ed. George Peter Murdock (Freeport, N.Y.: Books for Libraries Press, 1937), pp. 133–161.

25. Robert E. Dickinson, *City Region and Regionalism: A Geographical Contribution to Human Ecology* (New York: Oxford University Press, 1947).

26. Theodore Caplow, Sheldon Stryker, and Samuel E. Wallace, *The Urban Ambience: A Study of San Juan, Puerto Rico* (Totowa, N.J.: Bedminster Press, 1964).

27. Clifford R. Shaw, *Delinquency Areas* (Chicago: University of Chicago Press, 1929); facsimile edition (Ann Arbor: University of Michigan Press, 1967).

28. Eshref Shevky and Wendell Bell, *Social Area Analysis: Theory, Illustrative Application, and Computational Procedures* (Stanford,

Calif.: Stanford University Press, 1955). For an interesting attempt to apply the Shevky-Bell method to India's largest city, see Brian J. L. Berry and Philip H. Reese, "The Factorial Ecology of Calcutta," *American Journal of Sociology* 74, no. 5 (March 1969): 445–491.

29. Maurice D. Van Arsdol, Santo F. Camilleri, and Calvin F. Schmid, "The Generality of Urban Social Area Indexes," *American Sociological Review* 23, no. 3 (June 1958): 277–283.

30. U.S. Bureau of the Census, Department of Commerce, *Statistical Abstract of the United States, 1968* (Washington: Government Printing Office, published annually), table 17.

31. H. Kirk Danserau, "Some Implications of Modern Highways for Community Ecology," in Theodorson, *Studies in Human Ecology,* pp. 175–187.

32. *Statistical Abstract of the United States, 1968,* table 17.

33. *Ibid.,* tables 1086 and 1088.

34. Lee Taylor and Arthur R. Jones, Jr., *Rural Life and Urbanized Society* (New York: Oxford University Press, 1964), pp. 433–440.

35. For a wide survey of this field, see John Friedmann and William Alonso, *Regional Development and Planning: A Reader* (Cambridge, Mass.: M.I.T. Press, 1964).

36. The Tennessee Valley Authority (TVA) was the best-known regional planning agency.

37. *Statistical Abstract of the United States, 1968,* table 602.

38. LeCorbusier (pseudonym of Charles Edouard Jeanneret-Gris), *The Radiant City: Elements of a Doctrine of Urbanism to be Used as the Basis of Our Machine-Age Civilization* (New York: Orion Press, 1967), originally published 1933.

39. Ralph Borsodi, *Flight From the City: The Story of a New Way to Family Security* (New York: Harper & Row, 1933).

40. William H. Whyte, "Cities to Live In: Planning Versus the Inevitable," *Current,* no. 103 (January 1969): 48–58.

41. For an elegant presentation of their viewpoint, see Lewis Mumford, *The Culture of Cities* (New York: Harcourt Brace Jovanovich, 1938).

42. Clarence A. Perry, *The Rebuilding of Blighted Areas: A Study of the Neighborhood Unit in Replanning and Plot Assemblage* (New York: Regional Plan Association, 1933).

43. Jane Jacobs, *The Death and Life of Great American Cities* (New York: Random House, 1961).

44. *Ibid.,* pp. 38–39.

45. For an empirical study of the isolation of project residents, see Louis Kriesberg, "Neighborhood Setting and the Isolation of Public Housing Tenants, in *Urbanism, Urbanization and Change: Comparative Perspectives,* eds. Paul Meadows and Ephraim H. Mizruchi (New York: Addison-Wesley, 1969).

Stratification

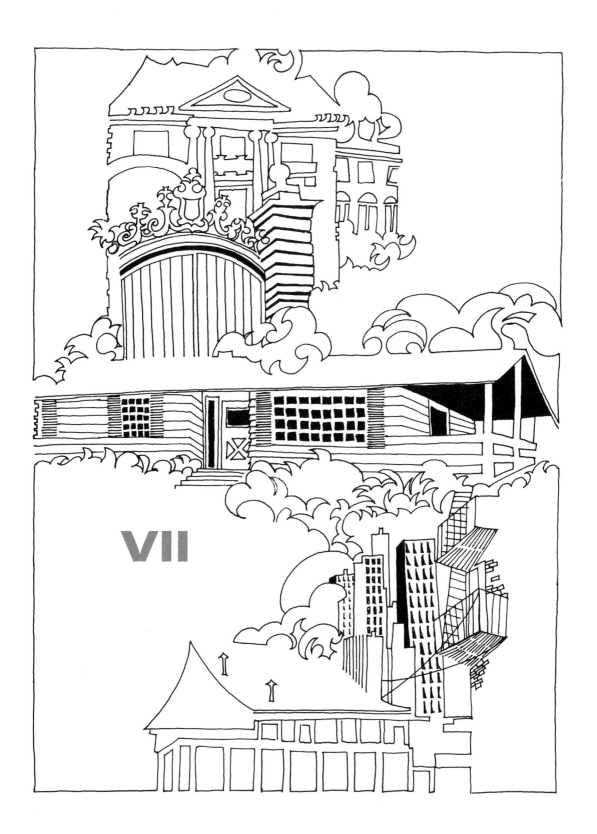

VII

Introduction

Stratification is the arrangement of the members of a social system in graded strata, with varying degrees of prestige, property, influence, and other status attributes. In current usage, the term stratification is mostly used to describe the distribution of status in a nation or a community. Such a distribution is called a *status order.* Although societies differ greatly with respect to the inheritance of status, the fundamental unit of stratification is the family rather than the individual.

A social class is a segment of a status order with a common identity recognized by its members and others. An estate is a legally recognized social class. A caste is a social class in which membership is hereditary and (in principle) unchangeable.

All modern societies, advanced and underdeveloped, capitalist and communist, large and small, have elaborate status orders. Whether all of them have social classes is a debatable question that will be considered at some length in this chapter.

The study of stratification is complicated by the fact that status orders have multiple bases and multiple consequences. Among the usual determinants of status in modern societies are occupation, education, property, lineage, ethnicity, religion, affiliations, and personal influence.

The consequences of occupying a given status are extremely numerous and complex. Broom and Selznick[1] present evidence from a number of recent studies showing that Americans of higher status have more years of education, more children attending college, less divorce, lower mortality, better dental care, and less chance of having a fat wife. High-status persons are more likely to vote conservatively, attend church, read a daily newspaper, have close friends, and say they are very happy. All of the empirical evidence on this topic indicates that people of higher status are better off *on the average* than people of lower status, with respect either to objectively measurable benefits or subjective reports of satisfaction. It goes without saying, of course, that these average differences conceal a great deal of individual variation and that some welfare clients are happier and healthier than some U.S. Senators.

The position of an individual and his family in a status order normally starts with some kind of social power—income, property, officeholding, personal influence, membership in valuable organizations, the possession of a rare skill, or access to rare goods. A given amount of power makes it possible to sustain a given style of life with appropriate housing, food, clothing, costume, rituals, and forms of recreation. A given style of life entitles its incumbents to a given amount of what Max Weber called "social honor"—prestige, esteem, or recognition. The satisfaction associated with high status is a mixture of material rewards (the captain eats better and more varied food than the crew) and social rewards (the captain likes giving orders more than the crew likes taking orders).[2]

Achieved vs. Ascribed Status

Achieved status is what an individual has as a result of his own actions; it is a social evaluation of those actions. One achieves a higher status, for example, by becoming a college graduate, a home-owner, a senior civil servant, the father of a boy, or a black-belt karate expert; and a lower status by becoming a prisoner, a skid row derelict, or a bankrupt.

Ascribed status is status awarded for attributes of the individual over which he has no control and which he is not expected to be able to change. Sex, race, age, origin, and appearance are the most common grounds on which status is ascribed.

In every known society status is determined both by achievement and by ascription, but most societies regard one of these methods of allocating status as more legitimate than the other. In the Hindu caste system, a family's status is *supposed* to be fixed by ascription and to remain unchanged from one generation to the next. In fact, achievement plays a considerable part in Hindu society, and empirical studies have shown a fair amount of mobility among Indian castes and sub-castes.[3] In American society, which claims to base status on achievement, the most superficial inquiry will show that ascription plays a very large part in determining status. Almost every industrialized nation (except the Republic of South Africa) is firmly committed to the juridical equality of its citizens before the law and to an ideology of equal opportunity. But these principles have very different meanings with the "Eastern" and "Western" types of national society, and even from one nation to another within these two categories.* In the Eastern system, all status is derived from occupations and must be confirmed by the state bureaucracy. Property, inherited or acquired, is specifically excluded as a source of status. The legal system makes it difficult to inherit any large amount of property, and the state under-

---

*Industrialized or semi-industrialized nations with "Eastern" systems include the Soviet Union, Czechoslovakia, Rumania, Hungary, Poland, Yugoslavia, China, and Cuba. Those with "Western" systems are more numerous although their total population is less. Besides the United States, Great Britain, France, West Germany, Italy, the Netherlands, Belgium and the Scandinavian countries, the category includes Canada, Australia, Israel, and a few of the Latin American countries. The Eastern countries are communist; the Western countries are capitalist or socialist or a mixture of both.

takes to undermine the position of those who have somehow acquired property. "The leading bodies and cooperatives," says the Little Red Book of Mao Tse-Tung, "must establish the dominant position of the poor peasants and the new lower-middle and the upper-middle peasants—whether old or new. ... There is a serious tendency toward capitalism among the well-to-do peasants. This tendency will become rampant if we in the slightest way neglect political work among the peasants. ... "[4]

There seem to be two varieties of occupational stratification in the Eastern system, one exclusively occupational, the other taking account of party membership. The ranking of occupations in the Eastern system is not distinctive except for the absence of private property as a factor in the assignment of persons to managerial positions. In the Eastern system, as in the Western, white-collar occupations rank higher than blue-collar occupations, and blue-collar industrial occupations are considered superior to service occupations. Supervisors have higher status than the people they supervise; white-collar occupations are stratified by the education required and the responsibility involved; and there is an elite of high-ranking functionaries in the state, the army, and the party who enjoy a luxurious style of life.[5]

With respect to descent and ethnicity, the workings of the Eastern system are more obscure. The attribution of status on the basis of individual lineage is of course taboo, but descent continues to play a part in several ways: first, in the provision of superior educational and recreational opportunities for the children of party members; second, in the distinction between good (worker and peasant) ancestry and bad (middle- or upper-class) ancestry; and third, in the persistence of discriminatory attitudes toward minority groups.

The Western system of stratification, by contrast, is a fantastic patchwork made up of bits and pieces that are partly historical, partly contemporary, sometimes real, and sometimes imaginary. Patterns of stratification vary greatly from one country to another and often from one town to the next. The inheritance of wealth, productive property, and social privileges is considered entirely legitimate, although subject to regulation by the state and tending to diminish over time. Personal lineage—descent from notables, the ability to trace a long chain of ancestors, residence in a particular place for several generations—are all positive status factors. Most of the western European countries, whether monarchical or republican, continue to recognize titles of nobility and other hereditary marks of distinction; the United States has evolved an elaborate system of private associations for establishing claims to status on the basis of descent from early settlers. Ethnicity and religion, sometimes separate and sometimes merged, are major factors in status ascription throughout the western system. To be a Welshman in London, a Sephardic Jew in New York, a Frieslander in Amsterdam, or a Bavarian Catholic in Berlin is to have a large part of one's status already determined.

Finally, race plays a very large part in the Western system of stratification wherever there are racially distinguishable populations. Indeed, this is the weak point of the Western system compared to the Eastern system.

The argument for the Eastern system is that it bases status on achievement alone. The argument against it is that, since the individual's status is totally dependent on the decisions of a monocratic government, he remains helpless and unfree regardless of the status he achieves. "All the animals are equal," wrote Orwell in *Animal Farm,* his parody of a totalitarian state, "but some are more equal than others."

The argument for the Western system is that it enlarges the scope of achievement by allowing the individual to transmit to his children and grandchildren some part of the status he achieves, while the element of ascription involved in the inheritance of property and prestige gives the individual a considerable degree of personal freedom by making it impossible for the state or any of its agencies to manipulate his status at will. It is not only in the twentieth century that men have perceived the state as a danger to themselves. The theory that private property is the best defense against the tyranny of the state was first set out by John Locke in the seventeenth century and has been one of the fundamental components of the democratic ideology ever since.

The reason why race is the weak point of the Western system wherever there are large minorities of non-European descent is that status based on skin color is pure ascription unsoftened by any element of achievement. What is even worse, it is a form of ascription without the flexibility that permits upwardly mobile persons elsewhere in the system to change their ethnicity, exaggerate the status of their ancestors, or develop new lineage claims. Blacks in the United States have recently begun to do all of these things, but so far, without much effect on the perceptions of the white population. The problem is compounded in the United States by the absence of centralized historical records and the freedom with which white persons can aggrandize the status of their ancestors as their own status improves. Ascription keeps pace, so to speak, with achievement. This is much more difficult for black persons to do if they are identified as the descendants of slaves, and little attention is paid to other components of their ancestry. With the shift of the black population from farm labor to diversified urban occupations, the incongruity between achieved status based on education and occupation and ascribed status based on race has increased to an almost insupportable degree. The people involved develop a profound sense of injustice and the legitimacy of the entire western system is called into question because of this flaw.

Historical Patterns of Stratification

The two related ideals of universal equality before the law and the grounding of family status on achievement are modern innovations, which appeared in Europe toward the end of the seventeenth century about the same time as the earliest bureaucracies and the beginnings of the Industrial Revolution. Practically all earlier societies had been composed of hereditary classes with unequal privileges recognized by law and accepted as right and proper.[6] The American and French Revolutions did not abruptly do away with the estate system, but did remove its legal and ideological basis so that the old estates were replaced by vaguely defined classes. The relationship between this new arrangement and the one it replaced was one of the first problems to be studied sociologically in the nineteenth century. As Raymond Aron remarks:

> Pre-Revolutionary society was composed of orders or estates. Before 1789 the French were not born free and equal; they did not all have the same rights; they were not all subject to the same obligations. Social heterogeneity was considered normal— heterogeneity not only of occupation, of income, and of living conditions but also of juridical status. Whatever social mobility there was, classes appeared hereditary; the juridical status of the noble like that of the non-noble was determined at birth. The French Revolution generated a society whose principles were fundamentally different. All the members of society became theoretically subject to the same legislation and, although limitations on the right of suffrage and the distinction between active and passive citizens were maintained in Western Europe for much of the last century, the accepted ideology recognized and proclaimed the universal extension of citizenship.[7]

VESTIGES OF THE ESTATE SYSTEM IN THE MODERN WORLD

The feudal society that flourished in Europe from about 900 A.D. to about 1400 was basically composed of knights, priests, townsmen, and peasants. Medieval society was marked by great diversity, and there were many variations of detail from one place and time to another, but the four estates just mentioned (plus perhaps a fifth estate of "strangers") were found everywhere. Each of them had its own laws, its own symbolism, and an elaborate internal stratification of its own. Certain cultural traits that are still conspicuous in the contemporary Western system of stratification can be traced directly back to the medieval estates, and vestiges of these ancient status orders are prominently displayed in events as diverse as real estate transactions, commencement ceremonies, county fairs, military parades, and Ph.D. examinations. The estates were organized as follows.[8]

KNIGHTS

The position of the medieval knight was based on land ownership, a monopoly of cavalry warfare, and service to an overlord, all three elements being closely related.

Land was held under the peculiar system called *vassalage,* whereby a knight held a village or a group of villages "in fee" from an overlord, who held his larger territory from a higher overlord and so on up to the king. A *fief,* as this kind of grant was called, was based in principle on a personal relationship between the lord and the vassal. Before entering into possession of his grant, the vassal took an oath of fealty in which he promised his lord loyalty and military service in exchange for protection. When fiefs became hereditary, as most of them eventually did, the new heir was still required to take a personal oath of fealty and to have his possession confirmed. Fiefs without male heirs often reverted to the grantor.

Since fiefs were personal relationships, all sorts of special arrangements were possible. A knight might hold fiefs from five or six different overlords. His status within the feudal hierarchy depended both on the amount of land he held and on the hierarchical level at which he held it. In the course of time, hereditary titles, hierarchically ordered, were attached to particular fiefs, but the inheritance of a title and the personal rank that went with it did not become automatic until the feudal system disappeared.

The entire structure of medieval society rested on the tactical superiority of the armored horseman over the foot soldier. Horsemanship and the use of the sword were very jealously monopolized, and could be taught only by knights to suitably sponsored candidates. In principle, the candidate had to demonstrate his military competence. Induction into knighthood was a solemn ceremony, normally preceded by many years of training and indoctrination. In an age where government consisted for the most part of military activity, and the king's court was the headquarters of an armed band rather than an administrative center, knighthood became a prerequisite for the major government offices also, although it was more often a matter of the king's servants acquiring knighthood than of knights entering the king's service.

With the passage of time, the ideology of knighthood became increasingly elaborate, including, among other elements, a code of gallantry toward women, an obligation of public service, and high standards of personal conduct. These ideals were probably more honored in the breach than in observance; modern research has disclosed that Sir Thomas Malory, who set down the legends of King Arthur and the Knights of the Round Table in their classic form, was a disgraced knight who spent much of his life in prison for rape and theft. Nevertheless, the ideal of the perfect knight evolved directly into the ideal of the perfect gentleman and is thus still influential in the Western system of stratification.

CLERICS

The clerical estate (the First Estate of the *ancien régime* in France) consisted of men and women in holy orders, monks, nuns, friars, deacons, priests, and bishops. They were relatively numerous—perhaps a third of the adult population in medieval Spain. Since most of them were vowed to celibacy throughout their lives, the status they acquired within the clerical estate was not transmitted to their descendants. But the clerical estate was by no means isolated from the other sectors of the medieval world. On the one hand, knightly status often conferred an advantage within the church. Some religious orders were limited to candidates of noble birth; appointments to many church benefices were controlled by noble families. A study of Roman Catholic saints finds that 78 percent of all the saints in the calendar had upper-class origins; the highest proportion (97 percent) in the eighth and tenth centuries and the lowest proportion (29 percent) in the nineteenth century.[9] On the other hand, the channels of vertical mobility in the church always remained open to talented individuals of humble origin. Beggars' sons rose to be cardinals and popes, raising the status of their relatives correspondingly.

Literacy was required for all but the lowest church offices. A clerk by definition was someone who could read and write, and the famous "benefit of clergy" was a reduced penalty for crimes committed by literate criminals. Reputation and advancement in the church were often based on what we would now call educational achievement, and modern institutions of higher education evolved from academies and universities that began as purely religious establishments.

TOWNSPEOPLE

In its earliest and simplest form, the medieval town grew around a market located at a river crossing or a road intersection under the protection of a neighboring castle, but most of these towns eventually made themselves independent of their feudal protectors. In some instances, their autonomy was so great that a serf who set foot within the city walls was automatically emancipated. Even without such privileges, the growth of towns was supported by a steady stream of peasants leaving the land for one reason or another, to become merchants, artisans, and urban laborers. As occupations and trades developed, they assumed the form of occupational organization known as a guild, which bore some resemblance to a labor union, a trade association, a producer's cooperative, and a religious fraternity, all at the same time. Under the guild system, occupations and trades were arrayed in an elaborate prestige order. Some guilds eventually rose so high in prestige that their members ceased to do manual work and their association with the trade became merely symbolic. Others declined so far that their members became pariahs and lived in segregated slums. Besides their occupational stratification, the towns were stratified by wealth, and most of them developed hereditary distinctions between patricians and plebians that sharpened over the course of centuries. Urban patricians, like those of Venice, often acquired land and feudal titles in the neighborhood of the city but continued to engage in trade and to participate in commercial enterprises.

PEASANTS

The peasants were by far the largest part of the population in medieval times, and continued to be so in most parts of Europe until the nineteenth or early twentieth century. Under the feudal system, most of the peasants were attached to the land and sold or transferred with it, whether as *serfs,* who were personally unfree, or as tenants, who were free but depended on a particular piece of land for their subsistence. The gradual abolition of serfdom that began in the thirteenth century and continued into the nineteenth had relatively little effect upon the peasant style of life; that style remained traditional, localistic, and self-sufficient. Peasant life continued without dramatic change from one generation to the next, governed by the seasons, the weather, and the requirements of a nearly stable technology. The peasantry was the population reservoir for the upper estates. As the feudal system disappeared and its place was taken by simpler forms of land tenure, a sharp cleavage developed in many peasant communities between rich peasants and poor peasants, a cleavage that sometimes persisted for generations. The children of peasants moved to the town and became burghers, or entered the church, or went to war and acquired wealth and knighthoods, but there was almost no movement *into* the peasantry from these other groups and very little movement of peasants from one region to another. Many a peasant village entered the modern era speaking a dialect unknown to outsiders and practicing customs unchanged since the Crusades. One of the principal features of modern European life is the diminution of the peasantry everywhere, as a changing agricultural technology encourages migration to the cities as well as the penetration of urban influences into village life. Pockets of peasant life with intact folklore, folk art, costumes, rituals, and dialects survive here and there in Europe and are likely to continue for some time, given the tenacity of peasant culture, but it is unlikely that their gradual disappearance will be arrested.

One of the principal differences between the North American and European systems of stratification is that there has never been a peasant class here. Land was always plentiful in North America, and its abundance was one of the principal incentives for immigration. From the beginning, the majority of Americans who tilled the soil were free farmers, owning their own land and living on their farms rather than in villages. Even among the tenant farmers of impoverished regions and among the liberated Negro slaves who remained on the land after the Civil War, nothing like the European peasant community ever developed.

THE DISAPPEARANCE OF THE ESTATES

The disappearance of the estates involved the extension of three kinds of rights to the entire body of citizens.[10] This movement occurred in approximately three successive stages:

Civil rights are mentioned in the American Declaration of Independence of 1776, and more particularly enumerated in the Bill of Rights appended to the U.S. Constitution in 1792. These rights include freedom of speech, belief, and religion; of assembly and petition; the right to justice and due process; personal liberty, the right to privacy, and immunity from unlawful searches and seizures; the right to bear arms; no taxation without representation; immunity from torture, from cruel and unusual punishment, and from self-incrimination; and equality before the law.

Political rights include the franchise, the right to join and leave a political party of one's own choosing, freedom from coercion in the exercise of the franchise, and the right to hold public office.

Social rights include the right to an education, to medical care, and to protection against physical hazards; freedom to migrate; protection against unemployment, disability, and old age; equal access to public services, equal opportunities for employment, and for upward mobility; and a guaranteed minimum subsistence.

Civil rights had been generally extended to citizens of European and American nations by the middle of the nineteenth century although with the continued exclusion of racial and religious minorities. Political rights were gradually extended to the entire populations of the same countries during the remainder of the nineteenth century and the early part of the twentieth, although again with certain exclusions —the suffrage was not granted to women in some of the major Western countries until after World War I.

Social rights became the business of national governments toward the end of the nineteenth century, and are still being elaborated and extended in most of the world's nations.

THE INDUSTRIAL REVOLUTION AND NEW FORMS OF STRATIFICATION

The Industrial Revolution, as it developed in England from the middle of the eighteenth century and a little later on the European continent and in North America, included the combination of several elements into a distinctively new mode of production. The most important of these elements were capitalism, manufacturing, and machinery.

Capitalism is an arrangement whereby private individuals and private associations have an unlimited right to acquire and manage natural resources and production facilities, to sell or exchange the commodities produced, and to use the proceeds for private luxury, for altruistic purposes, or to obtain additional wealth.

Manufacturing is the mass production of standardized useful commodities in large establishments by means of an elaborate division of labor under close supervision.

A *machine* (in the industrial sense) is a tool or set of tools used in production whose working energy is supplied by a motor utilizing some combination of natural forces.

Each of these elements appeared long before the Industrial Revolution. The origins of capitalism have been traced by some authorities as far back as the eleventh century, when certain poor peasants, dispossessed from the land, drifted into the towns and by trading and peddling built substantial fortunes in moveable property.[11] The earliest origins of manufacturing in Europe are somewhat obscure, but by 1500 sizable factories were turning out cloth, bricks, weapons, and paper in several countries. The mining of coal, iron, tin, and copper began to take on industrial proportions as early as the sixteenth century. By the middle of that century the principal mining districts of England were producing about 200,000 tons of coal annually, and by the end of the seventeenth century their production rose to about 3 million tons.[12] Machines driven by windmills and water power were familiar to the men of the Renaissance; some of those designed by Leonardo da Vinci are mechanically sophisticated even by modern standards. Ribbon-spinning machines seem to have been in use in Germany and Holland in the sixteenth century together with flour mills, sawmills, and drainage pumps. Steam pumps were in use in English coal mines around 1700, and by 1800 the steam engine was driving machinery in half a dozen different industries.[13]

However, the effective *combination* of these elements did not take place until nearly the end of the eighteenth century. The nearly simultaneous inventions of the spinning jenny, the cotton gin, and the power loom, and of the double-acting steam engine to run them, revolutionized the manufacture of textiles and launched a process of industrialization that has continued to expand into other regions, other continents, and other lines of production without interruption ever since. The pace of social change in the Industrial Revolution was rapid, compared to the rhythm of earlier historical developments. Industrialization had scarcely begun in Europe and America when the Napoleonic Wars (and the War of 1812) ended in 1815. Within less than a generation—by the 1830s—the new factories employed hundreds of thousands of workers and dominated the social landscape while the conflict between capitalists and industrial workers had already moved to the center of the political scene.

The Marxist Theory of Social Classes

The two new classes that appeared as industry developed were promptly identified by Marx and Engels as the major protagonists of modern history. The owners and organizers of the new factories were, for the most part, self-made men of obscure origin. Some of them were uneducated, and got their start in peddling, trading, and petty speculation. Others had been inventors, lawyers, or bankers before they glimpsed the opportunities offered by factory operation. In New England, a considerable number had been ship captains, a few were schoolteachers or ministers. Perhaps the best-known fact about the early capitalists is that many of them were pious Protestants belonging to strict Calvinistic or Evangelical sects. The relationship between the Protestant ethic and the spirit of capitalism is one of the favorite themes of historical sociology.[14]

Marx called these men the *bourgeoisie,* perhaps because the first European government that clearly represented capitalist interests was the "bourgeois monarchy" of Louis-Phillipe, installed in France in

1830; perhaps in contrast to the landowning aristocrats with whom they had to share power. The term "bourgeois" is still the fundamental Marxian epithet for capitalists. Because the same term is used in French-speaking countries (and increasingly in the United States) to denote the middle classes or anything appertaining to them, it often induces confusion. Marx himself distinguished between the capitalist bourgeoisie and the petit bourgeoisie of small proprietors and minor functionaries, but he had no class term for professional, technical, and white-collar workers (who were much less numerous in his time than they are now).

The new class of factory wage workers whom Marx labeled the *proletariat* after the Latin name for the Roman populace were, according to hundreds of contemporary accounts, thoroughly miserable. In Europe, they were drawn largely from the poorest stratum of the peasantry, driven off the land by changes in agricultural methods, the rapid increase of population, and the wars and revolutions of the late eighteenth century. In the United States, many of them were recent immigrants. Their working conditions were atrocious. Early factory owners saw nothing wrong in working small children 15 hours a day for seven days a week or harnessing pregnant women to treadmills. Wages were sometimes set so low that workers starved at their machines. Safety precautions were unheard of. The living accomodations of factory workers were repeatedly described by educated observers as worse than those of farm animals. The brazen inhumanity of the factory owners and the unpleasant contrast between the great fortunes they amassed and the desperate poverty of their employees evoked a storm of protest that did not subside for a hundred years, and that led to the abolition of capitalism in some countries, and to its regulation everywhere else.

The writings of Marx and Engels were part of a vast protest against the cruelty and injustice of industrial management in the nineteenth century. Marx's *Capital* contains hundreds of items like this:

> The manufacture of lucifer matches dates from 1833, from the discovery of the method of applying phosphorus to the match itself. Since 1845 this manufacture has rapidly developed in England, and has extended especially amongst the thickly populated parts of London as well as in Manchester, Birmingham, Liverpool, Bristol, Norwich, Newcastle and Glasgow. With it has spread the form of lockjaw, which a Vienna physician in 1845 discovered to be a disease peculiar to lucifer-matchmakers. Half the workers are children under thirteen, and young persons under eighteen. The manufacture is on account of its unhealthiness and unpleasantness in such bad odour that only the most miserable part of the laboring class, half-starved widows and so forth, deliver up their children to it, "the ragged, half-starved, untaught children."
> Of the witnesses that Commissioner White examined (1863), 270 were under 18, 50 under ten, ten only eight, and five only six years old. A range of the working day from 12 to 14 or 15 hours,

night-labour, irregular meal times, meals for the most part taken in the very workrooms that are pestilent with phosphorus. Dante would have found the worst horrors of his inferno surpassed in this manufacture.[15]

Reform legislation followed fairly quickly after the exposure of abuses, but remained for a long while ineffective. When Marx published the first edition of his book in 1867, nearly 40 years had elapsed in England since the passage of the first Parliamentary Acts intended to improve working conditions in factories, and practically no improvement was discernible. The pessimistic conclusion he drew was that industrial conditions could never be reformed under capitalistic management. This conclusion became an article of faith for his followers in the ensuing century, unshaken by the reduction of the work week to 40 hours or less, the elimination of child labor, the rise of factory wages far above subsistence levels and the transformation of the factory into a fairly safe and healthy workplace.

Marx never set down his theory of social classes in coherent form. Chapter 52 of *Capital,* which was to be devoted to that topic, breaks off on the second page; he did not live to complete the manuscript. In this fragment, he speaks of three great social classes—wage laborers, capitalists, and landlords—and begins to discuss the question whether physicians, officials, and other occupational groups constitute distinct classes. But elsewhere in his works[16] he seems to say that a class is a group of people in the same economic situation, whose interests are fundamentally opposed to those of another group, who are aware of this opposition and of their common identity and who are engaged or prepared to engage in conflict. *Class consciousness* and *class struggle* are the key terms in this theory. History is seen as a long struggle of the ruled against their rulers, which is to be terminated in a mystical fashion by the extinction of the capitalists, the last ruling class, and the victory of the proletarians, who will become the entire population without losing their identity as a social class.

Marx did not suppose that class consciousness was automatically produced by an individual's economic situation. Indeed, he took it for granted that it was not since, under his assumptions, a fully class-conscious society would be actively revolutionary. He pointed out many instances in which people in an occupational group failed to develop solidarity among themselves or hostility toward groups with opposing interests, and other instances in which people identified with a class to which they did not belong by birth or occupation. Both Marx and Engels were bourgeois in origin and in their style of life. But Marxism has always derived much of its persuasiveness from the joining of two apparently contradictory themes—on the one hand, the inevitability of the triumph of the proletariat; on the other hand, the need for professional (generally middle-class) revolutionaries to create class consciousness and to lead the proletariat to victory.

Weber's theory of social classes is partly a refutation of Marxism, especially of the Marxist proposition that modern systems of stratification are completely determined by the unequal distribution of property. Weber distinguished sharply between a *class,* by which he meant an aggregate of persons in the same economic situation, and a *status group,* by which he meant a group of people having an approximately uniform style of life and enjoying about the same level of prestige.

Weber's discussion of the relationship between classes and status groups[17] is a masterpiece of sociological analysis. (Translated into English, it seems less clear than it really is because Weber's definition of a status group is nearly identical with the usual definition of a class, and this creates some confusion.) Let us try to follow his analysis in some detail; it provides the best key to a general understanding of social stratification.

A class for Weber is composed of all persons in the same economic situation, that is, who have about the same probability of procuring goods, gaining a position in life, and gratifying their wants, insofar as this probability rests on the control of goods and services and the access to opportunities within a given economic system. Classes of slightly different kinds are created by differences in property, occupational differences, and unequal opportunities for vertical mobility. Some classes develop organizations and political parties to support their interests, some develop a consciousness of their own identity, and some engage in conflict with other solidary classes, but these developments are by no means inevitable. A privileged class may coexist with a much less privileged class without the development of any class antagonism at all—Weber cites the relationship of the plantation owners and the poor whites in the antebellum South. Any class struggle, when it does occur, may be nonrevolutionary and directed toward the redistribution of wealth or other privileges rather than toward a change in the economic system. Except at the bottom of the scale, where completely unskilled and propertyless persons are dependent on irregular employment, the identity of an economic situation with a class can only be approximate, because hardly any two persons have exactly the same life chances and these are highly variable over time.

Status groups are composed of persons having the same style of life and receiving about the same "social honor" from others. Persons in a status group tend to receive the same formal education, acquire the same manners, practice the same domestic customs, and teach their children the same values. The self-awareness of a status group is expressed by *connubium, the approval of intermarriage within the group and disapproval of marriage outside it,* and *commensalism, the willingness of persons in the group to eat with each other and to associate on an equal footing in other ways.* Status groups usually specify a range of appropriate vocations for their members and reject others as inappropriate or unworthy. In this process, a status group often comes to monopolize certain positions, to appropriate political power, and to claim hereditary superiority. Some status groups—pariah groups—have very low prestige and are treated with uniform contempt by outsiders. Such groups, according to Weber, are likely to develop internal value systems that confer a sense of dignity on individual members by reference to the hidden advantages they enjoy over outsiders or to a future destiny for which they are specially ordained.

Of course, Weber did not deny the existence of a relationship between classes and status groups or between an individual's economic situation and his status. What he tried to do was explain the relationship between them. "With some oversimplification," he wrote, "one might thus say that classes are stratified according to their relations to the production and acquisition of goods; whereas status groups are stratified according to the principles of their *consumption* of goods as represented by special styles of life."[18] This distinction enabled him to see many aspects of stratification in modern societies to which the simpler Marxist analysis is blind, for example, that wealth is not always convertible into high status and is not always essential for membership in a high-status group. The degree of connection between the economic system and the status order is not fixed or constant but varies from place to place and from time to time, being greatest in rapidly changing societies in periods of technical and economic transformation and least in societies dominated by religious or political values.

The social classes described in most of the American studies reviewed below would be called status groups in Weber's terminology. Although these studies disclose a great variety of local status orders, they are unanimous in showing that status in an American community is determined by race, religion, ethnicity, length of settlement, personal reputation, and conformity to standardized styles of life as well as by income, wealth, education, and occupation. The class consciousness that draws people together in defense of their common economic interests is a major factor in American politics, but its influence is intermittent and irregular. The class consciousness that leads the average citizen to categorize certain persons as suitable role partners in the various sectors of his life and other persons as unsuitable or dangerous is so pervasive an element in daily life that it goes almost unnoticed until it is called to public attention by a sociological study or a mass protest.

European Expansion as a Source of Stratification

Early in the fifteenth century, Portuguese captains sponsored by Prince Henry the Navigator began to probe southward along the Atlantic coast of Africa. Trading, exploring, and raiding coastal settlements, they moved further year by year until, in 1487, Bartholomeu Dias discovered the Cape of Good Hope. The exploration continued. In 1498, Vasco da Gama completed the circuit of Africa and landed at Calcutta, opening a sea route between Europe and India that was soon crowded with ships. Within the next generation, Portuguese ships explored the coasts of China and brought back the first authentic report of the half-mythical island of Japan. Meanwhile, Christopher Columbus had sailed to the West Indies in 1492 and explored the Caribbean region in three subsequent voyages. By 1525, European ships were plying the American coast from Labrador to Rio de Janeiro.

Before the end of the sixteenth century, the survivors of a Portuguese expedition had circumnavigated the globe and a regular passenger service had been established across the Pacific Ocean. The movement was remarkable both for its rapidity and for its unbroken success. Twenty years after Vasco da Gama's landing, there was hardly an Indian port of any importance that was not controlled by Europeans. Thirty years after Columbus sighted a speck of light on Watling Island in the Bahamas, the great empires of Mexico, Peru, and Guatemala were completely in the hands of the Spaniards, and their ships and those of the Portuguese, the English, the Dutch, the French, the Swedes, and the Danes were happily poking into every cove on the American coast in search of gold, silver, furs, fish, slaves, timber, or whatever else could be found. The peaceable Arawak Indians who had welcomed Columbus and his men were already nearly extinct. Not only settlements and forts but sizable cities had been founded in Hispaniola and Cuba and on the Spanish Main.

The Europeans who accomplished these military and engineering miracles were not necessarily more civilized than the people they conquered. Their engineering abilities were far inferior to those of the Incas; they knew less mathematics than the Hindus and less astronomy than the Mayas. The irresistible advantage they enjoyed wherever they went rested upon their possession of firearms and the means of transporting them by sea and land.[19] The cannon and muskets of the fifteenth century were crude and inaccurate, but against natives armed with spears and arrows the men who used them were invincible. By 1500, European ships were capable of crossing any ocean and finding their way back again. The small cannon they carried gave them absolute control of any harbor they entered. Their horses and musketeers enabled them to capture any inland city they could find before their horses died or their provisions ran out.

The world was theirs for the taking and they took it. Held prisoner by Pizarro, the last of the Incas raised his ransom by filling a large room with gold to a line on the wall as high as a tall man could reach. The Spaniards took the gold and killed him anyway. The candelabrum set up in the Cathedral of Seville to commemorate the return of the Cortez expedition was of solid Mexican silver and heavier than a modern locomotive. The governors of East Indian outposts returned to England or Holland with more wealth than any private citizen had ever possessed before. The cod and the halibut of the Grand Banks, the Canadian beaver, and the tall timber of Maine were less spectacular but equally important sources of new wealth.

Not all the booty was inanimate. Everywhere, the conquering Europeans took native women, and a population of mixed blood appeared within a few years after the first settlement. In the West Indies, the Indians were practically exterminated, partly by military action and partly by imported European diseases. In Central and South America, most of the Indians were enslaved by retired conquistadors who settled in the new countries with grants of land. After about a century of European occupation, the combined effects of disease, overwork, and social disorganization had greatly reduced the indigenous population in most of the settled areas. At the same time the area under cultivation was expanding, and the demand for agricultural products that could not be grown in Europe, like sugar and tobacco, appeared inexhaustible. The planters began to import Africans, drawing upon the already established slave markets of West Africa where young tribesmen, captured or bought in the distant interior, could be bought from local traders. The importation of slaves from Africa to America continued for more than 200 years; on a small scale at first, its volume increased sharply in the eighteenth century and reached a peak in the early 1800s, just before the importation of slaves was finally abolished by the United States (1809), the British West Indies (1816), and most of the Latin American countries (before 1821). A bootleg trade in slaves seems to have continued until about 1850.

By the time the slave trade was terminated, more than a third of the population in the American South (but only a negligible proportion in other regions) was of African descent,[20] as were the overwhelming majority of the population in the British West Indies and large minorities in the Spanish West Indies, Brazil, Guiana, Honduras, and Venezuela. In all of these countries, a considerable amount of biological amalgamation took place among the three major stocks represented—European, Amerindian, African.

In the United States, all persons of mixed descent were classified as Negroes by custom and law. In the British West Indies, the mulattoes gradually became a separate stratum distinct both from the whites, who retained their identity as Englishmen, and from the black villagers, who constituted the majority of the population. In some Latin American countries, especially Brazil and the small island of Puerto Rico, the three major stocks were so thoroughly mixed that color came to be regarded as a personal rather than a group characteristic. Although color was closely correlated with social status—and still is— no hard-and-fast lines were drawn between racial groups after the abolition of slavery. The contact of races led to still other outcomes in other countries. For example, the considerable number of African slaves imported into Guatemala were eventually absorbed into the other parts of the population and lost their distinctive identity, so that today, Guatemalans recognize only whites (entirely of European descent), ladinos (of mixed European and Indian descent), and Indians (descended from the original inhabitants). This classification, like the classification of whites and Negroes in the United States, is partly artificial. Persons who live in an Indian village and practice its rites and customs are classified as Indians even if, as occasionally happens, they have white skin, blue eyes, and blond hair. Indians who abandon the ancestral culture, move to the city, and rise in the social scale begin to be identified as ladinos, and a man belonging to an established upper-class family is regarded as white even when his features are typically Indian.

The European conquest of the world continued steadily throughout the eighteenth and nineteenth centuries as improvements in navigation, communication, and land transportation brought the remoter parts of the world within the reach of expeditions and guns. The westward movement of the frontier in the United States did not cease entirely until about 1910, when the last bits of unexplored territory were penetrated and the last hostile Indians subdued. That date was approximately the high-water mark of European influence in the world. By then, all the continents had been explored, Europeans had found the sources of the Nile and pacified the tribesmen of the Himalayan foothills; the North Pole had been reached, and an expedition was on its way to the South Pole. Every sizable country in the world, except for Japan and a few countries —like Ethiopia, Tibet, Yemen—too poor or remote to be worth conquering, was administered or in some way controlled by people of European descent. Then the tide turned and European influence began to recede, slowly at first, then very rapidly after World War II. By 1970, the English, French, German, Dutch, Spanish, and Portuguese empires had all dissolved, except for a few widely scattered outposts, like Angola, Curaçao, Réunion, and Hong Kong. The United States continued—at extremely high cost—to maintain a sort of protectorate over the Phillipines, Taiwan, South Korea, and South Vietnam and over Panama, Venezuela, and one or two other Latin American countries, but all of these arrangements appeared to be temporary and insecure.

Race and Social Class in the Modern World

The effects of the European conquest on systems of stratification around the world were far-reaching, and the retraction of that influence is certain to have consequences that cannot be foreseen now. Among the effects of the conquest were these:

1. About 40 multiracial national societies were established, and in all of them skin color and other racial traits became a basis for ascribing status.[21] Although the status orders of these societies differ in detail, as noted above, they invariably reflect the historic dominance of Europeans. Most of them fall into a pattern whereby "pure" whites are the highest stratum, "pure" Negroes or Indians are the lowest stratum, and the population of mixed ancestry has intermediate status. Arrangements of this kind have tended to outlast the political and social conditions from which they arose. For example, although the white population of Haiti was killed or driven away at the beginning of the nineteenth century, social status in modern Haiti is still closely linked to skin color, with lighter-skinned persons tending to have higher status.

2. In those countries that received a considerable number of European immigrants, priority of settlement became an important basis for ascribing status. In the United States and in South Africa, for example, the descendants of the seventeenth and eighteenth century settlers regard themselves as superior to the descendants of nineteenth century settlers, who in turn look down on recent immigrants. For more than 40 years, beginning just after World War I, American immigration laws distinguished between "desirable" immigrants—having the same national origins as the early settlers—and "undesirable" immigrants—from countries that were not heavily represented by the early settlers. In countries where priority of immigration is an important status indicator, priority of settlement plays a very large part in the status order of a locality, as numerous studies have shown.[22]

3. In India, China, Java, and some other densely populated countries with fully developed civilizations, European officials, merchants, planters, and missionaries occupied a privileged but segregated place in the status order during the colonial era. They associated with the highest-ranking class of indigenous families, but without conceding them full equality *or* being fully accepted as equal. Both groups strongly disapproved of intermarriage, each secretly considered the other inferior, and relatively little racial amalgamation occurred. European families in some cases remained in these countries for six or seven generations without losing their original national identity. Very few of them were able to remain after the colonized country regained its independence. By contrast, members of the indigenous population who had gained status because of their connections with the European administration usually found their privileges enhanced by national independence. Many, if not most, of the anticolonial revolutions were led by men educated in Europe or in the United States.

4. Another important effect of the European conquest was the establishment of a status order for the nations of the world, based on their relative wealth or degree of modernization or level of national development—all of which mean nearly the same thing. This status order emerged as the nations of the world began to participate in a global economy and communications network.[23] Highly developed countries have a large supply of mechanical energy, efficient industrial plants, extensive school facilities, ample food supplies, good roads, many telephones, automobiles, and so forth. Although nearly all the world's countries are developing rapidly and steadily, the differences among them are huge. It is very difficult for a poor country to close the gap that separates it from rich countries. Table 7–1, which compares the United States and Nigeria with respect to various indices of development, shows how dramatic such differences are. Nigeria is a typical underdeveloped country; in 1960 it ranked sixty-first in level of development among the 66 large countries of the world. Table 7–2 ranks all these countries with respect to development. The direct relationship between European expansion from 1500 to 1900 and the contemporary pattern of international stratification appears very plainly when we examine this table.

| *Table 7-1* | UNITED STATES-NIGERIA RATIOS WITH RESPECT TO VARIOUS INDICATORS OF DEVELOPMENT, 1960 |

Gross National Product per capita	35/1
Telephones per capita	345/1
Primary school enrollment per 1,000 population age 5-14	3/1
Secondary school enrollment per 1,000 population age 15-19	18/1
University enrollment per 1,000 population (including students studying abroad)	162/1
Hospital beds per capita	20/1
Calories consumed per capita	1.2/1
Grams of protein consumed per capita	2/1
Mileage of paved roads	55/1
Number of motor vehicles	240/1
Newspaper circulation per capita	40/1
Radio receivers per capita	240/1
Electricity consumption	475/1
Petroleum consumption	1160/1
Steel consumption	100/1
Per acre yields of grain crops	6/1

Source: Based on data from Profiles of National Development Project (New York: Columbia University, Bureau of Applied Social Research, 1965).

The 22 countries in the upper tercile—they may be called *developed* countries despite the vast differences among them—are all European or have populations of predominantly European origin except for Japan, the only country that succeeded in absorbing Western technology without submitting to foreign domination, and South Africa, a country with an official caste system, whose development rank is a composite of the high level of a white minority and the mediocre level of the black majority.

The 22 countries of the lower tercile in Table 7-2—they may be called *underdeveloped*—include the several large Asiatic countries with indigenous civilizations, in which European influence during the era of colonialism was nullified to a large extent by the persistence of traditional values and by new ideologies that sprang up in response to the external challenge. These countries—China, India, Pakistan, Indonesia, and Iran—contain more than a third of the world's population and are moving rapidly in an uncertain direction. Finally, the least developed of the underdeveloped countries are those that experienced little or no European influence before the present century. The last countries in the table—the Sudan, Ethiopia, Afghanistan, Nepal, and

Table 7-2   DEVELOPMENT RANK OF 66 MAJOR COUNTRIES, 1960

A. Developed Countries (Upper Tercile)		B. Developing Countries (Middle Tercile)		C. Underdeveloped Countries (Lower Tercile)	
Development Rank	Countries	Development Rank	Countries	Development Rank	Countries
1st	United States	23rd	Chile	45th	Ghana
2nd	United Kingdom	24th	Cuba	46th	Philippines
3rd	Belgium	25th	Greece	47th	Iran
4th	Switzerland	26th	Portugal	48th	India
5th	West Germany	27th	Rumania	49th	China
6th	Sweden	28th	Yugoslavia	50th	Madagascar
7th	Australia	29th	Venezuela	51st	Congo (Leopoldville)
8th	France	30th	Mexico	52nd	South Vietnam
9th	Canada	31st	Malaya—Singapore	53rd	Thailand
10th	Austria	32nd	Taiwan	54th	Indonesia
11th	East Germany	33rd	Brazil	55th	Uganda
12th	Netherlands	34th	Colombia	56th	Mozambique
13th	Czechoslovakia	35th	Rhodesia—Nyasaland	57th	Burma
14th	Italy	36th	Peru	58th	Saudi Arabia
15th	Japan	37th	Algeria	59th	Tanganyika
16th	Soviet Union	38th	Ceylon	60th	Pakistan
17th	Argentina	39th	Egypt	61st	Nigeria
18th	Hungary	40th	Morocco	62nd	Sudan
19th	Poland	41st	South Korea	63rd	Ethiopia
20th	Bulgaria	42nd	Turkey	64th	Afghanistan
21st	South Africa	43rd	Kenya	65th	Nepal
22nd	Spain	44th	Iraq	66th	Yemen

Source: *Development Rank: A New Method of Rating National Development.* (New York: Columbia University, Bureau of Applied Social Research, 1966).

Yemen—were isolated kingdoms that maintained their independence throughout most of the colonial era.

WORLD PROGRESS AND INEQUALITY

Ever since Merton and Rossi explained certain anomalous findings about the morale of soldiers in various military situations that had been reported in *The American Soldier*,[24] it has been an accepted principle of sociological theory that anyone's satisfaction or dissatisfaction with his position in a stratified social system is determined not so much by his objective situation as by the comparison he makes between his own situation and the situation of a reference group or reference individual. The mechanisms whereby reference groups and reference individuals are selected are not yet entirely understood, but it is well established that changes in reference can occur independently of changes in an actor's measurable rewards and deprivations. An individual's increasing affluence may be accompanied by increased satisfaction, decreased satisfaction, or unchanged satisfaction, depending on how he evaluates his own progress in relation to that of friends or neighbors or relatives or public figures with whom he compares himself. Collective actors, like social classes and nations, behave much like individuals in this respect, although the psychological reactions of a collectivity are more difficult to record than those of an individual, and the conclusions drawn from such observations are always a little uncertain.

So far as can be determined by statistical measures, there is no sizable country in the world that has not made significant progress in development since World War II. And since all of the components of national development are intercorrelated, this progress means that nearly everywhere on earth, the average family is better fed, better clothed, and better housed than a few years ago. Fewer babies die, more children learn to read, fewer illnesses occur and fewer of them go untreated. More homes are lighted by electricity, and a larger proportion of the population have bathrooms, central heating, automobiles, television, good shoes, and annual vacations.

The process of development enlarges the geographical and historical perspectives of a national population partly by exposing them to education and the mass media, partly by substituting a rational, technically oriented view of human society for more picturesque but less informative cosmologies. In July 1969, an audience estimated at 500 million persons saw the first moon landing on television; this was by far the largest audience ever to witness a single event. Both the nature of the event and the technology by which it was broadcast exerted some pressure on the vast audience to accept the scientific view of the world and to place themselves in a global frame of reference.

The combination of unequal levels of development, universal progress, and the enlarged perspectives attributable to development suffices to explain why the rising levels of affluence in many developing and underdeveloped countries has produced much dissatisfaction with the international hierarchy shown in Table 7–2.

A somewhat similar reaction can be discerned in many of the nations having a Western system of stratification, especially those like Great Britain and the United States, in which the ascription of status according to descent seems to take precedence over the achievement of status through education and occupational mobility. The rapid increase of affluence at every level of status and income does not produce as much satisfaction as might be expected when everyone's situation improves simultaneously and the individual gains no relative advantage. At the same time, the enlarged perspective that accompanies a rising standard of living under modern conditions enhances awareness of long-standing inequities and encourages resistance to them.

THE SOCIAL EFFECTS OF STRATIFICATION STUDIES

In a democratic but stratified society in which social classes have no legal standing, the boundaries between classes are vague and the criteria of membership in a class vary from one locality to another and from one generation to the next, so that the system as a whole may be pictured in quite different ways by different observers.

This imprecision is not merely a methodological problem, and it cannot be overcome through developing better questionnaires and scales to measure social status. The difficulty of delimiting social classes is inherent in the way a society like ours is stratified. The existing stratification is partly based on an unequal distribution of social qualifications and rewards—such as education, occupation, income, and property (see Tables 7–3 and 7–4)—partly on the changeable criteria that individuals use to identify a reference group of "people like ourselves," and partly on the even more erratic criteria they use to identify people "not like us." The individual's perception of his own class position is inherently subjective; if it were not, he would belong to an estate or a caste rather than to a class (it can be argued that blacks in the United States *do* belong to a caste). When, as often happens, a physician or a banker classifies himself on a questionnaire as "working class," it is futile for a sociologist to protest. The sociologist is on even shakier ground when he argues that his five-class model of the status order in an Indiana community is more accurate than a three-class model preferred by some of his respondents.

Because the division of a population into social classes has this built-in element of indeterminacy, the sociologist who proposes a model of satratification to describe a human society may persuade so many people to accept his image as their own that the fit between reality and the model improves in a dramatic way. Thus, the identification of "the poor" as a distinct social class in a series of popular sociological works that began to appear in the early 1960s[25] led very quickly to the appearance of scores of government agencies, private associations, and political movements representing, serving, or appealing to the millions of people who, for the first time, began to claim

Table 7-3   PERCENT OF PERSONS IN VARIOUS
                   CATEGORIES OWNING VARIOUS
                   KINDS OF CAPITAL, IN A NATIONAL
                   SAMPLE, 1964

	Rental Real Estate	Savings Bonds	Shares, Stocks, or Bonds in a Private Company	Cases (N)
		Percentage Having Each Kind of Item		
Education:				
College completed	19.2	55.6	57.6	99
Some college	17.0	50.9	47.2	106
High school completed	11.3	31.5	25.7	257
1-3 years of high school	15.9	20.9	13.6	220
8th grade completed	18.0	27.9	18.9	111
Less than 8th grade	8.5	16.2	6.9	130
Occupation:				
Professional	18.3	47.1	49.0	104
Managerial	18.7	47.2	47.9	144
Clerical	9.5	40.5	27.0	74
Sales	19.2	36.5	42.3	52
Craftsmen	11.9	27.8	17.9	151
Operatives	5.8	23.9	6.5	155
Service and private household	11.2	14.6	7.9	89
Laborers	21.8	14.5	10.9	55
All farm	18.6	18.6	20.0	70
Family income:				
Greater than $10,000	22.7	46.0	59.5	163
$7,000-$9,999	14.2	40.9	28.4	176
$5,000-$6,999	13.0	34.0	20.5	200
$3,000-$4,999	10.9	22.4	13.7	183
Less than $3,000	10.9	14.8	7.7	183

Source: Robert W. Hodge and Donald J. Treiman, "Class Identification in the United States," *American Journal of Sociology* 73, no. 5 (March 1968): p. 540, table 2.

a collective identity as the poor. For this reason, an account of the models used by sociologists to describe stratification in a modern society is more than a bibliographical record. It helps to explain some of the patterns of class consciousness that appear in that society.

The development of stratification models in the United States falls into two distinct periods—an earlier period of intensive community studies and a more recent period in which attempts have been made to describe the stratification of the nation as a whole. A few of the more influential models are briefly described below:

THE MIDDLETOWN TWO-CLASS MODEL

The first work to describe the class system of an American community on the basis of detailed empirical data was the Lynds' *Middletown*, published in 1929.[26] (See Chapter Three above.) One of its early chapters is entitled "The Dominance of Getting a Living." In that chapter the authors divided the families of Middletown into two classes, called the Working Class and the Business Class, according to the

---

Table 7-4	SOCIOECONOMIC CHARACTERISTICS OF FOUR-TEEN RELIGIOUS GROUPS IN A DETROIT SAMPLE

Religious Group	Total (N)	Median Family Income	Median Occupational Status[a]	Median School Years Completed
Congregational	10	$17,500	82.7	16.5
Episcopal	34	13,000	59.9	13.0
Presbyterian	75	11,667	60.3	13.5
Nondenominational Protestant	10	11,250	39.9	11.8
Methodist	93	10,703	45.0	12.1
Protestant, no denomination specified	32	9,727	48.8	11.5
Baptist	104	9,311	28.6	11.4
Church of Christ	16	8,636	23.3	11.5
Other fundamentalist	15	7,938	26.4	11.0
All Protestants	499	10,117	45.3	12.0
Roman Catholics	427	9,999	43.2	12.0
Eastern Orthodox	13	9,999	55.0	12.6
Jew	29	14,688	65.0	15.7
Total Sample	1,013	$10,177	45.2	12.0

[a] The current occupation of the respondent was first coded into the six-digit detailed occupation-industry code of the U.S. Bureau of the Census and then recoded by computer to the two-digit code of Duncan's Index of Socioeconomic Status (cf. Duncan, 1961).

Source: Edward O. Laumann, "The Social Structure of Religious and Ethno-religious Groups in a Metropolitan Community," *American Sociological Review*, 34, no. 2 (April 1969): 186, table 2.

occupation of the principal breadwinner. The two classes were described thus:

> Members of the first group, by and large, address their activities in getting their living primarily to *things,* utilizing material tools in the making of things and the performance of services, while the members of the second group address their activities primarily to *people* in the selling or promotion of things, services, and ideas. This second group supplies to Middletown the multitude of non-material institutional activities such as "credit," "legal contract," "education," "sale for a price," "management," and "city government" by which Middletown people negotiate with each other in converting the narrowly specialized product of their workaday lives into "a comfortable evening at home," "a Sunday afternoon out in the car," "fire protection," "a new go-cart for the baby," and all the other things that constitute living in Middletown.
> . . .
>
> While an effort will be made to make clear at certain points variant behavior within these two groups, it is after all this division into working class and business class that constitutes the outstanding cleavage in Middletown. The mere fact of being born on one or the other side of the watershed roughly formed by these two groups is the most significant single cultural factor tending to influence what one does all day long throughout one's life; whom one marries; when one gets up in the morning; whether one belongs to the Holy Roller or Presbyterian Church; or drives a Ford or a Buick; whether or not one's daughter makes the desirable high school Violet Club; or one's wife meets with the Sew We Do Club or with the Art Students' League; whether one belongs to the Odd Fellows or to the Masonic Shrine; whether one sits about evenings with one's necktie off; and so on indefinitely throughout the daily comings and goings of the Middletown man, woman, or child.[27]

Reclassifying occupational data from the 1920 census, the investigators concluded that 71 percent of the population belonged to the business class and 29 percent to the working class at that date, the two classes being separated by a twilight belt where they overlapped and merged. Figure 7–1 depicts this model.

Nowadays, it is customary to speak of "blue-collar" and "white-collar" workers or of the "middle class" and the "working class," but aside from these minor changes in nomenclature, the two-class model is still in use and is perhaps the most satisfactory and least ambiguous model that can be used to describe the status order of the average American community.

However, even the Lynds themselves found the two-class model too simple to describe the complexities of status in *Middletown.* In *Middletown in Transition,* the restudy they undertook a decade later (see Chapter Three), they identified an emerging upper class composed of a few wealthy manufacturers and bankers, the local managers of national corporations, and their relatives and associates. They went on

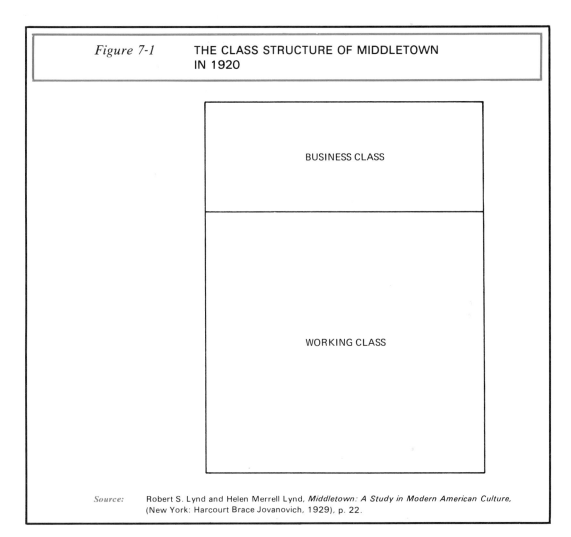

Source: Robert S. Lynd and Helen Merrell Lynd, *Middletown: A Study in Modern American Culture,* (New York: Harcourt Brace Jovanovich, 1929), p. 22.

Figure 7-1   THE CLASS STRUCTURE OF MIDDLETOWN IN 1920

BUSINESS CLASS

WORKING CLASS

to subdivide the business class into an upper stratum of substantial merchants, professionals, and executives and a lower stratum of retail proprietors, clerical workers and the like, and the working class into three strata—foremen and craftsmen at the top, machine operators and laborers in the middle, and "poor white" casual workers at the bottom. What the new model gained in detail it lost in precision, since it was no longer possible to specify the exact size of each class or to describe its culture with assurance.

THE YANKEE CITY SIX-CLASS MODEL

In revising their original model, the Lynds may have been influenced by Warner's study of Yankee City, whose findings began to be reported around 1933.[28] Warner used a six-class model—or a three-class model with two subdivisions in each class—to describe the status order of Yankee City(see Figure 7–2). His six classes were labeled upper-upper, lower-upper, upper-middle, lower-middle, upper-lower, lower-lower, and abbreviated as UU, LU, UM, LM, UL, and LL. Unlike the Middletown model, the Yankee City model was not based on occupation alone. A social class, in Warner's view, is a group of

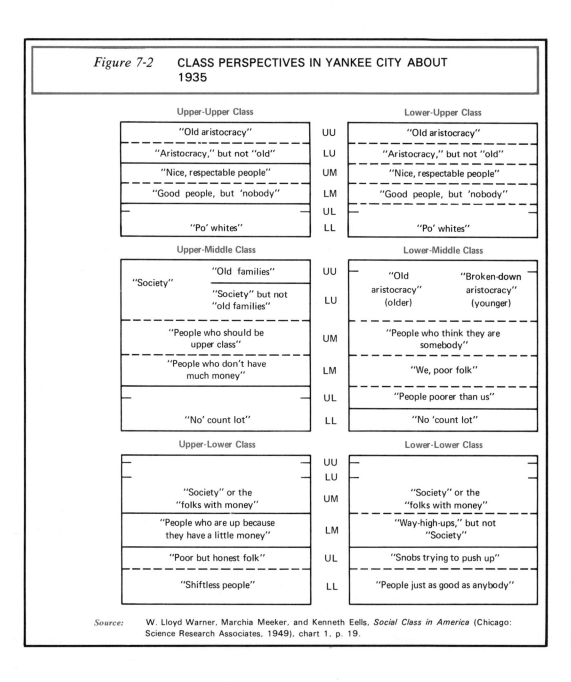

Figure 7-2   CLASS PERSPECTIVES IN YANKEE CITY ABOUT 1935

Upper-Upper Class

"Old aristocracy"	UU
"Aristocracy," but not "old"	LU
"Nice, respectable people"	UM
"Good people, but 'nobody"	LM
	UL
"Po' whites"	LL

Lower-Upper Class

"Old aristocracy"
"Aristocracy," but not "old"
"Nice, respectable people"
"Good people, but 'nobody"
"Po' whites"

Upper-Middle Class

"Society"	"Old families"	UU
	"Society" but not "old families"	LU
"People who should be upper class"		UM
"People who don't have much money"		LM
		UL
"No' count lot"		LL

Lower-Middle Class

"Old aristocracy" (older)	"Broken-down aristocracy" (younger)
"People who think they are somebody"	
"We, poor folk"	
"People poorer than us"	
"No 'count lot"	

Upper-Lower Class

	UU
	LU
"Society" or the "folks with money"	UM
"People who are up because they have a little money"	LM
"Poor but honest folk"	UL
"Shiftless people"	LL

Lower-Lower Class

"Society" or the "folks with money"
"Way-high-ups," but not "Society"
"Snobs trying to push up"
"People just as good as anybody"

Source: W. Lloyd Warner, Marchia Meeker, and Kenneth Eells, *Social Class in America* (Chicago: Science Research Associates, 1949), chart 1, p. 19.

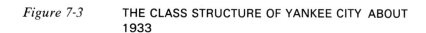

Figure 7-3   THE CLASS STRUCTURE OF YANKEE CITY ABOUT 1933

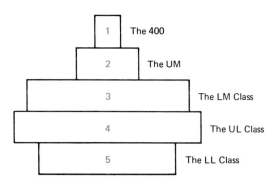

1	The 400
2	The UM
3	The LM Class
4	The UL Class
5	The LL Class

Source: W. Lloyd Warner, Marchia Meeker, and Kenneth Eells, *Social Class in America* (Chicago: Science Research Associates, 1949), chart II, p. 70.

people who are willing to associate with each other on a more or less equal footing. They also refuse to associate closely with the members of inferior or superior classes; in the former case, because they fear contamination, and in the latter case, because they might be snubbed or exploited. The six classes were described as hereditary groups differing in wealth and income, education, occupation, style of life, speech habits, sexual practices, and kinship arrangements. Vertical mobility between classes was said to be so strictly regulated in Yankee City that it was practically impossible for a person born locally to move upward or downward by more than one class in his lifetime.

This way of looking at stratification implies a high degree of class consciousness at all levels of the society, but Warner and his collaborators took pains to point out that the six-class system was perceived in different ways from different points in the hierarchy. Figure 7–3 shows how people whom the investigators identified as belonging to each of the six classes visualized the class system on the basis of their own experience.

The six-class model seems to reflect the peculiarities of Yankee City, a small New England seaport whose dominant families associated themselves with an era of departed commercial glory and whose low rates of migration and technological change restricted vertical mobility. However, investigators of the same persuasion reported finding "real" classes and a high degree of class consciousness in other parts of the country, notably in the small Indiana town that appears in the literature both as Elmtown and as Jonesville. In *Elmtown's Youth,*[29] A. B. Hollingshead describes the elaborate procedure of rating and comparison by which in 1941–1942 he was able to assign the families of

524 Elmtown high school students to one of five classes. Elmtown's five classes were very similar to the six classes of Yankee City; the principal difference was that the upper-upper and lower-upper classes were not separated in Elmtown.

In the Warner model, the upper-upper class has *both* wealth and lineage, enough inherited capital for most—but not all—of its members to support a dignified and expensive style of life and enough influence over community institutions to control the direction of social change insofar as it is locally controllable. They are a cohesive group whose members recognize each other personally and jealously restrict their interaction with outsiders. The lower-upper class is composed of active candidates for membership in the upper-upper class, often persons with more wealth but less lineage, who court and imitate the upper-uppers in the hope of eventually being accepted as equals.

The upper-middle class is composed of families whose heads have had successful careers and have reached positions of authority and responsibility by their own efforts without inherited wealth or notable ancestry. These are the doctors, the lawyers, the merchants, the executives, and the leaders of political and social organizations. Their status is based on personal achievement, not only in the occupational sphere, but also with respect to the education and good behavior of their children, the maintenance of their homes, volunteer service to the church and other voluntary associations, and approved hobbies and avocations. Their values are those of the good citizen.

Families of the lower-middle class accept the same values—respectability, solvency, educational and occupational achievement—but have not attained high incomes or other marks of worldly success. They are more familistic, more conservative, more religious, less secure, less influential and to all appearances, much less happy than the upper-middles. The occupations in which they are found are those that offer the least chance of upward mobility. As small retail proprietors, clerical workers, or skilled craftsmen, they are vulnerable to economic and personal crises and run more risk of downward mobility than other strata of the population.

The upper-lower class (in Elmtown) is described as "poor but honest, hard workers, who pay their taxes, raise their children properly, but never seem to get ahead financially. From the viewpoint of the Class I's and Class II's, they add little to the community beyond providing the labor that keeps the factories going, and customers in the stores. Their function is to work, to behave themselves, to keep things going. They are respected generally for what they are—hard workers who make their own way in life—and not for intellectual, political, economic, or social achievement."[30] The majority of blue-collar factory workers and the lower ranks of civil service employees, fall into this class together with truckdrivers, waitresses, and all sorts of laborers. A considerable proportion of the married women work fulltime. Family life is stable but not as stable as in the middle classes; there is much more divorce, separation, early marriage, and illegitimacy. Husbands and wives lead relatively separate social lives; children are disciplined more severely, brought up less carefully and emancipated earlier than in the middle classes. Ethnic and religious divisions *within* the upper and lower class are sharp, and often accompanied by extremist attitudes of one kind or another.

The lower-lower class, as described in Yankee City and Elmtown a generation ago, were outcasts, living wretched lives on the clam flats or down by the garbage dump, hated and despised by the rest of the population. They held only irregular or menial jobs, and their incomes were very low. Family life was unstable; adolescent promiscuity, illegitimacy, early child-bearing, wife-beating, and desertion were common among them. There was virtually no participation in church affairs or other organized public activities. Child-raising practices were casual to the point of neglect, school achievement low, and delinquency rates very high. Although the lower-lowers were only about a fourth of the total population, they accounted for most of the offenses known to the police and most of the expenses of public relief and private philanthropy.

In contrast to the slum populations of metropolitan cities, the lower-lowers of Yankee City and the Class V's of Elmtown were descended from old settlers of English stock; in their ethnic composition, they were closer to the upper-uppers than to any of the intervening classes.

THE CASTE-AND-CLASS MODEL

Studying stratification in a small Georgia community in the early 1930s, Dollard[31] described the caste boundary that divided the population into an upper (white) and a lower (black) caste between which vertical mobility was in principle impossible, and the class lines that separated both white and black populations into horizontal strata between which considerable mobility could and did occur. Even in the deep South, in the 1930s,

> ... certain Negroes outranked many whites or, to state the obverse, certain whites were, for given purposes, inferior to many Negroes, despite the fact that color caste operates strongly and is backed by very severe sanctions. Further inspection and analysis of this problem led us to the conclusion that, while all Negroes are considered socially inferior and are categorically subordinate to all whites in color caste, many of them are superior and superordinate by social-class position to many, if not most, whites.[32]

Figure 7–4 shows the caste-class situation as it was described, following this early model, by Myrdal in *An American Dilemma.* (See Chapter Three above.)

More than a generation after these old studies, the diagram continues to describe the situation of blacks in many American communities although a number of significant changes have occurred behind the diagram, so to speak. First, there has been a sharp increase in the proportion of middle-class families in the black population compared

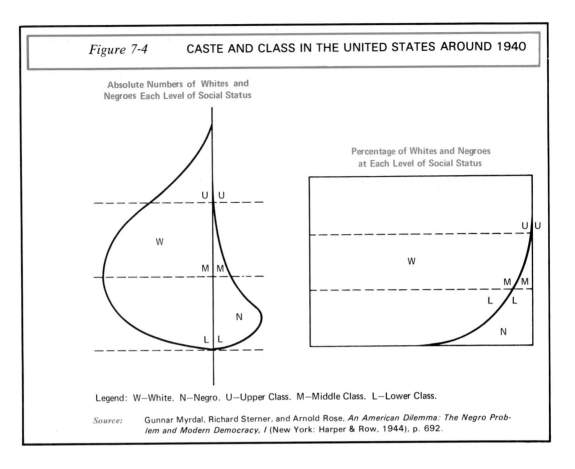

Figure 7-4   CASTE AND CLASS IN THE UNITED STATES AROUND 1940

Absolute Numbers of Whites and
Negroes Each Level of Social Status

Percentage of Whites and Negroes
at Each Level of Social Status

Legend: W—White. N—Negro. U—Upper Class. M—Middle Class. L—Lower Class.

Source: Gunnar Myrdal, Richard Sterner, and Arnold Rose, *An American Dilemma: The Negro Problem and Modern Democracy, I* (New York: Harper & Row, 1944), p. 692.

to the relative proportion of middle-class families in the white population. Figure 7–4 would have to be redrawn to describe the present distribution.

Second, a generation ago, the rules of color-caste were held sacrosanct by southern whites, and their legitimacy was acknowledged to some extent by blacks too. It was this element of *legitimacy* that allowed the arrangement to be described as a caste system. The Hindu caste system, the prototype of all others, is inseparable from the Hindu religion; although the lower castes appear to resent the disadvantages imposed on them, it is nearly impossible for low-caste Hindus to reject the whole idea of caste without abandoning their religion and a large part of their culture.[33]

The color-caste system in the United States had much less impressive origins. The detailed etiquette of discrimination ("Jim Crow") did not even go back to the days of slavery; some of its rules and customs had been invented as late as 1900, imposed on southern Negroes by force or threats and only outwardly accepted by them.[34] By the late

1960s, almost all of the local and state legislation that supported the color-caste system had been declared unconstitutional or repealed. The federal government had repeatedly committed itself to the long-range goal of racial equality.

The interplay of class and caste attitudes as been the subject of extensive research. Myrdal was struck by the fact that the color-caste line prevented white and black tenant farmers and agricultural laborers from making common cause against the landowners and bankers by whom both groups felt themselves to be exploited. In place of class consciousness based on common economic interests, the acute caste consciousness of lower-class whites froze them into a position of permanent hostility toward their black neighbors and into a position of permanent disadvantage in relation to other white groups. Caste consciousness and the intolerance associated with it were much weaker among upper-class whites, whose status could not be jeopardized by associating with blacks, than among the poor whites, whose social rewards were practically limited to those they could obtain by the assertion of white superiority. Myrdal saw this as a successful tactic whereby the former slaveholders were able to maintain their nearly feudal privileges in the southern economy after the overthrow of slavery. Other observers regard the development of the Jim Crow structure as an upper-class strategy that miscarried when the poor whites developed white supremacy into something like a religion and were able to impose it on the entire white population.

> ... the Southern conservatives, having purchased the support of the lower-class rural Whites, were now prisoners of their own policies. The Jim Crow laws bore most heavily upon the better educated more responsible Negroes. This suited the poor Whites, who were most opposed to any Negroes whose accomplishments refuted the idea of a natural status gap. It did not suit the upper-class Whites, who feared nothing from the Negro but were alarmed by the way in which some poorer members of their own racial group were prepared to use their power. ... Most of these men must have found the demands for solidarity on racial lines too imperious to be opposed.[35]

With respect to the black middle and upper classes, as Myrdal and other investigators observed them just before World War II, two characteristics seemed to militate against the erosion of the color-caste line: first, their partial adoption of white values with respect to skin color, so that higher status was ascribed to lighter-skinned persons and successful men tended to choose wives of lighter color than themselves; second, their realization that segregation protected them from competition with whites and enabled them to maintain a superior status and an admired style of life with resources that would have been insufficient in the white sector of the community.

The data of a 1966 survey reported by Brink and Harris[36] suggest that there was still a relationship between social class and racial attitudes among whites at that time but that the corresponding relationship among blacks was no longer apparent. As Table 7-5 shows, affluent whites were far more sympathetic to integration and civil rights than their poor white neighbors. Several explanations for this pattern have been offered. The simplest is that high-status whites would not be threatened by black competition for jobs, public services, or living space if the color-caste line were suddenly removed since the black population they would encounter on their own class level would continue to be relatively small. Lower-class whites would not only face enhanced competition from lower-class blacks if they were not protected by the caste line, but would also be forced to acknowledge the superior status of middle-class blacks. Like any simple explanation for a complex social phenomenon, this one is difficult to verify, but it does seem to account for the existing distribution of class and caste attitudes in an approximate way.[37]

Table 7-5a WHITE ATTITUDES TOWARD INTEGRATION, BY INCOME LEVEL, UNITED STATES, 1966

Objected to:	All Whites	Low Income Whites	Affluent Whites
Negroes living next door	51%	54%	41%
Negro child to supper	42	51	29
Sitting next to Negro on bus	16	25	9

Table 7-5b NEGRO ATTITUDES TOWARD INTEGRATION, BY INCOME LEVEL, NORTHERN STATES, 1966

Preferred:	All Negroes	Low Income Negroes	Affluent Negroes
Mixed working group	86%	93%	85%
Mixed neighborhood	79	78	80
Mixed school for one's children	82	78	83

In recent years, as previously noted, sociological attention has shifted from the class structures of selected small communities—although these continue to be studied—to the status order of the nation as a whole. The latter is much harder to describe than the former. Although it can be plausibly argued that the inhabitants of Yankee City or of Elmtown recognize a definite class system, even though their images of it are distorted and confused, it is nearly impossible to make the same assertion for the United States.

In some industrialized countries, like Great Britain, social status appears to be primarily hereditary, although considerable vertical mobility can occur between and within generations. The average adult takes his class status from his parents. It is expressed by a distinctive accent and recognizable mannerisms, and in the usual case it is reinforced by the schools he attends. Social status does not appear to be hereditary to the same extent in the United States. The absorption of foreign whites, that is, the progression of a family from "immigrant" to "foreign-born" to "ethnic" to "American" to "native American" is a continuous process that, even in the absence of occupational mobility, would assure discontinuity between the status of successive generations in millions of families.

In some industrialized countries, like France, there are well-marked boundaries between occupational strata although considerable mobility occurs between generations. The close relatives of a peasant are likely to be peasants; the close relatives of a factory worker are usually factory workers. A petit bourgeois family may be represented in a dozen occupations but it is not likely to be closely connected with the aristocracy, the grand bourgeoisie, or even the industrial working class. This limitation appears to be less usual in the United States, where white-collar and blue-collar workers, professional men and laborers, bankers and farm hands, are often found in the same family. The limited empirical evidence we have on this point indicates that occupational disparity of this kind somewhat decreases the frequency of interaction between close relatives but does not usually lead them to break off their relationship.[38]

In some industrialized countries, like Germany, the Netherlands, Belgium, and Switzerland, the population is divided into separate religious or linguistic compartments, among which there is relatively little intermarriage or close association. The individual's religious and linguistic identity, taken from his parents, is an important part of his status and rarely subject to change. In the United States, religion and ethnic identity are important elements in an individual's status but—at least in the white sector of the population—the boundaries between religious and ethnic groups are indistinct and are frequently crossed in all directions.

In many advanced countries, like France and Sweden, there are close correlations between education and occupational status and between occupational status and income. Admission to a career is a formal process, requiring the appropriate diplomas; most people remain in the same career throughout their lifetimes and their earnings are determined almost exclusively by their occupational progress. Although a few persons in these countries accumulate great wealth from private ventures, the opportunities for speculation and for extraoccupational earnings are relatively limited, and remuneration is standardized within occupations. The United States, by contrast, has a very high rate of interoccupational mobility, numerous opportunities for windfall earnings, many remunerative criminal and illicit enterprises, and unparalleled opportunities for private speculation. Even ordinary wages and salaries are relatively unstandardized in many sectors of the economy. As a result, the connection between an individual's occupational status on the one hand, and his income and style of life on the other, is rather tenuous. A factory worker's family with three employed adults may easily have a higher income than a banker's family in the same community. Undertakers, real estate agents, bookmakers, and traveling salesmen sometimes live in princely style. Speculative opportunities on the stock market, in real estate, and in commodity markets are open to all, and considerable fortunes are accumulated and spent by some people without any discernible change in their class identification or lack of it.

The regions of the United States differ greatly in the length of their histories (three and a half centuries for Massachusetts or Virginia, two centuries for Kentucky or Ohio, less than a century for North Dakota or Oklahoma), and the pattern of settlement and population growth has varied greatly from one place to another within the same region. These circumstances have produced an astonishing diversity of social structures and life styles, which hinders the transfer of status from one locality to another. The upper classes identified by sociologists in East Harlem, in Boston, in a Colorado mining town, or in rural South Carolina do not share a common culture or a common identity.

Aside from cultural differences, status ascriptions in the United States are qualified by community size and type. The upper-class individual moving from a small community to a metropolitan community (say, from Elmtown to Chicago) will not ordinarily be able to convert his upper-class status in the small community into upper-class status in the metropolis. Conversely, a lower-class individual moving in the same direction can shuck off the stigma of his low status in the small community. Upper-class individuals and families migrating from metropolitan centers to suburbs or to smaller communities can usually carry their status with them. Lower-class families migrating from metropolitan centers to suburban areas tend to redefine themselves as middle class.[39]

THE NO-CLASS MODEL OF THE NATIONAL SOCIETY

Attempts to measure the population of major social classes in the United States as a whole have been rather unsuccessful. When respondents in national surveys are asked to state their own social class, very few of them say "upper class" or "lower class"; the great majority describe themselves as "middle class." If respondents are offered a set of categories rather than allowed to use their own, the fractions classifying themselves as "upper class" and "lower class" are still tiny, but the remainder of the population divides itself almost evenly between "middle class" and "working class." On closer inspection, these ambiguous results turn out to be even more ambiguous than they seem, since a great many professionals, officials, and executives classify themselves as working class because they work hard, and a great many factory operatives and unskilled laborers classify themselves as middle class because they live respectably.[40]

Attempts at objective classification based on occupation, education, and income are even less satisfactory. The existence of stratification is plain, of course, but whether it divides the population into separate and distinct strata remains highly doubtful. One authority after a careful review of the research evidence decides on the following distribution:[41]

Social Classes	Percent of Population
Upper classes	3
Middle classes	37
Lower classes	60

Social Classes	Percent of Population
Upper classes	1
Upper-middle classes	9
Lower-middle classes	40
Working classes	40
Lower classes	10

Another authority, examining the same evidence, arrives at a quite different distribution.[42] Some sociologists maintain that the distribution of the national population into social classes is impossible because social class, although a reality in preindustrial societies, has now become a myth. Robert Nisbet, who holds this opinion, believes that the type of class structure discovered in Yankee City, Elmtown, and other small, rather isolated American communities are vestiges of preindustrial social arrangements that are certain to disappear as the influences of the modern world break into the last enclaves of traditional stratification. Nisbet writes:

> . . . In the same way that there has been a general disengagement of economic and political power, during the past century and more, from any homogeneous scale of stratification, leaving in its

wake plurality and dispersion, so has there been a general disengagement of social status itself from any clearly definable set of ranks. That scales of status exist in our society is incontestable, that they are often of driving concern to individuals is equally incontestable. But social status is at once too continuous within each of the numerous scales of status to make possible any identification of classes that have more than the most restricted or specialized acceptance.[43]

He suggests that class consciousness has been largely replaced by "level consciousness":

... Level consciousness makes for a high degree of individualism, with respect to aspirations and life chances; it does not promote feeling of identification or collective involvement. The principal motive of the level-conscious individual is to pass up and out of the level in which he finds himself. He is, so to speak, on the make.[44]

Nisbet insists that a social class is nothing if it is not a functioning part of a society. To be functional, it must have economic and political power;[45] the exercise of such power requires class consciousness and class solidarity as well as shared values and a more or less uniform style of life. In determining the presence or absence of social classes in a society, the problem of course is to decide how much of each of these features is required to constitute a class.

Programmatic Social Classes

If we define a social class as a large section of the population having relatively uniform statuses, an identifiable style of life, shared values, and awareness of a common identity, who are recognized by outsiders as having that identity and who—as a class—exercise social and economic power, then we are led to the interesting discovery that although the American population as a whole cannot be divided into a set of such classes, it is possible at any given historical moment to identify *some* classes that conform to the definition. These classes are called into being by political and social events, and they are likely to disappear when circumstances change. We might call them *programmatic classes,* because they nearly always appear in connection with a political or social program. At any given time, dozens of programmatic classes are offered to the public, so to speak, but only a few of them command wide acceptance. The mere mention of a programmatic class often tells us a great deal about the political opinions of the speaker. The ideology implied by a reference to "the urban poor," "Wall Street imperialists," "native Americans," "the jet set," "suburban squares," or "the toiling masses" is plain in each case. But only a few of these labels win sufficient favor so that the collectivity they denote is accepted as a reality by large numbers of people who identify themselves as belonging to the class in question. Whenever a programmatic class is accepted to that extent, important political consequences are certain to follow.[46]

Among the almost innumerable programmatic classes that have been proposed, a few stand out as especially influential. The section that follows briefly examines the *bourgeoisie* and the *proletariat* of Karl Marx, the *power elite* and the *new and old middle classes* of C. Wright Mills, and *the poor* of Michael Harrington.

THE BOURGEOISIE AND THE PROLETARIAT

The famous two-page incomplete last chapter of *Capital*[47] contains no reference to either the bourgeoisie or the proletariat. It begins with a bold statement that "wage laborers, capitalists and landowners" constitute the three great social classes, and breaks off in the middle of explaining how occupations that do not fit into these categories should be treated. However, the terms bourgeoisie and proletariat appear repeatedly throughout the 51 previous chapters of *Capital* and very frequently in other works by Marx and Engels, usually charged with the same connotations they have in Marxian literature today.

Part of the fascination of this pair of terms is that each of them has two meanings, one narrow and the other wide, which are often interchanged on the same page or within the same sentence. In the narrow sense, the bourgeoisie are the capitalists who control large-scale industry; they are people who own and operate factories. The proletariat are the propertyless wage-workers who get their living in the same factories. In the wide sense, the bourgeoisie includes all the managers, proprietors, and executives who have any share in the direction of a capitalist economy, the officials of government and private bureaucracies, professionals, technicians, artists, and even factory workers who are politically conservative. In the wide sense, the membership of the proletariat is expanded to include all manual workers, all farmers, and all the lower-ranking white-collar occupations. In countries that have had a Communist revolution, the bourgeoisie officially disappears but is resuscitated from time to time when the state identifies prosperous peasants or independent professionals or factory managers as "counterrevolutionary." Proletarian becomes a ceremonial term that applies to the entire population, or to that part of it that enjoys a clean bill of political health, including, on occasion, the high officials of the government and the armed forces, and the managerial cadres of heavy industry.

In democratic countries, the term bourgeoisie has a variety of pejorative meanings. In some contexts, it refers to the middle class in a three-class system; in other connections, it means "square" or unresponsive to avant-garde ideas in art, literature, and life style.

THE NEW MIDDLE CLASSES AND THE POWER ELITE

C. Wright Mills (1916–1962) occupied a unique place in American sociology. He was a rebel against the established order who described that order in elaborate and loving detail. It is often difficult to draw the line between statistical facts and poetical images in Mills' work—he had the habit of demonstrating a trend and then assuming that the trend had run its full course—but his description of stratification in the United States is one of the few serious attempts to comprehend American society as a whole. It is contained in two of his books: *White Collar,* published in 1951, and *The Power Elite,* published in 1956.[48]

White Collar describes the decline of the "old middle class" consisting of independent farmers, proprietors, and free professionals and the rise of the "new middle class" consisting of managers, salaried professionals, salespeople, and office workers.[49] Mills views the typical member of the new middle class, whom he sometimes calls the Little Man, with pity and contempt:

> He is more often pitiful than tragic, as he is seen collectively, fighting impersonal inflation, living out in slow misery his yearning for the quick American climb. He is pushed by forces beyond his control, pulled into movements he does not understand; he gets into situations in which his is the most helpless position. The white-collar man is the hero as victim, the small creature who is acted upon but does not act, who works along unnoticed in somebody's office or store, never talking loud, never talking back, never taking a stand.[50]

The misery of Mills' Little Man consists in his subjection to the large bureaucratic organizations by which he is employed, governed, entertained, and manipulated; whose workings he cannot understand and whose policies he cannot influence. According to Mills, the new middle class resembles a proletariat in being propertyless, exploited, and alienated. But unlike wage workers, the Little Men have no awareness of their own predicament and have remained politically inert.[51] Their values, according to Mills, are borrowed either from the old middle class, whose situation was profoundly different, or from the bureaucratic managers by whom they are manipulated:

> Under the system of explicit authority, in the round, solid nineteenth century, the victim knew he was being victimized, the misery and discontent of the powerless were explicit. In the amorphous twentieth century world, where manipulation replaces authority, the victim does not recognize his status. The formal aim, implemented by the latest psychological equipment, is to have men internalize what the managerial cadres would have them do, without their knowing their own motives. . . . [52]

In *White Collar,* these managerial cadres are not clearly visualized, although some distinctions are drawn between top managers who shape policy and the middle managers who exercise limited powers in the grip of the bureaucratic machine. But at that point Mills was more interested in the depersonalization of management than in the personal characteristics of the managers. Under the heading "the Managerial Demiurge," he discussed the bureaucratization of management, the "fetishization" of the enterprise and the shift from explicit authority to manipulation. He saw little difference between white-collar work and white-collar leisure, and he lamented the transition from rural to urban values.

> No longer is the framework within which a man lives fixed by traditional institutions. Mass communications replace tradition as a framework of life. Being thus afloat, the metropolitan man finds a new anchorage in the spectator sports, the idols of mass media, and other machineries of amusement. . . .
> The amusement of hollow people rests on their own hollowness and does not fill it up; it does not calm or relax them, as old middle-class frolics and jollifications may have done.[53]

In *The Power Elite,* the Managerial Demiurge is replaced by a small group of real people whom Mills identifies as the rulers of American society. These are the men who command the major hierarchies, run the machinery of the corporations and of the state, direct the military establishment, "occupy the strategic command posts of the social structure," and are rewarded by power, wealth, and celebrity beyond the dreams of ordinary men. The novelty of Mills' thesis lies in his insistence that the power elite is a unified social stratum that includes not only the top managers of the major public and private bureaucracies but also the family-conscious upper classes of the big cities, the celebrities of the stage and screen, heiresses, admirals, Congressmen and TV comedians. Social power in our time is said to be derived from large-scale bureaucratic institutions. The power elite are those who occupy the strategic posts in those institutions. They are supposed to exhibit psychological affinities, to move freely from top positions in one kind of structure to top positions in another, to share the same conservative biases, to participate in the same "higher immorality," and to profit in the same way from the complexity of institutional structures and the secrecy that surrounds decision-making at the upper levels.[54]

The Power Elite is a sermon against a system that awards power not to "representative men whose conduct and character constitute models," but to those who have found or been given the keys to a bureaucratic status order and who have "succeeded in the American system of organized irresponsibility." Coupled with Mills' disapproval of the institutional arrangements that award status on the basis of inheritance, luck, accident, or intrigue is his fascination with luxury and power:

> All over the world, like lords of creation, are those who, by travel, command the seasons and, by many houses, the very landscape they will see each morning and afternoon they are awakened. Here is the old whiskey and the new vice; the blonde girl with the moist mouth, always ready to go around the world; the silver Mercedes climbing the mountain bend, going where it wants to go for so long as it wants to stay. . . .

Here are the officials at the big desks with the four telephones, the ambassadors in the lounge-rooms, talking earnestly but somehow lightly. Here are the men who motor in from the airport with a secret service man beside the chauffeur, motorcycle outriders on either flank, and another tailing a block behind. Here are the people whose circumstances make them independent of the good will of others, never waiting for anyone but always waited upon.[55]

The central theme of *The Power Elite,* that all the holders of high status in American society are linked together in one vast coalition to maintain the status quo in general and their own advantages in particular, achieved wide currency some years after Mills' death when the term, "the Establishment" was introduced and became a shorthand expression of this theory. The Establishment is a wider, more flexible category than the power elite, to which it stands in somewhat the same relationship as does the bourgeoisie to the capitalists. That is, those identified with the Establishment include not only the rich, powerful, and famous people of the power elite but also anyone else who appears to support the status quo[56]—middle managers, newspaper reporters, conservative clergymen, or college deans, for example.

THE POOR AND THE URBAN POOR

The poor (and the urban poor) are the first programmatic classes to be officially recognized and enumerated in the United States. According to a news item in *The New York Times:*

> The government announced today some refinements in its methods of calculating poverty and discovered as a result that there were 1.6 million more poor persons in 1967 than had been thought.
> The new figure for 1967 is just under 27.8 million, including children. The present number of poor is not known but is probably lower.
> The new statistical definition revises upwards significantly the level of income at which non-foreign families are considered poor.
> The figure previously used was $3,335 annually for a family of four. That has been revised upwards to $3,410 for 1967 and, under the changes announced today, will work out to be a little more than $3,700 for 1969 because of the rise of prices.[57]

The official acceptance of the poor as a distinct category of persons and families, and the acknowledgement that their poverty presents a problem calling for governmental action, can be traced back to a single book by a nonacademic sociologist, Michael Harrington's *The Other America,* published in 1962.[58] Before its appearance, the poor had not been visualized as a distinct or permanent stratum of the American population. On the contrary, it was customary, in the Eisenhower years, to speak of the United States as an affluent society[59] in which the average level of living was higher than ever before or anywhere else, and was constantly rising so that whatever unmet needs remained were certain to be met sooner or later. The long-range problems of the affluent society were said to revolve around the imbalance between the prosperity of consumers and the relative impoverishment of public institutions and facilities.

The Other America demolished this complacent assumption without challenging the facts on which it had been based. Harrington identified between 40 and 50 million Americans, nearly a fourth of the total population, as poor. He admitted that they were not impoverished in the same way as the poor in nations where poverty is associated with starvation, but he maintained that some of them suffered from real hunger, that they lacked adequate housing, education, and medical care, and that perceiving their situation as hopeless, they were pessimistic and unhappy to a degree unsuspected by the rest of the population. Harrington accounted for the "invisibility" of the poor by their location in urban and rural slums off the beaten track, by the isolation of suburban dwellers from the city, by the standardization of clothing in the United States, and by the lack of political organization among the poor. The poor, he said, are those people who are immune to progress; indeed who suffer from progress because they lack the necessary education and skills to benefit from technological advancement. As the rest of the society moves ahead, their chances of obtaining normal jobs and incomes diminish. They are more tightly locked into a vicious circle of inadequate earnings and disorganized family life, leading to substandard education and occupational marginality for the next generation.

Harrington asserted that the resources of the affluent society were clearly adequate to raise this entire population out of poverty and that their continued presence was a national scandal. The poor, according to Harrington, fell into several types: migrant farm laborers and displaced farmers, those who remained behind in backward agricultural areas, the inhabitants of Negro ghettos in the large cities, the beats and Bohemians, who comprised the "intellectual poor," men on Skid Row, "urban hillbillies," old men and women living on inadequate pensions, and white slum families handicapped by unemployment, mental illness, alcoholism, illegitimacy and desertion, chronic illness, crime, ignorance, and the unwholesome living conditions of low-rent public housing projects. Some of these groups are relatively small and some are enormous. The total number of Skid Row men in the United States is probably not much over 100,000, but aged persons living on inadequate pensions may number 10 million or more.

Harrington's book aroused an almost instantaneous nationwide response. Less than three years later the first of a series of antipoverty programs had been launched by the federal government, and an economist could write, "I think it is fair to say that the outstanding fact about the problem of poverty in the United States today is our increased sensitivity to it."[60] The Johnson Administration was committed to a "war on poverty" and had created the Office of Economic Opportunity to direct it. Definitions of poverty had been developed by the Council of Economic Advisors, the Census Bureau, the Social Security Administration, and a number of private experts. And all of them confirmed that a sizable proportion (estimates ranged from 10 percent to 23 percent) of all families and an even higher proportion of single-person households were afflicted by poverty.[61]

The war on poverty reached its zenith with the passage of the Economic Opportunity Act of 1964, which included provisions for youth programs (the Job Corps, state-operated youth camps, work-training programs, work-study programs), urban and rural community action programs (general programs, adult basic education programs, the volunteer assistance program for needy children), rural antipoverty programs, employment and investment incentives, and work experience programs, together with provisions for the administration, coordination, and financing of all these activities.[62] It ran parallel to the involvement of the Johnson Administration in a vast campaign for civil rights, which reached its height with the passage of the Civil Rights Act of 1964 and the Voting Rights Act of 1965. Toward the end of 1966, the war on poverty began to be pushed aside by escalation of the war in Vietnam. Although existing antipoverty programs were continued, nothing new was done about poverty until President Nixon's proposal of a guaranteed minimum income in 1969.

Besides the stalemated war on poverty and the lost war in Vietnam, the decade of the 1960s saw an extremely rapid increase in the black proportion of the population in large metropolitan areas;[63] destructive riots in Watts, Detroit, Newark, and more than 200 other communities; the Black Power movement; the assassination of Dr. Martin Luther King; a fairly rapid expansion of the welfare population, and a series of dramatic changes in the structure of the civil rights movement. Nearly continuous exposure of these events on the front page and on the television screen changed the focus of attention from the poor into the *urban poor,* who were now understood to be black.

THE MOYNIHAN REPORT AND ITS CONSEQUENCES

In an address at Howard University in June 1965, President Johnson described the urban poor and offered a sociological analysis of their situation.

> Men and women of all races are born with the same range of abilities. But ability is not just the product of birth. Ability is stretched or stunted by the family you live with, and the neighborhood you live in, by the school you go to and the poverty or richness of your surroundings. It is a produce of a hundred unseen forces playing upon the child, the infant, and the man. . . .
>
> The number of Negroes in schools of higher learning has almost doubled in fifteen years. The number of non-white professional workers has more than doubled in ten years. The median income of Negro college women exceeds that of white college women. And there are also the enormous accomplishments of distinguished individual Negroes. . . .

These are proud and impressive achievements. But they tell only the story of a growing middle-class minority, steadily narrowing the gap between them and their white counterparts.

But for the great majority of Negro Americans—the poor, the unemployed, the uprooted and the dispossessed—there is a much grimmer story. They still are another nation. Despite the court orders and the laws, despite the legislative victories and the speeches, for them the walls are rising and the gulf is widening. . . . [64]

He went on to say that the rate of unemployment for Negroes was twice as high as for whites; that the ratio of average Negro family income to average white family income had declined from 57 percent to 53 percent in the previous decade; that infant mortality among Negroes had declined more slowly than among whites; and that the isolation of Negroes from the white community was increasing as they crowded into the central cities: more than 73 percent of the total black population lived in urban areas in 1965 compared to less than 70 percent of the whites. "Negro poverty," said the President, "is not white poverty. Many of its causes and many of its cures are the same. But there are differences. . . .

"Perhaps the most important—its influence radiating to every part of life—is the breakdown of Negro family structure. For this, most of all, white America must accept responsibility. It flows from centuries of oppression and persecution of the Negro man. It flows from long years of degradation and discrimination, which have attacked his dignity and assaulted his ability to provide for his family."[65]

The President's remarks were based on a report prepared by Daniel Patrick Moynihan, then Assistant Secretary of Labor, some weeks previously, which set forth the thesis that "family structure of lower-class Negroes is highly unstable, and in many urban centers is approaching complete breakdown."[66] Moynihan presented data to show that nearly a quarter of the Negro women living in cities who had ever been married were divorced, separated, or living apart from their husbands in 1960, and that among them, the proportion of married women with husbands present declined with age. The nonwhite illegitimacy ratio was eight times the white ratio and apparently increasing; nearly a fourth of Negro families were headed by women (see Table 7–6). Negro females, Moynihan showed, had a higher level of educational achievement than Negro males and achieved higher occupational status when employed. He went on to show that the intelligence scores and school achievement of Negro children were lower when they came from homes without fathers. Moreover, the disproportionately high crime rates of Negroes (at the time, they accounted for well over half the arrests in the nation), their high rate of failure on the armed forces mental test (almost four times as high as that of whites), and their high rates of narcotics addiction (more than half of all known narcotics addicts were Negro) could all be traced back to the weakness of the Negro family, its tendency toward ma-

	Table 7-6	THE DEMOGRAPHY OF POVERTY—SELECTED CHARAC-TERISTICS OF A SAMPLE OF NEVER MARRIED NEGRO WOMEN ON WELFARE IN NEW YORK CITY IN 1966

	Under 30	30-39	40 and Over
	Age of Respondent		
Community of rearing			
N.Y.C.-reared	45%	30%	14%
Another city	23	31	26
Town or farm	33	39	60
	101%	100%	100%
Childhood guardian			
Both parents	38%	41%	46%
Mother only	37	35	23
Other	25	24	31
	100%	100%	100%
Number of own siblings			
2 or less	38%	41%	57%
3 or 4	17	14	9
5 or more	45	45	34
	100%	100%	100%
Education			
Grade 8 or less	16%	45%	69%
Grade 9 to 11	57	35	26
High school graduate	27	20	6
	100%	100%	101%
Age at birth of first child			
Under 19 years	58%	42%	38%
19 or 20 years	20	19	12
21 years and over	23	39	50
	101%	100%	100%
Number of children borne			
2 or less	53%	28%	29%
3 or 4	35	31	23
5 or more	12	41	49
	100%	100%	100%
Number	(190)	(104)	(35)

Source: Based on Lawrence Podell, Families on Welfare in New York City, Preliminary Report No. 1, "Women, With and Without Husbands, on Welfare" (New York: City University of New York, Center for Social Research, November 22, 1967), table J, p. 27.

triarchy, and the fact that a large proportion, perhaps the majority, of Negro boys did not grow up under paternal authority.

The Moynihan Report raised a storm of controversy. It was excoriated by civil rights leaders as providing documentation for racism and as an attempt to hold Negroes responsible for their own disadvantaged position. It was attacked by welfare administrators and experts for seeming to hint that the welfare system had failed to relieve poverty and had contributed to the breakdown of the Negro family by offering a financial premium, in the form of aid to dependent children, to fatherless families. Finally, it was criticized by a number of sociologists for dramatic exaggeration, particularly for its assertion that the Negro family in the urban ghetto was "crumbling."

It is still difficult to determine the ultimate effect of the Moynihan Report and the discussion that followed. It may have contributed, in the late sixties, both to the "white backlash" and to the "black backlash." In any case, the urban poor have become a programmatic class almost unprecedented in American or even in modern European history, recognized by law, the object of innumerable public and private programs, increasingly class-conscious, and increasingly isolated from direct contact with other classes. The hope of erasing status distinctions based on race and integrating black Americans into a color-blind national society remains remote more than a hundred years after the guns fell silent at Appomattox.

1   Among the usual bases of stratification in modern societies are occupation, education, property, lineage, ethnicity, religion, affiliations, and personal influence. Occupation is the principal determinant of status in the Eastern (communist) system; property and ethnicity play a larger part in the Western (capitalist or socialist) system.

2   The Western system of stratification includes vestiges of the medieval estate system as well as important distinctions between white-collar and manual workers, and between owners and employees. Marx interpreted these differences in terms of "exploitation" and "class conflict." Max Weber provided a different explanation, which posited two separate class systems, one based on occupational differences and the other on life style.

3   The European exploration and conquest of the world that began in the fifteenth century and continued until early in the twentieth century led to the establishment of more than 40 multiracial national societies, and to many different patterns of stratification in which status is ascribed according to race. Another effect of European expansion was to establish a status order of nations, based on their unequal levels of modernization.

4   Various models of stratification have been proposed for American communities and for the United States as a whole, varying from a "no-class" model to models with six or more classes. None of these models commands universal agreement. There is no question that this society is heavily stratified, but it is difficult to obtain agreement as to where the boundaries of social classes should be placed.

5   Programmatic classes, sharing a common identity, are called into being by political and social events and the development of associated ideologies. Whenever a programmatic class is accepted as a reality by large numbers of people, important political consequences can be expected to follow.

Questions for Discussion / CHAPTER SEVEN

1 Can you explain why there is no peasant class in the United States?

2 The laws of some southern states forbidding interracial marriage have recently been declared unconstitutional. What does this signify from the standpoint of stratification?

3 How do you account for the fact that the countries of western Europe have higher levels of development, on the average, than the countries of eastern Europe? What would it take to change this situation?

4 "To study social classes is to change them." What does this statement mean?

5 Select the small community you know best and diagram its class system. What is the minimum number of classes that must be recognized?

6 Using whatever information is available about the same community, list as many correlates of class position as you can discover. What do you learn from this procedure?

7 Would you consider the principal of the high school you attended to be a member of the Establishment? Middle-class or upper-class? Powerful or powerless? How could you verify these answers?

8 Review your understanding of the following terms:

urban poor	status group
bourgeoisie	white-collar
caste	modernization
commensalism	ascription

Recommended Reading / CHAPTER SEVEN

Mayer, Kurt. *Class and Society,* rev. ed. New York: Random House, 1955. An excellent, brief introduction to the study of social stratification.

Bendix, Reinhard and Seymour Martin Lipset, eds., *Class, Status, and Power: Social Stratification in Comparative Perspective,* 2d ed. New York: Free Press, 1966; Roach, Jack L., Llewellyn Gross, and Orville R. Gursslin. *Social Stratification in the United States.* Englewood Cliffs, N.J.: Prentice-Hall, 1969. Both volumes present a miscellany of interesting information on stratification.

Mills, C. Wright. *The Power Elite.* New York: Oxford University Press, 1956; Keller, Suzanne. *Beyond the Ruling Class: Strategic Elites in Modern Society.* New York: Random House, 1963; and Rose, Arnold M. *The Power Structure: Political Process in American Society.* New York: Oxford University Press, 1967. Three different opinions about the relationship between stratification and political power in the United States.

Horowitz, Irving Louis. *Three Worlds of Development: The Theory and*

Practice of International Stratification. New York: Oxford University Press, 1966. One of the few systematic treatments of international stratification.

Notes / **CHAPTER SEVEN**

1. Leonard Broom and Philip Selznick, *Sociology,* 4th ed. (New York: Harper & Row, 1968), pp. 171–172.
2. This analysis follows Max Weber; see his *Economy and Society,* 3 vols., eds. Guenther Roth and Claus Wittich, vol. 2 (New York: Bedminster Press, 1968), pp. 926–939.
3. See Mysore N. Srinivas, *Social Change in Modern India* (Berkeley: University of California Press, 1966). For an interesting account of an entire Indian caste that succeeded in changing its status, see Lloyd I. Rudolph's account of the metamorphosis of the unclean Shanans of Madras into the relatively high-ranking Nadurs in "The Modernity of Tradition: The Democratic Incarnation of Caste in India," *American Political Science Review* 59, no. 4 (December 1965): 975–989.
4. *Quotations from Chairman Mao Tse-Tung* (New York: Praeger, 1967), chap. 3, pp. 16–17.
5. See David Granick, *The Red Executive: A Study of the Organization Man in Russian Industry* (Garden City, N.Y.: Anchor Books, 1961); Alex Inkeles, "Social Stratification and Mobility in the Soviet Union," in *Class, Status, and Power: Social Stratification in Comparative Perspective,* 2d ed., eds. Reinhard Bendix and Seymour Martin Lipset (New York: Free Press 1966), pp. 516–626; George Fischer, *The Soviet System and Modern Society* (New York: Atherton Press, 1968).
6. Civilized societies, that is. Some simple peoples have little or no stratification. The classic study is Leonard T. Hobhouse, G. C. Wheeler, and M. Ginsberg, *The Material Culture and Social Institutions of the Simpler Peoples: An Essay in Correlation* (New York: Humanities Press, 1965), originally published 1915. See also George Peter Murdock, *Social Structure* (New York: Macmillan, 1949).
7. Raymond Aron, "Social Class, Political Class, Ruling Class," in Bendix and Lipset, *Class, Status, and Power,* pp. 201–202.
8. For a fuller description of the European estate system, see Egon Ernest Bergel, *Social Stratification* (New York: McGraw-Hill, 1962).
9. Katherine George and Charles H. George, "Roman Catholic Sainthood and Social Status," in Bendix and Lipset, *Class, Status, and Power,* pp. 394–401.
10. This classification is based on T. H. Marshall, *Class, Citizenship and Social Development* (Garden City, N.Y.: Doubleday, 1964), pp. 71–72. For a summary of the historical development, see Reinhard

Bendix, *Nation-Building and Citizenship: Studies of Our Changing Social Order* (New York: John Wiley, 1964), pp. 74–104.

11. Henri Pirenne, "Stages in the Social History of Capitalism," in Bendix and Lipset, *Class, Status, and Power,* pp. 97–107.

12. John Ulric Nef, *The Rise of the British Coal Industry* (London: George Routledge and Sons, 1932).

13. One of the best historical accounts of the origins of industrial machinery is in Karl Marx, *Capital: A Critical Analysis of Capitalist Production* (New York: International Publishers, 1947), chap. 15. Originally published 1887.

14. Max Weber, *The Protestant Ethic and the Spirit of Capitalism,* trans. Talcott Parsons (New York: Scribner's, 1930); Richard H. Tawney, *Religion and the Rise of Capitalism* (Gloucester, Mass.: Peter Smith, 1963). Originally published 1926.

15. Marx, *Capital,* p. 230.

16. Especially in *The German Ideology* (with Friedrich Engels) (New York: International Publishers, 1939); and *The Eighteenth Brumaire of Louis Bonaparte* (New York: International Publishers, 1964).

17. Weber, *Economy and Society,* vol. 1, chap. 4, pp. 302–307; and vol. 2, chap. 9, pp. 926–940.

18. *Ibid.,* vol. 2, p. 937.

19. See Carlo M. Cipolla, *Guns and Sails in the Early Phase of European Expansion, 1400–1700* (London: Collins, 1965).

20. U.S. Bureau of the Census, *Historical Statistics of the United States: Colonial Times to 1957* (Washington: Government Printing Office, 1957), Series A95–122.

21. A summary of racial distributions in Western Hemisphere countries can be found in Marvin Harris, *Patterns of Race in the Americas* (New York: Walker, 1964), pp. 120–133; and for African countries south of the Sahara in Michael Banton, *Race Relations* (New York: Basic Books, 1967), pp. 214–221.

22. See, for example, W. Lloyd Warner and Leo Srole, *The Social Systems of American Ethnic Groups* (New Haven: Yale University Press, 1945).

23. For another description of international stratification, see Gustavo Lagos, *International Stratification and Underdeveloped Countries* (Chapel Hill: University of North Carolina Press, 1963).

24. Robert K. Merton and Alice S. Rossi, "Contributions to the Theory of Reference Group Behavior," pp. 279–334, in *Social Theory and Social Structure,* ed. Robert K. Merton, enlarged ed. (New York: Free Press, 1968).

25. The most influential of these works was Michael Harrington, *The Other America: Poverty in the United States* (New York: Macmillan, 1964). For evidence of the new class consciousness of the poor after 1963, see Lewis M. Killian, *The Impossible Revolution? Black Power and the American Dream* (New York: Random House, 1968).

26. Robert S. Lynd and Helen Merrell Lynd, *Middletown: A Study in*

American Culture (New York: Harcourt Brace Jovanovich, 1929).

27. *Ibid.,* pp. 22–24.

28. W. Lloyd Warner and Paul S. Lunt, *The Social Life of a Modern Community* (New Haven: Yale University Press, 1941); and *The Status System of a Modern Community* (New Haven: Yale University Press, 1942). See also the discussion of Warner's work in Chapter Three above.

29. August B. Hollingshead, *Elmtown's Youth: The Impact of Social Classes on Adolescents* (New York: John Wiley, 1949).

30. *Ibid.,* p. 103.

31. John Dollard, *Caste and Class in a Southern Town,* 2d ed. (New York: Harper & Row, 1949). Dollard's study was followed by several others, including Hortense Powdermaker, *After Freedom: A Cultural Study in the Deep South* (New York: Viking, 1939); Allison Davis, Burleigh B. Gardner, and Mary R. Gardner, *Deep South: A Social Anthropological Study of Caste and Class* (Chicago: University of Chicago Press, 1942, abridged ed., 1965). For a later and in some ways, more detailed description of caste and class in the rural South, see Morton Rubin, *Plantation County* (Chapel Hill, N.C.: University of North Carolina Press, 1951).

32. W. Lloyd Warner, *American Life: Dream and Reality* (Chicago: University of Chicago Press, 1953), p. 69.

33. An excellent discussion of the relationship between Hindu caste and American color-caste may be found in Banton, *Race Relations,* especially chap. 5, "Contact, Symbiosis and Acculturation."

34. The outward acceptance and inner rejection of color-caste etiquette is very clearly described in a white journalist's account of his travels through the South in 1959 disguised as a Negro. John Howard Griffin, *Black Like Me* (Boston: Houghton Mifflin, 1961).

35. Banton, *Race Relations,* p. 139.

36. William Brink and Louis Harris, *Black and White: A Study of U.S. Racial Attitudes Today* (New York: Simon & Schuster, 1967).

37. Some sociologists believe that intolerance and ethnic prejudice are normally prevalent in the lower strata of modern democratic societies. See the famous paper of Seymour Martin Lipset, "Democracy and Working-Class Authoritarianism," *American Sociological Review* 24, no. 4 (August 1959): 482–501.

38. Bert N. Adams, *Kinship in an Urban Setting* (Chicago: Markham, 1968).

39. This point can be disputed. For a fuller description of the issues involved, see William M. Dobriner, *Class in Suburbia* (Englewood Cliffs, N.J.: Prentice-Hall, 1963).

40. Richard Centers, *The Psychology of Social Classes: A Study of Class Consciousness* (New York: Russell and Russell, 1961). See also Jack L. Roach, Llewellyn Gross, and Orville R. Gurs-

slin, *Social Stratification in the United States* (Englewood Cliffs, N.J.: Prentice-Hall, 1969), chap. 3, pp. 74–149.

41. Bergel, *Social Stratification,* p. 277.
42. Joseph Alan Kahl, *The American Class Structure* (New York: Holt, Rinehart &Winston, 1957)
43. Robert A. Nisbet, *Tradition and Revolt: Historical and Sociological Essays* (New York: Random House, 1968), chap. 6, "The Decline and Fall of Social Class," p. 123.
44. *Ibid.,* p. 125.
45. For an excellent discussion of the relationship between social class and political power in communities, see William V. D'Antonio and William H. Form, *Influentials in Two Border Cities· A Study in Community Decision-Making* (Notre Dame, Indiana: University of Notre Dame Press, 1965), especially chap. 9.
46. For an exposition of American political history in terms of programmatic classes—although the author uses other terms for them—see Norbert Wiley, "America's Unique Class Politics: The Interplay of the Labor, Credit and Commodity Markets," *American Sociological Review* 32, no. 4 (August 1967): 529–541.
47. Marx, *Capital,* chap. 52.
48. C. Wright Mills, *White Collar: The American Middle Classes* (New York: Oxford University Press, 1951); *The Power Elite* (New York: Oxford University Press, 1956).
49. See Mills, *White Collar,* chap. 4, pp. 63–76; and *Historical Statistics of the United States,* Series D 123–572.
50. Mills, *White Collar,* p. xii.
51. An interesting attempt to describe psychological differences between the old middle class and the new middle class can be found in Joel I. Nelson, "Anomie: Comparisons Between the Old and the New Middle Class," *American Journal of Sociology* 74, no. 2 (September 1968): 184–192.
52. Mills, *White Collar,* p. 110.
53. *Ibid.,* p. 238.
54. Another, more neutrally toned attempt to identify a national upper class is E. Digby Baltzell, *The Protestant Establishment: Aristocracy and Caste in America* (New York: Random House, 1964). See also Stephen Birmingham, *The Right People: A Portrait of the American Social Establishment* (Boston: Little, Brown, 1968). A refutation of Mills' argument " . . . that there is a secret, hierarchical, and unified power structure in the United States . . . " was attempted by Arnold M. Rose, *The Power Structure: Political Process in American Society* (New York: Oxford University Press, 1967).
55. Mills, *The Power Elite,* pp. 92–93.
56. Empirical data on the relationship between status and participation in national politics can be found in William Kornhauser, *The Politics of Mass Society* (New York: Free Press, 1959); and in Herbert Tingsten, *Political Behavior: Studies in Election Statistics,* trans. Vilgot Mammerling (Totowa, N.J.: Bedminster Press, 1963), pp. 120–181.
57. *The New York Times,* August 16, 1969, p. C15.

58. Harrington, *The Other America.*
59. From John Kenneth Galbraith, *The Affluent Society* (Boston: Houghton Mifflin, 1958).
60. R. A. Gordon, "An Economist's View of Poverty," in *Poverty in America: Proceedings of a National Conference,* ed. Margaret S. Gordon (San Francisco: Chandler, 1965), p. 3.
61. Herman P. Miller, "Changes in the Number and Composition of the Poor," in *Ibid.,* pp. 81–101.
62. Public Law 88–452, 88th Cong., S.2642, August 20, 1964.
63. See Chapter Five above.
64. Remarks of President Lyndon B. Johnson at Howard University, June 4, 1965.
65. *Ibid.*
66. From Chap. 2 of the Moynihan Report, as reproduced in Lee Rainwater and William L. Yancey, *The Moynihan Report and the Politics of Controversy* (Cambridge, Mass.: M.I.T. Press, 1967), p. 51.

Work

Introduction

T*he sociology of work is the study of the social facts associated with the division of labor.* The fundamental concept in this branch of sociology is that of an occupation.

An occupation is a pattern of activities with a market value, which an individual pursues on a regular basis in order to obtain a livelihood.[1] Most people follow only a single occupation at a given time, although it is possible to have two or more. A man's principal occupation is usually a major factor in determining his general social status. A woman's social status is influenced both by her own occupation, if she has one, and by those of her father and husband at different stages of her life. After sex and age, occupation is perhaps the most important identifying characteristic that the sociologist needs to record for any subject he observes or interviews: it usually tells him more, for example, than the subject's place of birth, marital status, or education.

The labor force of any society consists of those persons who have occupations in the sense described above, whether or not they are working at a given time. In most industrial societies, the size of the labor force varies between 50 percent and 60 percent of the total population over 16. Of the remaining population, the largest number are women engaged in full-time housekeeping or child care; most of the rest are full-time students, elderly retired workers, or the inmates of institutions.

Division of Labor

All societies, even the simplest, have norms for assigning different kinds of work to their members according to sex and age, and all societies seem to have a few specialists, even those in which most adults do the same type of work.[2] In simple, rural societies, a surprising number of distinctive occupations are practiced, although the great majority of the population are engaged in a single primary occupation. In Tepoztlán, the Indian village in Mexico studied first by Redfield and then by Lewis, about 90 percent of the employed population were engaged in farming in 1948. The remainder were divided among 26 occupations, including rope makers, midwives, healers, masons, bakers, teachers, storekeepers, butchers, barbers, corn merchants, charcoal makers, tile and brick makers, bus employees, shoemakers, carpenters, ironworkers, silverworkers, millers, chauffeurs, druggists, plumbers, makers of fireworks and masks, and specialists in magic and traditional rituals.[3]

Both urbanization and modernization intensify the division of labor and are intimately connected with it. Why and how the division of a single occupation into a number of more specialized occupations increases productivity, even without new machinery, was first explained by Adam Smith in the famous pinmaking example in *The Wealth of Nations*.[4] The way in which the division of labor affects the entire structure of a modern society was analyzed more than a century later by Emile Durkheim,[5] who showed how the occupational specialization of a modernizing society leads to a type of solidarity based on mutual dependence in place of primitive social solidarity based on similarity (see Chapter Four).

A modern version of this theory is admirably stated by Everett Hughes:

> Division of labor, one of the most fundamental of all social processes, finds one of its most explicit expressions in occupations. The phrase, however, is but a poor term for differentiation of function in a social whole. It is poor because it emphasizes the division and neglects the integration, the relations among the functions so divided or differentiated. All organization of behavior consists of differentiation of function. Economic division of labor is but a special case, or a special aspect of it.
>
> An occupation, in essence, is not some particular set of activities; it is the part of an individual in any ongoing system of activities. The system may be large or small, simple or complex. The ties between the persons in different positions may be close or so distant as not to be social; they may be formal or informal, frequent or rare. The essential is that the occupation is the place ordinarily filled by one person in an organization or complex of efforts and activities. . . . The logic of the division and combination of activities and functions into occupations and of their allocation to various kinds of people in any system is not to be assumed as given but is in any case something to be discovered.[6]

CONSEQUENCE OF A PROGRESSIVE DIVISION OF LABOR

Under an advancing technology, a condition that now applies to most of the world's countries, the division of labor evolves continuously toward greater specialization of function and a more complex interdependence of productive tasks. This movement has certain seemingly inevitable consequences with respect to occupations.

In the first place, they become more numerous. New occupations develop in great numbers and existing ones are subdivided. The first occupational census of the United States, taken in connection with the decennial census of 1850, was able to cover the population satisfactorily with 323 occupations. The 1965 edition of the *Dictionary of Occupational Titles* listed 21,741 separate occupations.[7] Admittedly, the Dictionary recognizes finer subdivisions, but much of the increase is real.

Secondly, the rate of change within occupations—that is, the transformation of occupational tasks, the training required for them, and the conditions under which they are performed—greatly accelerates. One of the most interesting and important concomitants of a progressive division of labor is a decrease of competence in areas of life other than the occupational specialty one engages in:

> The modern urban dweller is perhaps the first man in history who would starve if placed in a fertile wilderness with appropriate tools. Even the expert, with some skill developed to a superlative degree, does not control any major fraction of current technology. Modern generals do not lead charges, and many a modern architect would be unable to construct a sturdy shed. Yet the speed and precision of thousands of human operations have been developed to an extent which would once have been regarded as humanly impossible.[8]

Classification of Occupations

The first occupational census of the United States in 1850 used a simple list of occupational titles such as farmer, merchant, cobbler. The 323 occupations in the alphabetical list were grouped into 15 economic categories: commerce; trade; manufacturing; mechanical arts and mining; agriculture; nonagricultural labor; army; sea and river navigation; law, medicine, and divinity; other pursuits requiring education; government and civil service; domestic services; other occupations. The first attempt to fit occupations into a status hierarchy was made in 1897 by William C. Hunt, who grouped all of the gainful workers reported by the Census of 1890 into four categories—the proprietor class, the clerical class, skilled workers, and the laboring class. This was the first in a long series of schemes for describing the stratification of the general population by means of an occupational distribution. Some of these scales were constructed through measurement of the intelligence of people in different occupations, or calculation of their average income, or determining by means of an opinion poll how much prestige was accorded to each occupation by the general public. The scale used by the Bureau of the Census, however, was developed without external verification by Alba Edwards for comparing the results of the census of 1940 with those of earlier censuses.[9] Although many details of the Edwards scale have since been changed, its general form has remained the same. Most of the information we have about occupational distribution, occupational mobility and occupational trends in the United States is expressed in terms of this scale, and every student of sociology should be thoroughly familiar with it.

In its original form, the Edwards scale had six major categories, described as "social-economic classes," and numbered as follows:

6. Professional persons

5. Proprietors, managers, and officials
    5a. farm owners and tenants
    5b. wholesale and retail dealers
    5c. other proprietors, managers, and officials

4. Clerks and kindred workers

3. Skilled workers and foremen

2. Semiskilled workers

1. Unskilled workers
    1a. farm laborers
    1b,c. nonfarm laborers   1d. service classes

Farm owners and tenants were classified as proprietors or managers; farm laborers as unskilled workers. There was no provision for separating domestic servants from workers in service businesses like restaurants or laundries. No distinction was made between office workers and salespeople. These and many other problems have been ironed out in the current form of the scale, which reads as follows:

White Collar
    Professional, technical, and kindred workers
    Managers, officials and proprietors (except farm)
    Clerical and kindred workers
    Sales workers

Blue Collar
    Craftsmen, foremen, and kindred workers
    Operatives and kindred workers
    Laborers (except farm)

Service
    Private household workers
    Other service workers

Farm
    Farm owners and managers
    Farm laborers and foremen

Table 8–1 shows the distribution of men and women employed in the United States in March 1967 by these occupational categories. In

Table 8-1	OCCUPATIONS OF EMPLOYED PERSONS IN THE UNITED STATES, 1968 (IN MILLIONS OF PERSONS)		
Occupational Group		Men	Women
White collar		(19.1)	(16.3)
Professional, technical, and kindred workers		6.4	4.0
Managers, officials, and proprietors (except farm)		6.5	1.2
Clerical and kindred workers		3.4	9.2
Sales workers		2.7	1.8
Blue collar		(21.9)	(4.6)
Craftsmen, foremen, and kindred workers		9.3	0.3
Operatives and kindred workers		9.6	4.2
Laborers (except farm)		3.0	0.1
Service		(3.3)	(6.1)
Private household workers		a	1.8
Other service workers		3.2	4.3
Farm		(2.8)	(0.5)
Total		(47.1)	(27.5)

aLess than 0.1.

Source: Based on *Statistical Abstract of the United States 1968*, table 324.

more extensive census tables, each of these major categories is broken down into finer subdivisions. For example, the major category of craftsmen, foremen, and kindred workers includes brick masons, stonemasons and stonesetters, carpenters, electricians, mechanics, and repairmen for air conditioning, heating, and refrigeration equipment, automobiles, and office machines; boilermakers, machinists, molders, toolmakers, diemakers, and toolsetters; and locomotive engineers and locomotive firemen, among many other trades.

SOME PROBLEMS OF OCCUPATIONAL CLASSIFICATION

The collection and analysis of occupational statistics involve many more problems than are involved, for example, in demographic statistics. Occupational designations are less valid and less reliable than designations of age, sex, or marital status and should always be handled with a certain caution. An occupation is not a fixed attribute of an individual, like his age. It can change from one day to the next. An individual may have more than one occupation; about 1 in 20 employed persons in the United States holds two or more jobs at any given time, and these may be in widely different occupations. Some occupations, like summer camp director, occupy the worker only a small part of the year, although they may provide most of his income. The occupation of an unemployed person may be literally impossible to determine, if he has held a variety of jobs in the past and is not looking for a specific type of job when questioned. Often, a single job has a multiple occupational character. The full-time driver of a farm truck may be considered either a truck driver or a farm laborer. The accountant managing a payroll office is both an accountant and an office manager. Even with the most elaborate classification, some occupations have no name or are unclassifiable for other reasons. The field supervisor of a public opinion survey belongs to an occupation —social science technician—that as yet has no place in the census classification. Illicit occupations, like bookmaker or call girl, are conventionally excluded from occupational classifications, presumably because of the difficulty of obtaining information about them.

Another group of problems has to do with the nature of an occupation as a social system. Some occupations, like the ministry, are almost worlds unto themselves. Others, like typing, are entirely unorganized and have hardly any trace of common norms and values. Some occupations, like locomotive engineer, have nearly standard working conditions and pay levels. Others, like entertainer, involve a vast range of working conditions and variations in earnings, running all the way from the highest levels in the economy down to negative income in cases where an entertainer's expenses exceed his pay. The occupation of farm owner has always been one of the most troublesome to classify, because it groups the half-starving operator of a one-acre tobacco farm in West Virginia with the millionaire manager and part owner of a 40,000-acre Texas ranch. Yet it is almost impossible to split this occupation by separating rich farmers from poor farmers without falling into other absurdities.

The occupational structure is itself in continuous flux. We can see the scale of the transformation by glancing at changes in occupational populations from one census to the next.[10] For example, between 1950 and 1960 there were seven occupational groups whose numbers more than doubled: industrial engineers, sales engineers, mathematicians, electrical and electronic technicians, other technicians, cashiers, and office machine operators. The electrical and electronic technicians, most of whom were located in the nearly brand-new electronics industry, increased by 679 percent in that decade. It is equally instructive to look at the declining occupations. The occupational groups whose numbers decreased by more than 10 percent from 1950 to 1960 were self-employed proprietors, carpenters, boilermakers, metal molders, locomotive engineers, locomotive firemen, and all categories of farmers. The number of farm owners and managers declined by 42 percent—an almost unbelievable rate, which nevertheless continued into the next decade. There was a further decline of 32 percent from 1960 to 1967, by which date the total population of independent farmers was less than 3 percent of the labor force and the total number of persons in farm occupations barely over 4 percent.

Most of the changes in occupational distribution that occur from year to year or from decade to decade are linked to long-term trends inherent in modern technology and social organization. Few of the changes that occur in this domain are entirely unexpected, and many of them can be predicted long in advance.

Table 8-2	GENERAL TRENDS IN OCCUPATIONAL DISTRIBUTION							

Occupational Group	Percent of Employed Persons in Each Occupational Group							
	1900	1910	1920	1930	1940	1950	1960	1968
White collar	17.6	21.4	24.9	29.4	31.1	36.6	43.1	46.8
Blue collar	35.8	38.2	40.2	39.6	39.8	41.1	36.3	36.3
Service	9.0	9.5	7.8	9.8	11.7	10.5	12.5	12.9
Farm	37.5	30.9	27.0	21.1	17.4	11.7	8.1	4.6
	99.9[a]	100.0	99.9[a]	99.9[a]	100.0	99.9[a]	100.0	99.6[a]

[a] Rounding errors.

Source: Based on *Historical Statistics of the United States*, 1957, Series D72-122; and *Statistical Abstract of the United States 1969*, table 322.

Table 8–2 shows the occupational distribution of the American labor force in each decade since 1900, using the four great categories of white-collar workers, blue-collar workers, service workers, and farm workers. The proportion of white-collar workers has increased in every decade. The proportion of blue-collar workers has fluctuated within a fairly narrow range and is now about the same as it was in 1900. The proportion of service workers has increased irregularly. The proportion of farm workers has decreased dramatically in each decade. Among the other trends that deserve notice are these:

1. The number of government employees (federal, state, and local) increased from about 2 percent of the labor force in 1910 to 15 percent of the labor force in 1966.[11] Since the great majority of civilian public employees hold white-collar positions, the expansion of governmental functions is one of the major factors accounting for the increase of the white-collar sector.

2. Throughout the twentieth century, there has been a steady movement out of *primary occupations (involving the production of raw materials, like farming, fishing, and lumbering)* into *secondary occupations (involving the subsequent processing of materials, like construc-*

tion and manufacturing) and a steady movement from secondary occupations into *tertiary occupations (involving the manipulation of symbols, like journalism or teaching.)* The net effect of this movement has been the depletion of the primary occupations and a great increase in the tertiary occupations, while the proportion of the labor force in secondary occupations has remained approximately the same. If the movement continues, there is every reason to expect that the secondary occupations will eventually be depleted too and that within a few decades a majority of the labor force will be found in the tertiary sector.

3. Within each occupational category, there has been a steady decline in the proportion of occupations requiring heavy muscular exertion, exposure to the elements, and personal subordination. Thus, the jobs of warehousemen, stevedores, hod carriers, and delivery men have been largely mechanized, while in service occupations, the proportion of private household workers has decreased from about 75 percent of all service workers in 1910 to less than 20 percent at the present time.

TRENDS IN LABOR FORCE PARTICIPATION

The *labor force participation rate is the percentage of persons in a population who are gainfully employed or seeking work at a given time.* Until 1967, the labor force participation rate in the United States was based on the population aged 14 and over. In 1967, the base was changed to the population aged 16 and over, but tables showing trends still use the old basis.

Labor force statistics are even less reliable than occupational statistics. It is often impossible to distinguish unemployed persons seeking work from those who have permanently left the labor force; an individual's position in this respect may be uncertain even to himself.

Table 8-3	LABOR FORCE PARTICIPATION RATE, UNITED STATES 1930-1965

Year	Percentage of Population 14 and Over in the Labor Force
1930	55.9%
1935	55.7
1940	55.3
1945	61.2
1950	57.7
1955	58.0
1960	57.0
1965	56.4

Source: Based on *Historical Statistics of the United States,* 1957, Series D1-12, and *Statistical Abstract of the United States, 1967,* table 3-16.

Certain categories are particularly troublesome. Married women who have worked in the past and are now found at home may or may not work again in the future. Students who work full-time during summer vacations are in and out of the labor force at different times of the year; those who hold a part-time job while attending school full time are even harder to classify. Under the current definition, all persons who work 15 hours or more per week as unpaid workers in a family enterprise are counted in the labor force. Since a family enterprise is very unlikely to keep time records for its unpaid employees, this category is especially doubtful.

For these and other reasons, labor force statistics must always be handled with caution, and often do not tell us what we want to know. For example, although there are figures on the participation rate of the population aged 14 to 19 going back to 1890, they show such dramatic inconsistencies that no trend at all can be derived from them.

Table 8–3 shows the participation rate for the entire population from 1930 to 1965. Except for the sharp increase during World War II, there has been little change in this rate during the past generation.

Table 8–4, which shows the participation rate by sex and color, and Table 8–5 which shows the participation rate of elderly persons, illustrate some of the divergent tendencies that underlie this stability. As Table 8–4 shows, the proportion of white males over 14 who are in the labor force fell by about six percentage points between 1950 and 1965, probably because of increased school attendance at the lower end of the age scale and earlier retirement at the upper end. Among nonwhite males, the participation rate decreased even faster. The decrease in male participation was offset, however, by an increase of more than five percentage points in the participation rate of white females. Among nonwhite females, who have had a higher participation rate than white females as far back as census information goes, the participation rate showed a significant, smaller increase. In general, the decrease in male employment was matched by a roughly equivalent increase of female employment. From 1950 to 1965, the labor force participation of *single* women dropped by about a fifth, presumably because of the combined effect of increased school attendance and earlier marriage. But at the same time, the labor force participation of married women living with their husbands increased by nearly half, and since there are many more married than single women, this produced a substantial net increase in the participation rate of women.

Table 8–5 shows another interesting pair of trends. From 1950 to 1965 the participation rate of men over the normal retirement age of 65 declined very sharply, whereas the much lower participation rate of elderly women remained almost unchanged. The somewhat shaky figures we have for earlier dates suggest that these trends have a long history. In 1890, the first year for which an estimate can be made, more than two-thirds of elderly men were still in the labor force, whereas the participation of elderly women was only a little below its present level.

Table 8-4 LABOR FORCE PARTICIPATION RATES BY SEX AND COLOR

Year	White Males	Nonwhite Males	White Females	Nonwhite Females
1950	83.3	83.5	31.4	42.1
1955	82.2	79.7	32.9	41.2
1960	80.0	77.0	35.0	45.5
1965	77.4	73.3	36.5	45.6

Source: Based on *Historical Statistics of the United States,* 1957, Series D13-25 and D26-35, *Statistical Abstract of the United States, 1967,* tables 316 and 324.

Table 8-5 LABOR FORCE PARTICIPATION OF MEN AND WOMEN OVER 65, UNITED STATES, 1950-1965

Year	Participation Rate	
	Men Over 65	Women Over 65
1950	44.7	9.5
1955	38.5	10.3
1960	32.2	10.5
1965	26.9	9.5

Source: Based on *Historical Statistics of the United States,* 1957, Series D13-25, and *Statistical Abstract of the United States, 1967,* table 316.

At the other end of the age scale, the most significant long-term trend has been the virtual disappearance of child labor. As recently as 1920 the labor force participation rate of boys 10 to 15 years old was 17 percent; it is now close to zero. In the next higher age groups, 16 to 19 and 20 to 24, the frequent occurrence of part-time and seasonal employment confuses the labor force statistics, but the massive upward trend in high school and college enrollment indicates that the average age of entrance into the full-time labor force has been rapidly rising for both boys and girls.

Measurement of Occupational Characteristics

Within the general labor force, each occupation has its own labor force consisting of those people employed in the occupation or seeking work in it or being trained for it. ~~These occupational labor forces~~ differ significantly among themselves with respect to the distribution of age, sex, race, education, and income, and differ also with respect to such features as stability of employment, internal regulation, and occupational solidarity. Let us look first at the elementary demographic characteristics of occupations.

AGE

Table 8–6 shows the median age of men in the major occupational groups of the United States in 1960. Both the oldest population, farm owners and managers, and the youngest, farm laborers and foremen, are engaged in the same type of work. Professionals are younger on the average than salesmen. Service workers are older than clerical workers.

Table 8-6   MEDIAN AGE OF MEN EMPLOYED IN VARIOUS OCCUPATIONS, UNITED STATES, 1960

Occupational Group	Median Age
White collar	
Professional, technical, and kindred workers	38.2
Managers, officials, and proprietors	45.4
Clerical and kindred workers	38.0
Sales workers	39.2
Blue collar	
Craftsmen, foremen, and kindred workers	41.8
Operatives and kindred workers	38.4
Laborers (except farm and mine)	37.4
Service	
Private household workers	a
Other service workers	43.4
Farm	
Farmers and farm managers	49.2
Farmhands and foremen	31.2

Source: aFew in this category.
Based on *Statistical Abstract of the United States, 1967,* table 330

These broad categories conceal much more striking age differences among particular occupations. Among the oldest male occupations are tailors and furriers, with a median age of 56; locomotive engineers, elevator operators, shoemakers, and real estate brokers, all with median ages over 50. Among the youngest are auto servicemen and parking attendants, with a median age of 26; and technicians, telephone linemen, shipping clerks, farm laborers, and elementary school teachers, all with median ages under 35. Such differences have various causes. Telephone linemen are young because the work requires a high degree of athletic ability, technicians because their occupation is nearly brand new, elementary school teachers because most of them move on to other occupations later in life. Locomotive engineers are elderly because of the long experience their job requires and also because theirs is a declining occupation with a small proportion of new recruits. Elevator operators are often men retired from more strenuous blue-collar occupations and chosen for steadiness and reliability. The real estate broker is often a man retired from another white-collar occupation and qualified for his work by extensive knowledge of a locality. The factors that affect the age distribution must be separately analyzed in the case of each occupation.

The occupations of women show similar divergences (Table 8–7). Among the oldest female occupations, dressmakers and seamstresses have a median age of 55; among the youngest, typists and office machine operators have a median age of 30.

Table 8-7	MEDIAN AGE OF WOMEN EMPLOYED IN VARIOUS OCCUPATIONS, UNITED STATES, 1960

Occupational Group	Median Age
White collar	
Professional, technical, and kindred workers	41.2
Managers, officials, and proprietors	47.6
Clerical and kindred workers	36.0
Sales workers	43.3
Blue collar	
Craftsmen, foremen, and kindred workers	43.6
Operatives and kindred workers	41.1
Laborers	a
Service	
Private household workers	44.8
Other service workers	41.7
Farm	
Farmers and farm managers	a
Farm laborers and foremen	40.0

Source: [a]Few in this category.

Based on *Statistical Abstract of the United States, 1967,* table 330.

Table 8–8 shows the proportion of women in each major occupational group in the United States in 1967. The variations are dramatic —from less than 3 percent of craftsmen and foremen to more than 97 percent of private household workers. The most important fact disclosed by Table 8–8 is that the occupational distribution of women is entirely different from that of men. Women are underrepresented in all the supervisory occupations—manager, proprietor, official, foreman, farm owner, and manager—but they are overrepresented in nonsupervisory white-collar occupations. Only about a third of employed men work at white-collar occupations, but nearly two-thirds of women do so. Among men there are more blue-collar workers than white-collar workers; among women, there were more than three times as many white-collar as blue-collar workers. Of the three million unskilled laborers in industry in 1967, less than 3 percent were women. Women might be said to cluster toward the middle of the occupational scale, with men nearly monopolizing both the highest and lowest occupations. The most important exceptions to this principle are household servants, nearly all women, and government officials, with a substantial representation of women in the lower and intermediate ranks.

Table 8-8   **PERCENT OF WOMEN IN VARIOUS OCCUPATIONS, UNITED STATES, 1967**

Occupational Group	% of Women
White collar	
Professional, technical, and kindred workers	37.7%
Managers, officials, and proprietors	16.4
Clerical and kindred workers	72.0
Sales workers	41.3
Blue collar	
Craftsmen, foremen, and kindred workers	2.8
Operatives and kindred workers	30.2
Laborers (except farm and mine)	2.8
Service	
Private household workers	97.4
Other service workers	57.0
Farm	
Farm owners and managers	5.5
Farm laborers and foremen	27.5
TOTAL LABOR FORCE	36.1

Source: Based on *Statistical Abstract of the United States, 1967*, table 327.

The apparently high representation of women among professional, technical, and kindred workers is deceptive. Schoolteachers and nurses account for the majority; all the other professional or technical occupations with a large representation of women—librarians, social workers, and dieticians, for example—are relatively low-ranking. The proportion of women in the major professions remains very small; fewer than 10 percent of physicians are women; fewer than 5 percent of lawyers and judges; and negligible proportions of architects, clergymen, dentists, and engineers. Indeed, men have recently invaded the minor professions traditionally reserved for women, such as nursing and librarianship, to a greater extent than women have been able to penetrate such traditionally male professions as architecture and dentistry. The proportion of women in the major professions has not advanced significantly since about 1910.

RACE

The proportion of nonwhites in each of the major occupational groups as of 1960 is shown separately for men and women in Table 8–9. There have been considerable changes since that date, but these somewhat out-of-date figures still show the general pattern of the distribution. Nonwhites (of whom the overwhelming majority were Negro) were underrepresented in all of the major white-collar categories among craftsmen and foremen and among farm owners and managers. There was, however, some nonwhite representation at every occupational level from the highest to the lowest. The closest approach to complete exclusion is found among managers and proprietors in manufacturing, and among locomotive engineers, each with a nonwhite representation of only 0.5 percent in 1960. The first case reflects the nearly total exclusion of nonwhites from the higher white-collar positions in private manufacturing enterprises of all kinds —a phenomenon related to the nearly total lack of nonwhite participation in the ownership of these companies. The case of the locomotive engineers has a long history going back to the nineteenth century practice of operating steam locomotives with a two-man crew consisting of a white engineer and a black fireman. As railroad technology evolved and railroad craft unions acquired direct influence over job assignments, the fireman's job was gradually taken over by whites while the locomotive engineers continued to maintain a "lily-white" union.

Among the white-collar occupations with relatively high nonwhite representation are clergyman, social worker, elementary school teacher, medical and dental technician, and mail carrier. The explanation is likely to be different in each case. The high proportion of nonwhite mail carriers, for example, represents a traditional segregation in some parts of the country between white inside employees and black outside employees of the Post Office. The high proportion of social workers and elementary school teachers represents equal opportunity policies respecting public employment that have been espe-

	Males	Females
Occupational Group	% Nonwhite	% Nonwhite

Table 8-9   PROPORTION OF NONWHITES IN VARIOUS OCCUPATIONS BY SEX, UNITED STATES, 1960

Occupational Group	Males % Nonwhite	Females % Nonwhite
White collar		
Professional, technical, and kindred workers	3.5%	7.2%
Managers, officials, and proprietors	2.0	3.9[a]
Clerical and kindred workers	6.8	3.6
Salesworkers	2.1	2.8
Blue collar		
Craftsmen, foremen, and kindred workers	4.9	7.3[a]
Operatives and kindred workers	11.1	10.6
Laborers (except farm and mine)	26.1	24.0[a]
Service		
Private household workers	48.4	54.5
Other service workers	21.5	19.5
Farm		
Farmers and farm managers	7.4	15.1[a]
Farm laborers and foremen	24.0	33.9
TOTAL LABOR FORCE	9.6	12.8

[a] Under 50,000 in this category.

Source: Based on *Statistical Abstract of the United States, 1967,* table 330.

cially effective in institutional areas where a large proportion of the client population (schoolchildren, social agency cases) is black.

Among manual occupations, nonwhites are overrepresented in a number of crafts (for example, plasterer, cement finisher, metal molder, mason, and tilesetter) and a number of skilled industrial occupations (crane, derrick, and hoist operator; furnaceman, smelterman, and pourer in a foundry, for example).

The large representation of black workers in foundry occupations goes back to a long-standing belief that blacks are better qualified to endure heat and to work in extreme conditions near furnaces and in foundries. In some other cases, among crane operators, and merchant seamen, for example, a large proportion of nonwhites is the result of the vigorous maintenance of a nondiscrimination policy by powerful unions ever since the early days of the New Deal. In still other occupations, like sawyer in a lumber mill and taxicab and bus driver, the large proportion of nonwhites is at least partly attributable to the location of the industry. A great many sawmills are located in the rural South, where a large proportion of the available labor force is black; and most of the bus and taxicab chauffeurs work in metropolitan cities where the same is true.

The many occupations that have a disproportionately low number of nonwhite workers—for example, lawyer and judge, mechanical engineer, insurance agent, manufacturing foreman, millwright, toolmaker, spinner, and weaver—reflect a number of interrelated factors that need to be examined separately in each case. Some of these are discrimination by employer, discrimination by unions, discrimination by schools and colleges, inability to meet qualification tests, the location of work places, the reluctance to put black professionals and officials in charge of white clients, and the partial monopoly of certain occupations by other ethnic groups.

Most of these factors seem to be diminishing in strength, and although the trends are often very slow-moving, the general pattern of occupational segregation in the United States has softened considerably in recent years.[12] Thus between 1950 and 1960 the percentage of the nonwhite labor force engaged in white-collar work more than doubled (from 10.2 percent to 22.9 percent), with spectacular increases in every white-collar category except that of managers, proprietors, and officials and salesworkers. Among nonwhite manual workers, the proportion of craftsmen and foremen increased from 5 percent to 8 percent, and the proportion of laborers declined from 14 percent to 11 percent during that decade. The proportion of the nonwhite labor force engaged in private household service declined sharply and the proportion engaged in farm work declined spectacularly. By 1966, as Table 8–10 shows, the proportions of the white labor force and of the nonwhite labor force in industrial and farm occupations were about equal, but a much higher proportion of whites were engaged in white-collar work and a much higher proportion of nonwhites in service work, and nonwhites were still conspicuously underrepresented in managerial and supervisory occupations. The progress achieved was highly significant, but it did not seem to foreshadow complete equalization in the near future.

Measurement of Occupational Status

The classification of occupations we have been using—a modified version of the socioeconomic scale devised by Edwards for the Bureau of the Census—was originally based on a common sense view of the occupational hierarchy. When this common sense view is analyzed, it turns out to involve six major assumptions:

1. white-collar work is better than manual work;
2. self-employment is better than being employed by others;
3. skilled occupations are better than unskilled occupations;
4. occupations that require higher educations are better than those that do not;

Table 8-10	PROPORTION OF WHITE AND NONWHITE LABOR FORCES FOLLOWING VARIOUS OCCUPATIONS, UNITED STATES, 1967		

Occupational Group	% of White Labor Force	% of Nonwhite Labor Force
White collar	(48.8)	(22.9)
Professional and technical workers	14.0	7.4
Managers, officials, proprietors	11.0	2.6
Clerical workers	17.2	11.2
Sales workers	6.6	1.7
Blue collar	(36.0)	(42.4)
Craftsmen and foremen	13.9	7.7
Operatives	18.1	23.5
Laborers	4.0	11.2
Service	(10.5)	(29.4)
Private household workers	1.4	10.4
Other service workers	9.1	19.0
Farm	(4.7)	(5.3)
Owners and managers	2.8	1.3
Laborers and foremen	1.9	4.0
TOTAL	100.0	100.0

Source: Based on *Statistical Abstract of the United States, 1908*, table 325.

5. the occupational rank of an owner or manager does not depend on the size of his enterprise or farm;
6. personal service is degrading.

It is obvious at a glance that these assumptions run counter to everyday experience in some cases and are inconsistent in other cases. Dentists, for example, are exclusively engaged in personal service. The president of a large corporation who is an employee does not on that account feel inferior to the self-employed operator of a corner grocery. Some very dirty jobs, like slicing up cadavers in a pathology laboratory, are highly respected. A toolmaker or master mechanic is seldom regarded as inferior to a white-collar timekeeper in the same shop.

One solution to problems of this kind is to group occupations in very broad categories that submerge inconsistencies. Another solution is to measure the status of an occupation directly by evaluating the attributes of its practitioners or by asking a sample of the general public how much prestige they attach to it.

It is interesting to examine the available information on the qualifications and rewards of the major occupational groups in the census classification. Table 8–11 shows the median years of schooling completed by persons who were in various occupations in the United States in 1962. Obviously, there is a rough correspondence between educational qualifications and this classification. The average professional had graduated from college; the average manager, proprietor, or salesman had graduated from high school; the average blue-collar and service worker had attended high school but not graduated; the average farmer had just a little more than an elementary education.

Table 8-11	EDUCATION OF MALES IN VARIOUS OCCUPATIONS, UNITED STATES, 1962	

Occupational Group	Median Years of Schooling
White collar	
Professionals	16.4
Managers	12.8
Proprietors	12.1
Salesmen	12.5
Blue collar	
Craftsmen, principally manufacturing	11.2
Craftsmen, construction	10.2
Operatives	10.0
Laborers	8.9
Service	10.3
Farm	
Farmers	8.8
Farm laborers	8.3

Source: Peter M. Blau and Otis Dudley Duncan, *The American Occupational Structure* (New York: John Wiley & Sons, 1967), table 2.1.

Figures on annual earnings are shown in Table 8–12. We can see at a glance the overlap in earnings between the lowest white-collar categories—clerical workers and retail salespeople—and the highest blue-collar categories of craftsmen and foremen. This table demonstrates the fundamental soundness of the census classification, at the same time masking the enormous diversity of occupations with respect to hourly wage rates, fringe benefits, working conditions, retirement provisions, security of tenure, and property rights.

Table 8-12	ANNUAL EARNINGS OF MALES IN VARIOUS OCCUPATIONS, UNITED STATES, 1965

Occupation Occupational Group	Median Earnings
White collar	
Professional, technical, and kindred workers:	
Self-employed	$11,790
Salaried	8,269
Managers, officials, and proprietors	7,895
Clerical and kindred workers	6,280
Sales workers:	
Retail	6,077
Other	7,721
Blue collar	
Craftsmen, foremen, and kindred workers	6,751
Operatives and kindred workers	5,782
Laborers (except farm and mine)	4,651
Service	
Private household workers	—
Other service workers	4,874
Farm	
Farms and farm managers	3,098
Farm laborers and foremen	2,274

Source: Based on *Statistical Abstract of the United States, 1967*, table 338. Figures refer to median earnings of year-round, full-time workers.

OCCUPATIONAL INTELLIGENCE

The effort to measure *occupational intelligence* began with the work of Yerkes, who published in 1921 the results of intelligence tests administered to Army recruits during World War I, including the average scores of soldiers coming from 55 civilian occupations.[13] Similar studies were carried out later and during World War II: the Yerkes study was replicated several times using the Army General Classification Test (AGCT), which was routinely administered to everyone inducted into the service. Table 8–13 shows the median AGCT score and the range of scores for men entering the Army Air Force from each of 74 civilian occupations.

Table 8–13 confirms the existence of the four-level occupational hierarchy we have been discussing, together with the overlap already noted between the higher blue-collar and lower white-collar occupations, and between the lower blue-collar and service occupations.

At first glance, the table seems to support the notion that differ-

Table 8-13	RANGE OF INTELLIGENCE SCORES OF 18,782 ARMY AIR FORCE WHITE ENLISTED MEN IN WORLD WAR II, BY CIVILIAN OCCUPATIONS

Occupation	Median I.Q.	Range
Accountant	128.1	94-157
Lawyer	126.8	96-157
Engineer	125.8	100-151
Public relations man	125.5	100-149
Auditor	125.5	98-151
Chemist	124.5	102-153
Reporter	125.7	100-157
Chief clerk	124.5	88-153
Teacher	123.7	76-155
Draftsman	121.7	74-155
Stenographer	121.4	66-151
Pharmacist	124.0	76-149
Tabulating machine operator	119.8	80-151
Bookkeeper	119.7	70-157
Manager, sales	120.7	90-137
Purchasing agent	119.2	82-153
Manager, production	117.0	82-153
Photographer	119.8	66-147
Clerk, general	117.9	68-155
Clerk-typist	117.3	80-147
Manager, miscellaneous	117.5	60-151
Installer-repairman, telephone and telegraph	116.8	76-149
Cashier	116.8	80-145
Instrument repairman	115.8	82-141
Radio repairman	116.5	56-151
Printer, job pressman, lithographic pressman	116.7	60-149
Salesman	116.2	60-153
Artist	115.4	82-139
Manager, retail store	116.2	52-151
Laboratory assistant	114.0	76-147
Toolmaker	111.6	76-143
Inspector	113.1	54-147
Stock clerk	113.0	54-151
Receiving and shipping clerk	113.4	58-155
Musician	112.8	56-147
Machinist	110.8	38-153
Foreman	111.4	60-151
Watchmaker	113.0	68-147
Airplane mechanic	110.5	66-147
Sales clerk	110.4	42-149
Electrician	110.6	64-149
Lathe operator	109.4	64-147
Receiving and shipping checker	108.9	52-151

Sheetmetal worker	108.1	62-153
Lineman, power and telephone and telegraph	108.8	70-133
Assembler	106.6	48-145
Mechanic	108.3	60-155
Machine operator	105.7	42-151
Auto serviceman	105.9	30-141
Riveter	105.3	50-141
Cabinetmaker	104.7	66-127
Upholsterer	105.8	68-131
Butcher	104.8	42-147
Plumber	104.8	56-139
Bartender	105.0	56-137
Carpenter, construction	104.1	42-147
Pipe fitter	105.2	56-139
Welder	103.6	48-147
Auto mechanic	101.8	48-151
Molder	105.5	48-137
Chauffeur	103.0	46-143
Tractor driver	101.6	42-147
Painter, general	100.1	38-147
Crane hoist operator	99.1	58-147
Cook and baker	99.5	20-147
Weaver	97.3	50-135
Truck driver	97.8	16-149
Laborer	97.7	26-145
Barber	98.1	42-141
Lumberjack	96.5	46-137
Farmer	93.4	24-147
Farmhand	94.0	24-141
Miner	92.0	42-139
Teamster	89.0	46-145

Source: Based on T.W. and M.S. Harrell, "Army General Classification Test Scores for Civilian Occupations," *Educational and Psychological Measurement*, 5 (1945): 231-232.

ences in occupational status are founded on differences in natural ability and to suggest that the mechanisms of social placement sort individuals into the occupations for which they are fitted. These conclusions should be taken with a grain of salt, however. In the first place, recent work in psychometrics has repeatedly shown that intelligence scores are affected by both heredity and early environment, instead of being purely genetic in character as was formerly supposed. In the second place, although the median scores decline sharply from accountants and lawyers down to miners and teamsters, and the lower scores in each range decline almost as regularly, there is only a slight and irregular decline in the maximum scores. What this means is that men of low intelligence are not found in high-ranking occupations, but men of high intelligence *are* found in low-ranking occupations. Since the distribution of occupational status is roughly pyramidal, and the low-ranking occupations are more heavily populated, they include a large proportion of the intellectually superior population despite the differences in average intelligence shown in the table. Using results from World War I, Lehman and Stoke were able to show that more than half of the "A category" men recruited to the Army came from manual occupations, although fewer than 2 percent of all manual workers recruited to the Army scored in the A category compared with 38 percent of the professional workers recruited.[14]

OCCUPATIONAL PRESTIGE

The first study involving direct measurement of occupational prestige was published by Counts in 1925.[15] Counts presented 45 familiar occupations to a sample of 450 students and teachers, who were asked to rate the occupations from 1 to 45 according to prestige. Individual ratings were then averaged to obtain an overall rating. Banker and college professor were first and second, street cleaner and ditch digger forty-fourth and forty-fifth. There have been numerous replications and partial replications of this study in the United States[16] and elsewhere; most of them have shown that prestige rankings are highly stable over time and do not differ much from one country to another.[17]

A study of occupational prestige conducted by the National Opinion Research Center (NORC) in 1947 introduced two improvements in method. The rating was done by a carefully drawn national sample of nearly 3,000 persons, and a longer list (90 occupations) was used. Each respondent was asked to express his "own personal opinion of the general standing that such a job has" by rating it on a five-point scale from Excellent to Poor and the ratings were then combined to produce an average score for each occupation.[18] The study was replicated by the same organization in 1963 with a somewhat smaller national sample. The results obtained were nearly identical with those of 1947, and indeed very close to the results of Counts' original study.[19] Table 8–14 shows the 1963 prestige ratings of the 90 occupations, from 1, United States Supreme Court Justice, to 90, shoeshiner. Blue-collar industrial occupations are somewhat lightly represented, but white-collar and service occupations are described in unusual detail. The rating method used has a tendency to produce ties, but the results are extremely clear.

By combining data from the 1947 NORC study and the 1950 census, Duncan was able to construct an occupational index that assigned a socioeconomic status score to every occupation enumerated in the decennial census.[20] This ingenious device has become one of the standard tools of sociological research and greatly simplifies the task of analyzing occupational mobility within an individual career. Table 8–15 shows the Duncan scores for the major occupational

Table 8-14   DISTRIBUTION OF OCCUPATIONAL PRESTIGE RANKS, UNITED STATES, 1963

Occupation	Rank
U.S. Supreme Court justice	1.0
Physician	2.0
Nuclear physicist	3.5
Scientist	3.5
Government scientist	5.5
State governor	5.5
Cabinet member in the federal government	8.0
U.S. representative in Congress	8.0
College professor	8.0
Chemist	11.0
Lawyer	11.0
Diplomat in U.S. Foreign Service	11.0
Dentist	14.0
Architect	14.0
County judge	14.0
Psychologist	17.5
Minister	17.5
Member of the board of directors of a large corporation	17.5
Mayor of a large city	17.5
Priest	21.5
Head of a department in a state government	21.5
Civil engineer	21.5
Airplane pilot	21.5
Banker	24.5
Biologist	24.5
Sociologist	26.0
Instructor in public schools	27.5
Captain in the regular army	27.5
Accountant for a large business	29.5
Public school teacher	29.5
Owner of a factory that employs about 100 people	31.5
Building contractor	31.5
Artist who paints pictures that are exhibited in galleries	34.5
Musician in a symphony orchestra	34.5
Author of novels	34.5
Economist	34.5
Official of an international labor union	37.0
Railroad engineer	39.0
Electrician	39.0
County agricultural agent	39.0
Owner-operator of a printing shop	41.5
Trained machinist	41.5
Farm owner and operator	44.0
Undertaker	44.0
Welfare worker for a city government	44.0

Newspaper columnist	46.0
Policeman	47.0
Reporter on a daily newspaper	48.0
Radio announcer	49.5
Bookkeeper	49.5
Tenant farmer—one who owns livestock and machinery and manages the farm	51.5
Insurance agent	51.5
Carpenter	53.0
Manager of a small store in a city	54.5
A local official of a labor union	54.5
Mail carrier	57.0
Railroad conductor	57.0
Traveling salesman for a wholesale concern	57.0
Plumber	59.0
Automobile repairman	60.0
Playground director	62.5
Barber	62.5
Machine operator in a factory	62.5
Owner-operator of a lunchstand	62.5
Corporal in the regular army	65.5
Garage mechanic	65.5
Truck driver	67.0
Fisherman who owns his own boat	68.0
Clerk in store	70.0
Milk route man	70.0
Streetcar motorman	70.0
Lumberjack	72.5
Restaurant cook	72.5
Singer in a nightclub	74.0
Filling station attendant	75.0
Dockworker	77.5
Railroad section hand	77.5
Night watchman	77.5
Coal miner	77.5
Restaurant waiter	80.5
Taxi driver	80.5
Farmhand	83.0
Janitor	83.0
Bartender	83.0
Clothes presser in laundry	85.0
Soda fountain clerk	86.0
Sharecropper—one who owns no livestock or equipment and does not manage farm	87.0
Garbage collector	88.0
Street sweeper	89.0
Shoeshiner	90.0

Source: Based on Robert W. Hodge, Paul M. Siegel, and Peter H. Rossi, "Occupational Prestige in the United States, 1925-1963," *American Journal of Sociology*, 70, no. 3 (November 1964): 286-302, table 1.

Table 8-15

DUNCAN STATUS SCORES FOR VARIOUS OCCUPATIONS, 1940

Occupational Group	Duncan Score
White collar	
Professional, technical, and kindred workers	75
Managers, officials, and proprietors	57
Sales workers	49
Clerical and kindred workers	45
Blue collar	
Craftsmen, foremen, and kindred workers	31
Operatives and kindred workers	18
Laborers (except farm and mine)	7
Service	
Private household workers	8
Other service workers	17
Farm	
Farmers and farm managers	14
Farm laborers and foremen	9

groups in the census classification. In contrast to the previous tables showing educational level and occupational earnings, these scores based on prestige show an enormous chasm between white-collar and blue-collar occupations. This effect may be due in part to the relative underrepresentation of factory occupations in the original NORC list, and in part to the tendency of white-collar raters to underestimate the qualifications for and rewards of blue-collar occupations with which they are relatively unfamiliar.

The extraordinary stability of prestige ratings is something of a puzzle in view of the considerable number of unstable elements that enter into a determination of prestige, including not only occupational qualifications and earnings, but also responsibility, the exercise of authority, the nature of the work, and its place in an organization. High-prestige occupations are difficult to enter, require frequent decisions with important consequences, and allow their practitioners to influence the lives of large numbers of people. Low-status occupations are easy to enter, require few decisions, and give very little influence to the individual worker.

As you will remember from Chapter One, vertical mobility is movement from one social position to another, involving a gain or a loss of status; horizontal mobility is movement from one job to another; and geographic mobility is movement from place to place. As if this were not complicated enough, each type of occupational mobility has several different modes, which demand separate attention.

Vertical mobility, for example, occurs in the following ways:

1. A movement to an occupation of higher or lower socio-economic status, as when a factory worker becomes a high school teacher or a high school teacher goes to work in a factory.
2. A promotion or demotion within the same occupation; as when the second mate of a ship becomes first mate, or a master takes a job as a mate.
3. A change in occupational level from one generation to the next, as when the plumber's son becomes an executive or the doctor's son becomes a truck driver.
4. The rise or decline of an entire occupational group whose position is changed in relation to other occupational groups, as when the prestige of psychologists increases or the influence of clergymen declines.

Horizontal mobility too may occur in a number of ways:

1. A change from one job to another, as when a factory worker becomes a plant guard.
2. A change from one industry to another, as when a construction worker gets a job in a factory. (Needless to say, a change from one job to another and a change from one industry to another often occur simultaneously.)
3. A movement between generations, as in the long-term movement of farmers' sons into urban occupations.
4. The shift of an occupation from one industry to another, as when journalists are employed by television networks instead of by newspapers.

The principal forms of geographic mobility are:

1. The movement of workers from one locality to another, as when southerners come north to look for work.
2. The successive changes of residence required by certain careers, as when foreign service officers are shifted from one country to another, after a two-year tour of duty.
3. The continuous travel that is a condition of employment in some occupations like railroading.

4. The seasonal movements of certain labor forces, such as migratory fruit pickers.

Needless to say, an occupational change often involves more than one type of mobility. Fortunately, occupational mobility is one of the most thoroughly studied topics in modern sociology and a great deal is known about it.

VERTICAL MOBILITY: FATHER TO SON

The pattern of occupational inheritance has been studied with special care in recent years because it provides direct information about the success or failure of industrial societies in providing equal opportunities for their citizens. Before the Industrial Revolution, as Sorokin showed in his *Social Mobility*,[21] traditional societies varied greatly in the extent to which they permitted or encouraged vertical mobility. Some set up occupational immobility as an ideal and treated any change of occupation from father to son as a form of deviance. As a medieval Portuguese proverb expressed it, "The good Lord who made the rich and the poor never intended that the poor should make themselves rich." Other early societies seem to have had extraordinarily high rates of vertical mobility. Ancient history, Occidental and Oriental, is full of slaves and slaves' sons who rose to wealth, eminence, and power. The history of the Western world from the end of the Crusades to the age of steam is the story, on the one hand, of hereditary monarchs and princes, on the other of a long series of great men risen from obscure origins: Dante, Leonardo da Vinci, Columbus, Luther, Shakespeare, Cervantes, Cromwell, Bach, Newton, Beethoven, Napoleon, and hundreds of others.

At the same time, it is nearly impossible to make any meaningful comparison of vertical mobility rates between earlier centuries and our own. For one thing, we lack the necessary data. For another, the structural differences between the largely rural societies of the past and the largely urban societies of today make it impossible to establish a common base. It does seem likely, however, that the occupational status of the average man in contemporary industrial societies is much less affected by that of his father than it was in earlier societies.[22]

The assessment of equality of opportunity is complicated by the difficulty of defining the concept. The negative end of a scale of equal opportunity is easily visualized. It would be represented by a caste society in which occupations were so rigidly stratified that no occupation had exactly the same rank as any other and everyone was compelled to follow the same occupation as his father. Such a system, of course, would be incompatible with a changing technology. The other extreme—completely equal opportunity—is harder to visualize because of alternate possibilities. It could be represented by a society in which all occupations were of equal status, but we have no reason to think that such a society is possible. Any division of labor seems to require a hierarchical arrangement of occupations, and the more complex the technology, the finer the gradations of status seem to become.

It is quite possible, of course, to abolish private property and the incomes derived from it. As of this writing, nearly half of the world's population lives under regimes that have done so. Such a system has a drastic effect on the distribution of wealth and income, but it does not necessarily affect the ranking of occupations. If anything, there is an opposite tendency. The gap between the highest and the lowest salaries seems to be greater in the government bureaus and factories of the Soviet Union and the Chinese People's Republic than in the United States or western Europe.[23]

Equality of opportunity may also be visualized as a situation in which there is no correlation between the occupational status of fathers and that of their sons. But unless we abandon the principle that occupations and occupational rewards ought to be distributed according to merit, that situation is unimaginable, because the abilities of fathers and sons, however measured, always show moderately high correlations. How much these correlations result from genetic inheritance and how much from environmental influence remains uncertain. But it appears that in all contemporary countries, the sons of men in higher-ranking occupations have, on the average, better school records than others and a better chance of being admitted to high-ranking occupations. Bordieu and Passeron, whose work is said to have stimulated the French student revolution of May 1968, go so far as to advocate the development of "a rational pedagogy whose principal purpose would be to neutralize, methodically and continuously, from the nursery school to the university, the influence of cultural inequality in the family environment of students."[24]

MEASUREMENT OF INTERGENERATIONAL MOBILITY

The measurement of the vertical mobility from father to sons in a modern economy is complicated by the fact that the average father and average son are likely to engage in several different occupations during their working lives, and the selection of the points in their occupational history to be compared is by no means self-evident. In the course of repeated studies, two schemes have become nearly standard. One is to compare the son's occupation at the time of the investigation to the occupation held by the father when the son first entered the labor force; the other is to compare the son's first full-time regular occupation with the father's occupation at the same time or with the father's last occupation, if the father left the labor force before the son entered it.

The most thorough and careful study of occupational mobility so far undertaken in the United States, by Blau and Duncan, makes use of both of these comparisons to describe intergenerational mobility.[25] Table 8–16, taken from their *American Occupational Structure,* shows the occupational distribution of the fathers of men in each of 17 occupational categories as of March 1962. It was based on a special survey carried out at their suggestion by the Bureau of the Census. The table is not easy to read at first sight, but it is worth the effort of study, because it contains a great deal of information and the data appear to be exceptionally reliable.

The table consists of inflow percentages, that is, it tells us what percentage of the sons in each occupational category had fathers in each occupational category. Reading down the first column, for example, we discover that 14.5 percent of the fathers of self-employed professionals had also been self-employed professionals, and 7.0 percent had been salaried professionals, so that more than a fifth of all professionals might be said to have "inherited" professional status. (Of course, the proportion inheriting any particular profession like medicine or law would be much less.) Reading down the last column, which represents men who were farm laborers, we discover that less than 1 percent of their fathers had been professionals, but 59.7 percent of them had been farmers and an additional 14.5 percent farm laborers. Of all the columns in the table, occupational inheritance is most conspicuous among farmers; more than four-fifths of their fathers were farmers also. The next highest category with respect to direct inheritance is very far behind; 16.3 percent of proprietors had fathers who were proprietors also. Thus, except among farmers and in certain specialized occupations that are too small to show up in the table, only a small minority of American men practice the same occupation as their fathers, or even a closely related occupation.

Occupational inheritance by broad categories is a much more important phenomenon. For example, 60 percent of self-employed professionals had fathers in white-collar occupations, whereas only 12 percent of the men in service occupations had fathers in white-collar occupations when they were growing up.

The table also tells us that both upward and downward mobility occur very frequently. Intergenerational movement from farming into every other occupational category was substantial. Movement from blue-collar to white-collar occupations occurred on a very large scale, and movement from white-collar to blue-collar occupations was by no means infrequent. The net amount of upward mobility between generations somewhat exceeded the downward mobility, in part because of the upgrading of the entire labor force noted above, and in part because some of the lower-ranking occupational groups of the previous generation had larger than average families.

Beginning with a matched set of national studies launched under the auspices of the International Sociological Association in 1951, a good deal of comparative work has been done on occupational mobility from one country to another.[26] The results are not always easy to interpret. In general, occupational mobility in the United States, the traditional land of opportunity, appears to be higher than in most other industrialized countries, but it is not as much higher as one might suppose. Comparing Australia, Italy, and the United States with respect to a three-level occupational distribution (manual, nonmanual, and farm), Broom and Jones found that 35 percent of the Italians, 42

Table 8-16

FATHER'S OCCUPATION FOR A SAMPLE OF AMERICAN—MEN, 25 TO 64 YEARS OLD, 1962

Father's Occupation	1	2	3	4	5	6	7	8	9	10	11	12	13	14	15	16	17
Professionals																	
1 Self-employed	14.5	3.9	1.5	3.8	0.8	0.8	1.1	0.3	0.3	0.6	0.3	0.3	0.4	0.2	0.6	0.5	0.6
2 Salaried	7.0	9.5	4.9	5.8	2.1	3.8	3.4	1.6	1.9	0.6	2.1	2.1	1.9	1.4	0.4	0.5	0.3
3 Managers	8.7	7.9	8.7	7.0	4.0	4.4	2.6	2.7	2.6	2.2	1.4	1.2	1.0	1.8	0.7	0.3	0.3
4 Salesman, other	5.6	3.4	5.2	8.1	2.6	1.7	4.4	0.8	1.5	0.8	0.5	1.0	0.6	0.0	0.4	0.4	0.3
5 Proprietors	18.5	9.6	16.5	13.2	16.3	7.1	15.2	3.5	5.2	5.7	3.7	3.4	3.7	1.6	2.0	1.5	1.6
6 Clerical	4.9	7.3	4.4	5.9	2.3	4.5	2.6	2.9	3.1	1.2	1.2	1.9	3.2	1.5	1.3	0.8	0.0
7 Salesman, retail	0.9	2.3	3.0	4.7	2.8	1.8	2.9	1.4	0.8	1.1	1.5	1.1	1.4	0.1	1.2	0.7	0.0
Craftsmen																	
8 Manufacturing	3.8	8.3	6.1	4.3	5.1	5.7	6.3	12.0	5.1	5.1	6.2	4.7	4.8	4.5	3.2	0.5	0.4
9 Other	4.0	7.0	7.4	7.9	6.0	8.0	6.1	6.9	11.0	5.8	5.3	7.8	5.4	3.8	4.1	1.2	1.2
10 Construction	3.0	3.2	4.4	4.1	5.8	6.2	2.6	6.9	5.5	13.7	3.6	3.9	4.6	2.6	4.9	0.8	1.8
Operatives																	
11 Manufacturing	5.2	6.4	5.1	6.5	6.1	7.5	7.1	12.9	7.7	4.9	13.7	6.9	7.1	14.5	6.3	1.2	2.8
12 Other	2.8	7.5	4.2	5.4	6.2	6.7	6.0	6.5	8.6	6.6	6.9	10.9	7.1	6.5	6.4	1.2	4.4
13 Service	2.3	3.7	4.0	4.8	3.7	6.3	5.3	4.8	3.9	4.7	5.1	4.6	8.2	5.4	3.3	0.8	0.6
Laborers																	
14 Manufacturing	0.0	1.0	1.2	0.4	0.8	1.3	0.8	2.6	1.5	1.0	3.2	2.2	3.0	5.9	2.4	0.6	0.9
15 Other	1.0	2.0	1.9	3.3	2.1	6.0	4.7	4.5	4.8	4.8	5.3	5.9	6.2	6.7	9.6	0.7	2.8
16 Farmers	11.2	10.8	13.3	10.1	24.3	18.3	17.6	20.1	24.4	30.4	26.6	29.4	22.8	29.5	32.6	82.0	59.7
16 Farm laborers	0.3	0.5	0.9	0.5	1.5	1.5	2.1	2.3	2.4	3.1	3.4	3.7	3.6	3.9	5.6	2.9	14.5
18 TOTAL [a]	100.0	100.0	100.0	100.0	100.0	100.0	100.0	100.0	100.0	100.0	100.0	100.0	100.0	100.0	100.0	100.0	100.0

Respondent's

[a]Columns as shown do not total 100.0, since men not reporting father's occupation are not shown separately.

Source: Based on Peter M. Blau and Otis Dudley Duncan, *The American Occupational Structure* (New York: John Wiley & Sons, 1967), table 2.8, p. 39

percent of the Australian, and 49 percent of the American sons were on a different level than their fathers. However, when these figures are corrected to take account of the differing proportions of fathers who were farmers in the three labor forces, the investigators conclude that the Australian occupational system is more open than the American, which is, in turn, more open than the Italian system.[27]

Another way of comparing occupational inheritance between countries is with respect to the recruitment of the elite—the upper professional and managerial occupations. The results of various national studies suggest that the chance that the only son of a father selected at random from the previous generation's labor force will rise to an elite occupation ranges from about 3 percent in Italy and Denmark to about 7 percent in France, Sweden, and Great Britain to more than 11 percent in Japan, the Netherlands, and the United States. The number of men rising from the lowest to the highest occupational level in one generation seems to be somewhat higher in the United States than in any other major country.[28] The rate of upward mobility of blue-collar sons into white-collar occupations in the United States, about 37 percent, appears to be exceeded by the rate in France and possibly in Switzerland. So far as historical trends are concerned, recent studies indicate no increasing rigidity in the American occupational structure.[29] Overall, the influence of social origins on the individual's career chances seems hardly to have changed at all in the past 40 years except that the basis of recruitment to the elite occupations has somewhat broadened.[30]

The foregoing summary does not reflect the special patterns of vertical mobility that apply to women, nonwhites, southerners, and immigrants. The vertical mobility patterns of women are very different from those of men and have been studied hardly at all. The discontinuous character of women's careers and the uncertainty whether their occupations should be compared with those of their mothers or their fathers has discouraged investigation of female intergenerational mobility, but the subject deserves exploration.

Recent studies have shown that men born in the South have less favorable chances of occupational advancement than men born in the North and that the difference is intensified rather than diminished when southerners migrate to the North. The inferior educational facilities of the South account for a large part but not all of this disadvantage. Blau and Duncan suggest that southern whites as well as southern blacks suffer from discrimination in northern labor markets.[31]

The black worker's chances of achieving upward vertical mobility are markedly inferior to the average white worker's, especially in the South. The difference is attributable both to lesser educational achievement than that of whites (and less adequate educational facilities at each level) and to various types of discrimination. Except for those who have graduated from college or have gone beyond it, education has less of an income-raising effect for blacks than for whites. This fact indicates that for the country as a whole, occupational discrimination against blacks is most acute at the intermediate educational levels and consequently most effective with regard to access to occupations of intermediate status.

In contrast to the rather bleak prospects for the equalization of occupational opportunities between whites and blacks,[32] equalization between native and foreign-born families seems to have been effectively achieved, according to the overall picture of intergenerational mobility. The evidence suggests that the occupational status of the native-born sons of foreign-born fathers is as high as, and for some immigrant groups slightly higher than, the average status of native-born sons of native-born fathers.

Most of the occupational movement between generations is to adjacent rather than distant occupational levels, and this movement occurs freely in all directions, except that relatively few sons of white-collar workers move down into blue-collar occupations and even fewer sons of blue-collar workers move sidewise into farming. Movement in these two directions is also relatively rare within the individual career.

Career Patterns

A career is the occupational life history of an individual, or a segment of it within a particular organization. It may involve vertical, horizontal, and geographical mobility in various combinations. The average American worker who retired from the labor force in the 1960s had been working for about 45 years, had held about 10 full-time jobs, and had changed occupations about four times.[33] As already noted, the amount of vertical mobility in the average American career is comparable with that in other industrialized countries. Horizontal mobility, however, appears to be much greater in the United States.

The averages are deceptive, however. The number of job changes in a career is partly a function of occupational status. In general, the higher a man's status, the less likely he will be to change his occupation when he changes jobs, and the fewer jobs he will hold in his lifetime. The least horizontal mobility is observed among self-employed professionals, like physicians and lawyers in private practice; many of them—by no means all—remain in the same occupation from the time they enter the labor force until the day they retire. At the other extreme of the scale, Skid Row drifters often hold 10 or more jobs within a single year. Neither of these extremes is typical. The important fact to remember for a broad view of American society is that most men do not pass their lives within a single occupation or at the same level of occupational status. Upward, downward, and crosswise movements occur very frequently.

The first classification of lifetime careers was developed by Miller and Form about 1950 and was based on the work histories of a representative sample of men in the Ohio labor force.[34] A career was divided into (1) an initial work period, including part-time and summer jobs held by adolescents; (2) trial jobs held for less than three years;

and (3) stable jobs, held for three years or more. The investigators identified career patterns in which occupational stability was achieved quickly, achieved slowly, never achieved, or achieved and lost.

This classification was modified by Gusfield, who added to it an "established career period," for workers who had been in the same job or occupation at least six years.[35] About 3 out of 10 of the men in his sample could be classified as having established careers, achieved either by early entry into a permanent job or occupation or by the gradual discovery of a permanent job or occupation after a period of shifting. Nearly the same proportion had either disestablished or unestablished careers, having either left a permanent occupation or not yet found one. The remainder of the sample showed what Gusfield called undirected work histories—frequent work changes with no prospect of an established career.

None of the available classifications of career patterns is entirely satisfactory, because careers are located within particular occupational milieus and these are always infinitely diverse. There are so many differences among, for example, the occupational milieus of a dermatologist, a circus performer, a long-haul truck driver, a piano tuner, and a naval officer—all skilled and self-respecting occupations by the way—that they almost defy rational grouping. Among the numerous characteristics that distinguish the career patterns of different occupations, the following deserve special attention.

1. In some occupations status normally increases with seniority up to a point in mid-career or later (college professor). In others, status remains level or nearly level throughout the career (elementary-school teacher). In others, the maximum status is usually achieved close to the beginning of a career, followed by a long decline thereafter (symphony orchestra musician).

2. Some occupations have definite career timetables. The ages of entry and retirement are set, and the individual can compare his status at any intervening point with the average status of his age peers to find out whether he is ahead of, even with, or behind the normal rate of advancement. Metropolitan policemen have careers of this kind. In other occupations, the timetable is less exact, but no less important. The performance of a mathematician or an executive is always evaluated in relation to his age. Some occupations have no timetable at all. Politics may be entered at any age from 21 to above 60, and a political career may terminate at any age from 22 to 95.

3. Some occupations virtually guarantee upward vertical mobility (army officer). Some offer a small chance of spectacular mobility (television actor) and others a large chance of moderate upward mobility (municipal employee).

4. Some occupational careers require the individual to establish close and friendly contact with people in the occupational milieu in order to get his work done (wholesale goods salesman). In other occupations, friendships within the milieu are not technically required but

are customary (railroading). In many occupations, after-hours fraternization is neither required nor expected (postal clerk).

And so on. The diversity of occupational milieus is nearly inexhaustible.[36] In many cases, entering an occupation means penetrating into a world virtually unknown to outsiders, governed by its own peculiar rules and customs and harboring its own heroes, myths, ceremonies, and signs of mutual recognition. Thus were railroaders described a generation ago by Cottrell[37] and jazz musicians more recently by Becker.[38] Some other occupations have only minimal institutions. Their incumbents share common viewpoints and have common problems, but have little contact with each other and are not well organized. Filling station operators fall into this category. Still other occupations are not autonomous in any respect and have no special culture at all. There are no mysteries in the comptometer operator's trade.

Some occupations, like medicine or plumbing, have only a single entrance. The educational and training requirements are fixed, and all those admitted to the occupation have undergone the same preparation. Other occupations permit different kinds of preparation (newspaper reporter) or permit the occasional entry of talented persons who have not had any formal training (commercial artist). Finally, there is a large group of occupations that require a given level of general education but no extended training (salesman).

Near the midpoint of the occupational status scale, where white-collar and manual levels overlap, there are a great many occupations that are often called "semiskilled" but cannot really be evaluated in terms of skill or even in terms of prior experience. Their common requirement is a high school diploma and some aptitude for the work. The typical period of training is less than a week. Long-term job stability is rare. Careers are not well defined. The work of men and women is nearly identical and receives equal compensation. Literacy, steadiness, dependability, and mechanical and arithmetical aptitude are the qualities principally valued, but workers are treated collectively and have little opportunity to distinguish themselves. Indeed, most studies of working groups at this level have discovered fairly elaborate systems for limiting and standardizing individual output in order to maintain a speed and style of work that is comfortable for everyone and allows the least rapid workers to keep up with the group. Machine operators in factories and clerical workers in large offices are the most typical representatives of these semiskilled occupations, but there are hundreds or thousands of others. Their relative importance tends to increase as the farmers, farmhands, laborers, and practitioners of old-fashioned crafts disappear from the labor force.

It is typically within these occupations that careers seem "undirected" or "unestablished." In the United States, industrial enterprises have retained the privilege of expanding and contracting their work forces to match the fluctuations in their production that occur in response to various market forces. Even in a year of full employment like 1966, the average rate of hiring in manufacturing industries ran 5 percent per month and the average rate of "separations" was 4.6 percent. About two-thirds of those who left their jobs did so voluntarily; the remainder were laid off.[39] It is not unusual for 5 percent of the manufacturing labor force to leave their jobs in a single month or for the same proportion, consisting partly of the same people, to get new jobs in a single month. One of the most curious aspects of the organization of large-scale production in the United States is the contrast between executives, who often remain with one employer for their entire working lives, and highly transient clerical workers and machine operators in the same companies.

Modern methods of job classification and personnel selection are designed to facilitate the movement of employees in and out of semiskilled occupations, partly by simplifying the operations of production so that they can be satisfactorily performed without extensive training, partly by accurate techniques of selection that make it easy to identify suitable candidates for a particular kind of work. In jobs of this type, personal relationships largely account for the workers' satisfaction or dissatisfaction, and management experts have developed elaborate ways of encouraging the formation of friendly relationships between supervisors and the people they supervise. The adjustment of real differences between employers and employees, on the other hand, is relegated for the most part to outside organizations—either mass-membership unions or government agencies.

The lack of opportunity that characterizes the semiskilled white-collar and blue-collar occupations has certain advantages for both the employer and the employee. The employer is able to enlarge and contract his working force as the exigencies of his business suggest. The employee, precisely because seniority in the plant gives him no real advantage, is free to pull up stakes and to move across the street or across the country to another job at the same level whenever he wishes to do so. But the worker who wants higher occupational status is not likely to find a ladder leading upward from the shop or office floor. He usually perceives—correctly—that his best chance for upward mobility is a transfer into a type of employment with more opportunities for promotion or into some type of small proprietorship.[40] Many semiskilled workers displace their ambitions onto the next generation, and hope to obtain by means of higher education a more favorable career for their children than they have had themselves.

Social Control of Occupational Performance

Among the nearly innumerable features of occupational milieus are those that have to do with the control of occupational behavior by various social agents: employers, supervisors, colleagues, peers, customers, clients, unions, inspectors, professional associations, instructors, licensing boards, and public officials. Among the first questions to be asked about any occupation are, Who controls the behavior of the workers in it, and who evaluates the quality of their work?

Because there are hundreds of different occupations with differing career patterns, no brief summary can possibly cover them all. In the following section, the discussion will be limited to the recruiting and promotion of workers in five types of occupation—independent professionals, corporation executives, unionized craftsmen, production line workers, and small retail proprietors. They are selected because they illustrate the astonishing diversity of career patterns that can exist simultaneously within the same occupational system and because each of them is important in its own right.

INDEPENDENT PROFESSIONALS[41]

The leading and most typical independent professions are law and medicine. What makes them "independent" is that the great majority of practitioners are in private practice, offering their services to the general public in return for fees fixed by mutual agreement. In both professions, a substantial minority hold salaried positions, but those who do are often entitled to engage in private practice on the side and are always entitled to return to private practice whenever they wish. Architecture and dentistry are professions with similar characteristics. Accountants, engineers, nurses, and social workers may also engage in private practice but are more likely to hold salaried positions in large organizations. Clergymen, teachers, and research scientists are professionals who engage in private practice only in exceptional cases.

A profession is an occupation that monopolizes a cluster of related work activities based on a large body of abstract knowledge, allowing considerable discretion to the practitioner and having serious social consequences. Theology, law, and medicine were the three faculties of the medieval university in which the original professions developed. Beginning with the nineteenth century, additional professions began to be added and professional status is now claimed with more or less success by a host of occupations—undertaking, forestry, journalism—that aspire to meet the criteria for a profession by requiring a long course of training at the university level, and by establishing a professional monopoly.

The distinctive marks of a professional monopoly are that certain work activities are reserved to qualified members of the profession, that other persons are forbidden to undertake these activities, and that membership in the profession is awarded and withdrawn by organizations controlled by the profession.

Until about 1910, access to the major professions required either a course of study in an appropriate faculty or a period of service in the office of a practicing professional. From that date onward, the educational requirement became dominant and increasingly elaborate. It is no longer possible to enter any independent profession in the United States without completing a course in a professional school preceded by three or four years of undergraduate education. Vestiges of the old system of office training survive in the form of internships in medicine and dentistry, clerkships in law, and required field experience in architecture, as well as in the continued separation of the qualifying degree, awarded by a professional school or college, and the license to practice, awarded after examination by official boards established by a state government but composed of eminent members of the profession. The right to practice the advanced subspecialties of each profession is awarded in a somewhat similar fashion.

At each level of training, the aspiring professional is carefully tested. Some candidates are rejected, either because they lack the knowledge and ability required at that stage or, in a few cases, for inappropriate behavior.

Although the qualifications of an independent professional are never reviewed except by other professionals, his success as a practitioner is measured by the number and kind of clients he attracts. Thus, in principle, it is professionals who determine that each practitioner is fully qualified, but it is laymen who decide which practitioner is better qualified than others. This arrangement involves two important assumptions: first, that any practitioner is perfectly qualified to perform any of the ordinary duties of the profession, and second, that no practitioner is ever interchangeable with another because of the elements of individuality in his work. It follows from the latter assumption that the value of professional services cannot be exactly measured in money, because the work of each professional is unique. This conclusion leads to setting the fee for important pieces of professional work according to the client's or patient's ability to pay. This principle sometimes has very questionable consequences, as when physicians charge higher fees to patients with medical insurance (because their ability to pay is greater) or when accident lawyers take the lion's share of the damages awarded to an injured client (because his ability to pay has been greatly increased by the award).

The ladder of formal advancement begins with admission to the professional school and terminates, in the case of physicians and dentists, with admission to practice a specialty; in the case of lawyers, with admission to practice before certain higher courts; in the case of architects, with admission to the leading institutes. Alongside this ladder is a vast informal system of recruiting and advancement somewhat differently structured in each profession but tending to the same purposes—the maintenance of control over professional careers in the hands of professionals rather than laymen and the conservation of certain acquired advantages by self-perpetuating professional groups.

In the case of law, a sharply graded prestige scale separates the best law schools from the good schools from the mediocre ones. Although the law school does not automatically determine the future careers of its students, it has a major effect upon them. "Making the Law Review" at one of the two or three best schools nearly insures a brilliant career. Mediocre grades at a mediocre school practically guarantee a slow start. The private practice of law is dominated by influential firms, themselves arranged in a prestige hierarchy. The Wall Street law firms studied by Smigel (cited above) are known nationally and internationally; their practices are vast, diversified, and lucrative. Organized as partnerships, some of them have scores of partners, associates, and junior lawyers. The latter are hired directly from law schools, mostly from the best law schools, and screened both for intellectual qualities and social presentability. Within a firm, advancement to a partnership depends upon attracting the notice and winning the approval of senior partners. Judgments of ability and personal sponsorship are closely interwoven. Similar firms, with somewhat narrower interests, dominate the practice of law in other metropolitan communities. The law school graduate who joins a minor firm or goes into practice with friends or hangs out his own shingle in the traditional way will almost certainly be restricted to marginal legal business, as Carlin's study (cited above) shows. However, political careers leading either to elective office or to judgeships offer an alternative career path for young lawyers outside the large firm.

In medicine, the majority of newly qualified physicians establish their own offices and practice individually throughout their working lives. Offices are sometimes shared with one or several colleagues for convenience, but without any semblance of a partnership. About one out of six physicians in private practice joins a team of specialists who treat patients in the same office or clinic and pool their fees. However, membership in a medical partnership is generally less prestigious, and less remunerative, than practicing alone. Given the shortage of physicians that has existed in the United States for several decades and is preserved by the limitation of enrollment in medical schools, it is relatively easy for a physician to open an office wherever he pleases, and he is almost sure to attract a considerable number of patients regardless of his personal qualities.

The institution that allocates prestige in the practice of medicine is the hospital. The number and quality of a doctor's hospital affiliations determines the type of patient he can accept in his office practice and, if he is a specialist, the number and types of patients who will be referred to him by other doctors. His position within the elaborate semivoluntary structure of the hospital determines how autonomously he can treat his patients there and how much influence and reputation he enjoys in the local medical community. These in turn have a direct effect upon the size and character of his practice. In the large cities, where the great majority of physicians are located, the practice of medicine is subdivided into ethnic compartments, each with its own hospital, its own system of mutual referrals, and its own professional community. Even a small city is likely to have some compartmentation between Christian and Jewish doctors. In a large metropolitan center there will be separate compartments, including a full complement of hospitals and associations, for Polish, Italian, and Ukrainian physicians as well as the major compartments occupied by Protestants, Catholics, and Jews; and a large compartment—with somewhat limited hospital facilities—for black physicians. Within each compartment, the individual's advancement in prestige and influence depends in varying measure on attracting the sponsorship of older colleagues and on the support of his peers, often reinforced by mutual referral and social contacts. Movement between compartments is difficult but not impossible; the doctor accomplishes it more easily by moving to another city than by changing hospitals in the same city.

The career patterns of dentistry and architecture have not yet been carefully studied but seem to include similar devices for adding informal to formal qualifications and for limiting the ability of laymen to influence the prestige of a practitioner by allocating prestige through occupational institutions controlled by professionals.

There is always a potential conflict in the professions (including the salaried professions) between competence and sponsorship and a danger that the able, friendless man will be overlooked in favor of someone with friends in the right places, or someone who had the luck or good judgment to enter the profession through one of its high-prestige channels. On the other hand, the importance of sponsorship in a profession proceeds from the nature of the work itself. The character and reputation of the professional, the extent to which he can call on his colleagues for assistance in a difficult case, are elements that contribute directly to the performance of professional tasks and cannot be separated from them. It is a curious feature of the professions that although they are proud of their independence, most practitioners are involved in an intricate network of social relations involving many other people in many other roles. For the lawyer in court, the doctor making rounds, or the architect on a building site, professional competence and professional reputation are different aspects of the same behavior.

The autonomy enjoyed by professionals, even salaried professionals, in regulating their own careers explains why the prospect of professionalization is so tempting for any occupation that requires or can be made to require university training and some of the necessary conditions for the establishment of an occupational monopoly. In some states, "realtor" and "social worker" are titles restricted by law to persons who can show certain credentials and have passed a qualifying examination, but the process of professionalization is not likely to be completed for such occupations in the near future. Although the title is legally monopolized the function is not; other persons continue to sell houses and investigate welfare clients. What is lacking in these marginal cases is the element of danger that attaches to the malperformance of a professional function. The unqualified practitioner is excluded from a profession by public authority, not ostensibly for the benefit of professionals, but because he can do grave harm by drawing a legal document improperly or undertaking a surgical operation for which he is untrained.

On the other hand, the professional monopoly creates its own dangers; necessary functions may go unperformed or practitioners may take advantage of their clients. The perception of these dangers is as ancient as the professions themselves and invariably leads to the development of a code of ethics, often embodied in an occupational oath or declaration to which all members of the profession subscribe. Such codes prohibit antisocial forms of practice, abuses against clients, unfair competition against colleagues, unprofessional activities of various kinds, and cooperation with unqualified practitioners. The Oath of Hippocrates, more than 2,000 years old, contains several of these themes; for example:

> Into whatever houses I enter, I will go into them for the benefit of the sick, and will abstain from every voluntary act of mischief and corruption; and, further, from the seduction of females or males, of freemen and slaves.

In addition to such general statements, professionals are governed by a great number of laws and regulations designed both to protect the public against the wayward professional and to protect the profession against hostile criticism.

The independent professions are more favorably situated with respect to retirement than any other sector of the labor force. The individual may choose his own moment to retire, and he retains his professional affiliations and his right to practice after retirement. Many physicians and lawyers remain active into their seventies and eighties. Some never retire at all but merely work a diminished number of hours and take longer vacations as they age. Even salaried positions held by members of the independent professions are partly exempt from the usual retirement rules. Judges and medical professors may continue to hold their positions 10 or 15 years after the usual age of civil service retirement.

CORPORATION EXECUTIVES[42]

Corporation executives are recruited primarily although not exclusively from among the sons of professionals, managers, and proprietors. The career of a corporation executive is usually stable and continuous, although it may involve mobility within and between companies. The vast majority of corporation executives are college graduates, with undergraduate degrees in arts and sciences or business or engineering. The vast majority are white, Protestant, Republican, married, fathers, and homeowners. Homosexuality, celibacy, drug addiction, absenteeism, radicalism, and mysticism are almost unknown among them. As a group they are homogeneous and disciplined.

The typical executive trainee is hired by a company representative who visits his college campus looking for men who have the standard social attributes, respectable academic records, ambition, and whatever special qualities—such as engineering aptitude—the company may require. There is no consistent preference in this hiring process for brilliant academic records or for the colleges of highest prestige. Some companies avoid students whose records seem excessively academic, and some prefer not to hire applicants from top-ranking colleges, who might form alumni cliques later in their careers.

In almost every company, the new recruit is placed in a training program where he remains from several months to several years, receiving more or less systematic instruction and acquiring familiarity with the company and industry, its geographical and social environment, and the procedures and folkways of corporate management.

Corporations differ greatly in their internal ideologies and in how seriously these are taken. In some companies, the trainee learns a pious reverence for the company and everything it stands for. In others, company policy as promulgated by higher management is treated with derision in the lower executive ranks. In either case, working conditions are comfortable, pay and fringe benefits are generous, and the trainee is required to show a fairly high degree of application to his work. Habitual lateness, drinking in the office, or disloyal remarks in the presence of outsiders would be almost unthinkable offenses.

The career of the corporation executive is an exercise in mobility. His legitimate goal is to rise as high as possible in the hierarchy of executive rank and income. A considerable amount of upward mobility is guaranteed for any man who follows an executive career. Normally, he will receive modest salary raises during the training period and fairly rapid promotion in the years immediately following. In companies with widely separated branches, promotions often involve a change of residence, a change of department or branch, or both. Horizontal moves are sometimes made without promotion but seldom without salary increase or some other benefit. When the executive reaches his middle thirties, the competition for promotion becomes far more intense and the job often becomes more demanding. At this stage some men begin to move toward positions in top management while others settle down to a slower, more comfortable pace of advancement. For men in their forties, the competition is almost decided. Some move sidewise into semiretirement, others become specialists, some leave for other companies, some move up to be regional managers, vice presidents, and directors. In his fifties, the executive who has reached the "policy-making level" may turn his energies to corporate acquisitions, intercompany relations, or government service. Virtually all corporation executives who are not owners retire in their sixties, sometimes continuing as directors or consultants but often breaking all ties with the company.

The almost monastic devotion of the American corporation executive to his work and to his company is an important feature of the industrial economy. There is nothing equivalent in the government service or in large-scale voluntary associations, although they have hosts of devoted and hard-working officials. The corporation executive is a man trained to get on with his subordinates, his superiors, and his colleagues with a minimum of stress and to leave them at a moment's notice without any sense of loss. "The tasks of social and occupational mobility," remarks William E. Henry, "are ones for which these men are singularly equipped. They can focus and concentrate their energies; they are under some compulsion to break off social relations and move into new ones; they are not distracted by either marked unconventionality or intensive investment in family or friends."[43]

Their capacity for mobility extends in all directions except downward. The corporation executive who moves from one company to another can be counted on to give his unstinted loyalty to the old company until the day of his departure and the same to his new company as soon as he arrives. In most large companies, the reorganization of executive positions and assignments is practically continuous, and remarkably untroubled.

The control of the executive's performance is simplified by the simplicity and clarity of the norms to which he is subject, and by his high visibility. As a candidate for promotion throughout most of his working life, he is constantly being tested, scrutinized, screened, and interviewed formally and informally. Annual or semiannual evaluations by superiors are part of his record. Any breach of the expectations that define the executive role is likely to be registered immediately by his fellow executives, and by executives in other companies too. For reasons that are not entirely clear, a considerable amount of external contact is built into the working life of the average executive. The necessity for this is self-evident in such activities as marketing, advertising, and purchasing, but it is notable that comptrollers, personnel men, and production engineers, whose work falls mostly within the enterprise, usually maintain a good deal of contact with their opposite numbers in competitive companies and with executives in related branches of business and industry. The taboo against fraternization with competitors that prevails in some European industries is almost totally lacking in the United States; indeed there might be said to be a taboo against nonfraternization. In some industries, like the pharmaceutical industry, where intercompany transfers are common, these contacts provide a market for executive talent and facilitate the development of industrywide attitudes and habits, but in others, like the automobile industry, where it is unusual for an executive to move to a competitor company, a high rate of external contact is maintained nevertheless.

UNIONIZED CRAFTSMEN[44]

The unionized craftsmen—the "aristocracy of manual labor"—belong to more than a hundred different trades with as many occupational traditions. Included among them are the craftsmen of the building trades: masons, bricklayers, electricians, plumbers, carpenters, and about two dozen others; of the foundry and metallurgical industries—molders, forgemen, and smeltermen, for example; of the railroads—locomotive engineers, firemen, boilermakers; of factories—millwrights, toolmakers, die setters, and many others; and such distinctive craftsmen as printers, diamond cutters, furriers, goldsmiths, and harbor pilots. Most of these trades inherit a long occupational tradition. Some of them are more or less directly descended from medieval guilds, and all of them preserve some vestiges of the guild system in their occupational institutions, such as formal apprenticeship, a distinction between masters and journeymen, and the privileges of seniority.

Like the professions, the craft unions attempt to monopolize the performance of certain occupational tasks and invoke the power of the state to help them do so. In most jurisdictions, for example, electricians and plumbers must be licensed in order to work on new construction, and it is not possible for anyone but a member of the craft union to meet the licensing requirements. Access to the craft is often through apprenticeship, and the union sets the qualifications for apprenticeship, limits the number of apprentices, and promotes them to journeymen. In some craft unions, every applicant for membership must be personally sponsored by a master of the craft. In all of them, sponsorship is an important element in selection; a considerable number of recruits are the sons, nephews, or cousins of men in the same craft. Additional sponsorship, in the form of character references or certificates of competence, are often required when an apprentice or helper presents himself to be qualified as a journeyman and again, in some trades, when the journeyman becomes a master or inspector or assumes supervisory duties. Craft unions tend to be closed groups; they are usually very slow in opening their doors to strangers. It is not unusual for nearly all the members of a local craft union to belong to the same ethnic group: Mohawk Indians in structural iron work; German Catholics in pianomaking; and Dutch Jews in diamond cutting, for example.

The craft union's occupational monopoly is much weaker than that of a profession, and the craftsman's credentials are not as readily transferable to another locality as the professional's. Sometimes they are not transferable at all. The control of qualifying examinations is not completely in the hands of the craft; outsiders, including engineers and other professionals who supervise craft work, usually sit on the licensing boards. In many crafts, apprenticeship has been replaced by vocational schooling under public control. Finally, the penalties for violation of the occupational monopoly in a craft are mild. An unlicensed plumber may be punished by the refusal of a certificate from the building inspector, but he will not be criminally prosecuted like an unlicensed surgeon.

The other great difference between the professions and the crafts is that craftsmen at the same level are considered to be absolutely interchangeable. Union contracts usually specify standard wages for craftsmen at each level, and seniority rules often dictate the assignment of craftsmen to particular jobs so that the employer has no opportunity to choose among individuals. In a well-regulated craft, formal and informal norms assure that both the quality and quantity of work performed by two equally qualified craftsmen under the same conditions will be substantially the same.

Some craftsmen, like pilots, change employers from day to day; others, like stonesetters, from month to month; others, like toolmakers, may remain with the same employer for many years. The length of employment has surprisingly little effect either on their conditions of work or their wages. Work rules are usually established by means of a master contract; they are readily enforceable because the work done by craftsmen is usually indispensable.

The typical craftsman's career shows comparatively little vertical mobility. As a journeyman, he works for many years at standard wages that rise a little faster than the earnings of other manual workers. In his middle years, he may seek upward mobility in activities peripheral to the craft, becoming a contractor, a government inspector, or a jobber-dealer without giving up his union card. Like professionals, craftsmen have the privilege of retiring early without losing their right to return to the trade and of continuing to work past the usual retirement age if they are capable of doing so.

The stability of a craft occupation as a social system is achieved through a system of formal norms that resists technological change and market pressures at the cost of some inefficiency and rigidity. Almost all crafts have elaborate written codes, often referred to as the "Rule Book." In the building trades these are likely to be set down in a building code. In other crafts, they are found in union by-laws, licensing regulations, master contracts and manuals. The essential elements of the Rule Book are the specification of acceptable tools and methods; hiring procedures and seniority rights; safety rules; the number of men required for a given type of job; standard working conditions; a standard hourly wage and standard modifications of that wage for overtime, weekends, idle time, travel, and hazardous conditions; the use of apprentices and helpers on the job; and the permitted and prohibited forms of cooperation with other crafts having overlapping jurisdiction.

PRODUCTION LINE WORKERS[45]

Recruiting for production line work is the responsibility of company personnel departments. Most production line workers belong to industrial unions, which, unlike craft unions, have no elaborate requirements for membership and are eager to enroll anyone hired within their jurisdiction. The usual form of labor contract in a mass production industry provides for a union shop, that is, an arrangement whereby nonunion members may be hired freely but are then required to join the union. Unlike the typical craft union, which is a relatively small, closed in-group, the typical industrial union is a large-scale, bureaucratized, somewhat impersonal organization whose major purpose is to negotiate wages, working conditions, and fringe benefits for its members and to assure a hearing for their grievances against management. The union contract may also guarantee rights to the employee based on his seniority with a particular employer. The usual provision is that workers with seniority in a given category must be laid off last and rehired first. A company's right to set whatever qualifications it wishes for production workers and to lay them off without notice is otherwise limited only by laws against discrimination on the grounds of race, color, or union membership.

The production line worker has no personal claim on his job. Except in a few companies, long-term job security is not available at this level, and opportunities for promotion are relatively scarce. Many factory workers remain at approximately the same occupational level from the beginning to the end of their working lives. Chinoy, in a 1948 study of automobile workers, described a more or less typical chrnology of aspirations among workers in a mass production industry:

1. Many young men who come to work in the factory define their jobs as temporary; they do not expect to remain in the ranks of factory labor.
2. Workers with the most clearly defined out-of-the-shop goals are married men in their late twenties or early thirties who have not acquired substantial seniority.
3. Workers are most likely to develop or sustain hope for promotion to supervision if while still relatively young they gain some form of advancement as wage workers, that is, if they secure jobs at the top of the hierarchy of desirability or if they move from non-skilled to skilled work.
4. The longer workers remain in the plant, the less likely are they to muster the initiative to leave, even if they continually talk of doing so.
5. As their seniority increases, workers can look forward to the possibility of individual wage increases (however small they may be) and of transfer to more desirable jobs.
6. The weight of increasing or already heavy family responsibilities keeps men with long seniority from seriously considering out-of-the-shop goals.
7. Workers who do not gain promotion to supervision before the age of forty or thereabouts quickly lose hope because of management's preference for younger men.
8. After workers reach the low wage ceiling at the top of the hierarchy of desirability, they may be satisfied with what they have achieved or, alternatively, they may become bitter and frustrated because of their inability to go further.
9. Some workers, as they approach the age of retirement, may become interested in out-of-the-shop goals as sources of income for their remaining years . . . [46]

The production line worker described by Chinoy is likely to regard his work as a practical necessity, pleasant or unpleasant as the case may be, rather than as an integral part of his life. The reasons are not hard to understand. He has no opportunity to acquire a vested interest either in his job or in the enterprise for which he works. He is unable to resist changes in his work imposed by technological innovation, as craftsmen do, or to adapt such changes to his own advantage, as professionals do. Even under the most enlightened management, his role in the productive process is more that of an instrument than that of an agent. Although there have been some interesting attempts, particularly in Europe, to enlarge the production line worker's job and to reverse the established trend toward the simplification of factory tasks, these have been limited in scope.[47] As a small cog in a large intricate mechanism, the production line worker has less autonomy in arranging and completing his work than almost anyone else in the labor force. On a fast assembly line, almost his entire workday may consist of making prescribed movements in a prescribed order at a prescribed speed. [48]

The company sets the daily and weekly calendar, the times and places for lunch and rest, and the penalties for absenteeism, lateness, and loitering. It restricts the worker's activities in the shop and tells him when he may or may not smoke, talk, leave his machine, go to the bathroom or enter another part of the plant. It often tells him what clothes to wear in the plant, and how often and where to have them laundered. It defines his responsibility with respect to company tools and materials and charges him for errors or losses; puts him under the authority of supervisors and sets penalties for disobedience; and requires his attendance at various times and places for medical examinations, training programs, and other forms of "processing."[49] Although companies vary greatly in the manner (and manners) of exercising this tight control, they never try to do away with it. Mass production is founded on the expectation that the activity of the production line worker will be closely controlled by technical requirements.

In addition to the control imposed by management, the production line worker is often subject to the informal but firm control of his peer group. The usual program of the peer group is to restrict output to a comfortable working pace, to equalize earnings and working conditions, and to resist those management controls that they regard as unreasonable.[50]

SMALL RETAIL PROPRIETORS[51]

These are the owners and operators of retail establishments (other than department stores, chain stores, and restaurants). The corner grocer, the haberdasher, the stationer, the hardware dealer, and the independent shoe merchant belong in this category. So does the neighborhood druggist, despite his professional training in pharmacy.

In recent years the number of small retail proprietors in the labor force has been declining almost as fast as the number of small independent farmers, largely owing to the competition of chain store enterprises with superior resources, the advantages of bulk purchasing, and more efficient management. Nevertheless, there are still more than half a million small proprietors and they are perhaps better equipped for survival than those who have been forced out of business. As in farming, a large minority of retail proprietors inherit their occupations either directly, by going into a family owned store as an assistant and taking it over when older relatives retire, or indirectly, by learning the trade in a family store and opening a similar store at some later point. There is not much horizontal mobility between retail trades (between the grocery business and the shoe business for example), but there is a great deal of mobility in and out of proprietorship. The number of new retail businesses founded every year is very high in proportion to the total in existence. Most of them are established on funds borrowed from banks or suppliers and have a short life expectancy. The failure of such an enterprise is not catastrophic for the proprietor, who normally sells his stock and fixtures and disposes of his lease as best he can without going through bankruptcy. Only to the extent that the unpaid debts of a failed business affect the proprietor's credit rating and reduce his ability to borrow does a failure affect his chance of future success.

Movement out of retail proprietorship also occurs at the other end of the scale, as retail enterprises develop into chain stores or department stores or supermarkets, or are purchased by larger retailers or sold to obtain capital for other business ventures. The larger retail organizations, having grown rapidly and uninterruptedly ever since World War II, are perennially short of personnel. Jobbers, distributors, and manufacturers always have a wide range of job openings for which familiarity with a particular line of retail business is a qualification. An experienced retail proprietor who is moderately young, moderately well-educated and geographically mobile can often exchange his proprietorship for a salaried job that has fewer risks, shorter hours and higher earnings. Thus, the growth of large-scale retail organizations tends to push the independent retailer out of his occupation by means of competitive pressures and to pull him out of it by irresistible inducements.

One of the principal attractions of independent proprietorship is "not being ordered around by anybody." The proprietor is not subject to the control of an organizational superior, because he has none, or to that of a peer group, because he is not expected or required to cooperate with his competitors. Nevertheless, his occupational performance is very closely controlled by local officials, suppliers, and creditors (often the same people), and customers.

The intervention of local officials in the retail market is one of the most constant features of urban life. Medieval towns regulated their markets minutely, fixing prices, setting standards of quality, inspecting weights and measures, and punishing adulteration, mislabeling and other types of mercantile fraud. Regulation of this type survives everywhere today; but in addition, the retailer is subject to many new types of government regulation as an employer, an advertiser, the occupant of a commercial building, and the keeper of a public place. The average commercial establishment must satisfy inspectors of weights, measures, and scales; sanitary and fire inspectors; building inspectors and tax inspectors. It must carry prescribed amounts of workmen's compensation and liability insurance and have suitable exits and entrances, ventilated storerooms and basements, and verified records of sales tax collection. It must refrain from discrimination in employment, illegal hours, obstruction of sidewalks or alleyways, and the sale of out of date products. In many cases, premises or proprietors or both must be specially licensed to sell a particular commodity like liquor, milk, meat, gasoline, or tobacco; in such cases, the continuation of a license depends upon conforming to an entire set of special regulations. Some of these, especially those having to do with tax accounting and insurance, create difficult problems for the independent proprietor, who has to follow complicated procedures designed for larger enterprises.

The regulations and the enforcement agencies to whom the retail proprietor is subject are so numerous and so poorly integrated that perfect compliance is literally impossible, and he is able to operate only because enforcement is slack. In some cities, this slackness is obtained through the payment of small standardized bribes to various inspectors. In other cases, it arises haphazardly because the retail proprietor is too small an offender for a tax office or employment commission to bother with.

The regulation of the retailer's behavior by his suppliers and other creditors is much more straightforward, and not so easily evaded. The first rule is prompt payment of financial obligations; delays in payment lead first to the loss of discounts, then to the restriction of credit and eventually to legal action. In many retail businesses, suppliers also fix the size of minimun orders; limit or prohibit the stocking of competitive brands; and set prices for their products under fair trade acts, franchise agreements, and other complicated arrangements. They may also insist that their merchandise be handled, displayed, or advertised in certain ways. In many cases, the supplier's representative automatically restocks the retailer's shelves as they empty and takes charge of the physical arrangement of merchandise and promotional displays. Under some agreements—filling stations are often run this way—the supplier loans the proprietor most of his operating capital but retains the right to dictate the operation of the business. It is often impossible to tell whether the supplier is assisting the retailer or coercing him. Modern methods of distribution involve a good deal of both.

Last but not least, the retail proprietor is under the partial control of his customers, upon whose good will his entire business depends. The increasing mobility of the customer and the decreasing autonomy of the retailer with respect to pricing increase his dependence on customer approbation and reinforce the conventional pattern of the merchant-customer relationship, whereby the retailer is expected to minimize his own status and exaggerate that of the customer by deferential manners, small personal attentions, and adherence to the formula that "the customer is always right." The usual penalty for violating these norms is the loss of the customer and perhaps of the customer's friends and relatives. The small retail store is usually a neighborhood enterprise; its customers are mostly drawn from those who live and work in the immediate vicinity. Lost customers are not easily replaced, and the loss of a few good customers may have a drastic effect on the cash balance. Here too, the small retail proprietor is at a competitive disadvantage compared to large-scale retail organizations whose sales clerks, having less personal stake in the business and dealing with a larger and less localized population, are not easily intimidated.

Paradoxically, the loss of influence that customers experience in moving from small-scale to large-scale retail stores is one reason why many of them prefer to deal with the small merchant even when his prices are somewhat higher and his stock more limited.

The Sociology of Wages

Of the $532 billion that Americans received as personal income in 1965, $355 billion was wages and salaries, $19 billion was other labor income like employers' contributions to private pension funds, and $56 billion was the income of business and farm proprietors.[52] In sum, about 80 percent of the dollars received by private persons are obtained from their occupations. (The remainder is divided between income from property, like dividends, and income from government programs, like welfare payments.) It is obvious that the social mechanisms that determine earnings in different occupations have important consequences for nearly everyone. They are very complicated mechanisms, and some of them are not completely understood.

FORMS OF PAYMENT

Almost every distinguishable occupation has its own rules for calculating the amount of work accomplished, for compensating the worker in money and other goods, and for the timing of these transactions. A worker's earnings may take the form of wages, salaries, fringe benefits, commissions, bonuses, receipts of sales, fees, honoraria, royalties, tips, percentages, subsistence, or payments in kind. He may be paid by the hour, the day, the week, the month, the year; by the piece, the pound, the ton, the word, the load, the trip, the mile, the column, the score, the square yard, or almost any other unit of measure. The price of his labor may be set by him, by an employer, by contract, by individual bargain, by custom, by legislation, by market processes, or by chance. It may fluctuate from hour to hour or remain unchanged for decades. All the workers in one occupation may earn exactly the same amount, whereas all those in another may earn different amounts. Some workers are paid less for what they do than for who they are or what they own. A few pay their employers for the privilege of holding a job that provides training or special opportunities. If we look again at the five occupational groups whose career patterns were discussed above, we discover that each of them has its own forms of remuneration, although these do not represent all the possibilities.

Independent professionals are paid directly by their clients or patients. The form of payment is a fee, and in theory, it is fixed by bargaining in each case. In practice, most independent professionals charge uniform fees for small, routine services, whereas in important cases, they set their fees in rough relation to the importance of the service, the amount of effort it requires, and the client or patient's ability to pay. This does not necessarily mean that the individual practitioner charges unequal fees for the same service, although it is not improper for him to do so. Some obstetricians set variable fees for the delivery of the baby depending upon the patient's income. Others set the same fee for all their private patients; if the fee is high their practice will be limited to high-income patients, and if it is especially low, they will attract a disproportionate number of low-income patients. The architect's fee is usually calculated as a flat percentage of the cost of the project he designs; it may be 10 percent for a house and somewhat less for industrial and commercial buildings. The professional's fee is almost always collected after the work is performed (there are a few exceptions in the practice of law), and some losses due to noncollection are certain to occur. Contingency fees, whereby the practitioner is entitled to be paid more if his intervention is successful, are accepted in the practice of law and are fairly common, although never officially recognized, in medicine, dentistry, and engineering.

Corporation executives are paid monthly salaries. This practice is so standard that it is doubtful whether anyone paid by the week can be described as an executive. In addition to their salaries, executives are paid substantial fringe benefits, rarely amounting to less than 25 percent of the salary and often to very much more. In the higher ranks they are remunerated by means of numerous perquisites, such as company cars, entertainment allowances, company-paid memberships in clubs, travel and vacation expenses for family members, the use of company planes for private errands and of company personnel for personal services, and many similar privileges. No hard-and-fast line can be drawn between a fringe benefit like the company's payment of college expenses for executives' children and a perquisite like the use of a company plane, except that fringe benefits are usually extended to a broad class of employees whereas perquisites are individually awarded. The third type of executive remuneration consists of financial rights in the company's business, profit-sharing plans, bonus plans, bonus stock, stock options, and a host of arrangements tailored to fit the tax laws. There are few, if any, large companies that do not reward executives by giving them shares in the equity or profits of the business or by making it easy for them to acquire such shares on easy terms. A stock option is often the most important part of the remuneration of a high-ranking executive and makes the amount of his salary nearly irrelevant. Because it is impossible to attach a precise value to an option issued in anticipation of a rise in the market price of the company's shares, statistics of executive compensation are likely to be uninformative or misleading. Only a handful of executives, most of them in family-owned companies, have salaries equal to those of movie stars or important country music singers, but they are much more likely to become rich.

Skilled craftsmen are paid hourly wages, with time-and-a-half for normal overtime and double- or triple-time for weekend or night work.

Under normal circumstances, all the craftsmen in a given trade in a given locality receive uniform wages and are expected to do approximately uniform work for it. The rate is always high compared to the hourly rate of clerical workers or operatives; it often exceeds the hourly rate paid to salaried professionals. However, in many industries, the craftsman is not sure of getting work five days a week or 50 weeks in the year. When work is scarce, it is usually distributed according to seniority, but wage rates are not affected. The craftsman's wage is negotiated annually or thereabouts between his union and an association representing many employers. It is usually binding on all local employers, whether or not they participate in the negotiations.

Production line workers may be paid either hourly wages or piece rates. Combinations of the two are common. Hourly wages are subject to various kinds of adjustment for seniority, shift, quality or quantity of output, down time, waiting time, penalties, and bonuses. Wages are paid by check, weekly or bimonthly. In some cases, the rate is set by the employer on a take-it-or-leave-it basis (subject of course to the minimum hourly rates set by federal and state legislation). More commonly, the base rate is based on a contract negotiated between a union and the employer for a fairly long period, with provision for introducing individual and seasonal variations when necessary.

As for retail proprietors, the requirements of the tax laws compel most of them to separate their personal accounts from those of the store, but the separation is more apparent than real. A retail proprietor with orderly habits will pay himself a fixed weekly salary for his own services, setting the figure low enough so that it can be met comfortably even when business is slow. An additional part of his earnings will be taken in services—free goods, family use of the delivery van, an apartment over the store. Additional earnings may be taken out in cash as needed, or used to pay off a mortgage, or put back into the business by the purchase of new fixtures or stock. Well-established retail stores are often organized as closely held corporations; this imposes additional bookkeeping on the proprietor, but allows him to deduct items of expenditure in which the business and personal elements are not easily separated. In the long run, a retail business survives if the proprietor is able to maintain or increase the value of his investment; it approaches liquidation as soon as he begins to dip into his working capital to pay his living expenses.

THE PROBLEM OF COMPARING WAGES

Even this brief survey of a few occupations illustrates why it is always difficult and sometimes impossible to compare earnings from one occupation to another. First, whenever earnings are taken in some form other than wages or salaries—in free goods, in perquisites, in stock options, in company services—it is nearly impossible to determine their cash value, yet such payments are conspicuous elements in the remuneration of two of the five occupational groups discussed above and many others also—salaried professionals, government officials, entertainers, restaurant workers, members of the armed services, farmers, and farm laborers, for example.

Second, a large part of the American labor force is engaged in systematic concealment of supplementary or marginal income in order to reduce income taxes. Most high incomes from work are taken in some form carefully worked out by tax lawyers and accountants to minimize tax liability. The usual formula for doing this is to convert income that would otherwise appear as wages, salaries, or fees into capital gains that are taxed at a much lower rate, and to convert personal expenses into business expenses that can be deducted from income. The line between tax avoidance, which is a legitimate and highly respectable activity, and tax evasion, which is illegal and sometimes criminal, shifts constantly. At one time, large numbers of motor yachts were owned by corporations for the use of their executives, the upkeep and maintenance being treated as business expense. The tax rules were then tightened so that it became nearly impossible for a yacht to satisfy the requirement of being "primarily used for business purposes"; most of the company yachts disappeared. During the same period, there was practically no restriction on the use of company airplanes for personal transportation. Corporate aviation throve accordingly. The rules for distinguishing between business and nonbusiness expense are often incredibly fine-spun. For a lunch between business acquaintances to be deductible, under the rules introduced in 1964 and still nominally in force, the participants must discuss business during the meal; in theory, a business discussion after dessert would not satisfy the requirement. All self-employed persons, professionals, business executives, retail proprietors, farm proprietors, and independent servicemen and a good many public officials, salaried professionals, and craftsmen are continuously involved with such subtle and uncertain rules. This is one reason why the sociological investigator usually finds it harder to obtain information from respondents about their incomes than about their sexual aberrations.

Third, the comparison of earnings is hampered by the technical obstacle that no single time unit will serve for all occupations. An hourly basis is obviously inappropriate for opera singers or burglars. A monthly basis misrepresents the earnings of seasonal and intermittent occupations like farming. An annual basis is not applicable to the numerous occupations that are held for only part of the year, or to the large numbers of persons—perhaps half the women and a third of the men in blue-collar occupations—who work less than 11 months in a given year.

The comparison of lifetime earnings in different occupations is hampered by changes in the value of money and in the structure of occupations over a period of years, as well as by the presence in the labor force of numerous occupations—like parking attendant and federal judge—that nobody holds for a lifetime. All in all, it hardly makes sense to consider differences in occupational earnings without taking into account the different systems of wage determination in the occupations to be compared.

Anyone who has taken a course in elementary economics will know that labor in a market economy may be regarded as a commodity, the price of which is determined by supply and demand, and will have learned something about the classic theories of wage determination. One of these, Ricardo's Iron Law, justified starvation wages on the grounds that any surplus wages would lead to a Malthusian increase in the supply of labor, which would in turn depress wages back to the starvation level. Marx's theory of surplus value also held that the average wages of an industrial population could not rise much above the cost of subsistence under a capitalist system, because the laborer being forced to sell his services in order to live, and the capitalist not forced to buy his services, the wage bargain would be struck near the worker's cost of subsistence and the "surplus value" he produced diverted to the capitalist. That is the proper meaning of the Marxist term *exploitation—the purchase of labor at a price far below its productive value to the employer.*

These theories appeared reasonable when they were announced, but subsequent events failed to confirm them. By the time Marx began work on *Capital,* the wages of factory workers had already risen sharply from the subsistence level of the first decades of the Industrial Revolution. In the century that has since elapsed, the wages of factory workers in all industrialized countries have risen far above the subsistence level; and in addition, the proportion of skilled workers, managers, supervisors and white-collar workers in the industrial force—all earning more than production line workers—has steadily increased, whereas the proportion of unskilled laborers has steadily declined. The margin by which the wages of production line workers exceed a subsistence wage is a fair measure of a country's development[53] and seems to be nearly independent of the form of ownership in its economy. In general, factory workers in the communist countries of eastern Europe are less advanced beyond the subsistence level than factory workers in the capitalist and capitalist-socialist economies of the western European countries, but this is more plausibly attributed to long-standing differences in levels of national development than to short-term wage policies. Neither the capitalist nor the commissar drives the hard bargain anticipated by Ricardo's Law. Both of them pay wages somewhere between the low level at which the worker and his family could barely survive and the high level at which the enterprise could barely survive. But in backward economies, where the productivity of the industrial worker is comparatively low and both agricultural products and manufactured goods are relatively scarce, the range between the lowest possible wage at which the worker can survive and the highest possible wage at which the enterprise can continue will be fairly small; as industrial technology progresses, the range continues to increase without apparent limit, permitting not only continuous wage increases but also the simultaneous shortening of work hours.

Paradoxical as it may seem, the most spectacular spread of earnings (the earnings fan) is likely to be found in a very poor country. In some parts of Central America, the domestic servants of rich families are able to keep servants of their own at home, but in California it is normal for a waitress to eat her off-duty meals in as good a restaurant as the one in which she serves. In the one case, the earnings fan is relatively open; in the other relatively closed. Between 1939 and 1965, the ratio of the farm laborer's median earnings to those of professional and technical workers rose from 0.16 to 0.27. The ratio of operative's wages to those of craftsmen and foremen rose from 0.64 to 0.71 during the same interval.[54]

The closing of the earnings fan in France from 1800 to 1948 was recorded for a large variety of occupations by Fourastié.

> The salary of a councilor of state increased by a factor of at least 40 from 1800 to 1948; the salary of a professor at the Collège de France by 100; the average salary of an office boy in a government agency by 220; the hourly wages of laborers in provincial cities by more than 400. The wage rate of workers without special job training had increased to 80 percent of the skilled-worker wage rate at the end of the period, compared to an average of about 50 percent before 1800. The wage rate of women has also been raised in comparison to that of men and the present difference is only about 20 percent . . .
>
> The Chief Justice of the Court of Accounts, assuming him to be the father of two dependent children, earned in 1948 not more than four and a half times as much as his office boy *by hour of work,* although the difference between these two positions was of the order of 50 to 1 in 1800.[55]

Two other factors contribute to the closing of the earnings fan. Minimum wage legislation tends to raise the average earnings of the lowest occupational groups. Income tax legislation tends to lower the average earnings of the highest occupational groups. In the United States, the former purpose has been more easily achieved than the latter. Other countries have various outcomes.

The closing of the earnings fan does not necessarily bring about the closing of the income fan in an economy where a large proportion of the highest incomes are based on returns from property and a large proportion of the lowest incomes are derived from pension and welfare programs. The available figures are fragmentary and not easy to interpret, but it appears that the distribution of total family income flattened steadily in the United States until about 1945, but has since changed very little. In 1965, the poorest fifth of American families received 5 percent and the richest fifth 41 percent of the aggregate income of the nation's families.[56]

Although the labor force participation of women has risen to the point where about half the entire female population between the ages of 18 and 24 and between the ages of 35 and 64 are found in the labor force at any given moment, the career patterns of women are very different from those of men.[57]

1. A woman's occupational career is not normally continuous. Whereas the average man is employed or looking for work between his departure from school around the age of 20 and his retirement around the age of 65, the average woman works intermittently, entering the labor force when she finishes her schooling, leaving it either at marriage or after the birth of her first child, entering again when her children are all in school or after divorce, leaving again when her husband retires or when her first grandchildren are born or for a second marriage, sometimes reentering when she becomes a widow, but generally retiring early. The higher her socioeconomic status the more likely a woman is to interrupt her career at marriage and not to return to work until her children are grown, but the pattern of intermittent employment appears at all status levels.

2. The vertical mobility of women is discouraged by the discontinuity of their careers, their supposed incapacity for exercising authority, and their exclusion from most closed, privileged occupational groups.

3. Women workers have much greater opportunity for horizontal mobility than men. Practically all the occupations they customarily follow are readily transferred from place to place, and continuity of experience is not a requirement for the maintenance of occupational credentials. The predominantly female profession of nursing is afflicted with a perennial problem of excessive turnover, described by one authority as follows: "What makes them different from workers migrating in search of greener job pastures is that, for them, a job is merely the way to support themselves decently while they see the sights, sample the social life, have a bit of fun and then move on. These nurses do not follow any orientation to work as a central focus of living; their attention is directed to values outside the job environment and they use their work as a means to other, unrelated ends."[58] In other instances, such as with the public school teachers described by Becker, women's careers are organized in terms of horizontal mobility between positions that are nominally on the same level but offer different degrees of comfort and convenience.[59]

4. Whereas most employed men support a family for most of their working lives, only a small minority of white women (and a somewhat larger minority of black women) do so. The average employed woman uses her earnings either for her own sole support or to supplement the earnings of her husband. Thus, although the slogan of equal pay for equal work is seldom challenged directly, it often appears unfair in particular cases because the obligations of an employed man are

likely to be much greater than those of his female colleague. In European countries, where the basic wage of the head of the family is supplemented by allowances for his dependents, the problem is less sharp and seems to encourage greater equality between men and women in the same enterprises.

5. The perennial movement of women in and out of the labor force has the effect of maintaining a labor reserve that can be called upon at almost a moment's notice to meet an increase in the demand for labor in any occupation in which women are numerous. This phenomenon has multiple effects. It tends to reinforce wage discrimination against women, and when direct discrimination is prohibited, to encourage various indirect forms like the denial of a promotion. It also tends to depress the wages and decrease the bargaining power of men in the same occupations. Thus, the occupations in which women predominate are relatively unorganized, for collective bargaining, and this lack of organization tends to reinforce the predominance of women in them.

In sum, the terms on which women are enlisted in our economy are highly favorable to family solidarity. Women have an opportunity to contribute to family support whenever they wish to, are allowed to interrupt their careers whenever they are more needed at home and are able to follow their husbands from place to place as his career requires without surrendering whatever occupational seniority they have acquired. The price of these advantages is almost complete exclusion from the arena in which men compete for promotion, wealth, and status. Only in a few special fields, like entertainment, literature, department store merchandising, social work, and espionage can women compete on nearly equal terms with men. The ambitious woman, who values a career more than the satisfactions of family life, must pick her ground with care.

Summary / CHAPTER EIGHT

1   Under modern conditions, the division of labor tends to become progressively more complex with the result that occupations become more numerous and occupational change accelerates. At the same time there is a steady movement from primary occupations that produce raw materials into secondary occupations that process materials and thence into tertiary occupations that manipulate symbols.

2   Recent trends in labor force participation include later entry into the labor force and earlier retirement for both sexes, a decrease in male employment and an increase in the employment of women (especially married women), and the virtual disappearance of child labor.

3   Occupational populations (those engaged in a particular occupation at a particular time) show dramatic differences in composition by age, sex, race, intelligence, and other characteristics. Some of these differences are attributable to the nature of the work, but more of them can be traced to the social history of individual occupations.

4   The study of occupational inheritance does not indicate increasing rigidity in the American occupational structure. Overall, the influence of an individual's social origins on his career chances has remained about the same in recent decades, except that recruitment to the professions and other elite occupations has become less restrictive.

5   Occupational performance is always socially controlled, but the agents of control, the modes of supervision, the devices for wage-setting, and the norms of performance vary from one type of occupation to another. They are markedly different for independent professionals, corporation executives, skilled craftsmen, production line workers, and small retail proprietors, for example.

6   The career patterns of women are very different from those of men; these patterns are marked in the typical case by discontinuity, lesser opportunity for vertical mobility, greater opportunity for horizontal mobility, somewhat lesser earnings, and concentration in unorganized occupations.

Questions for Discussion / CHAPTER EIGHT

1   "Although only about a third of employed men work at white-collar occupations, nearly two-thirds of women do so." How would you account for this striking difference?

2 Discuss whether it would make sense to classify *student* and *housewife* as occupations, when the activity is full-time.

3 On the basis of what you know about current trends, what census occupational groups are likely to increase fastest in the decade 1970–1980?

4 In what ways was your father's occupational choice influenced by your grandfather's occupation? In what ways is your occupational choice likely to be influenced by your father's occupation? Which case shows more influence?

5 Photographers have sought recognition as members of a profession without much success so far. Can you identify the features of the occupation that hinder its professionalization?

6 Obtain a complete work history from some friend or relative past 60; what do you learn from analyzing the career pattern in this case?

7 Policemen often claim (through their unions) to be entitled to higher pay than firemen in the same cities. Firemen usually insist that they are entitled to equal pay. What are the arguments on each side of this question? Which arguments do you find more persuasive?

8 One of the interesting discoveries of recent years is that the automation of industry has not led to widespread unemployment. What is the explanation?

9 Review your understanding of the following terms:

division of labor	profession
occupation	occupational inheritance
labor force	career pattern
participation rate	semiskilled work

Recommended Reading / **CHAPTER EIGHT**

Taylor, Lee. *Occupational Sociology.* New York: Oxford University Press, 1968; and Hall, Richard H. *Occupations and the Social Structure.* Englewood Cliffs, N.J.: Prentice-Hall, 1969. Two excellent textbooks of occupational sociology.

Friedmann, Georges. *The Anatomy of Work: Labor, Leisure, and te Implications of Automation,* trans. Wyatt Rawson. New York: Free Press, 1962; and Faunce, William A. *Problems of an Industrial Society.* New York: McGraw-Hill, 1968. Both volumes analyze the implications of automation and other major occupational trends.

Ferman, Louis A., Joyce L. Kornbluh and A. Miller, eds. *Negroes and Jobs: A Book of Readings.* Ann Arbor, Mich.: University of Michigan Press, 1968. Discusses the occupational problems of black workers from several points of view.

Firth, Raymond. *The Malay Fishermen: Their Peasant Economy,* 2d rev. ed. Hamden, Conn.: Archon Books, 1966. A fascinating study of work in a non-industrial society.

Notes / CHAPTER EIGHT

1. See Arthur Salz, "Occupation," *Encyclopedia of the Social Sciences,* ed. Edwin R. A. Seligman (New York: Macmillan, 1933), vol. 11, pp. 424–435; and William H. Form, "Occupations and Careers," *International Encyclopedia of the Social Sciences,* ed. David L. Sills (New York: Macmillan and Free Press, 1968), vol. 11, pp. 245–255, for the background of this definition.
2. See, for example, Hilda Kuper, *The Swazi: A South African Kingdom* (New York: Holt, Rinehart & Winston, 1963), pp. 45–48.
3. Oscar Lewis, *Tepoztlán: Village in Mexico* (New York: Holt, Rinehart & Winston, 1960).
4. Adam Smith, *An Inquiry into the Nature and Causes of the Wealth of Nations,* 6th ed., 2 vols. (London: Methuen, 1950), bk. 1, chap. 1. Originally published in 1776.
5. Émile Durkheim, *The Division of Labor in Society,* trans. George Simpson (New York: Free Press, 1960). Originally published 1893. See the summary of this work in Chapter Four above.
6. Everett Cherrington Hughes, "The Study of Occupations," in *Sociology Today: Problems and Prospects,* ed. Robert K. Merton, Leonard Broom, and Leonard S. Cottrell (New York: Basic Books, 1959), pp. 442–458. The quotation is from pp. 445–446.
7. U.S. Employment Service, *Dictionary of Occupational Titles,* 3d ed. (Washington, D.C.: Government Printing Office, 1965).
8. Theodore Caplow, *The Sociology of Work* (Minneapolis: University of Minnesota Press, 1954), and (New York: McGraw-Hill, 1964), p. 27.
9. Alba M. Edwards, *Comparative Occupational Statistics for the United States, 1870–1940* (Washington, D.C.: Government Printing Office, 1943), table 330.
10. U.S. Bureau of the Census, Department of Commerce, *Statistical Abstract of the United States* (Washington, D.C.: Government Printing Office, 1967).
11. Based on Gladys L. Palmer and Ann Ratner, *Industrial and Occupational Trends in National Employment 1910–1940, 1910–1948* (Philadelphia: University of Pennsylvania, Industrial Research Department, Wharton School of Finance and Commerce, research report no. 11, 1949).

12. *Statistical Abstract of the United States 1968,* table 325.
13. R. M. Yerkes, ed., "Psychological Examining in the U.S. Army," *Memoirs of the National Academy of Science* 15 (1921).
14. Stuart M. Stoke and Harvey C. Lehman, "Occupational Intelligence in the Army: A Postscript," *American Journal of Sociology* 36, no. 2 (September 1930): 221–232.
15. George S. Counts, "The Social Status of Occupations: A Problem in Vocational Guidance," *School Review* 33 (January 1925).
16. See, for example, Mapheus Smith, "An Empirical Scale of Prestige Status of Occupations," *American Sociological Review* 8, no. 2 (April 1943): 185–192; M. E. Day and D. G. Peterson, "Changes in Social Status of Occupations," *Occupations* 25 (January 1947); Alex Inkeles and Peter H. Rossi, "National Comparisons of Occupational Prestige," *American Journal of Sociology* 61, no. 4 (January 1956): 329–339; Lionel S. Lewis and Joseph Lopreato, "Functional Importance and Prestige of Occupations," *Pacific Sociological Review* 6, no. 2 (Fall 1963): 55–59.
17. For a summary of occupational prestige studies in 24 countries, see Robert W. Hodge, Donald J. Treiman, and Peter H. Rossi, "A Comparative Study of Occupational Prestige," in *Class, Status and Power: Social Stratification in Comparative Perspective,* ed. Reinhard Bendix and Seymour Martin Lipset, 2d ed. (New York: Free Press, 1966), pp. 309–334.
18. Albert J. Reiss, Jr., with Otis Dudley Duncan, Paul K. Hatt, and Cecil C. North, *Occupations and Social Status* (New York: Free Press, 1961).
19. Robert W. Hodge, Paul M. Siegel, and Peter H. Rossi, "Occupational Prestige in the United States, 1925–1963," *American Journal of Sociology* 70, no. 3 (November 1964): 286–302.
20. Otis Dudley Duncan, "A Socioeconomic Index for All Occupations," in Reiss et al., *Occupations and Social Status,* pp. 109–138.
21. Pitirim A. Sorokin, *Social Mobility* (New York: Harper & Row, 1927).
22. One of the rare studies that provides information on the occupational origins of factory workers in the early stages of industrialization shows a high proportion of hereditary workers. Arcadius Kahan, "The 'Hereditary Workers' Hypothesis and the Development of a Factory Labor Force in Eighteenth- and Nineteenth-Century Russia," in *Education and Economic Development,* eds. C. Arnold Anderson and Mary Jean Bowman (Chicago: Aldine, 1965), pp. 291–312.
23. Information on occupational differentials in China may be found in Hans Koningsberger, "China Notes—1," *The New Yorker,* April 23, 1966, pp. 57–125; for the Soviet Union, in Robert W. Campbell, *Soviet Economic Power: Its Organization, Growth and Challenge,* 2d ed. (Boston: Houghton Mifflin, 1966).
24. Pierre Bourdieu and Jean-Claude Passeron, *Les Héritiers* (Paris: Editions de Minuit, 1964).

25. Peter M. Blau and Otis Dudley Duncan, *The American Occupational Structure* (New York: John Wiley, 1967). Among other important studies of intergenerational mobility in the United States, see Percy E. Davidson and H. Dewey Anderson, *Occupational Mobility in an American Community* (Stanford, Calif.: Stanford University Press, 1937); Frank William Taussig and C. S. Joslyn, *American Business Leaders: A Study in Social Origins and Social Stratification* (New York: Macmillan, 1932); Natalie Rogoff, *Recent Trends in Occupational Mobility* (New York: Free Press, 1953); Elton F. Jackson and Harry F. Crockett, Jr., "Occupational Mobility in the United States: A Point Estimate and Trend Comparison," *American Sociological Review* 29, no. 1 (February 1964): 1–15; and W. Lloyd Warner and James C. Abegglen, *Occupational Mobility in American Business and Industry, 1928–1952* (Minneapolis: University of Minnesota Press, 1955).

26. Hodge, Treiman, and Rossi, "A Comparative Study of Occupational Prestige."

27. Leonard Broom and F. Lancaster Jones, "Father-to-Son Mobility: Australia in Comparative Perspective," *American Journal of Sociology* 74, no. 4 (January 1969): 333–342.

28. Based on S. M. Miller, "Comparative Social Mobility," *Current Sociology* 9 (1960).

29. Blau and Duncan, *American Occupational Structure.* For additional data, see Seymour Martin Lipset and Reinhard Bendix, *Social Mobility in Industrial Society* (Berkeley, Calif.: University of California Press, 1960).

30. Blau and Duncan, *American Occupational Structure,* p. 424; W. Lloyd Warner and James C. Abegglen, *Big Business Leaders in America* (New York: Harper & Row, 1955), p. 30.

31. Blau and Duncan, *American Occupational Structure,* pp. 213–219.

32. For a review of the available evidence on the occupational situation of Negroes, see Louis A. Ferman, Joyce L. Kornbluh, and J. A. Miller, eds., *Negroes and Jobs: A Book of Readings* (Ann Arbor, Mich.: University of Michigan Press, 1968).

33. Estimates based on several studies. For a summary of the statistical evidence—and slightly different conclusions—see Lee Taylor, *Occupational Sociology* (New York: Oxford University Press, 1968), pp. 75–80.

34. Delbert C. Miller and William H. Form, *Industrial Sociology: An Introduction to the Sociology of Work Relations* (New York: Harper & Row, 1951).

35. Joseph Gusfield, "Occupational Roles and Forms of Enterprise," *American Journal of Sociology* 66, no. 6 (May 1961): 571–580.

36. Harold L. Wilensky, "Work, Careers, and Social Integration," *International Social Sciences Journal* 12, no. 4 (1960): 543–560.

37. W. Fred Cottrell, *The Railroader* (Stanford, Calif.: Stanford University Press, 1940).

38. Howard S. Becker, *Outsiders: Studies in the Sociology of Deviance* (New York: Free Press, 1963).

39. *Statistical Abstract of the United States 1968,* table 343.

40. The best-known study of the occupational aspirations of semi-skilled workers is Ely Chinoy, *Automobile Workers and the American Dream* (Garden City, N.Y.: Doubleday, 1955).

41. Among the many studies of recruitment and promotion in the professions, the following are especially informative: Oswald Hall, "The Stages of a Medical Career," *American Journal of Sociology* 53, no. 5 (March 1948): 327–336; Oswald Hall, "Types of Medical Careers," *American Journal of Sociology* 55, no. 3 (November 1949): 243–253; Robert K. Merton, George G. Reader, and Patricia Kendall, eds., *The Student Physician: Introductory Studies in the Sociology of Medical Education* (Cambridge, Mass.: Harvard University Press, published for the Commonwealth Fund, 1957); Howard S. Becker et al., *Boys in White: Student Culture in Medical School* (Chicago: University of Chicago Press, 1961); Jerome E. Carlin, *Current Research in the Sociology of the Legal Profession* (New York: Columbia University Press, 1962); Erwin O. Smigel, *The Wall Street Lawyer: Professional Organization Man?* (New York: Free Press, 1964); Joel F. Handler, *The Lawyer and His Community: The Practicing Bar in a Middle-Sized City* (Madison, Wisc.: University of Wisconsin Press, 1967); Paul D. Montagna, "Professionalization and Bureaucratization in Large Professional Organizations," *American Journal of Sociology* 74, no. 2 (September 1968): 138–145; Robert Perrucci and Joel E. Gerstl, *Profession Without Community: Engineers in American Society* (New York: Random House, 1969).

42. Among studies of recruitment and promotion of corporation executives, see: Warner and Abegglen, *Big Business Leaders in America;* William H. Whyte, Jr., *The Organization Man* (New York: Simon and Schuster, 1956); Melville Dalton, *Men Who Manage: Fusions of Feeling and Theory in Administration* (New York: John Wiley, 1959); W. Lloyd Warner, "The Corporation Man," in *The Corporation in Modern Society,* ed. Edward S. Mason (Cambridge, Mass.: Harvard University Press, 1960), pp. 106–121; Vance Packard, *The Pyramid Climbers* (New York: McGraw-Hill, 1962).

43. William E. Henry, "Executive Personality," in *The Emergent American Society,* ed. W. Lloyd Warner, vol. 1, *Large-Scale Organizations* (New Haven: Yale University Press, 1967), pp. 266–275.

44. There have been very few studies of the recruitment and promotion of craftsmen, but see: Abraham Zaleznik, *Worker Satisfaction and Development: A Case Study of Work and Social Behavior in a Factory Group* (Boston: Harvard University Division of Research, Graduate School of Business Administration, 1956); U.S. Bureau of Apprenticeship, *Apprenticeship, Past and Present: A Story of Apprenticeship Training in the Skilled Trades Since Colonial Days,* rev. ed. (Washington, D.C.: Government Printing Office, 1962); and Robert Blauner, *Alienation and Freedom: The Factory Worker and His Industry* (Chicago: University of Chicago Press, 1964).

45. Among the studies of recruitment and promotion of production line workers, see: Chinoy, *Automobile Workers and the American Dream;* Robert H. Guest, "Work Career and Aspirations of Automobile Workers," in *Labor and Trade Unionism: An Interdisciplinary Reader,* ed. Walter Galenson and Seymour Martin Lipset (New York: John Wiley, 1960), pp. 319–328; Blauner, *Alienation and Freedom.* For descriptions of two industrial organizations where promotion was heavily influenced by ascribed status characteristics, see: Orvis Collins, "Ethnic Behavior in Industry: Sponsorship and Rejection in a New England Factory," *American Journal of Sociology* 51, no. 4 (January 1946): 293–298; and Melville Dalton, "Informal Factors in Career Achievement," *American Journal of Sociology* 56, no. 5 (March 1951): 407–415. In one of these organizations, candidates for managerial promotions were expected to be Masons, Protestant, of Anglo-Saxon or German descent, Republicans, and members of a local yacht club. In the second, executives were nearly all of Yankee stock and foremen nearly all Irish. Both studies are rather old; current discrimination arrangements in industry are likely to be less clear-cut.
46. Chinoy, *Automobile Workers and the American Dream,* pp. 110–111.
47. For a full description of the problems of excessive division of labor on the production line, and some of the attempted solutions, see Georges Friedmann, *The Anatomy of Work: Labor, Leisure, and the Implications of Automation,* trans. Wyatt Rawson (New York: Free Press, 1962).
48. Charles R. Walker, Robert H. Guest, and Arthur N. Turner, *The Foreman on the Assemblyline* (Cambridge, Mass.: Harvard University Press, 1956).
49. "Seen from below, the management is not a Who but a series of Theys. ... " C. Wright Mills, *White Collar: The American Middle Classes* (New York: Oxford University Press, 1956), p. 80.
50. As explained in Martin Meissner, *Technology and the Worker: Technical Demands and Social Processes in Industry* (San Francisco: Chandler, 1969).
51. One of the rare sociological studies of small retail enterprises is Monique Coornaert, "Le Commerce de Détail: Enquête Sociologique dans une Commune de la Banlieue Parisienne," *L'Année Sociologique* 17 (1966): 3–88.
52. U.S. Department of Commerce, Office of Business Economics, *Survey of Current Business* 46, no. 8 (August 1966).
53. See the tables in Chap. 1 of Jean Fourastié, *The Causes of Wealth,* trans. Theodore Caplow (New York: Free Press, 1960).
54. U.S. Bureau of the Census, *Historical Statistics of the United States: Colonial Times to 1957* (Washington, D.C.: Government Printing Office, 1957), Series G169–190; and *Statistical Abstract of the United States 1967,* table 338.
55. Fourastié, *The Causes of Wealth,* pp. 30–32.
56. *Historical Statistics of the United States,* Series G131–146, G99–

117. *Statistical Abstract of the United States 1967,* table 471. For a more extended discussion, see Simon S. Kuznets, *Six Lectures on Economic Growth* (New York: Free Press, 1959).

57. Extensive evidence on this point may be found in Francis Ivan Nye and Lois Wladis Hoffman, *The Employed Mother in America* (Chicago: Rand McNally, 1963).

58. Ruth H. Pape, "Touristry: A Type of Occupational Mobility," *Social Problems* 11, No. 4 (Spring 1964).

59. Howard S. Becker, "The Career of the Chicago Public School-teacher," *American Journal of Sociology* 57, no. 5 (March 1952): 470–477.

Organizations

IX

Introduction

An organization is a social system that has an unequivocal collective identity, an exact roster of members, an explicit program of activity and procedures for replacing members.

There are many different species of organization. They range in size from a membership of three persons, which is conventionally considered to be the minimum, to the more than 600 million members of the Roman Catholic church, the largest existing organization. (The United Nations is an organization of national states; it has no individual members.)

No one has ever counted all the organizations in the world or even in a single country; they are extremely numerous and extremely diverse. it is not unusual for a sociologist to devote his entire career to the study of a single type of organization and still to be troubled by the vastness of his subject. But all organizations, regardless of their size, purpose, or location, have important features in common.

Common Types of Organization

Before we turn to the basic principles of organizational analysis, it may be instructive to look at a list of some types of organization commonly encountered in the United States. Most of them would also be found in any other large country and in any civilized society of the past. The list is not intended to be exhaustive,[1] but it includes most of the common types.

Athletic teams	Denominations
Banks	Ethnic associations
Boards	Expeditions
Bureaus	Extended families
Churches	Factories
Civic associations	Federations
Clubs	Fraternities and sororities
Colleges	Gangs
Committees	Governments
Cooperatives	Honorary societies
Corporations	Hospitals
Courts	Hotels

Houses of prostitution	Political parties
Indian tribes	Pressure groups
Institutes	Prisons and jails
Juries	Professional associations
Labor unions	Public agencies
Learned societies	Recreational associations
Legislatures	Research laboratories
Lodges and brotherhoods	Restaurants
Markets	Retail stores
Merchant and naval ships	Schools
Military commands	Sects
Missions and settlement houses	Social agencies
Monasteries and convents	States
Museums and libraries	Summer camps
Nuclear families	Taverns and night clubs
Orphanages	Theatrical companies
Orchestras and bands	Trade associations
Partnerships	Universities
Plantations	Veterans' associations
Police and fire departments	Workshops

The description of organizational types is complicated by the fact that large organizations are always made up of component organizations, some of a different type from the parent organization. A university, for example, is composed of colleges, which in turn are composed of departments, but it may include many other types of organizations as well: athletic teams, clubs, fraternities, examining boards, administrative bureaus, libraries, museums, research laboratories, restaurants, workshops, political associations, a summer camp, a bookstore, a theatrical company, a military unit, an orchestra, or a fire department. Not to mention innumerable committees.

Each of these subdivisions is an organization in its own right, and it is not particularly useful to try to distinguish between autonomous and nonautonomous organizations. In modern societies, very few important organizations are really autonomous. Almost all those that appear to be so, like private corporations, turn out on closer analysis to be licensed or chartered by the state. Moreover, many organizations are closely linked with other organizations to which they do not stand in the simple relationship of parent organization and component organization.

Nonorganizations

Not all social systems are organized. One important use of the four identifying features mentioned in the definition above is to enable us to recognize "nonorganizations." For example, social classes in an open society do not have a clear-cut collective identity, nor do they have an exact roster of membership, definite membership procedures, or a program.

Races and ethnic groups are not organizations, although some of them (Negroes, "Wasps," or Polish-Americans, for example) have names and collective identities and something approaching a roster of membership. Sooner or later, all ethnic groups generate benevolent organizations and pressure groups to advance their interests, and these may be closely identified with the population they represent, but the image of an ethnic group as an organization is one of the errors of vision that accompanies and encourages bigotry. Even under conditions of great political excitement, races and ethnic groups are seldom sufficiently cohesive to be organized.

Cliques, circles of friends, residential neighborhoods, and children's play groups are usually unorganized, having neither an exact roster nor an explicit program. It does not take much, however, to transform an office clique into an organized peer group, or a circle of friends into a social club.

Political factions (as distinct from political parties) are often unorganized. Within any large organization, there are factions like the "Old Guard," the "Young Turks," or the "rank and file," which have collective identities and some elements of a program but lack exact rosters or membership procedures. They range from substantial, important, semipermanent groups that can easily be organized if the need arises to aggregations so vague that it may be impossible to estimate their strength or even to demonstrate that they lead a collective existence. No one can count the number of "old-fashioned Americans," "politically aroused college students," or "Parsonian sociologists," because there are no definite criteria for separating the members of such groups from nonmembers.

The conventional understanding that an organization must have at least three members has already been mentioned. (The ancient Romans had a phrase for it: *tres faciunt collegium*—"It takes three to make an organization"). A *dyad, or* two-person group, has no membership procedures. If it loses one of its two members, it cannot replace him and retain the same identity. A married couple is not considered an organization. If one spouse dies and the other marries again, the new couple does not seem to be a continuation of the old couple. However, the nuclear family *is* an organization. It can add new members by birth or adoption, and can survive the loss of one or more members.

The Community as an Organization

The community is a special type of organization based on residence within a bounded territory. Villages, towns, cities, provinces, and countries generally have an unequivocal collective identity, an exact roster of inhabitants, a calendar of daily and seasonal activities, and some sort of program for the defense of those interests that arise from their common residence.

Most sizable communities have governments, which are organizations in their own right and analytically distinct from the communities to which they correspond. The nation and the state, for example, are separate entities. The nation may survive, like Poland after its several partitions, when the state has been destroyed. The actions of the state may not represent the sentiments or the interests of the nation. States are readily combined or divided; nations are not. The two types of organization are closely related, but it is often important to keep them distinct.

Organizational Size

Organizations can be conveniently arranged in four categories of size as follows:

A small organization is small enough for every member to know every other and to interact with him directly. The upper limit is about 30 members, although a very durable small organization, like a primitive tribe, may be somewhat larger. The number of possible pair-relationships in a group of 30 persons is 435;[2] not all small organizations realize all their possible relationships.

A middle-sized organization is too large to permit the development of a relationship between every pair of members but small enough so that certain key members can interact directly with all the others. The upper limit is about a thousand members.

A large organization is too large for any member to interact directly with all of the others, but small enough for all or most of the members to be assembled at one time in one place. The upper limit of large organizations is variable, but lies in the neighborhood of 50,000 members.

The giant organization has too many members too widely dispersed for all of them ever to be assembled at one time and place. Its leaders are known to the rank and file through communication media, and no leader is personally acquainted with more than a small fraction of the membership.

An organization's chances of survival seem to increase directly with its size. For example, giant corporations are more likely to weather depressions than are large-sized corporations; small corporations are exceedingly fragile. Contrary to a widespread belief, large and giant organizations devote a smaller share of their resources to administration and other forms of self-maintenance than do small and medium-sized organizations. A well-known study of four industrial organizations by Mason Haire showed that the ratio of supervisors to employees declined sharply with increases in size, and there is confirmatory evidence from other sources.[3] Size and efficiency appear to be correlated also in types of organization whose efficiency is harder to measure than the business corporation's—schools, research institutes, and political parties, for example.

On the other hand, larger organizations are generally less effective in providing personal satisfaction to their members. *Alienation—the loss of interest in the purposes toward which one's own activity is directed—* is a perennial problem of large and giant organizations.

Indeed, it is doubtful whether these organizations could survive at all if the emotional needs of their members were not satisfied by small component organizations, many of them informal or illegitimate, that spring up wherever men are thrown into frequent face-to-face contact by the requirements of a large organization's program.

The Individual vs. the Organization

To understand why large and giant organizations, particularly those of the type called bureaucracies, are more efficient than small and medium-sized organizations in accomplishing their stated goals but less effective in keeping their members happy, we need to see what an organization is, what it does, and what its inherent limitations are.

Every organization may be considered as a mechanism for the achievement of collective goals that could not be achieved as easily, or could not be achieved at all, without it. But an organization consumes resources simply by continuing to exist. The cost of its operation must be balanced by some output to justify the continued expenditure of time, effort, money, and other scarce resources it requires. The effectiveness of an organization is almost never a matter of indifference to its members, and the institutional pattern that serves as a blueprint for a particular type of organization always includes devices for evaluating organizational performance.

There are all sorts of requirements that an organization must satisfy to stay in existence; one authority lists 17 of them.[4] The easiest way to visualize the problem of maintaining an organization—whether it be a household or a state, a factory or a football team, a stock exchange or a folk-singing group—is to separate its relationships with the external environment from the relationships of its members among themselves. The external problem is to maintain a steady flow of inputs *from* the environment and of outputs *to* the environment. The internal problem is to maintain the organizational structure.

Although an organization is something like a mechanism, its parts are human, not inert. They have private purposes that are never identical with the collective purposes of the organization, and they must usually be persuaded to carry out their organizational tasks. An organization that relies heavily on coercion is necessarily ineffective. In a prison run on old-fashioned lines, the motivation of prisoners is weak, and a large proportion of the available resources must be used to keep inmates under control; the organization does not satisfy the needs of either the prisoners or the guards, and therefore does not command their loyalty. The participation of one group must be bought with money and privileges; the participation of the other group is obtained by force or the threat of force. In neither case are the results very satisfactory. Pure coercion is a very expensive way of assuring cooperation.

Pure voluntarism is not much better. An organization that depends upon the voluntary efforts of its members, like a political party, may be highly effective in short bursts of activity, but it lacks staying power;

any member may reduce his participation if his enthusiasm fades, or if another interest calls him elsewhere. There is no way of assuring the orderly continuity of operations unless the division of labor is so simplified that individuals who withdraw are easily replaced. But since effectiveness in collective tasks normally requires an intricate division of labor, organizations that depend exclusively on voluntary participation are forced to operate at a low level of output. In many cases, this low-level output produces such unsatisfactory results that the morale of participants also suffers.

Virtually all durable organizations fall well between the two extremes of purely coercive and purely voluntary participation. Members are persuaded to participate in the common tasks by a variety of rewards and deprivations that have been incorporated into the organization's status order. Elements of voluntarism and coercion are present, but remain in the background, so to speak. The individual voluntarily assumes an organizational position that carries a whole set of duties, rights, and relationships with it. The organization reserves some coercive power to use against flagrantly defiant individuals, but the power of the organization is limited by contradictions between its goals and the purposes of its members.

It was Georg Simmel who first called attention to the fundamental incompatibility between "two logically contradictory characterizations of man—the characterization which is based on his function as a member ... ; and the opposing characterization which is based on his function as an autonomous being."[5] The demands of any organization on a member are generally excessive, because the organization sees the man only in terms of its own program and his specialized role within it. It demands of him a wholehearted, single-minded devotion to his role as a foreman, a soldier, a chairman, a husband, a juror, or a policeman, without taking full account of his private purposes in that role or of other purposes he derives from other roles. The soldier, for example, may be more interested in staying alive than in contributing to a successful invasion. The actor may be more involved in his backstage pursuit of the actress playing opposite him than in their scenes on the stage. The foreman may care more about his promotion than about the morale of the shop. And so forth.

Putting these oppositions so baldly falsifies the matter. There is nearly always an interplay of "official" and "private" goals in any organizational performance. The balance between them is delicate and fluctuating. Complete devotion to an organizational role is suspect and disturbing. It raises questions about the subject's mental health. Complete neglect of organizational obligations is equally disturbing. It signals the collapse of a portion of the social structure. One can understand the working balance between collective and individual purposes in a particular type of organization only by examining its hierarchical arrangements in detail. The congruence between organizational and private purposes is usually greatest at the top and least at the bottom of a hierarchy, but there are numerous exceptions.

PRODUCTIVITY AND MORALE

Productivity and morale are the terms used in analyzing the effectiveness of work groups in industry. The relationship between productivity and morale has been studied literally thousands of times in industrial settings.[6] Taken together, these studies seem to show that productivity and morale are not highly correlated. A contented worker is not necessarily efficient, and an inefficient worker is not necessarily discontented. Work groups with very low morale are not likely to be highly productive and the esprit de corps evoked by outstanding productivity is often favorable to morale, but between these extremes, within the normal range of work group performance, the correlations that can be established between productivity and morale are low and change from one situation to another. An interesting study by Seashore[7] of a company engaged in heavy industry showed that work groups with high morale were generally more effective in achieving their goals than work groups with low morale. However, some work groups had the goal of maximizing and others of minimizing output, so that morale was positively correlated with productivity in some cases and negatively correlated in other cases.

With respect to nonindustrial organizations, like armies, bureaucracies, or schools, the evidence is less coherent.[8] What there is again suggests that the relationship between morale and productivity is not constant, but that the two variables are very loosely related, so that organizations can be found with almost every possible combination of productivity and morale. The organization that achieves its collective goals does not necessarily make its members happy, and the organization whose members are happy is not necessarily well managed.

However, in general, the larger the organization and the more intricate its division of labor, the better its chances of achieving a high level of productivity; the smaller and simpler an organization, the likelier it is to develop a high level of morale. Close coordination of an organization's components improves productivity; making them as autonomous as possible raises morale.

Studies of American and of German combat units toward the end of World War II concluded that their morale was almost entirely dependent on the solidarity of small groups and related hardly at all to the political and ideological goals of the respective armies, or the nations they represented.[9] A study of German units by Shils and Janowitz concluded that "when the individual's immediate group, and its supporting formations, met his basic organic needs, offered him affection and esteem from both officers and comrades, supplied him with a sense of power and adequately regulated his relations with authority, the element of self-concern in battle, which would lead to disruption of the effective functioning of his primary group, was minimized."[10]

However, it would be premature to conclude, as some hasty commentators have done, that men never fight for good causes but only *for the good opinion of their buddies*. The World War II studies may tell us more about that particular war than about combat in general.

An earlier study of the Spanish Civil War by Dollard and Horton[11] indicated that soldiers in that war were strongly identified with a cause, which furnished their incentive to fight; and there is massive evidence to suggest that the efficient military units of the past were often pervaded from top to bottom by political and religious convictions. The extreme dependence of World War II soldiers on peer group solidarity in the later phases of the war may be taken as a sign of organizational breakdown, rather than as a general explanation of military behavior; indeed, in the case of the Wehrmacht, the breakdown was evident in many other ways. This is not to suggest that small-group solidarity would not be an important element of combat morale in any army, but only that the soldier's exclusive dependence on his peer group is equivalent to alienation from the larger military organization to which he belongs.

There is always more than one level of productivity and morale. The fact that large organizations are made up of component organizations, which in turn include still smaller organizations, introduces an unavoidable complication into organizational analysis. If we redefine productivity as an individual's contribution to the achievement of organizational goals and morale as a measure of his willingness to continue participating in the organizational program, it is immediately apparent that an individual may have different levels of morale with regard to the whole organization and to one or more of its components. He may, for example, be eager to leave the army at the first opportunity but also eager to remain with the same platoon for the duration of his military service. In the same way, he may have different levels of productivity with regard to different levels of the organization. The platoon, for example, has goals of its own, which are never completely consistent with those of the army. The platoon's predominant goal may be to minimize casualties, whereas the army's predominant goal is to win battles. These two goals being nearly contradictory, an officer who is highly productive from the army's standpoint may be grossly inefficient from the platoon's standpoint, and vice versa. For the organization as a whole, the problem of achieving both high productivity *and* high morale resolves itself into the reduction of value-conflicts between itself and its component organizations and individuals.

Tables of Organization

A table of organization is a chart showing the positions in an organization and the prescribed interactions among them. It usually consists of little boxes connected by vertical and horizontal lines. Each little box represents a position or a category of positions. Vertical lines represent the interaction of superiors and subordinates; horizontal lines show the interaction of equals. Figures 9–1 to 9–5 are examples of such charts: the organizations they depict are of very different types, but each table is constructed in the same way.

As a graphic device, the table of organization is of fairly recent

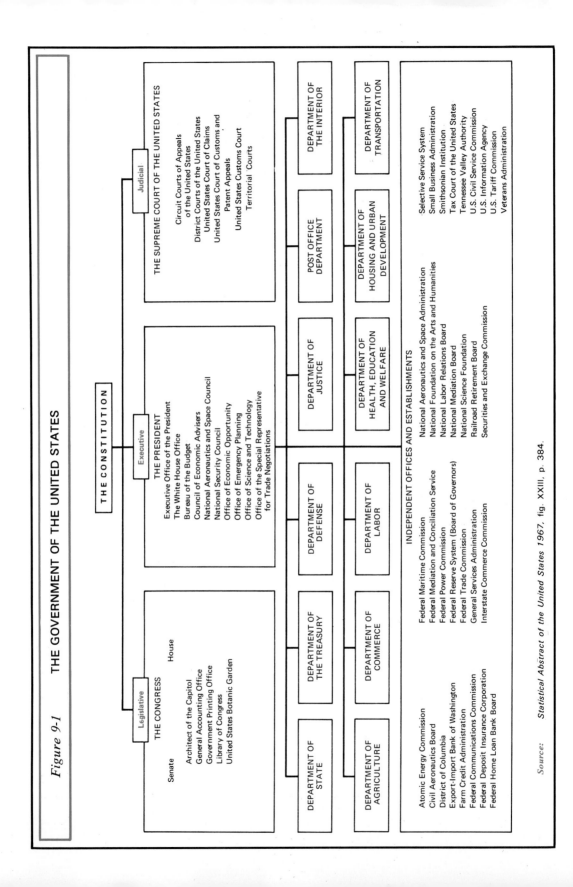

Figure 9-1   THE GOVERNMENT OF THE UNITED STATES

THE CONSTITUTION

Legislative

THE CONGRESS

Senate   House

Architect of the Capitol
General Accounting Office
Government Printing Office
Library of Congress
United States Botanic Garden

DEPARTMENT OF
STATE

DEPARTMENT OF
THE TREASURY

DEPARTMENT OF
AGRICULTURE

DEPARTMENT OF
COMMERCE

Executive

THE PRESIDENT

Executive Office of the President
The White House Office
Bureau of the Budget
Council of Economic Advisers
National Aeronautics and Space Council
National Security Council
Office of Economic Opportunity
Office of Emergency Planning
Office of Science and Technology
Office of the Special Representative
    for Trade Negotiations

DEPARTMENT OF
DEFENSE

DEPARTMENT OF
LABOR

DEPARTMENT OF
JUSTICE

DEPARTMENT OF
HEALTH, EDUCATION
AND WELFARE

Judicial

THE SUPREME COURT OF THE UNITED STATES

Circuit Courts of Appeals
of the United States
District Courts of the United States
United States Court of Claims
United States Court of Customs and
Patent Appeals
United States Customs Court
Territorial Courts

POST OFFICE
DEPARTMENT

DEPARTMENT OF
HOUSING AND URBAN
DEVELOPMENT

DEPARTMENT OF
THE INTERIOR

DEPARTMENT OF
TRANSPORTATION

INDEPENDENT OFFICES AND ESTABLISHMENTS

Atomic Energy Commission
Civil Aeronautics Board
District of Columbia
Export-Import Bank of Washington
Farm Credit Administration
Federal Communications Commission
Federal Deposit Insurance Corporation
Federal Home Loan Bank Board

Federal Maritime Commission
Federal Mediation and Conciliation Service
Federal Power Commission
Federal Reserve System (Board of Governors)
Federal Trade Commission
General Services Administration
Interstate Commerce Commission

National Aeronautics and Space Administration
National Foundation on the Arts and Humanities
National Labor Relations Board
National Mediation Board
National Science Foundation
Railroad Retirement Board
Securities and Exchange Commission

Selective Service System
Small Business Administration
Smithsonian Institution
Tax Court of the United States
Tennessee Valley Authority
U.S. Civil Service Commission
U.S. Information Agency
U.S. Tariff Commission
Veterans Administration

Source: *Statistical Abstract of the United States 1967,* fig. XXIII, p. 384.

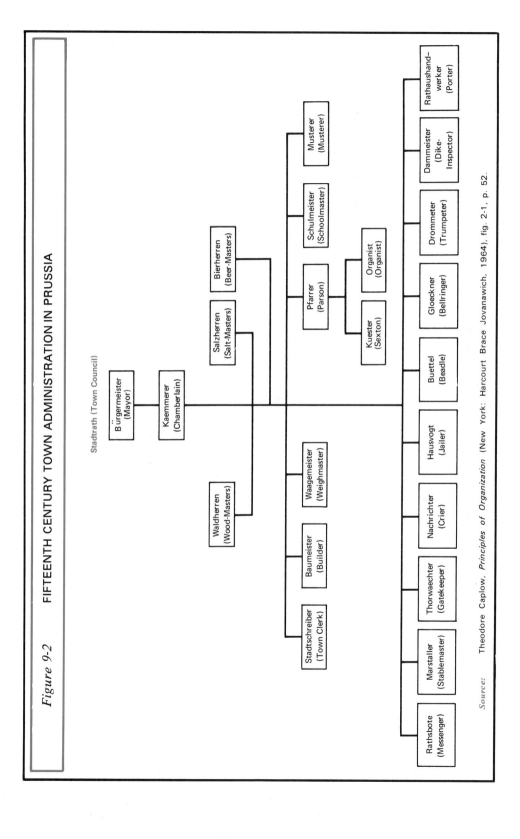

Figure 9-2   FIFTEENTH CENTURY TOWN ADMINISTRATION IN PRUSSIA

Source: Theodore Caplow, *Principles of Organization* (New York: Harcourt Brace Jovanovich, 1964), fig. 2-1, p. 52.

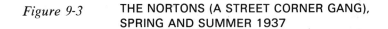

Figure 9-3   THE NORTONS (A STREET CORNER GANG), SPRING AND SUMMER 1937

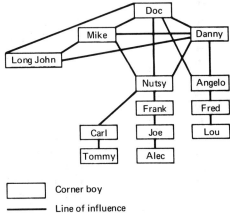

☐ Corner boy

—— Line of influence

Positions of boxes indicate relative status

Source: William Foote Whyte, *Street Corner Society: The Social Structure of an Italian Slum* (Chicago: University of Chicago Press, 1943), p. 13.

Figure 9-4   THREE DIFFERENT SHOP ORGANIZATION PATTERNS

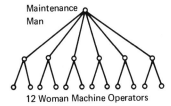

Maintenance Man

12 Woman Machine Operators

Maintenance Man

3 Woman Machine Operators

3 Woman Product Receivers

Maintenance Man

3 Woman Machine Operators

6 Woman Product Receivers

3 Male Laborers for Loading

Source: Michel Crozier, *The Bureaucratic Phenomenon* (Chicago: University of Chicago 1964), fig. 3, p. 95.

origin; it was first introduced about 1900. However, the idea behind it is much older,[12] and it is possible to reconstruct from documentary materials the tables of organization of ancient city-states, Roman corporations, Crusaders' armies, medieval guilds, and Renaissance bureaucracies.[13] So far as can be determined, no civilization that developed writing failed to develop the idea of an organization as a set of positions, differentiated by status and function, and describable without reference to the particular persons occupying the positions at a particular time; even preliterate societies often show familiarity with the concept of an organization as an abstraction composed of positions and relationships.

The expression of this concept by means of a two-dimensional chart was a simple but important invention; it has since become indispensable in the practical management of organizations and for sociological analysis. The preparation of a table of organization is usually the first step in an organizational study, and the preparation of a revised table of organization is often its last step. Indeed, it makes perfectly good sense to define an organization as any social system that can be described in a table of organization of conventional format. Although this format was developed to map large-scale organizations, it is equally useful to describe small organizations like committees or streetcorner gangs.

POSITIONS

Each of the little boxes in a table of organization represents a position. In the case of a large organization, most of the boxes near the top of the table (president, chairman, chief of staff, superintendent) represent positions with only a single incumbent, whereas most of the boxes near the bottom of the table represent positions with multiple incumbents (machine operators, infantrymen, delegates, classroom teachers). High-status members are less numerous and have more differentiated functions than low-status members.

A position is a category of membership in an organization whose incumbents are expected to act and interact according to a standard pattern that is part of the organizational program. In a two-dimensional table of organization, a position can be located vertically in the table by its status and horizontally by its function. The name of a position often specifies both elements, for example, substitute home economics teacher, chief gunner's mate. When an organization has branches in several places, a geographical coordinate may be added. Every position has a program and schedule of its own, which is part of the organization's program and schedule, and every position is a node in the network of communications that makes the organization a unit. Every position in an organization, except the highest, is permanently linked to at least one superior position with which interaction is prescribed; otherwise the position would be cut off from the organization and cease to function. When we study an organizational position we usually find that its incumbents are *required* to interact with

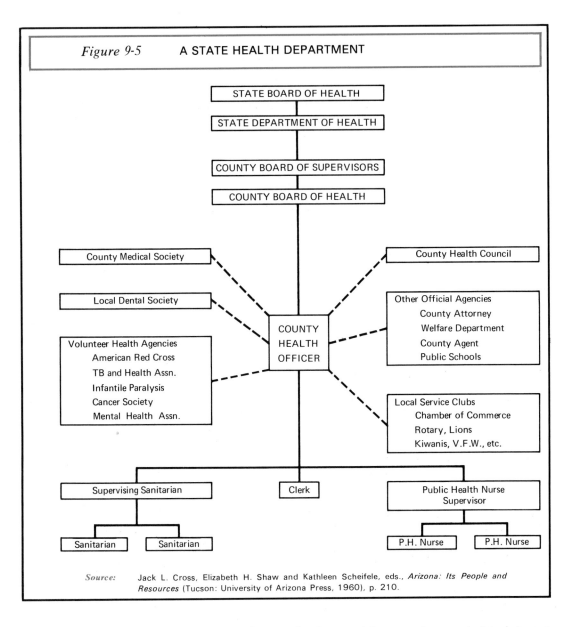

Figure 9-5   A STATE HEALTH DEPARTMENT

STATE BOARD OF HEALTH

STATE DEPARTMENT OF HEALTH

COUNTY BOARD OF SUPERVISORS

COUNTY BOARD OF HEALTH

County Medical Society

County Health Council

Local Dental Society

Other Official Agencies
County Attorney
Welfare Department
County Agent
Public Schools

COUNTY HEALTH OFFICER

Volunteer Health Agencies
American Red Cross
TB and Health Assn.
Infantile Paralysis
Cancer Society
Mental Health Assn.

Local Service Clubs
Chamber of Commerce
Rotary, Lions
Kiwanis, V.F.W., etc.

Supervising Sanitarian

Clerk

Public Health Nurse
Supervisor

Sanitarian

Sanitarian

P.H. Nurse

P.H. Nurse

Source: Jack L. Cross, Elizabeth H. Shaw and Kathleen Scheifele, eds., *Arizona: Its People and Resources* (Tucson: University of Arizona Press, 1960), p. 210.

the incumbents of several other positions, and *expected* to interact with the incumbents of several more. Many positions also include norms for interaction with outsiders. Soldiers, for example, are always told how to treat an enemy prisoner and how to behave if captured themselves.

In brief, every position includes one or more organizational roles. These are patterns of behavior prescribed for an incumbent of a given organizational position interacting with incumbents of other given po-

sitions with whom the organizational program requires him to interact. All the roles attached to one position are called a role-set, and this is what the sociologist generally studies when he wants to understand the behavior of a position-holder. The status of an organizational position is its place in the distribution of social power prescribed by the organization. Such a distribution is called a hierarchy, and every organization has one.

An inevitable outcome of all social organization, whenever and wherever it occurs, is the creation of social power. By ordering their social interactions and in fusing their relationships with common meanings, participants in social organizations collectively exercise power that none of them could exert individually. Whether these organizations be small groups, families, communities, formal associations, functional networks, or total societies, their actions and activities always involve the wielding of power in social life. Social power is generated through the process of social organization and is inseparable from it.[14]

ORGANIZATIONAL AND OTHER STATUSES

Because status is the most important concept in the sociology of organization, it is particularly important to distinguish organizational status from other kinds of status.

The term status sometimes refers to social class, the grouping of individuals and families in accordance with their income, possessions, descent, style of life, and affiliations. That sort of status was discussed in Chapter Seven. It resembles organizational status in some ways but is much less definite and has a much less certain effect on the interaction of individuals.

The term status is sometimes synonymous with prestige. *Prestige is a kind of public opinion, the average opinion of an audience about the relative preferability of competing persons, groups, or things.* Prestige is highly subjective, and a prestige rating is always affected by the characteristics of the audience whose opinions are sampled. Cellists have more prestige than trombonists among symphony musicians but less among jazz musicians. Most people assign higher prestige to the groups they belong to than outsiders do.

Both social class and prestige play a part in organizational activity, but they are quite distinct from organizational status, which is definite and objectively verifiable in most cases. There is room for argument about whether a family belongs to the upper, lower, or lower-middle class, or whether Italo-Americans are more respected than Polish-Americans, but there is no possible doubt about whether colonels are superior in status to lieutenant colonels.

Rank orders of social class and of prestige always show numerous gaps, ambiguities, and contradictions. The social class of a highly educated man in an unskilled occupation may be impossible to determine. A college may have high prestige in the eyes of its students and low prestige in the eyes of its faculty. The relative prestige of two unrelated occupations may be impossible to ascertain. There are bankers with low incomes and street beggars with high incomes. At the same cocktail party, *A* may snub *B, B* may snub *C,* and *C* may snub *A.*

An organizational hierarchy, by contrast, is an inclusive and orderly arrangement. The relative rank of any two colonels occupying identical positions is determined by seniority, as shown by the dates of their commissions. If their commissioning dates happen to be identical also, seniority is determined by age, and in the unlikely case that they have the same birthdate, there are additional rules to determine which of them outranks the other.

Status in a hierarchy is almost invariably transitive—that is, if *A* outranks *B* and *B* outranks *C,* then *A* must necessarily outrank *C.* Status indicators are generally consistent. We may assume with reasonable confidence that lieutenant colonels are paid less than colonels.

The Organizational Pyramid

The organizational pyramid is a diagram—somewhat resembling a population pyramid—which shows the number of status levels in a hierarchy and the number of members at each level.

A steep pyramid with many status levels and a sharply pointed top represents a highly centralized and probably autocratic organization. A shallow pyramid with fewer levels represents a more decentralized and probably more democratic form of organization. In large-scale organizations, which require a great deal of education and experience at the operating level, the organizational pyramid may be diamond-shaped. Most modern factories have more semiskilled machine operators than unskilled laborers, and some of them have more white-collar workers than machine operators.

A model developed by Warner[15] for normally constituted American corporations anticipates four levels of rank for a company with 100 production workers: 2 supervisors for each 25 workers, 1 coordinator for each 4 supervisors, and 1 superior coordinator at the top.

An expanded version of this model predicts that there will be 5 levels of rank in companies with 500 to 1,000 workers and 8 levels in companies with 50,000 to 100,000 workers, but empirical studies indicate that companies of this size tend to have 2 or 3 more levels than predicted. The largest company examined, with just under 500,-000 employees, had a 14-level hierarchy.[16]

Simple and Multiple Hierarchies

Some organizations have one hierarchy that encompasses all their positions. The Roman Catholic church, for example, can fit its entire vast membership into the hierarchy of layman-deacon-priest-bishop. All Catholics have certain duties and obligations in common, and may be said to share a common identity as members of the church, in addition to their differentiated positions in the hierarchy. Such a hierarchy is *simple,* regardless of its size.

A university, by contrast, exhibits *multiple* hierarchies: a student hierarchy of freshmen, sophomores, juniors, seniors, and professional and graduate students; an instructional hierarchy of assistants, instructors, and assistant, associate, full, and distinguished professors; an administrative hierarchy of administrative assistants, department chairmen, assistant and associate deans, deans, provosts, vice-presidents, and president or chancellor; a service hierarchy of guards, custodians, maintenance men, clerks, secretaries, foremen, and managers of various kinds; as well as an alumni hierarchy and such minor hierarchies as those that control intercollegiate athletics. No duties and obligations are shared by the members of all the organization's separate hierarchies, and there may not be *any* prescribed interactions between two positions in different hierarchies. In the relationship between sophomore and custodian for example, neither is legitimately superior or inferior. Even in the relationship between student and teacher, the separation of their two hierarchies is shown by the fact that the authority of the teacher vis-à-vis the student is not in principle affected by the teacher's rank in the faculty hierarchy or by the student's rank in any student hierarchy.

Status Schisms

Organizations sometimes split their hierarchies horizontally into strata that are isolated from each other by rules forbidding mobility and fraternization and imposing differences in life style. The distinction between officers and enlisted men in military organizations is a conspicuous example of a status schism. The phenomenon is found also in churches (between laity and clergy), factories (between management and labor), and even in such mild-mannered institutions as banks (between officers and employees).

A status schism transforms the table of organization by giving all members of the upper stratum some authority over all members of the lower stratum, whether or not their positions are normally connected. The terms and conditions of membership are manipulated to maximize social distance between the two strata, which are further distinguished by costume, insignia, manners, and perquisites. Friendship across the gap is always discouraged and sometimes prohibited. An incidental effect of this arrangement is an incongruous status relationship between the most senior members of the lower stratum and the most junior members of the upper stratum. A newly commissioned second lieutenant outranks an elderly master sergeant without any question, but his actual influence will probably be less.

Distortions in the Hierarchy

To say that the status order of an organization is definite, public, and clearly defined should not be taken to mean either that hierarchical arrangements always work as planned or that they are always planned in such a way as to be workable. Among the most common organizational phenomena are:

Usurpations of power by strategically placed individuals

The development of unforeseen inconsistencies between the status attached to a position and its actual importance in the organization's activity

The alternation of power relationships from one situation to another so that the leader in certain activities is a follower in others

Direct conflicts over status, often between two positions that are nearly equal, with the slightly superior position claiming more authority than the slightly inferior position is willing to concede.

The breakdown of a hierarchy may take the form of the displacement of an organizational program by the private programs of members. At the upper levels of the organization, members may use the organization's resources for private ends that have nothing to do with the organizational program, or that actually hinder it. Every large organization shows instances of corruption, malfeasance, nepotism, and abuse of privileges. At the lower levels of an organization, private interests are often collectively defended by an organized peer group with a program of its own; at intermediate levels, the formation of revolutionary coalitions against a common superior, or of improper coalitions between persons of widely separated rank, are likely to disrupt the status order.

Abuse of Authority

The abuse of authority may be said to occur whenever the holder of an organizational position uses his authority for private purposes that have nothing to do with the organization's program or that obstruct it (the executive who insists on sleeping with his secretary; the army officer who uses the freedom of movement conferred by his rank to avoid combat; the purchasing agent who accepts expensive gifts from suppliers; the official who blames his mistakes on subordinates). Some abuse of authority is likely to occur wherever there is authority to be abused; few organizations escape it.

Under ordinary circumstances, no one disputes that foremen ought to be paid more than the people they supervise or that professors should have more extensive library privileges than students. But how *much* more is the question. It usually falls to the highest-ranking members of an organization to distribute the available rewards, and they are very likely to overestimate the incentives required to maintain their own productivity and morale. A distribution of rewards may be characterized as abusive when members of an organization are unequally treated with respect to matters that fall entirely outside the organization's sphere of activity. The advancement of technology, the universalization of higher education, and the loss of belief in the legitimacy of class discrimination all tend to eliminate the traditional modes of abusing authority, but new forms of abuse spring up in their place. For example, the writer has observed a California engineering company that required the heads of its technical departments to undergo a monthly session with a psychoanalyst, the results of which were transmitted to their superiors.

Peer Groups

The organized peer group is composed of persons who occupy equal or nearly equal positions under a common superior and are brought into daily contact with each other. It is a primary group (every member interacts directly with every other) and an organization in its own right (it has a collective identity, a roster, a program of activity, and membership procedures), but it stands in a curious relationship to the parent organization, in whose table of organization it has no place and whose program it may actively oppose.

One of the first great discoveries of sociological research in industry was that productive enterprises were honeycombed with peer groups that made it their business to restrict the output of their members to a comfortable level, and to equalize output so as to eliminate the effect of individual differences in the competence of workers.[17] The peer group discovered in the Bank Wiring Observation Room of the Hawthorne experiments is a classic and familiar example. Later studies have shown that peer groups do more than resist the organization's program. Even while restricting output, the peer group may facilitate the accomplishment of the organization's program by sustaining the morale of its members, by providing channels for horizontal communication, by standardizing the rate and quality of work, and by "engineering from below" to correct the omissions and mistakes of higher authority.[18] The activities of peer groups range all the way from a sort of guerilla warfare against management to enthusiastic cooperation with it. Inevitably, the appearance of a peer group modifies the table of organization. The changes may not be observable from the outside and may be invisible even within the organization except at very close range. The sociologist studying an organization usually discovers that it does not operate as it is supposed to; this finding is usually linked to his discovery of active peer groups. Such phenomena are often described under the heading of *informal organization.* The term reminds us that every organization has important elements that are not derived from its table of organization or written down in its operating procedures.

We can understand the coalition process in organizations most readily by reducing situations to triadic form. *A triad is a social system containing three interrelated actors. A coalition is an alliance of two or more actors in opposition to other actors in the same system, and a coalition in a triad, of course, is the alliance of two members of the triad against the third member.* Coalitions that disrupt a hierarchy are most likely to occur in triads involving a superior and two subordinates, when the superior is more powerful than either subordinate alone, but the combined power of the subordinates equals or exceeds that of the superior. A successful coalition of subordinates against a superior is called a revolutionary coalition. To avoid domination by a revolutionary coalition, the superior may form an improper coalition (so called because it undermines the legitimate status orders) with one of his subordinates against the other. A revolutionary coalition lowers the "real" status of the superior against whom it is directed. An improper coalition lowers that of the excluded subordinate. In either event, the status relationships envisaged in the table of organization are considerably modified.

It is virtually impossible to design a table of organization that does not encourage revolutionary or improper coalitions at certain points. To endow each superior with enough power to withstand any possible coalition of his subordinates would require greater resources than most organizations command. In the normal course of events, the threat of a revolutionary coalition is met by a counter coalition of the superior with a peer or superior of his own, and the sequence of coalitions and counter coalitions may be long, complicated, and unpredictable. The distortion of hierarchical arrangements by coalitions is found in organizations of every size, from the nuclear family, where the coalition of mother and son against paternal authority is a standard feature of the institution,[19] to the national state, where the coalition of permanent civil servants against politically appointed cabinet ministers generally limits the possible scope of administrative reforms.[20]

Types of Legitimate Domination

"The Types of Legitimate Domination" is the title given by Max Weber to the famous chapter in which (having defined domination as the probability that certain commands would be obeyed by a given group of persons) he pointed out that every form of domination implies some degree of voluntary compliance and classified types of legitimate (that is, organizational) domination according to how voluntary compliance is obtained.

1. *Legal authority rests on the subject's commitment to the purposes of the organization and his belief that its rules and procedures are rationally related to its purposes and that the persons exercising au-*

thority do so in conformity with the rules and for organizational, rather than private, purposes. Accepting legal authority, one "salutes the uniform, not the man."

2. *Traditional authority rests on the subject's belief in the sanctity of tradition and the appropriateness of the power exercised in traditional roles.* The authority of a parent, a property owner, a teacher, or a priest seems natural and proper, even at times when the roles in question are changing.

3. *Charismatic authority rests on extraordinary personal qualities.* The followers of a charismatic leader accept his authority because they perceive him as different from and better than themselves. This is the authority of the founders of cults and the leaders of revolutions; of celebrities and Presidential candidates.

Weber's discussion of these three types of authority was mainly historical. He was particularly interested in the evolution of governments based on legal authority out of earlier forms of government based on traditional and charismatic authority. When he wrote (around 1910), charismatic authority had little importance in world politics, and Weber had no way of foreseeing the renewed importance it would soon acquire in the persons of Mussolini, Hitler, Stalin, Mao Tse-Tung, and the leaders of nationalist movements throughout the world. In any case, most of his attention was concentrated on a type of large-scale organization based on legal authority, which he called bureaucracy.

Bureaucracy: The Ideal Type

Although Weber traced the origins of bureaucracy far back in recorded history, he regarded it as a distinctively modern device that increases human control of the environment in much the same way as scientific technology does, and is closely related to it (see Chapter Four). Both bureaucracy and technology provide rational, impersonal modes of achieving large-scale collective projects, in contrast to the irrational and highly personalized forms of social action that predominated in preindustrial society. He explained how and why every type of large-scale organization in modern society tends to become bureaucratized.

> The development of the modern form of the organization of corporate groups in all fields is nothing less than identical with the development and continual spread of bureaucratic administration. This is true of church and state, of armies, political parties, economic enterprises, organizations to promote all kinds of causes, private associations, clubs, and many others. ... However many forms there may be which do not appear to fit this pattern, such as collegial representative bodies, parliamentary committees, soviets, honorary officers, lay judges, and what not, and however much people may complain about the "evils of bureaucracy," it would be sheer illusion to think for a moment that continuous

administrative work can be carried out in any field except by means of officials working in offices. The whole pattern of every-day life is cut to fit this framework. For bureaucratic administration is, other things being equal, always, from a formal, technical point of view, the most rational type. For the needs of mass administration to-day, it is completely indispensable. The choice is only that between bureaucracy and dilettantism in the field of administration. . . .

In this respect, it makes no difference whether the economic system is organized on a capitalistic or a socialistic basis. Indeed, if in the latter case a comparable level of technical efficiency were to be achieved, it would mean a tremendous increase in the importance of specialized bureaucracy.[22]

THE BUREAUCRATIC TABLE OF ORGANIZATION

A bureaucracy is a continuous hierarchy with each lower position under the control and supervision of a higher one and the conduct of each position (Weber calls it an *office*) governed by technical rules or norms. In order to be able to follow the complicated specifications that govern their conduct in office, officials must be extensively trained and only trained persons made eligible for appointment. Their work is impersonally evaluated, and they are promoted for both seniority and merit; the sequence of promotions constitutes a bureaucratic career. The officeholder is not allowed to own his office or any of the equipment associated with it. Organizational property is rigorously segregated from personal property. The office is supposed to be the official's sole occupation. It entitles him to a fixed monetary salary, fringe benefits, and retirement pay, sufficient to maintain a style of life appropriate for his status at each stage of his career. The office is separated from the home and official from private relationships.

Bureaucratic administration is supposed to be dominated by a spirit of formalism and impersonality, without love or hate, passion or enthusiasm, indeed with the least possible display of the official's personal feelings or preferences.

Empirical research on live bureaucratic organizations has provided us with a great deal more information about how they work than Weber has, without detracting from the usefulness of his description of the ideal type. What the studies have shown, above all, is a tendency for bureaucratic officials to resist bureaucratization and to find expression for their personal emotions, sentiments, and interests within the bureaucratic structure. Another important finding has been that bureaucratic structures usually have engineering problems—it is not so easy to design a workable table of organization along rational lines as Weber supposed.[23]

BUREAUCRATIC STRUCTURE AND PERSONALITY

The partial incompatibility between high productivity and high morale appears with special prominence in bureaucracies and generates increasingly serious problems as more and more types of social activity are bureaucratically administered. How to adapt to the demands of bureaucratic organizations, and how to defend one's own identity against the manipulations of bureaucratic agents, are problems of modern life. Protest movements in the industrially advanced countries often take the form of resistance to bureaucratization, especially in educational, religious, health, and welfare institutions.[24] An extensive sociological and popular literature laments the dehumanizing influence of bureaucracies.[25] It is not by accident that the word *bureaucrat* has been an epithet for more than a hundred years. It was Thorsten Veblen who coined the phrase "trained incapacity" to describe bureaucratic rigidity, formalism, and red tape in the face of circumstances demanding intelligent adaptation. The same theme was expressed in a famous essay by Merton, who noted that:

1. An effective bureaucracy demands reliability of response and strict devotion to regulations.
2. Such devotion to the rules leads to their transformation into absolutes; they are no longer conceived as relative to a set of purposes.
3. This interferes with ready adaptation under special conditions not clearly envisaged by those who drew up the general rules.
4. Thus, the very elements which conduce toward efficiency in general produce inefficiency in specific instances.[26]

CONTEMPORARY BUREAUCRATIC PATTERNS

Overconformity to the rules is still characteristic of bureaucracies, particularly of somewhat old-fashioned ones, but it is no longer as characteristic as it was. Recent improvements in communications equipment and office machinery—like the remote-control typewriter, the copying machine, and the multiple-console computer—have greatly speeded up bureaucratic procedures, and in many cases, have made them more flexible. Bureaucracies of modern design suffer more from acute impersonality than from red tape. This impersonality takes many forms: for example, the development of dialogues between men and machines, as when requests for information are met by recorded messages; the favoring of mechanical requirements over human preferences, as when numbers are substituted for names in telephone exchanges; the development of procedures that do not permit human intervention, as when supplies in a computerized warehouse become inaccessible except through the computer; and the substitution of automatic decision-making for good judgment, as when the less promising of two candidates for promotion is selected because of his higher psychometric scores.

The contemporary bureaucratic pattern is easily described, since government, industrial, educational, and philanthropic bureaucracies already look very much alike, and their resemblance tends to increase with every improvement in office machinery. The most salient features of the contemporary bureaucratic pattern are:

1. *Detailed Budgeting.* The table of organization and the ongoing program are combined in an annual budget that forecasts income, allocates funds to each department and section, and specifies the purposes for which the allocations are to be expended. A complete budget shows all the positions in an organization together with the salary and other expense items associated with each position, and incidentally provides the most complete and up-to-date version of the table of organization. It also includes items for all authorized activities and for various contingencies, thus providing a full description of the organizational program. Budgets are generally prepared on an annual basis, but are reviewed and revised at shorter intervals.

2. *Computerized Accounting.* Although the money on which a bureaucracy operates may be received in various forms, once inside the organization it becomes invisible and intangible and is handled only by high-speed machines. There is a payroll department that converts salary information on computer tapes or cards into checks and vouchers that are written and verified automatically. Depending on the field in which the organization is active, other centralized sections will handle records of production, inventory, traffic, enrollment, purchases, and other financially significant transactions in the same way.

3. *Personnel Procedures.* The fundamental personnel procedures are job classification, salary- and rate-setting, recruitment, intake-testing, on-the-job training, performance evaluation, maintenance of employee files, administration of retirement and other benefit programs, and employee counseling. The overall purpose of these related activities is to assure a continuous supply of suitably trained and qualified incumbents for all positions, to rationalize the distribution of incentives and rewards, and to make sure that no individual becomes indispensable to the organization.

4. *Standardized Communications.* Routine communications in a modern bureaucracy are generally transmitted on standardized forms designed for a specific purpose. They are prepared in duplicate, triplicate, quadruplicate, or more copies and "distributed" through predesignated "channels" for various types of "processing." It is virtually impossible to accomplish any significant act in a bureaucracy without the processing of a form. Among the important forms of processing are approval, authorization, countersigning, verification, coding, matching, estimation, programming, and filing. The last step is particularly important. Most bureaucracies file a copy of every form processed so that the transaction to which it refers can always be reconstructed at a later time.

5. *Operating Statistics.* A fully developed contemporary bureaucracy maintains a continuous and enormous flow of statistical information about the performance of its component units and subunits—down to individuals. A factory may generate daily or even hourly output figures for each department, section, and crew—sometimes for

each machine and worker. The president of a typical large university receives, among other operating statistics, periodic reports on faculty teaching load by college, department, and instructor, broken down by credit hours, student-contact hours, and type of instruction. In other reports, enrollment is broken down by college, school, department, instructor, and individual course; and information is provided on the age, sex, class standing, major subject, draft status, and grade average of the students in each category, together with comparative information for each of the five preceding years. These are only the routine reports; every administrator with access to a computer can obtain a steady flow of special reports at trivial cost.

The Bureaucratic Revolution

The bureaucratic type of large-scale organization is a complex invention whose appearance in western Europe (and subsequent diffusion to the rest of the world) paralleled the scientific revolution that began with the work of Newton, Boyle, and Lavoisier and the industrial revolution that began with the invention of the steam engine and the automatic loom. These three movements were inseparable aspects of the same social movement. The development of industrial machinery was made possible by the new scientific knowledge, much of which was conducted or encouraged by men working for early bureaucracies.

Weber was fascinated by certain examples of large-scale organization in the ancient world that included bureaucratic elements, especially the management of irrigation systems in ancient Egypt and the administration of the Roman legions in the later days of the Empire. This interest has caused some readers to overlook his insistence that full-fledged bureaucracies have appeared only in the modern world and that the development of bureaucratic administration has been closely linked with the development of mass production and of high-speed transportation and communication. The decisive reason for the advance of bureaucratic organization, he asserted, "has always been its purely *technical* superiority over any other form of organization. The fully developed bureaucratic apparatus compares with other organizations exactly as does the machine with the nonmechanical mode of production."[27]

THE ORIGINS OF BUREAUCRACY

Robert Merton's classic study of the relationship between pure science and practical invention in seventeenth century England shows a constant interplay between them. All the important English scientists of that era, among them Wren, Hooke, Newton, Boyle, Huyghens and Halley, he found, undertook some part of their scientific research in response to immediate, practical problems.

As a case in point, Merton [28] discusses the problem of devising an accurate astronomical method for ascertaining the longitude of ships at sea. Adequate methods of obtaining latitude by observation of the sun or of the pole star had been available since the early 1400s, but the problem of determining longitude by celestial observation is much more difficult, and every important astronomer of the seventeenth century seems to have attempted it at one time or another. (After a number of false starts, the invention of the marine chronometer with a balance spring instead of a pendulum provided a partial solution.) It was Sir Isaac Newton himself who persuaded Parliament to pass an act in 1714 offering a reward for a successful method of ascertaining longitude at sea, and he seems to have developed his theory of lunar movements partly because it promised to be useful for that same purpose. Newton and his colleagues of the Royal Society also worked on the theory of tides, the technique of shipbuilding, the development of standards for ship's timber, the measurement of speed through water, and the mechanics of sailpower. They devised diving bells and sea anchors and held numerous discussions about antifouling paint.

Some of these efforts were undertaken at the direct urging of the Royal Navy; others because the commissioners of the navy were known to be interested. During the seventeenth century, the Royal Navy expanded from a large to a giant organization. By the end of the century, it had become a full-fledged bureaucracy and may be considered the first in history. Although similar patterns were emerging on the Continent at about the same time, for example in the French system of provincial administration and in the Prussian army and civil service, the Royal Navy seems to have evolved first and fastest toward the ideal type of bureaucracy. Its table of organization showed a continuous series of official functions; it was governed by explicit rules called the Articles of War, which were read aloud to all personnel on major official occasions, and by a large set of subsidiary regulations. Each position had a definite sphere of competence, specified obligations, a specified degree of authority, and the means of compulsion to enforce it. A full-scale status schism had been developed between officers and men, with distinctive styles of life in each stratum. Service as an officer constituted a career, promotion from rank to rank was based ostensibly on merit, and advancement within each rank on seniority. The separation of personal from official property was virtually complete. Salaries and privileges were standardized, and even the booty obtainable when prizes were taken was distributed "according to the book."[29] The distinction between line and staff had already assumed an essentially modern form when Samuel Pepys, the famous diarist who was a staff official of the Royal Navy, wrote his secret diary toward the end of the century. In his preoccupation with appropriations, committees, personnel problems, and public relations, we hear for the first time the tone of voice of the modern executive. (Even such problems as excessive drinking at business luncheons were beginning to appear in Pepys' world.) A 1649 document describes the position (Clerk of the Acts) to which Pepys was appointed some years later in specifically bureaucratic terms:

The clarke of the Navye's duty depends principally upon rateing (by the Board's approbation) of all bills and recording of them, and all orders, contracts & warrants, making up and casting of accompts, framing and writing answers to letters, orders, and commands from Councell, Lord High Admirall, or Commissioners of the Admiralty, and he ought to be a very able accomptant, well versed in Navall affairs and all inferior officers' dutyes.[30]

Just as the first applications of scientific technology were limited to a few fields like warfare, textile manufacturing, and mining, bureaucratic organization was limited to nearly the same fields until about the end of the eighteenth century. When the United States Constitution went into effect in 1789, the War Department was the only large-scale component of the federal government, and there was not a single American manufacturing corporation; the first of them, the Society for Useful Manufactures of New Jersey, was founded two years later. But by 1820 there were hundreds of manufacturing corporations in the country and the Federal Post Office, with nearly 5,000 employees, had become the first large civilian agency of the government.

All through the nineteenth century, new inventions stimulated the growth of new types of large-scale organization, often very quickly. For example, in 1830 there were only 23 miles of railroad track in the United States, but this figure jumped to about 3,000 by 1840 and to 9,000 by 1850. In 1860, on the eve of the Civil War, there were more than 30,000 miles of railroad track. The railroad companies had grown correspondingly large and, of course, bureaucratic. The invention of the telegraph, the telephone, and electric lighting; new processes for mining, smelting, and refining metal; and new manufacturing techniques all had similar effects.

By 1900 nearly a third of the national wealth belonged to corporations, and the first billion-dollar corporation, United States Steel, was about to be founded by a syndicate of financiers. Although it was peacetime, the armed services totalled more than 100,000 men. The Post Office had 136,000 employees, and state and local governments were spending more than a billion dollars a year on education, roads, police and fire protection, hospitals, public assistance, and other services.[31] In that year, Henry Watterson wrote:

In 1800 we were a few millions of people and we loved liberty. In 1900 we are nearly a hundred millions of people and we love money. Most of this money is invested in what are called corporations. From a handful of individuals we have become a nation of institutions. The individual counts for less and less, organizations for more and more.[32]

Is the Process of Bureaucratization Endless?

The story recounted above forces this question on us whether we regard the prospect of increasing bureaucratization with horror or enthusiasm. There seems to be no limit to bureaucratization in capitalist societies, and socialist regimes are committed to the principle that the economic activity of a national society ought to be brought under a single, necessarily bureaucratic, management. Communism is distinguished from other forms of socialism by its insistence on extending bureaucratic management to noneconomic as well as economic activity, and in the case of the Maoist version of communism, to all human activity without limitation.

The Little Red Book of Chairman Mao holds up as an ideal the image of a national society transformed into one vast, well-integrated organization with a single set of accepted values and a single, common program. Every citizen is supposed to participate in formulating the program and to be bound by it in every moment of his life.

> To be able to carry on their production and studies effectively and to arrange their lives properly, the people want their government and those in charge of production and of cultural and educational organizations to issue appropriate orders of an obligatory nature. It is common sense that the maintenance of public order would be impossible without such administrative regulations. Administrative orders and the method of persuasion and education complement each other in resolving contradictions among the people.[33]

In the United States, there is neither an official nor a popular consensus about the optimum balance between bureaucracy on one hand, and individualism or small-scale organization on the other. There is an official commitment, embodied in antitrust legislation, to the principle that no industrial corporation should be allowed to grow large enough to monopolize the supply of an essential commodity. There is also a feeble commitment to the principle that the growth of the federal government ought not to go unchecked; this is expressed by a ceiling on the national debt, which is raised by Congress whenever the debt approaches it. There are various federal and state laws protecting families and private associations from outside intervention, and other laws that authorize government agencies to intervene under stated conditions. So far as can be determined, public opinion in the United States opposes the continued expansion of large-scale organizations, including government agencies, whenever the issue is put in general terms, but seldom opposes any particular step in that direction, such as the merger of large corporations, the expansion of government agencies, or the development of bureaucratic arrangements for the management of educational, philanthropic, scientific, artistic, welfare, and recreational activities.

Some sociologists believe that American society is already monocratically organized, or in other words, that a unified control over the whole system is exercised in a clandestine way by a small group of military officers, industrial executives, bankers, and politicians who occupy a network of interlocking influential positions in government, business, and other major institutions, and develop and impose national policies that protect the existing distribution of property and influence. This view of American society was eloquently presented and defended by C. Wright Mills.[34] The ruling group has been recently called "the Establishment" by those who believe in its existence and even by some of those who do not.[35]

Applied to American society in the last decade of the second century of national independence, the question whether bureaucratization is an endless process breaks down, upon closer examination, into three separate issues:

1. The number of civilian employees in the federal government increased from 239,000 in 1901 to 1,128,000 in 1940 and to 2,861,000 in 1966. The payrolls of state and local governments during the same period increased even faster, reaching the equivalent of 7,398,000 full-time jobs in 1966.[36] *What limits, if any, can be foreseen to the expansion of public bureaucracies?*

2. As of 1960, there were 4.7 million business firms in the United States. Of these, 754 companies had annual sales over $100 million which, taken together, totaled $318 billion. The number of firms employing at least 5,000 persons was 708.[37] *Will concentration of industry increase until all significant business activity is conducted by large corporations?*

3. Between 1950 and 1970 the growth of "client populations," the development of computers and other high-speed office machinery, and the increasing dependence of private institutions on government financial aid encouraged the bureaucratization of educational and cultural institutions, religious bodies, hospitals, social agencies, and other types of nongovernmental, nonbusiness organizations. *Will this trend continue until all cultural institutions are operated with the same impersonality as large-scale business?*

These issues are difficult to resolve with any degree of certainty, but they are not entirely inscrutable.

The movement toward the concentration of business enterprise is unlikely to be reversed, although its speed is variable. If there are no fundamental changes in the rules of the economic system, concentration will probably continue until virtually all significant business activity is conducted by large corporations, leaving only minor retail and service operations and a few marginal types of manufacturing in the hands of small companies and individual proprietors.

In the case of agriculture, the trends are more difficult to decipher. With the available machinery, the advantage of large farms over small farms is unmistakable, but whether the giant farm operated by a corporation has an economic advantage over the large farm operated by a proprietor is an unsettled point.

Similarly, although large companies, on the average, are unmistakably more effective than small companies, it is not equally certain that super-giant corporations enjoy any advantage over those that are already very large. Although successive studies of the 500 largest in-

Organizations

dustrial corporations show their combined share of the national wealth to be increasing, there is no discernible trend toward increasing concentration *among* these companies. From 1955 to 1965, for example, the sales of the 401st to 500th largest industrial corporations increased somewhat faster than the sales of the 100 largest and the sales of the 41st to 50th merchandising firms very much faster than those of the 10 largest.[38] Because few of the largest corporations ever fail, and the rank of a large company within its industry may remain unchanged for decades, the overall pattern of industrial bureaucratization in the United States appears to be relatively stable.

The question of whether there is any foreseeable limit to the expansion of government bureaucracies is somewhat harder to resolve. The expenditures of the federal government have increased much faster than the population or the national income in the present century, from less than a billion dollars a year just before World War I to more than $5 billion just before World War II to more than $200 billion in 1970. Expenditures of state and local governments have almost kept pace, rising from just over a billion dollars in 1902 to $95 billion in 1966.[39]

By 1966, total government expenditures amounted to about 27 percent of the Gross National Product and about $1,150 per capita. National defense, the postal service, public education, and Social Security accounted for about three-fourths of the grand total, the remainder being divided among dozens of different functions and activities. Among the federal agencies *outside* the regular executive departments that had more than a thousand employees in 1968 were the Atomic Energy Commission, the Civil Service Commission, the Federal Communications Commission, the Federal Deposit Insurance Corporation, the Federal Home Loan Bank Board, the Federal Power Commission, the Federal Soldiers' Home, the Federal Trade Commission, the General Services Administration, the Government of the Panama Canal Zone, the U.S. Information Agency, the Interstate Commerce Commission, the National Aeronautics and Space Administration, the National Labor Relations Board, the National Science Foundation, the Panama Canal Company, the Railroad Retirement Board, the Securities and Exchange Commission, the Selective Service System, the Small Business Administration, the Smithsonian Institution, the Tennessee Valley Authority, and the Veterans' Administration.[40]

The bulk of expenditures at all levels of government still goes for traditional government functions—war and defense, postal service, roads and bridges, schools. The only relatively new activity that compares in scale with these major items is the provision of Social Security and various forms of welfare assistance to the aged, the unemployed, dependent children, and the handicapped, but many programs in this category are self-supported by insurance payments. Direct public expenditures for welfare amount to under 10 percent of total government expenses in the United States—a relatively smaller proportion than in any other advanced industrial country.

The enormous and continuing increase in the costliness of government at all levels is due not so much to the proliferation of new activities as to the increasing costliness of old ones. Increasing expenditures on highways, for example, are necessitated by a continued rapid increase in the number of motor vehicles—from 49 million in 1950 to 96 million in 1967. This increase, in turn, rests partly on the increase of population, partly on suburbanization, and partly on its own momentum: increasing vehicular travel leads to the development of new traffic and parking facilities, which increase the propensity of the population to use their automobiles for short trips. From 1950 to 1966 the percentage of American families owning an automobile increased from 59 percent to 78 percent, while the percentage owning two or more automobiles increased from 7 percent to 25 percent.[41]

Similarly, the increase of educational expenditures—by far the largest item in the combined budgets of state and local governments—is due in part to an overall increase of population, in part to a disproportionate increase of the school-age population, and in even larger part to an increasing propensity to attend school. From 1950 to 1966, enrollment in the last year of high school more than doubled in the United States (from 1,134,000 to 2,560,000) and college enrollment rose nearly as fast (from 2,659,000 in 1950 to 4,491,000 in 1965). This expansion occurred at a time when facilities were becoming much more elaborate and the per-pupil cost of instruction, however measured, was rising very rapidly.

The case is somewhat different for military expenditures, which fluctuate with the size of the armed services, and of veterans' programs, which reflect the timing of war and peace. Military personnel on active duty increased from 12,000 in 1811 to 47,000 in 1814, the peak year of the War of 1812. By 1816, the figure was down to 17,000, and it did not rise much until the Mexican War, when it shot up to 60,000 and then declined to 23,000. The most spectacular increase of all occurred during the Civil War. The armed forces of the Union consisted of only 28,000 officers and men in 1860; by 1865 over a million men were in uniform. By 1866 there were only 77,000, and that number declined in subsequent years. The 44,000 of 1897 rose to 236,000 for the Spanish-American War of 1898. As a result of that war, the United States acquired its first overseas colonies, and perhaps as a result, the military population never again declined below 100,000. It was 166,000 in 1914 at the outbreak of World War I and rose to nearly 3 million in 1918, and the decline that took place after the war left it at a higher level than ever before in peace time. In the following two decades, the number did not drop below 240,000. It was 334,000 in 1939 when World War II broke out in Europe. By 1945, the number of men (and women) in the armed forces was more than 12 million, and the postwar plateau was in the neighborhood of 1.5 million. The Korean action of 1951–1952 raised this figure to 3 million, and in the ensuing period there was hardly any decline at all. Since 1951, and right through the Vietnam war, the military population on active duty has fluctuated in the neighborhood of 3 million.[42]

In addition to the change from a relatively small peacetime army before 1940 to a rather large one after 1945, the military part of the federal budget was changed in a fundamental way by the allocation of vast sums to research and development during and after World War II. Of course, there has always been a close relationship between military requirements and technology, and significant inventions have often resulted from the search for solutions to military problems.[43] We have already noted the connections between the requirements of naval warfare, large-scale organization, and the origins of modern science in seventeenth century England. The connection between military requirements and technology has been equally close in American history. The basic principles of mass production, including assembly-line methods and the interchangeability of parts, were introduced by Eli Whitney before 1800 in the manufacture of Army rifles. The early development of steam vessels and the later development of iron ships were largely underwritten by the Navy. The railroads were subsidized by the federal government partly because they enabled the Army to deal more effectively with hostile Indians on the frontier. Many of the early textile and shoe factories of New England got their start through military contracts.

The relationship has been equally close in the present century. For example, the development of civil aviation has consisted for the most part in adapting engines, airframes, and instruments developed for military purposes to civilian use. But not until the establishment of the Manhattan Project (the large organization of civilian scientists under military control that developed a practical method of making nuclear explosives) in 1942 was the support of scientific research institutionalized as a normal military activity. The sponsorship of pure and applied research not only in physics, mathematics, and chemistry, but also in botany and social psychology, is now a routine—and important—phase of military activity. Since World War II a whole set of new industries has been developed cooperatively by the military services, civilian scientists at universities, research institutes under military grants or contracts, and industrial firms involved in "defense procurement." This effort covers hundreds of fields from exploration of the ocean bottom to the development of lightweight heat-resistant metals. In each of the most important fields (for example, atomic energy, the exploration of space, and human biology) there is also a large civilian agency[44] that participates in the complex partnership of armed services, scientific laboratories, and industrial suppliers.

The "military-scientific-industrial complex," as it is popularly termed, is thus of very recent origin. It did not begin to take shape until World War II, and its spectacular growth in the two decades following the war was largely unplanned. The technological gains have been incalculably large; most of the specialized knowledge required to put men on the moon in 1969 was not even dreamed of in 1949. Nevertheless, the arrangement is makeshift, unsatisfactory to many participants, and much criticized by outside observers. The objections most often heard are that:

1. Priorities for research are set arbitrarily and haphazardly, without any necessary reference to the needs of the national society.

2. The arrangement is often very wasteful. About $7 billion is said to have been spent by the Department of Defense under Secretary Robert McNamara in developing a movable-wing aircraft, the usefulness of which was always in doubt.

3. Research under military auspices often takes directions that appear irresponsible; for example, the attempt to develop a new and deadlier form of bubonic plague for potential use in biological warfare.

4. Military research is usually kept secret, at least for a time, and this secrecy interferes with the normal progress of science and leads to widespread confusion and duplication of efforts.

5. The relationship among the military officers, government officials, scientists, and industrial executives involved in some of the new technological fields have not always been above suspicion. The possibility of corruption derives from the fact that, because of military secrecy, the only persons qualified to evaluate a project may be those already involved in it. Men who represent the government in negotiating with suppliers are often offered lucrative positions with those same suppliers when they leave the government's service.

These problems are so conspicuous that it is difficult to consider the present arrangements as permanent. The criticism of classified military research in the universities, which was a major theme of student protests in the late 1960s, had the immediate effect of weakening the linkage between military technology and civilian science. The gradual shift of responsibility for the space program from military to civilian control has a similar effect. It is likely that the federal government will continue to underwrite scientific research in the foreseeable future, but it is difficult to predict what form this collaboration will take.

The question of whether the bureaucratization of cultural, educational, religious, and recreational institutions will continue indefinitely is considerably easier to answer than it would have been a few years ago. Institutional bureaucracies have been growing very rapidly in the United States (and in other industrialized countries as well) under the multiple impetus of population growth, prosperity, increased mobility, and shortened working hours. Many educational and religious institutions have grown to unprecedented size, and their tables of organization have become increasingly complex. The first and most serious stirrings of disaffection with the bureaucratic pattern appeared in certain institutions like the University of California, the New York City school system, the Roman Catholic church, and the French radio and television network, in which rapid growth had been accompanied by dramatic bureaucratization.

The advantages of bureaucracy in lowering costs and increasing the speed and certainty of administration count for much less in an organization like a school or church, the primary goal of which is the benefit of individual members, than in a military or industrial organization. The protest movements of the 1960s used "participation" as an almost worldwide slogan, which was understood to imply the self-determination of small groups within large organizations and the simplification of formal procedures, even very ancient and sacred procedures like the liturgy of the Mass. The demand for participation seems to embody a deep-seated resistance to the bureaucratization of voluntary and semivoluntary associations. There has been much less demand from labor for participation in industrial management, and government officials have shown practically no interest in obtaining the right to increased participation in public administration. However, the mass support that extremist movements in educational, religious, and cultural institutions have been able to rally behind the demand for participation demonstrates that, at least for the time being, the tendency toward bureaucratization is no longer as strong as it was in those institutions and indeed, in some instances, may have been reversed.

Summarizing the research evidence about participation in voluntary associations, Berelson and Steiner write:

> Members tend to participate most when the association does not have a large salaried staff; when the members have considerable power relative to the officers; when the association is not large; when it is not highly specialized internally; and when the membership is homogeneous in character. . . . [45]

Sets of Organizations

A set of organizations consists of two or more organizations of the same type, which provide each other with models for mutual comparison. The families in a neighborhood; the leading companies in the electronics industry; the Episcopal churches of Baltimore; the midwestern state universities; the three major television networks; the leading symphony orchestras; the Chevrolet, Pontiac, Buick, Oldsmobile, and Cadillac divisions of General Motors; the teams in the National Hockey League; and the nations that have developed nuclear weapons of their own are each a set of organizations. Some of these sets, like the teams in the National Hockey League, are represented by a central organization, but this merely makes the operation of the set a little more orderly and predictable.

The identifying characteristics of a set are that each organization in it is visible to the members of every other organization, that they compete directly or indirectly, that they have similar tables of organization, and that their competition results in a prestige order that regulates the exchanges between them.

The prestige order of a set somewhat resembles a hierarchy, but the differences are as important as the similarities. Status in a hierarchy is assigned by an organization and involves a specified amount of power. The prestige of an organization in a set is composite of public opinion about its relative importance, goodness, productivity, and morale. These terms are nearly interchangeable when prestige is discussed, because it is one of the peculiarities of a prestige order in a set that no fine distinctions are drawn between different organizational qualities, and organizations with higher prestige are assumed to be *generally* superior to organizations with lower prestige.

Some organizations cannot function normally except within a set of similar organizations. Others are under no apparent constraint to maintain close relationship with similar organizations, but do so anyway. There is a tendency for the success of an organization in any field to be marked by an increase of contacts within various sets. The reverse effect, the increase of organizational complexity as a result of the organization's participation in a set, has been reported in one study of interorganizational relationships (in a set of social agencies):

> The involvement of staff in interorganizational relationships introduces them to new ideas, new perspectives, and new techniques for solving organizational problems. The establishment of collegial relationships with comparable staff members of other organizations provides them with a comparative framework for understanding their own organizations. This is likely to affect their professional activities—attendance at meetings of professional societies—as well as reinforce professional standards of excellence. In these ways the involvement of organizations in joint programs has the effect of increasing the complexity of the social and health welfare organizations.[46]

Among the functions of sets are the conservation and refinement of the institutional pattern, division of labor with respect to institutional experimentation, the allocation of scarce resources in the common environment, the provision of a market for trained personnel, and systematic self-appraisal.

The prestige of an organization in a set is what determines the exchange value, so to speak, of the statuses within that organization. Without some such device, the movement of individuals between organizations would be much more difficult to arrange. The prestige of the organization may be thought of as a kind of coefficient by which the individual's organization status is multiplied to obtain its value relative to a status in some other organization. Low status in a high-prestige organization may be more valuable than high status in a low-ranking organization. The star of a minor league team may be very glad to accept a place as a substitute in a major league team; the fourth engineer on an ocean liner may have better pay and prospects than the chief engineer of a tramp freighter.

The principal dysfunction of sets of organizations is that they reward equal performance unequally in different places. The brilliant student who does excellent work in a mediocre college will probably not be as well rewarded as if he had done the same work at a prestigious college. A military genius in the Panamanian Army cannot expect the worldwide recognition he might have won in the French Army.

An individual can compare his status in an organization with that of an offered position in another organization to determine whether moving would represent an advantage for him; whether, for example, becoming a divisional manager in the large X Company would represent upward or downward mobility from his present position as vice-president of the small Y Company.

Status Consistency[47]

There is a natural tendency for a social actor to demand consistency among the positions he holds simultaneously in different organizations and for the people around him to concur in that demand. Consistent positions are those that have the same exchange value. In a community where the distribution of status is generally consistent, A, if superior to B in one organization, will also be superior to him in any other organization to which they both belong, and if the same B is superior to C in any organization, A will be superior to C in any organization to which both of *them* belong.

The universal resistance to status inconsistency seems to be based on a universal experience that inconsistent relationships are uncomfortable. The research evidence suggests that persons holding inconsistent statuses are likely to develop dissatisfaction, cynicism, rebelliousness, and even illness.[48]

The Aggrandizement Effect

The aggrandizement effect is the tendency for the prestige of an organization in a set to be overestimated by its own members. In the typical case, the members of all the organizations in a set agree more or less about the total prestige order *except* with respect to their own organizations, to which most of them assign a higher rank than outsiders do. One study of a set of U.S. Air Force squadrons showed that more than half of them were ranked first in their sets by their own members. A study of the chairmen of a random sample of university departments showed that most of them ranked their own departments among the best five in the country. Similar effects have been found in many other types of organization.[49]

This leads to interesting consequences. If, as often happens, the amount of upward distortion is roughly constant throughout the set, the tendency of the members of each organization to overestimate its prestige will cancel out when their ratings are averaged, so that there may be a high degree of consensus with respect to the overall prestige order even though everyone is mistaken about his own place in it. Whenever two of the organizations of such a set are brought into contact, outside observers will agree about their relative prestige but the members of the interacting organizations will disagree, each claiming more than the other is willing to concede. Where the stakes of interaction are high, as in a set of nations, the aggrandizement effect sets the stage for very dangerous misunderstandings. Under less critical conditions, it enhances morale in each organization by exaggerating the value of membership and reducing the attractiveness of outside reference groups.

1. An organization is a social system that has an unequivocal collective identity, an exact roster of members, an explicit program of activity, and procedures for replacing members. Every organization is a device for achieving collective goals, and its effectiveness in doing so can always be measured in one way or another.

2. In order to maintain itself, an organization must establish an equilibrium in its exchanges with the environment and some sort of stability in its internal structure. It accomplishes these purposes partly by coercion, partly by enlisting voluntary cooperation.

3. There is always some strain between an organizational program and the private purposes of the individuals involved in it. For this reason, among others, the relationship between the effectiveness of an organization and the satisfaction of its members is highly variable. The authority exerted through the organizational hierarchy is always checked to some extent by the resistance of peer groups and other coalitions of subordinates.

4. A bureaucracy is a type of organization that handles a large volume of routine activity by means of impersonal standardized procedures. It is a characteristically modern type of organization, developing in conjunction with technological progress. The ideal type of bureaucracy was described by Max Weber. Contemporary bureaucracies rely on detailed budgeting, computerized accounting, standardized personnel procedures and communications, and a steady flow of operating statistics.

5. The expansion of government and business bureaucracies is not likely to be interrupted in the near future, but in the case of cultural institutions, certain countertrends to bureaucratization have recently appeared.

Questions for Discussion / CHAPTER NINE

1. How would you go about studying the relationship between productivity and morale on a college football team?

2. Can you draw a table of organization for the Beatles? The Mafia? All your relatives? The United Nations? Explain why or why not in each case.

3. You are told that an organization has 19 distinct status levels. What else does this figure tell you about that organization?

4 Under what circumstances is a peer group likely to engage in the systematic limitation of output?

5 What was the Bureaucratic Revolution? When did it start? When did it finish?

6 How would you expect a status schism to affect productivity and morale in the superior stratum? In the inferior stratum?

7 In which of the following types of organization would you expect to find the greatest aggrandizement effect: athletic teams, neighborhood gangs, amateur theatrical groups? Explain your answer.

8 How do you account for the fact that bureaucracies are famous both for efficiency and for inefficiency?

9 Find a concrete illustration of each of the following in your own experience:

a status schism	charismatic authority
a simple hierarchy	"trained incapacity"
abuse of authority	a set of organizations
a peer group	status inconsistency
a revolutionary coalition	pure coercion

Recommended Reading / **CHAPTER NINE**

Thompson, James D. *Organizations In Action: Social Science Bases of Administrative Behavior.* New York: McGraw-Hill, 1967; and Scott Greer, *Social Organization.* New York: Random House, 1965. Two short and readable textbooks on social organization.

Grimshaw, Austin, and John W. Hennessey, Jr. *Organizational Behavior: Cases and Readings.* New York: McGraw-Hill, 1960. Contains descriptions of organizational problems, designed for case analysis by students.

Barnard, Chester I. *The Functions of the Executive.* Cambridge, Mass.: Harvard University Press, 1938. The classic and still readable work on organizational theory.

Warner, W. Lloyd, ed. *The Emergent American Society,* vol. 1, *Large-Scale Organizations.* New Haven: Yale University Press, 1967. Brings together a great deal of descriptive information about contemporary business, labor, religious, educational, and governmental organizations in the United States.

Moore, Wilbert E. *The Conduct of the Corporation.* (New York: Random House, 1962. Describes the world of the big private enterprise.

Notes / CHAPTER NINE

1. Systematic classifications of organizational types are found in Peter M. Blau and W. Richard Scott, *Formal Organizations: A Comparative Approach* (San Francisco: Chandler, 1962), pp. 42–45; and Amitai Etzioni, *A Comparative Analysis of Complex Organizations: On Power, Involvement and Their Correlates* (New York: Free Press, 1961), pp. 66–67.
2. PR (possible pair relationships)   For a full discussion of the number of possible relationships in groups of varying size, see William H. Kephart, "A Quantitative Analysis of Intragroup Relationships," *American Journal of Sociology* 55, no. 6 (May 1950): 544–549.
3. Mason Haire, "Biological Models and Empirical Histories of the Growth of Organizations," in *Modern Organization Theory: A Symposium of the Foundation for Research on Human Behavior*, ed. Mason Haire (New York: John Wiley, 1959), pp. 272–306. See also Theodore R. Anderson and Seymour Warkov, "Organizational Size and Functional Complexity: A Study of Administration in Hospitals," *American Sociological Review* 26, no. 1 (February 1961): 23–28.
4. Marvin E. Olsen, *The Process of Social Organization* (New York: Holt, Rinehart & Winston, 1968), pp. 74–75.
5. Georg Simmel, "How is Society Possible?" in *Georg Simmel, 1858–1918,* ed. and trans. Kurt H. Wolff (Columbus, Ohio: Ohio State University Press, 1959): 350–351.
6. An important collection of such studies is in Rensis Likert, *New Patterns of Management* (New York: McGraw-Hill, 1961).
7. *Ibid,* pp. 31–32.
8. The intricate relationship of productivity and morale in nonindustrial organizations is illustrated in these two related studies, among others: Peter M. Blau, *The Dynamics of Bureaucracy: A Study of Interpersonal Relations in Two Government Agencies* (Chicago: University of Chicago Press, 1955, rev. ed., 1963); and Harry Cohen, *The Demonics of Bureaucracy: Problems of Change in a Government Agency* (Ames, Iowa: Iowa State University Press, 1965).
9. Samuel A. Stouffer et al., *Studies in Social Psychology in World War II,* vol. 2, table 20, p. 179; Edward A. Shils, "Primary Groups in the American Army," in *Continuities in Social Research: Studies in the Scope and Method of "The American Soldier,"* ed. Robert K. Merton and Paul F. Lazarsfeld (New York: Free Press, 1950), pp. 16–39.
10. Edward A. Shils and Morris Janowitz, "Cohesion and Disintegra-

tion in the Wehrmacht in World War II," *Public Opinion Quarterly* 12, no. 2 (Summer 1948): 280–315.

11. John Dollard with the assistance of Donald Horton, *Fear in Battle* (New Haven: Yale University Institute of Human Relations, 1943). For still another type of battlefield motivation, see Charles C. Moskos, Jr., "Why Men Fight: American Combat Soldiers in Vietnam," *Transactions* 7, no. 1 (November 1969): 13–23.

12. The first industrial expert to discuss tables of organization at length (but without presenting them in graphic form) was Charles Babbage, *On the Economy of Machinery and Manufactures* (London: C. Knight, 1832).

13. More information about early tables of organization can be found in Theodore Caplow, *Principles of Organization* (New York: Harcourt Brace Jovanovich, 1964), pp. 50–58.

14. Olsen, *The Process of Social Organization,* p. 171.

15. W. Lloyd Warner, ed., *The Emergent American Society,* vol. 1, *Large-Scale Organizations* (New Haven: Yale University Press, 1967).

16. *Ibid.,* p. 45.

17. A comprehensive summary of early studies describing the activities of industrial peer groups can be found in Morris S. Viteles, *Motivation and Morale in Industry* (New York: Norton, 1953).

18. For beautiful examples of "engineering from below," see Donald Roy, "Efficiency and 'the Fix': Informal Intergroup Relations in a Piecework Machine Shop," *American Journal of Sociology* 60, no. 3 (November 1954): 255–266.

19. Among them, the Irish farm family described by Conrad M. Arensberg and Solon T. Kimball, *Family and Community in Ireland,* 2d ed. (Cambridge, Mass.: Harvard University Press, 1968).

20. This theme runs throughout Weber's discussion of the types of legitimate domination. See Max Weber, *The Theory of Social and Economic Organization,* 5th ed., ed. Talcott Parsons and trans. A. M. Henderson (New York: Free Press, 1968).

21. *Ibid.,* pp. 324–423.

22. *Ibid.,* pp. 337–338.

23. Among the numerous studies of bureaucracy from which these two general conclusions are drawn, see especially, Philip A. Selznick, *TVA and the Grass Roots: A Study in the Sociology of Formal Organization* (Berkeley: University of California Press, 1949); Alvin W. Gouldner, *Patterns of Industrial Bureaucracy* (New York: Free Press, 1954); Roy G. Francis and Robert C. Stone, *Service and Procedure in Bureaucracy: A Case Study* (Minneapolis: University of Minnesota Press, 1956); Marshall Dimock, *Administrative Vitality: The Conflict with Bureaucracy* (New York: Harper & Row, 1959); Morris Janowitz, *The Professional Soldier: A Social and Political Portrait* (New York: Free Press, 1960); and Michel Crozier, *The Bureaucratic Phenomenon* (Chicago: University of Chicago Press, 1964).

24. It is paradoxical that some of the most vehement opponents of

bureaucratization are devotees of Chairman Mao, who advocates a totally bureaucratized society.

25. Among the most eloquent of these cries of distress have been: David Riesman, Reuel Denney, and Nathan Glazer, *The Lonely Crowd: A Study of the Changing American Character* (New Haven: Yale University Press, 1964); William H. Whyte, Jr., *The Organization Man* (New York: Simon & Schuster, 1956); Chris Argyris, *Personality and Organization: The Conflict between System and the Individual* (New York: Harper & Row, 1957); Alan Harrington, *Life in the Crystal Palace* (New York: Knopf, 1959); Georges Friedmann, *The Anatomy of Work: Labor, Leisure, and the Implications of Automation,* trans. Wyatt Rawson (New York: Free Press, 1962); Victor A. Thompson, *Modern Organization* (New York: Knopf, 1961); Vance Packard, *The Pyramid Climbers* (New York: McGraw-Hill, 1962); and long before any of these, Thorstein Veblen, *The Theory of Business Enterprise* (New York: Scribner's, 1904).

26. Robert K. Merton, *Social Theory and Social Structure,* enlarged ed. (New York: Free Press, 1968), chap. 8, p. 254.

27. Max Weber, *Economy and Society: An Outline of Interpretive Sociology,* ed. Guenther Roth and Claus Wittich, 3 vols. (New York: Bedminster Press, 1968), vol. 3, p. 973.

28. Merton, *Social Theory and Social Structure,* chap. 21, pp. 661–681.

29. For a full description of the bureaucratic structure of the Royal Navy in 1739–1748, see Daniel A. Baugh, *British Naval Administration in the Age of Walpole* (Princeton, N.J.: Princeton University Press, 1965).

30. E. Hallam Moorhouse, *Samuel Pepys: Administrator, Observer, Gossip* (London: Chapman and Hall, 1909), p. 34.

31. U.S. Bureau of the Census, *Historical Statistics of the United States: Colonial Times to 1957* (Washington, D.C.: Government Printing Office 1957), Series Y763–775, Y547–574, Y241–250.

32. Quoted in John P. Davis, *Corporations: A Study of the Origin and Development of Great Business Combinations and Their Relation to the Authority of the State* (New York: Capricorn Books, 1961), p. 4. Originally published 1905.

33. Mao Tse-Tung, *Quotations from Chairman Mao Tse-Tung* (New York: Bantam, 1967), p. 29.

34. C. Wright Mills, *The Power Elite* (New York: Oxford University Press, 1956).

35. The term "Establishment" did not acquire its current meaning until about 1966.

36. U.S. Bureau of the Census, Department of Commerce, *Statistical Abstract of the United States 1967,* tables 606 and 607. *Historical Statistics of the United States,* Series Y241–250.

37. Warner, *The Emergent American Society,* vol. 1, pp. 25–27.

38. *Statistical Abstract of the United States 1968,* table 695.

39. *Statistical Abstract of the United States 1967,* tables 580 and

606; and *Historical Statistics of the United States,* Series Y, various tables.

40. *Statistical Abstract of the United States 1968,* table 569.
41. *Ibid.,* tables 822 and 826.
42. *Ibid.,* sect. 9, various tables.
43. R. Buckminster Fuller et al., *World Design Science Decade 1965–1975,,* document 1, *Inventory of World Resources, Human Trends and Needs* (Carbondale, Ill.: Southern Illinois University, 1965–1967).
44. The Atomic Energy Commission, the National Aeronautics and Space Agency, and the National Institutes of Health, respectively. For a more thorough exploration of this issue, see Harold L. Wilensky, *Organizational Intelligence: Knowledge and Policy in Government and Industry* (New York: Basic Books, 1967).
45. Bernard Berelson and Gary A. Steiner, *Human Behavior: An Inventory of Scientific Findings* (New York: Harcourt Brace Jovanovich, 1964), p. 380.
46. Michael Aiken and Jerald Hage, "Organizational Interdependence and Intra-Organizational Structure," *American Sociological Review* 33, no. 6 (December 1968): 927.
47. Other terms sometimes used for the same concept are "status crystallization," "status congruency," and "status equilibration."
48. Elton F. Jackson, "Status Consistency and Symptoms of Stress," *American Sociological Review* 27, no. 4 (August 1962): 469–480; Seymour Parker, "Status Consistency and Stress," *Ibid.* 28, no. 1 (February 1963): 131–132; Irwin W. Goffman, "Status Consistency and Preference for Change in Power Distribution," *Ibid.* 22, no. 3 (June 1957): 275–280; and Everett E. Hagen, *On the Theory of Social Change: How Economic Growth Begins* (Homewood, Ill.: Dorsey Press, 1962).
49. Caplow, *Principles of Organization,* pp. 213–217.

The Family

The family is the most universal of social institutions and the source of the earliest and most powerful influences to which the normal individual in every society is exposed. Our discussion of the family will begin with the forms of kinship, a brief summary of what has been discovered about kinship systems in general, a description of the American kinship system and how it operates, and a few comments on the relation of kinship to other social institutions.

Next we shall consider the changing American family—changes in its structure, in its predominant values and attitudes, and in the amount of variation it permits. Then we shall describe and illustrate several ways of analyzing the nuclear family as a social system, each of which has its own type of data and its own characteristic results.

Kinship Systems

A kinship system is a set of relationships derived from descent and marriage, which includes a set of kinship terms linked to a set of behavior patterns and attitudes.[1] Every known human society, past or present, has such a system, and a surprising number of general statements can be made about them. In all (or nearly all) societies:

1. Most children are born into and raised in a nuclear family consisting of a father, a mother, and their children.
2. The nuclear family has sexual, reproductive, economic, and educational functions.
3. At some stage in the formation of a nuclear family, a marriage ceremony establishes new kinship relationships between a man and woman and between their respective relatives and determines some or all of the kinship relationships of their offspring.
4. Marriage is socially regulated, both by rules of exogamy that compel the individual to find his spouse outside certain kinship categories and by rules of endogamy that compel him to marry within his own group.
5. Although rules of exogamy vary greatly, they always include the prohibition of marriage between the members of an existing nuclear family.
6. The kinship position of a newborn child is established by a

ceremony soon after his birth. In all societies, someone is designated as the sociological father; he may or may not be the biological father.

7. There is no clear relationship between the forms of kinship and the technological level of a society. Some very backward peoples, like the Australian aborigines, have very complex kinship systems. The predominant kinship system in the United States is one of the simplest known.

The Nuclear Family

The modern emphasis on the nuclear family as the fundamental unit of kinship structure, owes much to the work of George Peter Murdock, whose *Social Structure*, published in 1949,[2] was an analysis of the family institutions of 250 human societies that had been studied at one time or another. This information, from a great variety of original sources, had been assembled in the files of the Cross-Cultural Survey (now called the Human Relations Area Files) at Yale University.

The overwhelming majority of the human race spend their early years in the presence of a pair of adults whom they call "mother" and "father" and of other offspring of the same adults whom they call "brother" or "sister." This is the *nuclear family*.[3] Murdock found the nuclear family in every one of his 250 societies, although in the majority of them, nuclear families are combined into larger aggregates. *The extended family consists of two or more nuclear families linked by common descent. The polygamous family consists of two or more nuclear families which have one parent in common.*

In every society studied by Murdock, sexual relationships between the married pair in the nuclear family are permitted and expected and all other sexual relationships within the nuclear family are severely prohibited. However, only a minority of societies resemble our own in regarding all sexual relationships between unmarried persons as illegitimate. In a large fraction of societies, unmarried, unrelated persons enjoy complete sexual freedom and in another large fraction, sexual intercourse is permitted between certain relatives (rather frequently, for example, between a married man and his wife's unmarried sister). Thus, as Murdock points out, the sexual relationship between spouses cannot be the principal explanation for the universality of the nuclear family. Its essential feature is the combination of four functions that are essential to the continuation of any society: the regulation of sexual relations, the provision of household labor, the physical care of offspring, and their education as social actors.

"By virtue of their primary sex differences," Murdock remarks, "a man and a woman make an exceptionally efficient cooperating unit."[4] Every society exhibits an elaborate division of labor by sex within the nuclear family. Some tasks are performed by the father, with real or play assistance from his sons; some tasks by the mother, helped by her daughters. Some tasks are carried out jointly and others may be undertaken by either sex. The distribution of tasks often seem arbitrary; in some tribes, where the women do the heavy work and the men cultivate graceful leisure activities, it may seem unnatural to us. In the great majority of societies, however, the division of labor is roughly analogous to our own. Men undertake the more strenuous tasks like construction and range further afield to hunt or trade. Women do most of the work of the household, prepare food, cultivate gardens, manufacture clothing and utensils, and are principally responsible for the care of infants and young children. In the course of his education in the nuclear family, the child acquires not only the culture of a particular society but also the subculture that goes with his family's status within that society, and a vast repertory of habits, attitudes, and skills for dealing with his immediate environment and the persons in it.

Rules of Marriage

In order to discuss this topic intelligently, we are going to need several new terms. *Monogamy is the marriage of one man with one woman. Polygamy is any form of plural marriage. Polygyny is the marriage of one husband with several wives; it occurs in many societies. Polyandry is the marriage of one wife with several husbands; it is rare. Group marriage would be the marriage of two or more husbands to two or more wives simultaneously; it is practically nonexistent.*

Of the 250 societies in Murdock's sample, 193 were polygynous, 43 were monogamous, and 2 were polyandrous. These figures are deceptive, however, since in most polygynous societies, only a few men of superior wealth or status can support two or more families and the great majority of marriages are monogamous. This necessarily is the case whenever the number of adult men and women in a society is approximately equal. Polyandry seems to occur only in societies where because of female infanticide or for other reasons, women are extremely scarce.[5] Polygyny often, and polyandry almost always, involve the plural marriage of siblings to the same spouse. That is, a man may marry two or more sisters or a woman may marry two or more brothers.

Most societies permit divorce, sometimes only at the husband's initiative or at the wife's; sometimes only for stated causes and sometimes at the free will of the parties. The terms vary too much to be briefly summarized. When the remarriage of divorced or widowed spouses is permitted, the rules and ceremonies applicable to first marriages are usually simplified. Many societies recognize several different classes of marriage. In a polygamous system, a first marriage may have more weight, require more ceremonies, and create wider kinship obligations than any subsequent marriage. In some cases, marriage may be contracted with varying degrees of formality. In Haiti, for example, marriage may take place in church, before a civil official, or by the announcement of the parties. The less formal marriages are more easily dissolved.

Exogamy refers to marriage outside one's own group. Endogamy refers to marriage within one's own group. All human societies have exogamous rules requiring the selection of marriage partners outside a specified group, and virtually all of them have endogamous rules also. In other words, the laws or the customs define for each individual a restricted number of suitable persons to marry. In some cases, the regulation is so lax that a man can marry any female in the tribe except his grandmother, mother, sister, daughter, or granddaughter. In others, it is so restrictive that he may be required, for example, to marry his mother's brother's oldest daughter and no other person.

The incest prohibition is an exogamous rule. It prohibits sexual relations—and thereby makes marriage impossible—between close relatives of opposite sex. The definition of a close relative varies greatly, even within sectors of the same family system. In some Christian societies, a man may not marry his first cousin's widow; in others he may be allowed to marry his own niece. Nevertheless, the prohibition of incest appears to be a universal social practice. Every currently existing society prohibits marriage between a parent and a child (or grandchild or great-grandchild) and between a brother and a sister.

Scholars have tried to explain the universality of the incest prohibition for more than a century without coming to a definite conclusion. The currently preferred theory is that a social system without an incest prohibition would not survive because of the disruption of the nuclear family by sexual jealousy and the disorganization of the kinship system by incompatible combinations of roles.

Rules of endogamy require the individual to select a spouse within a suitable category, that is, in such a way that the children born to the marriage will have an intelligible status. Rules of endogamy may require the individual to find a spouse within his own tribe, his own caste, or his own age group. Such rules are generally enforced either by the community's refusal to recognize the union with an outsider as marriage, or by the denial of social identity to the offspring.

Early students of kinship distinguished three types of marriage: marriage by capture, marriage by purchase, and marriage by free choice. Modern analysts regard every system of marriage as a network of social exchanges whereby family groups exchange women of childbearing age so as to maintain both social integration and biological continuity.[7]

Systems of Descent

Every normally situated individual in any society has a group of *kindred—persons with whom he has a socially recognized relationship based on descent or marriage. Consanguineal kin relationships are based on descent. Affinal kin relationships are based on marriage.*

When a newborn child enters a society, some of his parents' relatives become his relatives, but not all of them. If they did, his own kin group would be double the size of each of his parent's; the kin group of his children would be double the size of his own and, in a few generations, his descendants would have kin groups too large to be counted. Every society solves this structural problem by reckoning descent in a way that reduces the child's kin group to the same scale as his parent's. Although such rules appear arbitrary to an outsider, they usually operate by easy stages and seem perfectly natural to people who are used to them.

Patrilineal descent achieves the necessary reduction by affiliating the child to his father's consanguineal relatives and discarding his mother's kin group. Matrilineal descent affiliates the child with his mother's relatives and discards his father's kin. Double descent is an ingenious arrangement whereby each child acquires his father's patrilineal relatives and his mother's matrilineal relatives. In bilateral descent, the child is identically related to his father's and his mother's relatives and his kin group is reduced in size by dropping the remoter relatives of his parents. Of the 250 societies in Murdock's sample, 105 are patrilineal, 75 are bilateral, 52 are matrilineal, and 18 follow a rule of double descent.[8]

The predominant American system is considered bilateral, because relatives of the father and mother become relatives of the child without distinction, but it has certain patrilineal elements, and surnames are assigned as if the system were patrilineal.

Closely related to the rules of descent are the rules of residence and inheritance. *A family system is patrilocal if the wife normally goes to live with or near her husband's relatives, matrilocal if the husband normally goes to live with his wife's people, and neolocal if they are expected to set up a residence of their own.* There are some other alternatives also, such as residence with an uncle or division of the year between the mother's village and father's village. Inheritance may be patrilineal, with property descending in the male line, or matrilineal, with property descending in the female line, or bilateral, as it is with us. There is a definite linkage between patrilineal descent, patrilocal residence, and patrilineal inheritance, on the one hand, and matrilineal descent, matrilocal residence, and matrilineal inheritance, on the other; but it is by no means perfect and almost every conceivable combination of these elements is found somewhere.

The ethnologists for whom the study of kinship systems is a fascinating and inexhaustible game have been particularly interested in matrilineal societies like the Trobrianders studied by Malinowski,[9] where there is a curious transformation of parent-child relationships. Among the Trobrianders, a boy belongs to his mother's kin group and is under the authority of his mother's brother. There is not supposed to be either a legal or biological relationship between him and his father, although they are on close and friendly terms and he can always count on his father's support in a crisis. Under these conditions, it appears, some of the ambivalence aroused by the father's authority in other societies is transferred to the uncle, and the entire structure of the nuclear family is modified.

Patterns of Authority in the Nuclear Family

We must avoid the mistake of identifying matrilineal families as *matriarchal, which means wife-dominated.* In a matrilineal family, authority is usually exercised not by the wife but by her male relatives, and the status of women is not necessarily higher than in a patrilineal system. There is no known society in which husbands are normally placed under the authority of their wives or in which men are routinely dominated by women, although in a few societies—both patrilineal and matrilineal—old women may rule an extended family.

The great majority of family systems can be classified as patripotestal or equipotestal. *In the patripostestal family, the authority of the father cannot be challenged or overturned by any coalition of his wife and children. In the equipotestal family, husband and wife are not necessarily regarded as equal, but the father can be dominated by a mother-and-child coalition.* The patripotestal family is often associated with polygyny, bride purchase, patrilineal inheritance, and intense male jealousy, whereas the equipotestal family is more likely to be found with matrilineal or bilateral inheritance, monogamy, and sexual freedom.

The distribution of power in a particular nuclear family does not necessarily follow the socially accepted pattern. Henpecked husbands and domineering wives can be observed even in patriarchal family systems where the wife is supposedly on a par with her husband's cattle.[10] Instances of extreme domination by either father or mother are frequent in equipotestal family systems like our own.

Substitution and Extension of Kinship Relationships

Every kinship system includes machinery for moving persons from one kinship position to another without strict reference to biological relationships and for combining different biological relationships into a single category. An example of the first practice in our own system is the adoption by childless families of infants who are subsequently treated in every respect as if they had been born to their adoptive parents, sometimes even to the extent that the fact of their adoption is concealed from them. An example of the second type of practice is that most Americans designate their father's sister, their mother's sister, their father's brother's wife, and their mother's brother's wife as "aunt" and behave as if the four different relationships were more or less equivalent.

One important type of substitution is the designation of a sociological father *(pater)* who is not the biological father *(genitor)* of a child. This practice is widespread because some societies are ignorant or misinformed about biological paternity, because biological paternity can seldom be established with absolute certainty, and because a newborn child in any society is severely handicapped if he lacks a father of suitable status, age, and affiliation. Some of the systems for ascribing paternity that ethnologists have discovered are very peculiar indeed. In Tibetan families, the senior husband is ordinarily designated as the father of all children born to the wife; because, under certain circumstances, a widow can take the place of the senior husband as head of the household, it is possible for her to become the *father* of children born to the secondary wives of her junior husbands.[11] Among the Tiwi, an Australian tribe which insisted on the remarriage of all widows at their husband's funerals, the man who married a widow became the father of all her living children even when, as often happened, some of them were old enough to be his parents.[12]

The universal practice of combining closer and more distant relatives into a single category called by the same name and treated in the same way rests partly on the need to reduce the kinship network to manageable simplicity and partly on the need for substitutes to perform the roles of close kinsmen when the latter are missing or absent.

The tendency to classify kin is so marked among some primitive peoples that it was formerly thought to be the identifying characteristic of primitive kinship systems. Among the Tikopia studied by Firth, for example, there are 15 basic kinship terms, only 2 of which, husband and wife, describe a particular person. The word *tama*, for example, is used for a father, a father's brother, a father's father's brother's son, and for all the remoter relatives in approximately the same generation on the paternal side of the family. In everyday life, the relationship of an individual to his distant *tama* may be practically disregarded, but all *tamas* are expected to be present on the great occasions of his life; and if his father and his paternal uncles are dead, one or more remoter *tama* will take over some of their duties and responsibilities.[13]

The individual has a single set of rights and duties toward all of his *tamas* and they toward him, but the intensity of the obligation decreases as the relationship becomes more remote. We ourselves behave in a similar way toward cousins. The term "cousin" includes grandchildren of our own grandparents, who are fairly close relatives,[14] and other persons so distantly connected to us that it may be impossible to determine the exact relationship.

In addition to procedures that allow the substitution of one kinsman for another, practically all kinship systems have procedures for the assimilation of unrelated persons into the kin group by adoption or nomination. In many parts of Latin America, a newborn infant is assigned a pair of godparents to substitute for the parents if and when necessary. Sometimes affinal relatives are adopted as consanguineal —a brother-in-law may become a blood brother after a conventional ceremony. Quite often, the stranger who lives with a primitive people is assimilated into their kinship system by adoption, as Firth became the adopted son of a clan chief in Tikopia. In a small society like Tikopia, where everyone is somewhat related to everyone else, there may be no provision at all for friendly association with nonrelatives.

When we turn to the study of kinship in our own society, we are confronted with a divergence between the "American family" in general and the peculiarities of particular families. This divergence can sometimes be overlooked in discussing exotic societies,[15] but it is inescapable when we examine our own. In addition, it is plain that some sectors of the population—Appalachian mountaineers or Puerto Rican immigrants, for example—display variant forms of the family. Nevertheless, it is possible to describe the kinship system under which the majority of American families are organized, a system imposed in part by a common culture and in part by the state laws that regulate marriage, divorce, inheritance, dependency, and similar matters.

The standard family unit in the United States is a nuclear family consisting of a husband and wife and their young children, who form an autonomous household unit, share their income, take their meals in common, and are mutually responsible for each other's behavior. Children generally leave the parental home in early adulthood, whether or not they marry. The overwhelming majority do marry and form nuclear families of their own, before the age of 30. Marriage is monogamous, and all sexual activity outside the marriage relationship is theoretically prohibited although in practice a great deal of such activity occurs. Divorce is moderately easy and comparatively frequent, at the initiative of either spouse. About a third of all the marriages contracted are ultimately terminated by divorce, and about two-thirds of these divorces involve couples with children. The young children of a divorced couple ordinarily remain with their mother and continue the nuclear family in an incomplete form, but the father's obligation to support them is not terminated by divorce. Most divorced persons remarry and form new nuclear families consisting again of a husband and wife and their children or stepchildren. In the normal course of events, the nuclear family is again reduced to a married couple by the departure of the children, and ultimately extinguished by the death of either spouse.

Marriage does not involve either capture or purchase. Individuals select their own marriage partners according to the subjective criteria of romantic love. Incest prohibitions are established by law and somewhat modified by local custom. Each major religious denomination attempts to enforce a rule of religious endogamy, with partial success. Social classes and ethnic groups based on common descent enforce a considerable degree of endogamy, but do so by informal pressure rather than by formal rules. Racial endogamy is much more severely enforced; marriage between persons identified as white and persons identified as Negro was, until recently, prohibited by law in many states and still arouses intense social disapproval.

Although the newly married young couple may remain in the vicinity of either set of parents, they are expected to establish an autonomous household of their own with as little delay as possible. Parents and, in a minor way, other relatives may contribute money and goods toward the new household. The wife adopts her husband's surname at the time of marriage. Their male children, natural and adopted, carry the same surname through life; their female offspring carry it through childhood and adolescence but change it when they marry. For some occasions, the wife uses her husband's given name as well as his surname, prefixed by "Mrs." After a divorce, the wife may continue to use her husband's surname if she wishes, but not his given name. The given names of either the husband or wife and the abandoned family name of the wife may be assigned to the children as given names, but these practices are optional. The assignment of given names is the sole privilege of the parents, exercised soon after the birth of a child.

This patrilineal naming arrangement is a vestige of an older patrilineal system. Like most cultural vestiges, it still has a discernible function. The American nuclear family is expected to strive for upward mobility, and the principal avenue of achievement is the husband's occupation. The assignment of his name to all members of his nuclear family makes it easier for changes in his—and their—social status to be recognized and acknowledged.

Patrilineal naming makes the husband's ethnic and class affiliations somewhat more influential than the wife's in determining the joint status of the couple. If the husband's name is O'Reilly and he marries Miss Smith, their children and grandchildren are more likely to identify themselves as Irish than if the husband's name were Smith and the wife's O'Reilly. In the case of interreligious marriages, the religious identify of the offspring is often fixed in advance by agreement between the parents. In the case of interracial marriage, the special and peculiar rule that prevails in the United States defines the children as Negro if either parent was so defined, regardless of their appearance.

The nuclear family in the United States is clearly equipotestal, although the rights and duties of the spouses are not identical. The power distribution in each nuclear family is partly determined by local practice and partly by the interaction of individual personalities. A few families are ruled by a tyrannical father, others by a domineering mother, but the normal alternatives are that husband and wife have approximately equal influence, or one or the other is mildly dominant.[16] Parents are permitted to form coalitions with children, especially adolescent children, against the other parent. The rules of inheritance give spouses certain fixed rights in each other's property and provide for the even division of property among the surviving children of a marriage without regard to their age or sex. On the other hand, parents are free to distribute their property among their children in an unequal fashion by will, or to exclude them altogether from inheriting—a further demonstration of the independence and autonomy of the nuclear family under its dual leadership.

THE KIN NETWORK

There can be no serious question about the predominance of the nuclear family in contemporary American society. In 1966, 98.3 percent of the married couples in the United States had households of their own. Empirical studies have repeatedly demonstrated the isolation of the nuclear family from its past. A study by Codere of the genealogies of 200 Vassar College students, drawn largely from a privileged social stratum, disclosed that only 7 percent of them knew the name of a great-great-grandparent, fewer than half knew the name of *any* great-grandparent, and only 1 percent knew the names of all their great-grandparents. One out of 10 of their grandparents, 4 out of 5 of their great-grandparents, and 99 out of 100 of their great-great-grandparents had been completely forgotten.[17]

The extended family, either as a household organization or as a genealogical entity, seems to be very rare in the United States, but this does not mean that the nuclear family stands alone and without close connections to relatives. A whole series of recent studies has demonstrated the continued vitality of kin networks for urban families.[18] An individual's *kin network* is made up of those relatives whom he acknowledges and with whom he maintains some degree of contact. Although studies in different settings have found kin networks of different size, they are all in agreement on the following points:

1. Most urban families maintain relationships with some of their kin outside the nuclear family. These relationships involve sociability, joint activity, and mutual aid.
2. Kin networks are bilateral in character, including a mixture of paternal and maternal relatives, the relative numbers of which are determined by individual circumstances and choice.
3. Working-class kin networks are generally more concentrated geographically than middle-class kin networks and marked by sharper segregation of the sexes.
4. Females are more involved with their own kin than males and have somewhat more responsibility for the maintenance of kin networks than males.

THE ADAMS STUDY[19]

Bert N. Adams interviewed 797 men and women, all white, married, married only once and for 20 years or less, in Greensboro, North Carolina in 1963–1964. Of the more than 30,000 relatives known to the 797 respondents, 17 percent lived in the same community, 49 percent within a hundred miles, and 77 percent in the same three-state region. The frequency of interaction was greatly affected by proximity. Most of the respondents whose parents lived in the same community saw them more than once a week; none of those whose parents lived more than 100 miles away saw them as often as once a week. However, a fairly high rate of communication by letter and telephone was maintained with parents living elsewhere. Only 4 percent of those whose parents lived outside the region reported contact with them less than once a month. Most of these contacts were for pure sociability, but aid in either direction and joint participation in social activities and voluntary organizations were frequent. Very few respondents, however, had worked with a parent, or had even been employed in the same enterprise. Fifty-four percent of the men and 64 percent of the women reported themselves as affectionately close to their fathers; 59 percent of the men and 79 percent of the women were affectionately close to their mothers.

Eighty-eight percent of the respondents had at least one living sibling. Frequency of interaction was found to be strongly influenced by distance. When the sibling lived in Greensboro he was likely to be seen at least once a week; if he lived outside Greensboro, he was likely to be seen yearly or less often. Communication by letter and telephone with siblings was much less than communication with parents, and there was much less mutual aid and joint participation in voluntary organizations with siblings. Siblings with similar occupational positions were seen more often than those with dissimilar occupational histories. The relationship between siblings living close to each other was much closer when their parents also lived in the vicinity than when their parents were absent or dead.

The respondents were asked about their relationship with a "best-known cousin." There was a tendency for respondents to designate a cousin of the same sex, especially in blue-collar families, and the women of the sample showed a clear preference for a mother's sister's daughter, although the seven other types of first cousin were all well represented. There seemed to be a tendency for cousins to substitute for siblings. At any rate, respondents with no siblings, or with no siblings of the same sex, interacted more with their best-known cousins. Although the frequency of interaction was lower than with siblings, 60 percent of the respondents whose best-known cousins lived in Greensboro had some contact with them at least once a month. With greater distance, interaction and communication dropped off very sharply. Contact with cousins was virtually limited to sociability and ritual occasions, with practically no instances of mutual aid.

DEMOGRAPHIC TRENDS IN THE AMERICAN FAMILY

The principal long-term trends in the demography of the American family are: an increase in the prevalence of marriage, a tendency to marry earlier, a decreasing proportion of very large families, a decrease in average household size, a higher rate of home ownership, an increase in the duration of marriages broken by divorce, and an increasing tendency for divorced and widowed persons to remarry. The average duration of all marriages has been lengthening steadily, because of earlier marriage and greater survival.[20]

Some of these figures warrant closer attention. The United States Census distinguishes between a *household, composed of all persons who occupy a housing unit together,* and a *family,* which the Census defines as *a group of two or more persons related by blood, marriage, or adoption, and residing together.* There were about 50 million families in the United States in 1967. About 90 percent of them were headed by a husband and wife living together, and 56 percent of them included children under 18. The great majority of nuclear families lived alone without any relatives or unrelated persons in the same household.

The average household contained 3.38 persons in 1960, the number having slowly declined from 4.11 in 1930, 4.93 in 1890, and 5.28 in 1860.

The median age at first marriage in 1966 was 22.8 years for men and 20.5 years for women. It had been 24.3 for men and 21.3 for women in 1930, and 26.1 for men and 22.0 for women in 1890, the earliest year for which figures are available. About three out of four marriages are first marriages for both bride and groom.

Divorce statistics for the United States are exceptionally poor, but the divorce rate appears to have risen from a very low level in 1890 to a point within its present range in 1920, when the rate was 8 divorces per year per 1,000 married women. Since then it has fluctuated irregularly, going as low as 6.1 in 1932 and as high as 17.8 in 1946. The average rate in the 1960s was slightly under 10. Taking account of the probability that desertion—the "poor man's divorce"— is less common than formerly, the durability of marriage in the United States has probably not declined significantly in the past half-century. However, there is a trend for divorce to affect marriages of longer standing. In 1963, marriages broken by divorce had had a median duration of 7.5 years, and 72 percent of them involved children under 18. The majority of divorced persons remarry without much delay.

Not only does marriage occur at an earlier age; it has become nearly universal. Only 6.5 percent of the men and 5.7 percent of the women aged 45–54 were reported as single, never married, in 1966. The proportion married of the total male population (over 14) rose from 52 percent in 1890 to 68 percent in 1966; and the proportion married of the total female population over 14 rose from 55 percent in 1890 to 64 percent in 1966. These differences do not disappear when changes in the age distribution of the population between 1890 and 1966 are taken into account.

The proportion of owner-occupied dwelling units remained virtually unchanged, around 48 percent between 1890 and 1930 and then declined somewhat during the Great Depression. Since World War II the proportion has risen steadily, from 55 percent in 1950 to 62 percent in 1960 to an estimated 70 percent in 1970.

Thus, the statistical evidence suggests that the family institution in the United States is in thriving condition. The only country in the world that recorded a higher crude marriage rate than the United States in 1967 was the miniscule Republic of San Marino.[21] It is doubtful whether any other sizable country has ever had so large a proportion of the adult population married and living with a spouse as has the United States at the present time. Nevertheless, the prevailing tone of sociological comment about the family expresses alarm or anxiety much more often than satisfaction. To understand why this is so, we must go back to the family sociologists of the 1920s.

THE CHANGING FUNCTIONS OF THE FAMILY
ACCORDING TO OGBURN

William Fielding Ogburn (1886–1959) was an eminent sociologist who specialized in the study of social change. As chairman of a national commission appointed by President Hoover, he was responsible for the first comprehensive summary of social trends in the United States based on statistical evidence.[22]

Ogburn identified six major functions of the family; economic, protective, recreational, educational, religious, and "that family function which gives status to the individual." He maintained that all six functions were weakening[23] as the American family ceased to make its own soap and bake its own bread; as the protective function was transferred to the police and to insurance companies; as family recreation was replaced by commercial entertainment; as education was removed from the home to the school and the schoolteacher took over many parental responsibilities; as the influence of religion declined and religious rituals disappeared from the home; as the individual's status ceased to depend on his family; and as the choice of marriage partners became a matter of individual preference.

Comparing the urban family of the 1920s with the rural or semirural families of a generation before, Ogburn thought that all these trends were obvious. However, if we compare the urban family of the 1920s with the suburban family of the 1970s, the trends are not so clear. It is plain that the recreational function of the family has been expanding recently and possibly its relgious function also; that the transfer of educational responsibility from parent to teacher and of protective functions from the family to public agencies is no longer an unequivocal trend; and that some of the economic services mentioned by Ogburn as moving out of the home, such as laundering and handicrafts, have moved right back into it with modern appliances.

In addition to the six economic and social functions mentioned above, Ogburn identified a seventh function of the nuclear family: "furnishing media for the expression of affection," or the "affectional function." He was not sure whether it was declining. He saw some signs that its importance had been enhanced by increased emphasis on personal relationships and child development, and he supposed that the future stability of the family would depend on how well it performed the affectional function and provided psychological satisfaction for its members.

Ernest W. Burgess (1886–1966) was a contemporary and colleague of Ogburn. He developed and elaborated the description of the American family as a new type of institution that, having lost its extrinsic functions, such as economic production, education, religious training, and protection, now specialized in the development and enhancement of personal relationships. According to Burgess, writing in 1948, the American family showed the following trends:

1. *Modifiability and adaptability* in response to conditions of rapid social change.

2. *Urbanization,* not merely in the sense that the proportion of families living in the cities is increasing, but that rural, as well as urban, families are adopting the urban way of life.
3. *Secularization,* with the declining control of religion and with the increasing role of material comforts, labor-saving devices, and other mechanical contrivances like the automobile, the radio, and television.
4. *Instability,* as evidenced by the continuing increase in divorce, reaching in 1945 the proportion of one for every three marriages.
5. *Specialization* in the functions of giving and receiving affection, bearing and rearing of children, and personality development, which followed the loss of extrinsic functions such as economic production, education, religious training, and protection.
6. The *trend to companionship,* with emphasis upon consensus, common interests, democratic relations, and personal happiness of family members.[24]

Burgess concluded that with the rapid changes of modern society and the probable continuation of the trends described above, successful family life would come to depend more and more upon the mutual adaptability of husbands and wives, and of parents and children—their ability to make personal adjustments to each other and to abandon traditional attitudes and habits in favor of continuous innovation.

MARRIAGE AND FAMILY IN MIDDLETOWN

The Lynds' study of Middletown contrasted the family institutions they observed in Middletown in 1924 and 1925 with what they were able to reconstruct of the family institutions of Middletown around 1890.[25] Middletown families, they noted, shrank from an average of 4.6 persons in 1890 to 3.8 in 1920 because of a decrease in the number of children and of other dependents in the home. The married proportion of the adult population had increased and people were marrying at an earlier age, in part, said the Lynds, because of:

> the cessation of apprenticeship, which gives a boy of 18 a man's wages at a machine, the increased opportunities for wives to supplement the family income by working, the relatively greater ease and respectability of dissolving a marriage today, the diffusion of knowledge of means of contraception, and the growing tendency to engage in leisure time pursuits by couples rather than in crowds, the unattached man or woman being more 'out of it' in the highly organized paired social life of today than a generation ago when informal 'dropping in' was the rule.[26]

They noted a trend toward the secularization of marriage. The percent of Middletown marriages performed by a minister of religion had fallen from 85 percent in 1890 to 63 percent in 1923. The taboo on extramarital sexual relationships had been somewhat relaxed, although it was still very strong. The informal criteria for mate-selection did not seem to the Lynds to have changed much since the 1890s. Romantic love was regarded at both periods as the only valid basis for marriage, but in various ways parents encouraged the association of their children with young people considered suitable marriage partners. The chief qualifications sought by parents were, in a husband, the ability to provide a good living, and in the wife, the ability to "make a home" and to maintain their social contacts. Close companionship was not regarded as essential in marriage. The companionship between husband and wife varied greatly in different families, but the coming of the automobile appeared to have brought couples closer together in their leisure activities.

The divorce rate had increased very sharply. There were 9 divorces for each 100 licenses issued in the county in 1889 and 42 divorces for each 100 licenses issued in 1924. Cruel treatment was the usual legal complaint.

Contraception was a nearly universal practice in the Middletown business class around 1925. (Nothing is known about its use around 1890.) In the working class, only about half of the wives interviewed had any experience of birth control, and there was much ignorance and confusion about it.

At both periods, children were reared almost entirely in an individual home by their parents from birth to the age of 5 or 6; and from that age to 12 or 13, the home remained the dominant agency of socialization, supplemented by compulsory schooling, optional religious education, and the increasing influence of peers. Thereafter, the influence of the home began to recede. The adolescent was regarded as a kind of junior adult, increasingly independent of parental authority.

Sons were no longer likely to learn their father's trade directly from him, and high school instruction in domestic science had partly replaced the domestic training of daughters by their mothers. In the working class, children might be somewhat neglected if both parents worked.

The number of outside agencies drawing adolescents away from home had multiplied. Extracurricular school programs, the YMCA, the Boy Scouts, the movies, and auto-riding are listed among the activities of the 1925 adolescent that had been unknown to his parents in the 1890s. Use of the family automobile had become an important source of dissension between parents and children. The car was a necessity for participation in high school social activities in 1925: "A boy almost never takes a girl to a dance except in a car." In 1890, well-brought-up boys and girls were commonly forbidden to sit together in the dark, but motion pictures and the automobile had entirely lifted this taboo by 1925, making for much greater exclusiveness of individual couples. The incidence of "petting" had apparently increased, although no accurate information was available for 1890.

When Middletown mothers were asked to compare their emphases in training their children with those of their own mothers, they described "strict obedience" and "loyalty to the church" as their mothers' predominant values and also as important for themselves—but along with "independence" and "frankness." They believed that their families were far more democratic than those of their own parents had been.

Compared to families in 1890, families in 1925 were more likely to be specifically concerned with the technique of child-raising. A large literature on the subject had appeared, much of it especially directed to young mothers. In addition, shorter working hours had created more opportunities for fathers to engage in various activities with their children.

Schooling was compulsory in Middletown in 1924 and occupied children 4 to 6 hours a day, 5 days a week, 9 months of the year from the age of 6 to at least the age of 14. In 1890, education had not been compulsory, and when compulsory schooling was introduced a few years later, only 12 consecutive weeks of attendance were required. By 1924, public kindergartens permitted children of 4 and 5 to attend school also. Between 1890 and 1924, enrollment in the high schools increased three times as fast as the population, and the number of graduates increased five times as fast. By 1924 most of the children of Middletown were attending at least the first years of high school, and a considerable number were going on to college. The growth of extracurricular activities, particularly in the high school, had already developed a social world and a special culture that occupied nearly all the waking time of Middletown's adolescents.

It is plain from this brief summary that most of the characteristic features of the modern American family had already made their appearance by 1924, and it is possible that the changes that took place in the 34 years from 1890 to 1924 were more fundamental than any changes that have occurred since. On the other hand, it is apparent that even the changes from 1890 to 1924 were not as abrupt as is sometimes supposed. Many of the features of the 1924 family (or the 1970 family, for that matter) represent the continuation of trends that were already discernible in Middletown in 1890; for example, the increase of formal schooling and the softening of parental authority.

THE COURTING OF THREE GENERATIONS OF WOMEN

Another empirical study that demonstrated the slow, continuous character of social change in family institutions was Kohler's questionnaire study of courtship in a three-generation sample consisting of married, college-trained women around 1950, their mothers, and their maternal grandmothers.[27] As the investigator was quick to point out, the sample was not representative of the total population. Its members were mostly native-born, white, urban, Protestant, and prosperous to begin with, and only 43 percent of the questionnaires distributed were returned. There was probably a tendency for unconventional and unhappy courtship experiences to be omitted. Nevertheless, the results are interesting with respect to social change.

Most of the women in each generation claimed to have considered seriously only one possible husband, the man they finally married. Their mean age at the time of their first date with him was 19 for all three generations. The median frequency of dating was one date per week for the grandmothers, two per week for the mothers, and three per week for the daughters. In the overwhelming majority of cases, the men financed the dating activities, but whereas the grandmothers received gifts from their men and rarely gave any, the mothers gave gifts more freely, and some of the daughters gave more gifts to their men than they received in return. In all three generations the typical young couple visited the homes of both sets of parents once or twice a week during the later phases of their courtship. The grandmothers were engaged approximately nine months on the average, the mothers eight months, and the daughters seven months.

The discussion of problems connected with married life increased spectacularly: from 4 percent of the grandmothers who discussed marital problems with their men to 49 percent of the daughters who did so. On the other hand, the grandmothers were better acquainted with their men to begin with. Only 19 percent of them knew their future husbands for less than a year before their marriage, compared to 22 percent of the mothers and 29 percent of the daughters. The grandmothers made the acquaintance of men mostly at home or in local situations. The granddaughters were likely to meet them through school or outside activities. Somewhat unexpectedly, the grandmothers reported *less* chaperonage than either the mothers or the daughters.

Long-Term Trends in American Family Life

A steady annual increase in the duration and distribution of schooling has been a constant feature of American family life for at least a century, which is as far back as we have any useful information. The percentage of the population 5–17 years old enrolled in school increased from 57 percent in 1870 to over 70 percent in 1900 to over 80 percent in 1930 to over 95 percent in 1966. The ratio of high school graduates to the number of 17-year-olds in the population increased from 2 percent in 1870 to 6 percent in 1900 to 29 percent in 1930 to almost 70 percent in 1966.

Another long-term trend that strongly affects the American family is the increasing employment of married women in outside occupations. In 1890, only a little over 4 percent of married women living with their husbands were counted in the labor force. By 1940, the proportion had risen to 15 percent and by 1966 to 35 percent.

Discussions of modern trends in the family often hark back with perfect assurance to "the American family of yesterday," which one writer describes as:

... male-dominated, duty-bound, parent-centered, and fertile. It was made sturdy by the rigorous demands of an unrelenting work world where a man's status was measured no less by his time of rising in the morning and his industry than by his tangible possessions. It was unified in the mutual struggle for economic necessities. It gave little place to such values as happiness, personal expression, self-development, and individual rights. Life was family-centered, not individual-centered.[28]

But two interesting recent studies of earlier family patterns in the United States, one based on a content analysis of the magazines that circulated in New England during the second half of the eighteenth century, and the other based on the accounts of European travelers who visited the United States and commented on American family patterns during the first half of the nineteenth century, suggest that some of the characteristic features of the modern American family are not of recent origin. Popular literature, if not actual life, in the American colonies was dominated by the romantic love complex, and the wives of the men who signed the Declaration of Independence read stories and poems that emphasized the theme of *personal happiness* in nearly every discussion of courtship and marriage. The description of courtship practices in Colonial times does not ring too strangely on modern ears.

> ... the data suggest that the male had the power of choosing whom to court (or who was to court his daughter) but the female may have had control of the relationship through the threatened or actual withholding of affection and through "playing the coquette."[29]

By the early nineteenth century (1800–1850), it is evident from the accounts of foreign visitors that the free choice of mates was the prevailing pattern in the United States, and the norm throughout the country was that the choice of a spouse should be based on love. The foreign visitors were also struck by the American habit of early marriage and the freedom given to young women before marriage, including the freedom to leave home for extended periods, to travel alone, and to choose their own friends of the opposite sex.[30]

Marriage seemed to bring a considerable loss of freedom. Outside employment for married women was then unknown, and married women were rather secluded. On the other hand, several observers noted that women had considerable authority in household matters and a few were already anticipating the European myth that American men are dominated by their wives.

There was marked disagreement among the foreign observers about the integration of the American family. Some, like de Toqueville, believed that the atmosphere of equality and the absence of arbitrary authority developed a great deal of emotional solidarity among members of the nuclear family. De Toqueville, in effect, described the companionate family that Burgess saw "emerging" a hundred years later. Other foreign travelers believed that the American family was disintegrating and cited the fact that husbands often neglected their families for their work and spent most of their waking time away from home. Finally, nearly all the travelers commented on the permissive child-raising practices that were prevalent in America, although they disagreed about the consequences, some of them feeling that American children were pampered and undisciplined, whereas others approved their spontaneity and independence.

The principal features of the modern American family that are missing from these early nineteenth century accounts are the problems of divorce, the isolation of the aged, extramarital sexuality, and adolescent revolt. All these occurred but were not conspicuous or typical.

THE PATRIARCHAL MYTH

It is highly probable that the power of fathers and husbands over wives and children has declined considerably in the United States in the past century or so, both in the "native American" family and in various immigrant groups. The religious and legal concepts that govern American family life remotely descended from Greek, Roman, and Hebrew family institutions that were authentically patriarchal and that still give a patriarchal flavor to the language and rituals associated with the family, for example, in the custom of the father's "giving away" of the bride. But any description of paternal authority in the real patriarchal systems of ancient Greece and early Rome, for example, will show the enormous distance that separated the American family of even a hundred years ago from patriarchalism.

"Greek and Roman laws recognized in the father this unlimited power with which religion had at first clothed him. The numerous and diverse rights which these laws conferred upon him may be divided into three classes, according as we consider the father of a family as a religious chief, as the master of the property, or as a judge."[31] As religious chief, besides regulating all the details of domestic worship, the father had the right to recognize a child at its birth or to reject it, to repudiate his wife at will, to give his daughter in marriage, to permit or forbid his son's marriage, to exclude a son from the family, to adopt a stranger and, at his death, to name a guardian for his wife's children. As master of the family property, he was considered its sole owner, neither wife nor children having any part of it. His wife's dowry belonged to him without reserve; she could not own anything independently. The son's situation was the same; all that he might earn or might obtain in other ways belonged to his father, not to himself, and under some circumstances, his father could sell him without his consent.

The father alone could appear in court as plaintiff, defendant, or witness. He was considered responsible for the actions of the members of his family and had the right to judge them for most private and public offenses. If he condemned a wife or child to death, no authority could modify his sentence.

Except perhaps in tiny isolated sects, nothing like this has existed in the United States at any time in our history.

FAMILIAL VALUES

The stable and relatively permanent values that seem to be generally accepted in the United States and provide the foundation of our diverse family institutions were summarized more than 20 years ago by John Sirjamaki in eight succinct statements:

1. Marriage is a dominating life-goal for men as well as for women.
2. The giving and taking in marriage should be based on personal affection and choice.
3. The criterion of successful marriage is the personal happiness of husband and wife.
4. The best years of life are those of youth and its qualities are the most desirable.
5. Children should be reared in a child's world and shielded from too early participation in adult woes and tribulations.
6. The exercise of sex should be contained within wedlock.
7. Family roles of husband and wife should be based on a sexual division of labor, but with the male status being superior.
8. Individual, not familial, values are to be sought in family living.[32]

These statements were composed before 1948, but the values they express have not changed extensively in the interim, except perhaps that the prohibition of premarital sexual activity may have been somewhat relaxed and the insistence on superior male status within the family is no longer quite as strong.

It should not be supposed, by any means, that these values are absolutely held throughout all sectors of the population, much less that they are invariably followed in practice. But they do seem to underlie most of the diverse family patterns that have developed in the United States.

Diverse Family Patterns

The constant features of family life in our society are the autonomy of the nuclear family, the free choice of marriage partners validated by romantic love, the bilateral reckoning of kinship, relationships of friendship and mutual aid among secondary relatives, the disapproval of the extramarital sexual activity of married persons; formal disapproval but practical tolerance of the heterosexual activity of unmarried persons if they are of sufficient age and of appropriate status and no pregnancy results; the practices of supporting the nuclear family from a common purse and claiming an identical socioeconomic status for all its members; the relatively high incidence of divorce and remarriage and the consequent reorganization of nuclear families; together with a number of less important features.

The variable features are of two kinds. First, for the majority of the population, the relationships within the nuclear family are not specified in detail, so that there is an enormous range of acceptable variation in the relationships of husband and wife, parents and children, brothers and sisters. Second, in numerous subgroups of the population, especially those set apart by racial discrimination, poverty, isolation, or a combination of these factors, significant departures from the normal type of nuclear family can be observed.

VARIATIONS IN HUSBAND-WIFE RELATIONSHIPS

The range of possible variations in husband-wife relationships in families of high status is illustrated by Cuber and Harroff's study, *The Significant Americans.*[33] Their sample of 437 persons was "roughly representative . . . of the leadership echelon of decision-making, policy-forming people, the most successful as success is currently conceived." Information was obtained in structured interviews that lasted from three hours to several days and that seems to have elicited unusually frank responses. The five prevailing types of relationships among the couples are designated by the investigators as the *conflict-habituated,* the *devitalized,* the *passive-congenial,* the *vital,* and the *total.*

In the marriages of the conflict-habituated couples, there is much tension and conflict, although it is largely controlled. Their conflicts range from private quarrels more or less concealed from friends and relatives, to violent, public brawls. In these relationships, the need for controlling conflict and hostility comes to "preoccupy much of the action." In some cases, the satisfaction of a deep-seated need for conflict may be precisely what holds the marriage together.

The devitalized relationships are those whose quality and intensity have declined sharply from the earlier years of marriage. These people were once in love and closely identified with one another, but they have moved far apart emotionally while continuing to appear together, supervise their children together, and uphold their community responsibilities. Typically, there is little overt conflict between them, but their interaction has become apathetic and lifeless. People who live in such a relationship often believe that it is the appropriate or inevitable condition of a durable marriage in the middle years.

The passive-congenial relationship is similar except that it lacks the element of disillusion and emotional loss. These couples have little conflict, many common interests, and little emotional contact with one another. As the investigators remark, it is a mode of relationship that facilitates the achievement of other goals and enables people who desire personal autonomy to obtain it with a minimum of interference from their spouses.

In the vital relationship, husband and wife are intensely bound together in the important matters of their lives and the marital relationship is the center of their existence. As these couples move through their work, recreation, and family activities, they attach little importance to any activities that cannot be shared with the spouse. The intensity of their relationship may increase over time instead of declining. Couples with this sort of relationship recognize themselves as in a minority, although an appreciable one.

The total relationship is a more extreme form of the vital relationship in which husbands and wives share all their important attitudes and interests and spend most of their free time in each other's company. With regard to some relationships of this kind in the sample, it seemed to the investigators that neither spouse had a separate, private existence.

Blue-Collar Marriage, a notable study of working-class couples by Mirra Komarovsky,[34] suggests that the marital relationship shows a wide range of normal variation in this stratum also, although blue-collar marriage in general seems to be marked by greater social distance between men's activities and women's activities than is found among other classes. The Komarovsky study was based on extensive, partially structured interviews with both the husband and wife of 58 native, white, working-class couples. The husbands were mostly in semiskilled occupations. No respondent had more than a high school education. The proportion of respondents describing their marriages as happy, moderately happy, and unhappy fell into equal thirds.

The variability of their conceptions of marriage is illustrated by their reactions to a story told by the interviewer. It deals with companionship:

A couple has been married for seven years. The wife says that her husband is a good provider and a good man, but still she complains to her mother about her marriage. She says he comes home, reads the paper, watches T.V., but doesn't talk to her. He says he "doesn't like to gab just for the sake of talking." But she says he is not companionable and has nothing to say to her. *What do you think of this couple?*

In commenting upon the story, some interviewees referred to their own marriages, identifying with the fictitious couple: "Say, you know, I feel like that guy"; "That's home plate, that's right on the button"; "Why, that's a typical marriage. My husband is a lot like that, so is my cousin's husband and my sister's husband." One man asserted: "If my wife acted like that, I would straighten her out in short order."

Apart from such incidental references to personal experiences, three themes are expressed in the responses to this story. The first theme reflects the view that *the lack of husband-wife conversation in the story presents a genuine problem.* Of the 99 men and women who commented upon this story only 37 percent took this position. Not all of these blamed the husband—"Does *she* have anything interesting to say?" Some expressed resignation, while others proposed remedies. But whether pessimistic or "constructive" about the situation, these individuals share the view that it is deplorable. ...

In contrast with these attitudes, another 37 percent of the group *categorically denied that the wife in the story presents a legitimate grievance.* It is the wife who is criticized for her immaturity and selfishness—by women as well as their husbands. ...

Besides the two main types of responses, 11 percent of the interviewees read into the story a particular situation that ... is a source of great concern to women: "Maybe the husband's got something on his mind. She should leave him alone." When men appear worried, "poking at them only makes it worse. You let them alone and with time they'll come around."[35]

Responses to the story varied both with education and length of marriage. As might be expected, high school graduates were more likely to regard the lack of conversation as a genuine problem than those with less education. As might not be expected, long-married couples were more likely to regard the lack of conversation as a genuine problem than those who had been married only a few years.

Variations in Parent-Child Relationships

Much of the emphasis in the empirical investigation of parent-child relationships has been placed on differences between social classes rather than on variations among families of the same class. Kohn sums up the results of several studies by himself and others concerning class differences in parental attitudes:

> We, too, found that working-class parents value obedience, neatness, and cleanliness more highly than do middle-class parents, and that middle-class parents in turn value curiosity, happiness, consideration and—most importantly—self control more highly than do working-class parents. We further found that there are characteristic clusters of value choice in the two social classes: working-class parental values center on conformity to external proscriptions, middle-class parental values on *self*-direction. To working-class parents, it is the overt act that matters: the child should not transgress externally imposed rules; to middle-class parents, it is the child's motives and feelings that matter: the child should govern himself.[36]

Such differences are differences of degree, not differences of kind. What empirical evidence there is indicates very clearly that parent-child relationships are influenced, but not completely determined, by the social characteristics of the parents, the circumstances in which they themselves grew up, and the setting in which they raise their children.

A study of *Autocratic Family Ideology* by Glen H. Elder, Jr.[37] was based on a structured interview survey in which information about family ideology was collected from national samples of approximately 1,000 respondents in each of five countries. The dependent variable —autocratic ideology—is based on the response to a single question:

> In general, how much voice do you think children of 16 should have in family decisions?

> great deal ————————
> some   ————————

little	————————
one	————————
other	————————
don't know	————————

Respondents answering "little" or "none" were coded as having an autocratic family ideology.

The percentage of males holding an autocratic family ideology in the United States is far lower (22 percent) than in West Germany (41 percent), Great Britain (43 percent), Mexico (48 percent), or Italy (64 percent). In all these countries, the oldest members of the sample (those born before 1900) were significantly more autocratic than the youngest (born after 1930). This probably represents a long-term cultural trend, although it is conceivable that the attitudes of the older men simply became more autocratic with increasing age. In the American sample, only 31 percent of the old men and only 10 percent of the young men chose the autocratic ideology.

In all age groups there was an inverse relationship between educational attainment and the autocratic ideology; that is, better-educated persons of either sex were less likely to hold autocratic views, although this difference has recently been diminishing.

Among American male respondents, Catholics (31 percent) were more autocratic than Protestants (20 percent); migrants (25 percent) more autocratic than natives of the city (20 percent); those whose own parents had been authoritarian (28 percent) were much more autocratic than those whose parents had been democratic (16 percent). Farmers (32 percent) were more autocratic than manual workers (25 percent) or small businessmen (24 percent); respondents in professional occupations (20 percent) and white-collar workers (14 percent) were the least autocratic.

A Special Type of American Family: The Appalachian Mountaineer

In addition to the dominant family form we have been describing, there are dozens of special types that have been described by investigators studying various subpopulations in the United States. In general, distinctive family patterns are most likely to be found at the top of the class system and toward the bottom; among nonwhites; in ethnic groups that preserve some element of foreign culture; in groups with distinctive religious or ideological beliefs; and in isolated settlements. Indeed, from one point of view, there is hardly any subpopulation that does not display some departures from the dominant type, but some, of course, are more different than others. The contemporary Appalachian mountain family, as described by Jack E. Weller,[38] is a case in point.

The Appalachian mountaineers are a sizable, mostly rural population who occupy a block of mountain counties in Kentucky, West Virginia, Virginia, Tennessee, and North Carolina. They live by farming, soft-coal mining, and timbering, but mining and timbering have been declining for many years and are now nearly moribund industries. The mountain counties have low per capita incomes and high birth rates. The people are described as traditionalist, religious, and fatalistic. They are oriented to the present rather than to the future and to personal rather than impersonal relationships.

According to Weller, the social life of the mountaineer is centered on a reference group of persons of the same sex and approximately the same age who are his relatives or neighbors. The composition of this group changes very slowly over time, and it does not normally include his parents, children, or spouse.

The nuclear family is not as isolated in this region as elsewhere. Both sons and daughters want to settle near their parents. Neighbors are often kin, and the nuclear family is open enough to absorb relatives with apparent ease. The home is not a center of social activity. Meals, although generally eaten at home, are not family occasions; food is taken cafeteria-style.

Marriage is based on romantic love, but weddings are casual and unceremonious, and the romantic element disappears soon after marriage as husbands and wives lead separate lives side by side. Mutual activity, even visiting together, is rare. Spouses remain emotionally dependent on their parents and on the peer groups they joined as adolescents. There is little communication between the sexes and a minimum of heterosexual encounters.

Babies are always wanted and welcomed as giving meaning to their parents' (especially their mothers') lives. Even illegitimate children are welcomed and are seldom given up for adoption. However, children are not planned, and there is little planning for them. Their arrival does not modify the character of family life. While they are still babies, they are part of the adult world, but as they begin to grow, their parents cease to play with them and they begin to form their own reference groups. Mutual activities involving parents and children are even more unusual than those involving husbands and wives. There is little conscious training or discipline and parental authority tends to be, according to the investigator, both arbitrary and erratic. For the most part, children are raised permissively and allowed to do what they please, so long as they do not interfere directly with adults. In adolescence, the boys live their lives almost entirely in a group of other boys of about the same age and that group is a conservative solidary unit that inhibits the individual from developing any long-range goals. Girls spend more of their lives at home than boys do and are actively protected by their brothers. There is a good deal of restlessness and frustration among adolescents but little delinquency. Marriage occurs at a very early age, often because of a pregnancy.

Multiple Perspectives on the Family

The scientific study of the family is complicated by the fact that the family is a multifaceted institution, which touches in one way or another all the other institutions of any society, its total significance cannot be comprehended from any single point of view. No one theoretical model is likely to include all of the elements of family life that are legitimately interesting to social scientists. The student of the family must be familiar with a number of different models for describing how the nuclear family is organized, how it works, and what purposes it serves. It is both possible and useful, for example, to describe the family as a legal-juridical system, a stratifying system, a structural-functional system, a system of psychosocial interaction, and a dramatic system. Each of these distinctive models will be briefly described in turn.

The Family as a Legal-Juridical System

"The laws dealing with marriage," Clifford Kirkpatrick, the dean of American family sociologists, remarks, "reflect family traditions out of the past. One finds traces of the Christian doctrine reacting against the tradition of pagan Rome, Protestant-Catholic disputes of the Reformation period, the doctrine of marriage in the present tense, the teachings of both canon and common law, the assumptions of civil marriage, and vestiges of patriarchal authority."[39] The same may be said of the laws concerning annulment, divorce, custody, paternity, adoption, support, property, and inheritance—the principal subjects of family law.

This legal structure has a number of peculiarities that compound the confusion induced by its multiple sources. The most important peculiarity is that each of the 50 states has its own family laws and its own procedures for enforcing them. Thus, for example, there are no two states within which the requirements for a legal and valid marriage are exactly the same. On the other hand, Article 4, Section 1 of the federal Constitution provides that "full faith and credit shall be given in each State to the public acts, records and judicial proceedings of every other State." . . . This means that, with certain minor exceptions, marriages contracted, divorces obtained, and wills probated in any state are binding in every other state, including those in which a given marriage or divorce would have been impossible or illegal.

Another peculiarity of the laws regulating family life is that they are often unfamiliar to the general public and in conflict with the moral sense of the community. A study by Bates, Cohen, and Robson compared the Nebraska law on 17 "issues" of parent-child relationships with the moral opinions of a random sample of the state's population. The legal rules and the moral sense of the community disagreed sharply with respect to 10 of the 17 issues.[40]

This discordance goes far toward explaining why many of the laws regulating family life are unenforced and unenforceable. Adultery, for example, is a felony (a serious crime) in many states, but prosecutions for it are unknown, although conclusive evidence of adultery is presented to the courts of those same states in thousands of divorce cases. A study by Eckhardt of a sample of Wisconsin fathers placed under court order to support their minor children after a divorce showed that a majority of them were noncompliant within a year after the order was issued. By the end of five years, two-thirds of them had ceased payment entirely, and legal action against them had been virtually abandoned.[41]

Nevertheless, the laws of the several states agree on a sufficient number of points so that some general description is possible.[42]

MARRIAGE LAWS

All states permit marriage at a younger age with parental consent than without it. The minimum age with parental consent ranges from 15 to 18 for boys and from 14 to 16 for girls. The minimum age for marriages without parental consent ranges from 18 to 21 for both sexes. In all states both parties must freely consent, must be unmarried, must not be closely related, and must not be mentally incompetent. In all but a few states, persons with venereal disease may not marry, and a blood test to determine its presence is required before a wedding. In all but three states, the ceremony may be performed by a clergyman of any denomination or by any one of a great number of civil officials. Practically all states require a waiting period of a few days between the issuance of a license and the ceremony for the obvious purpose of discouraging hasty decisions; but in relation to the importance of its consequence, marriage is cheap and simple everywhere in the United States.

A marriage can generally be annulled at the instance of either spouse if, for one reason or another, it is never followed by sexual intercourse. Annulment cancels the marriage retroactively with no further consequences. Annulments are also possible, although by no means automatic, when it can be shown that one of the parties was not legally eligible to be married—for example, underage or already married—and in cases involving force or fraud.

A man who marries takes on an obligation to support his wife out of his earnings or other income in a style commensurate with his total income. This obligation remains in force for the duration of the marriage and sometimes longer, even if the wife has an adequate income of her own. Both spouses assume a binding obligation to recognize, protect, and educate any children born of the marriage and to provide them with the necessities of life until they are grown up. This obligation applies somewhat more particularly to the husband than to the wife because he is normally the breadwinner and because he is more likely to try to evade it. During childhood and adolescence parents have some rights to the earnings of their children, and under certain conditions—for example, when a husband is incapacitated and unable to work at his usual employment—he may have a certain dubious right to be supported by his wife.

Marriage gives each spouse certain rights in the property of the other. The wife, in most states, is entitled to a sizable share of her husband's estate at his death, and this right (called a dower right) cannot be changed by his will. In a few states, husbands have a corresponding automatic claim (called a curtsey right) on the estate of their wives. Real estate bought by either spouse, especially a family homestead, often becomes their joint property. In some states (called community-property states), any property acquired by either spouse after marriage must be jointly shared with the other. In contrast, children have no irremovable rights to their parents' property, but their claim to be supported while they are minors persists after the death of parents and may be asserted against a parental estate. A right to another kind of support arises whenever an adult becomes completely destitute. Under the laws of most states, he is then entitled to the support of any close relative.

A parent-child relationship can be established by adoption as well as by birth. The adoption of a child requires the consent of the natural parents and, except in the case of a baby, of the child himself. In most states, only a married couple of obvious respectability is allowed to adopt, and there are procedures for inspection and review before the state gives its consent. The act of adoption, which is ordered by a court, wipes out all the legal ties between the adopted child and his natural parents and replaces them by ties to his adopted parents, which have exactly the same weight in law as those established by birth. Indeed, in some states the court may order the preparation of a new and falsified birth certificate showing the child to have been born of his adoptive parents.

A kind of involuntary adoption occurs in paternity cases, when the natural father of an illegitimate child is officially identified and assigned the obligation for the child's support. It is a limited sort of adoption. The link is only financial, and the father is not given any rights of custody or guardianship of the child.

DIVORCE LAWS

The persons who contract a marriage undertake two closely related mutual obligations—to have sexual intercourse only with each other and to maintain a common household. The violation of the first obligation by either party is called adultery, and it is accepted as grounds for divorce in all 50 states. Violation of the second is called desertion and is also grounds for divorce. The other grounds recognized in a majority of the states are cruelty, nonsupport, alcoholism, impotence, and insanity.

Divorce in most of the states follows what is sometimes called an adversary model; that is, the law assumes an innocent party who sues the guilty party, alleging adultery, desertion, or one of the other grounds for divorce. If the accusation turns out to be justified, the court awards a divorce to the innocent party and assigns certain penalties to the guilty party—such as paying all the legal costs or (if the guilty party is the husband) paying damages to the innocent party in the form of cash, property, or a pension, called alimony. According to this model, a divorce cannot be granted unless it is possible to identify the innocent and guilty parties and adjudicate between them. Thus, if the guilty party can show that the other party is guilty also—for example, if both husband and wife have had extramarital affairs—the suit is ordinarily denied. Likewise, if it appears that both spouses want a divorce and have agreed on the means of obtaining it, the divorce will not be granted, because the law perceives a kind of conspiracy between persons who are supposed to be adversaries.

This aspect of family law represents a particularly sharp discrepancy between the moral sense of the community and the legal norm. In fact, the majority of divorces probably involve mutual consent, and a large proportion occur for reasons unrelated to the legal grounds that are offered in court. The widespread falsification of testimony accommodates the actual practices of the population to the requirements of the adversary model.

A majority of divorces involve minor children, and in all such cases, the court has the right to determine which parent shall have custody of the children and what visitation rights the other parent will enjoy. In doing so, it may choose to accept or reject the proposals of the parents themselves, which are often embodied in a contract called a separation agreement. The frequent instability of custodial arrangements has led the courts to adopt the general principle that the state is an interested party in all matters affecting the parental relationship and that it may intervene at any time to safeguard the health or interests of a child. Even the children of parents married and living together are considered to be, in a wide sense, wards of the state and can be taken from their parents if a court thinks it necessary.[43]

INEQUALITY IN FAMILY·LAW

The argument that America has two systems of family law, one for the poor and one for the rest of society, has been vigorously advanced by Professor Jacobus ten Broek of the University of California[44] and as vigorously denied by other legal experts.[45] This duality, according to ten Broek, has several sources, but including especially the laws and regulations concerning public welfare, which impose legal requirements on families receiving public assistance that are not imposed on self-supporting families. For example, he points out that although the state of California does not recognize common law marriage, the income of a man who lives with a woman in a free union is taken into account by the state in determining the eligibility of children in the household for financial assistance. His opponents maintain that the absence of such a rule would create a strong incentive for low-income couples to avoid a wedding ceremony, even though in all other respects they acted as if married.

The issue is complex and involves some highly technical points of law. It is part of a larger argument centering around the question of whether welfare recipients have a legal right to their benefit payments and, if they do, what kind of right it is.

The nuclear family is the primary unit of social class in the United States, because most of the population live in intact nuclear families and the members of an intact nuclear family are regarded as having the same social status whereas their remoter relatives may have very different statuses. It is the nuclear family that transmits the values of a particular class along with the other social values passed on to its children in their early years. With the class values go distinctive habits, attitudes, and ways of acting, although it is not always easy to determine just what these are.

Studies of the influence of social class on family life are not always easy to compare, although a vast amount of research has been done. Most American investigators have used a two-class system, composed of the middle (or business or white-collar) class and the working (or lower or blue-collar) class as their frame of reference. Middle-class breadwinners, according to one common criterion, work primarily with people and symbols; working-class breadwinners with tools and materials.

There are two important groups that cannot be fit into these two classes. We may call them the rich and the poor. The rich have large incomes that do not depend exclusively on their personal efforts, representing payments for ownership, economic control, political power, or popular fame. The poor have low incomes that likewise do not depend exclusively on their personal efforts, consisting in part of relief payments, rent and food subsidies, aid to dependent children, and pensions.

Both the rich and the poor are more numerous in the United States than in most of the other highly modernized countries, and their family patterns are distinctive enough so that it does not make too much sense to merge them into the middle and working classes, respectively. Four classes seem to be about the working minimum for an adequate description of family life in the United States. The boundaries between them must remain vague, however, and there is no reason why an investigator cannot use a frame of reference involving more numerous classes. (For some possible models of stratification, see Chapter Seven.) For example, studying one of the larger metropolitan centers of the United States, it is possible to distinguish 10 categories consisting of 6 white classes (upper-upper, lower-upper, upper-middle, lower-middle, upper-lower, lower-lower); and 4 black classes (upper-middle, lower-middle, upper-lower, lower-lower).

CORRELATES OF CLASS POSITION

Goode summarizes some of the notable correlations that have been found between class position and various traits related to family life as follows. Some of these correlations are worldwide. Others, as noted, apply only to the United States.

Toward the higher social strata, people are taller, heavier, and have higher I.Q.s.

Divorce rates and rates of juvenile delinquency are lower toward the upper strata.

The birth rate is lower toward the upper strata in most countries; but the differences between the bottom and the top strata are becoming smaller; within any *given* social stratum, the wealthier families have more children; and in some countries the upper strata may have had a higher birth rate.

The age at marriage is higher toward the upper social strata, but in the past in most countries, the nobility married *earlier.*

In the U.S., middle-class adolescents are more likely than lower-class adolescents to engage in petting; but the latter are more likely to engage in sexual intercourse.

The better-educated wives in the U.S. are more likely than the less educated to experience orgasm in sexual intercourse; but generally toward the upper social strata, the frequency of marital sexual intercourse is lower.

Middle- and upper-class husbands have greater authority over their wives and children than do lower-class husbands; in Western countries, nevertheless, the ideology and values of middle- and upper-class husbands are more likely to be permissive and egalitarian.

Upper- and middle-class families control more fully the social, dating, and courtship behavior of their children.

Toward the upper social strata, men and women travel greater distances on the average to obtain spouses.

Toward the lower social strata, a higher percentage of total social activity takes place within the kin network, but the upper social strata interact with a larger number of kin.[46]

CLASS DIFFERENCES IN CHILD-RAISING

This topic aroused widespread interest immediately after World War II, and a large number of empirical studies were carried out in the United States. Although their conclusions agreed on certain points, they were contradictory with respect to the principal issue. One set of studies seemed to show that middle-class parents placed their children under stricter discipline, with more frustration of their natural impulses, than did lower-class parents. Another set of studies seemed to show that middle-class parents were generally more permissive than lower-class parents and allowed their children more scope for the free expression of their impulses. In a famous paper published in 1958, Bronfenbrenner undertook to resolve the apparent contradiction.[47] The data of the 15 major studies he reviewed were drawn from various points in time and could be conveniently divided into two periods, before and after 1945. In the earlier period, breastfeeding and demand-feeding of infants, later weaning, and later bowel and bladder training were all characteristic of the working class; middle-class mothers consistently exerted more pressure on their infants to develop rapidly and in a prescribed way. In the later period, all these differences were reversed, and it was working-class mothers who made more demands on their babies. Bronfenbrenner then compared these curious trends with a content analysis of successive editions of the U.S. Children's Bureau *Bulletin on Infant Care,* which showed a shift of expert opinion from a pervasive emphasis on rapid training before 1945 to a contrary emphasis on permissiveness after 1945. Putting this together with other research findings that showed middle-class mothers to be more receptive to expert advice on child care than working-class mothers, Bronfenbrenner concluded that child-raising practices in the middle class were much more responsive to the expert opinions of physicians and child psychologists than child-raising prac-tices in the working class, and that middle-class mothers had been less permissive than working-class mothers in the early period and more permissive in the later. The results are somewhat similar with respect to the training of older children; middle-class parents showed a consistent shift toward permissiveness after 1945. On the other hand, their permissiveness with respect to the child's expression of his own needs and impulses was still accompanied by a high level of expectation; with certain exceptions, middle-class parents expected their young children to become independent and responsible for their own behavior at earlier ages than working-class parents did. With no exceptions, the studies show that the academic aspirations of middle-class parents for their children were higher on the average than those of lower-class parents. Putting this together with the finding that working-class parents made more frequent use of physical punish-ment, whereas middle-class parents were likely to use various forms of psychological discipline such as appeals to guilt, expressions of disappointment, and the use of symbolic rewards and punishments, Bronfenbrenner concluded that the apparent leniency of middle-class parents may conceal a greater degree of parental control than work-ing-class parents were able to exercise by the use of more direct meth-ods.

> Moreover, the compelling power of these practices, rather than being reduced, is probably enhanced by the more permissive treat-ment accorded to middle-class children in the early years of life. The successful use of withdrawal of love as a discipline technique implies the prior existence of a gratifying relationship; the more love present in the first instance, the greater the threat implied in its withdrawal.[48]

Throughout the entire period studied, parent-child relationships in the middle class were consistently reported as more egalitarian and ori-ented toward the development of the child than those in the working class, which were more authoritarian and oriented toward the maintenance of order and obedience. There was some evidence, however, that this difference had been diminishing.

Recent studies of child-raising practices among the poor have emphasized the black urban slum family, whose numbers and visibility increased very rapidly during the 1950s and 1960s in every large American city. Thirty-seven percent of nonwhite, nonfarm households were identified as poor by a government survey in 1965, compared to 15 percent of the comparable white population; 45 percent of these households were headed by a woman. According to Lee Rainwater:

> It seems very likely that as many as two-thirds of Negro urban poor children will not live in families headed by a man and a woman throughout the first eighteen years of their lives.[49]

The household, he says, is likely to include relatives outside the nuclear family. Many of them include three or four generations, with a grandmother or great-grandmother at the head. When a couple marry, they ordinarily establish their own household; when they break up, the wife either maintains the same household or moves back in with her mother or grandmother. Black slum families have more children than either white slum families or black working-class families. Thus, these families have maximum burdens and minimum resources with which to carry them. According to the same authority:

> ... we are suggesting that Negro slum children as they grow up in their families and in their neighborhood are exposed to a set of experiences—and a rhetoric which conceptualizes them—that brings home to the child an understanding of his essence as a weak and debased person who can expect only partial gratification of his needs, and who must seek even this level of gratification by less than straightforward means.[50]

Hyman Rodman, C. Wright Mills, and some other sociologists have said that the conventional description of lower-class family life as disorganized is an expression of middle-class bias. Rodman, for example, suggests that instead of viewing promiscuity, illegitimacy, and desertion as *problems* of the lower class, it would make better sense "to think of them as *solutions* of lower-class persons to problems that they face in the social, economic, and perhaps legal and political spheres of life."[51]

There is something to be said for this position, especially if one wants sociology to be completely value-free. It is certainly true that the middle-class observer of lower-class family life is likely to be influenced by the prejudices of his own milieu and to misinterpret much of what he sees. On the other hand, people brought up in lower-class families and directly exposed to the instability of lower-class family life seem to be as emphatic as middle-class observers in describing promiscuity, illegitimacy, and desertion as problems and in desiring more stable family relationships.[52]

UPPER-CLASS FAMILIES

Upper-class families are families whose claims to social privilege, influence, and political or economic power are partly hereditary. Such families exist in the United States, particularly in and around the larger cities of the Eastern Seaboard.[53] Unlike the English gentry, for example, this class has no official identity and its boundaries are not quite determinable. Of the American presidents who have held office in the twentieth century, four (the two Roosevelts, Taft, and Kennedy) were brought up in families of this type, and a fifth, Hoover, founded one of his own.

Child-raising practices in upper-class families have a number of distinctive characteristics, including emphasis on extended family relations; early exposure to European influences; early involvement in a long series of age-graded associations and the removal of children from home to boarding school in early adolescence; a rather intense athletic training for both boys and girls; and an elaborate and traditional pattern associated with courtship and intended to lead to an endogamous marriage within the same class.

THE NUCLEAR FAMILY AS A STRUCTURAL-FUNCTIONAL SYSTEM

In a long series of books and articles dating from 1942,[54] Talcott Parsons has developed a comprehensive structural-functional theory of the family. According to this theory, the institutions of a complex society change by a process of differentiation whereby some of the functions formerly carried out by a subsystem are taken over by newer and more specialized (that is, more highly differentiated) subsystems, while the original unit adapts itself more specifically to the performance of its remaining function. Parsons' view of modern society is essentially optimistic; he seems to assume that when exterior development, like industrialization, impose new demands on social institutions, these institutions evolve into new forms capable of satisfying the demands and create a new equilibrium for the system as a whole.

According to Parsons, the distinctive features of the American nuclear family are its relative isolation and its ability to move from one place to another and from one status level to another without disrupting its internal relationships. Industrialization and continuous technological change require a highly motivated labor force whose individual members are free to move from one occupation to another and who are motivated by the promises of advancement and threats of deprivation to produce as much as they can.

> Equally important to effective socialization in our society, is the maintenance by the individual of a certain level of anxiety with regard to the attainment of the required behavior for his status. This socialized anxiety plays a major role in propelling him along that cultural route prescribed by his family, school, and later by adult society at his cultural level ... with regard to upward status-mobility, in the sense of climbing the "democratic ladder," this anxiety motivation is entirely realistic and rational in our kind of

society. It is experienced both as an urge to flee from the deprivation of low status and as a pull toward the greater biological and social security of high status persons.[55]

The norms for evaluating occupational achievements are impersonal, objective, and technical. They are continuously transformed by the rationalization and improvement of productive methods. In sharp contrast, the family, having lost most of its former educational, recreational, productive, and protective functions to other specialized institutions, is now specialized in the socialization of the young and the provision of emotional support for its members. The norms of the nuclear family are sharply opposed to those of the occupational world. They are customary, habitual, and emotionally charged. In order for socialization to be carried out successfully, status within the family must be determined by age, sex, and biological relationship, rather than by industrial norms of efficiency.

The segregation of these two sets of incompatible norms is accomplished, according to Parsons, by permitting only one member of the nuclear family, the husband-father, to play a competitive role in the occupational system and by assigning other members of the nuclear family a social position based on his occupational achievement. To make this arrangement workable, the nuclear family must be separated from larger kinship units so that it can move freely in geographical and social space, and at the same time, the family role of the husband and father must be clearly segregated from his occupational role. The nuclear family, and particularly the marital relationship that is its core, must be protected against the threat of direct competition between members. This is how Parsons explains the exclusion of married women from full participation in the occupational system. Even when they work at full-time jobs, these tend to be noncompetitive, and the location and status of the family continues to be determined by the occupational position of the husband-father.

The minimization of competition within the nuclear family also requires that parents and their dependent children have the same class status. But this requirement poses a dilemma: although occupational norms call for the assignment of status on the basis of occupational achievement alone, the requirement that children have the same status as their parents means, according to Parsons, that they enter the occupational world with an initial advantage or disadvantage.

The Family as a Unit of Interaction

The study of the nuclear family as a unit of interaction within which the personality of the individual develops either normally or abnormally has two major but closely related sources: the psychoanalytic theory of Sigmund Freud and his followers and the symbolic interaction school of sociology, which traces its origins back to Georg Simmel and Charles H. Cooley. In recent research and discussion about the family, these two approaches have greatly influenced each other and intermingled to some extent.

THE PSYCHOANALYST'S PICTURE OF THE FAMILY[56]

Psychoanalysis is a theory about the development of personality and the motivation of behavior joined with a technique for treating personality disorders. The theory emphasizes the importance of the unconscious mind, of sexual factors, and of early childhood experience in determining an individual's behavior. The treatment of personality disorders involves the establishment of a close, continuous, long-term relationship between a patient and an analyst; the analyst's task is to help the patient recall his early childhood experience and to identify the elements in that experience that are still interfering with his adaptation to the social environment. Psychoanalysis envisages a human being as driven by instinct toward the gratification of (mostly sexual) desires and, at the same time, frustrated by cultural norms and social institutions that harness his energies for collective purposes. The collision between the individual's antisocial instincts and society's repressive mechanisms occurs with greatest force in infancy, when the core personality structure, which includes presocial instincts (the Id), a conscious social self (the ego), and internalized social norms (the superego), is developing.

From the psychoanalyst's viewpoint, a normal adult is one who has passed successfully through a normal sequence of development and achieved a working balance between his instinctual needs and the demands of his social environment. Development is divided into three principal stages: infancy, the latent period, and adolescence. Infancy extends from birth to age 5 or 6 and is regarded as a period of intense sexuality, divided into three substages: the oral stage, in which the mouth is the principal source of satisfaction; the anal stage, in which satisfaction is centered on the eliminative organs; and the phallic stage, in which it is attached to the genital organs. During the latent period, which runs from age 5 or 6 to the age of puberty, the individual's sexual development is more or less suspended. In the adolescent period, from puberty to about 18 or 20, sexual development involves the abandonment of the Oedipal complex, which is an unconscious desire for incestuous union with the parent of the opposite sex,[57] and the fixation of sexual desires on unrelated persons of the opposite sex, which permits the establishment of stable, satisfactory heterosexual relationships.

Psychoanalysis almost invariably seeks to explain the current emotional manifestations of its patients or subjects as expressions of emotions developed in infancy within the nuclear family and connected with the Oedipus complex and its ramifications. Thus, according to some psychoanalysts, falling in love involves identifying someone with the parent to whom one had an Oedipal attachment, on the basis of a real or imaginary resemblance, and the husband-wife relationship is based on the love or hate originally held for a parent and unconsciously transferred to the spouse.

The Family as a Unity of Interacting Personalities

The approach of the symbolic interactionists to family research has been traced back to Simmel, Cooley, and Mead,[58] but its slogan and rallying point has been a definition originally proposed by Ernest W. Burgess and later expanded by John Dollard, to wit: *the family is a unity of interacting personalities each with a history, in a given cultural milieu.*[59] What this means is that a nuclear family must be studied as a whole and within its own terms of reference. It cannot be completely understood by means of external observation, and the behavior of the whole is something more than the sum of the behavior of its parts. Any external influences that affect one member of the family will invariably affect each of the others, and the relationships of family members to each other and to outsiders are determined within the total network of relationships and shared meaning that constitute the family.

Closely linked to this perspective is the idea of a family culture, or rather of the nuclear family as an intermediate agent that transmits the general culture of a society to its children but always modifies it in the process so that each family comes to have something like a subculture of its own, with customs, value orientations, and ways of perceiving reality that are distinct from those of its neighbors.

An important practical application of these ideas is the finding of a whole series of recent studies that almost all persons suffering from schizophrenia, the most common form of insanity, come from families whose interaction patterns display certain peculiarities.[60] As described by Haley, the family of the schizophrenic is marked by a conspicuous failure to form an interaction network in which interaction is regulated by an internal status order and by the development of coalitions and alliances among family members. The schizophrenic family is leaderless, and its members are incapable of forming coalitions. Their actions often disqualify their words, or their words contradict their actions; and when they respond to each other, the responses are irrelevant to, or at cross-purposes with, the original communication.

FAMILY DRAMAS

In life or in the theater, a dramatic situation involves the resolution of a conflict in a group of emotionally related persons. Most stage plays take place within the setting of a family; this has been the case ever since the first appearance of Greek tragedy. The family is a breeding ground of intensely emotional relationships and of bitter differences of interest. There are bound to be points in the life cycle of a nuclear family when the interplay of love, hate, and material interests leads to a crisis and its resolution. The principal varieties of dramatic conflict are between spouses, between siblings, between parents and adolescent children, between parents and adult children, and among the survivors to a bereavement. Each of these situations may include third parties as the allies or opponents of family members.

SUBSTANTIAL CONFLICTS

Inside the family, as well as outside, most dramatic conflicts are *substantial; that is, they involve a dispute over the distribution of power, territory, possessions, affections, or other valuable things,* and the conflict is ultimately resolved by a redistribution or by a successful defense of the existing distribution. Needless to say, few conflicts are restricted to a single issue; as soon as closely related persons move into opposition, other elements of their relationship are brought into question.

In addition to resolvable conflicts over substantial issues, many family sociologists attach a good deal of importance to *unresolvable conflicts based on incompatibility of temperament, appetites, habits, and preferences. They are called tensions.*[61] Their importance in relation to substantial conflicts is difficult to gauge in the present state of knowledge, but it can hardly be doubted that substantial conflicts may be provoked or intensified by tensions between the parties and that such tensions often originate in the course of substantial conflicts.

The American nuclear family is particularly susceptible to conflicts about power because the power of the husband over the wife, which arises from his initial control of the family income, and the power of parents over children, which arises from the circumstances of infancy and early childhood, are not reinforced by social sentiments and religious values to the same extent as in other cultures. Power, in other words, is not fully legitimized as authority. A wife can attempt to gain dominance over her husband without violating social norms. The adolescent who defies his parents is not treated either as a criminal or as a sinner. In more general terms, the tendency of children to gain in power relative to their parents, as they grow older and larger, is not counterbalanced by social norms. Parents suffer a real and involuntary loss of power as their children mature, and the process may be hastened by a parent-child coalition directed at the other parent, or by a coalition of children against parents.[62]

Conflicts over territory are relatively unimportant in the modern nuclear family, since the collective control of the family over its physical territory (house, apartment, farm, boat, cabin, and so forth) is seldom challenged, and a member of the family who has possession of a portion of the territory may not completely exclude the others. Conflicts over symbolic territory occur more often, because the division of household labor between husband and wife, male and female, and older and younger children is somewhat variable.

Conflicts over possessions are likely to occur between siblings, and between parents and adolescent children. Young children in the American nuclear family receive a constant stream of gifts and other purchased objects—toys, books, appliances, furniture, clothing—to which they are expected to attach symbolic as well as practical value, but to which they have no secure and well-defined title. A parental fiat can deprive the child of any piece of his property at any time or compel him to share it with a sibling. The conflicts between parents and adolescent children over material property is another aspect of their unsettled authority relationship. In the normal course of events, the child progressing through adolescence claims more and more independence and accepts less and less parental authority. From the parents' standpoint, the adolescent's increasing independence ought to be matched by a decreasing claim on the family's material resources. As the adolescent sees it, an increasing allocation of resources is necessary to establish his autonomy (for example, a car of his own); and since his emancipation is favorably regarded by the environing society, his parents have an obligation, from his standpoint, to provide the necessary means.

Conflicts over love arise in the nuclear family partly because its norms are inconsistent. Most marriages in our family system are contracted by a man and a woman who are in love and expect to remain so. Marriage establishes mutual obligations that are permanent and that seem to the parties to imply the indefinite continuation of the love affair that led to their marriage. At the same time, according to the accepted cultural beliefs, love is spontaneous, arbitrary, unpredictable, and above all, not subject to the lover's control. If husband or wife fall out of love with each other or fall in love with a third person (these events are likely to be linked) the romantic norms on which the family was founded seem to justify the abandonment of the marriage in favor of the new relationship, whereas the social and legal norms governing family life demand the opposite behavior. Since the romantic criterion for "true love" is subjective, such cases usually invite a dispute over the facts. The outside love will probably appear spurious to the abandoned spouse and not entitled to the benefits of the romantic norms. On the other hand, falling out of love is also part of the romantic complex,[63] and a claim to have done so is hard to refute. Triangular conflicts of this kind provide the theme for an amazingly large proportion of all stage plays and films.

The norms of the nuclear family seem to require parents to love their children equally, regardless of differences in sex, age, and temperament—a requirement that is manifestly impossible. Another norm requires children to love both parents equally. Both requirements seem to contradict certain instinctive tendencies, for example, the tendency for members of a primary group to form permanent coalitions and the tendency for a division of labor to occur with respect to affective (that is, emotional) functions. Freudian theory goes much further than this and supposes a general tendency for fathers to prefer daughters and mothers to prefer sons and for these preferences to be reciprocated. The most destructive and dramatic forms of family conflict occur when the two foregoing themes are united in the same situation, that is, when a parent and child of opposite sex develop a romantic attachment that arouses the jealousy of the other parent and of other children. Another characteristic type of conflict occurs when an adolescent or young adult exercises his right of free romantic choice and falls in love with someone who appears disagreeable or threatening to other members of the nuclear family. Romeo's family are hereditary enemies of Juliet's family, and Romeo himself has done unforgivable harm to the Montagues. In ordinary life, equally intense passions can be aroused by the suitor who is too old, too young, of the wrong religion or the wrong color, or too high- or low-ranking to be trusted.

This type of conflict merges insensibly with the other conflicts that occur within nuclear families whose members belong to outside organizations that impinge on family life in various ways and arouse inconsistent loyalties. Families whose members belong to different churches or opposing political parties, or to any other hostile factions, cannot easily insulate the internal relationships of the family from the external conflicts involving family members. Although the majority of marriages are homogamous with respect to religion, race, and social class, and although most married couples move closer to each other in their affiliations and opinions in the course of married life, some couples diverge instead and develop new differences as they go along. And it is quite normal for adolescents to join causes and develop loyalties of which their parents disapprove.

In life, as on the stage, the outcome of a dramatic conflict is a resolution that may be tragic or comic or a mixture of both. In about a third of all nuclear families, the marital conflicts are ultimately too severe to contain, and the family is broken by divorce, separation, or abandonment. Where the marriage remains intact, intergenerational conflict is sometimes severe enough to prevent any close relationship between parents and their adult children. Needless to say, families that do not break up may conceal all sorts of private disasters in their cupboards.

On balance, the American family system cannot be described as a total success or as a failure. Most members of most nuclear families are able to lead normal lives and to perform the social roles assigned to them. Their happiness, however, is not guaranteed; it must be individually achieved.

1   Every known human society has a kinship system, including the social regulation of marriage and descent. In practically all societies, most children are born into and raised in a nuclear family that consists of a father, a mother, and their offspring; combines sexual, reproductive, economic, and educational functions; and embodies a customary division of labor by sex and age.

2   The conspicuous features of the contemporary American kinship system include the autonomy of the nuclear family; individual, romantic selection of marriage partners; partial religious and racial endogamy; a patrilineal naming system; and an equipotestal distribution of parental authority. There is considerable reliance on extended kin for sociability and mutual aid.

3   Among the principal long-term trends of the American family are increases in prevalence and duration of marriage, a decrease in average family size, and an increasing tendency for divorced and widowed persons to remarry, together with steady increases in the amount of schooling for children and in the employment of married women, and some loss of family functions to outside agencies. On the other hand, there is evidence that some of the values that characterize family life in the United States have remained almost unchanged for generations.

4   The total significance of the family cannot be comprehended from any single point of view. It can be approached, for example, in terms of law, stratification, structure and function, psychosocial interaction, or dramatic conflict. Each of these models generates a valid description of family institutions and emphasizes a distinct set of problems.

Questions for Discussion / **CHAPTER TEN**

1 King Solomon had a thousand wives, including the Queen of Sheba. Was he polygynous or polyandrous? Exogamous or endogamous? How would his wives be related to each other—consanguineally, affinally, or not at all?

2 Describe the division of labor by sex and age that prevailed in your own family when you were 10 years old.

3 According to Murdock, "By virtue of their primary sex differences, a man and a woman make an exceptionally efficient cooperating unit." Defend or criticize this statement.

4 What might be the novel features of a family system based on the principles of the Women's Liberation Movement?

5 List in three columns all the living first cousins, second cousins, and third cousins whose names you know. How many of each have you seen in the past year? What accounts for this pattern?

Recommended Reading / **CHAPTER TEN**

Kirkpatrick, Clifford. *The Family as Process and Institution,* 2nd ed. New York: Ronald Press, 1963; and William M. Kephart, *The Family, Society and the Individual,* 2nd ed. Boston: Houghton Mifflin, 1966. Two excellent textbooks on family sociology.

Lewis, Oscar. *The Children of Sanchez: Autobiography of a Mexican Family.* New York: Random House, 1961. One of the few thorough accounts of personal interaction in a single family.

Rainwater, Lee, and William L. Yancey. *The Moynihan Report and the Politics of Controversy.* Cambridge, Mass.: M.I.T. Press, 1967. Presents both sides of a controversy about the structure and function of the black, lower-class urban family.

Notes / **CHAPTER TEN**

1. Adapted from the definition in Fred Eggan, "Kinship," in *International Encyclopedia of the Social Sciences*, ed. David L. Sills, 8 (New York: Macmillan and Free Press, 1968): 390–401.
2. George Peter Murdock, *Social Structure* (New York: Macmillan, 1949), is the principal, although not sole, source of the generalizations in this section.
3. Although some of the details of Murdock's analysis have been challenged, and it is not certain that the nuclear family is the basic social unit in every society, the exceptions, if they exist, are rare and numerically unimportant. See, for example, William N. Stephens, *The Family in Cross-Cultural Perspective* (New York: Holt, Rinehart & Winston, 1963), pp. 12–33.
4. Murdock, *Social Structure*, p. 7.
5. The handful of exceptions known to history are very special cases: for example, brother-sister marriages in families considered to be of divine origin and not subject to human regulation, notably the Incas of Peru and the Pharaohs of ancient Egypt. Middleton has produced evidence from inscriptions that brother-sister marriage was also practiced among commoners in ancient Egypt, but the historical distance is too great to permit any explanation. See Russell Middleton, "Brother-Sister and Father-Daughter Marriage in

Ancient Egypt," *American Sociological Review* 27, no. 5 (October 1962): 603–611.

7. The authoritative statement of this viewpoint is found in Claude Lévi-Strauss, *Structural Anthropology,* trans. Claire Jacobson and Brooke Grundfest Schoepf (New York: Basic Books, 1963).

8. Murdock, *Social Structure,* p. 59.

9. Bronislaw Malinowski, *The Father in Primitive Society* (New York: W.W. Norton, 1927).

10. See, for example, the description of marital relationships in Thomas Rhys Williams, *The Dusun: A North Borneo Society* (New York: Holt, Rinehart & Winston, 1965).

11. Prince Peter of Greece, *A Study of Polyandry* (The Hague: Mouton, 1963).

12. Charles William Merton Hart and Arnold R. Pilling, *The Tiwi of North Australia* (New York: Holt, Rinehart & Winston, 1966).

13. Raymond Firth, *We, the Tikopia: A Sociological Study of Kinship in Primitive Polynesia* (London: George Allen & Unwin, 1936).

14. In a sample of 140 respondents, mostly college students, questioned by Robins and Tomanec, nearly 400 moderately close relationships with first cousins were reported. Lee N. Robins and Miroda Tomanec, "Closeness to Blood Relatives Outside the Immediate Family," in *Kinship and Family Organization,* ed. Bernard Farber (New York: John Wiley, 1966), pp. 134–141.

15. "For example, the family which time and time again has been described as *the traditional Chinese family* was certainly the ideal family of that society, but it was also certainly never the actual family of any except for a small proportion of the members of that society." Martin J. Levy, Preface to Ansley J. Coale, et al., *Aspects of the Analysis of Family Structure* (Princeton, N.J.: Princeton University Press, 1965), p. 9.

16. Empirical evidence for this statement can be found in Charles E. Bowerman and Glen H. Elder, Jr., "Variations in Adolescent Perception of Family Power Structure," *American Sociological Review* 29, no. 4 (August 1964): 551–567.

17. Helen Codere, "A Genealogical Study of Kinship in the United States," *Psychiatry* 18, no. 1 (February 1955): 65–79. For additional evidence on the limitation of family history to two or three ascending generations, see Alice S. Rossi, "Naming Children in Middle-Class Families," *American Sociological Review* 30, no. 4 (August 1965): 499–513.

18. Much of this research is summarized in two papers by Marvin B. Sussman and Lee G. Burchinal, "Kin Family Network: Unheralded Structure in Current Conceptualizations of Family Functioning," *Marriage and Family Living* 24, no. 3 (August 1962): 231–240; and "Parental Aid to Married Children: Implications for Family Functioning," *Marriage and Family Living* 24, no. 4 (November 1962): 322–332.

19. Bert N. Adams, *Kinship in an Urban Setting* (Chicago: Markham, 1968).

20. The detailed evidence for all these trends can be found in U.S. Bureau of the Census, *Historical Statistics of the United States: Colonial Times to 1957* (Washington, D.C.: U.S. Government Printing Office, 1957), secs. A and B; and U.S. Bureau of the Census, Department of Commerce, *Statistical Abstract of the United States* (Washington, D.C.: U.S. Government Printing Office, 1968) and later editions, secs. 1 and 2.

21. United Nations, Statistical Office, Department of Economic and Social Affairs, *Demographic Yearbook* (New York: United Nations, 1967), table 30.

22. President's Research Committee on Social Trends, *Recent Social Trends in the United States,* 2 vols. (New York: McGraw-Hill, 1933).

23. The description of declining family functions is found in several of his writings. The best source is William F. Ogburn, "The Changing Family," *Publications of the American Sociological Society* 23 (1929): 124–133.

24. Ernest W. Burgess, "The Family in a Changing Society," *American Journal of Sociology* 53, no. 6 (May 1948): 417–418.

25. Robert S. Lynd and Helen Merrell Lynd, *Middletown: A Study in American Culture* (New York: Harcourt Brace Jovanovich, 1929).

26. *Ibid.,* p. 111.

27. Marvin R. Koller, "Some Changes in Courtship Behavior in Three Generations of Ohio Women," *American Sociological Review* 16, no. 3 (June 1951): 366–370.

28. Paul H. Landis, "The Changing Family," *Current History* 19, no. 109 (September 1950): 151–153. The quotation is from p. 151.

29. Herman R. Lantz, Eloise C. Snyder, Margaret Britton, and Raymond Schmitt, "Pre-industrial Patterns in the Colonial Family in America: A Content Analysis of Colonial Magazines," *American Sociological Review* 33, no. 3 (June 1968): 413–426.

30. Frank F. Furstenberg, Jr., "Industrialization and the American Family: A Look Backward," *American Sociological Review* 31, no. 3 (June 1966): 326–337.

31. Numa Denis Fustel de Coulanges, *The Ancient City: A Study on the Religion, Laws, and Institutions of Greece and Rome* (Garden City, N.Y.: Doubleday, n.d.), pp. 90–94. The quotation is from p. 90. Originally published 1864.

32. John Sirjamaki, "Culture Configurations in the American Family," *American Journal of Sociology* 53, no. 6 (May 1948): 464–470.

33. John F. Cuber and Peggy B. Harroff, *The Significant Americans: A Study of Sexual Behavior Among the Affluent* (New York: Appleton-Century-Crofts, 1965).

34. Mirra Komarovsky, *Blue-Collar Marriage* (New York: Random House, 1962).

35. *Ibid.,* pp. 114–117.

36. Melvin L. Kohn, "Social Class and Parent-Child Relationships: An Interpretation," *American Journal of Sociology* 68, no. 4 (January 1963): 475.

37. Glen H. Elder, Jr., "Role Relations, Sociocultural Environments, and Autocratic Family Ideology," *Sociometry* 28, no. 2 (June 1965): 173–196.

38. Jack E. Weller, *Yesterday's People: Life in Contemporary Appalachia* (Lexington, Ky.: University of Kentucky Press, 1965). For descriptions of other variant forms of the family in the United States, see, among others: E. Franklin Frazier, *The Negro Family in the United States* (Chicago: University of Chicago Press, 1939); Kenneth B. Clark, *Dark Ghetto: Dilemmas of Social Power* (New York: Harper & Row, 1965); Clarence Senior, *The Puerto Ricans of New York City* (Washington, D.C.: Office of Puerto Rico, 1948).

39. Clifford Kirkpatrick, *The Family as Process and Institution,* 2nd ed. (New York: Ronald Press, 1963), p. 421.

40. Julius Cohen, Reginald A. H. Robson, and Alan Bates, *Parental Authority: The Community and the Law* (New Brunswick, N.J.: Rutgers University Press, 1958).

41. Kenneth W. Eckhardt, "Deviance, Visibility and Legal Action: The Duty to Support," *Social Problems* 15, no. 4 (Spring 1968): 470–477.

42. Kirkpatrick, *The Family as Process and Institution,* table 31, "Marriage Laws as of July 31, 1961," p. 424; and table 40, "Divorce Laws as of July 1, 1961," p. 596.

43. For a more extended discussion of the family as a legal system, see K. Imogene Dean and M. W. Kargman, "Is There a Legal Conceptual Framework for the Study of the American Family?" in *Emerging Conceptual Frameworks in Family Analysis,* ed. F. Ivan Nye and Felix M. Berardo (New York: Macmillan, 1966): 269–292.

44. Jacobus ten Broek, "California's Dual System of Family Law: Its Origins, Development, and Present Status," *Stanford Law Review,* 3 parts: 16, no. 2 (March 1964): 257–317; 16, no. 4 (July 1964): 900–981; 17, no. 4 (April 1965): 614–682.

45. Thomas P. Lewis and Robert J. Levy, "Family Law and Welfare Policies: The Case for 'Dual Systems'," *California Law Review* 54, no. 2 (May 1966): 748–791.

46. William J. Goode, *Family and Mobility: A Report to the Institute of Life Insurance* (mimeograph, 1964), pp. 4–5. An abbreviated version of this important study is reproduced in *Class, Status and Power: Social Stratification in Comparative Perspective,* ed. Reinhard Bendix and Seymour Martin Lipset, 2nd ed. (New York: Free Press, 1966), pp. 582–601.

47. Urie Bronfenbrenner, "Socialization and Social Class Through Time and Space," in *Readings in Social Psychology,* ed. Eleanor E. Maccoby, Theodore M. Newcomb, and Eugene L. Hartley, 3rd ed. (New York: Henry Holt, 1958), pp. 400–425.

48. *Ibid.,* p. 419.

49. Lee Rainwater, "Crucible of Identity: The Negro Lower-Class Family," in *The Negro American,* ed. Talcott Parsons and Kenneth B. Clark (Boston; Beacon Press, 1965), p. 169.

50. *Ibid.,* pp. 193–194.

51. Hyman Rodman, "Middle-Class Misconceptions About Lower-Class Families," in *Marriage, Family and Society: A Reader,* ed. Hyman Rodman (New York: Random House, 1965), pp. 219–230.

52. See, for example, the studies by Frazier, Clark, and Senior, cited above.

53. See, among many other sources, E. Digby Baltzell, *Philadelphia Gentlemen: The Making of a National Upper Class* (New York: Free Press, 1966); and for a more general discussion, Edward N. Saveth, "The American Patrician Class: A Field for Research," *American Quarterly* 15, no. 2, part 2 (summer supplement, 1963): 235–252.

54. Among Talcott Parsons' very numerous writings on the family, the most representative are, perhaps, "The Social Structure of the Family," in *The Family: Its Function and Destiny,* ed. Ruth N. Anshen, 2nd ed., (New York: Harper & Row, 1959); with Robert F. Bales, *Family, Socialization and Interaction Process* (New York: Free Press, 1955); "The Normal American Family," in *Man and Civilization: The Family's Search for Survival: A Symposium,* ed. Seymour M. Farber, Piero Mustacchi, and Roger H. L. Wilson (New York: McGraw-Hill, 1965), pp. 31–50.

55. Parsons, op cit.

56. For an admirably succinct introduction to the psychoanalytic view of the family, see Alan E. Bayer, "The Psychoanalytic Frame of Reference in Family Study," in *Emerging Conceptual Frameworks in Family Analysis,* ed. Nye and Berardo, pp. 152–175.

57. Freud used the term *Oedipus complex* for both son-mother and daughter-father attachments; some of his followers prefer *Electra complex* for the latter. Sigmund Freud, *General Introduction to Psychoanalysis,* rev. ed., trans. Joan Riviere (New York: Garden City Books, 1952), originally published 1917.

58. Sheldon Stryker, "The Interactional and Situational Approaches," in *Handbook of Marriage and the Family,* ed. Harold T. Christenson (Chicago: Rand McNally, 1964), pp. 125–170.

59. For a history of the influence of this definition, see Jay D. Schvaneveldt, "The Interactional Framework in the Study of the Family," in *Emerging Conceptual Frameworks in Family Analysis,* ed. Nye and Berardo, pp. 97–129.

60. Most of these studies are reported or referred to in Gerald Handel, ed., *The Psychosocial Interior of the Family* (Chicago: Aldine, 1967). See especially Jay Haley, "The Family of the Schizophrenic: A Model System," pp. 251–275.

61. Willard Waller, *The Family: A Dynamic Interpretation* revised by Reuben Hill (New York: Dryden Press, 1951), pp. 298–300.

62. For a discussion of coalitions in the nuclear family, see Theodore Caplow, *Two Against One: Coalitions in Triads* (Englewood Cliffs, N.J.: Prentice-Hall, 1968), chap. 6, pp. 62–94.

63. Romantic love seems to be a very widespread phenomenon, not a peculiarity of our own culture. See William J. Goode, "The Soci-

ology of the Family: Horizons in Family Theory," in *Sociology Today: Problems and Prospects,* ed. Robert K. Merton, Leonard Broom, and Leonard S. Cottrell, Jr. (New York: Basic Books, 1959), pp. 178–196.

Deviance

XI

Deviance is behavior that violates explicit social norms and elicits
corrective or punitive reactions from norm-enforcing agents. This definition is a little complicated at first glance but it is the result of many
years of effort by sociologists to describe certain social phenomena
with a minimum of personal and class bias.[1]

The study of deviance belongs to the larger field of *social problems,*
which inherits the preoccupation of early American sociologists with
"vice, crime and misery." This larger field has also been called *social
pathology* and *social disorganization.* It might be summarily defined
as the study of trouble, and of the ways individuals and social systems
get in and out of trouble. A recent book on social problems divides its
subject matter into four major categories: problems of the life cycle,
problems of deviance, problems of community and nation, and world
problems.[2] Included in the volume are papers on adolescence as a
social problem, work as a social problem, and on race relations, popular culture, housing, war, population, and national development as
social problems. All these applications of the term are familiar and
legitimate.

*A social problem is any aspect of any society that is designated by
anyone as a subject of public concern.* Leisure as well as work,[3] education as well as delinquency, and science as well as illiteracy are
nowadays often identified as social problems. In societies like our
own, with rapidly advancing technologies, rapidly growing populations, and high rates of horizontal and vertical mobility, many institutional changes occur. Nearly every institutional change makes some
people uncomfortable or apprehensive, thus creating innumerable social problems.

Deviance is always a social problem but not all social problems
involve deviance. The definition of a social problem is essentially arbitrary. You can make the increasing average height of the population
into a social problem if you are troubled by it and invite other people
to share your concern. But you can never demonstrate the existence
of a social problem to people who do not share your values and concerns. Deviance has a more objective character. Whether a particular
type of behavior is deviant in a given social system at a given moment
of time can be empirically determined. If the behavior violates a norm
that is codified in laws, rules, or customs; if it is recorded in predeter-

mined ways and there are social agents capable of enforcing the norm (whether or not they do so in the particular case), it can be *proved* in effect that the given behavior is deviant.

Anomie and Delinquent Subcultures

Despite its objective character deviance is a very complicated phenomenon. Most types of deviance are difficult to explain, even after prolonged study, and more difficult to cure. It is much too simple to regard the deviant as an individual who defies the rules of society and is punished if caught. There is a mountain of evidence to show that deviance is itself socially patterned. This means, among other things, that:

1. The force of a norm varies from time to time and from one position to another in a social system. When norms are weakened, for any combination of reasons, the amount of deviance rises. When norms are strengthened, the amount of deviance declines.
2. More often than not, deviant acts are committed by, or sponsored by, large groups of people rather than by isolated individuals. In some cases, the norms of a group *require* members to violate the norms of the larger society and punish those who fail to do so.
3. If a particular form of deviant behavior becomes more frequent, the legitimacy of the norm that forbids it is diminished until the norm disappears or is revived by new means of enforcement.

The loss of confidence in social norms is called anomie. The term was introduced by Durkheim and was one of the principal themes of his study of suicide.[4] According to Durkheim, the principal source of anomie is a disruption of the equilibrium between desire and fulfillment or, in modern terms, between aspiration and achievement. Any sudden change in social conditions, even a favorable change, induces anomie by disturbing the relationship between the routine activities of individuals and their life goals.

Robert Merton's famous paper on social structure and anomie,[5] first published in 1938, described the anomie induced in a society that places a high value on individual success but distributes opportunities for success unevenly. According to Merton, when people confront the fact that they are unable to achieve their culturally induced aspirations by conventional means, they may show one of four different reactions. They may "hold fast to the culturally emphasized goals while abandoning culturally approved ways of seeking them"; or "reluctantly abandon their aspirations while clinging perhaps on that account all the more tightly to the routines of their roles"; or "withdraw altogether from the struggle for place giving up both their hopes and the comparative safety of routinely abiding by the rules"; or "repudiate a range of culturally prescribed goals and means but . . . seek in concert to develop new ones having their own claims to legitimacy." These types of anomic reaction are labeled *innovation, ritualism, retreatism,* and *rebellion.*

This theory holds that deviant acts are more likely to be committed by anomic individuals than by fully socialized individuals who accept the legitimacy of the norms. (No one suggests that *all* deviant acts are committed by anomic individuals.) It further proposes that if the degree of anomie in a social system increases, the probability of deviant acts will increase both for anomic and nonanomic members of that system, but it will increase more for those who are anomic.

The great popularity of the foregoing theory as an explanation of deviant behavior in the United States may be related to certain aspects of American society that are not really shared with other technologically advanced countries. Among these are the concentration of crime and other forms of deviant behavior in urban slums inhabited by ethnic minorities (a situation that has prevailed ever since the great Irish immigration of the 1840s, although the minorities involved have changed several times) and the prevalence of illicit institutions. Some illicit institutions can be blamed on the American habit of enacting legislation to control the habits of the population in a manner that creates lucrative markets for illicit goods and services. Others are attributable to a tradition of lawlessness and a diversity of law enforcement agencies that allow dishonest business practices, and political corruption to flourish in many forms. Neither urban slums nor illicit institutions are unknown elsewhere, but they are not as conspicuous in any other technologically advanced country.

TRENDS IN ANOMIE AND DEVIANT BEHAVIOR

Durkheim viewed anomie as an intermittent interruption of the equilibrium between aspiration and achievement in a population, associated with cyclical events like financial crises and unique events like political revolutions. He did not suppose that anomie had any steady tendency to increase over time or that it was a function of modernization, although he attributed the egoistic type of suicide to the decline of the intense collective life that characterized traditional societies. The belief that anomie increases steadily with urbanization, population growth, and technological progress is an American amendment to Durkheim's theory that has gained wide acceptance without much empirical evidence. When empirical tests are made, the results seem to support Durkheim's opinion that increases of deviant behavior follow specific events that disturb the equilibrium of a national society. There does not seem to be any inexorable upward trend of deviant behavior in modern societies; several types of deviant behavior show long-term downward trends, as we will see. However, long-term trends in deviance are obscured by continuous changes in the substance of the norms, so that the norm violations of one era become innocuous in the next and vice versa. Public nudity or seminudity, for example, was permitted in 1970 to an extent that would have been inconceivable in 1900; but the use of narcotics was freely permitted in 1900, and severely punished in 1970. There are tides of fashion in norms, norm enforcement, and norm violation; and the force of these tides is now greatly enhanced by the constant attention of the mass media.

Most of the norms that a large civilized society takes seriously find expression in its laws. Most of the acts that can be identified as deviant are so defined by laws, and if these were repealed or fell into disuse, the behavior would no longer be clearly identifiable as deviant. For example, the practice of contraception and the dissemination of information about contraceptive methods were formerly prohibited in many parts of the United States; these prohibitions have now lapsed everywhere in the country. It would be absurd to classify the practice or diffusion of contraception as deviant behavior (except within those religious groups that have continued to enforce their own prohibitions of contraception.) Consequently, it is practical and convenient to identify some types of deviant behavior by reference to the laws that define them as deviant and the enforcement practices to which those laws give rise.

The forms of deviance to be discussed in this chapter are all recognized by law, as well as by widely held informal norms. They are old, relatively stable, and widely familiar types of behavior, found in every large social system, and can be classified for our present purposes as follows:

1. Crimes against persons and property
2. Suicide
3. Deviant sexual relationships
4. Deviant habits

OMITTED FORMS OF DEVIANCE

The foregoing classification by no means exhausts the catalog of deviant acts, or of culture complexes associated with deviant behavior. A comprehensive review of deviance in contemporary society would be too vast a project for the space available here, and so we have omitted any discussion of organized crime, that is, crime as a business; of deviant life styles, like those of the commune or the motorcycle gang; of traffic violations and other offenses that are handled by criminal procedures without arousing any moral sentiments; or of the riots, protests, sit-ins, and other public demonstrations that occur in large national societies when their political institutions are changing.

Mental disorder is another type of behavior that is sometimes classified as deviant. It will not be considered here, because the behavior of the schizophrenic or paranoid patient is generally perceived in our society as symptomatic of an illness, analogous to an infectious disease, rather than as a pattern of nonconformity to social norms. The distinction is admittedly hazy, however. On the one hand, mental patients are often treated punitively in and out of mental hospitals, and on the other hand, almost any type of deviance can be attributed to environmental factors and described in quasi-medical terms.

We have also omitted, because of space limitations, deviance from the specialized norms of particular organizations. There are several Protestant denominations for whom dancing is a form of deviant activity. Almost every occupation, social movement, peer group, association, and household has some such norms of its own and limited means of enforcing them.

Crimes Against Persons and Property

Murder, rape, and assault are crimes against persons. Burglary, theft, and embezzlement are crimes against property. Robbery is both.

These are ancient primeval crimes, known to the Old Testament and the Code of Hammurabi, defined as deviant by every society that has laws. The recognition and punishment of these basic offenses is a cultural universal,[6] but cultural variation enters to exempt certain acts and to discriminate degrees of severity.[7] Not all deliberate killings are murder. Most legal systems provide for deliberate killings that are not criminal at all, in self-defense and war, for example. The severity of an offense varies with the status of the offender and of the victim, their relationship, and other circumstances. In some societies, the murder of a guest is the most heinous of possible offenses, in others the murder of a parent, a priest, or a chief. Among ourselves, the murder of a child is regarded with special abhorrence and more severely punished than the murder of an adult. When property is stolen, the severity of the offense depends upon what is taken, from whom, by whom, and whence. In the United States the law distinguishes between the stealing of articles of greater value (grand larceny) and articles of lesser value (petit larceny). A theft is punished more severely if it involves trespassing (burglary) and still more severely if it involves a personal encounter with the victim (robbery). There is a tendency to punish theft from the government more severely than theft from private persons and theft from relatives or friends less severely than theft from strangers.

Human nature and social structure being what they are, every large society has a considerable amount of crime, a small number of habitual criminals, and a larger number of occasional offenders. The object of the criminal law is not to eliminate crime but to keep it at a tolerable level. What is tolerable varies from one time and place to another, but any sharp increase in the frequency of serious crime can be interpreted as a sign of strain in the social system within which it occurs and as a warning of the possible breakdown of essential social institutions.

How to determine when an increase of serious crime has occurred is more of a problem than most people suppose. Most criminal behavior is clandestine. The criminal attempts to conceal the crime or his part in it, and of course he often succeeds. It is not even theoretically possible to obtain a complete count of criminal acts; there are some perfect murders and undetected embezzlements, for example. In practice, it is seldom possible to get more than a very rough count, based on the number of offenses reported, the number of arrests made, or the number of convictions, for each given type of offense. Each of these sources of information is unreliable for different reasons. Offenses reported to the police are not always officially recorded. Some complaints are spurious, some are made more than once. In certain categories, like vandalism and fraud, the majority of offenses are not reported at all, because the victim expects no help from the police or wishes to avoid embroilment or has means of private settlement. The number of arrests made is greatly affected by the changing policies and practices of law enforcement agencies. It can vary dramatically without signaling any change in the rate of criminal activity. The number of convictions for particular crimes is a particularly unreliable index in the United States because, as studies have shown, a large proportion of criminal cases are settled by a process of bargaining whereby serious charges are exchanged for lighter charges in return for admissions of guilt that save the trouble of a trial.[8]

The analysis of trends in crime is further complicated by changes in the law and other changes in the social environment. Most of the world's advanced countries have reported dramatic increases in the frequency of car theft as the number of automobiles has increased. The incidence of grand larceny—defined as the theft of articles valued above a stated amount—would increase during a period of monetary inflation even if the propensity to steal remained constant. Such problems are compounded in the United States by the differing laws of the 50 states and the multiplicity of local jurisdictions. Despite all these obstacles, criminal statistics have been considerably improved in recent years, and sociologists who specialize in criminology can now answer a good many questions that were formerly unsettled.

THE INCIDENCE OF CRIME IN THE UNITED STATES[9]

As Table 11-1 shows, between 3 percent and 4 percent of the total American population[10] were arrested in the course of a recent year— the great majority of them for relatively minor offenses. Almost half the persons arrested were taken into custody for public drunkenness, driving under the influence of alcohol, violations of the liquor laws, and disorderly conduct due to drinking.

Table 11-2 shows the relative frequency of arrests for the seven serious crimes included in the FBI's national crime index. Fewer than 1 percent of the population were arrested for serious offenses. The great majority of these arrests were accounted for by three types of stealing: larceny, burglary, and car theft. Crimes against persons— willful homicide, aggravated assault, rape, and robbery—accounted for only about 3 percent of total arrests.

Of course, arrest rates do not give a full measure of criminal activity. Not all the crimes reported to the police lead to an arrest; the likelihood that an arrest will be made is much higher for offenses against persons than for offenses against property. Interview surveys of representative samples of the national population have demonstrated that a great many serious crimes are not reported at all, either because the

Table 11-1   ARREST RATES FOR THE 10 MOST FREQUENT OFFENSES, UNITED STATES, 1965

Rank	Offense	Rate per 100,000 Population	% of Total Arrests
1	Drunkenness	1,145	31.0%
2	Disorderly conduct	425	11.5
3	Larceny (over and under $50)	286	7.7
4	Driving under the influence of alcohol	180	4.9
5	Simple assault	155	4.2
6	Burglary	147	4.0
7	Liquor law violations	134	3.6
8	Vagrancy	90	2.4
9	Gambling	85	2.3
10	Motor vehicle theft	76	2.1
	TOTAL	2,723	73.7

Source: Based on U.S. President's Commission on Law Enforcement and the Administration of Justice, *The Challenge of Crime in a Free Society: A Report* (Washington, D.C.: Government Printing Office, 1967), chap. 2, table 2, p. 20.

Table 11-2   ARREST RATES FOR SEVEN SERIOUS OFFENSES, UNITED STATES, 1965

Offense	Rate per 100,000 Population	% of Total Arrests
Larceny	286	7.5%
Burglary	147	4.0
Auto theft	76	2.1
Aggravated assault	63	1.7
Robbery	34	0.9
Forcible rape	8	0.2
Willful homicide	5	0.1
	619	16.5%

Source: Based on *Statistical Abstract of the United States, 1967*, table 218.

Table 11-3	COMPARISON OF OFFENSE RATES OBTAINED FROM POLICE RECORDS AND OFFENSE RATES OBTAINED FROM INTERVIEW SURVEYS, 1965-1966

| | Rate per 100,000 Population | |
Offense	By Police Records	By Survey Data
Burglary	300	949
Larceny	267	606
Auto theft	226	206
Aggravated assault	107	218
Robbery	61	94
Forcible rape	12	43

Source: Based on U.S. President's Commission on Law Enforcement and the Administration of Justice. *The Challenge of Crime in a Free Society: A Report* (Washington, D.C.: Government Printing Office, 1967), chap. 2, table 4, p. 21.

victim does not believe the police could help him, as in many cases of burglary, or because he does not want to involve the offender with the law, as in many cases of assault, or because of unwillingness to disclose the crime, as in many cases of rape. Table 11–3 compares the frequency with which six of the seven serious crimes were reported to police with the frequency of the same crimes estimated from the findings of a national survey by the National Opinion Research Center (NORC). Most robberies seem to have been officially reported and auto thefts may be reported more often than they actually occur, but only a fraction of the burglaries, thefts, rapes, and serious assaults were reported.

THE CAUSES OF CRIME

The causes of crime are not difficult to identify, but they are extremely difficult to sort out. The combination of circumstances that produce high rates of juvenile delinquency and adult crime is well known. The difficulty that has haunted criminology since crime first began to be scientifically studied is that it is not possible to pick one or two principal causes out of the cluster of factors associated with delinquent behavior.

As one expert explains:

> ... the cause of delinquency, "other things being equal," is any one or more of the following: poor street lighting, alleys, immigration, paternal infidelity, differential association, neurotic acting out, broken homes, the American income distribution, lack of alter-

nate meaningful activities, advertising and display, failure to nail down prized objects, the slum, the ecological organization of the American city, materialism, its opposite; preoccupation with one's worth as a person, the law itself, the absurdity of society or the human condition; the want of religion, the nuclear family, the political system which needs crime which needs as a training ground prisons and reformatories; schools that engage few or no loyalties, the perversity of the individual delinquent, or his parents, or theirs; psychological ignorance, the unconscious wishes of those who deplore the activity or condemn the actors. "Choose your pick," as they say. There can hardly be a question that all are involved, and an infinity—literally—of other candidates for causal ascription besides. And each of these "causal factors" is also connected for the purposes of science with an infinity of other causes. The selection for reporting and hence attention of any one cause—say, the ghettoization of Negroes in the Black Belt, leading to rent extortion, leading to overcrowding, leading to heightened necessities for certain types of experiences and escapes—is as clear an act of judgment (in the legal sense) as if when a bridge collapsed a judge were to select a particular passenger over it as the cause of its downfall from the combined excessive weight of all of them on it at the time.[11]

Not only is it difficult to find a single underlying cause of criminal behavior, but it is even more difficult to explain why particular individuals in high-risk populations become delinquent whereas others, apparently exposed to the same deleterious influences, remain law-abiding.

Although simple explanations—and simple cures—are not available, crime shows important regularities that persist over large areas and for long periods of time. Some of them, indeed, appear to be universal. For example, there does not seem to be any human society in which women are as likely to commit murder as men.

In the United States, the frequency of serious offenses is strongly affected by community size and location, and by the age, sex, race, and income level of both offender and victim. In crimes against persons, the preexisting relationship between offender and victim is important also.

COMMUNITY SIZE AS A CRIME FACTOR

Table 11–4 shows offense rates by community size in the United States in 1965. As the figures demonstrate, serious crime is primarily a metropolitan phenomenon. There is much more crime in metropolitan cities than in middle-sized cities, and much more in middle-sized cities than in rural and suburban areas. Of the seven serious offenses described in the table, robbery is probably the best indicator of the real incidence of criminal acts, because it is usually committed by a stranger, seldom provoked by the victim, and almost always reported to the police. The probability of being robbed is about 8 times as high for metropolitan city dwellers as for surburban residents, more than

10 times as high as for small-town residents, and more than 22 times as high as for rural residents. It is possible that more crimes go unreported in smaller places, but this has not been demonstrated. Indeed, the reverse is a little more probable, and in that case, the true difference in rates between communities of different size would be even more than the large differences shown in the table.

COMMUNITY LOCATION AS A CRIME FACTOR

In addition to the general influence of community size, there are local and regional traditions with respect to crime. Chicago, long regarded as an especially crime-ridden city, reported 421 robberies per 100,000 population in 1965. Milwaukee, only 90 miles away but well known as a quiet city, reported only 28 robberies per 100,000 in that same year,[12] with similar methods of reporting. They had respectively the highest and lowest rates among the nation's largest cities. Such intercommunity differences may persist for long periods of time.

The southern states show much higher rates of homicide and assault than do the northern or western states. In 1965, for example, the South Atlantic states had a rate of 8.4 per 100,000 population for willful homicide compared to a national average of 5.1, and a rate of 165.8 for aggravated assault compared to a national average of 109.-5.[13] At the same time, the rates of crimes against property in the South are distinctly below the national average. A study by Hackney indicates that the greater inclination of southerners toward personal violence goes back at least to 1915, which is as far as the usable statistics go; that it is accompanied by the more widespread ownership and use of firearms in the South than in the North; and that it is not explicable by the racial composition of the southern population.[14] Both whites and blacks in the South are more likely to commit homicide and assault than their counterparts in the North and the West.

SEX AS A CRIME FACTOR

Delinquency and crime are predominantly male activities. Women and girls constitute less than 5 percent of the prison, jail, and reformatory population in the United States. The overwhelming majority of this small minority are confined for sexual delinquency, mostly prostitution or adolescent promiscuity. When women are involved in serious crimes, it is usually as accomplices of male criminals. Some women independently engage in murder, forgery, and shoplifting, but the proportion of such offenses committed by women is exceedingly small. Female delinquents are first arrested at a later age than male delinquents, they are less likely to be committed, and when committed they serve much shorter sentences.[15]

Women play a larger role as victims than as offenders, but even in this regard, they lag far behind men. Except for forcible rape, all the recognized victims of which are female, women are less likely than men to be the victim of any crime against persons.[16]

Table 11-4   OFFENSE RATES PER 100,000 POPULATION, BY COMMUNITY SIZE, UNITED STATES, 1965

Group	Willful Homicide	Forcible Rape	Robbery	Aggravated Assault	Burglary	Larceny $50 and Over	Motor Vehicle Theft
Cities over 1 million	10	26	221	246	930	734	586
500,000 to 1 million	10	20	165	182	1,009	555	640
250,000 to 500,000	7	15	122	142	1,045	550	468
100,000 to 250,000	6	11	73	151	871	556	353
50,000 to 100,000	4	8	49	85	675	492	297
25,000 to 50,000	3	6	33	71	562	443	212
10,000 to 25,000	2	6	19	67	462	309	141
Under 10,000	2	5	12	62	369	236	99
Rural	4	9	10	58	308	176	51
Suburban area	3	10	28	66	545	359	160
All places	5	12	61	107	605	420	251

Source: Based on U.S. President's Commission on Law Enforcement and the Administration of Justice. *The Challenge of Crime in a Free Society: A Report* (Washington, D.C.: Government Printing Office, 1967), chap. 2, table 8, p. 28.

Table 11-5

Age	Percent of All Arrests for Serious Offenses
Under 18	49%
18-19	14
20-24	12
Over 24	25
Total	100%

Table 11-5   ARRESTS FOR SERIOUS OFFENSES BY AGE OF PERSONS ARRESTED, UNITED STATES, 1965

Source: Statistical Abstract of the United States, 1967, table 219.

AGE AS A CRIME FACTOR

The popular belief that juvenile delinquency is a serious social problem, the severity of which increases from year to year, is well-founded. Table 11–5 shows the proportion of arrests for serious offenses (the seven crimes previously discussed) that involved youths and young adults in 1965. *Nearly half of all the serious offenders were under 18; three-quarters of them were under 25.* The frequency of serious offenses against persons was higher among children aged 11–14 than among men 45–49! Although the evidence is scattered and not conclusive, it appears that the proportion of major crimes committed by adolescents has been rising in the United States for a considerable time and is now greater than ever before.[17]

There is some evidence that the increase in juvenile criminality is a worldwide phenomenon. Startling increases in juvenile delinquency were reported in the 1950s and 1960s by countries as far apart and as different in their social structures as Sweden, Japan, and Israel.[18] It is noteworthy that these countries lack many of the conditions associated with juvenile delinquency in the United States. For example, Sweden has no slums, Israel has no problem of adolescent unemployment, and parental authority is still very strong in Japan. The increase in juvenile delinquency appears to be somehow related to certain social changes that have been occurring in all these countries, especially urbanization, which weakens the social control exercised by adults over adolescents; the increased specialization of labor, which retards the age of entrance into the labor force; and the increased affluence of urban societies, which makes it impossible for unemployed adolescents to eat without working and at the same time sharpens their appetite for luxuries.

CLASS AND RACE AS CRIME FACTORS

Both criminals and their victims are drawn in disproportionate numbers from the least privileged strata of urban society, and this appears to be the case nearly everywhere in the world where data are available. The offenses reported to the police are more likely to lead to arrest and punishment when the offender is identified by the authorities as poor or belonging to a minority group or coming from a "tough neighborhood" or belonging to a well-known gang.[19] The inmates of prisons and reformatories are drawn in disproportionate numbers from the unskilled, the uneducated, and the underprivileged segments of a population. Negroes are between three and four times as numerous among prison and reformatory inmates as in the general population;[20] the majority of prisoners in many states are black.

Since it has long been known that persons of higher social status, especially male adolescents, commit many serious offenses without being caught and often go unpunished when caught, it has sometimes been thought that the level of delinquency might be about the same in all social strata and the apparent difference due only to discrimination by law enforcement agencies. However, recent research seems to demonstrate that the inverse correlation between socioeconomic status and delinquency is real—although exaggerated in many instances by the selective treatment of offenders.[21] It is principally in disadvantaged urban areas that delinquent subcultures have been observed, that is, institutional patterns that prescribe a way of life which includes the commission of serious crimes.[22]

It is a less familiar but equally important fact that the impact of crime falls most heavily on the same segments of the population that produce a disproportionate number of offenders. This is especially true of violent crimes against the person. According to the NORC study, previously cited, persons with incomes under $3,000 were five times as likely to be robbed as persons with incomes over $10,000. They were also more likely to be raped or burglarized and even more likely to have their cars stolen. (Grand larceny and aggravated assault, however, were more likely to be perpetrated against the rich.) Nonwhites were shown by the same study to suffer about four times as much robbery and rape, nearly twice as much burglary and assault, and relatively more car theft than whites.[23]

THE OFFENDER-VICTIM RELATIONSHIP

The basis for the similarity between the socioeconomic characteristics of the offender and his victim is that in crimes of violence (except robbery), they are more likely to be acquaintances than strangers. Even property crimes, like burglary and car theft, are more likely to be committed by neighbors than by complete outsiders.

A Philadelphia study of criminal homicides from 1948 to 1952 disclosed that only 12 percent of murders were committed by strangers; in more than 50 percent of the cases studied, the murderer was a relative or close friend of the victim. Another study in the District of Columbia showed that only 36 percent of a series of rapes and only 19 percent of a series of aggravated assaults were committed by complete strangers. A Chicago study found that 93 percent of a sample of murders, 88 percent of rapes and 91 percent of aggravated assaults were intraracial, that is, involved an offender and victim of the same race. Robbery is the only violent crime that is very frequently interracial.[24]

WHITE-COLLAR CRIME

The term *white-collar crime* was invented by Edwin H. Sutherland. In a famous paper published in 1940,[25] he applied it to *the illegal acts committed by "respectable or at least respected business and professional men" in the course of their occupations.* Sutherland argued that conclusions about the high incidence of crime in the lower class are based on statistics which emphasized the kinds of crimes habitually committed by lower-class persons—murders, assaults, robberies, and so forth—but give little or no weight to such white-collar crimes as financial fraud, commercial bribery, misrepresentation, embezzlement, and professional malpractice. White-collar crime, he asserted, not only was underrepresented in criminal statistics but usually went unpunished, and in the rare instances when offenders were caught, was treated leniently.

Analyzing decisions by courts and commissions against the 70 largest corporations in the United States for violations of the antitrust laws, false advertising, infractions of labor laws, and the infringement of patent, copyrights, and trademarks, he found that every corporation in his sample had at least one adverse decision; the average was about eight. However, only 9 percent of these adverse decisions were made in a criminal court; Sutherland's problem was to show that the other 91 percent of them involved criminal behavior. He maintained that most of the acts involved were socially injurious and that the penalties provided by law for such acts were similar to those provided for ordinary crime.

Sutherland's demonstration that a great many illegal acts are committed by middle-class and upper-class persons in the practice of their professions or in their capacity as executives and officials is irrefutable. So is his contention that the economic cost of embezzlement, consumer fraud, product adulteration, political graft, and other forms of white-collar crime probably exceed is the economic cost of ordinary (or common law) crimes.[26] But his insistence that white-collar crime should be treated on the same footing as common law crime has been vigorously challenged by other criminologists.[27] They see a significant difference between common law crimes, which inflict pain and hardship on individual victims, and white-collar crimes, whose effects are diffuse and uncertain. The force of Sutherland's demonstration was blunted by his insistence that white-collar crime is "real crime" regardless of whether it is so classified by a court or only by a criminologist.

The fact remains that there is an extraordinary volume of illegal behavior in business and the professions in the United States[28]—far more, it appears, than in most other technologically advanced countries.

Mixed in with Sutherland's category of white-collar crimes are a number of offenses, like embezzlement and fraudulent conversion, that are also common law crimes. Offenders in these categories tend to be white, middle-aged, and respectable, and—as Cressey's interesting study of convicted embezzlers shows[29]—they often refuse to recognize the nature of their criminal acts as they commit them; the typical embezzler persuades himself that he is not stealing the funds entrusted to him but borrowing them for a worthy purpose.

Long-Term Trends in Criminality

The United States has thousands of local governments engaged in law enforcement. Until quite recently, many of them kept no systematic records, and those that did made no effort to keep them in a form that would permit comparisons with other districts. It was quite impossible to obtain reliable statistical data about criminality in the United States as a whole before 1933, when the Uniform Crime Reports began to be collected by the FBI. The national statistics that have been available since that date are distrusted by many experts. However, fairly reliable series that go back as far as the early 1800s are available in a few jurisdictions,[30] and analysis of these shows a long-term *declining* trend in serious crime, although with numerous fluctuations.

In a careful study of criminality in nineteenth century Massachusetts, Lane discovered that the incidence of serious crimes decreased by about two-thirds from 1840 to 1900, despite rapid urbanization and the development of urban slums during the same interval.[31] Data from the Uniform Crime Reports from 1933 to 1965 show slight downward trends in willful homicide and robbery and marked upward trends in burglary and larceny (but not in car thefts).[32] Most criminologists are critical of the FBI's regular, periodic announcements of sharp increases in crime. They point out that such increases are often attributable to changes in reporting procedures, or to inflation in the price of stolen articles, and do not necessarily indicate any increase in the average citizen's risk of being victimized. As late as 1967, the President's Commission on Law Enforcement and Administration of Justice could not say after an 18-month study whether the crime rate was higher than it had been before, or if Americans had become more criminal than their counterparts in earlier times. By 1969, however, another Presidential commission was convinced that the incidence of serious crime in the United States had begun to rise sharply in the late 1960s and would probably continue to do so for some years to come.[33] The conclusion was based on an unmistakable increase in the frequency of robbery, regarded by experts as the best indicator of the trend of criminality because it involves both persons and property and does not often involve a prior relationship between offender and victim. The rate of bank robbery, which is a particularly reliable indicator because *all* offenses are reported, increased by about 300 percent during the 1960s.

The reason for predicting a continued increase is that the segment of the population most likely to be involved in serious crime—underschooled, underemployed male adolescents in metropolitan centers—was growing in relation to the general population because of high birth rates in the 1950s, continued urbanization, minority group concentration in central cities, and the declining employability of unskilled adolescents. These factors would tend to raise the incidence of serious crime even in the absence of the "trend toward violence" so much discussed in the mass media. As the same report points out, however, the hazard of violent crime is probably somewhat less than the average law-abiding citizen imagines. A U.S. resident's chance of being killed in a car crash is almost 34 times the chances that he will be murdered by a stranger.

Compared to other countries, the United States occupies an intermediate position with respect to violence. The incidence of willful homicide—the only serious crime for which international comparisons can be made—is much higher in the United States than in most of the western European countries but much lower than in most of the countries of Latin America or those few countries of Africa and Asia for which information is available.

Suicide

From one standpoint, suicide may be considered the most extreme form of deviance, since it not only involves the violation of powerful social norms but amounts, in effect, to a total withdrawal from society. From another standpoint, suicide is a marginal form of deviance because few vestiges now remain of the sanctions that it formerly provoked in Christian countries—penalties imposed on the estate, the family, and the corpse of the successful suicide and the criminal prosecution of the unsuccessful suicide.

Suicide, as explained in Chapter Three, was the first topic selected for modern sociological research (by Durkheim). It has been a topic of perennial interest to sociologists and other social scientists; a recent bibliography lists more than 3,000 studies.[35] Nevertheless, some of the major theoretical questions in the sociology of suicide have not yet been satisfactorily answered.

Even before Durkheim, the two outstanding features of suicide rates had been discovered. First, they are fairly stable from year to year in a given population. Table 11–6 combines one of Durkheim's tables, which illustrated this stability in 11 European countries from 1866 to 1878, with data for 1965–1966 from the same countries. Even after the lapse of a century, some features of the original pattern remain unchanged, and in two countries, France and Norway, the actual rates remain approximately the same.

Second, if a population is subdivided by any of the major character-

			Period	
Country	1866-1870	1871-1875	1874-1878	1965-1966
Italy	30	35	38	54
Belgium	66	69	78	150
England	67	66	69	104
Norway	76	73	71	77
Austria	78	94	130	230
Sweden	85	81	91	201
Bavaria	90	91	100	—
France	135	150	160	150
Prussia	142	134	152	—
Denmark	277	258	255	190
Saxony	293	267	334	—
West Germany	—	—	—	200
United States	—	—	—	109

Source: Based on Emile Durkheim, *Suicide* New York: Free Press, 1951), table III, p. 50; and *Demographic Yearbook of the United Nations, 1967*, table 24.

istics that affect the social roles of individuals, the subpopulations will show significantly different suicide rates, and the direction of these differences is generally predictable. Suicide rates are strongly affected by age, sex, religion, race, marital condition, and occupation.

The most important and consistent correlations between suicide rates and demographic or social characteristics are these:

1. Male suicide rates are almost invariably higher than female suicide rates. The precise ratio varies from one country to another and from one subpopulation to another. Suicide is about three and one-half times more frequent among males than among females in the United States.

2. Suicide rates increase with age. In the United States, they are negligible for children under 15 and rise slowly from about 2.5 per 100,000 population in the age group 15–19 to about 25 per 100,000 in the over-60 age group.

3. Suicide rates are higher among Orientals than among Caucasians and higher among Caucasians than among Negroes. In the United States in 1960, the population of Chinese origin had a suicide rate twice as high as the white population, in which the rate in turn was three times as high as that of the black population.

4. Catholics and Jews have generally lower rates than Protestants living at the same time and place. In other parts of the world, Buddhists seem to have high rates and Moslems to have low rates.

5. Except at the youngest ages, married persons have much lower suicide rates than single persons, but the protection against suicide provided by marriage is relatively greater for husbands than for wives. In the unmarried population, divorced persons are more likely to commit suicide than single or widowed persons.

6. Suicide is especially prevalent in three types of occupation— those of highest status, those of lowest status, and those involving the use of weapons. Occupational differences have not been completely charted, but they are often of extreme magnitude.[36]

When several of the foregoing characteristics are combined, the differences are often staggering. For example, the annual suicide rate among single, nonwhite females under 20 in the United States in 1949–1951 was 0.3 per 100,000 population; the corresponding rate for divorced, white males over age 75 was 139.1.[37]

Some other factors that might be expected to influence suicide rates do not do so or have only an ambiguous influence. The incidence of suicide in a population is not closely correlated with other forms of violence; what correlation there is appears to be negative. It is not clearly related to modernization, technological development, or income level; and it shows *no* consistent tendency to increase under the stresses of an increasingly complex world. Although, as Table 11–6 shows, the suicide rate rose during the past century in most of the countries in the table, it fell sharply in Denmark and remained unchanged in Norway and France. Since about 1930 the general suicide rate in the United States has declined fairly steadily, from a level of about 16 per 100,000 to its present level of about 10.[38]

EXPLAINING DIFFERENCES IN SUICIDE RATES

Although suicide rates, like other public statistics, have their shortcomings, they seem to be more valid and reliable than most other indicators of social disorganization. That is why Durkheim chose them for his pioneering study. The differences between subpopulations are large and stable and reasonably consistent from one place to another, hence the continued efforts by sociologists to explain them.

Although Durkheim distinguished several different types of suicide, he reached the general conclusion that "suicide varies inversely with the degree of integration of the social groups of which the individual forms a part."[39] Recent scholars have elaborated and modified this explanation. For example, Henry and Short[40] maintain that the suicide rate of a population varies inversely with the strength of the relational system among its members (that is, their emotional involvement with each other). The strength of the relational system is said to depend upon external restraints or the degree to which behavior is required to conform to the expectations of other persons, and these in turn are said to vary inversely with status. Gibbs and Martin[41] propose that the suicide rate varies inversely with the degree of status integration in a population. By status integration, they mean the extent to which the various statuses of an individual are clustered, so that knowing one of his statuses enables an observer to guess the others. The theory seems to say that individuals who simultaneously hold two or more incongruent statuses will have a special propensity to suicide.

Deviant Sexual Relationships

The regulation of sexual relationships is one of the most fundamental aspects of social organization. It occurs in all known societies, even those that lack political institutions and have no trace of centralized authority. Every known society prohibits sexual relations between certain close relatives, makes some distinction between the permissible sexual behavior of married and unmarried persons, and imposes some restriction on unusual sexual acts.

Sumner's famous statement that "the mores can make anything right or anything wrong,"[42] is a forceful half-truth in relation to sexual behavior. The mores never make incest right, but they do define it in various ways, so that in one society a love affair between second cousins is incestuous and in another society a man is allowed to marry his niece. But the plasticity of definition is not unlimited; there is no living society that approves sexual relationships between parents and children, for example.

In this field as in others, we identify deviant behavior as behavior that violates explicit social norms and elicits repressive or punitive reactions from agents of norm enforcement. Behavior that is illegal but has ceased to be punished—like adult fornication in most American states—is not classified as deviant under this definition. However, it must be remembered that criminal prosecution is not the sole form of norm enforcement. The criminal statutes against adultery are dead letters, but the offense is still severely punished in the divorce courts. Homosexuality as such is often not prosecuted, but a public official, an athletic coach, or an industrial foreman accused of homosexuality is likely to lose his job.

GENERAL CONSIDERATIONS

The regulation of sexual relationships appears to be accomplished in every organized society by means of a normative system that permits certain types of sexual relationship, disapproves but usually tolerates other types of relationship, and punishes still other types of relationship with varying degrees of severity. Although the boundary between the first two of these categories—proper and improper relationships—is clearly marked in most social systems and slow to shift, the boundary between relationships that are merely improper and those that are seriously prohibited is much harder to trace and—particularly under modern conditions—is subject to shifting. Contrary to popular belief, such shifts are not always toward liberalization. Statutory rape, for example, was originally defined by the common law as a sexual relationship with a girl under the age of 10, but the age has been steadily raised until in some states, a sexual relationship with a girl of nearly 18 is punishable—and is often punished—by a prison term.

Our concern in this section is with *deviant* sexual relationships, that is, activities involving mutual consent and participation. Sexual violence, as in forcible rape or child molestation, belongs to another category. The laws of all 50 American states limit permissible sexual relationships to mutually consenting, legally married couples who are free from certain specified disabilities. These laws are quite restrictive compared to those of most of the unmodernized societies studied by anthropologists. In Murdock's survey of 250 representative human societies, only 43 societies in the sample limited themselves to monogamous marriage, and only 3 (and possibly a few others for which information is incomplete) attempt to enforce a prohibition of all sexual intercourse outside marriage.[43] Measured against the norms of modern large-scale societies, American laws are neither especially permissive, like those of the Scandinavian countries, nor especially restrictive, like those of the Soviet Union.

For convenience of discussion, the forms of deviant sexual relationship will be divided into three categories:

1. Those defined as major crimes—incest, bigamy and statutory rape.
2. Those defined as minor offenses—prostitution, juvenile promiscuity, homosexuality.
3. Those that elicit noncriminal but serious sanctions—extramarital affairs and illegitimacy.

INCEST

As noted in Chapter Ten, the laws of the 50 states prohibit marriage between primary relatives, like brother and sister, between secondary consanguineal relatives, like uncle and niece, and in a few cases, between secondary affinal like father- and daughter-in-law. However, criminal sanctions against incest are applied to sexual relationships rather than to marriage and almost exclusively to relationships between primary relatives. Prosecutions for brother-sister or mother-son relationships are rare, either because the behavior seldom occurs or because there is ordinarily no way for it to come to public notice. Prosecutions and convictions for father-daughter incest are not uncommon. Most of the offenders are unskilled industrial or agricultural workers with low incomes, little education, and few community ties. The wife is the usual complainant. The daughter, even if of age, is never prosecuted.[44]

This is one of the few numerically significant forms of deviance that is not regarded as a social problem, presumably because there is no incongruence between the community sentiment and the letter of the law. There does not appear to be any subculture that actively encourages incest. The anxieties aroused by illegitimacy or prostitution, because they present alarming trends or because they seem to reflect a discrepancy between public and private norms or a clash of values between social strata, are absent in this case.

BIGAMY

Bigamy is marriage with a new spouse by a man or woman whose former spouse is still living and has not been divorced. Although there are no reliable statistics about bigamy, case histories and other miscellaneous information indicate that it is widespread in the United States, perhaps more so than in any other monogamous country. Since the 50 states do not have uniform procedures for marriage or divorce and there are no central records of marriages and divorces, the marital status of separated couples is often ambiguous enough to permit either husband or wife to forget their marriage and to contract another. Under these circumstances, a later discovery of the fact is not likely to produce much societal reaction. In practice, bigamy prosecutions are reserved for the much rarer cases in which a man maintains two or more separate households simultaneously, each with a wife whom he has married legally and who does not suspect the existence of the other wife. This exotic pattern is apt to be punished harshly. It is always prosecuted as a felony, and conviction almost always leads to a prison term. Since it is practically impossible for a woman to maintain separate households with two unknowing husbands simultaneously, women are seldom, if ever, prosecuted for bigamy.

The severity of the reaction elicited by the special type of bigamy described above seems to be related to the severe punishment meted out to counterfeiters, mail robbers, and persons who impersonate government officials. The agencies of law enforcement react as if more provoked by the abuse of their own procedures than by similar acts involving other means. The bigamist's temerity in contracting a legal marriage illegally seems to account for the severity of punishment and the likelihood that he will be sent to prison, even if both wives plead for his release. The element of provocation is lacking in the much more numerous cases in which the status of a previous marriage is doubtful, and these are seldom prosecuted. A man who establishes a second household cannot be prosecuted at all if he and his partner announce themselves as married without going through the formality of a legal wedding.

STATUTORY RAPE

Statutory rape is a sexual relationship in which the female partner is under a certain age set by the law of a particular state usually 16, 17, or 18. Despite the name, there is very little similarity between statutory rape and real or forcible rape. Statutory rape is a curious technical offense that has evolved almost by accident. The common law, which set the female age of consent at 10, regarded a sexual relationship with a girl under that age as akin to rape, since she would be sexually immature and incapable of a meaningful consent. By raising the age of consent steadily higher and higher, American legislatures extend the same assumption to cover female adolescents, who may be both mature and sexually experienced. This leads to all sorts of anomalies. For example, if an adolescent prostitute is caught with an inexperienced younger boy, the boy may be convicted of statutory rape.

Skolnick and Woodworth[45] studied prosecutions for statutory rape in a medium-sized California city, which averaged about 12 cases a month in 1962–1963. California law sets the age of consent at 18, and during the period of the study, did not accept the excuse that the accused had reason to believe the girl to be older. Most of the cases studied involved girls between 14 and 18, since males involved with girls under 14 were usually charged with the more serious offense of child molesting. Of 250 males accused of statutory rape, 57 percent were arrested and prosecuted either as adult offenders or juvenile delinquents. Of 85 adults prosecuted, nearly half were allowed to plead guilty to statutory rape as a misdemeanor, a few were acquitted, and the remainder were held for a superior court where all but one individual were ultimately convicted of a felony or persuaded to plead guilty, the guilty pleas being about evenly divided between felonies and misdemeanors. Thus, the probability that a man or boy arrested for statutory rape would be prosecuted was fairly high, and the probability was overwhelming that if prosecuted he would be convicted.

Closer inspection of these cases revealed that behind this apparently irrational procedure was an explicable if not rational complex of procedures and sentiments. In the most frequent instance, the complaint of statutory rape is made by a division of the welfare department when an unwed mother applies for aid to dependent children. The next most frequent source of complaint is the girl's parents. In the disposition of such cases, the police play an important role, either by persuading the complainants to drop the charge or by inducing them to cooperate with it. Oddly enough, cases involving little or no age difference between the boy and girl are more likely to be prosecuted than those involving older men. The first type of case is unlikely to be reported at all unless a pregnancy results and welfare is applied for. The net effect is that "statutory rape is punished mainly among the poor who become visible by applying for maternity aid from welfare authorities."[46] Unlike incest and bigamy, statutory rape has the familiar profile of a social problem. First, the correspondence between the official norms and the moral sentiments of the community is imperfect. Second, the social benefits secured by the arrest and conviction of statutory rape offenders are debatable. Third, the societal reaction to this form of deviance appears to be biased against low-status persons.

Each of the foregoing types of sexual deviance, when detected, is pursued as a serious crime of a nonrepetitive character. The three types of sexual deviance to which we next turn our attention—prostitution, juvenile promiscuity, and homosexuality—show a quite different pattern. They belong to a larger category that has been labelled "status criminality" and "crime without victims." Although hundreds of individuals are arrested and punished every day for these offenses, the punishments are minor, in some cases merely symbolic, and are not realistically intended to prevent repetition of the offense. Indeed, it is somewhat unclear what intentions support such patterns of norm enforcement, but certain beliefs are commonly held regarding them: (a) penalties have a deterrent effect on a considerable number of persons who do not engage in the prohibited activity but might do so if it were not punished at all; (b) a large volume of arrests enables the authorities to maintain a constant surveillance of persons who, because of their deviant sexual behavior, are likely to be drawn into other types of antisocial activity; (c) the stigma attached to offenders by arrest, conviction, and minor punishment serves as a warning to other persons whom they might otherwise corrupt or deceive. For example, stigmatization restricts the prostitute's opportunity to retire and make a normal marriage, and it prevents the male homosexual from obtaining a job as a teacher or a policeman.

Those who oppose punishment for these widespread forms of sexual deviance argue that: (a) the law enforcement procedures are expensive and ineffective; they do not prevent recurrence of the same behavior, and they even encourage it; (b) the official stigmatization fixes individuals in a deviant way of life by making it difficult for them to redefine themselves as normal and by assuring that they will meet with external resistance if they attempt to do so; (c) the stigmatization of a given type of sexual behavior as criminal places it in an underworld outside the protection of the law and creates opportunities for more serious crimes; (d) the societal reaction to sexual deviance is often discriminatory, punishing low-status persons for acts committed with impunity by high-status persons.

On occasion, the foregoing arguments are replaced by the single sweeping assertion that the state has no legitimate interest in sexual activity, which is, or ought to be, a purely private matter. Although this viewpoint is widely accepted, it is not very plausible sociologically. Even if we could imagine a government that excluded sexual activity from its purview (thereby giving up, for example, the regulation of marriage), it is not easy to imagine a community without sexual norms or the means of enforcing them. Casual observers are often misled by the relaxation of certain norms and fail to observe contrary trends. Homosexuality is now treated more tolerantly almost everywhere in the Western world than it was two or three generations ago, but there is far less toleration of child marriage, for example.

PROSTITUTION

Prostitution is the sale of sexual favors to strangers for money or other valuables. It seems to occur in urban places everywhere and to have certain recurrent features, although the relative number of prostitutes may vary greatly from one city to the next.

Prostitutes seem always to be sharply stratified according to the price of their services and the social status of their customers. In some societies, like those of ancient Greece and modern Japan, this stratification may be institutionalized so that the different grades of prostitutes are trained in different ways and play quite different social roles. In nearly every society, the lowest strata of prostitutes are social outcasts with whom it is disgraceful for anyone to associate except for sexual purposes, whereas the highest strata enjoy considerable prestige and glamor. Male prostitution, for either homosexual or female clients, seems always to be relatively insignificant compared to female prostitution, and to be governed by a quite different institutional pattern.[47]

So far as can be determined, prostitution is illegal or partly illegal in every modernized nation today. (The nearest approach to an exception is Denmark, where it is not illegal for a female to take pay for a sexual contact *if* she has another paid occupation at the same time.) The degree of illegality varies. In some countries, as in the United States, the penalties are nominal but imposed frequently. In other countries, like the Soviet Union, they are severe but easily evaded. A number of European countries maintain an official or quasi-official system of inspection and licensing of prostitutes. Whatever the specific regulations, they identify the occupational role of the prostitute as semicriminal and involve her in a set of illicit relationships with policemen, detectives, inspectors, informers, and other intermediaries of law enforcement. The effect—which is not entirely unintended— is to restrict the prostitute's nonbusiness associations to an underworld, and to create barriers against her return to normal associations and activities.[48] The institution of pimping, whereby the prostitute turns over her earnings to a man by whom she is "protected" and to whom she may be emotionally attached, is regarded by most observers as a response to the circumstances that isolate the prostitute from normal relationships outside of her working hours and to the occupational norms that explicitly oppose any emotional involvement with clients.[49]

Prostitution in the United States conforms to the generalized description above. It is illegal everywhere but practiced in all urban places and is by far the most frequent cause of arrest for adult females. The penalty seldom exceeds a small fine or a few days in jail. The earnings of prostitutes are relatively high compared to those in most other women's occupations, and recruitment seems to be almost entirely voluntary. There is no evidence that girls are enticed or coerced into prostitution as they were reputed to be in the days of the celebrated "white slave trade."

The major strata within the status order of prostitution are streetwalkers, call girls, and party girls. Streetwalkers—the lowest grade of prostitutes—solicit their clients in public places. They are frequently arrested and are likely to contract venereal diseases. Call girls remain in their own apartments for business purposes, and make their appointments by telephone. Their clients are usually referred by other clients or by such agents as bellboys and taxi drivers. The call girl usually arranges immunity from arrest in one way or another. Party girls are the highest-ranking category of prostitutes and therefore not always identifiable as such. They are sufficiently presentable to appear in public with their clients and to offer temporary companionship as well as sexual contact. Party girls are often hired by business firms and other large-scale organizations as part of the hospitality offered to customers and official visitors, and the hospitality in such cases is considered to be more gracious if the girl is not recognized as a professional.[50]

There is no reliable information about the frequency of prostitution in the United States at any date, but evidence from the Kinsey Report suggests that its relative frequency had been declining for several decades before the 1940s and that this decline was attributable to a greater amount of premarital and extramarital sexual activity by respectable women. Among males born in 1910 and after, the proportion who had ever gone to a prostitute was the same as among males born in 1909 and before (about 70 percent), but the number of visits reported by the younger group was two-thirds to one-half fewer.[51] Since the total sexual activity reported by the older and younger males was approximately the same and female respondents showed an increase in nonmarital sexual activity,[52] it appears plain that prostitution had been partly replaced by other types of sexual relationship. The trend since the 1940s, when Kinsey's data were gathered, is unknown, but there are no indications at all that point to the gradual disappearance of commercial prostitution. Kingsley Davis notes that:

> Since the basic causes of prostitution—the institutional control of sex, the unequal scale of attractiveness, the presence of economic and social inequality between classes and between male and female—are not likely to disappear, prostitution is not likely to disappear either. However, the particular form and scope of the institution may change. One such alteration follows from the appearance of sex freedom among the women of the middle and upper classes. The greater the proportion of free, mutually pleasurable intercourse, the lesser is the demand for paid prostitution.[53]

JUVENILE PROMISCUITY

Adolescent prostitution is practically unknown in the United States, presumably because the clients of an adolescent prostitute would be subject to prosecution for statutory rape and anyone else involved in her activities might be charged with corrupting a minor. But promiscuity—sometimes called incorrigibility—is by far the most frequent type of delinquency among young girls. As previously noted, very few major crimes are committed by girls, although they sometimes figure as accessories.

Juvenile promiscuity is one of the most unmistakable forms of status criminality. Under the juvenile court system prevailing in the United States the charges against an offender need not be specified or supported by evidence of violation of a criminal statute. Female juvenile delinquents usually have a history of indiscriminate sexual intercourse, or sexual activity at an unusually precocious age, or sexual association with male delinquents, or runaways with adult men. Any of these activities, when they come to the notice of a juvenile court, are likely to lead to a reformatory commitment for a fairly long term. An unknown, but apparently considerable, proportion of girls adjudged delinquent graduate to prostitution after they pass the age of consent. The identification of female adolescents as promiscuous is heavily biased by socioeconomic status, more so than the identification of any other group of offenders; middle-class and upper-class girls are rarely charged.

By one of those odd quirks that characterize the American system of criminal justice, juvenile promiscuity is much less likely to be punished if it leads to an illegitimate pregnancy, because adolescent unmarried mothers are eligible for welfare payments and are not usually prosecuted for promiscuity if they have young children in their care.

HOMOSEXUALITY

Homosexuality is a much more complicated phenomenon than prostitution, and it is much less understood. Although individuals with homosexual tendencies can probably be found in any sizable population, the incidence of overt homosexual relationships varies sharply from one society to another and even from one occupation or neighborhood to another. In addition, female homosexuality is seldom regarded as equivalent to male homosexuality. Sexual relationships between males are defined as criminal and are actively prosecuted in most of the states;[54] those between females are not defined as criminal and seem to elicit only mild disapproval.

The evidence of recent studies suggests that the homosexual and the heterosexual populations are not as sharply separated as was formerly supposed. Intense emotional relationships between peers of the same sex are believed by some psychiatrists to be part of normal heterosexual development, and a considerable proportion of these involve some degree of homosexual experience. Some adults are bisexual, participating in both heterosexual and homosexual relationships either simultaneously or at different periods of their lives. Finally, in adult populations segregated by sex, as in prisons, there may be very high rates of homosexuality. One study of a women's prison estimated that about half of the inmates participated in homosexual relationships during their imprisonment and that these relationships were culturally patterned as imitations of heterosexual affairs, one inmate taking the masculine role of "butch" and another the role of "femme."[55] This prison may be exceptional, but studies of male prisoners also suggest a high incidence of homosexual behavior.[56]

The Kinsey Reports are the principal source of information about the incidence of homosexuality in the general population. Hooker summarizes the findings of Kinsey based on large, though imperfect, samples of white males and females in the United States:

For white males, the estimated incidence was indicated by the following: (1) 37 percent had at least one overt homosexual experience between the onset of adolescence and old age; (2) 10 percent were predominantly homosexual for at least three years between the ages of 16 and 55; (3) 4 percent were solely homosexual after the onset of adolescence. For white females, the estimated incidence was much lower: (1) 13 percent had at least one overt homosexual experience between adolescence and old age; (2) 28 percent had covert or overt experience; (3) a half to a third as many females were primarily or exclusively homosexual in any age period.[57]

Other findings from the same study were that the homosexual activity of males decreased with increasing education and occupational status, whereas that of females increased among the more educated. Homosexuality also appears to be correlated with community size and to be somewhat incompatible with religious participation.

The Kinsey interviews provided the data for Gagnon and Simon's study of the life experience of 550 white males with extensive histories of homosexuality.[58] Their most interesting finding was that the majority had experienced no trouble with the police, with their families, or at their places of work; in other words, they had been able to maintain the secrecy of their homosexual involvements, which were typically with casual partners and unrelated to their other social roles. They were more likely to encounter trouble with their partners than with the authorities. A large proportion of them had been rolled, robbed, or blackmailed.

Although there are signs of increasing public tolerance of male homosexuality, as evidenced, for example, by the formation of "homophile" associations to campaign for the removal of legal restrictions, there is no clear trend in the frequency or distribution of homosexual behavior.

Homosexuality is accepted in certain occupational settings, among dancers and hairdressers, for example, but the homosexual employed in a professional or managerial occupation lives in constant danger of disclosure. If he is arrested, the significant penalty is not the small fine or suspended jail sentence that a court will impose, but the damage that may be done to his various statuses by disclosure of his deviant identity.

In the section that follows we consider two widespread forms of sexual deviance that are not restricted at all by criminal sanctions but are restrained by other types of societal reaction.

EXTRAMARITAL AFFAIRS

It is quite impossible to estimate the numerical frequency of *extramarital affairs—that is, of relatively durable heterosexual relationships in which one or both partners are married to other persons*—but case history studies and surveys[59] indicate that such relationships are not uncommon. It is generally believed that their frequency has risen, if only because of the enhanced opportunities provided by modern mobility. Although statutes defining adultery as criminal are still on the books in most jurisdictions, they have entirely lost their force. A more active agent of norm enforcement is the family court, which accords a privileged status with respect to divorce, separation, support, or the custody of children to the married person who can prove that his spouse has had an extramarital affair. Another agent of enforcement is the "injured spouse," who is permitted by custom to take various punitive measures on his or her own behalf. Although the "unwritten law" that permitted a husband to kill his wife's lover (and in particularly provocative circumstances, his wife) no longer prevails anywhere in the United States, its influence is still felt in cases of homicide, assault, wife-beating, and eviction where the injured spouse is allowed some liberty to take the law into his own hands, and is treated with leniency when he does so.

ILLEGITIMACY

Illegitimacy is the bearing of children by unmarried women. A child is legitimate if the mother is married at the time of its birth even though she was unmarried at the time of its conception, and any child born to a married woman is legally presumed to be her husband's child.

Some illegitimacy occurs in all or nearly all societies for which records are available. Unlike some other forms of deviance, illegitimacy is difficult to conceal, and it is possible to make fairly reliable comparisons between countries and between eras.

The most useful measure of illegitimacy is the *illegitimacy ratio—the number of illegitimate births per 1,000 live births in a given population during a stated time interval.* (It is sometimes expressed as a percentage and often miscalled the illegitimacy rate.) Illegitimacy ratios reported by the United Nations for 1958 varied from a low of 4 (Israel) to a high of 739 (Panama). In general, illegitimacy is lowest in the countries on both the European and African sides of the Mediterranean and highest in the Latin American and Caribbean area. Among countries with illegitimacy ratios under 20 were Ireland, Greece, and Japan. Among those with illegitimacy ratios over 400 were Venezuela, Peru, Paraguay, and the Dominican Republic.[60]

Within most countries, illegitimacy seems to show a long-term upward trend accompanying modernization, with upward fluctuations during periods of prosperity and downward fluctuations during periods of depression. It is greater in the lower strata of a hierarchical social system (no exceptions to this principle are known), and when the lowest stratum of a hierarchy is racially differentiated from the higher strata, and upward mobility out of the lowest stratum is infrequent, a considerable volume of illegitimacy may be expected as a matter of course.

Statistics of illegitimacy in the United States are imperfect in several respects: a number of states protect illegitimate children by concealing the fact of illegitimacy on birth certificates; the recording procedures of other states are not entirely consistent; and the available series do not go back very far. Nevertheless, the long-term trend has been moving unmistakably upward. The illegitimacy ratio for the white population was 18 in 1940 and 44 in 1966. For the nonwhite population, it was 136 in 1940 and 276 in 1966. The overall illegitimacy ratio for the United States in 1966 was 81.[61]

Theoretical discussions of illegitimacy usually begin with the Principle of Legitimacy proposed by Malinowski as a universal social norm: "No child should be brought into the world without a man—and one man at that—assuming the role of sociological father, that is, guardian and protector, the male link between the child and the rest of the community."[62] Needless to say, Malinowski recognized that this norm, like most norms, would be violated.

The later discovery that legitimacy was comparatively rare in the Caribbean Islands, where most births are attributable to consensual union, that is, to couples living together unmarried, seemed at first to cast some doubt upon Malinowski's principle, but closer investigation disclosed that even in Caribbean areas where the great majority of births are illegitimate, there is a nearly unanimous preference for marriage and that both mother and child have higher status when the mother is legally married.[63]

On the basis of this evidence and comparative information from other parts of the world, Goode expanded Malinowski's principle into a much more comprehensive explanation of illegitimacy.[64] According to Goode, a basic function of marriage is to establish an appropriate status for the newborn child within a larger community. In order to maintain its own status order, a well-integrated community must enforce a norm of legitimacy in one way or another. But if a community is in the process of disintegration or is trapped in a situation where few rewarding statuses are available to any of its members, the norm of legitimacy, although still recognized, will be very weakly enforced.

Goode identifies several major areas of relatively high illegitimacy: northwestern Europe (especially Scandinavia), the urbanized parts of southern Africa, the Caribbean, and most of Latin America. The pattern of illegitimacy in northwestern Europe is quite different from the patterns found in the other areas, being a survival of the old peasant custom of deferring marriage until after the birth of one or more children to an established young couple. In other words, childbirth outside of marriage was strongly disapproved, but the timing of the wedding was not critical for a socially recognized marriage.

In the other areas, the prevalence of illegitimacy seems to be attributable to various defects in community integration. Goode describes a South African pattern thus:

> The natives in the African urban or industrialized locations have come from tribes in which elders were once powerful, marriages were arranged, and illegitimacy was rare. The skills and knowledge of the elders are not greatly respected in the urban areas, because they are no longer effective. Social control is therefore likely to be reduced to the formal controls of the outside, white society. Although there is some tendency for people from the same tribe to cluster together, as happened in urban ghettos in the United States, such groupings achieve less social control over the individual than do the economic and political imperatives of urban life, and at every turn the native is reminded that both his parental culture and community have no prestige and can be ignored. The kin lines that his family was once at pains to preserve need not be taken seriously. A young man need not worry that a girl's elders or male siblings will bring him to account for a pregnancy outside marriage. A girl need not wait until her sweetheart has saved enough for the bride price; nor is she, unprotected by a kin network, in any position to force him to wait. White governments in Africa, like those in the United States *antebellum* South, are little interested in maintaining legitimacy, since by caste definition African legitimacy has no relevance for white legitimacy.[65]

One of the few American studies to examine illegitimacy in its social context is a study by Short, Strodtbeck, and Cartwright[66] of parenthood in a Negro streetcorner gang observed in Chicago from 1959 to 1961. At the beginning of the inquiry, the gang consisted of 21 boys and one girl, all between the ages of 15 and 20. They were interviewed about relationships in their own families and about their conceptions of the ideal family and of the families they hoped to establish. Although *all* the respondents came from mother-centered families in which the fathers were absent or undependable, their view of the ideal family was highly conventional. It included such features as paternal dominance, family planning, job stability, and marital stability. Most of the respondents expressed the intention of founding such families.

Meanwhile, all the gang members without exception were involved in casual sex relations. At the time of the original inquiry, 5 of the 24 boys in the gang had fathered illegitimate children; two years later, 12 of them had done so. In none of these cases did the father establish a stable relationship with the mother, although one or two marriages took place, and other members had left the gang to marry. When investigators divided the gang into core and marginal members, they found about twice as much illegitimate paternity among the core members, but no other differences in personality, attitudes, or status could be discovered between fathers and nonfathers. The fathers were about 16 months older than the nonfathers on the average, and the investigators concluded that the difference between the two groups was accounted for by chance and the length of their exposure to the risk of paternity. They guessed that if the group continued to function as a unit, most of the nonfathers would soon father illegitimate children in their turn, given the existing pattern of sex relationships, the permissiveness of the adult community, the lack of interest in contraception, the inability of the boys to support a family when conception occurred, and the fact that an adolescent girl gained rather than lost status in the community when the birth of an illegitimate child led others to recognize her as a woman with adult responsibilities.

The future trend of illegitimacy in the United States and elsewhere is uncertain because of the coexisting influences with opposite effects. For example, a rising educational level and the development of nearly infallible contraceptive methods tend to lower illegitimacy, whereas increases in affluence, which simplifies the problem of supporting illegitimate children, tend to raise it.

Deviant Habits

Deviant habits include activities defined as illegal or immoral, which are nevertheless habitual for many people. To fall within the definition of deviance, an habitual activity must violate explicit norms and arouse a corrective response from norm-enforcing agents. Many habits that are clearly harmful, like excessive smoking, do not meet these criteria.

To a greater extent than in any other Western country, legislators in the United States have attempted to change widespread habits by passing laws, without much regard to the practicality of enforcing them. Much of this legislation has been worse than ineffective, not only failing to repress the undesired activities but also tending to corrupt the agencies of law enforcement and to promote the growth of organized crime. The Eighteenth Amendment to the Constitution, which was ratified in January 1919, prohibited the manufacture, sale, or transportation of intoxicating liquors for beverage purposes everywhere in the United States. (It was repealed by the Twenty-first Amendment in December 1933.) During the 15 years that Prohibition was in effect, liquor consumption in the United States continued at a high level, and an elaborate network of illegal and highly profitable enterprises sprang up to satisfy the continued demand. When Prohibition was repealed, many of the gangs and criminal syndicates it had created turned their attention to organized extortion, political racketeering, large-scale smuggling, and other substitute lines of business. A generation later, the attempt to prohibit the use of certain mood-changing drugs had somewhat similar results. The consumption of the prohibited products continued, and the business of supplying them became sufficiently profitable to support large criminal "empires."

In this section we shall discuss the three types of deviant habit that are most conspicuous in the United States at present—alcoholism, drug abuse, and gambling. Each has a very long history and an elaborate culture of its own.

The consumption of alcoholic beverages cannot in itself be considered a deviant habit. Most of the world's societies have developed some type of wine or beer for use on ritual and sociable occasions. Most technically advanced societies have developed one or more types of distilled spirit (whiskey, vodka, rum, cognac, arrack, and so on), which have a much higher alcoholic content than wine or beer and are used for the relief of anxiety, the promotion of sociability, and medicinal purposes.[67]

The effect of alcohol depends upon the type of beverage; the amount taken; the rate at which it is taken; whether it is preceded or accompanied by food; the size, health, and drinking experience of the consumer; and the customs and norms that regulate drinking. The latter vary enormously from one social system to another according to whether drinking is a daily routine or restricted to special occasions, whether it is restricted to adult males, and whether drunkenness is encouraged, tolerated, or disapproved.

In the United States, about two-thirds of all adults drink alcoholic beverages at least occasionally.[68] In the total population over 18, the annual per capita consumption in 1967 amounted to about 9 quarts of hard liquor, 6 quarts of wine, and 100 quarts of beer.[69] There are more male than female drinkers at every age. The adult drinking pattern is usually established in late adolescence, somewhat earlier than the minimum age set by law. Drinking habits vary significantly by income, education, social class, religion, ethnicity, and some other social characteristics.[70] There is some uncertainty about the long-term trend in alcoholic consumption. Hard drinking is known to have been frequent on the American frontier. Straus and Bacon present figures —for which no source is given—to show a considerable drop in per capita consumption of spirits from 1850 to 1950, with concurrent increases in the consumption of beer and wine. However, other data indicate that the per capita production of distilled spirits in the United States nearly doubled from 1870 to 1955[71] while amounts imported increased also. In the more recent decades for which reliable statistics are available, trends in alcohol consumption have been unmistakably upward. Between 1940 and 1967, the per capita consumption of distilled spirits, of beer, and of wine in the United States have each increased by about 50 percent.[72]

The proportion of drinkers generally increases from the bottom to the top of a status distribution. It appears to be higher among urban than among rural populations, higher among Catholics than among Protestants, and approximately the same for whites and blacks. The type of beverage and the manner of consumption vary from one social group to another. On the average, blue-collar workers consume more beer but less wine than white-collar workers. The cocktail lounge attracts customers of higher status than the neighborhood tavern.[73] Distinctive drinking patterns have been described for a number of ethnic groups in the United States, especially Jews, Irish, and Italians.[74] All three groups make extensive use of alcohol but the rates of alcoholism are very much higher among the Irish than among Jews and Italians, whose drinking practices appear to be better integrated with their dietary habits, family life, and religious beliefs. However, it has been observed that individuals who become alienated from the norms of groups in which alcoholism is rare become susceptible to particularly severe forms of alcoholism.

Although, as we have said, the consumption of alcohol cannot be considered a form of deviance in itself, alcoholism and drunkenness are the most important types of deviant behavior in the United States, measured by the number of persons and incidents involved, the direct social costs incurred, or the extent of restrictive efforts. *Alcoholism is a pattern of habitual heavy drinking that interferes with the drinker's ability to perform his assigned social roles. A distinction is sometimes made between spree alcoholism, which involves long periods of normal activity interspersed by bouts of uncontrollable drinking, and the addictive alcoholism of persons who have become dependent on alcohol and feel compelled to drink almost continuously. Drunkenness is the condition of a drinker who has lost control of his own behavior to the extent that he risks injury to himself or others.* Not all alcoholics get drunk—there are some who never do—and not all drunks are alcoholics; the majority of normal drinkers have probably experienced intoxication at one time or another. On the other hand, most of the persons arrested for public drunkenness can be identified as alcoholics, and alcoholics as a group have a very high incidence of drunken episodes.

There are said to be about five million alcoholics in the United States, that is, heavy drinkers whose drinking interferes with their routines and relationships and whose health has been, or will be, adversely affected by their drinking.[75] This estimate is necessarily imprecise, because the line between heavy drinkers and alcoholics cannot be drawn with certainty, but it seems to be of the right order of magnitude. It is based on a formula that estimates the number of alcoholics from the annual number of deaths from cirrhosis of the liver, a deteriorative disease closely associated with alcoholism. Alcoholism is typically a progressive condition and one of very long duration. It may take 20 years or more of steady drinking to induce physiological addiction. The life history of the alcoholic is typically marked by lost jobs and friendships, family crises, prolonged hospitalization, and other traumatic experiences directly attributable to drinking.

The social impact of alcoholism is directly reflected in the traffic casualty lists.[76] In the United States in 1967, the total number of deaths from motor vehicle accidents exceeded 53,000. After having declined slowly for many years, the death rate from motor vehicle accidents rose sharply from 21.3 per 100,000 population in 1960 to 27.1 in 1966,[77] and for each fatality, there were from 5 to 10 serious injuries. On all the available evidence a large proportion of these casualties can be attributed to alcoholic intoxication. The majority of drivers killed in motor vehicle accidents can be shown by post-mortem analysis to have been drinking, and since it is not always the drinking driver who is killed in such accidents, the proportion of fatal accidents involving alcohol is even higher, probably in the neighborhood of 75 percent. According to Morris and Hawkins, "At least half of all single vehicle mishaps in which the driver died and almost half the fatal multiple vehicle accidents were found to be the responsibility of the 1 to 4 percent of. American drivers who are heavy drinkers."[78]

Although drunken driving is punished with moderate severity when detected (license suspensions are common and jail sentences not unknown), attempts to restrict drunken driving by police inspection at highway checkpoints have met with massive public resistance. American sociability customs involve extensive drinking in what Clinard calls "public drinking halls"—bars, taverns, nightclubs, and so forth. There are more than 200,000 of these establishments in the United States. Relatively few of them are located within easy walking distance of their customers' homes. Sociability customs also involve serving liquor in private homes to guests who arrive and depart by automobile. Adolescent experimentation with drinking and driving occurs widely, often below the legal age fixed for either activity. The double inexperience of the novice driver who is also a novice drinker is particularly hazardous.

A third type of alcoholism is exemplified by homeless men who live in the Skid Row districts of large cities.[79] Their number is comparatively small—the total population of the New York Bowery, one of the largest and oldest Skid Row districts in the United States, was less than 7,000 in 1969—but Skid Row men are highly conspicuous because they spend most of their waking time in public places, often in a drunk and helpless condition. In addition to the homeless men on Skid Row, there is a much larger population of unaffiliated low-income males who are scattered through the city but exhibit some of the same behavior patterns as Skid Row men. The average homeless man is unmarried, middle-aged or elderly, with a history of irregular, low-level employment and very few family, community, religious, or political affiliations. Only a minority of the Skid Row men are alcoholics, but the majority participate in a drinking pattern, which involves the daily consumption of as much cheap sweet wine as they can obtain. Homeless men are very frequently arrested for public drunkenness or disorderly conduct, held overnight in jail, and either sentenced to a few days of imprisonment or released immediately. Many individuals in the Skid Row districts of large cities have records showing dozens and even hundreds of drunkenness arrests. Such arrests account for more than a third of all the police arrests made annually in the United States. The intended purposes of this strange pattern of law enforcement, which has been labelled "the Revolving Door," are unclear to most of the persons involved. Some cities are experimenting with "detoxification centers" to which public drunks can be taken for an overnight stay without arrest or trial. In other communities, arrests for drunkenness are no longer made unless some other offense, like molestation or property damage, has been committed.

There have been innumerable attempts to cure alcoholism, reduce the damage due to drunkenness, and rehabilitate homeless men. The national experiment with Prohibition was only the culmination of the various temperance movements that flourished through the United States throughout the nineteenth century; some of them remain active to this day. Prohibition is still maintained by local option in hundreds of cities and towns, and the sale and consumption of alcoholic beverages is extensively regulated by law in all 50 states, although no two states have identical regulations. Every state sets a minimum age (sometimes 18, but usually 21) for the purchase or consumption of alcoholic beverages. The hours, location, and internal arrangement of bars, taverns, and liquor stores are regulated everywhere. Special penalties are provided in most jurisdictions for violating any of the numerous regulations governing the sale or use of alcohol. The cure of alcoholics and the rehabilitation of homeless men is the business of dozens of agencies, ranging from old-fashioned revival missions to psychiatric clinics, and of dozens of organizations, of which Alcoholics Anonymous is the best known.

The results of these efforts have not, on the whole, been encouraging.[80] The long experience of Alcoholics Anonymous and of professionally staffed programs indicates that an alcoholic can give up drinking and return to a more normal pattern of social activity if his desire to do so is very strong. In any population of homeless men, a small minority can be helped by any serious program that enlists their active cooperation, but the large majorirty, who are not eager to change their way of life, participate in such programs only for limited, expedient purposes and are not much affected by them. The record of legislative restriction is equally poor. Although the regulation of drunken driving, adolescent drinking, and illegal sale cannot be dismissed as entirely ineffective, decades of legal experimentation have not produced satisfactory evidence that legislation or law enforcement can reduce alcoholism, discourage drunken driving, or control public drunkenness under the prevailing conditions.

DRUG ABUSE

A drug is a chemical substance that produces a definite desired effect when ingested by or applied to the human body. In addition to their desired effects, most drugs have undesired or *side* effects. Some drugs have a primary influence on physiological functions, others on mental functions, although it is probably the case that any drug with appreciable effect has some influence on both. A few of the drugs in use today have been known for centuries, but the greater number of them have been discovered in recent years. The use of drugs seems to increase with modernization, and among modernized countries, the United States—for reasons not well understood—shows the highest per capita consumption of drugs of all types.

For sociological purposes, the drugs in use in the United States today can be divided into three broad categories: prescription drugs, self-administered drugs, and illegal drugs.[81]

1. *Prescription drugs are those selected by a physician for an in-*

dividual patient and obtainable only with a prescription. This category, which has been expanding rapidly, includes a number of traditional substances like strychnine and belladonna, which are therapeutic in small amounts and poisonous in larger amounts, as well as the "miracle drugs" of recent decades, the sulfanilomides and antibiotics, insulin and insulin substitutes, the drugs that lower blood pressure and remove water from body tissues, the vaccines and the oral contraceptives. It also includes a group of drugs whose primary purpose is alteration of mood. They were first introduced in the 1950s. Some of these, like phenothiazine, have so powerful a quieting effect that they suppress psychotic symptoms and enable many patients who would formerly have remained in mental hospitals to lead a normal existence with sustained dosages. Other products, like meprobamate, have similar but much milder effects; they are frequently taken by nervous persons to cope with anxiety and depression. The total consumption of mood-changing pills in the United States is staggering, more than 10 *billion* pills annually.

Analgesics are used in surgical cases, for patients with severe injuries, and in painful illnesses. They fall into two major groups—barbiturates, used to induce sleep and relieve tension, and opiates, used to relieve severe pain by inducing partial or complete unconsciousness. Opiates fall into two groups: derivatives of the opium poppy, like morphine, and synthetic substitutes, like Dilaudid, but they all carry a risk of addiction. Heroin, the preferred drug of opiate addicts, was formerly a prescription drug, but can no longer be legally prescribed by a physician. The other opiates are used very extensively for medical purposes, but physicians are supposed to follow special regulations and procedures when prescribing them.

2. *Self-administered drugs include a host of products sold across the counter in drug stores and pharmacies and may also be considered to include nonpharmaceutical products like coffee, tea, and cigarettes, which have appreciable drug effects.* The drugs sold for self-administration include a great many traditional remedies, like castor oil, a number of modern synthetics, like vitamin drugs, whose side effects are believed to be negligible, and a few powerful drugs, like aspirin, that came into use before World War I when no drugs were under exclusive medical control. Although few, if any, new drugs are now released for self-administration, the widespread practice of writing "PRN" prescriptions, refillable at the patient's initiative, and the availability of black market sources, means that a good many prescription drugs are in fact available for self-administration, especially barbiturates, tranquilizers, and contraceptives.

3. *Illegal drugs are those that can neither be legitimately prescribed by a physician nor purchased for self-administration.*[82] The best-known examples in the United States at present are heroin, a partly synthetic derivative of opium, which can be sniffed, but is usually injected; marijuana, extracted from the Indian hemp plant and usually smoked like tobacco; and LSD, a synthetic chemical that is usually swallowed. Pure opium, another derivative of the hemp plant

called hashish, and a whole group of hallucinogenic drugs resembling LSD are also in this category.

Although the vast consumption of prescription and self-administered drugs in the United States may constitute a social problem, drug-taking within those categories cannot be classified as deviance, since it seldom violates social norms and elicits no significant reaction from norm-enforcing agents. The widespread concern about drug abuse is concentrated on illegal drugs, particularly those mentioned above.

Unlike the other types of deviant behavior we have discussed, this one is practically unique to the United States. Drug addiction is not a serious problem in any other highly developed country, and the patterns of drug consumption in undeveloped countries are quite dissimilar to ours. Moreover, illegal drug use in the United States excites more concern than other types of deviance that are much more important numerically. The number of known narcotic addicts in the United States in 1970 was less than 100,000, about half of them concentrated in New York City and most of the remainder in the metropolitan areas of Illinois, Texas, and California.[83] Yet there are few social problems that have recently engaged more of the public's attention or aroused so much controversy among experts. The reasons must be sought in the peculiar history of drug regulation in the United States and in the special linkages that have developed here among the several types of illegal drugs.

Opium is the dried juice of the opium poppy; it has been known to be used in various forms since antiquity. It contains two powerful alkaloids, morphine and codeine, which were isolated early in the nineteenth century. Morphine came into wide use about the time of the Civil War when the invention of the hypodermic needle provided a convenient means of administration. It was thought at first to be nonaddictive but soon recognized to be more addictive than opium. Heroin was developed in 1898 as a nonaddictive morphine substitute, which in turn proved even more addictive. A number of entirely synthetic narcotic drugs have since been developed, and these, too, are capable of producing addiction. Some pharmacologists maintain that any narcotic drug that reliably relieves pain and induces sleep in proportion to its dosage will necessarily be addictive, but the question is not entirely settled.

Opium and its derivatives have a cluster of familiar effects, which are not completely shared by the synthetic narcotics. When an opium product is administered regularly, (a) many recipients develop progressive tolerance, that is, they require increasing doses to obtain a constant effect; (b) a strong craving for the drug develops; and (c) physiological dependence—which makes it impossible to discontinue the drug without undergoing severe withdrawal symptoms—is established. The combination of (b) and (c) constitute addiction. Addiction to opiates can be established very quickly and without the user's intending to become addicted. It may even occur without the user's knowledge that he is taking an opiate; many of the patent medicines distributed in the United States in the nineteenth century contained substantial doses of an opium derivative called laudanum, and innocent users of these products often became addicted to them.

Once established, opium addiction is difficult to break, and after it is broken, it is easily reestablished. Careful studies of opiate addicts whose addiction has been interrupted at the Lexington hospital of the Public Health Service indicates that the great majority become readdicted within a few months. Even the most successful voluntary programs for the treatment of addiction, which accepts only addicts with a high motivation for cure, report more failures than successes. But although opiate addiction is a long-term condition, it is not necessarily lifelong. Some addicts become permanently abstinent after being cured and re-addicted several times. Others eventually give up the habit without any external help.

The other illegal drugs may be habituating but are not addictive. The users of marijuana and to a lesser extent the users of hallucinogens may rely on these drugs to alleviate the anxieties and tensions of daily life or may crave the repetition of drug experiences, but are not likely to become physiologically dependent on them or to suffer acutely if they are withdrawn (less so than the tobacco smoker, for example).

The use of opiates by physicians and laymen was completely legal in the United States until 1914, when Congress passed the Harrison Act as part of an international movement to control the traffic in opium and other addicting drugs. The act set an excise tax on these products, required persons handling them to register and to maintain exact records, and prohibited possession of the drugs except for legitimate medical purposes.

The apparent intentions of this law were soon much enlarged through the efforts of the Narcotics Division of the Treasury Department (later the Federal Bureau of Narcotics), which became and remains to this day a self-activated lobby for punitive drug legislation. The division vigorously prosecuted physicians who prescribed narcotics for addicts, even in the course of curing them, and obtained a number of court decisions that seemed to exclude the treatment of addicts from the "legitimate medical purposes" mentioned in the Harrison Act. Although these decisions were later reversed, their effect was permanent; physicians ceased to prescribe narcotics for known addicts or to regard addiction as a treatable condition.[84] An illegal traffic in opiates sprang up to supply the demand of the addicted population, and heroin became the drug of choice—except for addicted physicians, and other special groups. The price of opiates, which had formerly been quite moderate, rose to astronomical levels that generated huge profits for the illegal suppliers and made it necessary for the typical addict to engage in crime in order to obtain the means of supplying his habit, and to frequent an underworld milieu in order to remain in contact with drug suppliers.

The outcome has been an increasingly close connection between drug addiction and crime, a dramatic shift in the social characteristics

of the addict population, and a steady movement toward more punitive legislation. The manufacture of heroin was prohibited in 1924,
marijuana became an illegal drug in 1937, and the penalties for drug
offenses were greatly stiffened by the Boggs Amendment of 1951 and
by the Narcotic Drug Control Act of 1956. The latter set the minimum
federal penalty for mere possession at two years' imprisonment and
the maximum penalty for sale (of heroin to a person under 18 by a
person over 18) as death. In addition, by 1960 all but a handful of
states had passed a standard drug control law drafted by the Narcotics Bureau, and the main burden of drug law enforcement had shifted
from federal to state agencies. In 1961, for example, the total number
of federal narcotics prosecutions (excluding marijuana cases) was 1,-
436. The total number of state and local prosecutions was nearly 20
times as great.[85]

Although both federal and state laws impose severe penalties for
both the possession and sale of marijuana, these are so incongruous
with the prevailing attitudes of the public and of law enforcement
agencies that no serious attempt is made to enforce them except in
the case of wholesale smugglers and dealers. Most of the existing
legislation does not provide specific penalties for the use of LSD and
other hallucinogens. By the time such legislation began to be drafted
in the late 1960s, the use of these drugs had apparently diminished,
as the reports of harmful side effects came to be believed by users.

From 1965 to 1970 there was a great upsurge of interest in, and
discussion of, illegal drugs. Whether it was accompanied by a corresponding increase in the use of illegal drugs is difficult to determine.
The available evidence suggests that heroin addiction remained at
about the same level, rising in some localities but declining in others,
that marijuana use increased sharply, and that the use of hallucinogens increased very rapidly and then more slowly declined.

A number of sociologists who have specialized in the study of drug
problems attribute the unusual scale and persistence of addiction in
the United States to the isolation of the drug addict from medical aid
and the economic inducements created for dealers by attempted
prohibition. They point to the experience of other countries, especially
Great Britiain, as evidence that a more permissive, medically oriented
approach to drug problems yields a much smaller volume of drug use
than the futile attempt to suppress the use of opiates entirely.[86] Although the main outlines of this argument are fairly convincing, there
is some evidence that the use of opiates was more widespread in the
United States than in any European country back in the nineteenth
century when there was no regulation whatever. A careful study carried out in Michigan in 1878[87] estimated the number of "opium and
morphine eaters" in the United States as 117,000, based on the analysis of what appear to be fairly solid contemporary data. A 1915
study, using data obtained from the compulsory registration of addicts
in Tennessee,[88] estimated the national total as 269,000 and discussed
the growing use of the new drug, heroin, among adolescent males in
large cities.

On balance, punitive legislation should probably not be held solely responsible for narcotics addiction in the United States, although it has almost certainly increased the impact of addiction as a social problem and affected the social attributes of users. Before the passage of the Harrison Act the typical opium addict in the United States was a white middle-aged female. Today, male addicts outnumber female addicts by about five to one. The majority of them are young adults drawn from minority groups in metropolitan areas and are likely to be unemployed, engaged in illegal activities besides drug-taking, heavily involved in addict culture, and isolated from nonusers.

Some other types of opiate addiction also persist, but are much less important numerically than heroin addiction. Addiction is fairly common among physicians, but the typical physician addict contracts his habit in isolation, uses demerol rather than heroin, and ordinarily has no contact with other addicts or with the addict culture until he is caught.[89]

The relationship between opiate addiction and the use of other illegal drugs varies with time, place, and circumstances. In areas where heroin addiction is common, the use of marijuana by adolescents often precedes and leads to heroin addiction.[90] Among other marijuana-using groups, like jazz musicians and student radicals, the progression to heroin is virtually unknown, although marijuana usage appears to be connected with the use of hallucinogens and, in some instances, with a diffuse pattern of drug use that embraces a variety of products from benzedrine to opium. The principal social problem associated with marijuana usage is the conflict established between nonusers, who accept the legal prohibition as right and proper, and users, who insist that marijuana is neither addictive nor particularly harmful in any other way.

There is no serious question, however, about the incapacitating effects of heroin on its users or about the antisocial consequences of heroin under existing conditions, and enormous resources have been devoted to various treatment programs.[91] The most successful of these appear to be methadone maintenance and residential programs of the Synanon type. Methadone is a synthetic opiate that has relatively little effect on sensation or behavior but blocks out the effect of any heroin taken concurrently. By converting heroin addiction into methadone addiction, some clinic programs enable their patients to hold jobs, reestablish family relationships, and return to normal social roles. Some individuals are eventually able to give up the substitute drug also; others need to be maintained on a constant daily dosage. In programs of the Synanon type, the addict is allowed to join a residential group composed entirely of ex-addicts if he can persuade them of his sincerity in wanting to give up his addiction. The residential group acts like a large but intimate family in which the ex-addict is responsible to his fellows for every aspect of his daily behavior and is forced to reject all the norms and habits of the addict culture in order to remain in good standing and enjoy the emotional rewards offered by the group. The Synanon approach is appropriate only for people who are highly motivated to change their deviant status, but with some of these, it has near-miraculous results.[92]

ILLEGAL GAMBLING

The complex relationship between regulation and deviance in a modern society is even better illustrated by the case of gambling than by that of illegal drug-taking, since gambling has to a large extent been legalized in the United States but illegal gambling persists and thrives anyhow.

Gambling—making the transfer of money or other valuables contingent on the outcome of a future and uncertain event[93]—is as old and widespread a social practice as the use of alcohol, and has much more frequently aroused disapproval. It was outlawed by the laws of ancient Egypt, the Hindu code, the Talmud, and the Koran. Under English law, generally copied in the United States, a winner cannot recover a gambling debt by legal process. The gambling practices that are familiar today—betting on races and athletic contests; cards, dice, and roulette; and lotteries of all kinds—have been banned more often than they have been permitted, although such bans are seldom completely effective.

The laws about gambling are so diverse and arbitrary that they are difficult to summarize, but there seems to be a slow, irregular drift toward the legalization of gambling in the United States and other countries. Betting on horse races has always been legal in a few states, like Kentucky and New York. In recent years, the national wire services, which had made remote betting on horse races possible throughout the country, have been broken up by prosecution, but at the same time, more than half the states have legalized betting at racetracks.[94] Nevada in 1931 legalized all forms of gambling, and two of its towns, Reno and Las Vegas, have become major tourist centers because of their gambling facilities. Many states permit certain forms of gambling, under religious or charitable auspices, and several states, including New York and New Jersey, operate lotteries.

None of these legal arrangements permits a gambler to gamble daily or weekly with a chance of winning substantially, a pattern that appears to be preferred by the large (but unknown) proportion of the population who gamble. Such opportunities are provided by a network of illicit gambling arrangements. The principal forms of illicit gambling in the United States are the numbers; off-track betting on horse races; bookmaker betting on baseball, football, basketball, and elections; slot machines of various types, and undercover gambling houses. There are almost innumerable minor forms of illegal gambling, including punchboards, pool hall betting, and high-stake bridge and poker.

Gambling methods vary according to income, social class, and ethnicity. The numbers game is a daily lottery in which players bet small amounts on a 3-digit number they have picked; a winning number pays between 500 and 800 times the original bet. The game is widely played, and even more widely followed, in urban slum neighborhoods, especially by blacks, Puerto Ricans, and Mexican Americans. Off-track betting on horse races and betting on athletic contests are closely related activities, sometimes handled by the same bookmakers, but horseplayers are probably of somewhat lower socioeconomic status, on the average, than bettors on athletic events. In a local setting, each group may have its preferred pattern. One description of a working bookmaker in Brooklyn quotes him as saying, "The Jews like baseball and basketball, but especially baseball. That's the biggest play today. The big-money boys like the one-to-one situation of the starting pitchers. Guys today follow Koufax and Marichal like guys years ago would follow Man O'War and Dan Patch. The Irish and Italians like the horses and pro football. The Negroes and the Puerto Ricans, because they don't have the bread, play the numbers—sucker odds, 500-to-1. . . . "[95] Except for a few specialized gambling houses in some of the larger cities, there are no methods of illicit gambling designed for high-income customers; the stock market and commodity exchanges, although intended for other purposes, provide them with an almost infinite supply of legitimate gambling opportunities.

Illicit gambling has been less studied than any other major type of deviance. Estimates of the total number of persons involved, either as professionals or as customers, the volume of wagers, or the profitability of gambling enterprises are purely speculative. Unlike a prostitute or a drug addict, the professional gambler usually maintains a respectable appearance and reputation and is highly resistant to sociological inquiry; however, a few research findings may be noted:

1. The customer of an illegal gambling facility is seldom treated as a deviant; the application of antigambling laws is limited to the professional gambler.

2. Every known form of professional gambling is highly profitable. The professional gambler is almost invariably recruited from the same social level as his customers, but has a higher average standard of living; the poorer the community, the greater the relative advantage of the gambler and the more substantial the status claims he can make.[96] In slum neighborhoods, opportunities to enter gambling occupations are as eagerly sought as opportunities for vertical mobility in legitimate occupations.

3. In illicit gambling, the customer's only protection against being cheated is the personal reputation of the man who takes his bet. To establish such a reputation, the gambler must work in one locality and establish a network of personal contacts.[97] Operating in this way, he is unlikely to escape the attention of the police and other authorities and cannot expect to remain in business unless the police are bought off. Every system of illegal gambling seems to involve the corruption of public officials.

4. Because the gambler handles large sums of money while remaining outside the protection of the law, he is peculiarly vulnerable to force, whether applied by the strong-arm men of a criminal syndi-

cate or by policemen. Most professional gamblers are employed by, or operate under the control of, organizations that provide protection from both law enforcement agencies and criminal intruders along with financial backing and other services. Illegal gambling is the principal source of revenue for large-scale criminal syndicates in the United States, and it provides the capital for their forays into other fields of business.

Thus, as in the case of narcotics addiction, the secondary consequences of prohibiting a disapproved but widely desired activity are probably more disruptive of the institutional structure than the prohibited activity could be by itself. Once a pattern of regulation and evasion has been established, however, it is difficult to dismantle. Given an existing network of criminal organizations built on the profits of illegal gambling, the legalization of gambling is likely to present them with new opportunities for profitable fraud and the corruption of public officials. Although these obstacles have been overcome in some European and Latin American countries, where public lotteries are conducted sufficiently often to satisfy the habitual gambler and numerous safeguards insure fair play, it remains an open question whether such arrangements would be feasible in the United States, where discrepancies between the norms embodied in legislation and those expressed by private behavior appear to be greater than in most other countries.

Summary / CHAPTER ELEVEN

1. Deviance is behavior that violates explicit social norms and elicits corrective or punitive reactions from norm-enforcing agents. It is socially patterned; the force of norms varies according to time and place, deviant behavior is often group-sponsored, and a change in the frequency of deviant acts in a population modifies the applicable norms.

2. Contrary to popular belief, there does not seem to be a close correlation between modernization and deviance. Some forms of deviance increase with modernization, others show stable, declining, or irregular trends.

3. Crimes against persons and property are more frequent in the United States than in most other industrialized countries, and have recently been rising rapidly. Although it is difficult to find a single cause of criminality, the frequency of serious offenses is strongly affected by community size and location and by the age, sex, race, and income level of the persons involved. Serious crimes are concentrated in metropolitan cities generally, and certain cities in particular, and are committed predominantly by young males. The poor and nonwhites are heavily represented among both offenders and victims.

4. Suicide rates are remarkably stable in a given population from year to year, and if a population is subdivided by the major social characteristics of its members, the subpopulations show large and significant differences in their rates also. Males are more prone to suicide than females, older people than younger people, whites than blacks, single persons than married persons. In addition, religion, occupation, and personal relationships have marked effects upon the propensity to suicide.

5. Some deviant sexual relationships are defined as major crimes (incest, bigamy, and statutory rape), some as minor offenses (prostitution, juvenile promiscuity, homosexuality), and some as shameful but not criminal (extramarital affairs, illegitimacy). Each of these activities is socially patterned, but the patterns have little in common, and do not follow a single trend.

6. For reasons not clearly understood, the social control of deviant habits such as alcoholism, drug-taking, and illegal gambling has been less successful in the United States than in most other countries. The social impact of alcoholism is expressed in a large toll of traffic casualties. The use of mood-changing drugs in various forms has been spreading rapidly, and attempts to suppress addiction to narcotics and habituation to marijuana and hallucinogens by criminal sanctions have been ineffective. Illicit gambling persists despite the legalization of some forms of gambling.

1. Almost everyone has anomic reactions in some situations. Can you find examples of innovation, ritualism, retreatism, and rebellion in your own past behavior?

2. What does it mean to say, "Alcoholism (or homosexuality or delinquency) is a disease and should be treated, rather than punished"? What are the usual arguments for and against such statements?

3. Have you ever stolen a small article from a store or public place? If your answer is affirmative, did that make you a delinquent?

4. How do you account for the fact that women commit very few serious crimes, compared to men?

5. Does the increase of suicide with advancing age imply that older people are unhappier on the average than younger people?

6. Under what social conditions will the illegitimacy rate be very low? Under what conditions will it be very high?

7. Prostitutes, skid row derelicts, and drug addicts are sometimes described as occupying "stigmatized statuses." What do such statuses have in common?

8. Programs that have attempted to reduce drug abuse in schools and colleges by familiarizing students with the dangers of addiction and other side effects have not been conspicuously successful. Can you suggest a sociological explanation for this?

Recommended Reading / CHAPTER ELEVEN

McGee, Reece. *Social Disorganization.* San Francisco: Chandler, 1962. Describes the interplay of organizational norms and deviant behavior.

Blumberg, , Abraham S. *Criminal Justice.* Chicago: Quadrangle Books, 1967; David J. Bordua, ed. *The Police: Six Sociological Essays.* New York: John Wiley & Sons, 1967; David A. Ward and Gene G. Kassebaum. *Women's Prison: Sex and Social Structure.* Chicago: Aldine, 1965; David J. Pittman and C. Wayne Gordon. *Revolving Door: A Study of the Chronic Police Case Inebriate.* New York: Free Press,

1958; and Alvin W. Gouldner. *Patterns of Industrial Bureaucracy.* New York: Free Press, 1954. Readable studies of the pitfalls and problems of official norm-enforcement.

Cressey, Donald R., and David A. Ward, eds. *Delinquency, Crime and Social Process.* New York: Harper & Row, 1969; John H. Gagnon and William Simon, eds., *Sexual Deviance.* New York: Harper & Row, 1969; Morris E. Chafetz and Harold W. Demone, Jr.. *Alcoholism and Society.* New York: Oxford University Press, 1962; Alfred R. Linde-smith. *Addiction and Opiates.* Chicago: Aldine, 1968; Erich Goode. *Marijuana.* New York: Atherton Press, 1970. Authoritative works on particular aspects of deviance.

Notes / **CHAPTER ELEVEN**

1. An extended discussion of this concept and its evolution may be found in Simon Dinitz, Russell R. Dynes, and Alfred C. Clarke, *Deviance: Studies in the Process of Stigmatization and Societal Reaction* (New York: Oxford University Press, 1969), pp. 3–22; Earl Rubington and Martin S. Weinberg, eds., *Deviance: The Interactionist Perspective* (New York: Macmillan, 1968); Jack P. Gibbs, "Conceptions of Deviance: The Old and the New," in *Approaches to Deviance: Theories, Concepts and Research Findings,* ed. Mark Lefton, James K. Skipper, Jr., and Charles H. McCaghy (New York: Appleton-Century-Crofts, 1968), pp. 44–55.
2. Howard S. Becker, ed., *Social Problems: A Modern Approach* (New York: John Wiley, 1966).
3. Note, for example, Erwin O. Smigel, ed., *Work and Leisure: A Contemporary Social Problem* (New Haven: College and University Press, 1963).
4. Emile Durkheim, *Suicide: A Study in Sociology,* trans. John A. Spaulding and George Simpson (New York: Free Press, 1951), pp. 241–276; originally published 1897. See also the discussion in Chapter Four above.
5. Merton has suggested that the English form of the word *anomia* be used to describe the condition in individuals, and that the French form *anomie* be reserved for entire social systems, but they are often used interchangeably. Robert K. Merton, "Anomie, Anomia and Social Interaction: Contexts of Deviant Behavior," in *Anomie and Deviant Behavior: A Discussion and Critique,* ed. Marshall B. Clinard (New York: Free Press, 1964), pp. 213–242; see also Merton's chapter "Social Structure and Anomie," in *Social Theory and Social Structure,* enlarged ed. (New York: Free Press, 1968).
6. With the possible exception of a few peoples, like the Greenland

Eskimos, who had no formal organizations larger than the nuclear family.

7. For an illuminating description of a system of criminal law entirely different from our own, see the account of crime and punishment among the Comanche in Edward Adamson Hoebel, *The Law of Primitive Man: A Study in Comparative Legal Dynamics* (Cambridge, Mass.: Harvard University Press, 1954).

8. The workings of such arrangements are shown in detail in Abraham S. Blumberg, *Criminal Justice* (Chicago: Quadrangle Books, 1967); and in Donald J. Newman, "Pleading Guilty for Considerations: A Study of Bargain Justice," *Journal of Criminal Law, Criminology and Police Science* 46, no. 6 (March-April 1956): 780–790.

9. The principal source for this section is the President's Commission on Law Enforcement and the Administration of Justice, *The Challenge of Crime in a Free Society: A Report* (Washington, D.C.: U.S. Government Printing Office, 1967), chap. 2, pp. 17–53.

10. More precisely, the population of a national reporting area that included a little more than two-thirds of the population.

11. John R. Seeley, "Social Science? Some Probative Problems," in *Radical Perspectives on Social Problems: Readings in Critical Sociology,* ed. Frank Lindenfeld (New York: Macmillan, 1968), pp. 4–12. The quotation is from p. 8.

12. President's Commission, *The Challenge of Crime,* chap. 2, p. 30.

13. U.S. Bureau of the Census, Department of Commerce, *Statistical Abstract of the United States* (Washington, D.C.: U.S. Government Printing Office, 1968), table 213.

14. Sheldon Hackney, "Southern Violence," *American Historical Review* 74, no. 3 (February 1969): 906–925.

15. *Statistical Abstract of the United States 1967,* table 238.

16. For an excellent brief summary of what is known about female delinquency, see David A. Ward and Gene G. Kassebaum, *Women's Prison: Sex and Social Structure* (Chicago: Aldine, 1965), pp. 58–69.

17. *Statistical Abstract of the United States 1967,* tables 219 and 220.

18. Jackson Toby, "Affluence and Adolescent Crime," in *Delinquency, Crime and Social Process,* ed. Donald R. Cressey and D. A. Ward (New York: Harper & Row, 1969), pp. 285–311.

19. For a description of this pattern, see Carl Werthman and Irvin Piliavin, "Gang Members and the Police," in *The Police: Six Sociological Essays,* ed. David J. Bordua (New York: John Wiley, 1967), pp. 56–98; Richard A. Cloward and Lloyd E. Ohlin, *Delinquency and Opportunity: A Theory of Delinquent Gangs* (New York: Free Press, 1961).

20. *Statistical Abstract of the United States 1967,* table 238.

21. John P. Clark and Eugene P. Wenninger, "Socio-Economic Class and Area as Correlates of Illegal Behavior Among Juveniles," in

Cressey and Ward, *Delinquency, Crime and Social Process*, pp. 388–403.

22. This is one of the best studied topics in current sociology. See, among many other works, Albert K. Cohen, *Delinquent Boys: The Culture of the Gang* (New York: Free Press, 1963).
23. President's Commission, *The Challenge of Crime*. chap. 2, pp. 38–39.
24. *Ibid.,* pp. 39–40.
25. Edwin H. Sutherland, "White-Collar Criminality," *American Sociological Review* 5, no. 1 (February 1940): 1–12.
26. Edwin H. Sutherland, "Is White-Collar Crime Crime?" *American Sociological Review* 10, no. 2 (April 1945): 132–139.
27. Among others, Vilhelm Aubert, "White-Collar Crime and Social Structure," *American Journal of Sociology* 58, no. 3 (November 1952): 263–271; Paul W. Tappan, "Who Is the Criminal?" *American Sociological Review* 12, no. 1 (February 1947): 96–102.
28. Ample evidence for this assertion may be found in Gilbert Geis, ed., *White-Collar Criminal: The Offender in Business and the Professions* (New York: Atherton Press, 1968).
29. Donald R. Cressey, *Other People's Money: A Study in the Social Psychology of Embezzlement* (New York: Free Press, 1953).
30. Erikson has extracted from the court records of Essex County the rates of conviction of various offenses in seventeenth-century Puritan New England. They are not as low as one might expect. Converted to a comparable base, the annual rate of conviction for crimes against persons and property in 1651–1655 was 174 per 100,000 of the population. Kai Erikson, *Wayward Puritans: A Study in the Sociology of Deviance* (New York: John Wiley, 1966), table 3, p. 175.
31. Roger Lane, "Urbanization and Criminal Violence in the Nineteenth Century: Massachusetts as a Test Case," in *The History of Violence in America: Historical and Comparative Perspectives,* Report to the National Commission on the Causes and Prevention of Violence, ed. Hugh Davis Graham and Ted Robert Gurr (New York: Praeger, 1969), pp. 445–459.
32. President's Commission, *The Challenge of Crime,* figs. 3 and 4, pp. 22 and 23, respectively.
33. Fred P. Graham, "A Contemporary History of American Crime," in Graham and Gurr, *The History of Violence in America,* pp. 485–504.
34. *Ibid.,* 501.
35. One published bibliography lists 2,202 books and papers published from 1897 to 1957, and 1,267 more published between 1958 and 1967. Norman L. Farberow, *Bibliography on Suicide and Suicide Prevention 1897–1957, 1958–1967* (Chevy Chase, Md.: National Institute of Mental Health, 1969).
36. The data for these generalizations are nicely summarized in Jack P. Gibbs, "Suicide," in *Contemporary Social Problems,* ed. Robert K. Merton and Robert A. Nisbet, 2nd ed. (New York: Harcourt,

Brace & World, 1966), pp. 281–321; and in "Suicide," *Encylopedia Brittanica,* 14th ed., 21: 532–534.

37. Gibbs, "Suicide," table 10, p. 307.
38. *Statistical Abstract of the United States 1968,* table 239.
39. Durkheim, *Suicide,* p. 209.
40. Andrew F. Henry and James F. Short, *Suicide and Homicide: Some Economic, Sociological, and Psychological Aspects of Aggression* (New York: Free Press, 1954).
41. William Graham Sumner, *Folkways: A Study of the Sociological Importance of Usages, Manners, Customs, Mores, and Morals* (New York: Ginn, 1940); originally published 1906.
42. George Peter Murdock, *Social Structure* (New York: Macmillan, 1949).
43. S. Kirson Weinberg, *Incest Behavior* (New York: Citadel Press, 1955).
44. Jerome H. Skolnick and J. Richard Woodworth, "Bureaucracy, Information and Social Control: A Study of a Morals Detail," in Bordua, *The Police,* pp. 99–136.
45. *Ibid.,* p. 109.
46. A system of male prostitution is described in Albert J. Reiss, Jr., "The Social Integration of Queers and Peers," *Social Problems* 9, no. 2 (Fall 1961): 102–120.
47. John H. Gagnon, "Prostitution," in *International Encyclopedia of the Social Sciences,* ed. David L. Sills (New York: Free Press and Macmillan, 1968), vol. 12, pp. 592–598.
48. For an account of how this norm is taught and learned see James H. Bryan, "Apprenticeships in Prostitution," *Social Problems* 12, no. 3 (Winter 1965): 287–297.
49. Harold Greenwald, *The Call Girl: A Social and Psychoanalytic Study* (New York: Ballantine Books, 1965).
50. Alfred C. Kinsey, Wendell B. Pomeroy, and Clyde E. Martin, *Sexual Behavior in the Human Male* (Philadelphia: Saunders, 1948), pp. 595–609.
51. Alfred C. Kinsey et al., *Sexual Behavior in the Human Female* (Philadelphia: Saunders, 1953), pp. 298–302.
52. Kingsley Davis, "Sexual Behavior," in Merton and Nisbet, *Contemporary Social Problems,* pp. 322–373. The quotation is from p. 371.
53. Morris Ploscowe, *Sex and the Law* (Englewood Cliffs, N.J.: Prentice-Hall, 1951).
54. Ward and Kassebaum, *Women's Prison.*
55. Donald Clemmer, *The Prison Community* (New York: Holt, Rinehart & Winston, 1958); Gresham M. Sykes, *The Society of Captives: A Study of a Maximum Security Prison* (Princeton, N.J.: Princeton University Press, 1958).
56. Evelyn Hooker, "Sexual Behavior: Homsexuality," in *International Encyclopedia of the Social Sciences,* vol. 14 (1968), p. 229.
57. John H. Gagnon and William Simon, "Homosexuality: The Formulation of a Sociological Perspective," *Journal of Health and Social Behavior* 8, no. 3 (September 1967): 177–185.

58. See, for example, John F. Cuber and Peggy B. Harroff, *The Significant Americans: A Study of Sexual Behavior Among the Affluent* (New York: Appleton-Century-Crofts, 1965), with reference to a high-status sample; and Elliot Liebow, *Tally's Corner: A Study of Negro Streetcorner Men* (Boston: Little, Brown, 1967), with reference to a low-status sample.

59. United Nations, Statistical Office, Department of Economic and Social Affairs, *Demographic Yearbook* (New York: United Nations, 1959), table 10.

60. *Statistical Abstract of the United States 1968,* tables 55 and 60.

61. Bronislaw Malinowski, "Parenthood—the Basis of Social Structure," in *The New Generation: The Intimate Problems of Modern Parents and Children,* ed. V. F. Calverton and Samuel D. Schmalhausen (New York: Macauley, 1930): 137.

62. See Judith Blake, *Family Structure in Jamaica* (New York: Free Press, 1962).

63. William J. Goode, "Illegitimacy in the Caribbean Social Structure," *American Sociological Review* 25, no. 1 (February 1960): 21–30; and "Illegitimacy, Anomie and Cultural Penetration," *American Sociological Review* 26, no. 6 (December 1961): 910–925.

64. Goode, "Illegitimacy, Anomie and Cultural Penetration," p. 914.

65. James F. Short, Jr. and Fred L. Strodtbeck, *Group Process and Gang Delinquency* (Chicago: University of Chicago Press, 1965), chap. 2, pp. 27–46.

66. For a cross-cultural view of drinking patterns, see David J. Pittman and Charles R. Snyder, eds., *Society, Culture and Drinking Patterns* (New York: John Wiley, 1962).

67. This estimate is based on various studies, which are summarized and cited in Robert Straus, "Alcohol," in Merton and Nisbet, *Contemporary Social Problems,* pp. 236–280.

68. *Statistical Abstract of the United States 1968,* table 1122.

69. Most current discussions of group differences in drinking patterns lean heavily on a national questionnaire survey covering a sample of 16,000 college students in 1949–1951. Robert Straus and Seldon D. Bacon, *Drinking in College* (New Haven: Yale University Press, 1953).

70. U.S. Bureau of the Census, *Historical Statistics of the United States: Colonial Times to 1957* (Washington, D.C.: U.S. Government Printing Office, 1957), series P187–232.

71. *Statistical Abstract of the United States 1968,* table 1122.

72. There is a fairly extensive literature on the sociology of public drinking places. See, among others, Marshall B. Clinard, "The Public Drinking House and Society," in Pittman and Snyder, *Society, Culture and Drinking Patterns,* pp. 270–292; Sherri Cavan, *Liquor License: An Ethnography of Bar Behavior* (Chicago: Aldine, 1966).

73. Robert Freed Bales, "Cultural Differences in Rates of Alcoholism," *Quarterly Journal of Studies on Alcohol* 6, no. 4 (March 1946):

480–499; Charles R. Snyder, *Alcohol and the Jews: A Cultural Study of Drinking and Sobriety* (New York: Free Press, 1958); Giorgio Lolli et al., *Alcohol in Italian Culture: Food and Wine in Relation to Sobriety Among Italians and Italian Americans* (New York: Free Press, 1958).

74. Straus, "Alcohol," p. 267.

75. For a general discussion of the problem, see B. H. Fox and J. H. Fox, eds., *Alcohol and Traffic Safety,* Public Health Service Bulletin 1043 (Washington, D.C.: U.S. Government Printing Office, 1963).

76. *Statistical Abstract of the United States 1968,* table 72.

77. For a thorough discussion of drunken driving as the most prevalent type of violence in our society, and of possible means of controlling it, see Norval Morris and Gordon Hawkins, "From Murder and From Violence, Good Lord, Deliver Us," *Midway* 10, no. 1 (Summer 1969): 71.

78. Skid Row has been as extensively studied by sociologists as any sector of modern society. One of the most comprehensive reports is Donald J. Bogue, *Skid Row in American Cities* (University of Chicago: Community and Family Study Center, 1963). For an annotated bibliography of the literature on homelessness and disaffiliation, see Howard M. Bahr, ed., *Disaffiliated Man: Essays and Bibliography on Skid Row, Vagrancy, and Outsiders* (Toronto: University of Toronto Press, 1970).

79. Morris E. Chafetz and Harold W. Demone, Jr., *Alcoholism and Society* (New York: Oxford University Press, 1962).

80. For a general discussion of the use and abuse of drugs of all three types, see Bernard Barber, *Drugs and Society* (New York: Russell Sage Foundation, 1967).

81. The characteristics and effects of opiates are briefly and clearly described in Edwin M. Schur, *Narcotic Addiction in Britain and America: The Impact of Public Policy* (Bloomington, Ind.: Indiana University Press, 1962), pp. 18–35; and those of other illegal drugs in Richard M. Blum, "Mind-Altering Drugs and Dangerous Behavior," in U.S. Task Force on Narcotics and Drug Abuse, Task Force Report, *Narcotics and Drug Abuse: Annotations and Consultants' Papers* (Washington, D.C.: U.S. Government Printing Office, 1967), pp. 23–29.

82. for data supporting these estimates, see John A. O'Donnell and John C. Ball, eds., *Narcotic Addiction* (New York: Harper & Row, 1966), pp. 6–9.

83. See Joint Committee of the American Bar Association and the American Medical Association on Narcotic Drugs, *Drug Addiction: Crime or Disease?* Interim and Final Reports (Bloomington, Ind.: Indiana University Press, 1961).

84. The total number of state and local prosecutions in that year was 29,122, but 10 to 15 percent of these were marijuana cases. Alfred R. Lindesmith, *The Addict and the Law* (Bloomington. Ind.: Indiana University Press, 1965), pp. 112–113.

85. See Schur, *Narcotic Addiction,* and Lindesmith, *The Addict and the Law,* for the full development of these arguments.

86. O. Marshall, "The Opium Habit in Michigan," in O'Donnell and Ball, *Narcotic Addiction,* pp. 45–54.

87. Lucius P. Brown, "Enforcement of the Tennessee Anti-Narcotics Law," *ibid.,* pp. 34–45.

88. Charles Winick, "Physician Narcotic Addicts," *Social Problems* 9, no. 2 (Fall 1961): 174–186.

89. Daniel Glaser, James Inciardi, and Dean Babst, *Later Heroin Use by Adolescent Marijuana and Heroin Users, and by Non-Drug Using Adolescent Offenders* (new York State Narcotic Addiction Control Commission, Division of Research, mimeographed, September 1968).

90. The available methods are summarized in Appendix C to U.S. Task Force, *Narcotics and Drug Abuse.*

91. For an analytic description of the Synanon program, see Rita Volkman and Donald R. Cressey, "Differential Association and the Rehabilitation of Drug Addicts," *American Journal of Sociology* 69, no. 2 (September 1963): 129–142.

92. This definition follows that of Edward C. Devereux, Jr., "Gambling," *International Encyclopedia of the Social Sciences,* vol. 6 (1968), pp. 53–62.

93. The entire cultural complex associated with betting on horse races is described with loving care in Marvin B. Scott, *The Racing Game* (Chicago: Aldine, 1968).

94. Joe Flaherty, "Frankie Carlin, the Bookie," in *America's Troubles: A Casebook on Social Conflict,* ed. H. E. Freeman and N. R. Kurtz (Englewood Cliffs, N.J.: Prentice-Hall, 1969), p. 434.

95. A study of Negro numbers men incarcerated in a reformatory found that "the men presented themselves as respectable, middle class people who were churchgoers, homeowners, and fathers." Julian B. Roebuck, "The Numbers Man," in Dinitz, Dynes, and Clarke, *Deviance,* p. 79.

96. One of the few studies that show the numbers game and its associated activities in a larger community structure is Irving Spergel, *Racketville, Slumtown, Haulburg: An Exploratory Study of Delinquent Subcultures* (Chicago: University of Chicago Press, 1964).

Part Three

Macrosociology

The three chapters in this last part of Elementary Sociology are concerned with some of the major social issues that confront the world as a whole and that can be usefully studied by sociological methods.

Social Conflict

XII

Introduction

The containment of conflict is the crucial problem of modern civilization. The invention of nuclear explosives during World War II and the subsequent improvement and mass production of such weapons has created a universal emergency that puts the survival of humanity in question. The system of mutual deterrence, which has so far prevented nuclear war, appears to be too fragile a device to function indefinitely but more effective means of prevention have been slow to evolve, and every nation of the world carries on its affairs under a sword of Damocles.

In the United States, the long period of domestic tranquility that began with the New Deal of 1933 ended around 1965, when the Vietnam conflict divided the country more sharply than any other issue of the previous hundred years. The civil rights movement in many places became a hostile confrontation of whites and blacks, and a wave of rebellion broke out in colleges, churches, and other hitherto peaceful institutions.

The sociological importance of conflict hardly needs to be underlined for a student in today's world. The existing knowledge in this field[1] is plainly inadequate to meet existing needs. We do not know how to abolish war or racial prejudice or even how to contain them within tolerable limits, although a large majority of the population and an overwhelming majority of national leaders would like to do so, or say they would.

It is not entirely clear why the sociology of conflict appears so retarded in relation to other branches of sociology. A partial explanation is that the empirical study of conflict situations is difficult. There may be no place for a neutral observer to stand even when the opposing sides are willing to respect his neutrality. Another explanation is that elements of indeterminacy are built into every conflict situation. The strategist uses all the data available to him to simulate his antagonist's prediction of future events and then shapes a course of action calculated to invalidate that prediction. The strategist on the other side does the same. Unless the sociological observer has a great deal more data than either of them, which is unlikely, he may not be able to establish causal relationships under these circumstances.

The fundamental reason why so little progress has been made in the sociology of conflict, however, is probably theoretical rather than methodological. Conflict, for the sociologist, is not a flaw in the social machinery to be located and repaired but a basic social process, without which no large-scale social system could survive. It is one side of a coin, the other side of which is called cooperation. In order to reduce the incidence of conflict in a social system or to abolish a particular type of conflict, it may be necessary to transform that system profoundly. The resources for such a transformation may not be available to a would-be reformer, or for the time being, to anyone else.

How to Recognize Conflict

The minimum elements of a social conflict are two or more antagonists (either individuals or groups) on two opposing "sides," at least one scarce thing for which they contend, and some means whereby they can interact and influence each other's behavior. Each party to a conflict has some hope of winning and some fear of losing, and his activity is directed in a general way toward winning.

Social conflict is a process of interaction between persons or groups with incompatible goals. It should not be confused with psychological conflict, in which an individual is torn by conflicting motives, the conflict between curiosity and the urge to flight, for example. Social conflict should also be distinguished from impersonal forms of competition, like competitive examinations; from one-sided forms of aggression, like genocide; from the opposition of abstract or intangible forces, like the "conflict" between tradition and modernity; from systems of exploitation, like the Hindu caste system; and from mere differences of taste or opinion, like the opposition of those who prefer beer and those who prefer wine. Nor should contests between men and animals, like bullfights, be counted as social conflicts.

Types of Conflict

Rapaport classifies conflicts as fights, games, or debates,[2] depending on whether the object is to harm the opponent, to score over him, or to persuade him, but this distinction is sometimes hard to apply in a real conflict, which may have more than one purpose. The object of an election campaign may be to damage the opposing party, to win at the polls, and to convert opponents to one's own position—all at the same time.

Many common types of conflict are important and interesting enough to be studied for themselves, without much reference to general theories of conflict. Detailed studies have been made in this way of wars,[3] revolutions,[4] coups d'état,[5] gang fights,[6] riots,[7] community controversies,[8] political campaigns,[9] feuds,[10] strikes[11] and other familiar types of conflict.

Conflicts may also be classified in various other ways: for example, as large-scale or small-scale, as involving organized or unorganized groups, or as having various degrees of intensity. For analytical purposes, one of the most useful classifications is the following:

Episodic conflicts are recurrent conflicts regulated by rules that participants and witnesses accept as legitimate. The active phases of these conflicts occur at scheduled times and under set conditions; the weapons or instruments to be used are determined in advance, together with the rules for declaring winners and losers and for allocating rewards. Among the important types of episodic conflict are elections to office, legislative campaigns, lawsuits, games, races, and the negotiation of union contracts.

Continuous conflicts are unplanned conflicts within a stable social system. The object of the struggle is part of the situation. Often it is not very clearly defined. There are no scheduled episodes of conflict; the means to be used are not specified in advance or recognized as legitimate. It is generally impossible to identify a winner or a loser or to fix the exact moment when a conflict begins or ends. Continuous conflicts are found in all or nearly all organizations. Sibling rivalry and marital discord are types of continuous conflict; so are bureaucratic intrigue, "office politics," schisms in churches, factionalism in voluntary associations, commercial rivalry, and international relations in peacetime, as well as class, religious, and ethnic hostilities.

Terminal conflicts are conflicts in which one participant attempts to disable another permanently. War and revolution are the two outstanding examples of terminal conflict, but it occurs on a smaller scale in mutinies, feuds, gang fights, and the more extreme forms of bureaucratic intrigue and market competition.

These three types of conflict, although they are related and sometimes blend into each other, have very different consequences for the social systems in which they take place. In general, episodic conflict maintains the integration of the social system in which it occurs; the regular repetition of free elections in a democratic society or of athletic contests in a community seems to strengthen the social system under whose rules the contests are conducted. Episodic conflict is usually pleasurable for both participants and spectators, who derive a variety of satisfactions from their direct or vicarious participation. Spectator sports interested the ancient Romans and the men of the Middle Ages as much as ourselves; they are institutionalized in nearly all societies.

Continuous conflict, by contrast, is often a symptom of organizational breakdown. Quarreling between husband and wife or rivalry between siblings does not contribute to the cohesiveness of a family, but is much more likely to lead to its dissolution. The same may be said of departmental rivalry in a bureaucracy or antagonism between faculty and students in a university. Since continuous conflict is not anticipated in the institutional norms, its tactics have to be improvised and are necessarily illegitimate, and most situations of continuous conflict are pervaded by bad feeling. Both sides feel they have been treated unfairly and nurse their grudges. Neither side can defend itself without scanting its obligations to the larger system that includes both sides.

Terminal conflict has a different significance for individual than for collective actors. A man killed in a duel is effectively terminated, but a nation defeated in a terminal war becomes part of a new collectivity and is very likely to reappear in history at a later time.

The boundary between the parties in episodic conflicts is fixed in advance; in continuous conflict the boundary is irregular and fluctuating; but in terminal conflict the object of at least one side is to destroy the boundary altogether. Each side appears intensely threatening to the other, but believes itself to occupy a defensive position, protecting its vital interests against the inexhaustible malice of the enemy. For this reason, terminal conflict has an inherent tendency to get out of hand. The tensions generated by episodic conflict are quickly dissipated after each episode as emotions are redirected toward the next episode. The hostilities generated in continuous conflict are held in check by the need of the parties to continue collaborating within the larger social system to which they both belong and by the restraining influence of third parties whose interests are bound up with the maintenance of the larger system. The restraining influences in terminal conflict are much weaker, and the level of the hostility often continues to rise throughout the course of the conflict until the original issues are completely submerged.

The foregoing summary is only the barest introduction to the two central problems of the sociology of conflict which are:

1. What is the effect of conflict on the social system in which it occurs?
2. What is the relationship between hostile emotions and aggressive acts?

These questions were the special concern of Georg Simmel, and his writings on conflict[12] offer fairly detailed answers to both of them.

Simmel's Conflict Theory

Simmel's social theory was summarized in Chapter Four. As noted there, his view of human existence was essentially dualistic; he saw it as a combination of such opposite elements as conflict and cooperation, conformity and nonconformity, persistence and change. In keeping with this dualism, he believed that sympathy and hostility are basic to human relations and that the need for both of them is inborn —"part of the hereditary inventory of our species."[13]

Anticipating modern students of animal behavior by more than half a century, Simmel argued for the existence of an inborn aggressive instinct. He pointed out that serious intergroup conflicts often occur over the most trivial issues, that individuals and groups often invent issues for conflict or seek out enemies with whom conflict can be provoked, that hostility is more easily aroused than sympathy in ordinary social situations, that the relationships of primitive groups are normally hostile, and that antagonism is often practiced for its own sake, as in team sports. Nevertheless, he believed that aggressive impulses do not explain all types of social conflict and under some circumstances, hardly play a part at all. Conflict commonly results from real and substantial differences of interest. It is partly by means of conflict that aggregates of individuals are welded together into organized groups. Conflict plays a large part in fixing group boundaries, building status orders, codifying values, and establishing the points of reference that give continuity to the life of an individual and meaningful identity to an organized group.

In a general way, cooperation *within* groups results from conflict *between* groups, but Simmel was too much aware of the diverse combinations that enter into cooperation and conflict to imagine that internal peace must always be bought at the price of external war or that conflict is invariably beneficial, or that all forms of conflict serve the same function. He did think that a conflict-free society was unimaginable and a contradiction in terms. Human interaction on an intimate or on a grandiose scale always involves a mixture of sympathy and hostility. Pure love is as rare and unstable a reaction as pure hate. From the standpoint of an organized group, the most valuable type of conflict, according to Simmel, is a contest for socially approved goals under socially promulgated norms that are fully accepted by the antagonists; such conflicts strengthen the group and reinforce its common values. The most destructive and bitter conflicts take place between parties who formerly belonged to the same group and were united by bonds of solidarity. Each party then conceives itself to be fighting not only for its own interests but for the values of the larger system, which the other party has betrayed.

The effect of external conflict on the internal structure of groups was particularly interesting to Simmel. The approach of an enemy forces an organized group to tighten its structure and mobilize its resources. Internal interaction increases, the status order is strengthened, toleration for deviance declines. Sometimes, the process of mobilization takes unexpected turns. Latent dissensions may come to the surface and destroy the group before a shot has been fired. Unity is sometimes achieved by a deliberate reduction of size or territory, which leaves a hard core of fanatics ready to wage battle. In other cases, coalitions are formed with past and future enemies, on the sole basis of their current opposition to a common foe. Some of these temporary alliances unexpectedly become permanent and lead to new organizations. For Simmel, conflict and the unification of groups were virtually synonymous—practically all large organizations develop out of conflict situations, and practically all reorganizations are attributable to internal or external conflict.

Within a going organization, conflict continues to figure in two important ways. First, the willingness of members to accept internal discipline fluctuates with external threats. In general, internal authority is enhanced by the presence of an enemy who threatens the organizational boundary, and it may be undermined either by the defeat of the enemy, which removes the apparent need for internal discipline, or by the defeat of one's own organization, which weakens its hold on members.

Simmel also sees conflict as a means of adjustment and distribution, the indispensable instrument for ascertaining the relative strength of two organizations and allocating scarce resources between them. These functions of conflict account for the tendency of organizations to seek out new antagonists, to encourage the unification of enemy groups, and even to invent imaginary enemies when real ones are scarce.

The relationship between the instinctive and organizational components of conflict appears again in Simmel's discussion of the resolution of intergroup conflict. This, according to Simmel, is no less irrational than the commencement of conflict. Some struggles end because one of the parties has exhausted its strength, but others are resolved because the object of conflict has disappeared or has lost its importance to the participants, or has been displaced by other interests. The impulse to conciliation may be as irresistible as the impulse to aggression. The outcome of a conflict between former friends may be to knit them closer together or to leave them fixed in permanent hostility. In any case, the settlement of a large-scale conflict usually involves the development of new forms of organization.

Clues About Conflict from Animal Behavior

Ethology, the scientific study of the social behavior of animals,[14] is an important source of insights about the effect of conflict on patterns of social organization, and the relationship between hostile emotions and aggressive acts. Its best-known practitioner is Konrad Lorenz, an Austrian scientist born in 1903. Lorenz conducted many of the pioneer ethological experiments, founded the Institute for Behavioral Physiology at Altenburg, and has long been active in tracing connections between animal and human behavior, particularly with regard to aggression.

Ethologists study the behavior patterns of all sorts of animals— birds, mammals, reptiles, fish. Some of the behavior patterns of animals are unbelievably complex, and some of them resemble human behavior patterns. Geese, for example, fall in love and form monogamous unions that may last for a lifetime if not broken up by infidelity or desertion; sometimes a goose marriage is replaced by a homosexual attachment between two ganders.[15] The satin bowerbird of Australia has evolved a status order in which blue males outrank green males. The difference in plumage is acquired; as a bird becomes dominant, it turns blue. Bowerbirds collect blue objects—pebbles, bits of broken glass, feathers, flowers, or scraps of paper—which they display near their nests. Green bowerbirds collect blue objects with equal zeal but are invariably despoiled by the blues.[16] These reports appear to be reliable.

The ethologists consider aggression to be one of the four great instincts,[17] or basic drives, that determine animal behavior. (The other basic drives are reproduction, hunger, and fear; and there are innumerable minor instincts that shape the behavior of particular species.)

They distinguish two sorts of animal conflict: *interspecific, between individuals of different species; and intraspecific, between individuals of the same species.* Contrary to popular belief, interspecific conflict appears to be relatively rare in nature and of little importance from an evolutionary standpoint. The relationship of predator to prey is quite different from conflict, and does not normally arouse the same reactions. Animals usually ignore other species in whom they have no dietary interest when they meet them in the wild.

Intraspecific conflict, however, is a very common and very important behavior pattern. It occurs in nearly all species of mammals and birds, and in a great many species of fish, reptiles, and insects. According to Lorenz, it has three distinct evolutionary functions. It contributes to the preservation of the species by producing a balanced distribution of individuals over the available environment, by giving the strongest individuals more opportunity than weaker ones to reproduce, and by providing for defense of the helpless young. These functions are inseparably related, and a given pattern of intraspecific aggression emerges by natural selection over a very long period of time to meet the conditions of a particular environment. If the environment suddenly changes, the behavior patterns that formerly assured the survival of the species may bring about its extinction instead. Intraspecific aggression is closely linked to three other patterns that occur quite frequently in the animal kingdom—territoriality, dominance, and bonding. *Territoriality is the exclusive occupation of a clearly demarcated area by an animal or group of animals and the defense of the boundaries against intruders of the same species. Dominance is an undisputed superiority of one animal over another of the same species, which precludes conflict between them; it is often but not always based on the outcome of a prior conflict. Bonding is the establishment of exclusive, nonaggressive relationships between animals who recognize each other individually;* it is closely—perhaps invariably—associated with joint aggression against unrelated animals of the same species.

The importance of these behavior patterns in the animal world was quite unsuspected until a few years ago, and their discovery is one of the great achievements of modern science. Most of the data are still too new to be fully interpreted, and additional information on the social behavior of animals is being gathered at an astounding rate,[18] but the part played by aggression in building up certain types of society is already quite plain.

There are almost innumerable types of animal settlement. Some creatures lead hermit lives, some occupy individual domains where they remain from birth to death. Some have nests where they raise their young but commute to the hunting grounds where they find food. Some live in "towns" with half a dozen families of the same species, some in enormous aggregations with tens of thousands of neighbors. Many animals have one form of settlement during the breeding season and another during the rest of the year.

In the midst of all this diversity two great distinctions stand out: first, between flocking and territorial animals; second, among the territorial animals, between those that do and those that do not form associations larger than the breeding pair.

Thousands of animal species, as far removed from each other as dogs and tropical fish, occupy individual territories with well-marked boundaries, which they defend against intruders of the same species. The size of the territory varies according to the habit of the species and the strength of the proprietor; it may be only a few inches or hundreds of yards across. Some territories are occupied permanently, others only for breeding or nesting. Some are defended by adult males, others by females or by pairs, or by entire groups. The remarkable feature of territories in general is that in encounters between proprietors and intruders, the intruders are almost always driven off, even when they are stronger or more numerous than the proprietors.

The boundaries of the territory may be determined by repeated trials of strength and are subject to change with changing circumstances, but since the aggressiveness of the defender increases greatly as he is pushed back toward the center of his own territory, he is not likely to be completely displaced. The following interesting example is taken from Lorenz's observation of tropical fish.

> Four fish of this species [cichlids] were put into a large tank and at once the strongest male, A, occupied the left, back, lower corner and chased the other three mercilessly around the whole tank; in other words, he claimed the whole tank as his territory. After a few days, male B took possession of a tiny space immediately below the surface in the diagonally opposite right, front, upper corner. There he bravely resisted the attacks of the first male. . . . During succeeding days, the space defended by B grew visibly, expanding downward until he finally took his station in the right, front, lower corner, so gaining a much more satisfactory headquarters. Now at last he had the same chances as A, whom he quickly pressed so far back that their territories divided the tank into two almost equal parts. It was interesting to see how both fishes patrolled the border continuously, maintaining a threatening attitude. Then one morning they were doing this on the extreme right of the tank, again around the original headquarters of B, who could now scarcely call a few square inches his own. I knew at once what had happened. A had paired, and since it is characteristic of all large cichlids that both partners take part in territorial defense, B was subjected to double pressure and his territory had decreased accordingly. Next day the fish were again in the middle of the tank, threatening each other across the "border," but now there were four, because B had also taken a mate, and thus the balance of power with the A family was restored.[19]

Few animals are more aggressive toward members of their own species than rats. Unlike most other animals, they fight to kill. If rats from different localities are put into the same enclosure, they are likely to fight until only one animal or pair survives.

The fierce hostility of rats toward outsiders is accompanied by the mildest possible manners toward members of the same pack. There is no status order in the rat pack, because rats apparently do not recognize each other as individuals or develop "personal" relationships. Members of a pack apparently recognize each other by smell, and if an experimenter removes a rat from the pack, changes its smell, and returns it, it will be attacked and probably torn to pieces. The members of a pack are aroused to such fury by the presence of a stranger that they sometimes bite each other by accident during the lynching.

In contrast to rats, other animals that live in groups and defend a collective territory recognize each other as individuals and develop consistent status orders within their groups. Such arrangements have been observed among wolves, jackdaws, and many other species; they are particularly characteristic of monkeys.[20]

Among the apes, man's closest animal relatives, group life appears to be the universal mode. Primate groups range from the size of a nuclear family (gibbons) to troops of a hundred or more (baboons). All the apes, except the invulnerable and unaggressive gorillas, occupy exclusive territories that are closed to other members of the same species, but they do not seem to spend much time or energy on territorial defense. Hierarchy is the key to primate social organization. The hierarchical style varies from species to species—the benevolent despotism of the gorilla leader is quite different from the brutal oligarchism of dominant baboons or the casual stratification of the chimpanzees—but in nearly every group of apes, males dominate females; males in their prime dominate young and elderly males; and infants and young animals are both dominated and protected by all their adult relatives. Disputes over food and sexual opportunities are usually prevented by the status order or resolved in favor of the higher-ranking animal. Disputes over status are generally settled "psychologically" by confrontation. Fighting within the group occurs in some species and not in others; when it does occur, it is seldom very damaging. At worst, the loser may be driven out of the group. Apes of all species seem to recognize each other individually and to be capable of forming friendships and coalitions.[21]

The ethologists have not been slow to draft hypotheses about human aggression from their wealth of new information about animal aggression,[22] but they are hampered in proving them by two considerations: first, animals exhibit an astounding variety of aggressive social behavior; second, anatomical and physiological evolution does not seem to be matched by the orderly evolution of social relationships. Similar species may exhibit very dissimilar behavior patterns, and vice versa. The family life of geese has a much more human aspect than the family life of baboons, although baboons resemble men quite closely and geese do not.

Among the generalizations about aggression that can be drawn from animal studies in the present state of knowledge are these:

1. The occupation of territories and intraspecific aggression are instinctive forms of behavior that are closely linked in many animal species.
2. In territorial fights among animals, defenders have a marked advantage over intruders.
3. In the case of collectively defended territories, there appears to be

some connection between external aggression and internal cohesion. Groups that are especially hostile toward intruders are likely to show a high degree of internal solidarity.

4. In most species, intraspecific fights are relatively harmless. Carnivorous animals with lethal weapons—like lions and tigers—are instinctively restrained from using them against rivals of the same species.

5. The behavior pattern for intraspecific aggression appears to be instinctive in most species. It does not vary much among individuals and does not need to be learned. Morris summarizes the instinctive preparation for an aggressive encounter in the human body:

> ... adrenalin pours into the blood and the whole circulatory system is profoundly affected. The heart beats faster and blood is transferred from the skin and viscera to the muscles and brain. There is an increase in blood pressure. The rate of production of red blood corpuscles is rapidly stepped up. There is a reduction of the time taken for blood to coagulate. In addition there is a cessation in the processes of digesting and storing food. Salivation is restrained. Movements of the stomach, the secretion of gastric juices, and the peristaltic movements of the intestines are all inhibited. Also, the rectum and bladder do not empty as easily as under normal conditions. Stored carbohydrate is rushed out of the liver and floods the blood with sugar. There is a massive increase in respiratory activity. Breathing becomes quicker and deeper. The temperature-regulating mechanisms are activated. The hair stands on end and there is profuse sweating.[23]

6. The instinctive repertory in species that enage in intraspecific aggression usually includes patterns of submission or appeasement that terminate a fight by inhibiting the aggressive behavior of the winner before the loser is seriously injured. Status orders in animal groups appear to be established through the operation of these patterns.

7. Animals instinctively prepare for intraspecific fighting, having a need to exercise their aggressive instincts, so to speak. In the absence of a threatening rival, they will seek one out, and if none is to be found they may attack inappropriate objects, their mates, or even themselves.

8. Perhaps the most important conclusion that can be drawn from the observation of animal aggression is that conflict, like sexual reproduction, is not a cultural invention but a primitive mammalian response. The great causes of human conflict—struggles for prestige or dominance, sexual rivalry, conflict over territory and other forms of property, senseless hostility to strangers—all seem to be deeply rooted in animal nature.

However, the particular forms of aggression that occur in a particular human society are culturally determined. This fact greatly diminishes the usefulness of the general finding that aggression is instinctive, since we do not really know how much an instinctive behavior pattern can be modified by cultural influences. It is not yet clear whether *lethal* aggressiveness is an instinctive behavior pattern that differentiates men and rats from most other mammals, or whether the human habit of maiming and killing opponents is a culturally induced perversion of our instinctive nature. The question is more than a scholarly conundrum. Instinctive behavior, by definition, is behavior that cannot be changed in the short run. If man is instinctively lethal to his fellows, there is little prospect of a peaceful world, whereas if human nature is basically similar to the nature of the other great apes, the abolition of lethal forms of conflict is at least a theoretical possibility.

Although it is probably not possible to resolve this general question on the basis of present knowledge, some evidence that bears on it can be drawn from historical attempts to establish conflict-free human societies or utopias. The outcome of these experiments will be considered in the next section.

Clues About Conflict from Utopian Experimentation

A utopia is a rationally designed, conflict-free society.[24] Utopias are often regarded as impossible, and to call a project utopian is nearly the same as calling it foolish. The term has this connotation for conservatives, who like to describe egalitarian reforms as utopian, and also for radicals, who long ago abandoned "utopian socialism" for the "scientific socialism" of Marx and Engels. One of the most curious aspects of Marxist theory down to the present day is its lack of interest in the postrevolutionary society. Marx discussed in a vague and cursory fashion the disappearance of social classes from history and the "withering away" of the state, which were to follow the overthrow of capitalism, but he never showed any interest in the specific arrangements that would take the place of the state. Lenin developed the concept of the "dictatorship of the proletariat" as an intermediate stage of unknown duration between the corrupt prerevolutionary era and the perfect postrevolutionary era, but without showing much interest in the latter. The Little Red Book of Mao Tse-Tung refers to the eventual disappearance of the dictatorial state only to explain that this desirable objective must be deferred as long as imperialism exists outside China or there is any possibility of internal opposition within the country.[25]

Long before the appearance of either capitalism or socialism, a number of important writers attempted to describe the necessary conditions for a society without internal conflict. This literary tradition goes back to Plato's *Republic* (around 375 B.C.) and includes such classics as Thomas More's *Utopia* (1516), Francis Bacon's *New Atlantis* (1627), and James Harrington's *Oceania* (1656). It has continued in such works as Etienne Cabet's *Voyage en Icarie* (1842), Edward Bellamy's *Looking Backward* (1888), B. F. Skinner's *Walden Two* (1948), and innumerable pieces of science fiction. In the course of this tradition, there has been a constant interplay between theory and practice, fiction and fact. Plato apparently based his book on a real utopian experiment in Sparta; More seems to have been influenced by early accounts of Inca social organization. Some of Harrington's ideas were adopted in William Penn's constitution for Pennsylvania, and communes have been founded in various places to try out the ideas of Cabet, Bellamy, and Skinner.

Utopian experiments do not appear at random in history; they are connected with larger social movements. Early Christianity was a utopian movement, and convents and monasteries may still be described as utopian organizations. The Anabaptist movement that preceded the Reformation in Germany generated a utopian tradition that has survived to this day; the Amish and Hutterites belong to it.[26] The opportunities offered by the American frontier in the eighteenth and nineteenth centuries and the ferment of political and religious ideas that accompanied the settlement of the continent led to the founding of scores of utopian communities.[27] The Zionist migration to Palestine in the early twentieth century fostered a type of utopian community called the kibbutz; there are more than 200 of these communities in modern Israel.[28] In recent years, utopian colonies have been founded in the United States for such diverse purposes as sexual sharing, political indoctrination, the practice of Buddhism, and the rehabilitation of drug addicts.

If we treat these diverse projects, so widely distributed in space and time, as a single series of sociolocal experiments, the principal finding is that small communities practically free of internal conflict can be established and survive for long periods of time *if* they meet certain conditions. Whether a large utopian society is possible remains an unsettled question. None of the numerous attempts to found one has so far succeeded.

The conditions that permit the survival of a utopian community emerge so clearly from the historical evidence that we may almost speak of a utopian formula. In order for a utopian community to abolish internal conflict, it seems to be necessary for the principal objects of conflict to be removed or neutralized. Working back from the devices observed in successful utopian communities,[29] the principal objects of conflict can be roughly identified as (1) sexual opportunity, (2) property, (3) power and status, and (4) values and opinions.

Celibacy is the simplest device for eliminating sexual rivalry from a community. The longest-lasting of the American utopian movements, the Shakers, required complete celibacy, and married couples were permanently separated on admittance although both sexes lived in the same large house.

> Men and women had separate stairs. They were not allowed to
> pass on a stairway nor to speak to each other unless "a third party
> above the age of ten" be present. If a "world's person" offered his
> hand it was to be shaken "for civility," but if of the opposite sex

the Shaker was required to report the contact to elder or eldress "before attending meeting."[30]

Although celibacy is the simplest device for repressing sexual rivalry, other devices have worked in special circumstances. Among the Hutterites, for example, marriage is required for full membership in the community, but the slightest departure from strict monogamy is an unpardonable sin. Fertility is so much encouraged that almost all young married women are pregnant or caring for an infant. The individual passes his daily round in full view of the entire village. Adultery, desertion, and divorce are almost unheard of among the Hutterites; even family quarreling is said to be very rare. In the Israeli kibbutz, by contrast, marriage is successfully deemphasized. It can be contracted without ceremony and does not involve a change of name, a transfer of property, or a change of status for either party. Parents are not allowed to raise their own children, although they visit them frequently.[31]

A system of sexual sharing or absolute promiscuity ought theoretically to remove sexual rivalry; it was proposed for the guardians in Plato's *Republic* and has been tried occasionally in real-life communities but seems to be inherently unstable. Among the several American communities that attempted to do away with sexual exclusiveness, only the Oneida Community, which flourished in upper New York State in the mid-nineteenth century, persisted for any length of time. Its carefully regulated system can hardly be described as promiscuity. Any man might apply through an intermediary to sleep with any woman and she had the right to accept or reject him, but couples who showed signs of developing "exclusive affection" were separated. Affairs between adolescents were prohibited because girls were supposed to be initiated into sexual experience by elderly men and boys by older women. The Oneidans were fairly successful at contraception, and lovemaking was separated from procreation. The couples assigned to have children were selected by a committee of elders, who likened the process to the selective breeding of livestock, and showed some tendency to prefer themselves as fathers.[32]

Examination of other evidence suggests that the essential element of the utopian formula may be the abolition or neutralization of the nuclear family rather than the prevention of sexual rivalry. There does not seem to be any example of a successful utopian community, either in the United States or elsewhere, that permitted marriage and allowed a married couple to maintain a separate household, and raise their own children.

The elimination of property as a subject of conflict seems to require the substitution of communal for private property. The abolition of property in the utopian communities is much more sweeping than in socialist countries; not only the means of production are collectively owned but also the small objects of daily use. Convent nuns are taught to speak of "our toothbrush" instead of "my toothbrush." In the early form of the kibbutz, "no member of the kibbutz could claim ownership even to his own set of clothing, which after use, laundering and patching, would be placed in the general clothes bin and perhaps issued to another member."[33] Most of the successful American communities studied by Kanter required their members to sign over all their property when they joined, and to turn over any money or property they obtained later by inheritance, gift, or outside work. This stipulation seems to be a fixed part of the utopian formula wherever and whenever it appears. The first sign of breakdown in a modern utopian community often seems to be the private acquisition of articles of dress, appliances, and other attractive consumer goods, especially by younger members.

Conflict over power and status is minimized by one of two devices: absolute equality or an unchangeable status order. In practice, these two apparently opposite conditions are often combined. For example, the leader may be divinely appointed or otherwise endowed with such charisma that the survival of the community is bound up with the continued maintenance of his authority, while all other members are considered to be equal brothers and sisters (as among the early American Rappites). Some utopian communities ascribe unchangeable status to members on the basis of seniority, either by dividing them into broad strata by age, as in the otherwise egalitarian kibbutz, or by basing the status of each member on his personal seniority, as in some monastic orders. The utopian formula must exclude the possibility of vertical mobility except by the simple operation of time. A society that holds out a promise of achieved status to individuals is by definition no utopia, since it fosters competition, which is a form of conflict.

Conflict about values and opinions is avoided in utopian communities by the same device that prevents conflict about property—total sharing. Utopias are formed in the first place to embody a doctrine. They never encourage deviation from it. The utopian formula includes both positive measures for maintaining unanimity and negative measures for excluding new ideas and alien viewpoints. The positive measures include very frequent meetings, daily or oftener in most cases, constant repetition of the group creed, and the frequent performance of rituals of solidarity. The negative measures include public criticism of deviant members, penalties for innovation, and censorship. The Shakers excluded books and newspapers altogether to prevent ideological contamination. Members are usually forbidden to associate closely with outsiders. Many utopian communities have had the sociological good fortune to be surrounded by hostile neighbors with whom communication was difficult. Those that lacked this advantage have developed unusual costumes and customs to inhibit the contact of their members with outsiders, and especially with their former friends and relatives. Kanter quotes a Shaker hymn that went in part as follows:

Of all the relations that ever I see
My old fleshly kindred are furthest from me

So bad and so ugly, so hateful they feel
To see them and hate them increases my zeal.

The utopian formula seems to have been rediscovered again and again in the course of human history and to have been successful in many different settings. Human nature is not so aggressive as to prevent the establishment of thoroughly peaceful communities, especially when they can continue to engage in conflict with outside enemies hostile to their very existence. Nor is it impossible to raise healthy and happy children outside the nuclear family if the community substituted for the family is solidary enough. Why then does the utopian form of society remain so rare in a world in which so many people are made unhappy by interpersonal conflict?

The explanation appears to be twofold: first, a utopia is a relatively inefficient form of organization from an economic and technical standpoint; second, the utopian style of life is not satisfying in the absence of a set of transcendental values to which individuals are willing to subordinate their individual preferences. A great deal of the time and energy available to a utopian community must go into the maintenance of its own structure, and every technological improvement that it adopts threatens the continuity of that structure.[34]

Just as the study of animal behavior suggests that human conflict has an instinctive basis, so the study of utopias reminds us that most human conflicts are based on real, not imaginary, differences of interest, that such differences spring from the scarcity of things desired, and that a society can reduce scarcity either by increasing the availability of such things or by persuading its members to desire them less.

A Model of Conflict

We turn now to a more detailed examination of conflict-in-general, a subject that makes sense only because it is possible—and apparently useful—to apply a single model to all sorts of conflict situations. That model is described below in terms of its minimum elements, a typical sequence of events, and a set of measurable variables that affect the outcome of *any* conflict.

The minimum elements of a real conflict appear to be (a) two parties who are (b) aware of each other's identity; (c) able to injure each other; (d) willing to injure each other; and (e) uncertain about the outcome of their interaction. Conflict, in other words, necessarily involves risks for both sides. They may not be exactly equivalent risks, but they are appreciable enough to exclude the quite different types of social behavior that occur when one individual or group can persecute another with impunity or when two hostile parties are incapable of damaging each other at all.

Moreover, conflict is sequential. It follows a sequence of events or "scenario," which may take a form like this:

1. Hostile contacts
2. Mutual threatening
3. Mobilization
4. Confrontation and challenge
5. Further mobilization
6. Active fighting
7. Escalation and counterescalation
8. Retreat
9. Assessment of the outcome
10. Peacemaking and reorganization

Most conflicts, whether human or animal, between individuals or groups, organized or unorganized, continuous or episodic or terminal, follow a sequence resembling the one above, although stages of it can be combined, omitted, or repeated. One way of analyzing a particular type of conflict (strikes, football games, or revolutions, for example) is to describe the typical scenario of the type and to show when and how departures from it occur.

Another way of studying conflict is to compare the opposing parties with respect to certain variables that each party to an organized conflict measures for itself and estimates for its opponent. The most important of these variables are total resources, resources committed, level of hostility, cost, and tactical skill.[35] For the sake of clarity, the discussion that follows refers to conflict between organized groups, although the same model is applicable to conflicts involving individuals or unorganized groups.

RESOURCES

These include such things as manpower, territory, materiel, productive facilities, symbols, information, claims on allies, and the organizational structure itself. When the resources of two potential opponents are identical or nearly so, the outcome of a conflict between them may be unpredictable. This is the ideal situation for those forms of episodic conflict in which the excitement of the contest is valued for itself, as close contests are much more exciting than uneven contests. Equality between the potential opponents tends to discourage continuous or terminal conflict because neither side can count on winning cheaply. On the other hand, when resources are sufficiently unequal so that the outcome of a potential conflict is certain, the conflict is likely to be avoided. In episodic situations, the weaker party abandons the field or concedes. In continuous situations, it submits to exploitation by the stronger. In terminal situations, it allows itself to be annexed or dispersed.

It is often impossible, however, to ascertain the relative fighting strengths of antagonistic parties by comparing their resources. We need also to know what proportion of those resources will be committed, how much hostility will be aroused, and what costs the organization is willing to sustain. One of the principal functions of conflict, as

Simmel pointed out, is to determine the relative power of groups whose estimates of their relative power do not agree.

COMMITMENT OF RESOURCES

It often happens that an organization that has extensive resources but commits only a small proportion of them to an engagement is badly beaten by an enemy with trivial resources that are fully committed. The pirates who sack a city, the terrorist band that holds a region in subjection, and the little mob of conspirators who strike down a government by a coup d'état all illustrate this pattern. If the struggle lasts long enough, the organization with larger resources will probably develop adequate means of self-defense, often by copying the methods of its attackers. But in many episodes, this reaction is too little or too late.

LEVEL OF HOSTILITY

The outcome of a conflict between two organized groups is not merely a function of the resources that each side is able to use against the other. Many conflicts appear to be decided by the relative hostility of the parties. Hostility may be defined as the desire to fight a particular enemy; in various circumstances it is called "toughness" or "high morale," "ferocity" or "discipline," "fanaticism" or the "will to win." In every case, it stands for the mobilization of emotions against an opponent. As it appears from animal studies and from the common observation of human behavior, hostility and fear are alternative reactions to the same stimuli. A show of hostility may evoke a reaction of counter-hostility or of fear, or very commonly a mixture of both. In some species that exhibit mixed reactions, an increase of hostility in one confronting animal normally evokes an increase of fear in the other. Conversely, an expression of fear by one animal enhances the hostility of its opponent. But in other species, for reasons not clearly understood, the expression of fear or submissive behavior by one animal in a confrontation inhibits the hostility of the opponent and prevents it from attacking. Human behavior seems to exhibit both of these patterns. In some circumstances, the helplessness of an opponent will protect him from harm, whereas in other circumstances it will expose him to unlimited attack. The pages of history are crowded with stories of armies that were treated kindly because they surrendered without fighting and others that were butchered without mercy for the same reason. Neither students of animal behavior nor those of human behavior are able at this point to explain the bewildering difference between the two patterns.

A finding from animal studies is that, as previously noted, the animals defending a territory against intruders of the same species are normally more aggressive than the intruders and that the difference increases the closer the intruders come to the center of the defended territory. Similar processes seem to be at work in human conflict, where they are obscured by the complexity of social and cultural systems. Although the modern technology of war favors attack over defense, and invasions may succeed initially, a people defending a national territory against a foreign army seem to be nearly always successful in the long run, even when their resources are vastly inferior. It has become an accepted principle of modern warfare that an occupying army cannot hold unfriendly territory indefinitely or stamp out a resistance movement without assistance from the civilian population.

COSTS OF CONFLICT

One possible explanation for the aggressiveness of animals and people defending their own territory is that the potential cost of defeat is much greater for the defender, who stands to lose whatever he has, than for the intruder, who can withdraw and look for easier pickings elsewhere. Even the intangible costs of defeat are greater for the defender: his humiliation is witnessed by his neighbors and relatives. A defeated intruder, on the other hand, can always save face at home with a story about wizards and dragons.

The cost of engaging in conflict is usually a matter of advance calculation. There are two major calculations that are seldom omitted in organized conflict: the relative costs of fighting and refusing to fight, and the relative costs of the conflict to the parties. The costs of the conflict include resources consumed in attack and defense as well as losses directly inflicted by the opponent. In a conflict between two parties with very unequal resources, the cost of the conflict to the richer side may easily exceed the total resources of the poorer side. This sort of disparity can affect the outcome of a conflict in several different ways. An aggressive organization with superior resources can sometimes buy a victory by incurring costs that the opponent cannot match. In the classic pattern of business conflict called cutthroat competition, a firm with large resources reduces the price of its goods or services below cost and incurs severe operating losses in order to drive weaker firms out of business. Under other circumstances, the cost of conflict for an organization with large resources may be so great that it prefers to pay tribute and even to leave itself open to further attack rather than to incur them.

Great disparities of cost are characteristic of terminal conflict; they are unusual in continuous conflict, and in episodic conflicts, the costs to each party are supposed to be roughly equal, and this equality is maintained by limiting the preparations of the parties, by prohibiting tactics that might inflict excessive losses, and by avoiding unequal matches.

TACTICAL SKILL

Tactical skill is another variable that should be included in any theoretical model of conflict. In some conflict situations, it is the *only* significant variable. (In a friendly game of chess, for example, both players start with the same resources and may be presumed about equal in the value they attach to winning.) Tactical skill is always a very important element in episodic conflict—in team sports and political elections, for example. Its significance in a continuous or terminal conflict depends on the freedom of maneuver afforded by a particular situation. Military and diplomatic history provide innumerable examples of improbable victories and unexpected defeats that can only be attributed to differences in tactical skill, and the appearance of a tactical genius in any field of organized conflict may change the entire distribution of power in a relatively short time.

In the study of military action, a distinction is often made between strategy and tactics. *Strategy refers to the overall planning of a campaign and tactics to the execution of its separate operations.* One of the most typical patterns of warfare is that in which the defending side has a great superiority of resources but the attacking side begins hostilities with a larger commitment of resources and with leaders of greater tactical skill. In the initial phases of such a war, the attackers will follow a basic strategy of concentrating their forces, moving them rapidly from place to place and trying to achieve local superiority on battlefields of their own choosing. This strategy may lead to initial successes, but if the war continues, the defenders will gradually widen the scope and increase the scale of hostilities until the reserves of the attackers become so thin that victories diminish their strength nearly as much as defeats. This basic pattern appeared in the Napoleonic Wars, the American Civil War, World War I, and World War II. In each of these cases, the superior commitment and tactical skill of one side was ultimately overwhelmed by the greater resources of the other. In each case, too, shifting coalitions with neutral powers affected the course of the war and the strategical calculations of both sides from beginning to end. The coalition process is one of the most important aspects of conflict and more often than not determines the outcome.

The Coalition Process

A coalition is a combination of two or more actors (individuals or groups) who join forces against an opponent in a conflict.

With only a few exceptions, organized conflicts are witnessed by "third parties" who are capable of joining the fight on one side or the other or intervening to impose a settlement. The social field of a conflict, from the standpoint of a protagonist, is divided into three sectors: his own side, the opposing side, and third parties. His own side may, of course, be divided into factions, but it must be more or less unified in its action against the opponent if it is to have any chance of success, and this is generally recognized by everyone engaged in a serious conflict. Hence, serious conflicts seldom remain three- or four-sided; when three or more potentially hostile parties are brought together, they usually form coalitions that reduce the situation to a two-sided conflict.

The coalition process is governed by certain "rules of transitivity" that seem to spring from the nature of social relationships. In a situation of conflict, or potential conflict:

1. My friend's friend is friendly to me.
2. My friend's enemy is hostile to me.
3. My enemy's enemy is friendly to me.
4. My enemy's friend is hostile to me.[36]

It is convenient to visualize the occurrence of such relationships in the three-sided situation that sociologists call a triad (introduced in Chapter Nine)—a social system containing three interrelated actors.[37] Triads are very common in real life, occurring all the way from the level of family interaction to the level of international affairs. An interesting feature of many triadic situations is that although the parties differ in strength, a coalition of any two of them will be stronger than the third party against whom the coalition is directed. When there are differences or potential differences of interest among the parties in this configuration, the formation of a coalition is nearly certain, because each party faces defeat if a coalition is formed against it and hastens to prevent that possibility. The fundamental "rule" governing coalition formation under such circumstances, according to William Gamson, is that "an actor in a triad tends to select the weaker of two possible partners with whom winning coalitions can be formed."[38]

The reasons for this are not hard to understand. A coalition partner is simultaneously a potential opponent *within* the coalition, and it is obvious why each party prefers the less formidable of two possible partners, provided that he brings enough strength to the coalition to dominate its opponent. Other things being equal, A in Figure 12–1 will seek to form a coalition with C, B will also seek to form a coalition with C, and C will seek to form a coalition with B. Since B and C choose each other, the expected coalition in a triad of this type is BC.

The consequences of this principle are far-reaching. They are felt in every status order and in every political arena. Note that A in Figure 12–1 is virtually certain to be defeated because of his superior strength. C, although his weakness assures him a place in the winning coalition, is subject to domination by his coalition partner. In general, the configuration of power shown in Figure 12–2 favors B.

The geometry of coalitions is full of such surprising outcomes, wherein strength is transformed to weakness and weakness to strength.[39] Figures 12–3 and 12–4 illustrate other situations in which such a transformation is likely to occur. In Figure 12–2, B and C are equal and each is weaker than A, but their combined strength exceeds his. According to the rule stated above, B and C prefer each other to A as coalition partners, and A's strength is again the cause of his defeat.

Figure 12–3 represents a more extreme situation. B and C are equally strong and A is much weaker. By virtue of his weakness, A may be able to control the situation permanently because both B and

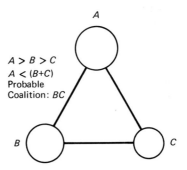

Figure 12-1   A TRIAD WITH UNEQUAL MEMBERS

A > B > C
A < (B+C)
Probable
Coalition: *BC*

A

B   *C*

Source: Based on Theodore Caplow, *Two Against One: Coalitions in Triads* (Englewood Cliffs, N.J.: Prentice-Hall, 1968), fig. 1-4, p. 6.

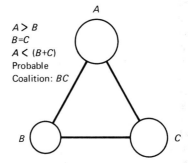

Figure 12-2   A TRIAD WITH TWO WEAK MEMBERS

A > B
B=C
A < (B+C)
Probable
Coalition: *BC*

A

B   *C*

Source: Based on Theodore Caplow, *Two Against One: Coalitions in Triads* (Englewood Cliffs, N.J.: Prentice-Hall, 1968), fig. 1-4, p. 6.

C want him as a coalition partner, and under appropriate circumstances, he may be able to exercise considerable pressure against his much stronger partner by threatening to change his allegiance and join the opponent. A minority party can sometimes dominate a legislature in this way, if the two major parties are about equal in voting strength.

The principle of preference for the weaker of two potential partners applies only to winning coalitions, of course. In a choice between a

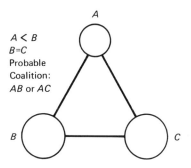

Figure 12-3   A TRIAD WITH TWO STRONG MEMBERS

A < B
B = C
Probable
Coalition:
AB or AC

Source: Based on Theodore Caplow, *Two Against One: Coalitions in Triads* (Englewood Cliffs, N.J.: Prentice-Hall, 1968), fig. 1-4, p. 6.

winning and a nonwinning coalition, the winning coalition will normally be chosen even if it means accepting the stronger of two possible coalition partners. Figure 12–4 illustrates a situation of this kind. It is similar to the situation shown in Figure 12–1 but with a highly significant difference—the combined strength of B and C is just equal to that of A, so that BC would not be a winning coalition in this case. According to expectation, A will prefer C as the weaker of the two possible partners that will give him a winning coalition, B will prefer A because BC is not a winning coalition, and C will prefer A for the same reason. Since A and C reciprocate each other's choices, the expected coalition is AC. It is B, this time, whose initial advantage of strength (in relation to C) spells his undoing.

The principle of preference for the weaker of two potential allies with whom a winning coalition can be formed is essential for understanding large-scale organized conflict as represented, for example, in international war. It is this form of conflict that will probably determine the future direction of social change, and to which we now turn our attention.

The Sociology of War

As a type of social action, international war is a large-scale armed conflict between governments or would-be governments, which lasts for a considerable time and results in considerable loss of life. As a legal condition, international war is a relationship between two governments or would-be governments that encourage their subjects to attack each other's persons and property.[40]

International war is a phenomenon that occurs within an *interna-*

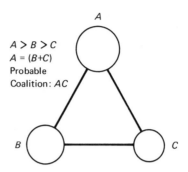
tional system, a set of governments that maintain continuous relationships with each other.[41] According to Aron,[42] international systems may be either *homogeneous* or *heterogeneous. A system is homogeneous if all the states belonging to it are organized in the same way, accept similar political values, and define their national interests by the same criteria.* The international system in which World War I broke out was a homogeneous system. Although some of its states were monarchies and others were republics, and some were liberal and some despotic, they did not disagree fundamentally about how the world should be organized.

In a heterogeneous international system, the states are organized in different ways that reflect their incompatible values. The international system in which World War II broke out was heterogeneous. It included fascist states committed to a policy of conquering and annexing weaker states whenever possible, communist states committed to the transformation of all noncommunist states by revolution, and a much larger set of states more or less committed to defend the integrity of existing national boundaries.

Although war in a homogeneous system can be exceedingly destructive, it is a normal event for which the system provides a full set of rules and procedures. War in a heterogeneous system has a somewhat different character; it involves a possible transformation of the system.

International systems may also be classified as multipolar or bipolar. *In a multipolar system, the powerful states are sufficiently numerous and sufficiently strong to make possible many different coalitions, and winning coalitions are quickly formed against any state that attempts to dominate the system.* The international system centered in

Europe was multipolar from the end of the Middle Ages to the end of World War II. *In a bipolar system, two of the states are much more powerful than any others, and each of them heads a large semipermanent coalition.* The modern international system was clearly bipolar from 1945 to about 1965, when the rift between Russia and China and the increasing independence of America's allies in western Europe began to reestablish the multipolar condition.

International law is a body of rules, customs, and agreements by which the interaction of sovereign states is supposed to be governed. It is quite different from the national (or domestic) law, which each state enforces within its own territory. National law is promulgated by a legislative body, applied by government officials, and enforced by police and courts. The citizens of a state obey its laws partly because they want to—the laws are an expression of their government—and partly because they are compelled to—the government can legitimately use violence against lawbreakers. The relative proportions of voluntarism and coercion that account for obedience to national law vary from one state to another; but even under an unpopular dictatorship, there is considerable voluntarism, and even under the most enlightened democracy, considerable coercion. A government that cannot apply force against persons who disobey its legitimate orders is no longer a government.

International law resembles national law in many respects—much of it is codified, and there are several international courts—but the differences are more important than the similarities. International laws are not promulgated by an organization that uses force to obtain compliance when it is not obtained voluntarily. There is no such organization in today's world. International law is obeyed only when it suits the interests of a sovereign state to do so or when compliance is enforced by stronger states pursuing their own interests. It is especially ineffective in a heterogeneous system, in which states do not take for granted one another's right to exist, and also especially ineffective in a bipolar system, where no enforcement action can be taken unless the two superpowers are in agreement.

The League of Nations covenant of 1920 obligated member nations not to resort to war until peaceful procedures for the settlement of disputes had been exhausted, and the Kellogg-Briand Pact of 1928 obliged its 63 signatories to renounce war altogether as an instrument of national policy. Although some minor disputes were resolved by these formulae, they had no effect whatever on the series of conflicts that led to World War II or on the conduct of that war. The United Nations Charter provides elaborate procedures for determining the aggressor nation in an armed conflict and for organized collective sanctions against aggressors. These measures have been moderately successful in some minor cases, but have failed to control the major conflicts in which the interests of the United States and the Soviet Union have been directly or indirectly opposed.

Perhaps the principal achievement of the United Nations has been to regulate the expansion of what used to be the European international system but now covers the entire world. At the beginning of the twentieth century, the nations of western Europe controlled most of the world's territory and dominated the international system; the United States was a marginal participant. Japan entered the system after its defeat of Russia in 1904; the United States became a major participant during World War I. Between the two world wars the system expanded rapidly. After World War II the colonial empires of the European nations in Africa, Asia, Asia Minor, and Oceania were replaced by independent nations, and a worldwide system based on the European concept of international relations appeared. The essential principles of this system are these:

1. All habitable territory should be under the control of a sovereign state.
2. Any state that maintains effective control over a territory is entitled to be recognized by other states.
3. All sovereign states are juridically equal, whether they have populations of 200 million or 20,000. The rights extended to foreign states by any state should be extended to all of them without distinction.
4. Any sovereign state is free to coin its own money, reorganize its own economic system, redistribute property within its territory, and make any rules it wishes for its own citizens.
5. No state is entitled to interfere in the relationships of another state with its own citizens.
6. All sovereign states are expected to have armed forces and to use them against other sovereign states in case of war and against their own populations in case of insurrection.

These norms are generally accepted by the states that make up the modern international system, and they are respected insofar as the formalities of travel, trade, diplomatic representation, and other forms of routine contact among nations are concerned. However, like all the norms of the international system, they are enforced only by voluntary agreement, and violations often occur. For example, a state may withhold recognition of a government that exercises effective control over a territory on the grounds that some small part of the territory is disputed, as the United States withholds recognition from Communist China, or a state may intervene in the internal affairs of another state on the basis of an obviously fictitious appeal for help, as did the Soviet Union in Czechoslovakia in 1967 and 1968.

International law takes no account of two very important features of the international system—the existence of spheres of influence within which the great powers feel entitled to intervene freely in the internal affairs of other states, and the possibility of changing boundaries. The boundaries of all states are supposed to be respected by other states so long as effective authority is maintained within them, but in the case of a boundary disputed by neighboring states or in the case of a region attempting to secede and establish its independence, other states are free to take either side. In a bipolar system, it is virtually certain that any local dispute that lasts long enough will attract foreign intervention on both sides.

It is plain that the international system, as presently constituted, does not include any very effective mechanisms for the prevention of war. The probability of armed conflict between nations or segments of nations does not seem to have been reduced since the international system expanded to take in the entire world. The reasons for identifying the persistence of war as the gravest social problem of our time will be apparent from the following brief summary of long-term trends in the incidence and intensity of war.

TRENDS IN WAR

Pitirim Sorokin assembled figures to show the frequency of war, the size of the armies involved, the number of casualties, and the ratios of involvement and of casualties to the total populations of nine European countries from 1101 A.D. to 1925. The data are fairly complete for four countries—France, England, Austria-Hungary, and Russia—and somewhat spotty for the others. For all nine countries, the base populations of the earlier centuries must be estimated, and the reliability of these figures is dubious. Nevertheless, the trends shown are of such magnitude as to be convincing, particularly because Sorokin presents all the raw data on which his tabulations are based, and explains how his estimates were made.[44]

In this period of a little more than eight centuries, the *frequency* of war showed no particular trend. The percent of all years in which the four countries were at war (for at least part of the year) varied from 40 percent for Austria to 56 percent for England. Similar results were obtained for other European countries with less complete information: on the average, about half the years in their total history had been peaceful.

If we turn to the size of armies and the number of casualties, definite and even dramatic trends appear. As Table 12–1 shows, the size of armies rose sharply from each century to the next, except for a decline in the nineteenth century, but casualties rose much faster. The proportion of casualties rose from about 1 in 40 soldiers in the twelfth century to about 2 in 5 in the twentieth century.

The most striking thing about the figures for the twentieth century is that they refer only to its first quarter; they do not include World War II, with its 50 million casualties, or all the smaller wars from 1925 to 1939 and from 1945 to the present. Nevertheless, the number of war casualties suffered by the four countries in the first quarter of the twentieth century exceeded their total military casualties in the previous eight centuries. It can be determined from other sources that the casualties sustained by the same countries in the *second* quarter of the twentieth century exceeded the combined total of the first quarter *plus* the previous eight centuries.

Table 12-1	WAR AND WAR CASUALTIES IN FOUR EUROPEAN COUNTRIES, 1101-1925 A.D.		

Period	Soldiers Mobilized	Casualties (Number)	Casualties (Percent)
1101-1200	1,161,000	29,940	2.5
1201-1300	2,372,000	68,440	2.9
1301-1400	3,867,000	166,729	4.6
1401-1500	5,000,000	285,000	5.7
1501-1600	9,758,000	573,020	5.9
1601-1700	15,865,000	2,497,170	15.7
1701-1800	24,849,000	3,622,140	14.6
1801-1900	17,869,800	2,912,771	16.3
1901-1925	41,465,000	16,147,550	38.9%

Source: Pitrim Sorokin, *Social and Cultural Dynamics*, vol. 3, *Fluctuation of Social Relationships, War and Revolution* (New York: Bedminster Press, 1962), tables 15 and 17.

These figures are subject to an important qualification. It is possible, although by no means certain, that the proportion of indirect casualties (due to disease and starvation in the wake of war) was greater in earlier centuries. On the other hand, the occasional massacres of civilians in earlier wars were insignificant compared to the large-scale civilian casualties inflicted by air raids in the present century.

When casualties are related to total population rather than to military forces, there seems to have been a relative decline in European casualties during the nineteenth century, preceding the spectacular increases of the twentieth century,[45] but this is somewhat deceptive. By the beginning of the nineteenth century, European weapons were being widely used in other parts of the world, and it so happened that the three bloodiest wars of the nineteenth century—the American Civil War, the Taiping Rebellion in China, and the López War of Paraguay —were fought on the periphery of the then-existing international system and are not represented in the table.

Discussing World War I, Sorokin points out that although its duration was only about four years, its effective duration was much greater than that of any earlier war, say the Hundred Years' War, because fighting in World War I was nearly continuous, whereas earlier wars consisted of long periods of inactivity interrupted by brief battles.

The evolution of military technology is often discussed in terms of a shifting balance between offensive and defensive tactics. For example, the advantage shifted from the offense to the defense when the medieval knight adopted full-body armor and back to the offense when cannon were brought onto the battlefield in the late fourteenth century. The trench warfare of World War I demonstrated the temporary superiority of defensive measures; the introduction of tanks late in that war began to shift the advantage back to the offense; and the blitzkrieg tactics that opened World War II showed that offensive tactics were overwhelmingly superior at that moment in time.

Although this is a useful way for the military historian to look at the evolution of military technology, it is more or less irrelevant for the sociologist. From the sociological standpoint, the important thing to know about the evolution of military technology is that it runs parallel to the development of industrial technology and is inseparable from the mainstream of technological evolution. The steady increase in casualties throughout European history reflects the steady improvement of weapons. Regardless of defensive measures, it is quicker and easier to kill a man with a crossbow than with a lance, with a musket than with a crossbow, with a rifle than with a musket, with a machine gun than with a rifle. In addition, improvements in agricultural technology have made it possible to keep larger and larger armies in the field for longer periods of time. As recently as the Civil War, some troops had to be sent home for planting and harvest if the army was to continue to eat, but modern armies are drawn from predominantly urban populations. Improvements in transportation and communication have made it possible for military forces to operate further from their home bases and on wider fronts. The development of land, sea, and air vehicles of steadily increasing size and of projectiles of steadily increasing power has brought more and more of the civilian population within the reach of an enemy's weapons. As matters now stand, the casualty rates are often greater among civilians in key cities than among soldiers at the front. Regardless of the fluctuating balance between defense and offense, the capacity of armies to destroy people and artifacts has increased continuously since the twelfth century and at an unprecedented and accelerating rate in recent years. It has more than kept pace with the increases of productive capacity in industry and agriculture that are traceable to the same causes—scientific progress, population expansion, and large-scale organization.

Further evidence of the increasing frequency and severity of war in modern times is found in the statistical tabulations of Quincy Wright[46] and of Lewis F. Richardson.[47] In the period from 1484 to 1945 there seem to have been between 25 and 30 large wars (each costing over 100,000 lives) out of some 278 wars recorded throughout the world. The number of large wars cannot be precisely determined, because it is sometimes impossible to say when one war ends and another begins and because it is always difficult to determine the exact number of casualties, but in round numbers, a large war occurred every 20 years between 1484 and 1945. Since 1945, this rate has been greatly exceeded. In the 20 years from 1946 to 1965 there were at least seven large wars: in India, Korea, Indochina, Colombia, China, Algeria, and the Congo. The secession of Biafra from Nigeria and the involvement of the United States in Vietnam added two more big wars between 1965 and 1970. Except for their frequency and severity, recent wars do not follow a single pattern. Some have been over boundaries (India-Kashmir) and some for colonial self-determination (Algeria); some have been civil wars over internal issues (Colombia); and some have been civil wars involving the political interests of outsiders (the Congo). The desire for national independence was an issue in most of these wars, but not in Kashmir, Colombia, or China. Revolutionary communism was an issue in most of them but not in Kashmir, Algeria, or Biafra. Most of these conflicts were closely linked to the Cold War between the United States and the Soviet Union, but not those in Kashmir, Colombia, Algeria, or Biafra. Plainly, the large wars of this era do not depend on a single set of issues and do not fall into a uniform pattern.

NUCLEAR WEAPONS

Nuclear explosives obtain their energy from the natural forces that bind the nuclei of atoms. They are immensely more powerful than explosives like dynamite or TNT, whose energy is derived from rapid combustion. The explosion of a pound of TNT has sufficient force to wreck a small building and to kill everyone in it, but it is neglible compared to the force of a nuclear explosion; the explosive force of a thousand tons of TNT (a kiloton) is the smallest unit used to measure the power of nuclear weapons.

Atomic bombs were developed by a large team of American scientists working in great haste and secrecy, in what was called the Manhattan Project, throughout most of World War II. They did not reach their objective until after Germany had surrendered. The first bomb was tested on July 16, 1945 at Alamagordo, New Mexico. Three weeks later, on August 16, a bomb with the power of 20 kilotons of TNT was dropped without warning on the city of Hiroshima in Japan, killing about 66,000 people and wounding about 69,000. More than two-thirds of the city's structures were destroyed or severely damaged. A similar bomb was dropped on Nagasaki three days later. It killed about 39,000 civilians and wounded about 25,000. As of this writing, these two weapons are the only ones that have been used in actual warfare, although many more have been exploded for test purposes and tens of thousands have been manufactured. In 1951, the United States developed and tested an improved type of atomic weapon known as a hydrogen bomb. The first one tested had 250 times the explosive force of the Hiroshima bomb. Since then, even more powerful models of these weapons have been developed and great stockpiles of them have been assembled. Each bomb is capable of smashing a metropolitan city and killing most of its population.[48]

The American monopoly of atomic weapons was relatively brief. The Soviet Union produced and tested an atomic bomb of its own as early as 1949, and within a few years Great Britain, France, and China had also succeeded in developing atomic arsenals, although on a much smaller scale. Estimates differ as to the exact destructive power of the weapons maintained in readiness by the United States and the Soviet

Union for use against each other, but it appears that since the early 1960s, each superpower has had the capacity to smash the other's major cities beyond immediate repair and to kill a third or more of the other's population, even if it is attacked first. The capabilities of the minor nuclear powers are less well known, but it appears that each of them would be able to destroy the major cities of any other country by surprise. Even a brief war fought with nuclear weapons might involve more destruction of life and property than all the previous wars of mankind, and there is at least a theoretical possibility that such a war would lead to the extinction of life by poisoning the atmosphere with radioactive particles.

The danger facing humanity is quite real, and unlike any previous danger known to history, it is a common threat to all men everywhere. Several possible solutions have been explored.

NUCLEAR DISARMAMENT

The scale of destruction imposed by nuclear weapons and the fact that they are better adapted for use against civilian populations than against military forces led many people to suggest, almost as soon as these weapons were invented, that the existing stocks of them ought to be destroyed and their use prohibited by treaty. A more or less permanent conference of the nuclear powers meets intermittently at Geneva to explore this possibility. These meetings are not expected to lead to literal disarmament, but they enable the nuclear powers to deal with some aspects of their own confrontation that present special hazards. For example, as it became apparent in the 1950s that the testing of nuclear explosives released enough radioactivity to injure the health of large populations far away from the test sites,[49] a test ban was discussed and finally arranged. After a three-year moratorium the United States, the Soviet Union, and Great Britain bound themselves by treaty in 1963 not to test nuclear explosives in the atmosphere or in the sea. Underground testing continued to be permitted. The two states that had just begun their testing programs at that time, France and China, refused to sign the treaty and continued to stage a limited number of tests in the atmosphere.

The prospects for disarmament within the existing international system are poor, because each nuclear power apprehends that if it did away with its nuclear arsenal, it would lie entirely at the mercy of any hostile state or party that secretly saved or manufactured a few weapons. A system of international inspection and control adequate to prevent such violations would have to reach into every citizen's life and every corner of the globe. It would not be an inspection system but a world government.

Obstacles to World Government

The unification of the entire world under a single government is advocated by many individuals and groups in democratic countries, but they have never been able to establish an influential political movement. The handful of organizations campaigning for world government find it difficult to devise a program that attracts mass support in any country, let alone throughout the world. The obstacles are formidable. The peaceful formation of a world government would require some 200 sovereign states to abdicate their sovereignty voluntarily, and even the most hopeful internationalists do not find it easy to visualize this event. Nationalism has turned out to be perhaps the strongest force in the contemporary world. Almost every definable nation that is not now independent, including some like the Welsh and the Bretons that have been merged in larger states for centuries, has an independence movement. Several states with populations of less than half a million have been accepted for membership in the United Nations.[50] Regional experiments involving the restriction of national sovereignty have not been conspicuously successful. Even under the very favorable conditions prevailing in western Europe after World War II—relative homogeneity of race, culture, and religion, a common history, a common enemy, and a more or less integrated economy— the states of western Europe, having formed a permanent military alliance, a customs union, a joint agency for heavy industry, and an international parliament, were unable to proceed toward further unification. In eastern Europe, the general tendency was the same. The countries of the Warsaw Pact, although sharing the same communist ideology, and united for defense and economic development, have not moved toward a merger. On the contrary, they have asserted their separateness at every opportunity and developed divergent national policies as far as outside pressures permitted.

In a heterogeneous international system the advocates of a world government face a painful dilemma. If such a government were established peacefully, it could only be as a federation of sovereign states. The essential feature of a federal constitution is the ability of the central government to guarantee the territorial integrity and internal constitutions of its constituent states. No sovereign state would be tempted to surrender its means of self-defense without very firm guarantees that its boundaries and institutions would be protected by the central government. When the United States was founded as a federation of 13 formerly sovereign states, the new government guaranteed the existing frontiers of each state and the republican institutions they already possessed. These arrangements have never since been seriously questioned except over the issue of slavery, which the framers of the Constitution left unsettled because they could not agree about it. In a bipolar international system, where the institutions of democratic and communist countries differ profoundly and the majority in each camp regards the institutions of the other as wicked and impermanent, it is very difficult to obtain mass support for the project of preserving and protecting those institutions forever.

In the communist countries, interest in world government takes a special form. The official ideology of Marxism-Leninism envisages the ultimate overthrow of all noncommunist regimes by internal revolution with help and support from established communist states and the ultimate unification of communist states in a worldwide coalition. In the original form of the doctrine, nationalism and international war were identified as part of the social pathology of capitalism and were expected to disappear after the triumph of the proletariat. In the generation after World War II, observers on both sides were startled to discover that nationalism had retained its appeal within the solid bloc of communist nations that now stretched from the Danube to the China Sea and that war between communist states was not only possible but probable. The division of the bloc into two hostile factions headed by Russia and China finally dispelled the illusion that world unification would automatically follow the spread of revolutionary movements.

The establishment of a world state by conquest, rather than by federation, is a dream still cherished by extremists here and there, but as it would require either new and unimaginable weapons or the acceptance of hundreds of millions of casualties as the price of unification,[51] this alternative has not figured largely in the calculations of reasonable men in recent years.

MUTUAL DETERRENCE

Although the invention of nuclear weapons transformed the fundamental conditions of the international system by making it impossible for any state to protect its citizens against a determined enemy, and unwise for any powerful state to risk a full-scale war, the international system was not transformed in response to these changes. Instead, the strategists of the nuclear powers found a way of excluding such weapons from international disputes, at least temporarily. This arrangement, known as mutual deterrence, made it possible for large wars to be fought with conventional weapons and for the international system to continue more or less unchanged.[52]

The strategy of mutual deterrence is visualized as a "two-player game" by the mathematical strategists who explore its ramifications and whose public statements, carefully studied by the experts of other countries, are part of the apparatus by which the players are able to maintain a common perspective and avoid disastrous moves.[53] Following a strategy of mutual deterrence, each of the two opposing powers defines its vital interests as clearly as possible for the benefit of the other and promises that it will use its nuclear weapons if necessary to defend those interests against hostile actions by the other. Vital interests include the territory of the nuclear power and its official allies, and their armed forces when operating within their own territory (units trespassing on hostile or disputed territory are fair game for the other side). One objective of each side in a game of mutual deterrence is to maintain *first strike credibility*—in other words, to convince the other side that vital interests will be defended by nuclear weapons regardless of the ultimate cost. The maintenance of first strike credibility requires occasional confrontations, such as the Cuban missile crisis of

1963, in which one side tests the determination of the other to un-
leash a first strike if sufficiently provoked. In areas where the two
sides have opposing but nonvital interests, like the Near East or South
Vietnam, disputes can be resolved without recourse to serious nuclear
threats by diplomacy, espionage, economic assistance, and military
intervention, neither power being held responsible for the actions of
its allies or satellites.

The other main objective of each power in a game of mutual deterrence is to maintain its *second strike capability,* which means that if
a surprise nuclear attack should be delivered by the opponent with his
maximum force, it would be possible to reply with a counterattack that
would inflict more damage on the opponent than he is willing to risk.
The theory of mutual deterrence presumes that no nuclear war will
occur as long as each side is convinced that any interference with the
vital interests of the other will elicit a first strike against itself. It therefore avoids such interference, while at the same time it refrains from
launching a surprise first strike, knowing that the losses it would suffer from the opponent's second strike capability would outweigh any
possible gain.[54]

It may seem strange that the safety of great nations should depend
on such subtle and apparently fragile arguments, yet the fact is that
the strategy of mutual deterrence has so far prevented any use of
nuclear weapons during a period of turmoil marked by great hostility
between the two dominant powers and by bitter local wars in which
they and their allies were involved. Moreover, the strategy of mutual
deterrence is the only safeguard against mass destruction of cities
and civilian populations that is presently available. For the time being,
there is nothing else to take its place.

Although there are precedents for the strategy of mutual deterrence,
the current situation contains some novel elements that make it difficult or impossible to base predictions on historical experience. One
novel element is that the rulers of large states, their families, and their
friends are directly and personally threatened in a nuclear confrontation. Another novel element is that nuclear technology has lowered
the cost of destroying buildings and other artifacts so far below the
cost of reconstructing them that a rich state cannot hope to realize
any economic profit by winning a nuclear war.

These factors, together with the demonstrated success of mutual
deterrence so far, might justify some optimism about the long-term
avoidance of nuclear war, except for certain disturbing elements for
which the accepted strategical model makes no provision. Visualized
as a game, mutual deterrence is intended for two players, and the
mechanism of deterrence cannot be counted upon if the game is enlarged to include additional, independent players. In a two-player
game, each side loses more than it gains by launching an unprovoked
first strike or by provoking the other side to do so. In a game of mutual
deterrence with three or more players, however, any player stands to
gain in relative strength if he can induce two other players to attack
each other, for example, by launching a first strike against one of them

that is deceptively identified as coming from the other. In a game of mutual deterrence with a large number of players, say 10 or more, it might not even be necessary to employ deception. Any first strike from an unexpected quarter would have the same effect.

By 1970, five nations had developed and tested hydrogen devices, and although the United States, Great Britain, and the Soviet Union agreed about the desirability of preventing the further proliferation of such weapons, France and China had refused to accept any limitations on their programs, and half a dozen other states were known to be pursuing nuclear projects of their own, which the superpowers had no way of halting. Since the technology of producing fissionable and fusionable materials was continuously being simplified, all signs pointed to the conversion of mutual deterrence into a game with a dozen or more players and quite unpredictable outcomes.

Another serious flaw in the strategy of mutual deterrence was demonstrated in the 1960s by the catastrophic and unprofitable American intervention in Vietnam, by the Russian invasion of Czechoslovakia to overthrow a popular communist regime, and by several other episodes. The strategy of mutual deterrence requires the two dominant powers in a bipolar international system to maintain order in and defend the boundaries of their respective blocs. By the late 1960s, both the Soviet Union and the United States—for somewhat different reasons—were finding it impossible to carry out these tasks. Although a solid bloc of communist countries still covered the larger part of Eurasia, the Russians had lost all semblance of control over its internal affairs, being opposed almost to the point of war by China and Albania, defied with varying degrees of success by Yugoslavia, Rumania, Poland, and Czechoslovakia, and almost ignored by North Korea and North Vietnam.

The United States, for its part, was more severely divided by its intervention in Vietnam than by any previous issue since its own Civil War. The dissension aroused by the Vietnam War penetrated and weakened all of the country's major institutions—schools, churches, political parties, communities, and even the armed forces. Although the United States intervened in Vietnam in keeping with the strategy of mutual deterrence, the built-in assumptions of that strategy no longer matched—even approximately—the facts of the international system. In 1965, when massive American intervention began in Vietnam, the communist bloc could no longer be visualized as a single political unit, controlled by Moscow and pursuing a common goal of world domination, and the United States was no longer the head of an alliance defending the united democracies of Europe, southern Asia, Latin America, and Oceania against the threat of communist invasion. From France to India, the noncommunist nations were pursuing diverse policies of their own within an international system that was again becoming multipolar. In these circumstances, the American attempt to defend a segment of the boundary of its bloc that ran through the former territory of French Indochina appeared more and more irrational with the passage of time.

In the decades that followed the first atomic explosion, it became increasingly clear that the institutions of the international system would not automatically adjust to the great change in military technology that had overtaken them. Nor had the attitudes and practices surrounding research been much affected by the revelation that the norms of science do not prohibit or even discourage the scientific development of antihuman devices. Not only nuclear explosives, but new and deadlier epidemic diseases and marvelous new poisons were being prepared in the laboratories. In theory, there seem to be only two alternatives to a universal disaster in the fairly near future: either the abandonment of the institutions of the present international system in favor of a world system involving national self-determination without unlimited sovereignty, or the invention of institutions for controlling technological development and inhibiting the use of science for antihuman purposes. Either of these alternatives implies the application on a very large scale of sociological knowledge that we do not now possess, but which might be acquired if the urgent need for it were sufficiently recognized.

Summary / CHAPTER TWELVE

1
Simmel's conflict theory explains how cooperation within groups results from conflict between groups, and describes conflict as indispensable for ascertaining the relative strength of groups, allocating resources among them, and stimulating the development of new types of organization.

2
Some insight into human conflict is provided by ethology, the modern study of animal behavior. Intraspecific conflict occurs widely among animals and appears to have several evolutionary functions. Many species of animals defend territories and develop stable hierarchies based on the outcome of previous conflicts. The fundamental patterns of human conflict seem to be deeply rooted in animal nature.

3
An adequate sociological model of conflict should take account of its sequential character, of a number of variables (such as resources and tactical skill) that each party to an organized conflict must estimate for itself and its opponent, and of the tendency for distributions of power to be modified by coalitions of the weak against the strong.

4
Experimental utopian communities have been founded from time to time with the goal of suppressing internal conflicts entirely, and some of them have been quite successful. The utopian formula involves the resolution of disputes over property by collective ownership, of sexual rivalry by celibacy or sexual sharing, of status rivalry by the prohibition of vertical mobility, and of differences of opinion by intensive indoctrination. The cost of maintaining a utopian structure, however, is very high.

5
War is a type of conflict that takes place within an international system, which operates on the assumption of unrestricted sovereignty rather than by international law. The international system as now constituted does not include effective mechanisms for the prevention of war or for the limitation of its severity.

6.
According to empirical studies, the *frequency* of war shows no definite long-term trend, but the *severity* of war, measured either by the proportion of the population directly engaged or the proportion of those engaged who are killed and wounded, has been increasing at a rapid and accelerating rate.

> The development of nuclear weapons threatens to raise the severity of war to unprecedented levels. In the absence of practicable means of achieving world government or disarmament, the fragile device of mutual deterrence provides limited protection against the potential destructiveness of nuclear warfare.

Questions for Discussion / **CHAPTER TWELVE**

1. Is it possible to engage in conflict without any feelings of hostility toward one's opponent? If your answer is affirmative, find a specific example.

2. "In territorial fights among animals, defenders have a marked advantage over intruders." Can you show that this principle applies to humans?

3. In what respects do the collective farms of the Soviet Union follow the utopian formula? In what respects do they differ from it?

4. Select an organized conflict that you have observed first-hand or with whose details you are familiar, and examine its sequence to see how well it fits the 10-stage "scenario" of conflict described in this chapter.

5. Find a revolutionary coalition in your own experience, and analyze its effect on the distribution of power in the system in which it occurred.

6. Can you account for the expansion of the European international system to the entire world after World War II?

7. What sort of research, if any, would be relevant to the problem of preventing nuclear war?

8. Review your understanding of the following terms:

continuous conflict	tactics
ethology	triad
aggression	sovereignty
hostility	second strike capability

Recommended Reading / **CHAPTER TWELVE**

Coser, Lewis A. *The Functions of Social Conflict.* New York: Free Press, 1964. Summarizes and amplifies the conflict theory of Georg Simmel.

Coleman, James S. *Community Conflict.* New York: Free Press, 1957; Martin Meyerson and Edward C. Banfield. *Politics, Planning and the*

Public Interest: The Case of Public Housing in Chicago. New York: Free Press, 1955; Alexander Leighton. *The Governing of Men: General Principles and Recommendations Based on Experience at a Japanese Relocation Camp.* Princeton, N.J.: Princeton University Press, 1945; Muzafer Sherif, "Experiments in Group Conflict," *Scientific American* 195, no. 5 (November 1956): 54–73; R. D. Accinelli. *A Study of the World Court Fight 1923–1935.* Ph.D. dissertation, University of California, 1968; Gordon McKay Stevenson, Jr. *To Insure Domestic Tranquillity: An Analysis of the Political Subsystem of Jet Aircraft Noise Abatement.* Ph.D. dissertation, Columbia University, 1970. Interesting case studies of organized conflict.

Aron, Raymond. *Peace and War: A Theory of International Relations,* trans. Richard Howard and Annette Baker Fox. Garden City, N.Y.: Doubleday, 1966; Charles Yost. *The Insecurity of Nations: International Relations in the Twentieth Century.* New York: Praeger, 1968. Two authoritative analyses of tne existing international system.

Graham, Hugh Davis, and Ted Robert Gurr, eds. *The History of Violence in America: Historical and Comparative Perspectives,* Report of the National Commission on the Causes and Prevention of Violence. (New York: Praeger, 1969. Contains a mine of information on the history of violent conflict in the United States and elsewhere.

Tavares de Sá, Hernane. *The Play Within the Play: The Inside Story of the UN.* New York: Knopf, 1966. Describes the United Nations and its peacekeeping activities in an informal but informative way.

Notes / **CHAPTER TWELVE**

1. For overall views of modern conflict, see Raymond W. Mack, "The Components of Social Conflict," *Social Problems* 12, no. 4 (Spring 1965): 388–397; and Robin M. Williams, Jr., "Conflict and Social Order: Some Complex Propositions for Sociologists Who Live in Interesting Times," paper presented to the Sociological Research Association annual meeting, San Francisco, September 1969.
2. Anatol Rapaport, *Fights, Games and Debates* (Ann Arbor, Mich.: University of Michigan Press, 1960); for other classifications of conflict, see Arnold M. Rose, *Sociology: The Study of Human Relations* (New York: Knopf, 1956); George Levinger, "Kurt Lewin's Approach to Conflict and Its Resolution: A Review with Some Extensions," *Journal of Conflict Resolution* 1, no. 4 (December 1957): 329–339; Lawrence M. Ephron, "Group Conflict in Organizations: A Critical Appraisal of Recent Theories," *Berkeley Journal of Sociology* 6, no. 1 (Spring 1961): 53–72.
3. For example, Quincy Wright, *A Study of War,* 2nd ed. (Chicago: University of Chicago Press, 1965).
4. For example, Crane Brinton, *The Anatomy of Revolution,* rev. and expanded ed. (New York: Vintage Books, 1965).

5. For example, D. J. Goodspeed, *The Conspirators: A Study of the Coup d'État* (New York: Viking Press, 1962).

6. For example, Elton McNeil, "Personal Hostility and International Aggression," *Journal of Conflict Resolution* 5, no. 3 (September 1961): 279–290.

7. For example, Morris Janowitz, *The Social Control of Escalated Riots* (Chicago: University of Chicago, Center for Policy Study, 1968).

8. For example, Martin Meyerson and Edward C. Banfield, *Politics, Planning and the Public Interest: The Case of Public Housing in Chicago* (New York: Free Press, 1955).

9. For example, Bernard R. Berelson, Paul F. Lazarsfeld, and William N. McPhee, *Voting: A Study of Opinion Formation in a Presidential Campaign* (Chicago: University of Chicago Press, 1954).

10. For example, Margaret Hasluck, "The Albanian Blood Feud," in *Law and Warfare: Studies in the Anthropology of Conflict,* ed. Paul Bohannan (Garden City, N.Y.: Natural History Press, 1967), pp. 381–408.

11. For example, Alvin W. Gouldner, *Wildcat Strike* (Yellow Springs, Ohio: Antioch Press, 1954).

12. Georg Simmel, *Conflict,* published with his *The Web of Group Affiliations* in one volume, trans. Kurt H. Wolff (New York: Free Press, 1955). Nicholas T. Spykman, *The Social Theory of Georg Simmel* (Chicago: University of Chicago Press, 1925). An extensive commentary on Simmel's theory of conflict is Lewis A. Coser, *The Functions of Social Conflict* (New York: Free Press, 1964). See also his *Continuities in the Study of Social Conflict* (New York: Free Press, 1967).

13. Simmel, *Conflict,* p. 32.

14. An excellent account of Lorenz's life and work is Joseph Alsop, "A Condition of Enormous Improbability," *The New Yorker,* March 8, 1969, pp. 39–93. See also Konrad Lorenz, *On Aggression* (New York: Harcourt, Brace Jovanovich, 1963).

15. Lorenz, *On Aggression,* pp. 180–215.

16. Robert Ardrey, *The Territorial Imperative: A Personal Inquiry into the Animal Origins of Property and Nations* (New York: Atheneum, 1966), pp. 174–179.

17. The terms *instinct* and *drive* are almost interchangeable in discussing animal behavior, but represent opposing viewpoints in human psychology. See Anthony Storr, *Human Aggression* (New York: Atheneum, 1968), especially chap. 2, pp. 11–20.

18. Some ideas of recent progress in the study of primates (apes and monkeys) may be obtained from Irven DeVore, ed., *Primate Behavior: Field Studies of Monkeys and Apes* (New York: Holt, Rinehart & Winston, 1965).

19. Lorenz, *On Aggression,* pp. 36–37.

20. See C. R. Carpenter, *A Field Study of the Behavior and Social Relations of Howling Monkeys* (Baltimore, Md.: Johns Hopkins University Press, 1934).

21. Evidence for these generalizations may be found in DeVore, *Primate Behavior.*

22. The works of Lorenz, Ardrey, and Storr, cited above, are largely devoted to establishing connections between animal and human patterns of aggressive behavior. Another interesting attempt to do so is Desmond Morris, *The Naked Ape: A Zoologist's Study of the Human Animal* (New York: McGraw-Hill, 1967), especially pp. 146–186.

23. *Ibid.*, p. 149.

24. The word utopia comes from a book by Sir Thomas More, *Utopia,* first published in 1516. See *The Complete Works of St. Thomas More,* vol. 4 (New Haven: Yale University Press, 1966).

25. *Quotations from Chairman Mao Tse-Tung* (New York: Bantam Books, 1967), chap. 3, "Socialism and Communism."

26. For the background of this movement, see Karl Mannheim, *Ideology and Utopia: An Introduction to the Sociology of Knowledge,* trans. Louis Wirth and Edward A. Shils (New York: Harcourt Brace Jovanovich, 1959). Descriptions of contemporary pietist communities are found in Charles S. Rice and Rollin C. Steinmetz, *The Amish Year* (New Brunswick, N.J.: Rutgers University Press, 1956); Lee Emerson Deets, *The Hutterites: A Study in Social Cohesion* (Gettysburg, S.D.: Times and News Publishing Co., 1939); Joseph W. Eaton and Robert J. Weil, *Culture and Mental Disorders: A Comparative Study of the Hutterites and Other Populations* (New York: Free Press, 1955). These peaceful and quiet communities began in wildly excited movements about the time of the Reformation. An account of these movements is given by Norman Cohn, *The Pursuit of the Millennium: Revolutionary Messianism in Medieval and Reformation Europe and Its Bearing on Modern Totalitarian Movements,* 2nd ed. (New York: Harper & Row, 1961).

27. An overall view of this movement can be obtained from William A. Hinds, *American Communities and Co-operative Colonies,* 2nd ed. (Chicago: Charles H. Kerr, 1908); Everett Webber, *Escape to Utopia: The Communal Movement in America* (New York: Hastings House, 1959); and Mark Holloway, *Heavens on Earth* (New York: Dover, 1966).

28. See Henrik F. Infield, *Co-operative Living in Palestine* (New York: Dryden Press, 1944); Gideon Baratz, et al., *A New Way of Life: The Collective Settlements of Israel* (London: Shindler and Golomb, 1949); Melford E. Spiro, *Kibbutz: Venture in Utopia* (Cambridge, Mass.: Harvard University Press, 1956); Boris Stern, *The Kibbutz that Was* (Washington, D.C.: Public Affairs Press, 1965).

29. A Study by Kanter of 91 utopian communities founded in the United States between 1780 and 1860 finds striking differences between 11 successful communities, which retained their utopian character from 33 to 180 years and 21 unsuccessful communities, which broke up soon after their founding. See Rosabeth Moss Kanter, "Commitment and Social Organization: A Study of Com-

mitment Mechanisms in Utopian Communities," *American Sociological Review* 33, no. 4 (August 1968): 499–517.

30. Webber, *Escape to Utopia,* p. 59.

31. Yonina Talmon, "Mate Selection in Collective Settlements," *American Sociological Review* 29, no. 4 (August 1964): 491–508. "We have not come across even one love affair or one instance of publicly known sexual relations between members of the same peer group who were cosocialized from birth or through most of their childhood" (p. 493).

32. Allan Westlake, *The Oneida Community* (London: Red Way, 1900).

33. Stern, *The Kibbutz That Was,* p. 54.

34. This point is well-explained in Joseph W. Eaton, "Controlled Acculturation: A Survival Technique of the Hutterites," *American Sociological Review* 17, no. 3 (June 1952): 331–340.

35. This formulation is partly derived from the arms race model of Lewis F. Richardson. See his *Arms and Insecurity: A Mathematical Study of the Causes and Origins of War,* ed. Nicolas Rashevsky and Ernesto Trucco (Pittsburgh: Boxwood Press, 1960). A brief summary of this model is found in R. P. Cuzzort, *Humanity and Modern Sociological Thought* (New York: Holt, Rinehart & Winston, 1969), pp. 115–130; and another summary in Kenneth Boulding, *Conflict and Defense: A General Theory* (New York: Harper & Row, 1962), pp. 227–247.

36. These principles are involved in a fascinating branch of mathematical social psychology called "balance theory," originally developed by Fritz Heider. See his "Attitudes and Cognitive Organization," *Journal of Psychology* 21 (1946): 107–112; and *The Psychology of Interpersonal Relations* (New York: John Wiley, 1958). See also Julian O. Morrisette, John C. Jahnke, and Keith Baker, "Structural Balance: A Test of the Completeness Hypothesis," *Behavioral Science* 11, no. 2 (March 1966): 121–125.

37. The rules governing the choice of coalition partners are similar in situations involving four or more parties, but the process of choice is somewhat more complicated. For discussion of coalitions in situations having more than three parties, see Richard H. Willis, "Coalitions in the Tetrad," *Sociometry* 25, no. 4 (December 1962): 358–376; and William H. Riker, *The Theory of Political Coalitions* (New Haven: Yale University Press, 1962).

38. An experimental demonstration of this principle is reported in William A. Gamson, "A Theory of Coalition Formation," *American Sociological Review* 26, no. 3 (June 1961): 373–382.

39. The subject is discussed at length in Theodore Caplow, *Two Against One: Coalitions in Triads* (Englewood Cliffs, N.J.: Prentice-Hall, 1968).

40. These definitions are taken, with some modifications, from Quincy Wright, "The Study of War," *International Encyclopedia of the Social Sciences,* ed. David L. Sills (New York: Macmillan and Free Press, 1968), vol. 16, pp. 453–468.

41. This definition is taken, with some modification, from Raymond Aron, *Peace and War: A Theory of International Relations,* trans. Richard Howard and Annette Baker Fox (Garden City, N.Y.: Doubleday, 1966).

42. *Ibid.,* pp. 99–104.

43. Despite the exclusion of the Chinese People's Republic from the United Nations, that state participates actively in the international system.

44. Pitirim A. Sorokin, *Social and Cultural Dynamics,* ol. 3, *Fluctuations of Social Relationships, War, and Revolution* (New York: Bedminster Press, 1962), part 2, pp. 259–380.

45. *Ibid.,* p.341.

46. Wright, "The Study of War," pp. 458–459. See also, Quincy Wright, *A Study of War,* 2nd ed. (Chicago: University of Chicago Press, 1965).

47. Lewis F. Richardson, *Statistics of Deadly Quarrels,* ed. Quincy Wright and C. C. Lienau (Pittsburgh: Boxwood Press, 1960).

48. R. Philip Hammond, "Atomic Energy," *Encyclopaedia Brittanica,* 14th ed., vol. 2 (1967), pp. 716–721.

49. For example, it is alleged that the first atomic explosion at Alamagordo produced a significant increase in infant mortality for several years thereafter in the states downwind of the test site. Ernest J. Sternglass, "Nuclear Testing and Infant Deaths," *Current,* no. 110 (September 1969): 12–15. This appears to be questionable, however.

50. The island of Anguilla, part of a former British colony in the Caribbean, with a population of 5,000, formed its own government in 1967 and solemnly requested membership in the United Nations.

51. Some highly original reflections on this dilemma are found in Boulding, *Conflict and Defense,* chap. 16.

52. For a detailed account of how this arrangement works, see Charles Yost, *The Insecurity of Nations: International Relations in the Twentieth Century* (New York: Praeger, 1968).

53. The rules of mutual deterrence are explained at length in Herman Kahn, *On Thermonuclear War,* 2nd ed. (Princeton, N.J.: Princeton University Press, 1961); and in Thomas C. Schelling and Morton H. Halperin, *Strategy and Arms Control* (New York: Twentieth Century Fund, 1961). For a more up-to-date summary, see Herbert Scoville, Jr. "The Limitation of Offensive Weapons," *Scientific American,* 224, no. 1 (January 1971).

54. For an attempt to visualize the effects of a nuclear war on American society, see Robert A. Dentler and Phillips Cutright, "Social Effects of Nuclear War: On People, On Democratic Society—Lessons of the Last War," in *Major American Social Problems,* ed. Robert A. Dentler (Chicago: Rand McNally, 1967), pp. 69–84.

Social Change

XIII

Introduction

S*ocial change is the process whereby measurable differences appear in a social system over a given interval of time.* The differences may appear in the scale, the form, or the content of such a system or to its relationship with other systems.

Social change may be spontaneous or planned, gradual or revolutionary, linear or cyclical; and, of course, it may be either short term or long term. (For the purposes of the present chapter, the long term is a period of at least 100 years, counting back from the present.)

Social change may be viewed as essentially beneficial—it is then called progress—or as essentially noxious—when it is called decline or decay. In nearly every social system, large or small, there is a tendency to view the history of the system in one or the other of these ways, either as a continuing development toward a future that will be better than anything in the system's past, or as a continuing decline from a golden age that can never return.

In his comprehensive review of the theories of social change held by Western social philosophers since the ancient Greeks, Nisbet shows that theories of progress have dominated some periods whereas theories of degeneration have held sway at other times. The mid-nineteenth century, in which the foundations of modern social science were laid, was an era of almost unbroken optimism among social theorists. Comte, Marx, and Spencer all believed that "the recent history of the West could be taken as evidence of the direction in which mankind as a whole *would* move and, flowing from this, *should* move."[1] In the twentieth century, the doctrine of the inevitability of progress has been frequently challenged, but according to Nisbet, some version of it is still accepted by most social theorists.

Theories of inevitable progress and of inevitable decay can be combined in interesting ways. The official Marxism that is taught in countries of the Soviet bloc includes a theory of inevitable progress for socialist societies and of inevitable decay in capitalist societies. The prevailing Chinese doctrine maintains that progress is inevitable only for those socialist societies organized "along correct lines."

Wherever men are free to theorize independently, opinions about the inevitability of progress have been held with less conviction in recent decades than formerly. The commission of history's most extensive and heartless massacres by the nationals of a highly modernized

European country during the Nazi era invalidated the correlation between technological progress and moral progress that had been taken for granted from the Renaissance to about 1910. The belief that the predetermined path of social change was a steady upward climb from barbarism to civilization was shared by nearly all educated men two generations ago. The political and military events of the twentieth century have undermined this confidence.

Not only has the doctrine of inevitable progress lost many of its adherents, but its inevitability has become conditional since the development of nuclear weapons. A few resolute optimists insist that everything will come out all right after World War III has demonstrated the foolishness of full-scale nuclear warfare,[2] but the majority of those who now attempt to predict the future course of social change must take into account the possibility that the development of technology may be decisively interrupted at some future moment and that the resources remaining after such an event may not be sufficient for it to resume.[3]

Despite the new uncertainty that attends consideration of the future, there have been few eras in human history when interest in the future was as intense as it is today, or as much intelligent effort was devoted to discerning its probable shape.[4]

The Sociology of the Future

Although patterns of social change can be studied with exclusive reference to the past—either to account for particular historical events, or to clarify the relationship between variables in changing systems[5]—most studies of social change are undertaken with the hope of partially unlocking the future. Generally speaking, the simplest way of going about this is the extrapolation of existing trends.

THE EXTRAPOLATION OF SOCIAL TRENDS

To extrapolate a trend is to carry it forward from the known past into the unknown future. The assurance with which a trend can be extrapolated, that is, the probability that the extrapolated values will approximate the actual values later observed, depends upon the length and regularity of the previous trend and on how well its causes are understood. The trend for the population of metropolitan areas to grow faster than the population of smaller communities is at least 150 years old and has maintained a roughly constant rate for all of that time. Even though its causes are not completely understood, it can be extrapolated into the future with considerable confidence. The trend toward a shortened work week has been established only for the past 50 years, and its course during that period has been fairly irregular. Nevertheless, its causes—increased per capita productivity and a widespread preference for dividing increments of productivity between additional leisure and additional income—are so well known that this trend too can be extrapolated with a reasonable degree of confidence.

Needless to say, any extrapolation at all carries with it a host of assumptions about other things remaining equal or other trends remaining constant. The development of a new form of high-speed personal loco-motion might shift population away from the larger metropolitan areas. A cessation of the rising trend of per capita productivity, or for that matter an acceleration of that trend, would undo our predictions of working hours in future years.

Even when an established trend is not interrupted by some abrupt change, the error of any extrapolation can be expected to increase sharply as the trend moves away into the future. The predicted size of a school's enrollment or a firm's volume of production two or three years from now may be nearly as accurate as this year's actual fig-ures, but an extrapolation of the same series for a 20-year period would be highly speculative and for a 50-year period, essentially worthless. The assumption that other things will remain equal is work-able only for relatively short intervals. Longer intervals produce unex-pected configurations of familiar elements as well as new elements and combinations. It is instructive to recall that eminent demogra-phers of the 1930s were concerned about the prospect of a world-wide population decline or that one of the most frequently discussed problems of American education in the 1950s was the political apathy of students. Even technological change, which follows a more regular course than social change, abounds in the totally unexpected.

> Suppose you went up to any scientist in the late nineteenth cen-tury and told him: "Here are two pieces of a substance called uranium 235. If you hold them apart, nothing will happen. But if you bring them together suddenly, you will liberate as much en-ergy as you could obtain by burning ten thousand tons of coal." No matter how farsighted and imaginative he might be, your pre-twentieth century scientist would have said: "What utter non-sense! That's magic, not science. Such things can't happen in the real world." Around 1890, when the foundations of physics and thermodynamics had (it seemed) been securely laid, he could have told you exactly why it was nonsense.[6]

Although knowledge of the future is necessarily uncertain, and ev-ery attempt to foretell the future is doomed to at least partial failure, the sociology of the future is an important field of social research. Social action is oriented toward the future, and many acts are intelligi-ble only in terms of the pictures of the future held by the actors. People who build a school, buy insurance, read a burial service, float a bond issue, plant a row of trees, campaign for civil rights, distribute revolutionary tracts, or collect antique automobiles, as well as those who matriculate, marry, or migrate, have a field of action that extends into the future; one cannot understand the meaning of what they do without taking their predictions into account. Such predictions are usually based on a rough extrapolation of trends observed in the past. The young couple who marry assume that their standard of living will rise during the time their children are growing to maturity, extrapolating trends observed in the careers of their parents and older acquaintances. The founders of a suburban school count on the continuation of several trends observed in the past: population increase, urban decentralization, and a continuously rising demand for education. It is hardly necessary to point out how fragile such extrapolations are when extended over a long period, but there is no way the future can be kept out of our personal and collective calculations, and we must make do with what information we have.

The investigator can sharpen his predictions of the future to some extent by careful study of past trends provided that he is not tempted by such exercises to regard social and cultural systems as closed or to underestimate the surprises that the future holds in store. The element of surprise was excluded by the three great precursors of modern sociology—Comte, Marx, and Spencer—when they attempted to explain all social change, past and present, by means of such grand concepts as social evolution and dialectical materialism. More recent scholars, like Toynbee and Sorokin, have attempted the same feat without greater success. Such theories either are on too large a scale to tell us anything about the immediate future of a social system, or are expressed in terms too abstract to describe particular social events. For the time being, at least, the extrapolation of statistical series based on quantitative data remains our best instrument, however inadequate, for peering into the future.

Fifteen Long-Term Trends

The long-term trends to be discussed in this section have each persisted for a century or more, and can be extrapolated into the future with reasonable confidence, assuming (a) that other things remain more or less equal and (b) that the course of history is not drastically modified by a nuclear war, a global epidemic, an invasion from space, the prolongation of the human life span, or some other event that changes the conditions of human existence enough to invalidate predictions based on the experience of the past. Most of the 15 trends listed below were touched on in earlier chapters. They refer simultaneously to the world as a whole, and to the United States. Each trend has now persisted for at least a hundred years, most of them much longer:

1. Technological progress
2. Technological diffusion
3. Increase of goods
4. Increase of services
5. Increase of symbols and images
6. Population expansion
7. Occupational specialization
8. Decreasing work effort
9. Equalization of the sexes
10. Urbanization and suburbanization

11. Intensified spatial mobility
12. Erosion of traditional cultures
13. Expansion of government
14. Increasing severity of war
15. Decreasing autonomy of the natural environment

A glance at this list suggests that it deals with multiple aspects of a single historical movement, and that the list could be extended without changing its unitary character. Any two of these trends are connected by a whole network of direct and indirect linkages. Urbanization, for example, depends on technological progress; technological progress is facilitated by urbanization; and each of these phenomena is both a cause and a result of occupational specialization. At the same time, each of these trends is an important topic in itself.

TECHNOLOGICAL PROGRESS

Technology is systematic knowledge applied to practical tasks. Every social system has a technological aspect, and the great civilizations of the past—ancient Egypt, imperial Rome, medieval China— all had extensive technologies that enabled them to do remarkable things. But modern technology, which emerged in Europe and North America around the beginning of the nineteenth century after many centuries of preliminary development,[7] has two unique features that distinguish it from any previous technology. First, it is closely linked with those special methods of acquiring and arranging information that we call science; second, it specializes in "high-energy converters," or devices for obtaining large amounts of usable energy from natural processes. The water mills that appeared all over Europe in the eleventh century and the windmills that came into use about a hundred years later were the original high-energy converters in this line of development. They were followed by the sailing ship and ultimately the steam engine, the electric turbine, and the atomic pile. Figure 13–1 describes the successive stages of this technology and its principal components.

The total horsepower of all prime movers (power sources) in the United States was estimated at 8.5 million in 1850, nearly 70 percent provided by work animals. By 1967, it had risen to 17,051 million, of which less than .01 percent was obtained from work animals.[8] Technically speaking, the trend of increasing available horsepower is not accelerating—the percentage increment varies from year to year and was greater in the 1920s than in any decade before or since, but the absolute amounts involved are now very large. The annual *increase* of available energy in the United States is about equal to the *total supply* of available energy in all of the Latin American countries combined, or in all of the Scandinavian countries combined.[9]

Buckminster Fuller, the designer of Figure 13–1, suggests an "energy slave" unit based on the average output of one man doing 150,-

Figure 13-1. STAGES OF TECHNOLOGY

① First Technological Revolution — The Discovery and Use of the Wheel

- Tusk, horn, and bone hand tools
- All-purpose stone and wood fist axes
- Special purpose stone and wood hand tools

Second Technological Revolution — The Discovery of Methods for Smelting Ores and for Making Alloys and Forged Tools and Weapons

- Metal hand-tools with energy supplied by man and animals
- Bronze / Iron Age

Third — The Industrial Revolution	Fourth — Chemicals and Chemical Engineering	Fifth — Electrical Transmission and Telecommunications	Sixth — Transportation	Seventh — Limitless Age
End of Franco-Prussian war	World War	World War		Controlled atomic fission

②

STAGE V	AUTOMATION
STAGE IV	MECHANIZATION
STAGE III	DIVERSIFICATION
STAGE II	DOMESTICATION
STAGE I	ADAPTATION

DEVELOPED SOCIETIES — Industrial Economics of Abundance
UNDERDEVELOPED SOCIETIES — Agriculturally Based Marginal Economics

Time axis: 10^6 5×10^5 10^5 5×10^4 10^4 5×10^3 2000 B.C. 965 A.D. 1000 — 10 11 12 13 14 15 16 17 18 19 1965

— 1965 Years Before Present —

THE LINE OF HIGH ADVANTAGE MOBILE ENVIRON CONTROL DEVELOPMENT WHICH GOES FROM SHIP, TO AIRPLANE, TO ROCKET, TO MANNED SPACE VEHICLE

MODE	Sailing Ships							Clippers	Steam Ships		Airplanes		Saturn V Rocket
TIME PERIOD	2500 B.C.	500 B.C.	1000 A.D.	1400	1500	1600	1700	1800	1900	1940	1940	1950	1965
AVERAGE TONNAGE	150	250	30	300	100–500	1000	1000	2100	2500	4500	propeller	jet	3000 tons
HORSEPOWER	80	120	30–90	150–250	—	500	750		1400		3500	12000	200,000 lbs. thrust
AVERAGE SPEED	8 knots	8 knots	12 knots	10 knots	11 knots	12 knots	16 knots	17–22 knots	20 knots	300 m.p.h.	600 m.p.h.	25,000 m.p.h.	

---

③

DOMINANT AGES	MODERN CRAFT 1000–1784	MACHINE AGE 1785–1869	POWER AGE 1870–1952	ATOMIC AGE 1953–1965
POWER	Human and animal muscle, wind and water	Multiple horse teams and steam engines	Gasoline engines and electric motors	Atomic energy and fossil fuel-burning equipment used to produce electric power and heat-fuel cells
TOOLS	Hand-wrought iron and wooden	Machine-wrought iron and steel	Multiple machine tools and automatic machines	Cybernated factories with computer closed feedback control loops
WORK SKILLS	All-around skilled craftsmen and unskilled manual workers	Subdivided manufacturing processes replace skilled craftsmen with semiskilled machine operators	Human feeder or tender replaced by skilled inspector-mechanic	Highly trained engineer-designers and skilled maintanance technician, systems specialist and programmer
MATERIALS	Wood, iron, and bronze	Steel and copper	Alloyed steels, light alloys, and aluminum	Plastics and super alloys (32 new metals used, notably magnesium and titanium)
TRANSPORTATION	Walking, use of animals by dirt road or via waterways by sailboat	Horse and buggy, steam trains via steel rails, and steam ships via ocean ways	Automobile via paved highways, diesel trains and ships, and airplane via world airways	Rocket and jet vertical takeoff aircraft, atomic ships, ground effect craft, helicopters and automobiles
COMMUNICATION	Word of mouth, drum, smoke signals, messenger and newspaper	Mail by train and ship, mechanically printed newspaper, telegraph, and telephone.	AM and FM radio, movies, television, magnetic tape, trans-ocean telephone, and microfilm	Videophone, dataphone, telstar and syncom, world wide communication satellites, "graphic" computers

Source: R. Buckminster Fuller, *World Design Decade 1965-1975*, Document I, "Inventory of World Resources, Human Trends and Needs." 1963, p. 63; copyright R. Buckminster Fuller; reprinted by permission.

000 foot-pounds of work per eight-hour day and working 250 days per year. Using this measure, the average number of energy slaves available per capita to the population of the entire world in 1960 was 34.[10] By 1970, it was approximately 75. Needless to say, these increases of energy are accompanied by innumerable improvements in the design and the capabilities of technical devices. According to Fuller,

> ... it must be noted that "energy slaves," though doing only the foot pounds of humans, are enormously more effective because they can work under conditions intolerable to man, e.g. 5,000° F., no sleep, ten-thousandths of an inch tolerance, one million magnification, 400,000 pounds per square inch sinuosity, 168,000 [miles] per second alacrity, etc.[11]

TECHNOLOGICAL DIFFUSION

The Industrial Revolution, as well as the long development that preceded it, took place in a western European framework. Innovations were most likely to be introduced in England, but they were copied quickly in adjacent parts of the continent and more slowly in countries as far away as Sweden or Austria. With the passage of time, the area of diffusion for this technology widened until it now covers the entire globe, although very unevenly and with some local exclusions. Technological differences are now better expressed as time lags than as absolute differences. The per capita consumption of energy in Asia is much lower than in the United States, but it is considerably higher than the per capita American consumption of 1920. Telephones and typewriters, trucks and airplanes are used in every country, and the number of countries able to produce their own versions of these items increases every year. Of the 68 countries of the world that had sizable populations (over five million) in 1960, all but Indonesia showed both absolute and per capita increases in energy consumption between 1960 and 1965.[12] Even in those countries whose populations were increasing more rapidly than any human population had ever increased before, the invisible population of "energy slaves" was more than keeping pace.

INCREASE OF GOODS

The most obvious result of technological progress is an apparently limitless increase in the amount, complexity, and diversity of material goods. The production of iron—which can be taken as a rough indicator of the production of tangible commodities—amounted to about 30 pounds per capita in the United States in 1830. In 1966, it was around 700 pounds per capita. For the entire world, including underdeveloped areas, iron production in 1966 was about 200 pounds per capita, roughly half a ton of new iron for each household.[13] The average modern family in every country has much larger supplies of the goods their ancestors had—more food, clothing, furniture and hand tools, for example—plus new kinds of goods unknown to previous generations—radios, toilets, typewriters, refrigerators, power tools, and so forth. As the per capita supply of energy from nonhuman sources increases, its value in relation to human labor necessarily declines; hence the cost of manufactured goods of all kinds has a tendency to decline in the long term. This tendency is often accelerated by the discovery of ways to make a device smaller, lighter, or of cheaper materials. In the case of newly invented products, the decline of prices as the volume of production grows and as the methods of production are improved is usually very rapid, but even old products show marked declines. Wall mirrors have not changed very much in form or function since the days of Louis XIV, but tracing the cost of mirrors over a 250-year period, Fourastié was able to show that in relation to the average worker's earnings, the price of mirrors was about 250 times less in 1955 than in 1702.[14]

It follows from what has been said about technological diffusion that the massive increase in man's stock of tangible, more or less useful objects is now worldwide. Some idea of the pattern of increase in tangible goods may be obtained from Table 13–1 which describes changes in the world production of a number of major commodities during the three-year period 1963–1966. In this short interval, the output of a single commodity—coffee—declined; many other food products showed small increases, some showed substantial increases, and the output of wheat, one of the world's two leading grain crops, increased by more than 25 percent. All the important industrial metals

Table 13-1	CHANGES IN THE TOTAL WORLD PRODUCTION OF CERTAIN GOODS FROM 1963 TO 1966		
No Increase	Small Increase (Under 10%)	Substantial Increase (10-25%)	Large Increase (Over 25%)
Cotton	Cocoa	Barley	Wheat
Oats	Peanuts	Fish	Iron
Rice	Corn	Sugar	Steel
Rye	Potatoes	Beer	Aluminum
Tobacco	Wool	Copper	Nickel
	Lumber	Tin	Petroleum
	Meat	Zinc	Paper
	Natural rubber	Synthetic fibers	Merchant ships
	Wine	Cement	Electrical energy
	Coal	Motor vehicles	Radios
			Television receivers
			Fertilizers

Source: *Statistical Yearbook of the United Nations, 1967,* table 1.

showed substantial (more than 10 percent) or major (more than 25 percent) increases in this brief interval, as did *all* the categories of manufactured products for which worldwide data could be obtained. Although the distribution of goods among individuals and families, and between private and public consumers, varies from one country to another, the process of accumulation is rapid and continuous nearly everywhere in the world.

The rates of output in agriculture normally lag behind rates in extractive industries, which in turn lag behind those in manufacturing industries, but the years immediately after 1966 witnessed a spectacular worldwide increase in agricultural production (based on new hybrid seeds), which was labeled the Green Revolution.

INCREASE OF SERVICES

The increase of tangible goods is invariably accompanied by an increase in what economists call services, intangible products that satisfy definite human needs. In practice, goods and services are intermingled. Consumers usually obtain their goods from merchants who provide transportation, storage, and credit services, for example. The performance of a service like a surgical operation or a piano lesson requires a supply of tangible goods. It is the availability of large per capita supplies of tangible goods that makes it possible for many workers to enter occupations that have no tangible product; and conversely, the large-scale production of tangible goods is made possible by the availability of such services as research and planning.

The services especially interesting to sociologists are those that can be grouped under the general heading of social welfare: education, medical care, public health, family protection and assistance, scientific research, legal advice, and social planning. Although all these services show long-term increases, some of them are rather difficult to measure. Only for education and medical care do we have roughly adequate information covering long periods of time and large geographic areas.

In the past century, the number of persons attending school at all levels has greatly increased throughout the world as has nearly every other measure of educational effort: the length of the school year, the average educational level achieved, the cost per student, the teacher-student ratio, the variety of courses available, and the effect of education on an individual's life chances.

One of the best indicators of the total volume of educational effort in the United States is the ratio of high school graduates to the total number of persons 17 years old. Expressed as a percentage, this figure increased from 2 percent in 1870, the earliest year for which there is information, to about 6 percent in 1900, 29 percent in 1930, 65 percent in 1960 and more than 80 percent in 1970.[15] During the same interval, the number of degrees earned at institutions of higher education increased at an equally spectacular rate—from about 9,000 in 1870 to more than 900,000 in 1970.[16]

In many other countries, the growth of the educational system has been even more precipitous, because it has been crowded into a shorter period. As of 1965, most European countries had fewer high school and college graduates in proportion to their adolescent populations than the United States did, but their enrollments were increasing so much more rapidly than U.S. enrollments that practically all of them might be expected to reach the American level before 1980 if recent rates were maintained.

Primary education has become nearly universal in all of the industrialized countries. By 1965, many developing countries—South Korea, the Philippines, Ghana, Thailand, Ceylon, Kenya, and Colombia, among others—had more than half of their children aged 5-14 in school full time. Even the most underdeveloped of the world's large countries—Nepal, Saudi Arabia, Afghanistan, Yemen, and Ethiopia—had, taken together, more than 10 percent of their school-age population in school in 1965 and had approximately doubled their enrollments in the previous five years.[17]

There is every reason to suppose that these remarkable trends will continue. However, the nearly worldwide wave of student rebellions and protests, centered in the universities of the advanced countries but extending into secondary schools and into less developed countries too, indicate that educational institutions have not successfully adapted to the rapid growth of their enrollment and the shift from elite to mass education.

The expansion of health services has been a much more closely regulated process than the expansion of education. Unlike other educational institutions, medical schools have been relatively unresponsive to increased public demand. For example, the ratio of physicians to total population in the United States was nearly the same in 1970 as it had been in 1870 (about 150 per 100,000),[18] but the availability of medical service was probably *lower* in 1970, because only about two-thirds of all qualified physicians were then in active private practice. This extraordinary restriction of supply in the face of a continuously rising demand has given physicians higher incomes than any other occupational group in the American labor force. However, the relative size of other occupations engaged in health care has increased substantially. The per capita supply of dentists jumped from 20 per 100,000 of the population in 1870 to nearly 60 in 1970. The supply of active professional nurses increased from 55 in 1910, the earliest year for which figures are available, to around 300 in 1970.[19] The auxiliary health occupations—practical nurses, hospital attendants, medical social workers, laboratory technicians, pharmaceutical workers—expanded even faster.

Elsewhere in the world, the increase of medical services was somewhat more rapid. The Soviet Union, Czechoslovakia, Argentina, Roumania, Poland, Venezuela, and Yugoslavia, among the relatively developed countries, and Egypt, South Korea, Iran, Nigeria, Pakistan, Uganda, Ghana, Mozambique, Afghanistan, Indonesia, the Sudan, Nepal, Ethiopia, and Yemen among the underdeveloped countries—all increased their relative supply of physicians by more than 50 percent between 1950 and 1965. The median for the world as a whole increased in that 15-year period from around 28 to around 42 per 100,000 population, and this increase was accomplished despite the fact that decolonized countries like Algeria, Morocco, Burma, and the Congo experienced sharp declines as European physicians left or were forced out.

During the same period, the effectiveness of medical services improved almost immeasurably as such serious epidemic diseases as infantile paralysis, typhoid fever, pneumonia, malaria, and tuberculosis were brought under control by new drugs and vaccines and numerous improvements were made in surgical and therapeutic techniques. The precipitous decline of death rates in all major countries in the 1950s and 1960s, described in Chapter Five, can be attributed in large part to the improvement of health services.

INCREASE OF SYMBOLS AND IMAGES

The invention of printing was one of the critical events in the long preliminary development that led to the Industrial Revolution. Although printing with movable type seems to have originated, like gunpowder, in China, its use in China was limited by the complexity of the Chinese alphabet. In Europe, the introduction of printing in the late fifteenth century increased the number and circulation of newly written books at least a thousandfold within a few years. Once started, this trend was never interrupted. The number of books, the average circulation of books, and the proportion of the world's population that reads books have increased steadily ever since. In the United States, for example, the number of new books and new editions published annually increased from about 2,000 in 1880 to nearly 29,000 in 1967,[21] about two and a half times faster than the rate of population growth.

When daily newspapers appeared in the early nineteenth century, their circulation began to grow with similar vigor. Far from discouraging the production of books, as might be expected, newspaper reading seems to have the opposite effect. The same effect occurred when illustrated magazines came into wide circulation later in the nineteenth century, and it has characterized the successive new "media" introduced in the twentieth century—the movies, radio, news magazines, television. Each has encouraged its predecessors. For example, the advent of television, beginning in 1946, did not spell the end of radio broadcasting. Although the content of radio broadcasts was somewhat modified, the proportion of radios per capita and the number of programs broadcast continues to rise from year to year. The modern appetite for symbols and images is apparently insatiable. Twenty years after the introduction of television, 94 percent of American households had at least one television set, 25 percent had two or more,[22] and the average viewing time per household was estimated at four hours per day! Yet throughout this period the per capita readership of books and magazines, along with the absorption of symbols and images in other forms, continued to rise.

The world as a whole seems to have the same appetite. The 1960s saw the spread of television to nearly all the countries of the world, including such faraway places as Yemen, Ethiopia, Upper Volta, and the Ryuku Islands, yet this had no dampening effect on radio broadcasting or cinematic production. Moviemaking, originally an American monopoly, has become a worldwide industry; among the countries making more than 50 full-length feature films annually by 1965 were Burma, Czechoslovakia, England, France, West Germany, Greece, Hong Kong, India, Italy, Japan, Korea, Mexico, Pakistan, the Philippines, Spain, and the Soviet Union.[23]

The distribution of symbols and images to more specialized audiences has proceeded at a similar pace. In 1850, the number of scientific journals in the world was small enough so that an assiduous reader could keep abreast of scientific developments by reading or skimming through most of them. By 1900, it was still possible to keep abreast of the journals written in one major language, like English or German. By 1960, even the most determined reader was unable to keep up with any significant fraction of the scientific literature. In medicine and related fields alone, more than 6,000 journals were regularly published. A relatively small field like sociology was reported in hundreds of journals in many languages.

Other devices for producing symbols and images for limited audiences—still photography, home movies, mimeograph and copying machines, teleprinters, closed-circuit television, teaching machines, videotape, data retrieval systems—are all coming into wider use, undergoing apparently limitless improvement, and spilling out an ever-rising flood of words, sounds, and pictures.

Although some observers attribute the social disturbances of the 1960s to a kind of perceptual indigestion, and others expect these new devices to produce profound cultural and social transformations, there is no solid evidence on these points. Numerous efforts to show a connection between children's television viewing and their later behavior as adolescents or adults have not been conspicuously successful. It is not even certain that patterns of political behavior have been fundamentally transformed by the intrusion of the mass media into every phase of the political process. The hypotheses that have been raised about such influences are fascinating but difficult to prove.[24]

POPULATION EXPANSION

In Chapter Five, we described the rapid increase in the population of the world (including all six continents and all but two or three countries) that is called the population explosion, and we examined the factors that brought it about. Although it has only recently become the subject of wide concern, the upward trend of the world's population is emphatically long-term; it can be traced back at least to the seventeenth century, and with a little less assurance, back to antiquity.

The expansion of a territorial population is always accompanied by a corresponding expansion of institutional and organizational populations. For example, an increase of national population is likely to bring about an increase in the number of factories and an increase in the size of the largest factories. Not only productive enterprises but churches, armies, government bureaus, voluntary associations, transportation systems, audiences and cemeteries become gigantic with reference to their historic counterparts, and keep right on growing. It is not surprising that the changes of scale are often accompanied by changes in structure and function, some of them entirely unanticipated. The common threads in these transformations are bureaucratization and depersonalization.

OCCUPATIONAL SPECIALIZATION

The intensification of the social division of labor, or occupational specialization, is as well-established a long-term trend as technological progress. Indeed, technological progress is unthinkable without occupational specialization, which involves a steady increase in the number of occupations and in the distinctness of related occupations. The fragmentation of professions like medicine and law into a cluster of specialties, which gradually become professions in their own right and begin to fragment into subspecialties, is a familiar example. At lower levels of occupational status, the pattern of specialization is a little harder to follow, but no less important. Each traditional craft is eventually replaced by a cluster of occupations, which carry out modernized versions of the same function by means of a complex division of labor. A few of these derivative occupations may be more skilled than the parent occupation, but the great majority require only a brief period of training added to a specified level of general education. Among occupations with the same educational requirements, mobility becomes easier as the number of occupations grows, but among occupations with varying educational requirements, it becomes more difficult.

Another feature of this process is the rapid obsolescence that overtakes skilled occupations as technology, work methods, and the scale of production change. Not only do the traditional skills of the craftsman age faster than the man himself, but technically grounded skills —like those of the research scientist or the tax lawyer—become obsolete even faster. At all levels of the occupational hierarchy, education becomes an increasingly important element in the occupational career, and individuals spend a large proportion of their working lives undergoing education in one form or another. The signs of this trend are manifold and can be observed in every country on earth. The average age of entry into the labor force for young people rises from year to year. For some professionals, like psychiatrists, the normal age of entry into the labor force may be deferred past the age of 30. Even for manual workers, it has risen from 12 or younger at the beginning of this century, to 19 or older now. As a result, a large part of the active population remains suspended in a condition sociologically intermediate between adolescence and adulthood.

The return to school at later points in the occupational career becomes obligatory in many occupations and the duration of such episodes lengthens until, in some careers, more time is spent in educational preparation than in occupational performance. Meanwhile, the age of retirement is slowly but steadily reduced, partly because technological progress dissociates seniority and competence, partly because workers elect to take some of their productivity gains in the form of leisure.

DECREASING WORK EFFORT

Individual workers often choose leisure in preference to additional income, as when civil service employees retire in early middle age after 20 or 25 years of service. In other instances, the same choice is made for them by the organizations that plan and manage work activities. The shortening span of the individual's career, compressed between a later start and earlier retirement, is accompanied by a steady curtailment of the number of hours in the workday, the workweek, and the workyear, and by the gradual elimination of physically strenuous jobs and uncomfortable working conditions. The standard workday in industry in the United States decreased from about 11 hours in 1860 to about 7.5 hours in 1969, the median workweek from 6–7 days to 4–5 days, and the workyear from around 310 to around 225 days. Similar curtailments of working time have been recorded nearly everywhere; they may temporarily cancel out gains in productivity.[25]

There are also offsetting factors. In some cases, physically strenuous work has been replaced by overmechanized tasks that are more disagreeable and exacting, like certain types of assembly-line work. In certain countries, the shortening of workdays in offices and factories does not fully compensate for the lengthening of the workyear that occurs when seasonal farmers or herdsmen move to the city. In a few —probably very few—occupations, the intensification of the division of labor imposes greater strain and lengthened work hours on people whose work consists largely of coordinating the work of others.

EQUALIZATION OF THE SEXES

Of the 15 major trends selected for discussion here, this one is the least certain and the most obscured by exceptions and countertrends. However, women's participation in the labor force, in politics, in education, and in the arts seems to have increased nearly everywhere during the past century. The causes of this movement are rather diverse and intricate. The increase of goods and services that accompanies modernization tends to release women from direct dependence on a supporting male. The improvement of contraceptives releases women from the constraints formerly imposed on their sexual behavior by the risk of an unwanted pregnancy and on their participation in the labor force by their lack of control over family size. The general shift from outdoor to indoor jobs, and away from strenuous work, removes most of the disadvantage that women formerly suffered because of their inferior muscular strength. The erosion of traditional cultures weakens male dominance in many societies.

On the other hand, family patterns that imply the inequality of the sexes seem to be persisting successfully in a number of countries, like Italy and Brazil, where social change has been exceptionally rapid in other respects. In other countries, like the United States, the apparent equalization of roles within the family is partly counterbalanced by a sharper separation of home and workplace, which tends to reduce the participation of wives in the larger social systems in which their husbands are active.

URBANIZATION AND SUBURBANIZATION

Since about the year 1000, there has been a steady movement of farmers and peasants off the land and into the towns in every region subject to technical progress, and since about 1800, there has been a proportionately faster movement of town dwellers into large metropolitan cities. Since around 1860, the populations of large metropolitan cities have been dispersing outward from their centers toward suburban peripheries that expand with each improvement of transportation facilities. (These movements were described in detail in Chapter Six.)

Although these trends are long established and now prevail in all countries of the world, some other urban phenomena are distinctly new. The spectacular increase in the number of metropolitan cities in recent years[26] has created an international network of great cities with a pool of common culture traits, quite in contrast to the preceding situation in which international exchanges were dominated by a handful of great cities in Europe and America or the situation of earlier centuries, when few cities had more than a regional sphere of influence.

Another novel aspect of city life is its military insecurity. In earlier centuries, towns offered protection against the armed intrusions that were a perennial threat in the open countryside. Even in World War II, when many cities were devastated by bombing, cities were defensible strongholds in ground action. But in a war conducted with nuclear weapons, the residents of metropolitan cities would be more exposed to enemy attacks than front-line soldiers. Every modern metropolis is a hostage to potential enemies.

Another unique feature of the modern urban condition is the traffic congestion that is often described as "strangling our cities." It develops when the private automobile is substituted for the omnibus. Although no metropolitan city has so far collapsed because of vehicular congestion, the delay, noise, accident risk, and air pollution resulting from excessive traffic have degraded the urban environment everywhere. By the early 1970s, daily traffic jams of crisis severity occurred in many Asiatic and African cities, in many cities of eastern Europe, and in all the metropolitan centers of western Europe, Latin America, and North America. Moreover, the volume of traffic was *not* beginning to level off in any of these places—neither in American cities where suburbanization continued to increase the average daily mileage of automobile-owning families, nor in remote Asiatic cities, where the introduction of private vehicles was just getting under way.

With urbanization go a host of subsidiary trends: the wider diffusion of literacy and plumbing, the displacement of local styles in dress, food, architecture, furniture, and entertainment by cosmopolitan styles slightly adapted to local preferences, and the application of imported political ideologies to local systems of stratification.

INCREASED SPATIAL MOBILITY

This is another multi-faceted trend that is now long established and apparently universal. It holds regardless of which indicator we select —residential movement from one address to another, intercity or interregional migration, volume of daily commuting traffic, domestic or foreign tourist travel, domestic or foreign business travel, daily mileage traveled by individuals, lifetime mileage traveled by individuals, the average speed of travel, or the average speed of trips between fixed points. Wherever we look, the trend is toward higher mobility. The only partial exceptions are migrations across national boundaries, which are subject to political control and do not show a consistent pattern, and the speed of local travel, which may decline here and there because of acute traffic congestion.

Otherwise, the increase in the volume, speed, and extensity of human locomotion is continuous, universal, and, so far, unlimited. In the United States, for example, the total mileage of motor vehicle travel doubles about every 15 years, and this rate of increase has not changed very much since 1925.[27] Before that date, with the automobile still in its introductory phase, the rate of increase was greater, as it is today in many countries. The total number of motor vehicles in use *outside* the United States increased from 36 million in 1953 to nearly 100 million in 1966, and so far as can be determined, the rate of increase of vehicles exceeded the rate of population growth in every country of the world except Haiti.[28] At this point in human history, the demand for locomotion is apparently insatiable, and there is no sign of its leveling off.

EROSION OF TRADITIONAL CULTURES

References to the disappearance of local customs and peculiarities were fairly frequent in the reports of eighteenth century travelers and social observers. By the late nineteenth century, there was hardly any account of life in the known parts of the world that did not refer to the gradual disappearance of local dialects, beliefs, practices, styles, and artifacts when the isolation of the locality was breached by mechanized communications and machine-made products. This type of erosion has continued into our own time, but for reasons that are not entirely clear, it has become far more destructive in recent years. Instead of the slow dilution of a local cultural system by the introduction of imported traits, we now see whole cultures swept away almost overnight. Firth's study of Tikopia in 1928–1929, reviewed in Chapter Three, discovered a large body of traditional rituals and beliefs that remained almost intact after more than a century of casual contact with European culture. By the time of Firth's last field trip in 1952, the entire culture complex, with its elaborate mythology and its annual cycle of ceremonies, had been abandoned and nearly forgotten.[29] An even more drastic transformation was observed by Margaret Mead in field studies of a New Guinea tribal society, the Manus, in 1928 and 1953.[30] Between these two dates, the Manus had lived and worked in close proximity to an American military base, and that contact changed their values to such an extent that they deliberately destroyed their old social institutions and invented new patterns of family interaction, religious belief, stratification, public health, and community action based on their image of life in a modernized society.

A close observer of life in the Balkans reports the disappearance of the local cultures of that region in the brief period between 1948 and 1963:

> ... the old Balkans were a good deal more than a disorderly world, or merely comic one. They were the quintessential mountain world, dark, passionate, replete with violence, a place of incomprehensible offenses and terrible nationalism, a land of obscure races, each proclaiming a dark and messianic destiny. ... Here was an archaic conceptual world, of peasants and shepherds, of uneasy cities, of brutal personal destinies. ...
>
> But all this is gone, or going fast, there are factories now, dirtying the sky with smoke, in the old lost valleys of the Rhodopes. In much of the Balkans now the commissars and technicians have had their way; the furrows on the collective farms reach to the far horizon. ... In the magic Bosnian evening or on the flat plains of the Dobrudja, along the mouths of the Danube, the muezzin still climbs the narrow stone stairway of the minaret and calls out the ancient cry, "I say there is no God but God," but no one comes to pray. The village costumes are gone; the women are unveiled. The young girls and boys drink too much, fornicate freely, and go at night to dance to inexpert jazz played in the village cafe or in the state-subsidized House of Culture. ... [31]

Another nostalgic observer describes the disappearance of an American subculture as of 1961:

> Now the people who inhabit the Kentucky mountains came into that region nearly two centuries ago, bringing with them what

many students affirm to be survivals of Elizabethan culture, and even Chaucerian speech. These they modified somewhat, of course, in the new situation, but a considerable part of the inheritance they preserved, and naturally they added something of their own until they had one of the most distinctive or individually flavored cultures in the United States. The whole culture complex—their special way of looking at life and in doing things—was kept intact right down to the most recent times: their speech, their balladry, their music, their social codes, and their religiosity. ... Then came the radio and the television, and the Kentucky mountaineer was no more.[32]

Exposure to a large quantity of external symbols and images seems to dissolve local cultures much faster than the importation of foreign tools and artifacts (which can be assimilated into existing culture complexes) or the appearance of foreigners (who can be assigned special roles without disturbing the existing pattern of social relationships). But the symbols and images carried by the radio, the cinema, and television are irresistible; they reshape the imagination so that old beliefs and values suddenly lose all their power.

Coupled to these cultural effects are the new patterns of mobility and population distribution. Although traditional societies were often more mobile than a casual observer might suppose, most of them were permanently attached to one small territory. Even town dwellers, in past centuries, bore strong local markings and expressed a kind of local patriotism that is rapidly becoming extinct. The world's metropolitan cities now contain a large and growing number of people who have entirely lost that sense of hereditary attachment to a locality which was one of the principal constituents of social identity throughout history.

In the typical case, the erosion of local traditions arouses remarkably little sentiment among the people directly involved. The native fisherman who exchanges his picturesque lateen sails (of a design unchanged during 20 centuries) for a diesel engine seems to do so without the slightest twinge of regret. But no matter how such acts are evaluated, they are irreversible. Like the species of birds and animals that have been extinguished by unconcerned hunters with automatic rifles, the cultures that are now being extinguished by rapid modernization will be absent from the world from now on—forever.

EXPANSION OF GOVERNMENT

As local cultures disappear and local social systems are absorbed into larger territorial units, many of the social functions that were formerly handled locally, traditionally, and informally are taken over by the bureaucratically organized governments that administer these larger territories—for example, education, the protection of the young, the regulation of marriage and divorce, the adjudication of disputes, the maintenance of order, and the operation of community services. In addition, technological progress, population expansion, urbanization, and related trends give rise to a host of new governmental functions; for example, regulation of the monetary supply, enforcement of international agreements, and conservation of the natural environment. With the passage of time, both old and new functions are continuously elaborated. As a result, in all modern countries, without apparent exception, there is a tendency for the proportion of the civilian labor force employed by the government, and the government's share of the gross national product, to rise indefinitely.

Warner[33] has listed and classified the functions performed by each department, agency, or bureau of our federal government into such broad categories as protection of rights, law enforcement, health and medical protection, social services, regulation of business, conservation, national defense, foreign relations, and intergovernmental services, and into such subcategories as civil rights, patents and copyrights, and Indian services. Table 13-2 shows the rise in the number of these services performed by each level of government in successive periods of American history. The total number of functions performed by the federal government rose from 27 in the early period to 112 in the recent period, and there were equivalent increases in the number of functions performed at the state and local levels of government.

Impressive as these increases are, the United States stands relatively low in relation to other countries with respect to both the number of government functions and the proportion of the labor force directly employed by the government. In the communist countries of eastern Europe, the great majority of the labor force consists of government employees, and government agencies are in direct charge of most large-scale offices, factories, and farms. In the Chinese People's Republic, all employed persons are government employees, and government regulation extends without any constitutional limit to every

| Table 13-2 | NUMBER OF FUNCTIONS PERFORMED AT EACH LEVEL OF GOVERNMENT IN THE UNITED STATES AT VARIOUS PERIODS |

| | Number of Functions | | |
Level of Government	Early Period (1790-1830)	Middle Period (1830-1900)	Recent Period (1900-1960)
Federal	27	46	112
State	13	17	58
Local	20	21	56

Source: W. Lloyd Warner, ed., *The Emergent American Society*, vol. I, *Large-Scale Organizations* (New Haven: Yale University Press, 1967), p. 579.

aspect of organized social life. Even in western European countries that favor the private ownership of productive facilities and place no limits on the private accumulation of wealth, like Great Britain, France, and the Netherlands, the proportion of economic and social activity under direct government control is higher than in the United States.

The existence of these variations suggests that although the trend toward expansion of governmental functions is universal, the rate of expansion is variable and is highly dependent upon the political values to which a national community is committed. Moreover, although all modern governments reach out to extend their control over all types of organized social activity, the mode of control may vary from a minimum degree of surveillance and the regulation of some obvious abuses to an unlimited right of the state to direct the activities of its citizens and to allocate all the resources in its territory.

INCREASING SEVERITY OF WAR

Discussing international systems in Chapter Twelve, we saw that the trend toward the expansion of governmental functions within nation-states has been matched in this century by the proliferation of new states, some in territories formerly under colonial rule and some created by secession from existing states. In that same chapter, we noted the increasing severity of war over the past several centuries and particularly in the twentieth century, as measured by the proportion of the population directly engaged, the casualty rates among soldiers and civilians, and the destruction of resources. The scope of the existing international system and the range of modern weapons is such that no inhabited region is protected against unwilling involvement in a war that may have arisen in a distant part of the world.

The increasing severity of war may be regarded as the key to social change in the immediate future. If the trend is not reversed soon, it is highly probable that technological progress, population growth, urbanization, and the other trends enumerated above will soon be interrupted, either temporarily or permanently. If the spiral of increasing ferocity *is* interrupted, most of the other trends associated with modernization are likely to continue at least for another century. The concern that was formerly felt about the possible exhaustion of energy sources has been dispelled by recent discoveries of new sources,[34] and the fear that the world's population would outrun the food supply in the near future has begun to disappear because of the so-called Green Revolution.[35] In the longer run, however, the increasing severity of war is only one of several hazards that threaten technological progress and its concomitant trends.

DECREASING AUTONOMY OF THE NATURAL ENVIRONMENT

Until about 1800, the earth was so sparsely populated by man and the amount of energy under human control was so feeble compared to natural forces that, except for the conversion of forest, marsh, or desert land into arable fields and the reversion of abandoned fields, the balance of nature remained largely unaffected by human presence. For example, only a few species of animals had been extinguished by half a million years or so of human hunting, although many animals had been driven out of densely settled regions. After 1800, the growth of population, the improvement of weapons and traps, the substitution of engines for sails, and extensive hunting and fishing in uninhabited regions began to make substantial inroads on the animal kingdom. Some very numerous species, like the passenger pigeon, and some very rare species, like the sea cow, were hunted to extinction in a few years. Others, like the bison, were reduced to a few specimens preserved as curiosities. The populations of many species were drastically reduced, with unanticipated effects on the populations of other species. In the recent decades, these disturbances have increased in speed and in scale. The population of great whales in all the oceans of the world was reduced so sharply by overfishing in the 1950s and 1960s that their survival became doubtful, and the use of DDT and other powerful insecticides virtually wiped out some of the bird species that formerly kept the insect population in balance.

The conversion of energy and the production of artifacts on an unprecedented scale in the twentieth century threatened to upset other balances in the natural environment. For example, the operation of tens of thousands of furnaces and millions of gasoline engines in the metropolitan cities released waste products into the atmosphere in quantities that exceeded the cleansing capacity of atmospheric circulation. As a result, some cities have developed permanent canopies of dust, smoke, and chemical vapors, which become dangerous in certain weather conditions. The release of combustion by-products continues on a scale that may cause irreversible changes in the earth's climate. Some meteorologists believe that the continued discharge of carbon dioxide into the atmosphere at existing rates will eventually reduce the rate at which the sun's heat is reflected into space and induce a rise in land and sea temperatures that will have far-reaching—and mostly harmful—effects.

The pollution of lakes, rivers and even seas is another problem traceable to technological progress, population expansion, and urbanization. Throughout the world, the predominant method of disposing of sewage and garbage is to dump them into a body of water. The volume of sewage increases more or less evenly with the human population, and the volume of garbage keeps pace with the increase of goods. When the regenerative capacity of streams and rivers is exceeded, the living organisms in them begin to disappear, and their ability to handle waste products diminishes dramatically. All the ecological relationships that connect the rivers with the seas, the life cycles of salmon and eels for example, are damaged or destroyed.

Most water pollution can be prevented by available means and without unreasonable expense. Hence, the large-scale pollution of the waters adjacent to settled areas can reasonably be described as a breakdown of social organization. Certain types of water pollution pose new problems, however. Modern technology produces an increasing volume of indestructible materials, some merely ugly, like polyethylene containers, and some very dangerous, like radioactive wastes, and these are being thrown almost indiscriminately into the ocean depths. There, unlike earlier types of garbage, they remain indefinitely without breaking down into their constituents.

Not only are the internal balances of the natural environment shaken by the various activities of high-energy societies, but population expansion and increased spatial mobility tend to deprive men of the direct experiences of an autonomous natural environment by multiplying intrusions upon it. For example, national and state forests, parks, and seashores have been established throughout the United States to preserve the original character of the environment in sites of exceptional beauty and interest, but nearly all such areas have their purposes somewhat defeated by overvisiting, as enormous crowds assemble to enjoy the solitude of the wilderness. Attendance at all sites of the national park system increased 349 percent (to 140 million visitors) from 1950 to 1967, while the total acreage of the system increased by only 22 percent.[36]

As with the erosion of local cultures, the erosion of the natural environment represents a permanent change in the human condition, the implications of which are still obscure. The world of the future, in either its cultural or its natural aspects, will have a smaller variety of sights, sounds, shapes, and patterns than the world of the past, but it is impossible to foretell whether this attrition of human experience will be compensated for by the expansion of experience in other, unforeseen directions.

Unconfirmed Trends

The 15 long-term trends discussed in the preceding section seem to be demonstrable beyond reasonable doubt by empirical (mostly quantitative) evidence. They will not necessarily continue into the future, even into the near future—the history of social change is full of surprises—but they have prevailed for a century or more and are not now restricted to particular societies or to particular regions of the world. The *unconfirmed* trends to be briefly reviewed in this section are frequently cited by popular commentators on social change, but they are not demonstrable to the same extent as the others, either because the empirical evidence is lacking, or because it is unsatisfactory, or because it does not show long-term continuity, or because contrary trends can be found in various parts of the world. Among those most often mentioned are the following:

1. Increasing anxiety
2. Breakdown of social values
3. Increasing anomie
4. Increasing deviance
5. Increasing political violence
6. Decline of the family

7. Decline of religion
8. Status equalization
9. Cultural homogenization
10. Global interdependence
11. Accelerating rates of social change

INCREASING ANXIETY

The supposed increase of anxiety is attributed to a variety of factors: the conflicting demands of inconsistent norms, the impersonality of large-scale organizations, the "pace" of urban life, the abandonment of religious beliefs, shifting standards of personal success, and so forth. The supporting evidence, however, is insufficient. The best index of increasing anxiety would be an increase in mental disorders, but Goldhamer and Marshall,[37] after a careful statistical comparison of nineteenth and twentieth century admissions rates to mental hospitals in Massachusetts and New York (presumably as anxious as any other regions of the modern world), found no evidence for a significant increase except among persons over 50. With respect to other indicators of anxiety, like suicide, opiate addiction, and alcoholism, the data, as we saw in Chapter Eleven, are inconclusive with respect to long-term trends.

BREAKDOWN OF SOCIAL VALUES

It is often alleged that modern man, in general, and Americans, in particular, are losing or have lost the consensus about basic values that bound men together in the simpler societies of the past. According to this view, the erosion of traditional cultures leaves a kind of moral vacuum, which a mass society cannot fill. There is very little evidence for the universality of this trend. On the contrary, modern totalitarian societies have a passion for unanimity hardly matched by any society of the past, and even in countries that encourage or pretend to encourage free value choices, studies of public opinion generally show a majority consensus with respect to fundamental values and wide participation in public discussions in which new values are formed.[38] Of course this does not prevent acute dissension in times of political crisis such as appeared in Germany in the 1920s or in the United States in the 1960s, but such crises are usually of limited duration.

INCREASING ANOMIE

Although there is a large literature on the relation between anomie and deviant behavior, the connection between the two phenomena has not been established with sufficient precision so that the amount of anomie in a society at a given time can be measured. Although such a trend is plausible, it cannot be proved or disproved in the present state of knowledge.

INCREASING DEVIANCE

The evidence we have about long-term trends in deviant behavior was reviewed in Chapter Eleven, and as we saw there, it is somewhat contradictory. Even if we restrict our attention to the United States and to recent decades, we find some forms of deviance increasing and others fluctuating, declining, or remaining stable. If the perspective is extended to the entire world, there seems to be evidence for a nearly universal increase in juvenile delinquency since World War II but not prior to that time, and other forms of deviance do not exhibit a consistent trend.

INCREASING POLITICAL VIOLENCE

The wave of political demonstrations and of both nonviolent and violent protests that shook the United States in the 1960s over the great issues of the Vietnam War, black civil rights, and student participation; the parallel occurrences in Europe, Latin America, and Japan over a variety of issues; the widespread violence that marked the Great Cultural Revolution in China; and the aftermath of the Six Day War of 1967 in the Middle East, have persuaded many observers that increasing political violence is an established trend, but other evidence does not support this conclusion. Political violence appears cyclical and episodic, although some countries are habitually more violent than others. The 1840s and the 1890s, for example, were marked by widespread political violence in Europe and in the United States. Although some of the political demonstrations of the 1960s were on an unprecedented scale and involved novel challenges to authority, the amount of violence, measured by the number of persons killed or wounded, was only moderate compared to that of earlier periods.[39]

DECLINE OF THE FAMILY

The announcement of a decline in the family or in selected aspects of family life often accompanies the discussion of family problems as a rhetorical flourish. But, as we saw in Chapter Ten, a better case can be made for an upward trend. The proportions of the adult population who are married, have children, and maintain a common household and the average duration of marriage have been steadily increasing in the United States and apparently in most other countries, although the information is fragmentary for parts of the world. Divorce rates in the United States are now relatively stable; they follow various courses in other countries. Illegitimacy rates are as likely to trend downward as upward.

DECLINE OF RELIGION

No other institutional area shows as sharp a discordance between the statistical evidence and common sense impressions. The belief in the decline of organized religion is almost an article of faith among the religious and the irreligious alike; but the available evidence indicates a steady growth in religious affiliation and activity in the United States and many other technologically advanced countries outside the communist bloc, where religious practice *has* declined. In 1890, 33 percent of the total American population were counted as church members; the proportion rose to 49 percent in 1940 and to 64 percent in 1960, since then it has been approximately stable.[40] The growth of religious activities, as measured by expenditures, has consistently outrun the growth of population and of national income.

Although accurate figures are difficult to come by, none of the world's major religious denominations is known to be declining in absolute numbers or even in relation to population. It is not inconceivable that increasing religious affiliation and activity are accompanied by a decrease in religious belief, but it is highly unlikely. What seems to be happening instead is the very gradual abandonment of nonscientific explanations of human phenomena and the belief in various sorts of miracles, in favor of ethical, social, and mystical doctrines that are more compatible with modern technology.

STATUS EQUALIZATION

The evidence for a general trend toward status equalization in modern societies is, at first glance, rather substantial.[41] Hardly any observer of organized religion would deny that the authority of the clergy over the laity has recently declined, and almost all family sociologists agree about the decline of parental authority. The decline of authority in the teacher-student relationship is too familiar to require documentation, and the ascendancy of upper over lower social classes has been weakened or destroyed in a great many countries since the beginning of the twentieth century. The sole reason for questioning this trend is that it is not quite universal. There is no evidence for example, of a long-run decline of authority in military or bureaucratic organizations, and there are numerous exceptions to the declining ascendancy of upper classes. As was noted in Chapters Seven and Eight, it is very difficult to establish a trend of decreasing or increasing stratification in either the class system or the occupational hierarchy in the United States. Examples of intensified stratification, like the apartheid system in South Africa, are not especially hard to find in the contemporary world. The diminishing importance of old bases of stratification like land ownership and ancestry is counterbalanced in many countries by the increasing importance of new bases of stratification, like education and party membership. Nevertheless, the argument for a general trend toward equalization is nearly convincing.

CULTURAL HOMOGENIZATION

The erosion of traditional cultures, together with the striking similarities in bureaucratic organizations among technologically advanced nations, raises the question whether the world is developing a single culture in which artifacts, art forms, and attitudes will eventually be indistinguishable from Iceland to Timor. The recent spread of certain standardized items—Coca Cola, public opinion surveys, transistor radios—into all corners of the known world lends some support to this idea. However, there seem to be a number of countervailing tendencies. Whereas technological progress homogenizes clothing or kitchen equipment, it has a diversifying effect on styles of work. In some respects, traditional societies that were overwhelmingly agricultural probably resembled each other more than modern industrial societies do.[42]

In addition, modern political movements, like Chinese communism, have created new cultural differences on a very large scale. The cultural similarities between contemporary China and the United States do not seem measurably greater than between the China and America of 50 or 100 years ago; communication between the two systems is probably more difficult now than then. Elsewhere in the world—in Ireland, Africa, the Near East, and India, for example—political movements have revived and intensified ancient differences of language, religion and, to some extent, life styles. Without any doubt, there are fewer independent cultural systems in today's world than formerly but it is highly premature to announce the merger of those that remain.

GLOBAL INTERDEPENDENCE

No modern phenomenon is more evident than the inclusion of the entire world in a single network of transportation and communication facilities. The observation that nations are being absorbed willy-nilly into a single world community has become equally commonplace, but it is not completely supported by the available data. If we examine the interaction of nations as expressed by international trade, or the exchange of students, mail, movies or official representatives, we discover that (a) most pairs of countries show no significant volume of interaction; (b) formidable barriers to interaction are maintained between political and regional blocs of nations; (c) the ratios of foreign trade to domestic trade, or of other foreign exchanges to internal exchanges, which are direct measures of international interdependence, seem to have increased throughout the nineteenth century but to have either oscillated or declined since about 1910,[43] although there is no single pattern that describes all types of exchange.

ACCELERATING SOCIAL CHANGE

It is an accepted platitude of popular sociology that social change is now more rapid than ever before and has been rapidly "accelerating," but it is not really clear what this statement means. Some of the trends we discussed earlier in the chapter, if plotted as graphs, would show an increasing slope—population expansion, for example. Others, like urbanization, show a decreasing slope and must continue to decelerate as the reservoir of rural population is emptied. It is doubtful whether the velocity of change—if we knew how to measure it—would be closely correlated with technological level. The changes recorded among some of the primitive peoples who have been closely observed in this century seem to be more sweeping than the changes that have occurred in any modernized society since the French Revolution. (The examples of the Manus and the Tikopia have already been mentioned.)

Much of modern history suggests that social change is a discontinuous process with a very uneven velocity. When we examine the development of an institutional complex over time, we often find short periods of drastic change interspersed with long intervals of relative stability. For example, the banking system in the United States was transformed between 1932 and 1935. It has not changed very much since. The structure of American universities changed dramatically from 1968 to 1970, after many years of relative stability. The suburban style of life based on the single-family residence, zoning, and the automobile appeared in the United States between 1918 and 1920; it was admirably and completely described by Sinclair Lewis as early as 1922,[44] but has remained essentially unchanged in the succeeding half-century. The operation of county jails in the United States has not changed significantly since the 1870s,[45] but the operation of mental hospitals was completely transformed when the phenothiazine tranquilizers were introduced in the late 1950s. As we saw in Chapter Ten, some of the distinctive features of the American family date back to colonial times. Innumerable other examples suggest that a social or cultural system is not analogous to an organism that matures and ages at a fixed rate, or to a machine whose parts all reflect the same level of technology. The elements of a social system are of varying age and origin and subject to different internal and external pressures. Therefore change in one part of such a system may occur at a different rate than change in other parts, and even the best-established trends do not maintain a constant velocity or a predictable rate of acceleration.

> 1 Social change may be spontaneous or planned, gradual or revolutionary, linear or cyclical, short-term or long-term. Most studies of social change are undertaken for the purpose of partially predicting the future. The simplest way of doing this is to extrapolate established long-term trends.

> 2 The extrapolation of a trend carries with it many assumptions about other things remaining equal or other trends remaining constant. Even under the most favorable conditions, the error of extrapolation can be expected to increase sharply as the trend moves away into the future. Despite the uncertainty of social predictions, the act of predicting is an essential component of ordinary social actions, and its accuracy can be considerably sharpened by careful, statistical analysis.

> 3 Among the major trends of social change that have now persisted for at least a hundred years and are likely—other things remaining equal —to extend into the future are technological progress; technological diffusion; the increase of goods, services, symbols and images; population expansion, occupational specialization, and decreasing work effort; equalization of the sexes; urbanization and suburbanization; intensified spatial mobility; the erosion of traditional cultures; the expansion of government and the increasing severity of war; and the decreasing autonomy of the natural environment.

> 4 Trends that are often mentioned in discussions of social change, but are *not* confirmed by the available evidence, include increasing anxiety; the progressive breakdown of social values; increasing anomie, deviance, and political violence; the decline of the family and of religion; status equalization; cultural homogenization; a trend toward global interdependence; and a general acceleration of social change.

Questions for Discussion / **CHAPTER THIRTEEN**

1 Suppose you were a sociologist living in the year 1900 and attempted to predict the course of change in the first half of the twentieth century by the extrapolation of established long-term trends. What correct predictions might you have made? What incorrect predictions?

2 What was the most recent social activity in which you participated that involved assumptions about the relatively distant future (more than 10 years hence)? Can you determine how those assumptions were arrived at?

3 How many powered mechanical devices can you enumerate that belong to you or to members of your immediate family (automobiles, radios, electric shavers, and so forth)? How many of these would have been owned by the average American family in 1900?

4 At what point would you expect the rising mileage of motor vehicle travel in the United States to level off? At what point might it be expected to decline?

5 Describe the erosion of distinctive culture traits in some locality or group known to you personally. How does it affect the people involved?

6 "Technological progress is unthinkable without occupational specialization." What does this statement mean? Can it be demonstrated? If so, how?

7 How do you account for the discrepancy between the widespread belief that the institutions of the family and of organized religion are declining and the statistical evidence that seems to show them as flourishing?

8 Can the overall velocity of social change be measured? What empirical facts would appropriately illustrate your answer?

Recommended Reading / **CHAPTER THIRTEEN**

Brown, Harrison. *The Challenge of Man's Future: An Inquiry Concerning the Condition of Man During the Years that Lie Ahead.* New York: Viking Press, 1954; Raymond W. Mack. *Transforming America: Patterns of Social Change.* New York: Random House, 1967. Two interesting attempts by social scientists to predict the future by extrapolating past trends.

Fourastié, Jean. *The Causes of Wealth.* trans. Theodore Caplow. New York: Free Press, 1960. A good basic explanation of the processes involved in economic and social development.

Mead, Margaret. *New Lives for Old: Cultural Transformation in Manus, 1928–1953.* New York: William Morrow, 1956. Gives a vivid account of rapid social change in a small society.

Lerner, Daniel. *The Passing of Traditional Society: Modernizing the Middle East.* New York: Free Press, 1964; and Neil J. Smelser, *Social Change in the Industrial Revolution: An Application of Theory to the British Coal Industry.* Chicago: University of Chicago Press, 1959. Two thorough and analytical case studies of social change.

1. Robert A. Nisbet, *Social Change and History: Aspects of the Western Theory of Development* (New York: Oxford University Press, 1969). The quotation is from pp. 190–191.

2. See, for example, Burnham Putnam Beckwith, *The Next 500 Years: Scientific Predictions of Major Social Trends* (New York: Exposition Press, 1967).

3. The reasons why it might not be possible for technological development to resume after a nuclear war are explained in Harrison Brown, *The Challenge of Man's Future: An Inquiry Concerning the Condition of Man During the Years That Lie Ahead* (New York: Viking Press, 1954).

4. A good sampling of current speculation about the future may be found in Daniel Bell, ed., *Towards the Year 2000: Work in Progress,* special issue of *Daedalus* (Boston: Houghton Mifflin, 1967).

5. A magnificent study of social change concerned entirely with the past is Lynn Townsend White, Jr., *Medieval Technology and Social Change* (Oxford: Clarendon Press, 1962).

6. Arthur C. Clarke, *Profiles of the Future: An Inquiry into the Limits of the Possible* (New York: Harper & Row, 1962), p. 19.

7. The earlier part of this development is carefully described by White, *Medieval Technology and Social Change;* and the entire sequence by W. Fred Cottrell, *Energy and Society: The Relation Between Energy, Social Change and Economic Development* (New York: McGraw-Hill, 1955).

8. U.S. Bureau of the Census, *Historical Statistics of the United States: Colonial Times to 1957* (Washington, D.C.: U.S. Government Printing Office, 1957), series S1-14; and U.S. Bureau of the Census, Department of Commerce, *Statistical Abstract of the United States* (Washington, D.C.: U.S. Government Printing Office, 1968), table 753.

9. United Nations, Statistical Office, *United Nations Statistical Yearbook* (New York: United Nations, 1967), table 142.

10. R. Buckminster Fuller et al., *World Design Science Decade 1965–1975,* document 1, *Inventory of World Resources, Human Trends and Needs* (Carbondale, Ill.: Southern Illinois University, 1965–1967), p. 29.

11. Ibid.

12. *Statistical Yearbooks of the United Nations,* 1961–1968.

13. *Ibid.,* 1967, table 126; and *Historical Statistics of the United States,* series M195–210.

14. Jean Fourastié, *The Causes of Wealth,* trans. Theodore Caplow (New York: Free Press, 1960), p. 37.

15. *Historical Statistics of the United States,* series H223–233; and *Statistical Abstract of the United States 1968,* table 183. The estimate for 1970 is extrapolated from the latter.

16. *Ibid.,* series H327–338 and table 199 respectively; 1970 estimate extrapolated from table 199.

17. Columbia University, Bureau of Applied Social Research, Profiles of Development Project, 1968.

18. *Historical Statistics of the United States,* series B180–194; *Statistical Abstract of the United States 1968,* table 88.

19. *Ibid.,* 1970 estimates extrapolated from table 88.

20. See footnote 17 above.

21. *Historical Statistics of the United States,* series R165–168; and *Statistical Abstract of the United States 1968,* table 749.

22. *Ibid.,* table 743.

23. *United Nations Statistical Yearbook 1967,* table 209.

24. Among the most interesting attempts to grasp the total significance of the rise in symbols and images are David Riesman, Reuel Denney, and Nathan Glazer, *The Lonely Crowd: A Study of the Changing American Character* (New Haven: Yale University Press, 1964); Jacques Barzun, *The House of Intellect* (New York: Harper & Row, 1959); Kenneth E. Boulding, *The Image: Knowledge in Life and Society* (Ann Arbor: University of Michigan Press, 1961); Marshall McLuhan, *Understanding Media: The Extensions of Man* (New York: McGraw-Hill, 1964).

25. Fourastié, *The Causes of Wealth,* pp. 164–174.

26. United Nations, Statistical Office, Department of Economic and Social Affairs, *Demographic Yearbook* (New York: United Nations, 1957), table 5; and 1967, table 6.

27. *Statistical Abstract of the United States 1968,* table 802; and *Historical Statistics of the United States,* series Q321–327.

28. *United Nations Statistical Yearbook 1967,* table 152.

29. Raymond Firth, *Social Change in Tikopia: Re-Study of a Polynesian Community after a Generation* (New York: Macmillan, 1959).

30. Margaret Mead, *New Lives for Old: Cultural Transformation in Manus, 1928–1953* (New York: William Morrow, 1956).

31. Edmund Stillman, "Farewell to the Balkans," *Harper's Magazine,* January 1963, pp. 84–89. The quotation is from pp. 85–86.

32. Richard M. Weaver, *Life Without Prejudice and Other Essays* (Chicago: Henry Regnery, 1966).

33. W. Lloyd Warner, ed., *The Emergent American Society,* vol. 1, *Large-Scale Organizations* (New Haven: Yale University Press, 1967), pp. 577–586.

34. Brown, *The Challenge of Man's Future,* pp. 149–186.

35. For a brief history of the Green Revolution, see Richard Critchfield, "Feeding the Hungry," *New Republic,* October 25, 1969, pp. 16–19.

36. *Statistical Abstract of the United States 1968,* table 288.

37. Herbert Goldhamer and Andrew W. Marshall, *Psychosis and Civilization: Two Studies in the Frequency of Mental Disease* (New York: Free Press, 1953).

38. For data supporting this assertion, see, for example, Gabriel A. Almond and Sidney Verba, *The Civic Culture: Political Attitudes and Democracy in Five Nations* (Princeton, N.J.: Princeton University Press, 1963).

39. See "A Historical Overview of Violence in Europe and America," in Hugh Davis Graham and Ted Robert Gurr, eds., *The History of Violence in America: Historical and Comparative Perspectives,* report submitted to the National Commission on the Causes and Prevention of Violence (New York: Praeger, 1969), especially pp. 28, 29, and 85.

40. *Historical Statistics of the United States,* series H528; *Statistical Abstract of the United States 1968,* table 51.

41. According to a widely held economic theory, technological progress necessarily tends in the long run to equalize incomes, thus encouraging status equalization. See Fourastié, *The Causes of Wealth.*

42. The economic historian, R. H. Tawney, remarked to a friend with whom he was traveling in China in the 1930s that the English workman of the eighteenth century "would have been very much at home in the economy as well as in the living conditions we have just been observing, but so also would the Frenchman from Paris or the Italian from Florence. The farmers would have wondered at some of the crops raised here, but they would have understood the Chinese methods of cultivation and the care given to the soil." Quoted in Warren S. Thompson, "Population," *Scientific American* 182, no. 2 (February 1950): 11–15. Quotation from p. 12.

43. A full review of the available data is found in Kurt Finsterbusch, *International Integration: Amounts, Geographic Loci, Patterns* (Ph.D. dissertation, Columbia University, 1969).

44. Sinclair Lewis, *Babbitt* (New York: Grosset and Dunlap, 1922).

45. Hans W. Mattick and Alexander B. Aikman, "The Cloacal Region of American Corrections," *Annals of the American Academy of Political and Social Science* 381 (January 1969): 109–118.

Prospects
of Social Technology

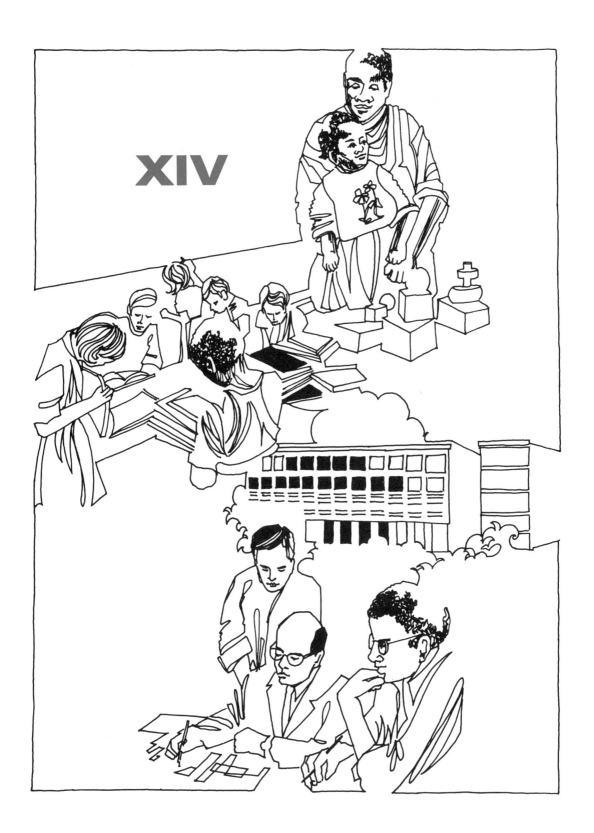

Introduction

S*ocial technology is the application of scientific knowledge to the solution of social problems.* The improvement of social technology is or ought to be a principal aim of sociology as a scientific discipline.

> What does science aim to do? The answer, as we piece it together from the writings of many authorities, seems to be that science seems to give man an understanding, a power of prediction, and a power of control, beyond that which he can achieve through his own unaided common sense.[1]

To regard science as an intellectual activity independent of the everyday world is to disregard its history, which has consisted of a continuous interplay between theory and practice, knowledge and application, laboratory methods and engineering. The evolution of the physical sciences cannot be understood at all without reference to the constant influence of practical questions and the tendency for investigators to follow lines of research suggested by outside organizations. In Chapter Nine, we saw how certain practical problems of navigation generated the first wave of scientific research in the seventeenth century. An equally close connection between science and technology can be demonstrated for each succeeding era; it is illustrated by the intimate two-way relationship between science and technology in the exploration of space.

The founders of modern sociology, as we saw in Chapter Four, expected that an effective social technoloy would automatically follow the accumulation of sociological knowledge. If they could return to earth today, they might be puzzled by the relatively backward condition of social technology. Research has provided a mountain of information about social phenomena, and an understanding of social processes that could not have been achieved by intuition or common sense, but it has not yet given anyone a significant power of control over social problems. As the body of sociological knowledge continues to expand, its failure to support a corresponding technology becomes more and more puzzling.

The improvement of social technology is probably essential for the survival and future welfare of humanity under the strange new conditions that have followed from the application of technology to agriculture, manufacturing, transportation, communication, and other types of collective endeavor. The eighteenth-century belief in an "invisible hand" that would regulate human affairs perfectly if not hampered by well-meaning interference is no longer plausible. The nineteenth-century belief (summed up in the magic word *progress*[2]) that all social problems would be automatically solved by modernization is not very convincing nowadays. The utopian conditions that were supposed to follow proletarian revolutions have failed to materialize; socialist as well as capitalist countries struggle with such problems as juvenile delinquency, bureaucratic impersonality, anomie, and ethnic conflict. Attempts to solve social problems "technocratically," by taking goals for granted, have not been notably successful, and attempts to solve problems by "participatory democracy," without the intervention of experts, have been even less fruitful.

It is unlikely that order can be imposed on the global society by force or by propaganda. It is not a question of persuading people to accept the obvious solutions to the problems that torment them. The solutions are not obvious; they are mostly unknown. The principal requirements for effective programs of social action are: (1) the sequential approach, and (2) practicable goals.

The Sequential Approach

The sequential approach may be illustrated by what happens when a dam is built across a river to impound water for hydroelectric power and irrigation. The engineer's competence is established in the first instance by a combination of theoretical and practical credentials. He has studied the appropriate physical sciences and understands their relevance to the job in hand, but the technology of dam-building is not entirely derived from physics and hydraulics. The engineer must know something about the folklore and tradition of dam-building, as well as the empirical characteristics of materials and machines. He must also have some systematic knowledge—even if in rough form—about the behavior of technicians and workmen.

When we say that every dam-building engineer uses a sequential approach, we mean that unlike a beaver or a small boy playing in a brook, he starts with the specification of an end-condition to be achieved. Indeed, in the typical case, the work of the dam-builder starts at an even earlier point, when he delineates for the client (whoever claims to speak for potential users of the dam) the various end-conditions that can be achieved with the existing technology, informs him of the advantages and disadvantages of each end condition, and estimates the time, money, and other resources required to reach each of the feasible end conditions in the particular setting. This interaction between engineer and client is an essential part of the sequential approach. It allows a reconciliation of the objectives envisioned by the client, and the possibilities described by the engineer. Almost invariably, the client must modify his initial objectives to take account of limitations in the technology. Surprisingly often, the engineer revises his initial statement of possibilities, enlarging the technology by research or by borrowing in order to achieve objectives that at first seemed impracticable. In some instances, of course, communication between the client and the engineer reveals that the objectives desired by the client cannot be achieved with the resources available. But in the normal case, the engineer and client agree on a detailed description of the desired end condition.

After discussion with the client, the engineer is able to describe the desired end-condition in detail. Then he works *backward* from the end condition to the present, establishing detailed descriptions of the intermediate conditions between the beginning and the end of the project. These descriptions are based on a large number of quantitative estimates, measurements, and calculations, and it is known in advance what tests and measurements will be appropriate at intermediate points to compare the actual course of the project with its predicted course. If the work moves from each intermediate condition to the next without deviating seriously from the predictions, as occurs in most routine engineering projects, then the actual end-condition will necessarily resemble the planned end-condition. Any observed deviation from the predicted measurements at an intermediate point is a signal that something has gone wrong in the planning or the execution of the work and that the predicted end-condition cannot be achieved without modifying the plan or its execution.

The difference between this procedure and the traditional approach of a social reformer to a social problem is especially clear in the early stages of a project. The social reformer does not feel compelled to describe an end-condition with any precision. He gives his clients only a vague, nonquantitative statement of his objectives, so that it may be quite impossible to determine at a later time whether the project has succeeded or failed. In the rare project in which an end-condition is described in quantitative terms and a date is fixed for its realization, the reformer is not likely to specify the intermediate conditions, and the evaluation of results may be delayed so long that it becomes irrelevant.

One result of this defective procedure is that ineffectual programs of social action are launched, expanded, and widely imitated before their futility is discovered. Legislatures and social agencies frequently adopt methods for the solution of complex problems that are either of unknown efficacy, like indeterminate sentences for young criminals, or known in advance to be ineffective, like the hospitalization of narcotics addicts. Such programs seldom provide for continuous recording of results and they rarely have precise goals or a definite time schedule. It is customary for their promoters to attribute poor results to insufficient financing and to use the evidence of a program's failure as an argument for expanding it.

The sequential approach, by contrast, involves continuous attention to the question of success or failure. It includes: (1) careful, complete, relevant quantitative reporting, that is, the counting of time, money, people, and results at every stage of a program; (2) the refusal to adopt any unproven solution for a social problem except experimentally on a small scale; (3) the refusal to apply measures on a large scale that have proved ineffective on a small scale; (4) continuous attention to the unanticipated consequences that always appear in any sequence of planned social action; (5) the step-by-step scheduling of activities in real calendar time, and the specification of as many intermediate conditions as possible; (6) the establishment in advance of measurable minimum criteria for a program's success. Thus, the minimum criteria for a local antipoverty program might read something like this:

1. Decent, safe and sanitary housing for all assisted families, within two years
2. Average school achievement equal to the 30th percentile of the general population within three years
3. 80 percent of assisted families to achieve financial autonomy within five years
4. The percentage of intact families to be maintained at the intake level or higher during the entire duration of the program

An agency adopting such criteria accepts the responsibility for achieving definite objectives in a limited population. The sequential approach envisages each program as a closed system, designed to achieve certain results for certain clients. A program that fails to meet its goals (that is, to satisfy the minimum criteria established in advance) is regarded as worse than none at all because it absorbs resources that might otherwise be available for more effective programs.

Practicable Goals

Even without a sequential approach, some parts of contemporary social technology must be counted as partly successful, if only because of the impetus provided by the steady per capita increase of mechanical energy everywhere in the world. The modernization of cities, the diffusion of literacy, and the reduction of infant mortality are goals that have been successfully realized in a hundred countries. Many of the programs of social action that fail are burdened with incompatible or self-contradictory goals, as if an engineer had undertaken to widen the channel of a river and increase the speed of its current at the same time. A good many social problems arise in the first place out of incompatible or self-contradictory goals—the maximization of productivity *and* the maximization of morale, for example—and if the social reformer is not forced into rationality by the sequential approach, he is likely to propose solutions that embody the same contradictions as the original problem.

The best way to demonstrate that a given set of goals is practicable is to show that they have actually been realized under similar conditions and with similar means. All useful technology rests partly on pragmatic experience and on the assumption that what has worked before can be made to work again. Every social system, however primitive, exhibits a great deal of successful social planning, which consists for the most part of establishing new organizations—families, hunting parties, monasteries, or factories—according to a pattern which has been tried many times before. From the standpoint of social technology, one successful pilot study that realizes its goals is worth a thousand plausible projects without practicable goals.

Social Technology and the Moral Order

There is a virtual unanimity among sociologists that future social systems will be unlike those of the present and past but considerably less agreement about the nature of the expected transformation. Mannheim, in a classic defense of social planning, discussed the possibility of a planned mass society with individual freedom as its principal goal.[2] Sorokin believed that the production, accumulation, and distribution of "love-energy" could accomplish the altruistic transformation of man's universe if it were undertaken with the same organized rationality as the production and distribution of mechanical energy.[3]

Some pessimistic observers see an inevitable descent toward a gloomy society of ant-men drudging away under the control of a monstrous, all-encompassing state.[4] Some optimistic observers believe that most of our current social problems will disappear by themselves and an era of unprecedented human freedom will be ushered in as soon as the potentialities of existing physical technology are fully grasped.[5] The consistent optimists are even rarer than the absolute pessimists, however. The vision that most sociologists hold of the future is that humanity is confronted with an almost immediate choice between catastrophe and triumph.[6] The seeds of catastrophe are nuclear weapons, the population explosion, environmental pollution, and the extension of bureaucratic control over individuals. The seeds of triumph are unlimited energy, the expansion of knowledge, the conquest of disease, the means to explore the universe, and the tendency for humanity to become conscious of itself as a single collectivity with common interests.

If this picture is correct, twentieth-century man stands at a crossroads trying to choose between the lady and the tiger, unlimited progress or unlimited misery. Both the threat of catastrophe and the hope of triumph are attributable to an industrial technology that can be used either for benign projects like the production of goods or for malign projects like the destruction of cities. An effective social technology would be similarly capable of both good and evil, and might be used either to enlarge the freedom and autonomy of individuals or to reduce them to perfect subjugation. But the dangers ought not to discourage us from the pursuit of sociological knowledge. The best cure for the abuse of knowledge is more knowledge. Social technology has a long way to go before it becomes capable of saving the world, but a small beginning has been made.

Summary / CHAPTER FOURTEEN

1. Science and technology are different aspects of the same effort. The founders of scientific sociology took for granted that they were laying the basis for a technology capable of solving social problems and improving social institutions. The delayed development of social technology is something of a puzzle.

2. The first steps toward any effective social technology involve (a) the sequential approach and (b) practicable goals.

3. Using a sequential approach, the people involved agree after discussion on the desired end condition and estimate the time and resources required to achieve it, then work backward from the end condition to the present, establishing detailed descriptions of the intermediate conditions, which later serve to measure progress and correct errors.

4. One can best demonstrate the practicability of the goals set for a program of social improvement by showing that similar goals have been realized before under similar conditions and with similar means. Social technology, like any other technology, must rely heavily on what has been learned from previous experience.

5. Modern man stands at a crossroads in history, facing a choice between unlimited progress and unlimited misery. Social technology has a long way to go before it becomes capable of saving the world, but its prospects are not hopeless.

Questions for Discussion / CHAPTER FOURTEEN

1. What is meant by "the intimate two-way relationship between science and technology in the exploration of space?"

2. Illegitimacy has been as closely studied as almost any social phenomenon, and a great deal is known about how and why illegitimacy occurs, but almost nothing is known about how to prevent illegitimacy. How can this be explained?

3. Why is the expectation that all social problems will be solved automatically by industrial progress no longer convincing today?

4. In a program for improving the administration of a public welfare system, who corresponds to "the engineer?" Who corresponds to "the client?" Who else might be actively involved?

5. What is the usual justification for adopting methods for the solution of social problems that are known in advance to be ineffective, like teaching high school students about the dangers of drug abuse in order to prevent them from experimenting with drugs?

6. The Puritans of the seventeenth century were accused of objecting to the cruel sport of bear-baiting not because it gave pain to the bear but because it gave pleasure to the spectators. Do you see a parallel in some current approaches to social problems?

7. Find an example in your own experience of a program of social improvement with two or more incompatible goals.

8. Review your understanding of the following terms:

> technology
> social planning
> closed system
> social improvement

Notes / **CHAPTER FOURTEEN**

1. Gordon W. Allport, *The Use of Personal Documents in Psychological Science* (New York: Social Science Research Council, Bulletin 49, 1942), p. 148.
2. Karl Mannheim, *Man and Society in an Age of Reconstruction: Studies in Modern Social Structure,* trans. Edward A. Shils (New York: Harcourt Brace Jovanovich, 1940), especially pp. 369–381.
3. Pitirim A. Sorokin, *The Basic Trends of Our Times* (New Haven: College and University Press, 1964), especially pp. 194–208.
4. See, for example, Roderick Seidenberg, *Posthistoric Man: An Inquiry* (Chapel Hill, N. C.: University of North Carolina Press, 1950).
5. See, for example, Marshall McLuhan, *Understanding Media: The Extensions of Man* (New York: McGraw-Hill, 1964).
6. For a thorough and cool-headed consideration of these alternatives, see Harrison Brown, *The Challenge of Man's Future: An Inquiry Concerning the Condition of Man During the Years that Lie Ahead* (New York: Viking Press, 1954).

GLOSSARY

ACCOMMODATION stable, mutual adjustment of groups with incompatible goals

ACT any speech or gesture with an ascertainable social meaning

AGGRANDIZEMENT EFFECT tendency for the prestige of an organization in a set to be overestimated by its own members

ALCOHOLISM pattern of habitual heavy drinking which interferes with the drinker's ability to perform his assigned social roles

ALIENATION loss of interest in the purposes toward which one's own activity is directed

ANALYSIS, CONTENT analysis of themes in written or spoken communications

ANOMIE loss of confidence in social norms

ASSIMILATION merger of two groups so that they no longer have separate goals

ATTITUDE an idea predisposing one to act in a given way in a given situation

AUTHORITY power supported by norms that are accepted by those over whom the power is exercised

BIRTH RATE, CRUDE number of births per thousand living persons in the total population of a given territory in a calendar year

BIRTH RATE, REFINED OR ADJUSTED birth rate based on some other population than the one in which the births occurred

BIRTH RATE, SPECIFIC number of births per thousand living persons of designated age, sex, and/or family status in a given population in a calendar year

BONDING establishment of exclusive, nonaggressive relationships between animals who recognize each other individually

BUREAUCRACY continuous hierarchy with each lower position under the control and supervision of a higher one and the conduct of each position governed by technical rules

CAPITALISM an arrangement whereby private individuals and private associations have an unlimited right to acquire and manage natural resources and production facilities, to sell or exchange the commodities produced, and to use the proceeds for private luxury, for altruistic purposes, or to obtain additional wealth

CAREER occupational life history of an individual, or a segment of it within a particular organization

CASTE   social class in which membership is hereditary and (in principle) unchangeable

CITY   a large, permanent assemblage of buildings and people that is at the same time a commercial, productive, political, cultural, and ceremonial center

COALITION   alliance of two or more actors in opposition to other actors in the same system

COALITION IN A TRIAD   alliance of two members of a triad against the third member

CODING   reduction of the information gathered in the field to a standardized form

COMMUNITY   special type of organization based on residence within a bounded territory

COMPETITION   impersonal struggle of groups having similar goals

CONFLICT   struggle over values, status, power, or scarce resources, in which the aims of the conflicting parties are not only to gain an advantage but also to subjugate their rivals

CONFLICT, CONTINUOUS   unplanned conflict within a social system to which the contending parties belong and in which they expect to remain for the foreseeable future

CONFLICT, EPISODIC   recurrent conflict regulated by rules that both participants and witnesses accept as legitimate

CONFLICT, SOCIAL   process of interaction between persons or groups with incompatible goals

CONFLICT, TERMINAL   conflict in which at least one party aims to prevent further conflict by permanently disabling or subjugating its opponent

CULTURE   socially acquired and transmitted patterns of activity and the objects associated with them

CULTURE TRAITS   small bits of culture

DEATH RATE   number of deaths in a calendar year per 1,000 persons alive in a given population at the beginning or the middle of that year

DEMOGRAPHIC TRANSITION   worldwide process whereby preindustrial populations with high mortality and fertility are transformed into modernized populations with low mortality and fertility, after passing through an intermediate phase of rapidly declining mortality and slowly declining fertility accompanied by spectacular natural increase

DEMOGRAPHY   scientific study of population

DEPENDENCY RATIO   ratio of the economically dependent population that needs to be supported to the economically active population capable of supporting dependents

DEVIANCE   behavior that violates the norms of a social system and provokes corrective efforts by agents of that system

DISORGANIZATION, INDIVIDUAL   loss of an individual's ability to organize his life for the realization of his own goals

DISORGANIZATION, SOCIAL   decrease of the influence of group norms upon individual members of a group

DOCUMENT, ATTESTED   document with which special pains have been taken to guarantee the accuracy of information recorded and to ensure its preservation

DOCUMENT, PRIMARY   document containing information the writer obtained from personal experience or first-hand observation

DOCUMENT, SECONDARY   document containing information derived from other documents

DOMINANCE   undisputed superiority of one animal over another of the same species which precludes conflict between them

DRUG   chemical substance that produces a definite, desired effect when ingested or applied to the body

DRUG, ILLEGAL   drug that can be neither legitimately prescribed by a physician nor purchased for self-administration

DRUNKENNESS   condition of a drinker who has lost control of his own behavior to the extent that he risks injury to himself or others

ECOLOGY, URBAN   study of the relationship between the city as a social system and the city as a landscape

EMIGRATION   migration from one country to another, viewed from the former country

ENDOGAMY   marriage within one's own group

ENUMERATION   count or measurement of the incidence of a specified phenomenon in a particular population at a stated time or during a stated time interval

ESTATE   legally recognized social class

ETHOLOGY   scientific study of the social behavior of animals

EXOGAMY   marriage outside one's own group

FAMILY   permanent group of two or more persons related by blood, marriage, or adoption

FAMILY, EXTENDED   two or more nuclear families linked by common descent

FAMILY, NUCLEAR   a pair of adults and their offspring, residing together

FUNCTION   the part played by any element of a social system in maintaining the system

FUNCTION, LATENT   function of an element of a social system that is *not* recognized by actors in that system

FUNCTION, MANIFEST   function of an element in a social system that *is* recognized by actors in that system

GROUP   social system consisting of a number of individuals who interact with each other and engage in some joint activities

HIERARCHY   distribution of social power prescribed by an organization

HYPOTHESIS   statement of a possible relationship between elements in a system, stated in a form suitable for testing by empirical research

ILLEGITIMACY   bearing of children by unmarried women

ILLEGITIMACY RATIO   number of illegitimate births per 1,000 live births in a given population during a stated time interval

IMMIGRATION   migration from one country to another, viewed from the receiving country

INFLUENCE   power that is exercised informally and without definite mechanisms for overcoming resistance

INFORMATION, HARD   information that has an objective character, does not change from one day to the next, and can be empirically verified

INFORMATION, SOFT   information that is subjective, changeable, and impossible to verify

INSTITUTION   distinctive pattern of social activity and values centered upon some major human need and accompanied by distinctive modes of social interaction; the term is also used for any large establishment with a permanent staff of workers or inmates under its roof

INSTITUTION, TOTAL   large establishment whose workers or inmates are subject to a fixed discipline throughout the 24 hours of the day

INTEGRATION   fitting together of the parts of a social system to make a unified whole

INTERACTION   process by which communicating individuals influence each other's thoughts and activities

INTERNATIONAL LAW   body of rules, customs, and agreements by which the interaction of sovereign states is supposed to be governed

INTERNATIONAL SYSTEM   set of governments that maintain continuous relationships

INTERNATIONAL WAR   large-scale armed conflict between governments or would-be governments, which lasts for a considerable time and results in considerable loss of life

INTERVIEW, STRUCTURED   interview for which the wording and order of questions has been partly or wholly designed in advance

INTERVIEW, UNSTRUCTURED   interview for which the wording and order of questions has not been determined in advance

KINSHIP SYSTEM   set of relationships derived from descent and marriage, which includes a set of kinship terms linked to a set of behavior patterns and attitudes

LABORATORY   room or other enclosed space under the control of an investigator, containing equipment for carrying out the procedures and measurements required in a particular type of scientific research

LABOR FORCE PARTICIPATION RATE   percentage of persons in a population who are gainfully employed or seeking work at a given time

LIFE EXPECTANCY   estimate of the average survival of a cohort of individuals of the same age if the specific mortality rates observed at a given date prevail throughout their lives

LIFE SPAN   maximum age that can be reached by an individual who lives his entire life in wholesome conditions and ultimately dies of old age

Glossary

MACHINE (INDUSTRIAL)   tool or set of tools used in production whose working energy is supplied by a motor utilizing some combination of natural forces

MANUFACTURING   mass production of standardized useful commodities in large establishments by means of an elaborate division of labor under close supervision

MIGRATION   change of residence from one place to another

MOBILITY   movement of individuals, families, and groups from one social position to another

MOBILITY, HORIZONTAL   movement from one social position to another at the same status level

MOBILITY, VERTICAL   movement from one social position to another involving a gain or loss of status

MODEL, SCIENTIFICALLY USEFUL   one that enables us to make sense out of a great many facts and to generate significant new questions to guide the gathering of additional facts

MODEL, PRACTICALLY USEFUL   one that suggests ways of applying sociological knowledge to the solution of social problems

MODERNIZATION   process whereby a contemporary society improves its control of the environment by means of an increasingly competent technology applied by increasingly complex organizations

MONOGAMY   system of marriage in which, at a given time, each husband is allowed only one wife and each wife only one husband

NORM   formal or informal rule governing the behavior of actors in a given social system

OBSERVER, COVERT   observer who is not identified as such within the situation or system he is studying

OBSERVER, DETACHED   observer who remains outside the situation or system he is studying

OBSERVER, PARTICIPANT   observer who engages in social activity within the situation or system he is studying

OCCUPATION   pattern of activities with a market value which an individual pursues on a regular basis in order to obtain a livelihood

ORGANIZATION   persistent social system with an explicit collective identity, an unequivocal roster of members, a program of repetitive activity directed toward the achievement of explicit goals, and procedures for the appointment of new members

ORGANIZATIONAL PYRAMID   diagram that shows the number of status levels in a hierarchy and the number of members at each level

PILOT STUDY   a small-scale dress rehearsal for a research project, complete with its own data-collection procedures and a miniature final report

POLYANDRY   marriage of one wife with several husbands

POLYGAMY   any form of plural marriage

POLYGYNY   marriage of one husband with several wives

POPULATION   an aggregate of persons identified by one or more characteristics which all of them have in common

POPULATION DRIFT   tendency for residential mobility within a territory to produce a net displacement of population in certain directions

POPULATION PYRAMID   diagram that shows the relative number of
persons at each age level in a population, usually divided by sex

POSITION   category of membership in an organization whose incumbents are expected to act and interact according to a standard
pattern that is part of the organizational program

POWER probability that an actor in a social relationship will be able
to carry out his own will despite resistance

PRESTIGE   average opinion of an audience about the relative preferability of competing persons, groups, or things

PROFESSION   occupation that monopolizes a cluster of related work
activities, based on a large body of abstract knowledge, allowing considerable discretion to the practitioner, and having serious social
consequences

PROSTITUTION   sale of sexual favors to strangers for money or other
valuables

RELATIONSHIP, AFFINAL   kin relationship based on marriage

RELATIONSHIP, CONSANGUINEAL   kin relationship based on descent

RELIABILITY   ability of an instrument to deliver an unchanged measurement when applied repeatedly to an unchanged phenomenon

REPRODUCTION RATE   measure of the replacement of a generation
of childbearing women by their childbearing daughters

RESPONDENT   person who responds voluntarily to a research inquiry with the understanding that his answers will be anonymous and
will have no personal consequences

ROLE   pattern of behavior expected of the incumbent of a given
social position when interacting with the incumbents of other given
positions

ROLE, ORGANIZATIONAL   pattern of behavior prescribed for an incumbent of a given organizational position vis-à-vis other persons
with whom the organizational program requires him to interact

SAMPLE, RANDOM   group of individuals selected to represent a
population by means of some prodceure that gives every individual in
the population an identical chance of being selected

SEX RATIO   number of males per 100 females in a given population

SOCIAL CHANGE   process whereby measurable differences appear
in a social system over a given interval of time

SOCIAL CLASS   large section of a population having relatively uniform statuses, an identifiable style of life, shared values, and an awareness of a common identity

SOCIALIZATION   process whereby an individual qualifies to participate in the activity of a group by learning the norms and roles expected
and approved by the group

SOCIAL RESEARCH   systematic observation and recording of human
behavior in social systems for the purpose of developing and testing
social theories

SOCIAL SYSTEM   group of living people engaged in some type of collective activity and related to each other in various ways

SOCIETY   self-sufficient, self-perpetuating social system, including persons of both sexes and all ages

SOCIOLOGY   scientific study of human relationships and their consequences

STATUS   place of a person or position in the rank order of influence in a social system

STATUS, ASCRIBED   status awarded for attributes of the individual over which he has no control and which he is not expected to be able to change

STATUS, ORGANIZATIONAL   place of an organizational position in the distribution of social power prescribed by the organization

STATUS SCHISM   horizontal split of an organizational hierarchy into strata that are isolated from each other by rules forbidding mobility and fraternization and imposing differences in life style

STATUTORY RAPE   sexual relationship in which the female partner is under a certain age set by the law of a particular state, usually 16 17, or 18

STRATIFICATION   arrangement of the members of a social system in graded strata, with varying degrees of prestige, property, influence, and other status attributes

SURVEY   study using standardized interviews or questionnaires

TABLE OF ORGANIZATION   chart showing the functions and statuses of positions in an organization and the prescribed interactions among them

TABULATION   arrangement of data according to two or more codes simultaneously

TECHNOLOGY   scientific knowledge applied to practical tasks

TECHNOLOGY, SOCIAL   application of scientific knowledge to the solution of social problems

TRANSFER SHEET   form on which the verbatim answers to an interview question are assembled for further analysis

TRIAD   social system containing three interrelated actors

URBANIZATION   movement of population from farms to cities and from small cities to larger cities

UTOPIA   rationally designed, conflict-free society

VALIDITY   ability of a research instrument to measure what it purports to measure

VALUE   conception of what is desirable which influences the social behavior of the holder

WORK, SOCIOLOGY OF   study of the social facts associated with the division of labor

Mass media, 636-7
Mass transit, 291-2
Matrilineal societies, 480
Mayo, Elton, 113
McNamara, Robert S., 463
Mead, George Herbert, 162, 184
Mead, Margaret, 110, 512, 642
Median age, 202, 204, 205; at marriage, 487, 489, 506
Medical sociology, 30
Men: addiction among, 565; age of, 228; age-specific death rate of, 207; U.S. and Peruvian (1961), criminal activity of, 535; life expectancy of, 218; middle-class, authority of, 506; suicides among, 542
Mencken, H. L., 107
Mental Hospital (Stanton and Schwartz), 142
Merton, Robert K., 157, 186-8, 330, 453, 455-6, 527-8
Middle class, 319-20, 334, 336, 338; black population entering, 339-40; child-rearing by, 507; kin networks of, 485; as major identification, 345; new, 347-50; parent-child relationship of, 507-8; and working class, 347; *see also* Upper class
Middle-range theories, 186-7
Middletown (Lynd and Lynd), 107-10, 117, 333
Middletown in Transition (Lynd and Lynd), 108-10, 334
Migrations: immigration as, 240, 247-50; models of, 239-40; political resettlement as, 240, 250-1; population drift as, 240, 244-7; *see also* Urbanization
Military-scientific-industrial complex, 461-3
Military technology, 608-9
Mill, John Stuart, 57, 165
Miller, Delbert C., 397
Mills, C. Wright, 168, 347, 459, 508
Mind and Society: A Treatise on General Sociology (Pareto), 170
Mobility, 6; geographic, 391; horizontal, 106, 391-2; intergenerational, 116; in urban environment, 105; residential, 239, 244; seasonal, 239; spatial, 641; vertical, 106, 391, 392-7, 406-9; *see also* Migrations, Status
Models, 41-2; of conflicts, 596-600; of ideal bureaucracy, 182-4; of migrations, 239-40; of stratification, 333-5, 339-42, 344-46
Monogamy, 478, 483
Monopoly, legislation against, 458
Montesquieu, 185
Moral order, social technology and, 664-5
Morale, productivity and, 438-9
More, Sir Thomas, 592
Morphine, 562, 564
Morris, Norval, 559, 591
Mortality, 205-14, 216; differential, 230-35; reduced, 211-14
Moynihan, Daniel Patrick, 353
Moynihan report, consequences of, 352-5
Mumford, Lewis, 298
Murders, 530, 538-9
Murdock, George Peter, 477, 478, 480, 545
Mussolini, Benito, 451
Mutual deterrence, 613-15
Myrdal, Gunnar, 123-6, 339, 341

Nagel, Ernest, 9
National Opinion Research Center study (NORC study), 387-8
National Recovery Act (1933), 292
Nationalism, 612
Negroes. *See* Blacks
Neighborhood Unit Plan (Perry), 298-300
Neolocality, 480
New Atlantis (Bacon), 592
New middle class, 347-50
Newspapers, 636
Newton, Sir Isaac, 456
Nicomachean Ethics (Aristotle), 159
Nisbet, Robert, 345-6, 626
Nonorganizations, 433-4
Nonvalidity of instrument, 65
Nonverbal tests, 62
NORC study (National Opinion Research Center study), 387-88
Norms, 8, 21-22
Note-taking: during interviews, 77; during observation, 79-80
Nuclear disarmament, 611
Nuclear family, 477; division of labor in, 477-8; patterns of authority in, 481; as standard family unit, 483-5; in utopian communities, 594; *see also* American family
Nuclear war, 610-11

Observation, gathering data by, 51-3, 78-80
Occupational distribution, long-term trends in, 372-5
Occupational performance, 400-14; of executives, 405-7; of workers, 409-11; of professionals, 401-5; of retail proprietors, 411-14; of craftsmen, 407-9
Occupational status, 381-87
Occupations, 366, 370-2; and age, 376-7; classification of, 368-72; and race, 379-81; and by sex, 378-9; suicide and, 543
Oceania (Harrington), 592
Offender-victim relationship, 538-9
Ogburn, William Fielding, 488
Old populations, 227-8
Operational definitions, 63-4
Opium addiction, 561-5
Oral history, 56
Organizational pyramid, 446
Organizational roles, 444-5
Organizations, 18, 432; authority in, 448-9; coalitions in, 450; collective identity of, 432; community as, 434-5; conflicts in, 586; individual vs., 436-9; informal, 449; internal, 116; large, 435, 457, 459; middle-sized, 435; sets of, 464-7; size of, 435-6; tables of, 18, 439-46; types of, 432-3; 596; *see also* Bureaucracy
Orwell, George, 313
Osborn, Frederick, 129, 130
Other America (Harrington), 350, 351

Paradoxes of power, 27
Parent-child relationship: in American family, 498-9; middle-class, 507-8
Parent-DuChatelet, Alexandre B., 98
Parental authority in Middletown, 491
Parents. *See* Family
Pareto, Vilfredo, 113, 115, 157; influence of, 185; Marx's influence on, 168; rise of fascism and, 184; social theories of, 170-2
Park, Robert E., 103, 177, 184, 267, 269

Parsons, Talcott, 137, 157, 185-6, 509-10
Participant observation, 51-3
Partisanship, 11
Passeron, Jean-Claude, 393
Pathological social conditions, 175
Pathology, social, 526
Patriarchal myth in American family, 494-95
Patrilineal descent, 480
Patrilineal naming, 484
Patrilocality, 480
Patripotestal family, 481
Patterns of Industrial Bureaucracy (Gouldner), 141
Pearson, Karl, 235
Peer groups, 449
People's Choice (Lazarsfeld), 126-29
Pepys, Samuel, 456
Permissiveness, 507
Perry, Clarence, 298-99
Personnel procedures, 454
Physical and Moral State of Workmen Employed in the Manufacture of Cotton, Linen and Silk (Villermé), 98
Physical sciences, 5-6
Piaget, Jean, 113
Pill, the, 225-6
Plainville, U.S.A. (West), 54
Planned cities, 280
Planning. *See* City planning, Social planning
Plato, 157-8, 592, 593
Polish Peasant in Europe and America, The (Thomas and Znaniecki), 86, 100-3
Political Arithmetik, 98
Political rights, 318
Political sociology, 30
Political violence, 649
Politics (Aristotle), 159-60
Pollution, 646-7
Polyandry, 478
Polybius, 160
Polygamy, 478
Poor, the, as programmatic class, 331, 350-5
Population, 198-9; age distribution of, 201-5; ancestry of, 237-8; research on, 30; young and old, 227-30; *see also* Age, Age distribution, Birth rate, Birth sex ratio, Dependency ratio, Divorce, Fertility, Life expectancy, Migrations, Mortality, Population distribution, Population growth, Rural population, Urban population, Urbanization
Population distribution, 198-9; of blacks, 246; density of, 253; in cities, 277; in metropolitan areas, 274; by regions, 244
Population drift, 240, 244-47
Population growth, 251-8; causes of, 253-4; of client population, 459; economic growth and, 256-7; fertility and, 255-6; and social change, 637-38; rate of, 251, 252, 254; of urban, 627
Population pyramid, 202
Power, 6-27; social, 445; *see also* Authority, Coercion, Dominance, Hierarchy, Leaders
Power elite, 347-50
Power Elite (Mills), 348, 349-50
Predictions, self-modifying, 10
Pregnancy, Birth and Abortion, 135
Prestige, 445; occupational, 387-8; order of, in sets of organizations, 464-5; *see also* Status
Principle of Population (Malthus), 163

28-30; pseudo-scientific beliefs about, 2-3; purpose of, 4-5; scientific, 6; specialization in, 30; as study of social facts, 173; vocabulary of, 13-28
Socioeconomic status, voting patterns and, 127
Sociometric status, 5
Socrates, 157, 158
Soft information, 47
Solidarity, 174; mechanical, in rural life, 270; organic, in cities, 270
Sorokin, Pitirim, 106-7, 184, 607, 608, 629, 664
Soziologie (Simmel), 177
Specialization and social change, 638-9
Spencer, Herbert, 156, 166-68, 171, 184, 626, 629
Spheres of influence, 606-7
Srole Scale of Anomie, 66-7
Stalin, Josef, 451
Standard Metropolitan Statistical Areas (SMSA), 273
Stanford-Binet Intelligence Test, 64
Stanton, Alfred H., 142
State, the: Marxist view of, 169; social technology and growth of, 664
Statistical Abstract of the United States, 44, 235
Statistics: maintenance of, by bureaucracies, 454-5; used in gathering data, 44-45
Status, 4-5; achieved vs. ascribed, 311-13; ambivalent character of, 178-9; consistency of, 466; equalization of, 650; marital, 234, 543; occupational, 381-7; organizational, 445-6; of participant observers, 53; rural society based on, 270; sociometric, 25; voting patterns and socioeconomic, 127; within family, 510
Status groups, 322-3
Status order, 310, 590, 595
Status schisms, 447
Status sets, 187
Steiner, Gary A., 465
Sterilization, 226
Sterner, Richard, 123
Stoke, Stuart M., 387
Stouffer, Samuel A., 129-33, 240
Strabo, 160
Strategy, 600; of mutual deterrence, 613-15
Stratification, 14-15, 25-6, 310; achieved vs. ascribed status and, 311-13; European expansion as source of, 323-27; historical patterns of, 313-19; models of, 333-42; among prostitutes, 549; social effects of studies in, 331-2; *see also* Social classes
Straus, Robert, 557
Street Corner Society (Whyte), 119-23
Strodtbeck, Fred L., 58, 555
Structure and Process in Modern Societies (Parsons), 185
Structure of Social Action (Parsons), 185
Studies in Social Psychology in World War II (Stouffer), 129-33
Study of Sociology (Spencer), 166
Subculture: delinquent, anomie and, 527-8; of metropolitan communities, 105
Subjectivity, 11-12
Substitution, 481-2
Suburbanization, 640-1
Suburbs: white, black ghettos and, 290-91; city planning and, 296-7
Succession, 103
Suicide (Durkheim), 173, 175

Suicide, 175-6, 541-44; social characteristics and, 541-44; rates of, 543
Sumner, William Graham, 21, 184, 544
Superiority: biological, 236; technical, 455
Surplus value, 418
Sutherland, Edwin H., 539
Symbiosis, 103
Synanon, 565-6

Tables of organization, 8, 439-46; in bureaucracy, 452; positions in, 443-45; organizational status in, 445-6
Taboo, 176,479
Tabulation, 82-4
Tactics, 600
Taft, William Howard, 509
Tama, 482
Tawney, 110
Technological progress, social change and, 630-31
Technology, social, 660; moral order and, 664-5; practicable goals of, 663-4; sequential approach to, 661-3
Television, 636-7
Terminal conflicts, 584; boundaries of, 585; individual and collective, 584-5
Territoriality, 588-9
Territory, 513
Thales, 160
Theft, 530
Thematic Apperception Test (TAT), 62
Theoretical models, 41-2
Theory of Moral Sentiments (Smith), 161-62
Thomas, William I., 100-3, 184
Thurstone scale, 67-8
Tikopia Ritual and Belief (Firth), 110
Time, scientific conception of, 8-9
Tönnies, Ferdinand, 270
Toqueville, Alexis de, 493
Total institutions, 20
Totem, 176
Towards a General Theory of Action (Parsons and Shils), 185
Toynbee, Arnold, 629
Traditional authority, 451
"Traditional and modern," 270
Traffic accidents, 558-9
Transfer sheets, 82
Triads, 140, 601

Unemployment, black, 353
Unidimensionality of scales, 67
Universe, scientific view of, 7-9
Unobtrusive Measures: Nonreactive Research in the Social Sciences (Webb), 62
Unreliability of research instruments, 63
Upper class, 336, 338; biological superiority of, 236; black, 341; families in, 509; *see also* Middle class
Urban community, 268-69
Urban ecology, 269, 279-85; Burgess model, 282-4; of Chicago, 103-6; of crescive and planned cities, 280; of Latin American cities, 284-5; of North American cities, 281-2
Urban life: drug addiction and, 562; mobility and, 105; social distance in, 105; theories of, 267-9
Urban population: by cities, 243; differential fertility of, 232; growth of, 627; U.S. and world, 241; voting patterns of, 127
Urban renewal, city planning and, 292-3

Urbanization, 240-4; automobile and, 245, 277; division of labor and, 367; juvenile delinquency and, 537; as long-term social change, 640-1; of modern American family, 489; *see also* Cities
Utopia (More), 592
Utopian experimentation, 592-6

Validity: of coding, 81; of research instruments, 63-5
Value judgments, 181
Values, 20; in American families, 495; breakdown of, 648; importance of, 181; local and cosmopolitan, 121; personal, and biases, 10-11; rational actions in support of, 181-2
Vassalage, 314
Veblen, Thorstein, 168, 184, 453
Verification of scientific analysis, 7-8
Vertical mobility, 6, 106, 391; of executives, 406-7; of craftsmen, 408-9; as intergenerational mobility, 392-7; *see also* Status
Villerme, Louis, R., 98
Violence, political, 649; *see also* Crimes, War
Vocabulary of sociology, 13-28
Voting patterns, 126-9
Voting Rights Act (1965), 352
Voyage en Icarie (Cabet), 592

Wages, 414-19; determining systems of, 418-19; forms of payment of, 414-16; problem in comparing, 416-17; *see also* Earnings, Earnings fan, Fees
Walden Two (Skinner), 592
Walker, Francis A., 235, 236
War, 603-11; casualties of 607, 609, 610; ending, 616; frequency of, 609; in international systems, 604-7; nuclear, 610-11; severity of, 609, 645; trends in, 607-10
War on Poverty, 351-2
Ward, Lester F., 184
Warner, W. Lloyd, 28, 116-19, 335, 336, 644
Watterson, Henry, 457
We, the Tikopia (Firth), 110-12
Wealth of Nations (Smith), 161-63, 367
Weapons, nuclear, 610; disarmament and, 611
Weber, Adna Ferrin, 276
Weber, Max, 25, 141, 157; on legitimate domination, 450-1; on Marx's influence on, 168; social class theory of, 322-3; on social honor, 311; social theories of, 180-5; urban life theories of, 267-9
Weller, Jack E., 499
White Collar (Mills), 348
White-collar crimes, 539-40
White suburbs, black ghettos and, 290-1
Whitehead, T.H., 113
Whitney, Eli, 462
Why We Fight (film series), 132
Whyte, William Foote, 119-23
Wife-husband relationship, variations in, 496-8
Wilkie, Wendell, 126
Willcox, Walter F., 276
Wirth, Louis, 267-9
Women: addiction among, 565; arrests of, 549; career patterns of, 420-1; criminal activity of, 535; early 19th century American, 493; in abor force, 378-79, 492; life span of, 217; in kinship networks, 485; suicide among, 542